CUDA Programming

A Developer's Guide to Parallel Computing with GPUs

Contents

Preface

Over the past five years there has been a revolution in computing brought about by a company that for successive years has emerged as one of the premier gaming hardware manufacturers—NVIDIA. With the introduction of the CUDA (Compute Unified Device Architecture) programming language, for the first time these hugely powerful graphics coprocessors could be used by everyday C programmers to offload computationally expensive work. From the embedded device industry, to home users, to supercomputers, everything has changed as a result of this.

One of the major changes in the computer software industry has been the move from serial programming to parallel programming. Here, CUDA has produced great advances. The graphics processor unit (GPU) by its very nature is designed for high-speed graphics, which are inherently parallel. CUDA takes a simple model of data parallelism and incorporates it into a programming model without the need for graphics primitives.

In fact, CUDA, unlike its predecessors, does not require any understanding or knowledge of graphics or graphics primitives. You do not have to be a games programmer either. The CUDA language makes the GPU look just like another programmable device.

Throughout this book I will assume readers have no prior knowledge of CUDA, or of parallel programming. I assume they have only an existing knowledge of the C/C++ programming language. As we progress and you become more competent with CUDA, we'll cover more advanced topics, taking you from a parallel unaware programmer to one who can exploit the full potential of CUDA.

For programmers already familiar with parallel programming concepts and CUDA, we'll be discussing in detail the architecture of the GPUs and how to get the most from each, including the latest Fermi and Kepler hardware. Literally anyone who can program in C or C++ can program with CUDA in a few hours given a little training. Getting from novice CUDA programmer, with a several times speedup to 10 times–plus speedup is what you should be capable of by the end of this book.

The book is very much aimed at learning CUDA, but with a focus on performance, having first achieved correctness. Your level of skill and understanding of writing high-performance code, especially for GPUs, will hugely benefit from this text.

This book is a practical guide to using CUDA in real applications, by real practitioners. At the same time, however, we cover the necessary theory and background so everyone, no matter what their background, can follow along and learn how to program in CUDA, making this book ideal for both professionals and those studying GPUs or parallel programming.

The book is set out as follows:

Chapter 1: A Short History of Supercomputing. This chapter is a broad introduction to the evolution of streaming processors covering some key developments that brought us to GPU processing today.

Chapter 2: Understanding Parallelism with GPUs. This chapter is an introduction to the concepts of parallel programming, such as how serial and parallel programs are different and how to approach solving problems in different ways. This chapter is primarily aimed at existing serial programmers to give a basis of understanding for concepts covered later in the book.

Chapter 3: CUDA Hardware Overview. This chapter provides a fairly detailed explanation of the hardware and architecture found around and within CUDA devices. To achieve the best performance from CUDA programming, a reasonable understanding of the hardware both within and outside the device is required.

Chapter 4: Setting Up CUDA. Installation and setup of the CUDA SDK under Windows, Mac, and the Linux variants. We also look at the main debugging environments available for CUDA.

Chapter 5: Grids, Blocks, and Threads. A detailed explanation of the CUDA threading model, including some examples of how the choices here impact performance.

Chapter 6: Memory Handling with CUDA. Understanding the different memory types and how they are used within CUDA is the single largest factor influencing performance. Here we take a detailed explanation, with examples, of how the various memory types work and the pitfalls of getting it wrong.

Chapter 7: Using CUDA in Practice. Detailed examination as to how central processing units (CPUs) and GPUs best cooperate with a number of problems and the issues involved in CPU/GPU programming.

Chapter 8: Multi-CPU and Multi-GPU Solutions. We look at how to program and use multiple GPUs within an application.

Chapter 9: Optimizing Your Application. A detailed breakdown of the main areas that limit performance in CUDA. We look at the tools and techniques that are available for analysis of CUDA code.

Chapter 10: Libraries and SDK. A look at some of the CUDA SDK samples and the libraries supplied with CUDA, and how you can use these within your applications.

Chapter 11: Designing GPU-Based Systems. This chapter takes a look at some of the issues involved with building your own GPU workstation.

Chapter 12: Common Problems, Causes, and Solutions. A look at the type of mistakes most programmers make when developing applications in CUDA and how these can be detected and avoided.

A Short History of Supercomputing

1

INTRODUCTION

So why in a book about CUDA are we looking at supercomputers? Supercomputers are typically at the leading edge of the technology curve. What we see here is what will be commonplace on the desktop in 5 to 10 years. In 2010, the annual International Supercomputer Conference in Hamburg, Germany, announced that a NVIDIA GPU-based machine had been listed as the second most powerful computer in the world, according to the top 500 list (*http://www.top500.org*). Theoretically, it had more peak performance than the mighty IBM Roadrunner, or the then-leader, the Cray Jaguar, peaking at near to 3 petaflops of performance. In 2011, NVIDIA CUDA-powered GPUs went on to claim the title of the fastest supercomputer in the world. It was suddenly clear to everyone that GPUs had arrived in a very big way on the high-performance computing landscape, as well as the humble desktop PC.

Supercomputing is the driver of many of the technologies we see in modern-day processors. Thanks to the need for ever-faster processors to process ever-larger datasets, the industry produces ever-faster computers. It is through some of these evolutions that GPU CUDA technology has come about today.

Both supercomputers and desktop computing are moving toward a heterogeneous computing route—that is, they are trying to achieve performance with a mix of CPU (Central Processor Unit) and specialist processors such as GPU (Graphics Processor Unit) technology. Two of the largest worldwide projects using GPUs are BOINC and Folding@Home, both of which are distributed computing projects. They allow ordinary people to make a real contribution to specific scientific projects. Contributions from CPU/GPU hosts on projects supporting GPU accelerators hugely outweigh contributions from CPU-only hosts. As of November 2011, there were some 5.5 million hosts contributing a total of around 5.3 petaflops. This is around half that of the world's fastest super-computer, in 2011, the Fujitsu "K computer" in Japan.

The replacement for Jaguar, currently the fastest U.S. supercomputer, code-named Titan, was brought on-line in 2012. It uses almost 300,000 CPU cores and up to 18,000 GPU boards to achieve between 10 and 20 petaflops of performance. With support like this from around the world, GPU programming is set to jump into the mainstream, both in the HPC industry and also on the desktop.

You can now put together or purchase a desktop supercomputer with several teraflops of performance. At the beginning of 2000, some 12 years ago, this would have given you first place in the top 500 list, beating IBM ASCI Red with its 9632 Pentium processors. This just shows how much a little over a decade of computing progress has achieved and opens up the question about where we will be a decade from now. You can be fairly certain GPUs will be at the forefront of this trend for some time to come. Thus, learning how to program GPUs effectively is a key skill any good developer needs to acquire.

VON NEUMANN ARCHITECTURE

Almost all processors work on the basis of the process developed by Von Neumann, considered one of the fathers of computing. In this approach, the processor fetches instructions from memory, decodes, and then executes that instruction.

A modern processor typically runs at anything up to 4 GHz in speed. Modern DDR-3 memory, when paired with say a standard Intel I7 device, can run at anything up to 2 GHz. However, the I7 has at least four processors or cores in one device, or double that if you count its hyperthreading ability as a real processor.

A DDR-3 triple-channel memory setup on a I7 Nehalem system would produce the theoretical bandwidth figures shown in Table 1.1. Depending on the motherboard, and exact memory pattern, the actual bandwidth could be considerably less.

Table 1.1 Bandwidth on I7 Nehalem Processor		
QPI Clock	**Theoretical Bandwidth**	**Per Core**
4.8 GT/s (standard part)	19.2 GB/s	4.8 GB/s
6.4 GT/s (extreme edition)	25.6 GB/s	6.4 GB/s
Note: QPI = Quick Path Interconnect.		

You run into the first problem with memory bandwidth when you consider the processor clock speed. If you take a processor running at 4 GHz, you need to potentially fetch, every cycle, an instruction (an operator) plus some data (an operand).

Each instruction is typically 32 bits, so if you execute nothing but a set of linear instructions, with no data, on every core, you get 4.8 GB/s ÷ 4 = 1.2 GB instructions per second. This assumes the processor can dispatch one instruction per clock on average*. However, you typically also need to fetch and write back data, which if we say is on a 1:1 ratio with instructions, means we effectively halve our throughput.

The ratio of CPU clock speed to memory speed is an important limiter for both CPU and GPU throughput and something we'll look at later. You will find most applications, with a few exceptions on both CPU and GPU, are often memory bound and not processor cycle or processor clock/load bound.

CPU vendors try to solve this problem by using cache memory and burst memory access. This exploits the principle of locality. It you look at a typical C program, you might see the following type of operation in a function:

```
void some_function
{
 int array[100];
 int i = 0;
```

---

*The actual achieved dispatch rate can be higher or lower than one, which we use here for simplicity.

```
for (i=0; i<100; i++)
{
  array[i] = i * 10;
}
}
```

If you look at how the processor would typically implement this, you would see the address of array loaded into some memory access register. The parameter i would be loaded into another register. The loop exit condition, 100, is loaded into another register or possibly encoded into the instruction stream as a literal value. The computer would then iterate around the same instructions, over and over again 100 times. For each value calculated, we have control, memory, and calculation instructions, fetched and executed.

This is clearly inefficient, as the computer is executing the same instructions, but with different data values. Thus, the hardware designers implement into just about all processors a small amount of cache, and in more complex processors, many levels of cache (Figure 1.1). When the processor would fetch something from memory, the processor first queries the cache, and if the data or instructions are present there, the high-speed cache provides them to the processor.

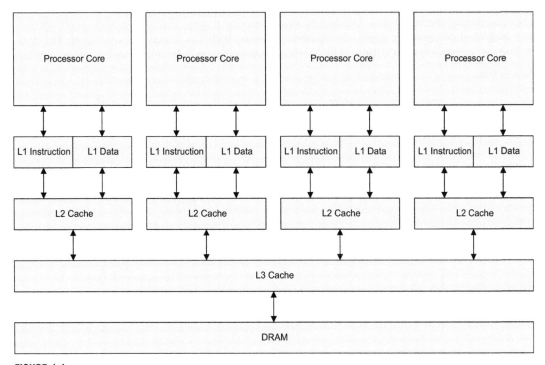

FIGURE 1.1

Typical modern CPU cache organization.

If the data is not in the first level (L1) cache, then a fetch from the second or third level (L2 or L3) cache is required, or from the main memory if no cache line has this data already. The first level cache typically runs at or near the processor clock speed, so for the execution of our loop, potentially we do get near the full processor speed, assuming we write cache as well as read cache. However, there is a cost for this: The size of the L1 cache is typically only 16 K or 32 K in size. The L2 cache is somewhat slower, but much larger, typically around 256 K. The L3 cache is much larger, usually several megabytes in size, but again much slower than the L2 cache.

With real-life examples, the loop iterations are much, much larger, maybe many megabytes in size. Even if the program can remain in cache memory, the dataset usually cannot, so the processor, despite all this cache trickery, is quite often limited by the memory throughput or bandwidth.

When the processor fetches an instruction or data item from the cache instead of the main memory, it's called a cache hit. The incremental benefit of using progressively larger caches drops off quite rapidly. This in turn means the ever-larger caches we see on modern processors are a less and less useful means to improve performance, unless they manage to encompass the *entire* dataset of the problem.

The Intel I7-920 processor has some 8 MB of internal L3 cache. This cache memory is not free, and if we look at the die for the Intel I7 processor, we see around 30% of the size of the chip is dedicated to the L3 cache memory (Figure 1.2).

As cache sizes grow, so does the physical size of the silicon used to make the processors. The larger the chip, the more expensive it is to manufacture and the higher the likelihood that it will contain an error and be discarded during the manufacturing process. Sometimes these faulty devices are sold cheaply as either triple- or dual-core devices, with the faulty cores disabled. However, the effect of larger, progressively more inefficient caches ultimately results in higher costs to the end user.

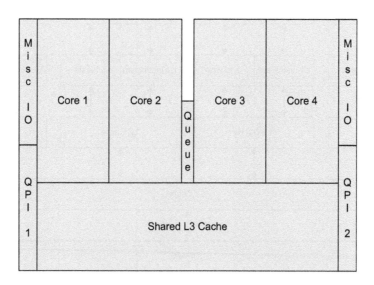

FIGURE 1.2

Layout of I7 Nehalem processor on processor die.

CRAY

The computing revolution that we all know today started back in the 1950s with the advent of the first microprocessors. These devices, by today's standards, are slow and you most likely have a far more powerful processor in your smartphone. However, these led to the evolution of supercomputers, which are machines usually owned by governments, large academic institutions, or corporations. They are thousands of times more powerful than the computers in general use today. They cost millions of dollars to produce, occupy huge amounts of space, usually have special cooling requirements, and require a team of engineers to look after them. They consume huge amounts of power, to the extent they are often as expensive to run over several years as they cost to build. In fact, power is one of the key considerations when planning such an installation and one of the main limiting factors in the growth of today's supercomputers.

One of the founders of modern supercomputers was Seymour Cray with his Cray-1, produced by Cray Research back in 1976. It had many thousands of individual cables required to connect everything together—so much so they used to employ women because their hands were smaller than those of most men and they could therefore more easily wire up all the thousands of individual cables.

These machines would typically have an uptime (the actual running time between breakdowns) measured in hours. Keeping them running for a whole day at a time would be considered a huge

FIGURE 1.3

Wiring inside the Cray-2 supercomputer.

achievement. This seems quite backward by today's standards. However, we owe a lot of what we have today to research carried out by Seymour Cray and other individuals of this era.

Cray went on to produce some of the most groundbreaking supercomputers of his time under various Cray names. The original Cray-1 cost some $8.8 million USD and achieved a massive 160 MFLOPS (million floating-point operations per second). Computing speed today is measured in TFLOPS (tera floating-point operations per second), a million times larger than the old MFLOPS measurement (10^{12} vs. 10^6). A single Fermi GPU card today has a theoretical peak in excess of 1 teraflop of performance.

The Cray-2 was a significant improvement on the Cray-1. It used a shared memory architecture, split into banks. These were connected to one, two, or four processors. It led the way for the creation of today's server-based symmetrical multiprocessor (SMP) systems in which multiple CPUs shared the same memory space. Like many machines of its era, it was a vector-based machine. In a vector machine the same operation acts on many operands. These still exist today, in part as processor extensions such as MMX, SSE, and AVX. GPU devices are, at their heart, vector processors that share many similarities with the older supercomputer designs.

The Cray also had hardware support for scatter- and gather-type primitives, something we'll see is quite important in parallel computing and something we look at in subsequent chapters.

Cray still exists today in the supercomputer market, and as of 2013 held the top 500 position with their Titan supercomputer at the Oak Ridge National Laboratory (*http://www.olcf.ornl.gov/titan/*). I encourage you to read about the history of this great company, which you can find on Cray's website (*http://www.cray.com*), as it gives some insight into the evolution of computers and as to where we are today.

CONNECTION MACHINE

Back in 1982 a corporation called Thinking Machines came up with a very interesting design, that of the Connection Machine.

It was a relatively simple concept that led to a revolution in today's parallel computers. They used a few simple parts over and over again. They created a 16-core CPU, and then installed some 4096 of these devices in one machine. The concept was different. Instead of one fast processor churning through a dataset, there were 64 K processors doing this task.

Let's take the simple example of manipulating the color of an RGB (red, green, blue) image. Each color is made up of a single byte, with 3 bytes representing the color of a single pixel. Let's suppose we want to reduce the blue level to zero.

Let's assume the memory is configured in three banks of red, blue, and green, rather than being interleaved. With a conventional processor, we would have a loop running through the blue memory and decrement every pixel color level by one. The operation is the same on each item of data, yet each time we fetch, decode, and execute the instruction stream on each loop iteration.

The Connection Machine used something called SIMD (single instruction, multiple data), which is used today in modern processors and known by names such as SSE (Streaming SIMD Extensions), MMX (Multi-Media eXtension), and AVX (Advanced Vector eXtensions). The concept is to define a data range and then have the processor apply that operation to the data range. However, SSE and MMX are based on having one processor core. The Connection Machine had 64 K processor cores, each executing SIMD instructions on its dataset.

Processors such as the Intel I7 are 64-bit processors, meaning they can process up to 64 bits at a time (8 bytes). The SSE SIMD instruction set extends this to 128 bits. With SIMD instructions on such a processor, we eliminate all redundant instruction memory fetches, and generate one sixteenth of the memory read and write cycles compared with fetching and writing 1 byte at a time. AVX extends this to 256 bits, making it even more effective.

For a high-definition (HD) video image of 1920×1080 resolution, the data size is 2,073,600 bytes, or around 2 MB per color plane. Thus, we generate around 260,000 SIMD cycles for a single conventional processor using SSE/MMX. By SIMD cycle, we mean one read, compute, and write cycle. The actual number of processor clocks may be considerably different than this, depending on the particular processor architecture.

The Connection Machine used 64 K processors. Thus, the 2 MB frame would have resulted in about 32 SIMD cycles for each processor. Clearly, this type of approach is vastly superior to the modern processor SIMD approach. However, there is of course a caveat. Synchronizing and communication between processors becomes the major issue when moving from a rather coarse-threaded approach of today's CPUs to a hugely parallel approach used by such machines.

CELL PROCESSOR

Another interesting development in supercomputers stemmed from IBM's invention of the Cell processor (Figure 1.4). This worked on the idea of having a regular processor act as a supervisory

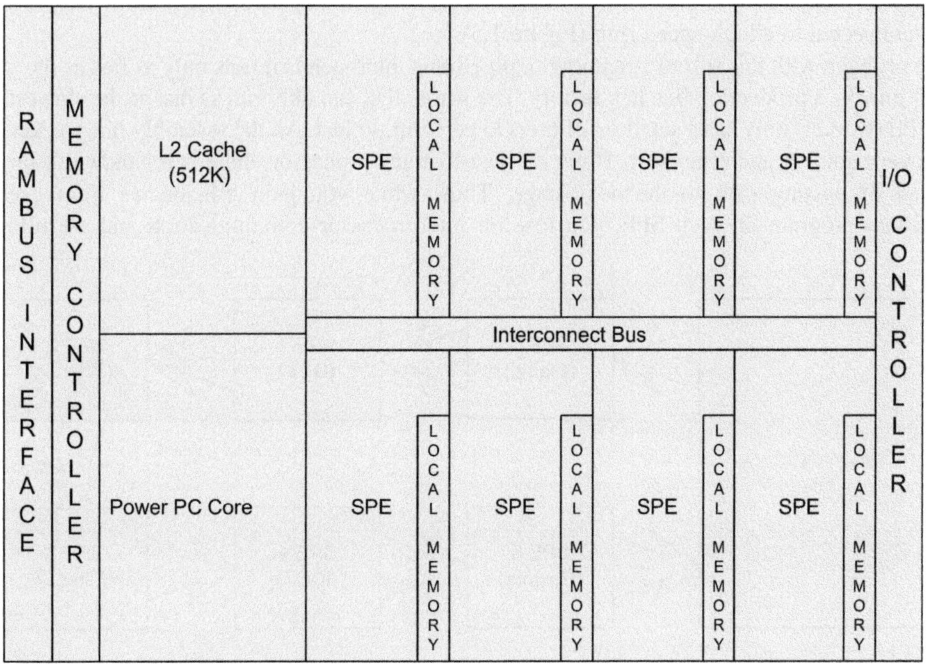

FIGURE 1.4

IBM cell processor die layout (8 SPE version).

processor, connected to a number of high-speed stream processors. The regular PowerPC (PPC) processor in the Cell acts as an interface to the stream processors and the outside world. The stream SIMD processors, or SPEs as IBM called them, would process datasets managed by the regular processor.

The Cell is a particularly interesting processor for us, as it's a similar design to what NVIDIA later used in the G80 and subsequent GPUs. Sony also used it in their PS3 console machines in the games industry, a very similar field to the main use of GPUs.

To program the Cell, you write a program to execute on the PowerPC core processor. It then invokes a program, using an entirely different binary, on each of the stream processing elements (SPEs). Each SPE is actually a core in itself. It can execute an independent program from its own local memory, which is different from the SPE next to it. In addition, the SPEs can communicate with one another and the PowerPC core over a shared interconnect. However, this type of hybrid architecture is not easy to program. The programmer must explicitly manage the eight SPEs, both in terms of programs and data, as well as the serial program running on the PowerPC core.

With the ability to talk directly to the coordinating processor, a series of simple steps can be achieved. With our RGB example earlier, the PPC core fetches a chunk of data to work on. It allocates these to the eight SPEs. As we do the same thing in each SPE, each SPE fetches the byte, decrements it, and writes its bit back to its local memory. When all SPEs are done, the PC core fetches the data from each SPE. It then writes its chunk of data (or tile) to the memory area where the whole image is being assembled. The Cell processor is designed to be used in groups, thus repeating the design of the Connection Machine.

The SPEs could also be ordered to perform a stream operation, involving multiple steps, as each SPE is connected to a high-speed ring (Figure 1.5).

The problem with this sort of streaming or pipelining approach is it runs only as fast as the slowest node. It mirrors a production line in a factory. The whole line can only run as fast as the slowest point. Each SPE (worker) only has a small set of tasks to perform, so just like the assembly line worker, it can do this very quickly and efficiently. However, just like any processor, there is a bandwidth limit and overhead of passing data to the next stage. Thus, while you gain efficiencies from executing a consistent program on each SPE, you lose on interprocessor communication and are ultimately

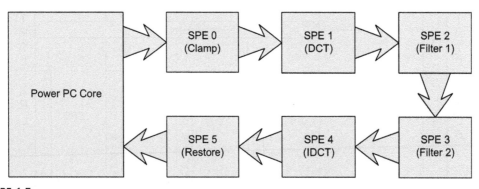

FIGURE 1.5

Example routing stream processor routing on Cell.

limited by the slowest process step. This is a common problem with any pipeline-based model of execution.

The alternative approach of putting everything on one SPE and then having each SPE process a small chunk of data is often a more efficient approach. This is the equivalent to training all assembly line workers to assemble a complete widget. For simple tasks, this is easy. However, each SPE has limits on available program and data memory. The PowerPC core must now also deliver and collect data from eight SPEs, instead of just two, so the management overhead and communication between host and SPEs increases.

IBM used a high-powered version of the Cell processor in their Roadrunner supercomputer, which as of 2010 was the third fastest computer on the top 500 list. It consists of 12,960 PowerPC cores, plus a total of 103,680 stream processors. Each PowerPC board is supervised by a dual-core AMD (Advanced Micro Devices) Opteron processor, of which there are 6912 in total. The Opteron processors act as coordinators among the nodes. Roadrunner has a theoretical throughput of 1.71 petaflops, cost $125 million USD to build, occupies 560 square meters, and consumes 2.35 MW of electricity when operating!

MULTINODE COMPUTING

As you increase the requirements (CPU, memory, storage space) needed on a single machine, costs rapidly increase. While a 2.6 GHz processor may cost you $250 USD, the same processor at 3.4 GHz may be $1400 for less than a 1 GHz increase in clock speed. A similar relationship is seen for both speed and size memory, and storage capacity.

Not only do costs scale as computing requirements scale, but so do the power requirements and the consequential heat dissipation issues. Processors can hit 4–5 GHz, given sufficient supply of power and cooling.

In computing you often find the law of diminishing returns. There is only so much you can put into a single case. You are limited by cost, space, power, and heat. The solution is to select a reasonable balance of each and to replicate this many times.

Cluster computing became popular in 1990s along with ever-increasing clock rates. The concept was a very simple one. Take a number of commodity PCs bought or made from off-the-shelf parts and connect them to an off-the-shelf multi-port Ethernet switch and you had up to N times the performance of a single box. Instead of paying $1600 for a high performance processor, you paid $250 and bought six medium performance processors. If your application needed huge memory capacity, the chances were that maxing out the DIMMs on many machines and adding them together was more than sufficient. Used together, the combined power of many machines hugely outperformed any single machine you could possible buy with a similar budget.

All of a sudden universities, schools, offices, and computer departments could build machines much more powerful than before and were not locked out of the high-speed computing market due to lack of funds. Cluster computing back then was like GPU computing today—a disruptive technology that changed the face of computing. Combined with the ever-increasing single-core clock speeds it provided a cheap way to achieve parallel processing within single-core CPUs.

Clusters of PCs typically ran a variation of LINUX with each node usually fetching its boot instructions and operating system (OS) from a central master node. For example, at CudaDeveloper we have a tiny cluster of low-powered, atom-based PCs with embedded CUDA GPUs. It's very cheap to buy and set up a cluster. Sometimes they can simply be made from a number of old PCs that are being replaced, so the hardware is effectively free.

However, the problem with cluster computing is it's only as fast as the amount of internode communication that is necessary for the problem. If you have 32 nodes and the problem breaks down into 32 nice chunks and requires no internode communication, you have an application that is ideal for a cluster. If every data point takes data from every node, you have a terrible problem to put into a cluster.

Clusters are seen inside modern CPUs and GPUs. Look back at Figure 1.1, the CPU cache hierarchy. If we consider each CPU core as a node, the L2 cache as DRAM (Dynamic Random Access Memory), the L3 cache as the network switch, and the DRAM as mass storage, we have a cluster in miniature (Figures 1.6 and 1.7).

The architecture inside a modern GPU is really no different. You have a number of streaming multiprocessors (SMs) that are akin to CPU cores. These are connected to a shared memory/L1 cache. This is connected to an L2 cache that acts as an inter-SM switch. Data can be held in global memory storage where it's then extracted and used by the host, or sent via the PCI-E switch directly to the memory on another GPU. The PCI-E switch is many times faster than any network interconnect.

The node may itself be replicated many times. This replication within a controlled environment forms a cluster. One evolution of the cluster designs are distributed applications. Distributed

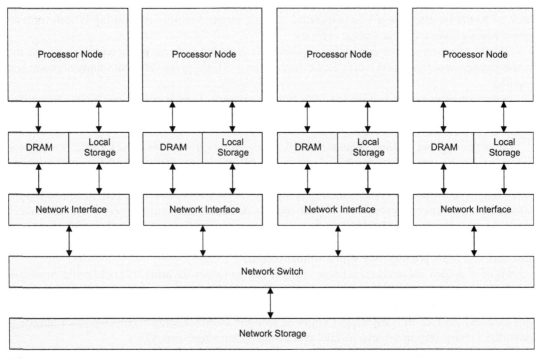

FIGURE 1.6

Typical cluster layout.

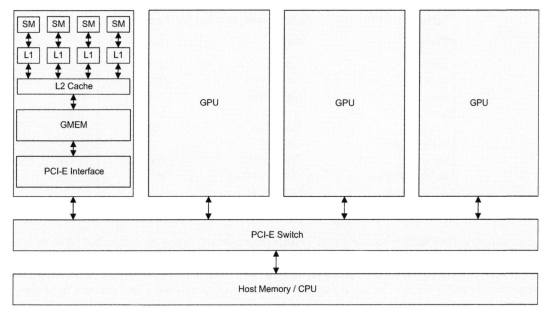

FIGURE 1.7

GPUs compared to a cluster.

applications run on many nodes, each of which may contain many processing elements including GPUs. Distributed applications may, but do not need to, run in a controlled environment of a managed cluster. They can connect arbitrary machines together to work on some common problem, BOINC and Folding@Home being two of the largest examples of such applications that connect machines together over the Internet.

THE EARLY DAYS OF GPGPU CODING

Graphics processing units (GPUs) are devices present in most modern PCs. They provide a number of basic operations to the CPU, such as rendering an image in memory and then displaying that image onto the screen. A GPU will typically process a complex set of polygons, a map of the scene to be rendered. It applies textures to the polygons and then performs shading and lighting calculations. The NVIDIA 5000 series cards brought for the first time photorealistic effects, such as shown in the Dawn Fairy demo from 2003.

Have a look at *http://www.nvidia.com/object/cool_stuff.html#/demos* and download some of the older demos and you'll see just how much GPUs have evolved over the past decade. See Table 1.2.

One of the important steps was the development of programmable shaders. These were effectively small programs that the GPU ran to calculate different effects. No longer was the rendering fixed in the GPU; through downloadable shaders, it could be manipulated. This was the first evolution of

Table 1.2 GPU Technology Demonstrated over the Years		
Demo	**Card**	**Year**
Dawn	GeForce FX	2003
Dusk Ultra	GeForce FX	2003
Nalu	GeForce 6	2004
Luna	GeForce 7	2005
Froggy	GeForce 8	2006
Human Head	GeForce 8	2007
Medusa	GeForce 200	2008
Supersonic Sled	GeForce 400	2010
A New Dawn	GeForce 600	2012

general-purpose graphical processor unit (GPGPU) programming, in that the design had taken its first steps in moving away from fixed function units.

However, these shaders were operations that by their very nature took a set of 3D points that represented a polygon map. The shaders applied the same operation to many such datasets, in a hugely parallel manner, giving huge throughput of computing power.

Now although polygons are sets of three points, and some other datasets such as RGB photos can be represented by sets of three points, a lot of datasets are not. A few brave researchers made use of GPU technology to try and speed up general-purpose computing. This led to the development of a number of initiatives (e.g., BrookGPU, Cg, CTM, etc.), all of which were aimed at making the GPU a real programmable device in the same way as the CPU. Unfortunately, each had its own advantages and problems. None were particularly easy to learn or program in and were never taught to people in large numbers. In short, there was never a critical mass of programmers or a critical mass of interest from programmers in this hard-to-learn technology. They never succeeded in hitting the mass market, something CUDA has for the first time managed to do, and at the same time provided programmers with a truly general-purpose language for GPUs.

THE DEATH OF THE SINGLE-CORE SOLUTION

One of the problems with today's modern processors is they have hit a clock rate limit at around 4 GHz. At this point they just generate too much heat for the current technology and require special and expensive cooling solutions. This is because as we increase the clock rate, the power consumption rises. In fact, the power consumption of a CPU, if you fix the voltage, is approximately the cube of its clock rate. To make this worse, as you increase the heat generated by the CPU, for the same clock rate, the power consumption also increases due to leakage properties of the silicon. This conversion of power into heat is a complete waste of energy. This increasingly inefficient use of power eventually means you are unable to either power or cool the processor sufficiently and you reach the thermal limits of the device or its housing, the so-called power wall.

Faced with not being able to increase the clock rate, making forever-faster processors, the processor manufacturers had to come up with another strategy. The two main PC processor manufacturers, Intel and AMD, have had to adopt a different approach. They have been forced down the route of adding more cores to processors, rather than continuously trying to increase CPU clock rates and/or extract more instructions per clock through instruction-level parallelism. We have dual, tri, quad, hex, 8, 12, and soon even 16 and 32 cores and so on. This is the future of where computing is now going for everyone, the GPU and CPU communities. The GPU is effectively already an 8 to 32 device in CPU terms.

There is a big problem with this approach—it requires programmers to switch from their traditional serial, single-thread approach, to dealing with multiple threads all executing at once. Now the programmer has to think about two, four, six, or eight program threads and how they interact and communicate with one another. When dual-core CPUs arrived, it was fairly easy, in that there were usually some background tasks being done that could be offloaded onto a second core. When quad-core CPUs arrived, not many programs were changed to support it. They just carried on being sold as single-thread applications. Even the games industry took years to move to quad-core programming, which is the one industry you'd expect to want to get the absolute most out of today's technology.

In some ways the processor manufacturers are to blame for this, because the single-core application runs just fine on one-quarter of the quad-core device. Some devices even increase the clock rate dynamically when only one core is active, encouraging programmers to be lazy and not make use of the available hardware.

There are economic reasons too. The software development companies need to get the product to market as soon as possible. Developing a better quad-core solution is all well and good, but not if the market is being grabbed by a competitor who got there first. As manufacturers still continue to make single- and dual-core devices, the market naturally settles on the lowest configuration, with the widest scope for sales. Until the time that quad-core CPUs are the minimum produced, market forces work against the move to multicore programming in the CPU market.

NVIDIA AND CUDA

If you look at the relative computational power in GPUs and CPUs, we get an interesting graph (Figure 1.8). We start to see a divergence of CPU and GPU computational power until 2009 when we see the GPU finally break the 1000 gigaflops or 1 teraflop barrier. At this point we were moving from the G80 hardware to the G200 and then in 2010 to the Fermi evolution. This is driven by the introduction of massively parallel hardware. The G80 is a 128 CUDA core device, the G200 is a 256 CUDA core device, and the Fermi is a 512 CUDA core device.

We see NVIDIA GPUs make a leap of 300 gigaflops from the G200 architecture to the Fermi architecture, nearly a 30% improvement in throughput. By comparison, Intel's leap from their core 2 architecture to the Nehalem architecture sees only a minor improvement. Only with the change to Sandy Bridge architecture do we see significant leaps in CPU performance. This is not to say one is better than the other, for the traditional CPUs are aimed at serial code execution and are extremely good at it. They contain special hardware such as branch prediction units, multiple caches, etc., all of which target serial code execution. The GPUs are not designed for this serial execution flow and only achieve their peak performance when fully utilized in a parallel manner.

In 2007, NVIDIA saw an opportunity to bring GPUs into the mainstream by adding an easy-to-use programming interface, which it dubbed CUDA, or Compute Unified Device Architecture. This

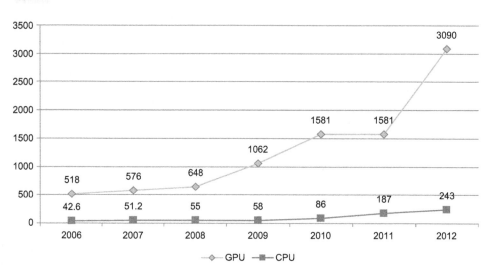

FIGURE 1.8

CPU and GPU peak performance in gigaflops.

opened up the possibility to program GPUs without having to learn complex shader languages, or to think only in terms of graphics primitives.

CUDA is an extension to the C language that allows GPU code to be written in regular C. The code is either targeted for the host processor (the CPU) or targeted at the device processor (the GPU). The host processor spawns multithreaded tasks (or kernels as they are known in CUDA) onto the GPU device. The GPU has its own internal scheduler that will then allocate the kernels to whatever GPU hardware is present. We'll cover scheduling in detail later. Provided there is enough parallelism in the task, as the number of SMs in the GPU grows, so should the speed of the program.

However, herein hides a big problem. You have to ask what percentage of the code can be run in parallel. The maximum speedup possible is limited by the amount of serial code. If you have an infinite amount of processing power and could do the parallel tasks in zero time, you would still be left with the time from the serial code part. Therefore, we have to consider at the outset if we can indeed parallelize a significant amount of the workload.

NVIDIA is committed to providing support to CUDA. Considerable information, examples, and tools to help with development are available from its website at *http://www.nvidia.com* under CudaZone.

CUDA, unlike its predecessors, has now actually started to gain momentum and for the first time it looks like there will be a programming language that will emerge as the one of choice for GPU programming. Given that the number of CUDA-enabled GPUs now number in the millions, there is a huge market out there waiting for CUDA-enabled applications.

There are currently many CUDA-enabled applications and the list grows monthly. NVIDIA showcases many of these on its community website at *http://www.nvidia.com/object/cuda_apps_flash_new.html*.

In areas where programs have to do a lot of computational work—for example, making a DVD from your home movies (video transcoding)—we see most mainstream video packages now supporting CUDA. The average speedup is 5 to 10 times in this domain.

Along with the introduction of CUDA came the Tesla series of cards. These cards are not graphics cards, and in fact they have no DVI or VGA connectors on them. They are dedicated compute cards aimed at scientific computing. Here we see huge speedups in scientific calculations. These cards can either be installed in a regular desktop PC or in dedicated server racks. NVIDIA provides such a system at *http://www.nvidia.com/object/preconfigured_clusters.html*, which claims to provide up to 30 times the power of a conventional cluster. CUDA and GPUs are reshaping the world of high-performance computing.

GPU HARDWARE

The NVIDIA G80 series processor and beyond implemented a design that is similar to both the Connection Machine and IBM's Cell processor. Each graphics card consists of a number of SMs. To each SM is attached eight or more SPs (Stream Processors). The original 9800 GTX card has eight SMs, giving a total of 128 SPs. However, unlike the Roadrunner, each GPU board can be purchased for a few hundred USD and it doesn't take 2.35 MW to power it. Power considerations are not to be overlooked, as we'll discuss later when we talk about building GPU servers.

The GPU cards can broadly be considered as accelerator or coprocessor cards. A GPU card, currently, must operate in conjunction with a CPU-based host. In this regard it follows very much the approach of the Cell processor with the regular serial core and N SIMD SPE cores. Each GPU device contains a set of SMs, each of which contain a set of SPs or CUDA cores. The SPs execute work as parallel sets of up to 32 units. They eliminate a lot of the complex circuitry needed on CPUs to achieve high-speed serial execution through instruction-level parallelism. They replace this with a programmer-specified explicit parallelism model, allowing more compute capacity to be squeezed onto the same area of silicon.

The overall throughput of GPUs is largely determined by the number of SPs present, the bandwidth to the global memory, and how well the programmer makes use of the parallel architecture he or she is working with. See Table 1.3 for a listing of current NVIDIA GPU cards.

Which board is correct for a given application is a balance between memory and GPU processing power needed for a given application. Note the 9800 GX2, 295, 590, 690, and K10 cards are actually dual cards, so to make full use of these they need to be programmed as two devices not one. The one caveat GPU here is that the figures quoted are for single-precision (32-bit) floating-point performance, not double-precision (64-bit) precision. Also be careful with the GF100 (Fermi) series, as the Tesla variant has double the number of double-precision units found in the standard desktop units, so achieves significantly better double-precision throughput. The Kepler K 20, yet to be released, will also have significant double precision performance over and above its already released K10 cousin.

Note also, although not shown here, as the generations have evolved, the power consumption, clock for clock, per SM has come down. However, the overall power consumption has increased considerably and this is one of the key considerations in any multi-GPU-based solution. Typically, we see dual-GPU-based cards (9800 GX2, 295, 590, 690) having marginally lower power consumption figures than the equivalent two single cards due to the use of shared circuitry and/or reduced clock frequencies.

NVIDIA provides various racks (the M series computing modules) containing two to four Tesla cards connected on a shared PCI-E bus for high-density computing. It's quite possible to build your own GPU cluster or microsupercomputer from standard PC parts, and we show you how to do this later in the book.

Table 1.3 Current Series of NVIDIA GPU Cards

GPU Series	Device	Number of SPs	Max Memory	GFlops (FMAD)	Bandwidth (GB/s)	Power (Watts)
9800 GT	G92	96	2GB	504	57	125
9800 GTX	G92	128	2GB	648	70	140
9800 GX2	G92	256	1GB	1152	2 x 64	197
260	G200	216	2GB	804	110	182
285	G200	240	2GB	1062	159	204
295	G200	480	1.8GB	1788	2 x 110	289
470	GF100	448	1.2GB	1088	134	215
480	GF100	448	1.5GB	1344	177	250
580	GF110	512	1.5GB	1581	152	244
590	GF110	1024	3GB	2488	2 x 164	365
680	GK104	1536	2GB	3090	192	195
690	GK104	3072	4GB	5620	2 x 192	300
Tesla C870	G80	128	1.5GB	518	77	171
Tesla C1060	G200	240	4GB	933	102	188
Tesla C2070	GF100	448	6GB	1288	144	247
Tesla K10	GK104	3072	8GB	5184	2 x 160	250

The great thing about CUDA is that, despite all the variability in hardware, programs written for the original CUDA devices can run on today's CUDA devices. The CUDA compilation model applies the same principle as used in Java—runtime compilation of a virtual instruction set. This allows modern GPUs to execute code from even the oldest generation GPUs. In many cases they benefit significantly from the original programmer reworking the program for the features of the newer GPUs. In fact, there is considerable scope for tuning for the various hardware revisions, which we'll cover toward the end of the book.

ALTERNATIVES TO CUDA

OpenCL

So what of the other GPU manufacturers, ATI (now AMD) being the prime example? AMD's product range is as impressive as the NVIDIA range in terms of raw computer power. However, AMD brought its stream computing technology to the marketplace a long time after NVIDIA brought out CUDA. As a consequence, NVIDA has far more applications available for CUDA than AMD/ATI does for its competing stream technology.

OpenCL and Direct compute is not something we'll cover in this book, but they deserve a mention in terms of alternatives to CUDA. CUDA is currently only officially executable on NVIDIA hardware. While NVIDIA has a sizeable chunk of the GPU market, its competitors also hold a sizeable chunk. As developers, we want to develop products for as large a market as possible, especially if we're talking about the consumer market. As such, people should be aware there are alternatives to CUDA, which support both NVIDIA's and others' hardware.

OpenCL is an open and royalty-free standard supported by NVIDIA, AMD, Intel and others. It sets out an open standard that allows the use of compute devices. A compute device can be a GPU, CPU, or other specialist device for which an OpenCL driver exists. As of 2012, OpenCL supports all major brands of GPU devices, including CPUs with at least SSE3 support.

Anyone who is familiar with CUDA can pick up OpenCL relatively easily, as the fundamental concepts are quite similar. However, OpenCL is somewhat more complex to use than CUDA, in that much of the work the CUDA runtime API does for the programmer needs to be explicitly performed in OpenCL.

You can read more about OpenCL at *http://www.khronos.org/opencl/*. There are also now a number of books written on OpenCL. I'd personally recommend learning CUDA prior to OpenCL as CUDA is somewhat of a higher-level language extension than OpenCL.

DirectCompute

DirectCompute is Microsoft's alternative to CUDA and OpenCL. It is a proprietary product linked to the Windows operating system, and in particular, the DirectX 11 API. The DirectX API was a huge leap forward for any of those who remember programming video cards before it. It meant the developers had to learn only one library API to program all graphics cards, rather than write or license drivers for each major video card manufacturer.

DirectX 11 is the latest standard and supported under Windows 7. With Microsoft's name behind the standard, you might expect to see some quite rapid adoption among the developer community. This is especially the case with developers already familiar with DirectX APIs. If you are familiar with CUDA and DirectCompute, then it is quite an easy task to port a CUDA application over to Direct-Compute. According to Microsoft, this is something you can typically do in an afternoon's work if you are familiar with both systems. However, being Windows centric, we'll exclude DirectCompute from many high-end systems where the various flavors of UNIX dominate.

Microsoft have also launched C++ AMP, an additional set of standard template libraries (STLs), which may appeal more to programmers already familiar with C++-style STLs.

CPU alternatives

The main parallel processing languages extensions are MPI, OpenMP, and pthreads if you are developing for Linux. For Windows there is the Windows threading model and OpenMP. MPI and pthreads are supported as various ports from the Unix world.

MPI (Message Passing Interface) is perhaps the most widely known messaging interface. It is process-based and generally found in large computing labs. It requires an administrator to configure the installation correctly and is best suited to controlled environments. Parallelism is expressed by spawning hundreds of processes over a cluster of nodes and explicitly exchanging messages, typically over high-speed network-based communication links (Ethernet or InfiniBand). MPI is widely used and taught. It's a good solution within a controlled cluster environment.

OpenMP (Open Multi-Processing) is a system designed for parallelism within a node or computer system. It works entirely differently, in that the programmer specifies various parallel directives through compiler pragmas. The compiler then attempts to automatically split the problem into N parts, according to the number of available processor cores. OpenMP support is built into many compilers, including the NVCC compiler used for CUDA. OpenMP tends to hit problems with scaling due to the underlying CPU architecture. Often the memory bandwidth in the CPU is just not large enough for all the cores continuously streaming data to or from memory.

Pthreads is a library that is used significantly for multithread applications on Linux. As with OpenMP, pthreads uses threads and not processes as it is designed for parallelism within a single node. However, unlike OpenMP, the programmer is responsible for thread management and synchronization. This provides more flexibility and consequently better performance for well-written programs.

ZeroMQ (0MQ) is also something that deserves a mention. This is a simple library that you link to, and we will use it later in the book for developing a multinode, multi-GPU example. ZeroMQ supports thread-, process-, and network-based communications models with a single cross-platform API. It is also available on both Linux and Windows platforms. It's designed for distributed computing, so the connections are dynamic and nodes fail gracefully.

Hadoop is also something that you may consider. Hadoop is an open-source version of Google's MapReduce framework. It's aimed primarily at the Linux platform. The concept is that you take a huge dataset and break (or map) it into a number of chunks. However, instead of sending the data to the node, the dataset is already split over hundreds or thousands of nodes using a parallel file system. Thus, the program, the reduce step, is instead sent to the node that contains the data. The output is written to the local node and remains there. Subsequent MapReduce programs take the previous output and again transform it in some way. As data is in fact mirrored to multiple nodes, this allows for a highly fault-tolerant as well as high-throughput system.

Directives and libraries

There are a number of compiler vendors, PGI, CAPS, and Cray being the most well-known, that support the recently announced OpenACC set of compiler directives for GPUs. These, in essence, replicate the approach of OpenMP, in that the programmer inserts a number of compiler directives marking regions as "to be executed on the GPU." The compiler then does the grunt work of moving data to or from the GPU, invoking kernels, etc.

As with the use of pthreads over OpenMP, with the lower level of control pthreads provides, you can achieve higher performance. The same is true of CUDA versus OpenACC. This extra level of control comes with a much higher level of required programming knowledge, a higher risk of errors, and the consequential time impact that may have on a development schedule. Currently, OpenACC requires directives to specify what areas of code should be run on the GPU, but also in which type of memory data should exist. NVIDIA claims you can get in the order of 5×plus speedup using such directives. It's a good solution for those programmers who need to get something working quickly. It's also great for those people for whom programming is a secondary consideration who just want the answer to their problem in a reasonable timeframe.

The use of libraries is also another key area where you can obtain some serious productivity gains, as well as execution time speedups. Libraries like SDK provide Thrust, which provides common functions implemented in a very efficient way. Libraries like CUBLAS are some of the best around for linear algebra. Libraries exist for many well-known applications such as Matlab and Mathematica. Language bindings exist for Python, Perl, Java, and many others. CUDA can even be integrated with Excel.

As with many aspects of software development in the modern age, the chances are that someone has done what you are about to develop already. Search the Internet and see what is already there before you spend weeks developing a library that, unless you are a CUDA expert, is unlikely to be faster than one that is already available. We look at libraries in chapter 10.

CONCLUSION

So maybe you're thinking, why develop in CUDA? The answer is that CUDA is currently the easiest language to develop in, in terms of support, debugging tools, and drivers. CUDA has a head start on everything else and has a huge lead in terms of maturity. If your application needs to support hardware other than NVIDIA's, then the best route currently is to develop under CUDA and then port the application to one of the other APIs. As such, we'll concentrate on CUDA, for if you become an expert with CUDA, it's easy to pick up alternative APIs should you need to. Understanding how CUDA works will allow you to better exploit and understand the limitations of any higher-level API.

The journey from a single-thread CPU programmer to a fully fledged parallel programmer on GPUs is one that I hope you will find interesting. Even if you never program a GPU in the future, the insight you gain will be of tremendous help in allowing you to design multithread programs. If you, like us, see the world changing to a parallel programming model, you'll want to be at the forefront of that wave of innovation and technological challenge. The single-thread industry is one that is slowly moving to obsolescence. To be a valuable asset and an employable individual, you need to have skills that reflect where the computing world is headed to, not those that are becoming progressively obsolete.

GPUs are changing the face of computing. All of a sudden the computing power of supercomputers from a decade ago can be slotted under your desk. No longer must you wait in a queue to submit work batches and wait months for a committee to approve your request to use limited computer resources at overstretched computing installations. You can go out, spend up to 5000–10,000 USD, and have a supercomputer on your desk, or a development machine that runs CUDA for a fraction of that. GPUs are a disruptive technological change that will make supercomputer-like levels of performance available for everyone.

Understanding Parallelism with GPUs

2

INTRODUCTION

This chapter aims to provide a broad introduction to the concepts of parallel programming and how these relate to GPU technology. It's primarily aimed at those people reading this text with a background in serial programming, but a lack of familiarity with parallel processing concepts. We look at these concepts in the primary context of GPUs.

TRADITIONAL SERIAL CODE

A significant number of programmers graduated when serial programs dominated the landscape and parallel programming attracted just a handful of enthusiasts. Most people who go to university get a degree related to IT because they are interested in technology. However, they also appreciate they need to have a job or career that pays a reasonable salary. Thus, in specializing, at least some consideration is given to the likely availability of positions after university. With the exception of research or academic posts, the number of commercial roles in parallel programming has always been, at best, small. Most programmers developed applications in a simple serial fashion based broadly on how universities taught them to program, which in turn was driven by market demand.

The landscape of parallel programming is scattered, with many technologies and languages that never quite made it to the mainstream. There was never really the large-scale market need for parallel hardware and, as a consequence, significant numbers of parallel programmers. Every year or two the various CPU vendors would bring out a new processor generation that executed code faster than the previous generation, thereby perpetuating legacy serial code.

Parallel programs by comparison were often linked closely to the hardware. Their goal was to achieve faster performance and often that was at the cost of portability. Feature X was implemented differently, or was not available in the next generation of parallel hardware. Periodically a revolutionary new architecture would appear that required a complete rewrite of all code. If your knowledge as a programmer was centered around processor X, it was valuable in the marketplace only so long as processor X was in use. Therefore, it made a lot more commercial sense to learn to program x86-type architecture than some exotic parallel architecture that may only be around for a few years.

However, over this time, a couple of standards did evolve that we still have today. The OpenMP standard addresses parallelism within a single node and is designed for shared memory machines that contain multicore processors. It does not have any concept of anything outside a single node or box. Thus, you are limited to problems that fit within a single box in terms of processing power, memory capacity, and storage space. Programming, however, is relatively easy as most of the low-level threading code (otherwise written using Windows threads or POSIX threads) is taken care of for you by OpenMP.

The MPI (Message Passing Interface) standard addresses parallelism between nodes and is aimed at clusters of machines within well-defined networks. It is often used in supercomputer installations where there may be many thousands of individual nodes. Each node holds a small section of the problem. Thus, common resources (CPU, cache, memory, storage, etc.) are multiplied by the number of nodes in the network. The Achilles' heel of any network is the various interconnects, the parts that connect the networked machines together. Internode communication is usually the dominating factor determining the maximum speed in any cluster-based solution.

Both OpenMP and MPI can be used together to exploit parallelism within nodes as well as across a network of machines. However, the APIs and the approaches used are entirely different, meaning they are often not used together. The OpenMP directives allow the programmer to take a high-level view of parallelism via specifying parallel regions. MPI by contrast uses an explicit interprocess communication model making the programmer do a lot more work.

Having invested the time to become familiar with one API, programmers are often loathe to learn another. Thus, problems that fit within one computer are often implemented with OpenMP solutions, whereas really large problems are implemented with cluster-based solutions such as MPI.

CUDA, the GPU programming language we'll explore in this text, can be used in conjunction with both OpenMP and MPI. There is also an OpenMP-like directive version of CUDA (OpenACC) that may be somewhat easier for those familiar with OpenMP to pick up. OpenMP, MPI, and CUDA are increasingly taught at undergraduate and graduate levels in many university computer courses.

However, the first experience most serial programmers had with parallel programming was the introduction of multicore CPUs. These, like the parallel environments before them, were largely ignored by all but a few enthusiasts. The primary use of multicore CPUs was for OS-based parallelism. This is a model based on *task parallelism* that we'll look at a little later.

As it became obvious that technology was marching toward the multicore route, more and more programmers started to take notice of the multicore era. Almost all desktops ship today with either a dual- or quad-core processor. Thus, programmers started using threads to allow the multiple cores on the CPU to be exploited.

A thread is a separate execution flow within a program that may diverge and converge as and when required with the main execution flow. Typically, CPU programs will have no more than twice the number of threads active than the number of physical processor cores. As with single-core processors, typically each OS task is time-sliced, given a small amount of time in turn, to give the illusion of running more tasks than there are physical CPU cores.

However, as the number of threads grows, this becomes more obvious to the end user. In the background the OS is having to context switch (swap in and out a set of registers) every time it needs to switch between tasks. As context switching is an expensive operation, typically thousands of cycles, CPU applications tend to have a fairly low number of threads compared with GPUs.

SERIAL/PARALLEL PROBLEMS

Threads brought with them many of the issues of parallel programming, primarily that of shared resources. Typically, sharing done with a semaphore, which is simply a lock or token. Whoever has the token can use the resource and everyone else has to wait for the user of the token to release it. As long as there is only a single token, everything works fine.

Problems occur when there are two or more tokens that must be shared by the same threads. In such situations, thread 0 grabs token 0, while thread 1 grabs token 1. Thread 0 now tries to grab token 1, while thread 1 tries to grab token 0. As the tokens are unavailable, both thread 0 and thread 1 sleep until the token becomes available. As neither thread ever releases the one token they already own, all threads wait forever. This is known as a deadlock, and it is something that can and will happen without proper design.

The opposite also happens—sharing of resources by chance. With any sort of locking system, all parties to a resource must behave correctly. That is, they must request the token, wait if necessary, and, only when they have the token, perform the operation. This relies on the programmer to identify shared resources and specifically put in place mechanisms to coordinate updates by multiple threads. However, there are usually several programmers in any given team. If just one of them doesn't follow this convention, or simply does not know this is a shared resource, you may appear to have a working program, but only by chance.

One of the projects I worked on for a large company had exactly this problem. All threads requested a lock, waited, and updated the shared resource. Everything worked fine and the particular code passed quality assurance and all tests. However, in the field occasionally users would report the value of a certain field being reset to 0, seemingly randomly. Random bugs are always terrible to track down, because being able to consistently reproduce a problem is often the starting point of tracking down the error.

An intern who happened to be working for the company actually found the issue. In a completely unrelated section of the code a pointer was not initialized under certain conditions. Due to the way the program ran, some of the time, depending on the thread execution order, the pointer would point to our protected data. The other code would then initialize "its variable" by writing 0 to the pointer, thus eliminating the contents of our "protected" and thread-shared parameter.

This is one of the unfortunate areas of thread-based operations; they operate with a shared memory space. This can be both an advantage in terms of not having to formally exchange data via messages, and a disadvantage in the lack of protection of shared data.

The alternative to threads is processes. These are somewhat heavier in terms of OS load in that both code *and* data contexts must be maintained by the OS. A thread by contrast needs to only maintain a code context (the program/instruction counter plus a set of registers) and shares the same data space. Both threads and processes may be executing entirely different sections of a program at any point in time.

Processes by default operate in an independent memory area. This usually is enough to ensure one process is unable to affect the data of other processes. Thus, the stray pointer issue should result in an exception for out-of-bounds memory access, or at the very least localize the bug to the particular process. Data consequently has to be transferred by formally passing messages to or from processes.

In many respects the threading model sits well with OpenMP, while the process model sits well with MPI. In terms of GPUs, they map to a hybrid of both approaches. CUDA uses a grid of blocks. This can be thought of as a queue (or a grid) of processes (blocks) with no interprocess communication. Within each block there are many threads which operate cooperatively in batches called *warps*. We will look at this further in the coming chapters.

CONCURRENCY

The first aspect of concurrency is to think about the particular problem, without regard for any implementation, and consider what aspects of it could run in parallel.

If possible, try to think of a formula that represents each output point as some function of the input data. This may be too cumbersome for some algorithms, for example, those that iterate over a large number of steps. For these, consider each step or iteration individually. Can the data points for the step be represented as a transformation of the input dataset? If so, then you simply have a set of kernels (steps) that run in sequence. These can simply be pushed into a queue (or stream) that the hardware will schedule sequentially.

A significant number of problems are known as "embarrassingly parallel," a term that rather underplays what is being achieved. If you can construct a formula where the output data points can be represented without relation to each other—for example, a matrix multiplication—be very happy. These types of problems can be implemented extremely well on GPUs and are easy to code.

If one or more steps of the algorithm can be represented in this way, but maybe one stage cannot, also be very happy. This single stage may turn out to be a bottleneck and may require a little thought, but the rest of the problem will usually be quite easy to code on a GPU.

If the problem requires every data point to know about the value of its surrounding neighbors then the speedup will ultimately be limited. In such cases, throwing more processors at the problem works up to a point. At this point the computation slows down due to the processors (or threads) spending more time sharing data than doing any useful work. The point at which you hit this will depend largely on the amount and cost of the communication overhead.

CUDA is ideal for an embarrassingly parallel problem, where little or no interthread or interblock communication is required. It supports interthread communication with explicit primitives using on-chip resources. Interblock communication is, however, only supported by invoking multiple kernels in series, communicating between kernel runs using off-chip global memory. It can also be performed in a somewhat restricted way through atomic operations to or from global memory.

CUDA splits problems into grids of blocks, each containing multiple threads. The blocks may run in any order. Only a subset of the blocks will ever execute at any one point in time. A block must execute from start to completion and may be run on one of N SMs (symmetrical multiprocessors). Blocks are allocated from the grid of blocks to any SM that has free slots. Initially this is done on a round-robin basis so each SM gets an equal distribution of blocks. For most kernels, the number of blocks needs to be in the order of eight or more times the number of physical SMs on the GPU.

To use a military analogy, we have an army (a grid) of soldiers (threads). The army is split into a number of units (blocks), each commanded by a lieutenant. The unit is split into squads of 32 soldiers (a warp), each commanded by a sergeant (See Figure 2.1).

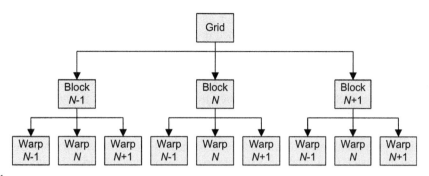

FIGURE 2.1

GPU-based view of threads.

To perform some action, central command (the kernel/host program) must provide some action plus some data. Each soldier (thread) works on his or her individual part of the problem. Threads may from time to time swap data with one another under the coordination of either the sergeant (the warp) or the lieutenant (the block). However, any coordination with other units (blocks) has to be performed by central command (the kernel/host program).

Thus, it's necessary to think of orchestrating thousands of threads in this very hierarchical manner when you think about how a CUDA program will implement concurrency. This may sound quite complex at first. However, for most embarrassingly parallel programs it's just a case of thinking of one thread generating a single output data point. A typical GPU has on the order of 24 K *active* threads. On Fermi GPUs you can define $65{,}535 \times 65{,}535 \times 1536$ threads in total, 24 K of which are active at any time. This is usually enough to cover most problems within a single node.

Locality

Computing has, over the last decade or so, moved from one limited by computational throughput of the processor, to one where moving the data is the primary limiting factor. When designing a processor in terms of processor real estate, compute units (or ALUs—algorithmic logic units) are cheap. They can run at high speed, and consume little power and physical die space. However, ALUs are of little use without operands. Considerable amounts of power and time are consumed in moving the operands to and from these functional units.

In modern computer designs this is addressed by the use of multilevel caches. Caches work on the principle of either spatial (close in the address space) or temporal (close in time) locality. Thus, data that has been accessed before, will likely be accessed again (temporal locality), and data that is close to the last accessed data will likely be accessed in the future (spatial locality).

Caches work well where the task is repeated many times. Consider for the moment a tradesperson, a plumber with a toolbox (a cache) that can hold four tools. A number of the jobs he will attend are similar, so the same four tools are repeatedly used (a cache hit).

However, a significant number of jobs require additional tools. If the tradesperson does not know in advance what the job will entail, he arrives and starts work. Partway through the job he needs an additional tool. As it's not in his toolbox (L1 cache), he retrieves the item from the van (L2 cache).

Occasionally he needs a special tool or part and must leave the job, drive down to the local hardware store (global memory), fetch the needed item, and return. Neither the tradesperson nor the client knows how long (the latency) this operation will actually take. There may be congestion on the freeway and/or queues at the hardware store (other processes competing for main memory access).

Clearly, this is not a very efficient use of the tradesperson's time. Each time a different tool or part is needed, it needs to be fetched by the tradesperson from either the van or the hardware store. While fetching new tools the tradesperson is not working on the problem at hand.

While this might seem bad, fetching data from a hard drive or SSD (solid-state drive) is akin to ordering an item at the hardware store. In comparative form, data from a hard drive arrives by regular courier several days later. Data from the SSD may arrive by overnight courier, but it's still very slow compared to accessing data in global memory.

In some more modern processor designs we have hardware threads. Some Intel processors feature hyperthreading, with two hardware threads per CPU core. To keep with the same analogy, this is equivalent to the tradesperson having an assistant and starting two jobs. Every time a new tool/part is required, the assistant is sent to fetch the new tool/part and the tradesperson switches to the alternate job. Providing the assistant is able to return with the necessary tool/part before the alternate job also needs an additional tool/part, the tradesperson continues to work.

Although an improvement, this has not solved the latency issue—how long it takes to fetch new tools/parts from the hardware store (global memory). Typical latencies to global memory are in the order of hundreds of clocks. Increasingly, the answer to this problem from traditional processor design has been to increase the size of the cache. In effect, arrive with a bigger van so fewer trips to the hardware store are necessary.

There is, however, an increasing cost to this approach, both in terms of capital outlay for a larger van and the time it takes to search a bigger van for the tool/part. Thus, the approach taken by most designs today is to arrive with a van (L2 cache) and a truck (L3 cache). In the extreme case of the server processors, a huge 18-wheeler is brought in to try to ensure the tradesperson is kept busy for just that little bit longer.

All of this work is necessary because of one fundamental reason. The CPUs are designed to run software where the programmer does not have to care about locality. Locality is an issue, regardless of whether the processor tries to hide it from the programmer or not. The denial that this is an issue is what leads to the huge amount of hardware necessary to deal with memory latency.

The design of GPUs takes a different approach. It places the GPU programmer in charge of dealing with locality and instead of an 18-wheeler truck gives him or her a number of small vans and a very large number of tradespeople.

Thus, in the first instance the programmer must deal with locality. He or she needs to think in advance about what tools/parts (memory locations/data structures) will be needed for a given job. These then need to be collected in a single trip to the hardware store (global memory) and placed in the correct van (on chip memory) for a given job at the outset. Given that this data has been collected, as much work as possible needs to be performed with the data to avoid having to fetch and return it only to fetch it again later for another purpose.

Thus, the continual cycle of work-stall-fetch from global memory, work-stall-fetch from global memory, etc. is broken. We can see the same analogy on a production line. Workers are supplied with baskets of parts to process, rather than each worker individually fetching widgets one at a time from the store manager's desk. To do otherwise is simply a hugely inefficient use of the available workers' time.

This simple process of planning ahead allows the programmer to schedule memory loads into the on-chip memory before they are needed. This works well with both an explicit local memory model such as the GPU's shared memory as well as a CPU-based cache. In the shared memory case you tell the memory management unit to request this data and then go off and perform useful work on another piece of data. In the cache case you can use special cache instructions that allow prefilling and/or locking of the cache with data you expect the program to use later.

The downside of the cache approach over the shared memory approach is eviction and dirty data. Data in a cache is said to be dirty if it has been written by the program. To free up the space in the cache for new useful data, the dirty data has to be written back to global memory before the cache space can be used again. This means instead of one trip to global memory of an unknown latency, we now have two—one to write the old data and one to get the new data.

The big advantage of the programmer-controlled on-chip memory is that the programmer is in control of when the writes happen. If you are performing some local transformation of the data, there may be no need to write the intermediate transformation back to global memory. With a cache, the cache controller does not know what needs to be written and what can be discarded. Thus, it writes everything, potentially creating lots of useless memory traffic that may in turn cause unnecessary congestion on the memory interface.

Although many do, not every algorithm lends itself to this type of "known in advance" memory pattern that the programmer can optimize for. At the same time, not every programmer wants to deal with locality issues, either initially or sometimes at all. It's a perfectly valid approach to develop a program, prove the concept, and then deal with locality issues.

To facilitate such an approach and to deal with the issues of algorithms that did not have a well-defined data/execution pattern, later generations of GPUs (compute 2.x onward) have both L1 and L2 caches. These can be configured with a preference toward cache or shared memory, allowing the programmer flexibility to configure the hardware for a given problem.

TYPES OF PARALLELISM

Task-based parallelism

If we look at a typical operating system, we see it exploit a type of parallelism called *task parallelism*. The processes are diverse and unrelated. A user might be reading an article on a website while playing music from his or her music library in the background. More than one CPU core can be exploited by running each application on a different core.

In terms of parallel programming, this can be exploited by writing a program as a number of sections that "pipe" (send via messages) the information from one application to another. The Linux pipe operator (the | symbol) does just this, via the operating system. The output of one program, such as grep, is the input of the next, such as sort. Thus, a set of input files can be easily scanned for a certain set of characters (the grep program) and that output set then sorted (the sort program). Each program can be scheduled to a separate CPU core.

This pattern of parallelism is known as *pipeline parallelism*. The output on one program provides the input for the next. With a diverse set of components, such as the various text-based tools in Linux, a huge variety of useful functions can be performed by the user. As the programmer cannot know at the outset everyone's needs, by providing components that operate together and can be connected easily, the programmer can target a very wide and diverse user base.

This type of parallelism is very much geared toward *coarse-grained parallelism*. That is, there are a number of powerful processors, each of which can perform a significant chunk of work.

In terms of GPUs we see coarse-grained parallelism only in terms of a GPU card and the execution of GPU kernels. GPUs support the pipeline parallelism pattern in two ways. First, kernels can be pushed into a single stream and separate streams executed concurrently. Second, multiple GPUs can work together directly through either passing data via the host or passing data via messages directly to one another over the PCI-E bus. This latter approach, the peer-to-peer (P2P) mechanism, was introduced in the CUDA 4.x SDK and requires certain OS/hardware/driver-level support.

One of the issues with a pipeline-based pattern is, like any production line, it can only run as fast as the slowest component. Thus, if the pipeline consists of five elements, each of which takes one second, we can produce one output per second. However, if just one of these elements takes two seconds, the throughput of the entire pipeline is reduced to one output every two seconds.

The approach to solving this is twofold. Let's consider the production line analogy for a moment. Fred's station takes two seconds because his task is complex. If we provide Fred with an assistant, Tim, and split his task in half with Tim, we're back to one second per stage. We now have six stages instead of five, but the throughput of the pipeline is now again one widget per second.

You can put up to four GPUs into a desktop PC with some thought and care about the design (see Chapter 11 on designing GPU systems). Thus, if we have a single GPU and it's taking too long to process a particular workflow, we can simply add another one and increase the overall processing power of the node. However, we then have to think about the division of work between the two GPUs. There may not be an easy 50/50 split. If we can only extract a 70/30 split, clearly the maximum benefit will be 7/10 (70%) of the existing runtime. If we could introduce another GPU and then maybe move another task, which occupied say 20% of the time, we'd end up with a 50/30/20 split. Again the speedup compared to one GPU would be 1/2 or 50% of the original time. We're still left with the worst-case time dominating the overall execution time.

The same issue applies to providing a speedup when using a single CPU/GPU combination. If we move 80% of the work off the CPU and onto the GPU, with the GPU computing this in just 10% of the time, what is the speedup? Well the CPU now takes 20% of the original time and the GPU 10% of the original time, but in parallel. Thus, the dominating factor is still the CPU. As the GPU is running in parallel and consumes less time than the CPU fraction, we can discount this time entirely. Thus, the maximum speedup is one divided by the fraction of the program that takes the longest time to execute.

This is known as Amdahl's law and is often quoted as the limiting factor in any speedup. It allows you to know at the outset what the maximum speedup achievable is, without writing a single line of code. Ultimately, you will have serial operations. Even if you move everything onto the GPU, you will still have to use the CPU to load and store data to and from storage devices. You will also have to transfer data to and from the GPU to facilitate input and output (I/O). Thus, maximum theoretical speedup is determined by the fraction of the program that performs the computation/algorithmic part, plus the remaining serial fraction.

Data-based parallelism

Computation power has been greatly increasing over the past couple of decades. We now have teraflop-capable GPUs. However, what has not kept pace with this evolution of compute power is the access time for data. The idea of data-based parallelism is that instead of concentrating on what tasks have to be performed, we look first to the data and how it needs to be transformed.

Task-based parallelism tends to fit more with coarse-grained parallelism approaches. Let's use an example of performing four different transformations on four separate, unrelated, and similarly sized arrays. We have four CPU cores, and a GPU with four SMs. In a task-based decomposition of the problem, we would assign one array to each of the CPU cores or SMs in the GPU. The parallel decomposition of the problem is driven by thinking about the tasks or transformations, not the data.

On the CPU side we could create four threads or processes to achieve this. On the GPU side we would need to use four blocks and pass the address of every array to every block. On the newer Fermi and Kepler devices, we could also create four separate kernels, one to process each array and run it concurrently.

A data-based decomposition would instead split the first array into four blocks and assign one CPU core or one GPU SM to each section of the array. Once completed, the remaining three arrays would be processed in a similar way. In terms of the GPU implementation, this would be four kernels, each of which contained four or more blocks. The parallel decomposition here is driven by thinking about the data first and the transformations second.

As our CPU has only four cores, it makes a lot of sense to decompose the data into four blocks. We could have thread 0 process element 0, thread 1 process element 1, thread 2 process element 2, thread 3 process element 3, and so on. Alternatively, the array could be split into four parts and each thread could start processing its section of the array.

In the first case, thread 0 fetches element 0. As CPUs contain multiple levels of cache, this brings the data into the device. Typically the L3 cache is shared by all cores. Thus, the memory access from the first fetch is distributed to all cores in the CPU. By contrast in the second case, four separate memory fetches are needed and four separate L3 cache lines are utilized. The latter approach is often better where the CPU cores need to write data back to memory. Interleaving the data elements by core means the cache has to coordinate and combine the writes from different cores, which is usually a bad idea.

If the algorithm permits, we can exploit a certain type of data parallelism, the SIMD (single instruction, multiple data) model. This would make use of special SIMD instructions such as MMX, SSE, AVX, etc. present in many x86-based CPUs. Thus, thread 0 could actually fetch multiple adjacent elements and process them with a single SIMD instruction.

If we consider the same problem on the GPU, each array needs to have a separate transformation performed on it. This naturally maps such that one transformation equates to a single GPU kernel (or program). Each SM, unlike a CPU core, is designed to run multiple blocks of data with each block split into multiple threads. Thus, we need a further level of decomposition to use the GPU efficiently. We'd typically allocate, at least initially, a combination of blocks and threads such that a single thread processed a single element of data. As with the CPU, there are benefits from processing multiple elements per thread. This is somewhat limited on GPUs as only load/store/move explicit SIMD primitives are supported, but this in turn allows for enhanced levels of *instruction-level parallelism* (ILP), which we'll see later is actually quite beneficial.

With a Fermi and Kepler GPUs, we have a shared L2 cache that replicates the L3 cache function on the CPU. Thus, as with the CPU, a memory fetch from one thread can be distributed to other threads directly from the cache. On older hardware, there is no cache. However, on GPUs adjacent memory locations are coalesced (combined) together by the hardware, resulting in a single and more efficient memory fetch. We look at this in detail in Chapter 6 on memory.

One important distinction between the caches found in GPUs and CPUs is cache coherency. In a cache-coherent system a write to a memory location needs to be communicated to all levels of cache in all cores. Thus, all processor cores see the same view of memory at any point in time. This is one of the key factors that limits the number of cores in a processor. Communication becomes increasingly more expensive in terms of time as the processor core count increases. The worst case in a cache-coherent system is where each core writes adjacent memory locations as each write forces a global update to every core's cache.

A non cache-coherent system by comparison does not automatically update the other core's caches. It relies on the programmer to write the output of each processor core to separate areas/addresses. This supports the view of a program where a single core is responsible for a single or small set of outputs. CPUs follow the cache-coherent approach whereas the GPU does not and thus is able to scale to a far larger number of cores (SMs) per device.

Let's assume for simplicity that we implement a kernel as four blocks. Thus, we have four kernels on the GPU and four processes or threads on the CPU. The CPU may support mechanisms such as hyperthreading to enable processing of additional threads/processes due to a stall event, a cache miss, for example. Thus, we could increase this number to eight and we might see an increase in performance. However, at some point, sometimes even at less than the number of cores, the CPU hits a point where there are just too many threads.

At this point the memory bandwidth becomes flooded and cache utilization drops off, resulting in less performance, not more.

On the GPU side, four blocks is nowhere near enough to satisfy four SMs. Each SM can actually schedule up to eight blocks (16 on Kepler). Thus, we'd need $8 \times 4 = 32$ blocks to load the four SMs correctly. As we have four independent operations, we can launch four simultaneous kernels on Fermi hardware via the streams feature (see Chapter 8 on using multiple GPUs). Consequently, we can launch 16 blocks in total and work on the four arrays in parallel. As with the CPU, however, it would be more efficient to work on one array at a time as this would likely result in better cache utilization. Thus, on the GPU we need to ensure we always have enough blocks (typically a minimum of 8 to 16 times the number of SMs on the GPU device).

FLYNN'S TAXONOMY

We mentioned the term SIMD earlier. This classification comes from Flynn's taxonomy, a classification of different computer architectures. The various types are as follows:

- SIMD—single instruction, multiple data
- MIMD—multiple instructions, multiple data
- SISD—single instruction, single data
- MISD—multiple instructions, single data

The standard serial programming most people will be familiar with follows the SISD model. That is, there is a single instruction stream working on a single data item at any one point in time. This equates to a single-core CPU able to perform one task at a time. Of course it's quite possible to provide the illusion of being able to perform more than a single task by simply switching between tasks very quickly, a technique called time-slicing.

MIMD systems are what we see today in dual- or quad-core desktop machines. They have a work pool of threads/processes that the OS will allocate to one of N CPU cores. Each thread/process has an independent stream of instructions, and thus the hardware contains all the control logic for decoding many separate instruction streams.

SIMD systems try to simplify this approach, in particular with the data parallelism model. They follow a single instruction stream at any one point in time. Thus, they require a single set of logic inside the device to decode and execute the instruction stream, rather than multiple-instruction decode paths. By removing this silicon real estate from the device, they can be smaller, cheaper, consume less power, and run at higher clock rates than their MIMD cousins.

Many algorithms make use of a small number of data points in one way or another. The data points can often be arranged as a SIMD instruction. Thus, all data points may have some fixed offset added, followed by a multiplication, a gain factor for example. This can be easily implemented as SIMD instructions. In effect, you are programming "for this range of data, perform this operation" instead of "for this data point, perform this operation." As the data operation or transformation is constant for all elements in the range, it can be fetched and decoded from the program memory only once. As the range is defined and contiguous, the data can be loaded en masse from the memory, rather than one word at a time.

However, algorithms where one element has transformation A applied while another element has transformation B applied, and all others have transformation C applied, are difficult to implement using SIMD. The exception is where this algorithm is hard-coded into the hardware because it's very common. Such examples include AES (Advanced Encryption Standard) and H.264 (a video compression standard).

The GPU takes a slightly different approach to SIMD. It implements a model NVIDIA calls SIMT (single instruction, multiple thread). In this model the instruction side of the SIMD instruction is not a fixed function as it is within the CPU hardware. The programmer instead defines, through a kernel, what each thread will do. Thus, the kernel will read the data uniformly and the kernel code will execute transformation A, B, or C as necessary. In practice, what happens is that A, B, and C are executed in sequence by repeating the instruction stream and masking out the nonparticipating threads. However, conceptually this is a much easier model to work with than one that only supports SIMD.

SOME COMMON PARALLEL PATTERNS

A number of parallel problems can be thought of as patterns. We see patterns in many software programs, although not everyone is aware of them. Thinking in terms of patterns allows us to broadly deconstruct or abstract a problem, and therefore more easily think about how to solve it.

Loop-based patterns

Almost anyone who has done any programming is familiar with loops. They vary primarily in terms of entry and exit conditions (`for`, `do...while`, `while`), and whether they create dependencies between loop iterations or not.

A loop-based iteration dependency is where one iteration of the loop depends on one or more previous iterations. We want to remove these if at all possible as they make implementing parallel algorithms more difficult. If in fact this can't be done, the loop is typically broken into a number of blocks that are executed in parallel. The result from block 0 is then retrospectively applied to block 1, then to block 2, and so on. There is an example later in this text where we adopt just such an approach when handling the prefix-sum algorithm.

Loop-based iteration is one of the easiest patterns to parallelize. With inter-loop dependencies removed, it's then simply a matter of deciding how to split, or partition, the work between the available processors. This should be done with a view to minimizing communication between processors and maximizing the use of on-chip resources (registers and shared memory on a GPU; L1/L2/L3 cache on a CPU). Communication overhead typically scales badly and is often the bottleneck in poorly designed systems.

The macro-level decomposition should be based on the number of logical processing units available. For the CPU, this is simply the number of logical hardware threads available. For the GPU, this is the number of SMs multiplied by the maximum load we can give to each SM, 1 to 16 blocks depending on resource usage. Notice we use the term *logical* and not physical hardware thread. Some Intel CPUs in particular support more than one logical thread per physical CPU core, so-called hyperthreading. GPUs run multiple blocks on a single SM, so we have to at least multiply the number of SMs by the maximum number of blocks each SM can support.

Using more than one thread per physical device maximizes the throughput of such devices, in terms of giving them something to do while they may be waiting on either a memory fetch or I/O-type operation. Selecting some multiple of this minimum number can also be useful in terms of load balancing on the GPU and allows for improvements when new GPUs are released. This is particularly the case when the partition of the data would generate an uneven workload, where some blocks take much longer than others. In this case, using many times the number of SMs as the basis of the partitioning of the data allows slack SMs to take work from a pool of available blocks.

However, on the CPU side, over subscribing the number of threads tends to lead to poor performance. This is largely due to context switching being performed in software by the OS. Increased contention for the cache and memory bandwidth also contributes significantly should you try to run too many threads. Thus, an existing multicore CPU solution, taken as is, typically has far too large a granularity for a GPU. You will almost always have to repartition the data into many smaller blocks to solve the same problem on the GPU.

When considering loop parallelism and porting an existing serial implementation, be critically aware of hidden dependencies. Look carefully at the loop to ensure one iteration does not calculate a value used later. Be wary of loops that count down as opposed to the standard zero to max value construct, the most common type of loop found. Why did the original programmer count backwards? It is likely this may be because there is some dependency in the loop and parallelizing it without understanding the dependencies will likely break it.

We also have to consider loops where we have an inner loop and one or more outer loops. How should these be parallelized? On a CPU the approach would be to parallelize only the outer loop as you have only a limited number of threads. This works well, but as before it depends on there being no loop iteration dependencies.

On the GPU the inner loop, provided it is small, is typically implemented by threads within a single block. As the loop iterations are grouped, adjacent threads usually access adjacent memory locations. This often allows us to exploit locality, something very important in CUDA programming. Any outer loop(s) are then implemented as blocks of the threads. These are concepts we cover in detail in Chapter 5.

Consider also that most loops can be flattened, thus reducing an inner and outer loop to a single loop. Think about an image processing algorithm that iterates along the X pixel axis in the inner loop and the Y pixel axis in the outer loop. It's possible to flatten this loop by considering all pixels as a single-dimensional array and iterating over pixels as opposed to image coordinates. This requires a little more thought on the programming side, but it may be useful if one or more loops contain a very small number of iterations. Such small loops present considerable loop overhead compared to the work done per iteration. They are, therefore, typically not efficient.

Fork/join pattern

The fork/join pattern is a common pattern in serial programming where there are synchronization points and only certain aspects of the program are parallel. The serial code runs and at some point hits a section where the work can be distributed to P processors in some manner. It then "forks" or spawns N threads/processes that perform the calculation in parallel. These then execute independently and finally converge or join once *all* the calculations are complete. This is typically the approach found in OpenMP and OpenACC, where you define a parallel region with pragma statements. The code then splits into N threads and later converges to a single thread again.

In Figure 2.2, we see a queue of data items. As we have three processing elements (e.g., CPU cores), these are split into three queues of data, one per processing element. Each is processed independently and then written to the appropriate place in the destination queue.

The fork/join pattern is typically implemented with static partitioning of the data. That is, the serial code will launch N threads and divide the dataset equally between the N threads. If each packet of data takes the same time to process, then this works well. However, as the overall time to execute is the time of the slowest thread, giving one thread too much work means it becomes the single factor determining the total time.

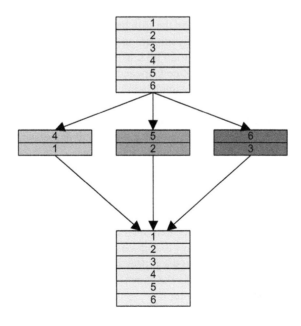

FIGURE 2.2

A queue of data processed by N threads.

Systems such as OpenMP also have dynamic scheduling allocation, which mirrors the approach taken by GPUs. Here a thread pool is created (a block pool for GPUs) and only once one task is completed is more work allocated. Thus, if 1 task takes 10x time and 20 tasks take just 1x time each, they are allocated only to free cores. With a dual-core CPU, core 1 gets the big 10x task and five of the smaller 1x tasks. Core 2 gets 15 of the smaller 1x tasks, and therefore both CPU core 1 and 2 complete around the same time.

In this particular example, we've chosen to fork three threads, yet there are six data items in the queue. Why not fork six threads? The reality is that in most problems there can actually be millions of data items and attempting to fork a million threads will cause almost all OSs to fail in one way or another.

Typically an OS will apply a "fair" scheduling policy. Thus, each of the million threads would need to be processed in turn by one of perhaps four available processor cores. Each thread also requires its own memory space. In Windows a thread can come with a 1 MB stack allocation, meaning we'd rapidly run out of memory prior to being able to fork enough threads.

Therefore on CPUs, typically programmers and many multithreaded libraries will use the number of logical processor threads available as the number of processes to fork. As CPU threads are typically also expensive to create and destroy, and also to limit maximum utilization, often a thread pool of workers is used who then fetch work from a queue of possible tasks.

On GPUs we have the opposite problem, in that we in fact need thousands or tens of thousands of threads. We have exactly the thread pool concept we find on more advanced CPU schedulers, except it's more like a block pool than a thread pool. The GPU has an upper limit on the number of *concurrent* blocks it can execute. Each block contains a number of threads. Both the number of threads per block and the overall number of concurrently running blocks vary by GPU generation.

The fork/join pattern is often used when there is an unknown amount of concurrency in a problem. Traversing a tree structure or a path exploration type algorithm may spawn (fork) additional threads when it encounters another node or path. When the path has been fully explored these threads may then join back into the pool of threads or simply complete to be respawned later.

This pattern is not natively supported on a GPU, as it uses a fixed number of blocks/threads at kernel launch time. Additional blocks cannot be launched by the kernel, only the host program. Thus, such algorithms on the GPU side are typically implemented as a series of GPU kernel launches, each of which needs to generate the next state. An alternative is to coordinate or signal the host and have it launch additional, concurrent kernels. Neither solution works particularly well, as GPUs are designed for a static amount of concurrency. Kepler introduces a concept, dynamic parallelism, which addresses this issue. See chapter 12 for more information on this.

Within a block of threads on a GPU there are a number of methods to communication between threads and to coordinate a certain amount of problem growth or varying levels of concurrency within a kernel. For example, if you have an 8×8 matrix you may have many places where just 64 threads are active. However, there may be others where 256 threads can be used. You can launch 256 threads and leave most of them idle until such time as needed. Such idle threads occupy resources and may limit the overall throughput, but do not consume any execution time on the GPU whilst idle. This allows the use of shared memory, fast memory close to the processor, rather than creating a number of distinct steps that need to be synchronized by using the much slower global memory and multiple kernel launches. We look at memory types in Chapter 6.

Finally, most GPUs support fast atomic operations and synchronization primitives that communicate data between threads in addition to simply synchronizing. We look at some examples of this later in the text.

Tiling/grids

The approach CUDA uses with all problems is to require the programmer to break the problem into smaller parts. Most parallel approaches make use of this concept in one way or another. Even in huge supercomputers problems such climate models must be broken down into hundreds of thousands of blocks, each of which is then allocated to one of the thousands of processing elements present in the machine. This type of parallel decomposition has the huge advantage that it scales really well.

A GPU is in many ways similar to a symmetrical multiprocessor system on a single device. Each SM is a processor in its own right, capable of running up multiple blocks of threads, typically 256 or 512 threads per block. A number of SMs exist on a single GPU and share a common global memory space. Together as a single GPU they can operate at peak speeds of up to 3 teraflops/s (GTX680).

While peak performance may be impressive, achieving anything like this is not possible without specially crafted programs, as this peak performance does not include things such as memory access, which is somewhat key to any real program. To achieve good performance on any platform requires a good knowledge of the hardware and the understanding of two key concepts—concurrency and locality.

There is concurrency in many problems. It's just that as someone who may come from a serial background, you may not immediately see the concurrency in a problem. The tiling model is thus an easy model to conceptualize. Imagine the problem in two dimensions—a flat arrangement of data—and simply overlay a grid onto the problem space. For a three-dimensional problem imagine the problem as a Rubik's Cube—a set of blocks that map onto the problem space.

CUDA provides the simple two-dimensional grid model. For a significant number of problems this is entirely sufficient. If you have a linear distribution of work within a single block, you have an ideal decomposition into CUDA blocks. As we can assign up to sixteen blocks per SM and we can have up to 16 SMs (30 on some GPUs), any number of blocks of 256 or larger is fine. In practice, we'd like to limit the number of elements within the block to 128, 256, or 512, so this in itself may drive much larger numbers of blocks with a typical dataset.

When considering concurrency, consider also if there is ILP that can be exploited. Conceptually it's easier to think about a single thread being associated with a single output data item. If, however, we can fill the GPU with threads on this basis and there is still more data that could be processed, can we still improve the throughput? The answer is yes, but only through the use of ILP.

ILP exploits the fact that instruction streams can be pipelined within the processor. Thus, it is more efficient to push four add operations into the queue, wait, and then collect them one at a time (push-push-push-push-wait), rather than perform them one at a time (push-wait-push-wait-push-wait-push-wait). For most GPUs, you'll find an ILP level of four operations per thread works best. There are some detailed studies and examples of this in Chapter 9. Thus, if possible we'd like to process N elements per thread, but not to the extent that it reduces the overall number of active threads.

Divide and conquer

The divide-and-conquer pattern is also a pattern for breaking down large problems into smaller sections, each of which can be conquered. Taken together these individual computations allow a much larger problem to be solved.

Typically you see divide-and-conquer algorithms used with recursion. Quick sort is a classic example of this. It recursively partitions the data into two sets, those above a pivot point and those below the pivot point. When the partition finally consists of just two items, they are compared and swapped.

Most recursive algorithms can also be represented as an iterative model, which is usually somewhat easier to map onto the GPU as it fits better into the primary tile-based decomposition model of the GPU.

Recursive algorithms are also supported on Fermi-class GPUs onwards, although as with the CPU you have to be aware of the maximum call depth and translate this into stack usage. The available stack can be queried with API call `cudaDeviceGetLimit()`. It can also be set with the API call `cudaDeviceSetLimit()`. Failure to allocate enough stack space, as with CPUs, will result in the program failing. Some debugging tools such as Parallel Nsight and CUDA-GDB can detect such stack overflow issues.

In selecting a recursive algorithm be aware that you are making a tradeoff of development time versus performance. It may be easier to conceptualize and therefore code a recursive algorithm than to try to convert such an approach to an iterative one. However, each recursive call causes any formal parameters to be pushed onto the stack along with any local variables. GPUs and CPUs implement a stack in the same way, simply an area of memory from the global memory space. Although CPUs and the Fermi-class GPUs cache this area, compared to passing values using registers, this is slow. Use iterative solutions where possible as they will generally perform much better and run on a wider range of GPU hardware.

CONCLUSION

We've looked here at a broad overview of some parallel processing concepts and how these are applied to the GPUs in particular. It's not the purpose of this text to write a volume on parallel processing, for there are entire books devoted to this subject. We want readers to have some feeling for the issues that parallel programming bring to the table that would not otherwise be thought about in a serial programming environment.

In subsequent chapters we cover some of these concepts in detail in terms of practical examples. We also look at parallel prefix-sum, an algorithm that allows multiple writers of data to share a common array without writing over one another's data. Such algorithms are never needed for serial based programming.

With parallelism comes a certain amount of complexity and the need for a programmer to think and plan ahead to consider the key issues of concurrency and locality. Always keep these two key concepts in mind when designing any software for the GPU.

CUDA Hardware Overview

PC ARCHITECTURE

Let's start by looking at the Core 2 architecture we still find today in many PCs and how it impacts our usage of GPU accelerators (Figure 3.1).

Notice that all GPU devices are connected to the processor via the PCI-E bus. In this case we've assumed a PCI-E 2.0 specification bus, giving an effective transfer rate of 5 GB/s. PCI-E 3.0 had just become available at the time of this writing and should significantly improve the bandwidth available.

However, to get data from the processor, we need to go through the Northbridge device over the slow FSB (front-side bus). The FSB can run anything up to 1600 MHz clock rate, although in many designs it is much slower. This is typically only one-third of the clock rate of a fast processor.

Memory is also accessed through the Northbridge, with peripherals routed through the Northbridge and Southbridge chipset. The Northbridge deals with all the high-speed components like memory, CPU and PCI-E bus connections. The Southbridge chip deals with the slower devices such as hard disks, USB, keyboard, network connections, etc. Of course, it's quite possible to connect a hard-disk controller to the PCI-E connection, and in practice, this is the only true way of getting RAID high-speed data access on such a system.

PCI-E (Peripheral Communications Interconnect Express) is an interesting bus as, unlike its predecessor, PCI (Peripheral Component Interconnect), it's based on guaranteed bandwidth. In the old PCI system each component could use the full bandwidth of the bus, but only one device at a time. Thus, the more cards you added, the less available bandwidth each card would receive. PCI-E solved this problem by the introduction of PCI-E lanes. These are high-speed serial links that can be combined together to form X1, X2, X4, X8, or X16 links. Most GPUs now use at least the PCI-E 2.0, X16 specification, as shown in Figure 3.1. With this setup, we have a 5 GB/s full-duplex bus, meaning we get the same upload and download speed, at the same time. Thus, we can transfer 5 GB/s to the card, while at the same time receiving 5 GB/s from the card. However, this does not mean we can transfer 10 GB/s *to* the card if we're not receiving any data (i.e., the bandwidth is not cumulative).

In a typical supercomputer environment, or even in a desktop application, we are dealing with a large dataset. A supercomputer may deal with petabytes of data. A desktop PC may be dealing with as little as a several GB high-definition video. In both cases, there is considerable data to fetch from the attached peripherals. A single 100 MB/s hard disk will load 6 GB of data in one minute. At this rate it takes over two and a half hours to read the entire contents of a standard 1 TB disk.

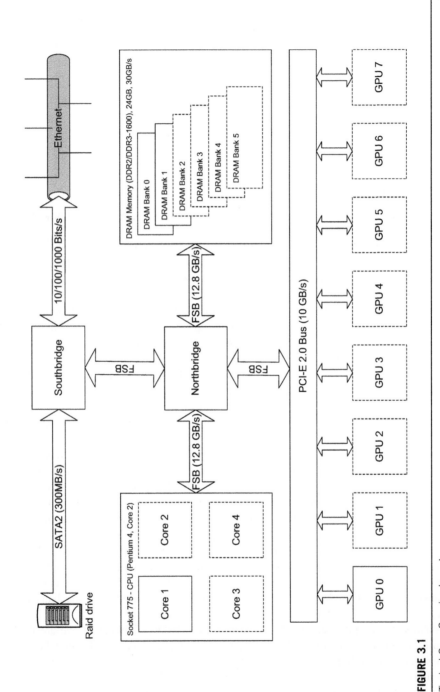

FIGURE 3.1

Typical Core 2 series layout.

If using MPI (Message Passing Interface), commonly used in clusters, the latency for this arrangement can be considerable if the Ethernet connections are attached to the Southbridge instead of the PCI-E bus. Consequently, dedicated high-speed interconnects like InfiniBand or 10 Gigabit Ethernet cards are often used on the PCI-E bus. This removes slots otherwise available for GPUs. Previously, as there was no direct GPU MPI interface, all communications in such a system are routed over the PCI-E bus to the CPU and back again. The GPU-Direct technology, available in the CUDA 4.0 SDK, solved this issue and it's now possible for certain InfiniBand cards to talk directly to the GPU without having to go through the CPU first. This update to the SDK also allows direct GPU to GPU communication.

We saw a number of major changes with the advent of the Nehalem architecture. The main change was to replace the Northbridge and the Southbridge chipset with the X58 chipset. The Nehalem architecture brought us QPI (Quick Path Interconnect), which was actually a huge advance over the FSB (Front Side Bus) approach and is similar to AMD's HyperTransport. QPI is a high-speed interconnect that can be used to talk to other devices or CPUs. In a typical Nehalem system it will connect to the memory subsystem, and through an X58 chipset, the PCI-E subsystem (Figure 3.2). The QPI runs at either 4.8 GT/s or 6.4 GT/s in the Extreme/Xeon processor versions.

With the X58 and 1366 processor socket, a total of 36 PCI-E lanes are available, which means up to two cards are supported at X16, or four cards at X8. Prior to the introduction of the LGA2011 socket, this provided the best bandwidth solution for a GPU machine to date.

The X58 design is also available in a lesser P55 chipset where you get only 16 lanes. This means one GPU card at X16, or two cards at X8.

From the I7/X58 chipset design, Intel moved onto the Sandybridge design, shown in Figure 3.3. One of the most noticeable improvements was the support for the SATA-3 standard, which supports 600 MB/s transfer rates. This, combined with SSDs, allows for considerable input/output (I/O) performance with loading and saving data.

The other major advance with the Sandybridge design was the introduction of the AVX (Advanced Vector Extensions) instruction set, also supported by AMD processors. AVX allows for vector instructions that provide up to four double-precision (256 bit/32 byte) wide vector operations. It's a very interesting development and something that can be used to considerably speed up compute-bound applications on the CPU.

Notice, however, the big downside of socket 1155 Sandybridge design: It supports only 16 PCI-E lanes, limiting the PCI-E bandwidth to 16 GB/s theoretical, 10 GB/s actual bandwidth. Intel has gone down the route of integrating more and more into the CPU with their desktop processors. Only the socket 2011 Sandybridge-E, the server offering, has a reasonable number of PCI-E lanes (40).

So how does AMD compare with the Intel designs? Unlike Intel, which has gradually moved away from large numbers of PCI-E lanes, in all but their server line, AMD have remained fairly constant. Their FX chipset, provides for either two X16 devices or four X8 PCI-E devices. The AMD3+ socket paired with the 990FX chipset makes for a good workhorse, as it provides SATA 6 GB/s ports paired with up to four X16 PCI-E slots (usually running at X8 speed).

One major difference between Intel and AMD is the price point for the number of cores. If you count only real processor cores and ignore logical (hyperthreaded) ones, for the same price point, you typically get more cores on the AMD device. However, the cores on the Intel device tend to perform better. Therefore, it depends a lot on the number of GPUs you need to support and the level of loading of the given cores.

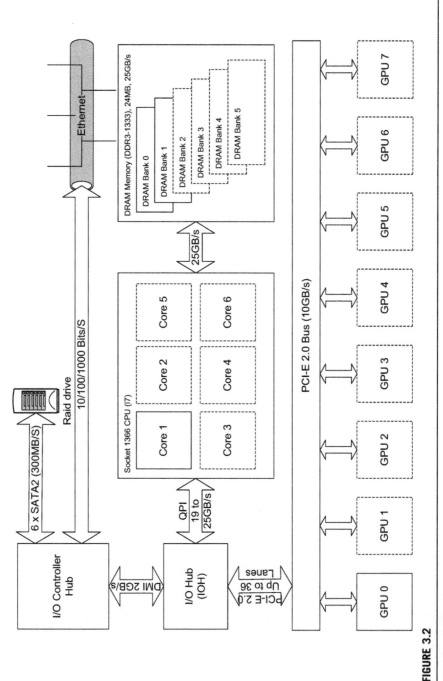

FIGURE 3.2

Nehalem/X58 system.

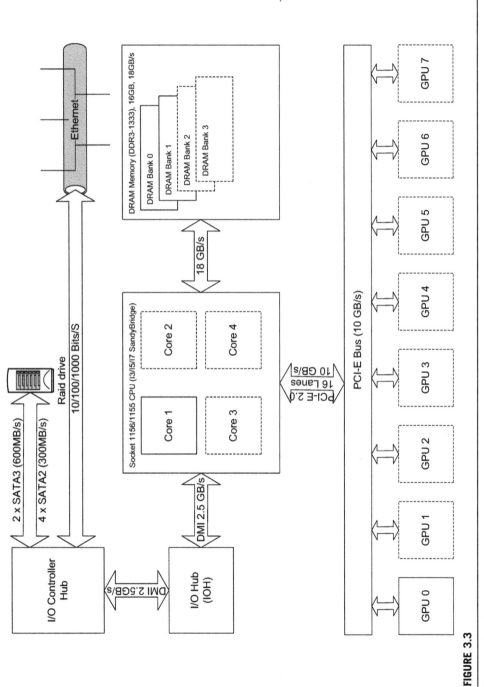

FIGURE 3.3

Sandybridge design.

As with the Intel design, you see similar levels of bandwidth around the system, with the exception of bandwidth to main memory. Intel uses triple or quad channel memory on their top-end systems and dual-channel memory on the lower-end systems. AMD uses only dual-channel memory, leading to significantly less CPU host-memory bandwidth being available (Figure 3.4).

One significant advantage of the AMD chipsets over the Intel ones is the support for up to six SATA (Serial ATA) 6 GB/s ports. If you consider that the slowest component in any system usually limits the overall throughput, this is something that needs some consideration. However, SATA3 can very quickly overload the bandwidth of Southbridge when using multiple SSDs (solid state drives). A PCI-E bus solution may be a better one, but it obviously requires additional costs.

GPU HARDWARE

GPU hardware is radically different than CPU hardware. Figure 3.5 shows how a multi-GPU system looks conceptually from the other side of the PCI-E bus.

Notice the GPU hardware consists of a number of key blocks:

- Memory (global, constant, shared)
- Streaming multiprocessors (SMs)
- Streaming processors (SPs)

The main thing to notice here is that a GPU is really an array of SMs, each of which has N cores (8 in G80 and GT200, 32–48 in Fermi, 8 plus in Kepler; see Figure 3.6). This is the key aspect that allows scaling of the processor. A GPU device consists of one or more SMs. Add more SMs to the device and you make the GPU able to process more tasks at the same time, or the same task quicker, if you have enough parallelism in the task.

Like CPUs, if the programmer writes code that limits the processor usage to N cores, let's say dual-core, when the CPU manufacturers bring out a quad-core device, the user sees no benefit. This is exactly what happened in the transition from dual- to quad-core CPUs, and lots of software then had to be rewritten to take advantage of the additional cores. NVIDIA hardware will increase in performance by growing a combination of the number of SMs and number of cores per SM. When designing software, be aware that the next generation may double the number of either.

Now let's take a closer look at the SMs themselves. There are number of key components making up each SM, however, not all are shown here for reasons of simplicity. The most significant part is that there are multiple SPs in each SM. There are 8 SPs shown here; in Fermi this grows to 32–48 SPs and in Kepler to 192. There is no reason to think the next hardware revision will not continue to increase the number of SPs/SMs.

Each SM has access to a register file, which is much like a chunk of memory that runs at the same speed as the SP units, so there is effectively zero wait time on this memory. The size of this memory varies from generation to generation. It is used for storing the registers in use for the threads running on an SP. There is also a shared memory block accessible only to the individual SM that can be used as a program-managed cache. Unlike a CPU cache, there is no hardware evicting cache data behind your back—it's entirely under programmer control.

Each SM has a separate bus into the texture memory, constant memory, and global memory spaces. Texture memory is a special view onto the global memory, which is useful for data where

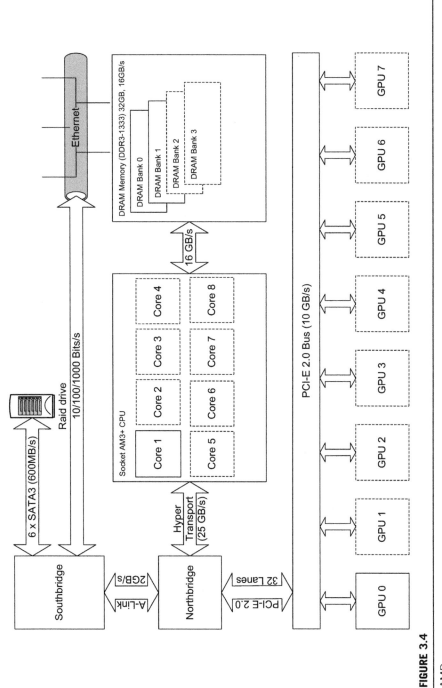

FIGURE 3.4

AMD.

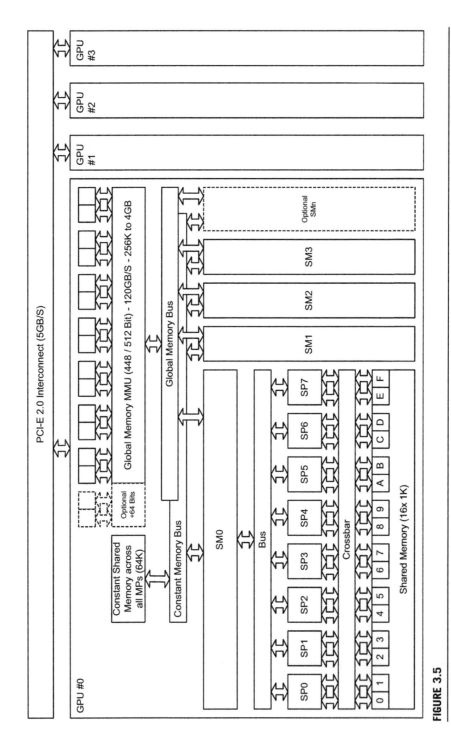

FIGURE 3.5

Block diagram of a GPU (G80/GT200) card.

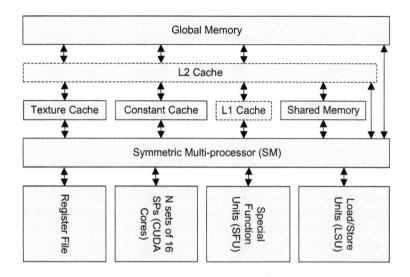

FIGURE 3.6

Inside an SM.

there is interpolation, for example, with 2D or 3D lookup tables. It has a special feature of hardware-based interpolation. Constant memory is used for read-only data and is cached on all hardware revisions. Like texture memory, constant memory is simply a view into the main global memory.

Global memory is supplied via GDDR (Graphic Double Data Rate) on the graphics card. This is a high-performance version of DDR (Double Data Rate) memory. Memory bus width can be up to 512 bits wide, giving a bandwidth of 5 to 10 times more than found on CPUs, up to 190 GB/s with the Fermi hardware, 288 GB/s with Kepler.

Each SM also has two or more special-purpose units (SPUs), which perform special hardware instructions, such as the high-speed 24-bit sin/cosine/exponent operations. Double-precision units are also present on GT200 and Fermi hardware.

CPUS AND GPUS

Now that you have some idea what the GPU hardware looks like, you might say that this is all very interesting, but what does it mean for us in terms of programming?

Anyone who has ever worked on a large project will know it's typically partitioned into sections and allocated to specific groups. There may be a specification group, a design group, a coding group, and a testing group. There are absolutely huge benefits to having people in each team who understand completely the job of the person before and after them in the chain of development.

Take, for example, testing. If the designer did not consider testing, he or she would not have included any means to test in software-specific hardware failures. If the test team could only test hardware failure by having the hardware fail, it would have to physically modify hardware to cause such failures. This is hard. It's much easier for the software people to design a flag that inverts the hardware-based error flag in software, thus allowing the failure functionality to be tested easily. Working on the testing team you might see how hard it is to do it any other way, but with a blinkered view of your own discipline, you might say that testing is not your role.

Some of the best engineers are those with a view of the processes before and after them. As software people, it's always good to know how the hardware actually works. For serial code execution, it may be interesting to know how things work, but usually not essential. The vast majority of developers have never taken a computer architecture course or read a book on the subject, which is a great shame. It's one of the main reasons we see such inefficient software written these days. I grew up learning BASIC at age 11, and was programming Z80 assembly language at 14, but it was only during my university days that I really started to understand computer architecture to any great depth.

Working in an embedded field gives you a very hands-on approach to hardware. There is no nice Windows operating system to set up the processor for you. Programming is a very low-level affair. With embedded applications, there are typically millions of boxes shipped. Sloppy code means poor use of the CPU and available memory, which could translate into needing a faster CPU or more memory. An additional 50 cent cost on a million boxes is half a million dollars. This translates into a lot of design and programming hours, so clearly it's more cost effective to write better code than buy additional hardware.

Parallel programming, even today, is very much tied to the hardware. If you just want to write code and don't care about performance, parallel programming is actually quite easy. To really get performance out of the hardware, you need to understand how it works. Most people can drive a car safely and slowly in first gear, but if you are unaware that there are other gears, or do not have the knowledge to engage them, you will never get from point A to point B very quickly. Learning about the hardware is a little like learning to change gear in a car with a manual gearbox—a little tricky at first, but something that comes naturally after awhile. By the same analogy, you can also buy a car with an automatic gearbox, akin to using a library already coded by someone who understands the low-level mechanics of the hardware. However, doing this without understanding the basics of how it works will often lead to a suboptimal implementation.

COMPUTE LEVELS

CUDA supports a number of compute levels. The original G80 series graphics cards shipped with the first version of CUDA. The compute capability is fixed into the hardware. To upgrade to a newer version users had to upgrade their hardware. Although this might sound like NVIDIA trying to force users to buy more cards, it in fact brings many benefits. When upgrading a compute level, you can often move from an older platform to a newer one, usually doubling the compute capacity of the card for a similar price to the original card. Given that NVIDIA typically brings out a new platform at least every couple of years, we have seen to date a huge increase in available compute power over the few years CUDA has been available.

A full list of the differences between each compute level can be found in the NVIDIA CUDA Programming Guide, Appendix G, which is shipped as part of the CUDA SDK. Therefore, we will only cover the major differences found at each compute level, that is, what you need to be aware of as a developer.

Compute 1.0

Compute level 1.0 is found on the older graphics cards, for example, the original 8800 Ultras and many of the 8000 series cards as well as the Tesla C/D/S870s. The main features lacking in compute 1.0 cards are those for atomic operations. Atomic operations are those where we can guarantee a complete operation without any other thread interrupting. In effect, the hardware implements a barrier point at the entry of the atomic function and guarantees the *completion* of the operation (add, sub, min, max, logical and, or, xor, etc.) as one operation. Compute 1.0 cards are effectively now obsolete, so this restriction, for all intents and purposes, can be ignored.

Compute 1.1

Compute level 1.1 is found in many of the later shipping 9000 series cards, such as the 9800 GTX, which were extremely popular. These are based on the G92 hardware as opposed to the G80 hardware of compute 1.0 devices.

One major change brought in with compute 1.1 devices was support, on many but not all devices, for overlapped data transfer and kernel execution. The SDK call to `cudaGetDeviceProperties()` returns the `deviceOverlap` property, which defines if this functionality is available. This allows for a very nice and important optimization called double buffering, which works as shown in Figure 3.7.

To use this method we require double the memory space we'd normally use, which may well be an issue if your target market only had a 512 MB card. However, with Tesla cards, used mainly for scientific computing, you can have up to 6 GB of GPU memory, which makes such techniques very useful. Let's look at what happens:

Cycle 0: Having allocated two areas of memory in the GPU memory space, the CPU fills the first buffer.

Cycle 1: The CPU then invokes a CUDA kernel (a GPU task) on the GPU, which returns immediately to the CPU (a nonblocking call). The CPU then fetches the next data packet, from a disk, the network, or wherever. Meanwhile, the GPU is processing away in the background on the data packet provided. When the CPU is ready, it starts filling the other buffer.

Cycle 2: When the CPU is done filling the buffer, it invokes a kernel to process buffer 1. It then checks if the kernel from cycle 1, which was processing buffer 0, has completed. If not, it waits until this kernel has finished and then fetches the data from buffer 0 and then loads the next data block into the same buffer. During this time the kernel kicked off at the start of the cycle is processing data on the GPU in buffer 1.

Cycle N: We then repeat cycle 2, alternating between which buffer we read and write to on the CPU with the buffer being processed on the GPU.

GPU-to-CPU and CPU-to-GPU transfers are made over the relatively slow (5 GB/s) PCI-E bus and this dual-buffering method largely hides this latency and keeps both the CPU and GPU busy.

Compute 1.2

Compute 1.2 devices appeared with the low-end GT200 series hardware. These were the initial GTX260 and GTX280 cards. With the GT200 series hardware, NVIDIA approximately doubled the

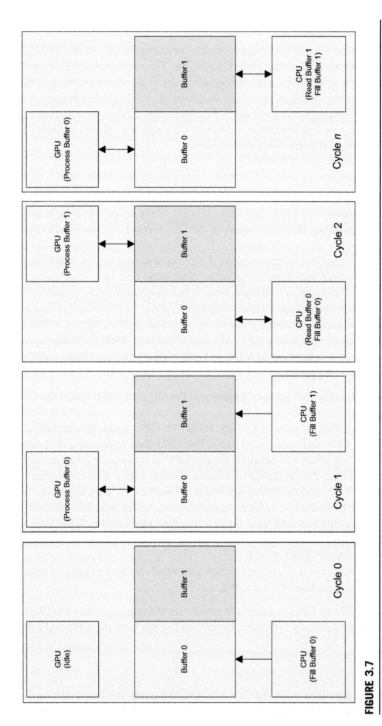

FIGURE 3.7

Double buffering with a single GPU.

number of CUDA core processors on a single card, through doubling the number of multiprocessors present on the card. We'll cover CUDA cores and multiprocessors later. In effect, this doubled the performance of the cards compared to the G80/G92 range before them.

Along with doubling the number of multiprocessors, NVIDIA increased the number of concurrent warps a multiprocessor could execute from 24 to 32. Warps are blocks of code that execute within a multiprocessor, and increasing the amount of available warps per multiprocessor gives us more scope to get better performance.

Issues with restrictions on coalesced access to the global memory and bank conflicts in the shared memory found in compute 1.0 and compute 1.1 devices were greatly reduced. This make the GT200 series hardware far easier to program and it greatly improved the performance of many previous, poorly written CUDA programs.

Compute 1.3

The compute 1.3 devices were introduced with the move from GT200 to the GT200 a/b revisions of the hardware. This followed shortly after the initial release of the GT200 series. Almost all higher-end cards from this era were compute 1.3 compatible.

The major change that occurs with compute 1.3 hardware is the introduction of support for limited double-precision calculations. GPUs are primarily aimed at graphics and here there is a huge need for fast single-precision calculations, but limited need for double-precision ones. Typically, you see an order of magnitude drop in performance using double-precision as opposed to single-precision floating-point operations, so time should be taken to see if there is any way single-precision arithmetic can be used to get the most out of this hardware. In many cases, a mixture of single and double-precision operations can be used, which is ideal since it exploits both the dedicated single-precision and double-precision hardware present.

Compute 2.0

Compute 2.0 devices saw the switch to Fermi hardware. The original guide for tuning applications for the Fermi architecture can be found on the NVIDIA website at http://developer.nvidia.com/cuda/nvidia-gpu-computing-documentation.

Some of the main changes in compute 2.x hardware are as follows:

- Introduction of 16 K to 48 K of L1 cache memory on each SP.
- Introduction of a shared L2 cache for all SMs.
- Support in Tesla-based devices for ECC (Error Correcting Code)-based memory checking and error correction.
- Support in Tesla-based devices for dual-copy engines.
- Extension in size of the shared memory from 16 K per SM up to 48 K per SM.
- For optimum coalescing of data, it must be 128-byte aligned.
- The number of shared memory banks increased from 16 to 32.

Let's look at the implications of some of these changes in detail. First, let's pick up on the introduction of the L1 cache and what this means. An L1 (level one) cache is a cache present on a device and is the fastest cache type available. Compute 1.x hardware has no cache, except for the texture and constant memory caches. The introduction of a cache makes it much easier for many programmers to write programs that work well on GPU hardware. It also allows for applications that do not follow a known memory pattern at compile time. However, to exploit the cache, the application either needs to have a sequential memory pattern or have at least some data reuse.

The L2 cache is up to 768 K in size on Fermi and, importantly, is a unified cache, meaning it is shared and provides a consistent view for all the SMs. This allows for much faster interblock communication through global atomic operations. Compared to having to go out to the global memory on the GPU, using the shared cache is an order of magnitude faster.

Support for ECC memory is a must for data centers. ECC memory provides for automatic error detection and correction. Electrical devices emit small amounts of radiation. When in close proximity to other devices, this radiation can change the contents of memory cells in the other device. Although the probability of this happening is tiny, as you increase the exposure of the equipment by densely packing it into data centers, the probability of something going wrong rises to an unacceptable level. ECC, therefore, detects and corrects single-bit upset conditions that you may find in large data centers. This reduces the amount of available RAM and negatively impacts memory bandwidth. Because this is a major drawback on graphics cards, ECC is only available on Tesla products.

Dual-copy engines allow you to extend the dual-buffer example we looked at earlier to use multiple streams. Streams are a concept we'll look at in detail later, but basically, they allow for N independent kernels to be executed in a pipeline fashion as shown in Figure 3.8.

Notice how the kernel sections run one after another in the figure. The copy operations are hidden by the execution of a kernel on another stream. The kernels and the copy engines execute concurrently, thus making the most use of the relevant units.

Note that the dual-copy engines are physically available on almost all the top-end Fermi GPUs, such as the GTX480 or GTX580 device. However, only the Tesla cards make both engines visible to the CUDA driver.

Shared memory also changed drastically, in that it was transformed into a combined L1 cache. The L1 cache size is 64 K. However, to preserve backward compatibility, a minimum of 16 K must be allocated to the shared memory, meaning the L1 cache is really only 48 K in size. Using a switch, shared memory and L1 cache usage can be swapped, giving 48 K of shared memory and 16 K of L1 cache. Going from 16 K of shared memory to 48 K of shared memory is a huge benefit for certain programs.

Alignment requirements for optimal use became more strict than in previous generations, due to the introduction of the L1 and L2 cache. Both use a cache line size of 128 bytes. A cache line is the *minimum* amount of data the memory can fetch. Thus, if your program fetches subsequent elements of

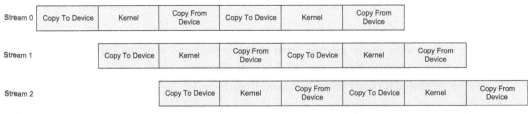

FIGURE 3.8

Stream pipelining.

the data, this works really well. This is typically what most CUDA programs do, with groups of threads fetching adjacent memory addresses. The one requirement that comes out of this change is to have 128-byte alignment of the dataset.

However, if your program has a sparse and distributed memory pattern per thread, you need to disable this feature and switch to the 32-bit mode of cache operation.

Finally, one of the last major changes we'll pick up on is the increase of shared memory banks from 16 to 32 bits. This is a major benefit over the previous generations. It allows each thread of the current warp (32 threads) to write to exactly one bank of 32 bits in the shared memory without causing a shared bank conflict.

Compute 2.1

Compute 2.1 is seen on certain devices aimed specifically at the games market, such as the GTX460 and GTX560. These devices change the architecture of the device as follows:

- 48 CUDA cores per SM instead of the usual 32 per SM.
- Eight single-precision, special-function units for transcendental per SM instead of the usual four.
- Dual-warp dispatcher instead of the usual single-warp dispatcher.

The x60 series cards have always had a very high penetration into the midrange games market, so if your application is targeted at the consumer market, it is important to be aware of the implication of these changes.

Noticeably different on the compute 2.1 hardware is the sacrifice of dual-precision hardware to increase the number of CUDA cores. For single-precision and integer calculation–dominated kernels, this is a good tradeoff. Most games make little use of double-precision floating-point data, but significant use of single-precision floating-point and integer math.

Warps, which we will cover in detail later, are groups of threads. On compute 2.0 hardware, the single-warp dispatcher takes two clock cycles to dispatch instructions of an entire warp. On compute 2.1 hardware, instead of two instruction dispatchers per two clock cycles, we now have four. In the hardware, there are three banks of 16 CUDA cores, 48 CUDA cores in total, instead of two banks of 16 CUDA cores. If NVIDIA could have just squeezed in another set of 16 CUDA cores, you'd have an ideal solution. Maybe we'll see this in future hardware.

The compute 2.1 hardware is actually a superscalar approach, similar to what is found on CPUs from the original Pentium CPU onwards. To make use of all the cores, the hardware needs to identify instruction-level parallelism (ILP) within a *single* thread. This is a significant divergence from the universal thread-level parallelism (TLP) approach recommended in the past. For ILP to be present there need to be instructions that are independent of one another. One of the easiest ways to do this is via the special vector class covered later in the book.

Performance of compute 2.1 hardware varies. Some well-known applications like Folding at Home perform really well with the compute 2.1 hardware. Other applications such as video encoding packages, where it's harder to extract ILP and memory bandwidth is a key factor, typically perform much worse.

The final details of Kepler and the new compute 3.0 platform were, at the time of writing, still largely unreleased. A discussion of the Kepler features already announced can be found in Chapter 12, under 'Developing for Future GPUs'.

Setting Up CUDA

4

INTRODUCTION

This chapter is here for anyone who is completely new to CUDA. We look at how to install CUDA on the various OSs, what tools you can use, and how CUDA compiles. Finally, we look at how to have the API help you identify the coding and API errors everyone makes.

CUDA is supported on three major OSs: Windows, Mac, and Linux. By far the easiest platform to use and learn CUDA with is the OS you are most familiar with using for programming development. For an absolute beginner, the Windows OS in conjunction with Microsoft Visual C++ is likely to be the best choice. Both the Windows and Mac installations are fairly much point and click. Both provide fairly standard integrated development environments that work well with CUDA.

INSTALLING THE SDK UNDER WINDOWS

To install CUDA onto a PC running Windows, you'll need to download the following components from the NVIDIA developer portal at *http://developer.nvidia.com/cuda-toolkit-41*. Note by the time this book hit the press release 5 of the toolkit was in its release candidate phase. Please check the NVIDIA website for the latest version.

You will need an already installed version of Microsoft Visual Studio 2005, 2008, or 2010. The first step is to download and install the latest set of NVIDIA development drivers for your relevant operating system from the previous link. Then you will need either the 32- or 64-bit version of the CUDA toolkit and GPU computing and SDK code samples. Make sure you pick the correct version for your OS. Install them in this order:

1. NVIDIA development drivers
2. CUDA toolkit
3. CUDA SDK
4. GPU computing SDK
5. Parallel Nsight debugger

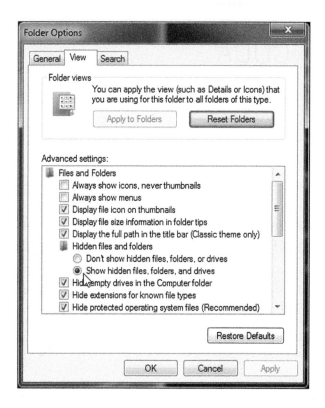

FIGURE 4.1

"Folder Options" to see hidden files.

Under Windows 7, the SDK installs all of its files into "ProgramData," which is a hidden directory of the C drive. To view the files you either need to always go via the CUDA SDK icon created on the desktop or go to "Folder Options" in Windows and tell it to show hidden files (Figure 4.1).

VISUAL STUDIO

CUDA supports Visual Studio versions from 2005 to 2010 including, for the most part, the express versions. The express versions are available free of charge from Microsoft. The professional versions are also available to registered students free of charge via the DreamSpark program at *https://www. dreamspark.com.*

To register all you need to do is supply your university or college details and identification numbers and you can download Visual Studio and many other programming tools. The program is also not just restricted to U.S.-based academic institutions, but available to students worldwide.

On the whole, Visual Studio 2008 has the best support for CUDA and compiles somewhat quicker than Visual Studio 2010. Visual Studio 2010 has, however, one very useful feature, which is automatic syntax checking of source code. Thus, if you use a type that is not defined, it underlines the error in red, just as Microsoft Word underlines spelling errors. This is an incredibly useful feature as it saves a lot of unnecessary compilation cycles for obvious issues. Thus, I'd recommend the 2010 version, especially if you can download it for free from DreamSpark.

Projects

One quick way of creating a project is to take one of the SDK examples, remove all the unnecessary project files, and insert your own source files. Note your CUDA source code should have a ".cu" extension so that it will be compiled by the NVIDIA compiler instead of Visual C. However, as we see later, you can also simply create a basic project framework using the project template wizard.

64-bit users

When using Windows 64-bit version, be aware that some of the project files are set up to run as 32-bit applications by default. Thus, when you try to build them you may get the error message: Fatal Error LNK1181: cannot open input file 'cutil32D.lib'.

This was not installed, as you most likely installed only the 64-bit version of the SDK along with the 64-bit version of Windows. To correct this issue all we have to do is set the target from 64 bits to 32 bits, which we do using the Build menu in Visual Studio, and then change the platform to X64 as shown in Figure 4.2.

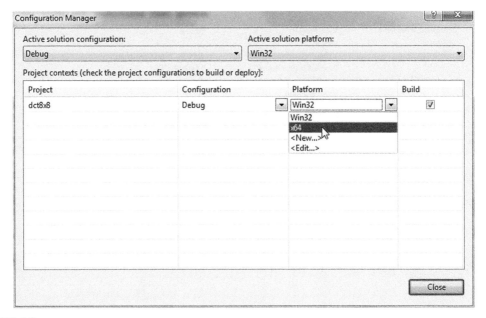

FIGURE 4.2

Visual C platform selection.

You may be prompted at the point you initiate a rebuild to save the project. Just add "_X86" to the end of the project name and save. The project will then build under a 64-bit environment and link in the correct library files.

You may also find an issue with a missing library, such as "cutil32.lib," for example. When the SDK is installed, it sets an environment variable, $(CUDA_LIB_PATH). This is usually set to: C:\Program Files\NVIDIA GPU Computing Toolkit\CUDA\v4.1\lib\X64.

You may find the path setup in the default project files may not have $(CUDA_LIB_PATH) as one of the entries. To add it, click on the project and then select "Project→Properties." This brings up the dialog box shown in Figure 4.3.

Clicking on the "…" button on the far right brings up a dialog where you can add the library path (Figure 4.4). Simply add "$(CUDA_LIB_PATH)" as a new line and the project should now link.

If you wish to build both 64-bit CUDA applications and 32-bit CUDA applications, both the 32- and 64-bit CUDA toolkits need to be installed. The samples from the SDK also require both the 32- and 64-bit versions of the SDK to be installed to be able to build both 32- and 64-bit versions of the samples.

You can build the necessary libraries by going to the following directories and building the solution files:

C:\ProgramData\NVIDIA Corporation\NVIDIA GPU Computing SDK 4.1\C\common
C:\ProgramData\NVIDIA Corporation\NVIDIA GPU Computing SDK 4.1\shared

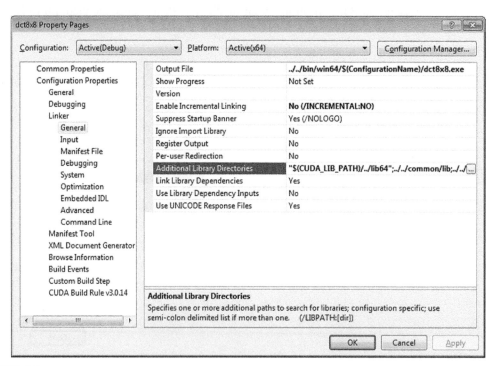

FIGURE 4.3

Additional library path.

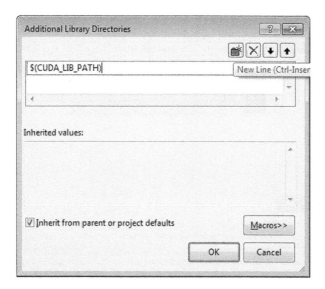

FIGURE 4.4

Adding library directories.

You will find the necessary libraries in

C:\ProgramData\NVIDIA Corporation\NVIDIA GPU Computing SDK 4.1\C\common\lib\X64.

You can also add these manually to any project that is missing them. Unfortunately, the SDK samples are not set up so they automatically build the necessary libraries when needed. The binaries for the libraries also are not supplied, which makes actually building the SDK samples a little frustrating.

Creating projects

To create a new CUDA-enabled application, simply create a CUDA application using the "File → New → Project Wizard" as shown in Figure 4.5. The wizard will then create a single project containing the file "kernel.cu," which contains a mix of code, some of which executes on the CPU and some of which executes on the GPU. The GPU code is contained in the function addKernel. This function simply takes a pointer to a destination array, c, and a couple of pointers to two input arrays, a and b. It then adds the contents of the a and b arrays together and stores the result in the destination array, c. It's a very simple example of the framework needed to execute a CUDA program.

Also included is the basic code to copy data to a device, invoke the kernel, and copy data back from the device to the host. It's a very useful starter project to get you compiling something under CUDA. We cover the standard framework needed to get a CUDA program working later in the text. It's useful to look at the code and try to understand it if you can. However, don't worry at this stage if it doesn't make sense as we'll build gradually on how to write programs for CUDA.

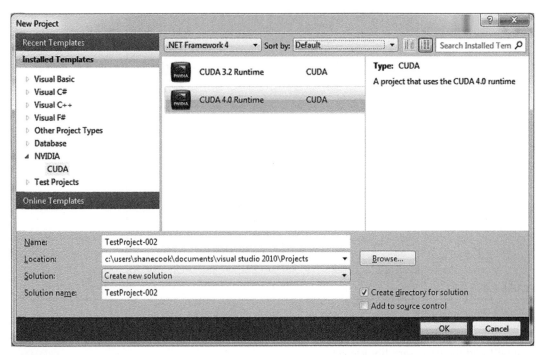

FIGURE 4.5

CUDA Project Wizard.

LINUX

CUDA is supported for the following Linux distributions. The supported versions will vary depending on which version of the CUDA toolkit you are installing.

- Fedora 14
- Redhat 6.0 and 5.5/CentOS 6.2 (the free version of Redhat)
- Ubuntu 11.04
- OpenSUSE 11.2

The first step in installing CUDA on a Linux platform is to make sure you have the latest set of kernel software. Use the following command from a terminal window to do this:

```
sudo yum update
```

The `sudo` command will log you in as the administrator. The `yum` command is a standard installation tool for the Linux RPM package. You are simply asking it to check for all installed packages and see if any updates are available. This ensures your system is fully up to date before installing any drivers. Many of the GUI-based installations also have GUI-based versions of the software updates that replace the older command line update interface.

Once the kernel has been updated to the latest level, run the following command:

```
sudo yum install gcc-c++ kernel-devel
```

This will install the standard GNU C++ environment as well as the kernel source you'll need to rebuild the kernel. Be aware that package names are case-sensitive. This will prompt you for around a 21 MB download and take a couple of minutes to install. Again, if you prefer, you can install the package via the GUI software installer for the particular OS.

Finally, as you are likely to be drawing some graphical output, you'll need an OpenGL development environment. Install this with the following command:

```
sudo yum install freeglut-devel libXi-devel libXmu-devel
```

Now you're ready to install the CUDA drivers. Make sure you install at least version 4.1 of the CUDA toolkit. There are a number of ways to install the updated NVIDIA drivers. NVIDIA does not release the source code to the drivers, so by default most Linux distributions install a very basic graphics driver.

Kernel base driver installation (CentOS, Ubuntu 10.4)

The CUDA releases should be used with a specific set of *development* drivers. Installing drivers by methods other than the one listed here may result in CUDA not working. Note the versions of the OS supported for the given version of the CUDA toolkit. These may not be the latest version of the particular Linux distribution. Using a later distribution will likely *not* work. Thus, the first installation step is to replace any existing drivers with the version specified for your specific Linux distribution. See Figure 4.6.

Once the download is complete, you need to boot Linux in text-only mode. Unlike Windows, which is always in graphics mode, text mode is required to install the drivers under Linux. You can make the system boot into text on most distributions using the following command from a Terminal window (usually under the Systems menu in the GUI):

```
sudo init 3
```

This will reboot the Linux machine and bring it back up in text mode. You can use `sudo init 5` to restore the graphics mode later.

If you get an error such as "User <user_name> is not in sudoers file," login as root using the `su` command. Edit the "/etc/sudoers" file and append the following line:

```
your_user_name ALL=(ALL) ALL
```

Be careful to replace `your_user_name` with your login name.

Certain distributions (e.g., Ubuntu) insist on booting to the GUI, regardless of the `init` mode. One method of resolving is as follows, from a text window. Edit the grub startup file:

```
sudo chmod +w /etc/default/grub
sudo nano /etc/default/grub
```

Change the following lines:

```
GRUB_CMDLINE_LINUX_DEFAULT="quiet splash"
GRUB_CMDLINE_LINUX_DEFAULT=""
```

to

```
# GRUB_CMDLINE_LINUX_DEFAULT="quiet splash"
GRUB_CMDLINE_LINUX_DEFAULT="text"
```

CUDA DOWNLOADS

CUDA TOOLKIT 4.2

CURRENT PRODUCTION RELEASE

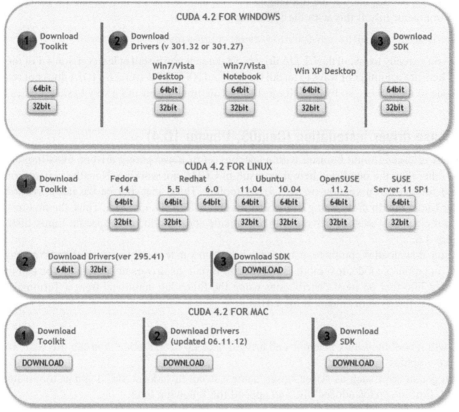

FIGURE 4.6

Supported Linux downloads and supported driver versions as of September 2012.

Now update grub using

```
sudo update-grub
```

Finally, reboot your machine and it should come up in text-only mode. Use the original lines to boot to the GUI again once the drivers are installed.

Now navigate to the area you stored the ".run" file you downloaded from the NVIDIA website. Then type

```
sudo sh NVIDIA-Linux-x86_64-285.05.33.run
```

The exact version of the driver you download will of course be different. You will be asked to agree to the NVIDIA license and will then have to wait a few minutes while everything installs. During this process the installer will attempt to replace the default Nouveau driver with the necessary NVIDIA drivers. If asked if you want to do this, select "Yes." This is an error-prone process and not every distribution works out of the box. If the NVIDIA installer is unable to remove the Nouveau driver then it may be necessary to blacklist the driver so the NVIDIA installer can install the correct drivers.

When you have the NVIDIA drivers installed correctly, type

```
sudo init 5
```

The machine will then reboot into the regular graphics mode. See earlier for Ubuntu.

The next task is to install the toolkit. There are a number available—select Fedora, Red Hat, Ubuntu, OpenSUSE, or SUSE depending on your distribution. As before, simply navigate to where you installed the SDK and run it by typing

```
sudo sh <sdk_version>.run
```

where <sdk_version> is the file you downloaded. It will then install all the tools needed and print a message saying the installation was successful. It then mentions you have to update the PATH and LD_LIBRARY_PATH environment variables, which you have to do by hand. To do this, you need to edit the "/etc/profile" startup file. Add the following lines:

```
export PATH=/usr/local/cuda/bin:$PATH
export LD_LIBRARY_PATH=/usr/local/cuda/lib:$LD_LIBRARY_PATH
```

Note that the file has to be writable. Use the "sudo chmod +w /etc/profile" to make it writable if required. You can edit this file with your favorite editor using such a command as "sudo nano/etc/profile".

Now log out and log back in again and type

```
env
```

This will list all of the current environment variable settings. Check for the two new entries you just amended. CUDA is now installed into the "/usr/local/bin" directory.

Next we'll need the GNU C++ compiler. Install the package "g++" from whatever software installer you are using on your system.

The next step is to install the SDK sample codes, so we have something to build and test. Download these from the NVIDIA site and run them, again using the sh sdk_version.run command (replace sdk_version with the actual one you download). Do *not* run this install as root as you will otherwise have to be logged in as root to build any of the samples.

By default the SDK will install to a subdirectory of your user account area. It may complain it can't find the CUDA installation and will use the default directory (the same one CUDA was installed to earlier). You can safely ignore this message.

Once the GPU computing SDK is installed, you then need to go to the "Common" subdirectory and run make to create a set of libraries.

Once this is done the SDK samples should build, allowing you to execute your first CUDA program in Linux and of course see if the driver is working correctly.

MAC

The Macintosh version is available, as with the other versions, from *http://developer.nvidia.com/cuda-toolkit-41*. Simply download and install the packages in the following order:

- Development drivers
- CUDA toolkit
- CUDA tools SDK and code samples

CUDA 4.1 requires Mac OS release 10.6.8 (Snow Leopard) or later. The latest release (10.7.x) or Lion release is available as a download from the Apple store or via a separate purchase from Apple.

The SDK installs into the "GPU Computing" directory under the "Developer" higher-level directory. Simply browse the "Developer/GPU Computing/C/bin/darwin/release" directory and you will find precompiled executables. Running the deviceQuery tool is useful to verify you have correctly installed the drivers and runtime environment.

To compile the samples, you will need XCode installed. This is the equivalent of GCC (GNU C Compiler) for the Mac. XCode can be downloaded from the Apple store. It's not a free product, but is available free of charge to anyone on the Apple Developer program, which includes both development of Macintosh and iPhone/iPad applications. It was also released shortly after the Lion OS as a free download for Lion OS owners.

Once XCode is installed, simply open a terminal window. To do this, go to Finder, open Utilities, and then double-click on the Terminal window. Type the following:

```
cd /Developer/'GPU Computing/C/src/project'
make-i
```

Replace project with the name of the particular SDK application you wish to compile. If you receive compilation errors, you have either not downloaded the XCode package or have an older version than is required.

INSTALLING A DEBUGGER

CUDA provides a debug environment called Parallel Nsight on the Windows and Linux platforms. This provides support for debugging CPU and GPU code and highlights areas where things are working less than efficiently. It also helps tremendously when trying to debug multithreaded applications.

Nsight is completely free and is a hugely useful tool. All it requires is that you register as a CUDA-registered developer, which is again entirely free. Once registered, you will be able to download the tool from the NVIDIA website.

Note that you must have Visual Studio 2008 or later (not the express version) and you must have installed Service Pack 1. There is a link within the release notes of Nsight to the SP1 download you need to install. The Linux version integrates into Eclipse.

Parallel Nsight comes as two parts, an application that integrates itself into Visual Studio as shown in Figure 4.7, and a separate monitoring application. The monitoring application works in conjunction with the main application. The monitor is usually resident, but does not have to be, on

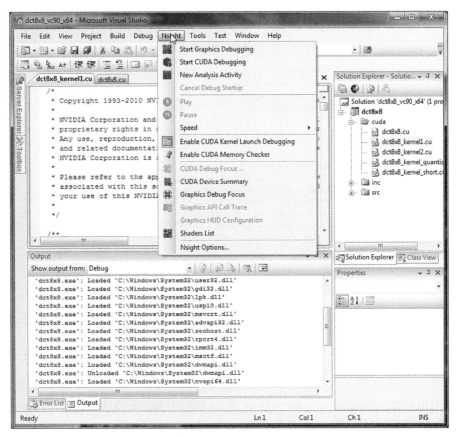

FIGURE 4.7

Nsight integrated into Microsoft Visual Studio.

the same machine as the development environment. Parallel Nsight works best with two CUDA capable GPUs, a dedicated GPU to run the code on and one to use as the regular display. Thus, the GPU running the target code cannot be used to run a second display. As most GPU cards have dual-monitor outputs, you can simply run two monitors off the display card should you have a dual-monitor setup. Note in the latest release, 2.2, the need for two GPUs was dropped.

It's also possible to set up the tool to acquire data from a remote GPU. However, in most cases it's easier to buy a low-end GPU and install it into your PC or workstation. The first step needed to set up Parallel Nsight on Windows is to disable TDR (Figure 4.8). TDR (Timeout Detection and Recovery) is a mechanism in Windows that detects crashes in the driver-level code. If the driver stops responding to events, Windows resets the driver. As the driver will halt when you define a breakpoint, this feature needs to be disabled.

To set the value, simply run the monitor and click on the "Nsight Monitor Options" hyperlink at the bottom right of the monitor dialog box. This will bring up the dialog shown in Figure 4.8. Setting the

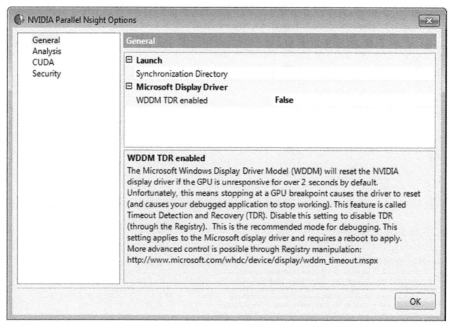

FIGURE 4.8

Disabling Windows kernel timeout.

"WDDM TDR enabled" will modify the registry to disable this feature. Reboot your PC, and Parallel Nsight will no longer warn you TDR is enabled.

To use Parallel Nsight on a remote machine, simply install the monitor package only on the remote Windows PC. When you first run the monitor, it will warn you Windows Firewall has blocked "Public network" (Internet based) access to the monitor, which is entirely what you want. However, the tool needs to have access to the local network, so allow this exception to any firewall rules you have set up on the monitor machine. As with a local node, you will have to fix the TDR issue and reboot once installed.

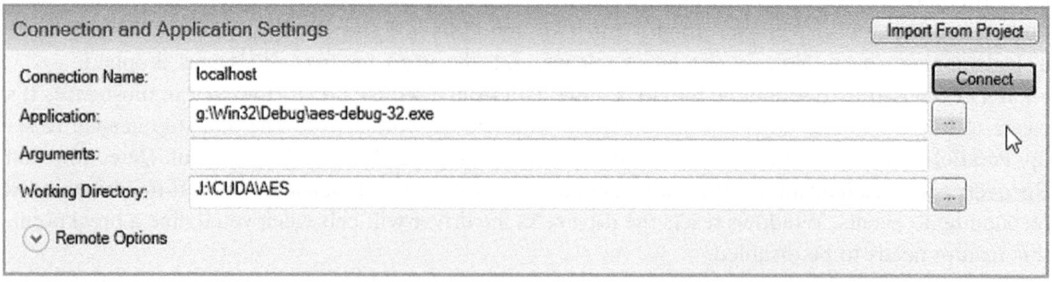

FIGURE 4.9

Parallel Nsight remote connection.

Connection and Application Settings		Import From Project
Connection Name:	ShaneCook-PC	Disconnect
Application:	g:\Win32\Debug\aes-debug-32.exe	...
Arguments:		
Working Directory:	J:\CUDA\AES	...
⌄ Remote Options		

FIGURE 4.10

Parallel Nsight connected remotely.

The next step is to run Visual Studio on the host PC and select a new analysis activity. You will see a section near the top of the window that looks like Figure 4.9. Notice the "Connection Name" says localhost, which just means your local machine. Open Windows Explorer and browse the local network to see the name of the Windows PC you would like to use to remotely debug. Replace localhost with the name shown in Windows Explorer. Then press the "Connect" button. You should see two confirmations that the connection has been made as shown in Figure 4.10.

First, the "Connect" button will change to a "Disconnect." Second, the "Connection Status" box should turn green and show all the possible GPUs on the target machine (Figure 4.11). In this case we're connecting to a test PC that has five GTX470 GPU cards set up on it.

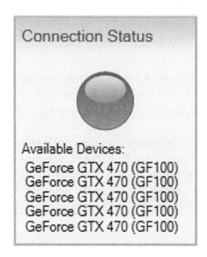

FIGURE 4.11

Parallel Nsight connection status.

Clicking on the "Launch" button on the "Application Control" panel next to the "Connection Status" panel will remotely launch the application on the target machine. However, prior to this all the necessary files need to be copied to the remote machine. This takes a few seconds or so, but is all automatic. Overall, it's a remarkably simple way of analyzing/debugging a remote application.

You may wish to set up Parallel Nsight in this manner if, for example, you have a laptop and wish to debug, or simply remotely run, an application that will run on a GPU server. Such usage includes when a GPU server or servers are shared by people who use it at different times, teaching classes, for example. You may also have remote developers who need to run code on specially set up test servers, perhaps because those servers also contain huge quantities of data and it's not practical or desirable to transfer that data to a local development machine. It also means you don't need to install Visual C++ on each of the remote servers you might have.

On the Linux and Mac side the debugger environment is CUDA-GDB. This provides an extended GNU debugger package. As with Parallel Nsight it allows debugging of both host and CUDA code, which includes setting a breakpoint in the CUDA code, single step, select a debug thread, etc. Both CUDA-GDB and the Visual Profiler tools are installed by default when you install the SDK, rather than being a separate download as with Parallel Nsight. As of 2012, Parallel Nsight was also released under the Eclipse environment for Linux.

The major difference between Windows and Mac/Linux was the profiling tool support. The Parallel Nsight tool is in this respect vastly superior to the Visual Profiler. The Visual Profiler is also available on Windows. It provides a fairly high-level overview and recommendations as to what to address in the code, and therefore is very suited to those starting out using CUDA. Parallel Nsight, by contrast, is aimed at a far more advanced user. We cover usage of both Parallel Nsight and Visual Profiler later in subsequent chapters. However, the focus throughout this text is on the use of Parallel Nsight as the primary debugging/analysis tool for GPU development.

For advanced CUDA development I'd strongly recommend using Parallel Nsight for debugging and analysis. For most people new to CUDA the combination of the Visual Profiler and CUDA-GDB work well enough to allow for development.

COMPILATION MODEL

The NVIDIA compiler, NVCC, sits in the background and is invoked when a CUDA source file needs to be compiled. The file extensions shown in Table 4.1 are used to define files as with CUDA source files or regular source files. This determines which compiler will be invoked, NVCC or the host compiler.

The generated executable file, or fat binary, contains one or more binary executable images for the different GPU generations. It also contains a PTX image, allowing the CUDA runtime to do just-in-time (JIT) compilation. This is very similar to Java byte code where the target is a virtual architecture, and this is compiled to the actual target hardware at the point the program is invoked. The PTX JIT

Table 4.1 Different CUDA File Types		
File Extension	**Meaning**	**Processed By**
.cu	Mixed host and device source file.	NVCC
.cup	A preprocessed expanded version of .cu file.	NVCC
.c, .cc, .cpp	A host C or C++ source file.	Host compiler
.ptx, .gpu	Intermediate virtual assembly files.	NVCC
.cubin	Binary image of GPU code.	NVCC

compilation only happens if the executable does not contain a binary image that is identical to the GPU in use. Consequently, all future architectures are backward compatible with the basic-level virtual architecture. Even GPUs for which the program was not compiled will execute legacy GPU code by simply compiling, at runtime, the PTX code embedded in the executable.

Just as with Java, code depositories are supported. Defining the environment variable CUDA_DEVCODE_CACHE to point to a directory will cause the runtime to save the compiled binary for later use, thus avoiding the startup delay necessary to compile the PTX code for the unknown GPU variant every time it is invoked.

We cover in the later chapters how you can view the real target assembly code, the result of the PTX to target translation.

ERROR HANDLING

Error handling in CUDA, as with C in general, is not as good as it could be. There are few runtime checks performed, and if you do something stupid, the runtime will usually allow it. This results in GPU programs that exit strangely. If you are lucky, you will get an error message which, like compiler errors, you learn to interpret over time.

Almost all function calls in CUDA return the error type cudaError_t, which is simply an integer value. Any value other than cudaSuccess will indicate a fatal error. This is usually caused by your program not setting up something correctly prior to use, or using an object after it has been destroyed. It can also be caused by the GPU kernel timeout present in Microsoft Windows if the kernel runs for more than a few seconds and you have not disabled this when installing tools such as Parallel Nsight (see previous section). Out-of-bounds memory accesses may generate exceptions that will often print various error messages to stderr (standard error output).

As every function returns an error code, every function call must be checked and some handler written. This makes for very tiresome and highly indented programming. For example,

```
if (cudaMalloc(...) == cudaSuccess)
{
 if (cudaEventCreate(&event) == cudaSucess)
  {
  ...
  }
}
else
{
...
}
```

To avoid this type of repetitive programming, throughout the book we will use the following macro definition to making calls to the CUDA API:

```
#define CUDA_CALL(x) {const cudaError_t a = (x); if (a != cudaSuccess) { printf("\nCUDA
Error: %s (err_num=%d) \n", cudaGetErrorString(a), a); cudaDeviceReset(); assert(0);} }
```

What this macro does is to allow you to specify x as some function call, for example,

```
CUDA_CALL(cudaEventCreate(&kernel_start));
```

This then creates a temporary variable a and assigns to it the return value of the function, which is of type cudaError_t. It then checks if this is not equal to cudaSuccess, that is, the call encountered some error. If there was an error detected, it prints to the screen the error returned plus a short description of what the error means. It also uses the assert macro, which identifies the source file and line in which the error occurs so you can easily track down the point at which the error is being detected.

This technique works for all the CUDA calls except for the invocation of kernels. Kernels are the programs you write to run on the GPU. These are executed using the ⟨⟨⟨ and ⟩⟩⟩ operators as follows:

```
my_kernel <<<num_blocks, num_threads>>>(param1, param2,...);
```

For error checking of kernels, we'll use the following function:

```
__host__ void cuda_error_check(const char * prefix, const char * postfix)
{
  if (cudaPeekAtLastError() != cudaSuccess)
  {
    printf("\n%s%s%s", prefix, cudaGetErrorString(cudaGetLastError()), postfix);
    cudaDeviceReset();
    wait_exit();
    exit(1);
  }
}
```

This function should be called immediately after executing the kernel call. It checks for any immediate errors, and if so, prints an error message, resets the GPU, optionally waits for a key press via the wait_exit function, and then exits the program.

Note that this is not foolproof, as the kernel call is asynchronous with the CPU code. That is, the GPU code is running in the background at the time we call cudaPeekAtLastError. If there has been no error detected *at this time*, then we see no error printed and the function continues to the next code line. Often that next code line will be a copy back from GPU memory to CPU memory. The error in the kernel may cause a subsequent API call to fail, which is almost always the next API call after the kernel call. Surrounding all calls to the API with the CUDA_CALL macro will flag the error at this point.

You can also force the kernel to complete prior to the error checking by simply inserting a call to cudaDeviceSynchronize prior to the cudaPeekAtLastError call. However, only do this on the debug version of the program or where you want the CPU to idle while the GPU is busy. As you should understand by the end of this text, such synchronous operation is good for debugging, but will harm performance, so you should be careful these calls do not remain in production code if they were inserted solely for debugging.

CONCLUSION

You should now have a working installation of the CUDA SDK, including the GPU computing SDK samples and a debugging environment. You should be able to build a simple GPU SDK sample, such as the deviceQuery project, and have it identify the GPUs in your system when run.

Grids, Blocks, and Threads

5

WHAT IT ALL MEANS

NVIDIA chose a rather interesting model for its scheduling, a variant of SIMD called SPMD (single program, multiple data). This is based on the underlying hardware implementation in many respects. At the heart of parallel programming is the idea of a thread, a single flow of execution through the program in the same way a piece of cotton flows through a garment. In the same way threads of cotton are woven into cloth, threads used together make up a parallel program. The CUDA programming model groups threads into special groups it calls warps, blocks, and grids, which we will look at in turn.

THREADS

A thread is the fundamental building block of a parallel program. Most C programmers are familiar with the concept if they have done any multicore programming. Even if you have never launched a thread in any code, you will be familiar with executing at least one thread, the single thread of execution through any serial piece of code.

With the advent of dual, quad, hex core processors, and beyond, more emphasis is explicitly placed on the programmer to make use of such hardware. Most programs written in the past few decades, with the exception of perhaps the past decade, were single-thread programs because the primary hardware on which they would execute was a single-core CPU. Sure, you had clusters and supercomputers that sought to exploit a high level of parallelism by duplicating the hardware and having thousands of commodity servers instead of a handful of massively powerful machines. However, these were mostly restricted to universities and large institutions, not generally available to the masses.

Thinking in terms of lots of threads is hard. It's much easier to think in terms of one task at a time. Serial programming languages like C/C++ were born from a time when serial processing speed doubled every few years. There was little need to do the hard parallel programming. That stopped almost a decade ago, and now, like it or not, to improve program speed requires us to think in terms of parallel design.

Problem decomposition

Parallelism in the CPU domain tends to be driven by the desire to run more than one (single-threaded) program on a single CPU. This is the task-level parallelism that we covered earlier. Programs, which are data intensive, like video encoding, for example, use the data parallelism model and split the task in N parts where N is the number of CPU cores available. You might, for example, have each CPU core calculate one "frame" of data where there are no interdependencies between frames. You may also choose to split each frame into N segments and allocate each one of the segments to an individual core.

In the GPU domain, you see exactly these choices when attempting to speed up rendering of 3D worlds in computer games by using more than one GPU. You can send complete, alternate frames to each GPU (Figure 5.1). Alternatively, you can ask one GPU to render the different parts of the screen.

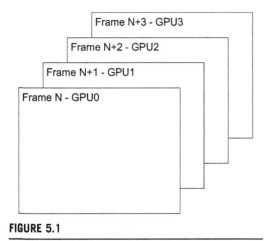

FIGURE 5.1

Alternate frame rendering (AFR) vs. Split Frame Rendering (SFR).

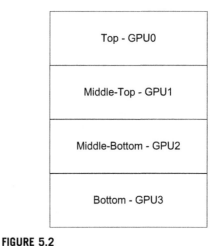

FIGURE 5.2

Coarse-grained parallelism.

However, there is a trade off here. If the dataset is self-contained, you can use less memory and transfer less data by only providing the GPU (or CPU) with the subset of the data you need to calculate. In the SFR GPU example used here, there may be no need for GPU3, which is rendering the floor to know the content of data from GPU0, which is probably rendering the sky. However, there may be shadows from a flying object, or the lighting level of the floor may need to vary based on the time of day. In such instances, it might be more beneficial to go with the alternate frame rendering approach because of this shared data.

We refer to SFR type splits as coarse-grained parallelism. Large chunks of data are split in some way between N powerful devices and then reconstructed later as the processed data. When designing applications for a parallel environment, choices at this level seriously impact the performance of your programs. The best choice here is very much linked to the actual hardware you will be using, as you will see with the various applications we develop throughout this book.

With a small number of powerful devices, such as in CPUs, the issue is often how to split the workload evenly. This is often easier to reason with because you are typically talking about only a small number of devices. With huge numbers of smaller devices, as with GPUs, they average out peaks in workload much better, but suffer from issues around synchronization and coordination.

In the same way as you have macro (large-scale) and micro (small-scale) economics, you have coarse and fine-grained parallelism. However, you only really find fine-grained parallelism at the programmer level on devices that support huge numbers of threads, such as GPUs. CPUs, by contrast, also support threads, but with a large overhead and thus are considered to be useful for more coarse-grained parallelism problems. CPUs, unlike GPUs, follow the MIMD (Multiple Instruction Multiple Data) model in that they support multiple independent instruction streams. This is a more flexible approach, but incurs additional overhead in terms of fetching multiple independent instruction streams as opposed to amortizing the single instruction stream over multiple processors.

To put this in context, let's consider a digital photo where you apply an image correction function to increase the brightness. On a GPU you might choose to assign one thread for every pixel in the image. On a quad-core CPU, you would likely assign one-quarter of the image to each CPU core.

How CPUs and GPUs are different

GPUs and CPUs are architecturally very different devices. CPUs are designed for running a small number of potentially quite complex tasks. GPUs are designed for running a large number of quite simple tasks. The CPU design is aimed at systems that execute a number of discrete and unconnected tasks. The GPU design is aimed at problems that can be broken down into thousands of tiny fragments and worked on individually. Thus, CPUs are very suitable for running operating systems and application software where there are a vast variety of tasks a computer may be performing at any given time.

CPUs and GPUs consequently support threads in very different ways. The CPU has a small number of registers per core that must be used to execute any given task. To achieve this, they rapidly context switch between tasks. Context switching on CPUs is expensive in terms of time, in that the entire register set must be saved to RAM and the next one restored from RAM. GPUs, by comparison, also use the same concept of context switching, but instead of having a single set of registers, they have multiple banks of registers. Consequently, a context switch simply involves setting a bank selector to switch in and out the current set of registers, which is several orders of magnitude faster than having to save to RAM.

Both CPUs and GPUs must deal with stall conditions. These are generally caused by I/O operations and memory fetches. The CPU does this by context switching. Providing there are enough tasks and the runtime of a thread is not too small, this works reasonably well. If there are not enough processes to keep the CPU busy, it will idle. If there are too many small tasks, each blocking after a short period, the CPU will spend most of its time context switching and very little time doing useful work. CPU scheduling policies are often based on time slicing, dividing the time equally among the threads. As the number of threads increases, the percentage of time spent context switching becomes increasingly large and the efficiency starts to rapidly drop off.

GPUs are designed to handle stall conditions and expect this to happen with high frequency. The GPU model is a data-parallel one and thus it needs thousands of threads to work efficiently. It uses this pool of available work to ensure it always has something useful to work on. Thus, when it hits a memory fetch operation or has to wait on the result of a calculation, the streaming processors simply switch to another instruction stream and return to the stalled instruction stream sometime later.

One of the major differences between CPUs and GPUs is the sheer number of processors on each device. CPUs are typically dual- or quad-core devices. That is to say they have a number of execution cores available to run programs on. GPUs have up to 30 SMs, which can be thought of a lot like CPU cores. CPUs often run single-thread programs, meaning they calculate just a single data point per core, per iteration. GPUs run in parallel by default. Thus, instead of calculating just a single data point per SM, GPUs calculate 32 per SM. This gives a 4 times advantage in terms of number of cores (SMs) over a typical quad core CPU, but also a 32 times advantage in terms of data throughput. Of course, CPU programs can also use all the available cores and extensions like MMX, SSE, and AVX. The question is how many CPU applications actually use these types of extensions.

GPUs also provide something quite unique—high-speed memory next to the SM, so-called shared memory. In many respects this implements the design philosophy of the Connection Machine and the Cell processor, in that it provides local workspace for the device outside of the standard register file. Thus, the programmer can leave data in this memory, safe in the knowledge the hardware will not evict it behind his or her back. It is also the primary mechanism communication between threads.

Task execution model

There are two major differences in the task execution model. The first is that groups of N SPs execute in a lock-step basis (Figure 5.3), running the *same* program but on different data. The second is that, because of this huge register file, switching threads has effectively *zero* overhead. Thus, the GPU can support a very large number of threads and is designed in this way.

Now what exactly do we mean by lock-step basis? Each instruction in the instruction queue is dispatched to every SP within an SM. Remember each SM can be thought of as single processor with N cores (SPs) embedded within it.

A conventional CPU will fetch a separate instruction stream for each CPU core. The GPU SPMD model used here allows an instruction fetch for N logical execution units, meaning you have $1/N$ the instructions memory bandwidth requirements of a conventional processor. This is a very similar approach to the vector or SIMD processors found in many high-end supercomputers.

However, this is not without its costs. As you will see later, if the program does not follow a nice neat execution flow where all N threads follow the same control path, for each branch, you will require additional execution cycles.

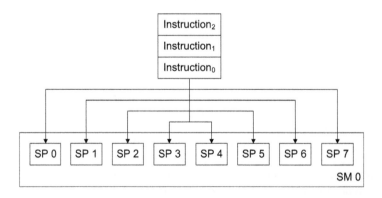

FIGURE 5.3

Lock-step instruction dispatch.

Threading on GPUs

So coming back to threads, let's look at a section of code and see what this means from a programming perspective.

```
void some_func(void)
{
  int i;

  for (i=0;i<128;i++)
  {
    a[i] = b[i] * c[i];
  }
}
```

This piece of code is very simple. It stores the result of a multiplication of b and c value for a given index in the result variable a for that same index. The for loop iterates 128 times (indexes 0 to 127). In CUDA you could translate this to 128 threads, each of which executes the line

```
a[i] = b[i] * c[i];
```

This is possible because there is no dependency between one iteration of the loop and the next. Thus, to transform this into a parallel program is actually quite easy. This is called loop parallelization and is very much the basis for one of the more popular parallel language extensions, OpenMP.

On a quad-core CPU you could also translate this to four blocks, where CPU core 1 handles indexes 0–31, core 2 indexes 32–63, core 3 indexes 64–95, and core 4 indexes 96–127. Some compilers will either automatically translate such blocks or translate them where the programmer marks that this loop can be parallelized. The Intel compiler is particularly good at this. Such compilers can be used to create embedded SSE/AVX instructions to vectorize a loop in this way, in addition to spawning multiple threads. This gives two levels of parallelism and is not too different from the GPU model.

In CUDA, you translate this loop by creating a kernel function, which is a function that executes on the GPU *only* and cannot be executed directly on the CPU. In the CUDA programming model the CPU handles the serial code execution, which is where it excels. When you come to a computationally intense section of code the CPU hands it over to the GPU to make use of the huge computational power it has. Some of you might remember the days when CPUs would use a floating-point coprocessor. Applications that used a large amount of floating-point math ran many times faster on machines fitted with such coprocessors. Exactly the same is true for GPUs. They are used to accelerate computationally intensive sections of a program.

The GPU kernel function, conceptually, looks identical to the loop body, but with the loop structure removed. Thus, you have the following:

```
__global__ void some_kernel_func(int * const a, const int * const b, const int * const c)
{
  a[i] = b[i] * c[i];
}
```

Notice you have lost the loop and the loop control variable, i. You also have a __global__ prefix added to the C function that tells the compiler to generate GPU code and not CPU code when compiling this function, and to make that GPU code globally visible from within the CPU.

The CPU and GPU have separate memory spaces, meaning you cannot access CPU parameters in the GPU code and vice versa. There are some special ways of doing exactly this, which we'll cover later in the book, but for now we will deal with them as separate memory spaces. As a consequence, the global arrays a, b, and c at the CPU level are no longer visible on the GPU level. You have to declare memory space on the GPU, copy over the arrays from the CPU, and pass the kernel pointers to the GPU memory space to both read and write from. When you are done, you copy that memory back into the CPU. We'll look at this a little later.

The next problem you have is that i is no longer defined; instead, the value of i is defined for you by the thread you are currently running. You will be launching 128 instances of this function, and initially this will be in the form of 128 threads. CUDA provides a special parameter, different for each thread, which defines the thread ID or number. You can use this to directly index into the array. This is very similar to MPI, where you get the process rank for each process.

The thread information is provided in a structure. As it's a structure element, we will store it in a variable, thread_idx for now to avoid having to reference the structure every time. Thus, the code becomes:

```
__global__ void some_kernel_func(int * const a, const int * const b, const int * const c)
{
  const unsigned int thread_idx = threadIdx.x;
  a[thread_idx] = b[thread_idx] * c[thread_idx];
}
```

Note, some people prefer idx or tid as the name for the thread index since these are somewhat shorter to type.

What is happening, now, is that for thread 0, the thread_idx calculation returns 0. For thread 1, it returns 1, and so on, up to thread 127, which uses index 127. Each thread does exactly two reads from memory, one multiply and one store operation, and then terminates. Notice how the code executed by each thread is identical, but the data changes. This is at the heart of the CUDA and SPMD model.

In OpenMP and MPI, you have similar blocks of code. They extract, for a given iteration of the loop, the thread ID or thread rank allocated to that thread. This is then used to index into the dataset.

A peek at hardware

Now remember you only actually have N cores on each SM, so how can you run 128 threads? Well, like the CPU, each thread group is placed into the SM and the N SPs start running the code. The first thing the GPU does after extracting the thread index is fetch a parameter from the b and c array. Unfortunately, this doesn't happen immediately. In fact, some 400–600 GPU clocks can go by before the memory subsystem comes back with the requested data. During this time the set of N threads gets suspended.

Threads are, in practice, actually grouped into 32 thread groups, and when all 32 threads are waiting on something such as memory access, they are suspended. The technical term for these groups of threads is a warp (32 threads) and a half warp (16 threads), something we'll return to later.

Thus, the 128 threads translate into four groups of 32 threads. The first set all run together to extract the thread ID and then calculate the address in the arrays and issue a memory fetch request (see

Figure 5.4). The next instruction, a multiply, requires both operands to have been provided, so the thread is suspended. When all 32 threads in that block of 32 threads are suspended, the hardware switches to another warp.

In Figure 5.5, you can see that when warp 0 is suspended pending its memory access completing, warp 1 becomes the executing warp. The GPU continues in this manner until all warps have moved to the suspended state (see Figure 5.6).

Prior to issuing the memory fetch, fetches from consecutive threads are usually coalesced or grouped together. This reduces the overall latency (time to respond to the request), as there is an overhead associated in the hardware with managing each request. As a result of the coalescing, the memory fetch returns with the data for a whole group of threads, usually enough to enable an entire warp.

These threads are then placed in the ready state and become available for the GPU to switch in the next time it hits a blocking operation, such as another memory fetch from another set of threads.

Having executed all the warps (groups of 32 threads) the GPU becomes idle waiting for any one of the pending memory accesses to complete. At some point later, you'll get a sequence of memory blocks being returned from the memory subsystem. It is likely, but not guaranteed, that these will come back in the order in which they were requested.

Let's assume that addresses 0–31 were returned at the same time. Warp 0 moves to the ready queue, and since there is no warp currently executing, warp 0 automatically moves to the executing state (see Figure 5.7). Gradually all the pending memory requests will complete, resulting in all of the warp blocks moving back to the ready queue.

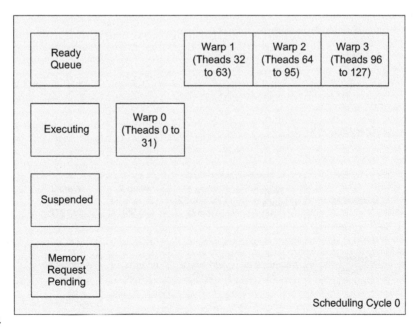

FIGURE 5.4

Cycle 0.

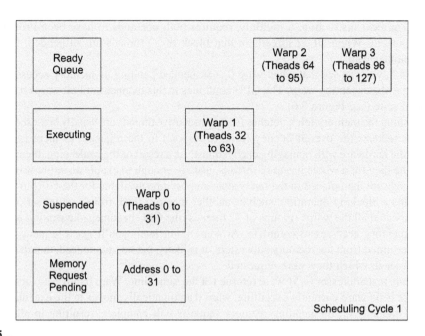

FIGURE 5.5

Cycle 1.

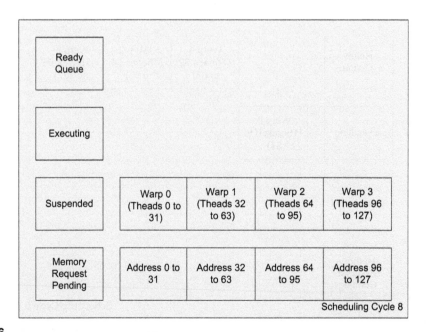

FIGURE 5.6

Cycle 8.

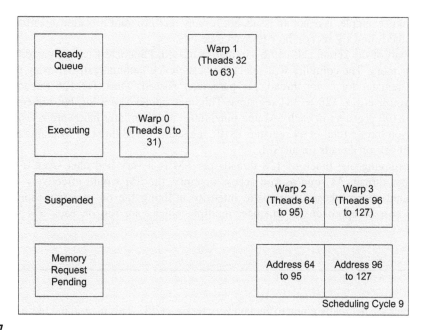

FIGURE 5.7

Cycle 9.

Once warp 0 has executed, its final instruction is a write to the destination array a. As there are no dependent instructions on this operation, warp 0 is then complete and is retired. The other warps move through this same cycle and eventually they have all issued a store request. Each warp is then retired, and the kernel completes, returning control to the CPU.

CUDA kernels

Now let's look a little more at how exactly you invoke a kernel. CUDA defines an extension to the C language used to invoke a kernel. Remember, a kernel is just a name for a function that executes on the GPU. To invoke a kernel you use the following syntax:

```
kernel_function<<<num_blocks, num_threads>>>(param1, param2, ...)
```

There are some other parameters you can pass, and we'll come back to this, but for now you have two important parameters to look at: num_blocks and num_threads. These can be either variables or literal values. I'd recommend the use of variables because you'll use them later when tuning performance.

The num_blocks parameter is something you have not yet covered and is covered in detail in the next section. For now all you need to do is ensure you have at least one block of threads.

The num_threads parameter is simply the number of threads you wish to launch into the kernel. For this simple example, this directly translates to the number of iterations of the loop. However, be aware that the hardware limits you to 512 threads per block on the early hardware and 1024 on the later hardware. In this example, it is not an issue, but for any real program it is almost certainly an issue. You'll see in the following section how to overcome this.

The next part of the kernel call is the parameters passed. Parameters can be passed via registers or constant memory. The compiler will select the best choice automatically. If using registers, you will use one register for every thread, per parameter passed. Thus, for 128 threads with three parameters, you use $3 \times 128 = 384$ registers. This may sound like a lot, but remember that you have at least 8192 registers in each SM and potentially more on later hardware revisions. So with 128 threads, you have a total of 64 registers (8192 registers ÷ 128 threads) available to you, *if* you run just one block of threads on an SM.

However, running one block of 128 threads per SM is a very bad idea, even if you can use 64 registers per thread. As soon as you access memory, the SM would effectively idle. Only in the very limited case of heavy arithmetic intensity utilizing the 64 registers should you even consider this sort of approach. In practice, multiple blocks are run on each SM to avoid any idle states.

BLOCKS

Now 512 threads are not really going to get you very far on a GPU. This may sound like a huge number to many programmers from the CPU domain, but on a GPU you usually need thousands or tens of thousands of concurrent threads to really achieve the throughput available on the device.

We touched on this previously in the last section on threads, with the num_blocks parameter for the kernel invocation. This is the first parameter within the <<< and >>> symbols:

```
kernel_function<<<num_blocks, num_threads>>>(param1, param2,.....)
```

If you change this from one to two, you double the number of threads you are asking the GPU to invoke on the hardware. Thus, the same call,

```
some_kernel_func<<< 2, 128 >>>(a, b, c);
```

will call the GPU function named some_kernel_func 2×128 times, each with a different thread. This, however, complicates the calculation of the thread_idx parameter, effectively the array index position. This previous, simple kernel needs a slight amendment to account for this.

```
__global__ void some_kernel_func(int * const a, const int * const b, const int * const c)
{
  const unsigned int thread_idx = (blockIdx.x * blockDim.x) + threadIdx.x;

  a[thread_idx] = b[thread_idx] * c[thread_idx];
}
```

To calculate the thread_idx parameter, you must now take into account the number of blocks. For the first block, blockIdx.x will contain zero, so effectively the thread_idx parameter is equal to the threadIdx.x parameter you used earlier. However, for block two, blockIdx.x will hold the value 1. The parameter blockDim.x holds the value 128, which is, in effect, the number of threads you requested per block in this example. Thus, you have a 1×128 thread base addresses, before adding in the thread offset from the threadIdx.x parameter.

Have you noticed the small error we have introduced in adding in another block? You will now launch 256 threads in total and index the array from 0 to 255. If you don't also change the size of the array, from 128 elements to 256 elements, you will access and write beyond the end of the array. This array out-of-bounds error will not be caught by the compiler and the code may actually run, depending on what is located after the destination array, a. Be careful when invoking a kernel that you do not access out of bounds elements.

For this example, we will stick with the 128-byte array size and change the kernel to invoke two blocks of 64 threads each as shown in Figure 5.8:

```
some_kernel_func<<< 2, 64 >>>(a, b, c);
```

Notice how, despite now having two blocks, the thread_idx parameter still equates to the array index, exactly as before. So what is the point of using blocks? In this trivial example, absolutely nothing. However, in any real-world problem, you have far more than 512 elements to deal with. In fact, if you look at the limit on the number of blocks, you find you have 65,536 blocks you can use on Fermi and prior generations.

At 65,536 blocks, with 512 threads per block, you can schedule 33,554,432 (around 33.5 million) threads in total. At 512 threads, you can have up to three blocks per SM. Actually, this limit is based on the total number of threads per SM, which is 2048 in Kepler, 1536 in Fermi hardware, and as little as 768 in the original G80 hardware.

If you schedule the maximum of 1024 threads per block on the Fermi hardware, 65,536 blocks would translate into around 64 million threads. Unfortunately, at 1024 threads, you only get one thread block per SM. Consequently, you'd need some 65,536 SMs in a single GPU before you could not allocate at least one block per SM. Currently, the maximum number of SMs found on any card is 30. Thus, there is some provision for the number of SMs to grow before you have more SMs than the number of blocks the hardware can support. This is one of the beauties of CUDA—the fact it can scale to thousands of execution units. The limit of the parallelism is only really the limit of the amount of parallelism that can be found in the application.

With 64 million threads, assuming one thread per array element, you can process up to 64 million elements. Assuming each element is a single-precision floating-point number, requiring 4 bytes of data, you'd need around 256 million bytes, or 256 MB, of data storage space. Almost all GPU cards support at least this amount of memory space, so working with threads and blocks alone you can achieve quite a large amount of parallelism and data coverage.

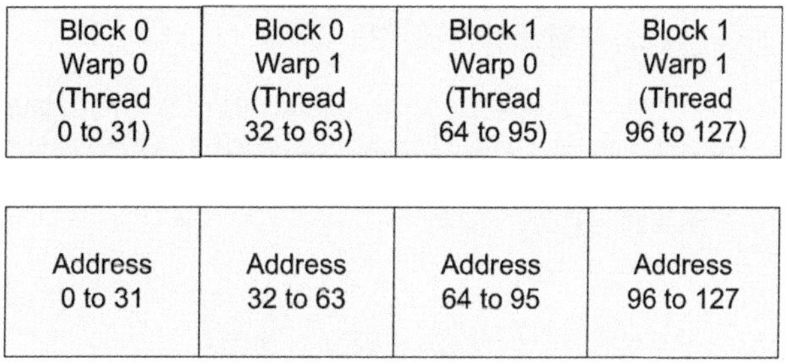

Block 0 Warp 0 (Thread 0 to 31)	Block 0 Warp 1 (Thread 32 to 63)	Block 1 Warp 0 (Thread 64 to 95)	Block 1 Warp 1 (Thread 96 to 127)

Address 0 to 31	Address 32 to 63	Address 64 to 95	Address 96 to 127

FIGURE 5.8

Block mapping to address.

For anyone worried about large datasets, where large problems can run into gigabytes, terabytes, or petabytes of data, there is a solution. For this, you generally either process more than one element per thread or use another dimension of blocks, which we'll cover in the next section.

Block arrangement

To ensure that you understand the block arrangement, we're going to write a short kernel program to print the block, thread, warp, and thread index to the screen. Now, unless you have at least version 3.2 of the SDK, the `printf` statement is not supported in kernels. So we'll ship the data back to the CPU and print it to the console window. The kernel program is thus as follows:

```
__global__ void what_is_my_id(unsigned int * const block,
                              unsigned int * const thread,
                              unsigned int * const warp,
                              unsigned int * const calc_thread)
{
  /* Thread id is block index * block size + thread offset into the block */
  const unsigned int thread_idx = (blockIdx.x * blockDim.x) + threadIdx.x;

  block[thread_idx] = blockIdx.x;
  thread[thread_idx] = threadIdx.x;

  /* Calculate warp using built in variable warpSize */
  warp[thread_idx] = threadIdx.x / warpSize;

  calc_thread[thread_idx] = thread_idx;
}
```

Now on the CPU you have to run a section of code, as follows, to allocate memory for the arrays on the GPU and then transfer the arrays back from the GPU and display them on the CPU.

```
#include <stdio.h>
#include <stdlib.h>
#include <conio.h>

__global__ void what_is_my_id(unsigned int * const block,
            unsigned int * const thread,
            unsigned int * const warp,
            unsigned int * const calc_thread)
{
  /* Thread id is block index * block size + thread offset into the block */
  const unsigned int thread_idx = (blockIdx.x * blockDim.x) + threadIdx.x;

  block[thread_idx] = blockIdx.x;
  thread[thread_idx] = threadIdx.x;

  /* Calculate warp using built in variable warpSize */
  warp[thread_idx] = threadIdx.x / warpSize;

  calc_thread[thread_idx] = thread_idx;
}
```

```
#define ARRAY_SIZE 128
#define ARRAY_SIZE_IN_BYTES (sizeof(unsigned int) * (ARRAY_SIZE))

/* Declare statically four arrays of ARRAY_SIZE each */

unsigned int cpu_block[ARRAY_SIZE];
unsigned int cpu_thread[ARRAY_SIZE];
unsigned int cpu_warp[ARRAY_SIZE];
unsigned int cpu_calc_thread[ARRAY_SIZE];

int main(void)
{
  /* Total thread count = 2 * 64 = 128 */
  const unsigned int num_blocks = 2;
  const unsigned int num_threads = 64;
  char ch;

  /* Declare pointers for GPU based params */
  unsigned int * gpu_block;
  unsigned int * gpu_thread;
  unsigned int * gpu_warp;
  unsigned int * gpu_calc_thread;

  /* Declare loop counter for use later */
  unsigned int i;

  /* Allocate four arrays on the GPU */
  cudaMalloc((void **)&gpu_block, ARRAY_SIZE_IN_BYTES);
  cudaMalloc((void **)&gpu_thread, ARRAY_SIZE_IN_BYTES);
  cudaMalloc((void **)&gpu_warp, ARRAY_SIZE_IN_BYTES);
  cudaMalloc((void **)&gpu_calc_thread, ARRAY_SIZE_IN_BYTES);

  /* Execute our kernel */
  what_is_my_id<<<num_blocks, num_threads>>>(gpu_block, gpu_thread, gpu_warp,
                                             gpu_calc_thread);

 /* Copy back the gpu results to the CPU */
  cudaMemcpy(cpu_block, gpu_block, ARRAY_SIZE_IN_BYTES,
            cudaMemcpyDeviceToHost);
  cudaMemcpy(cpu_thread, gpu_thread, ARRAY_SIZE_IN_BYTES,
            cudaMemcpyDeviceToHost);
  cudaMemcpy(cpu_warp, gpu_warp, ARRAY_SIZE_IN_BYTES,
            cudaMemcpyDeviceToHost);
  cudaMemcpy(cpu_calc_thread, gpu_calc_thread, ARRAY_SIZE_IN_BYTES,
            cudaMemcpyDeviceToHost);

  /* Free the arrays on the GPU as now we're done with them */
```

```
    cudaFree(gpu_block);
    cudaFree(gpu_thread);
    cudaFree(gpu_warp);
    cudaFree(gpu_calc_thread);

    /* Iterate through the arrays and print */
    for (i=0; i < ARRAY_SIZE; i++)
    {
      printf("Calculated Thread: %3u - Block: %2u - Warp %2u - Thread %3u\n",
        cpu_calc_thread[i], cpu_block[i], cpu_warp[i], cpu_thread[i]);
    }
    ch = getch();
}
```

In this example, what you see is that each block is located immediately after the one before it. As you have only a single dimension to the array, laying out the thread blocks in a similar way is an easy way to conceptualize a problem. The output of the program is as follows:

```
Calculated Thread: 0 - Block: 0 - Warp 0 - Thread 0
Calculated Thread: 1 - Block: 0 - Warp 0 - Thread 1
Calculated Thread: 2 - Block: 0 - Warp 0 - Thread 2
Calculated Thread: 3 - Block: 0 - Warp 0 - Thread 3
Calculated Thread: 4 - Block: 0 - Warp 0 - Thread 4
...
Calculated Thread: 30 - Block: 0 - Warp 0 - Thread 30
Calculated Thread: 31 - Block: 0 - Warp 0 - Thread 31
Calculated Thread: 32 - Block: 0 - Warp 1 - Thread 32
Calculated Thread: 33 - Block: 0 - Warp 1 - Thread 33
Calculated Thread: 34 - Block: 0 - Warp 1 - Thread 34
...
Calculated Thread: 62 - Block: 0 - Warp 1 - Thread 62
Calculated Thread: 63 - Block: 0 - Warp 1 - Thread 63
Calculated Thread: 64 - Block: 1 - Warp 0 - Thread 0
Calculated Thread: 65 - Block: 1 - Warp 0 - Thread 1
Calculated Thread: 66 - Block: 1 - Warp 0 - Thread 2
Calculated Thread: 67 - Block: 1 - Warp 0 - Thread 3
...
Calculated Thread: 94 - Block: 1 - Warp 0 - Thread 30
Calculated Thread: 95 - Block: 1 - Warp 0 - Thread 31
Calculated Thread: 96 - Block: 1 - Warp 1 - Thread 32
Calculated Thread: 97 - Block: 1 - Warp 1 - Thread 33
Calculated Thread: 98 - Block: 1 - Warp 1 - Thread 34
Calculated Thread: 99 - Block: 1 - Warp 1 - Thread 35
Calculated Thread: 100 - Block: 1 - Warp 1 - Thread 36
...
Calculated Thread: 126 - Block: 1 - Warp 1 - Thread 62
Calculated Thread: 127 - Block: 1 - Warp 1 - Thread 63
```

As you can see, the calculated thread, or the thread ID, goes from 0 to 127. Within that you allocate two blocks of 64 threads each. The thread indexes within each of these blocks go from 0 to 63. You also see that each block generates two warps.

GRIDS

A grid is simply a set of blocks where you have an X and a Y axis, in effect a 2D mapping. The final Y mapping gives you $Y \times X \times T$ possibilities for a thread index. Let's look at this using an example, but limiting the Y axis to a single row to start off with.

If you were to look at a typical HD image, you have a 1920×1080 resolution. The number of threads in a block should *always* be a multiple of the warp size, which is currently defined as 32. As you can only schedule a full warp on the hardware, if you don't do this, then the remaining part of the warp goes unused and you have to introduce a condition to ensure you don't process elements off the end of the X axis. This, as you'll see later, slows everything down.

To avoid poor memory coalescing, you should always try to arrange the memory and thread usage so they map. This will be covered in more detail in the next chapter on memory. Failure to do so will result in something in the order of a five times drop in performance.

To avoid tiny thread blocks, as they don't make full use of the hardware, we'll pick 192 threads per block. In most cases, this is the *minimum* number of threads you should think about using. This gives you exactly 10 blocks across each row of the image, which is an easy number to work with (Figure 5.9). Using a thread size that is a multiple of the X axis and the warp size makes life a lot easier.

Along the top on the X axis, you have the thread index. The row index forms the Y axis. The height of the row is exactly one pixel. As you have 1080 rows of 10 blocks, you have in total $1080 \times 10 = 10,800$ blocks. As each block has 192 threads, you are scheduling just over two million threads, one for each pixel.

This particular layout is useful where you have one operation on a single pixel or data point, *or* where you have some operation on a number of data points in the *same* row. On the Fermi hardware, at eight blocks per SM, you'd need a total of 1350 SMs (10,800 total blocks ÷ 8 scheduled blocks) to run out of parallelism at the application level. On the Fermi hardware currently available, you have only 16 SMs (GTX580), so each SM would be given 675 blocks to process.

This is all very well, but what if your data is not row based? As with arrays, you are not limited to a single dimension. You can have a 2D thread block arrangement. A lot of image algorithms, for

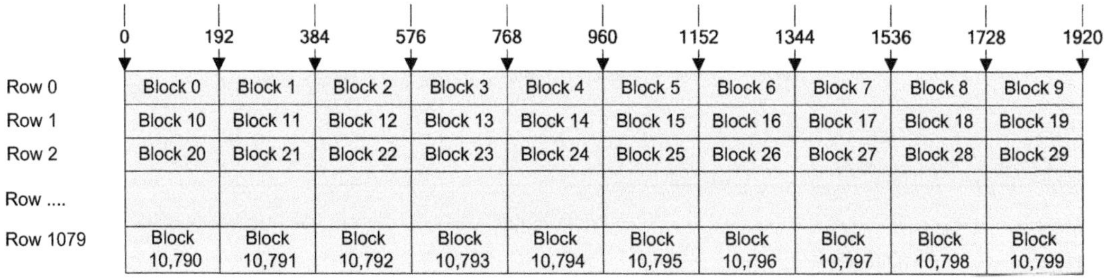

	0	192	384	576	768	960	1152	1344	1536	1728	1920
Row 0	Block 0	Block 1	Block 2	Block 3	Block 4	Block 5	Block 6	Block 7	Block 8	Block 9	
Row 1	Block 10	Block 11	Block 12	Block 13	Block 14	Block 15	Block 16	Block 17	Block 18	Block 19	
Row 2	Block 20	Block 21	Block 22	Block 23	Block 24	Block 25	Block 26	Block 27	Block 28	Block 29	
Row											
Row 1079	Block 10,790	Block 10,791	Block 10,792	Block 10,793	Block 10,794	Block 10,795	Block 10,796	Block 10,797	Block 10,798	Block 10,799	

FIGURE 5.9

Block allocation to rows.

example, use 8 × 8 blocks of pixels. We're using pixels here to show this arrangement, as it's easy for most people to conceptualize. Your data need not be pixel based. You typically represent pixels as a red, green, and blue component. You could equally have x, y, and z spatial coordinates as a single data point, or a simple 2D or 3D matrix holding the data points.

Stride and offset

As with arrays in C, thread blocks can be thought of as 2D structures. However, for 2D thread blocks, we need to introduce some new concepts. Just like in array indexing, to index into a Y element of 2D array, you need to know the width of the array, the number of X elements. Consider the array in Figure 5.10.

The width of the array is referred to as the stride of the memory access. The offset is the column value being accessed, starting at the left, which is always element 0. Thus, you have array element 5 being accessed with the index [1][5] or via the address calculation (row × (sizeof(array_element) × width))) + ((sizeof(array_element) × offset)). This is the calculation the compiler effectively uses, in an optimized form, when you do multidimensional array indexing in C code.

Array Element 0 X = 0 Y = 0	Array Element 1 X = 1 Y = 0	Array Element 2 X = 2 Y = 0	Array Element 3 X = 3 Y = 0	Array Element 4 X = 4 Y = 0
Array Element 5 X = 0 Y = 1	Array Element 6 X = 1 Y = 1	Array Element 7 X = 2 Y = 1	Array Element 8 X = 3 Y = 1	Array Element 9 X = 4 Y = 1
Array Element 10 X = 0 Y = 2	Array Element 11 X = 1 Y = 2	Array Element 12 X = 2 Y = 2	Array Element 13 X = 3 Y = 2	Array Element 14 X = 0 Y = 2

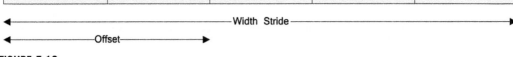

←————————————————— Width Stride ——————————————————→

←—————————Offset—————————→

FIGURE 5.10

Array mapping to elements.

Now, how is this relevant to threads and blocks in CUDA? CUDA is designed to allow for data decomposition into parallel threads and blocks. It allows you to define 1D, 2D, or 3D indexes ($Y \times X \times T$) when referring to the parallel structure of the program. This maps directly onto the way a typical area of memory is set out, allowing the data you are processing to be allocated to individual SMs. The process of keeping data close to the processor hugely increases performance, both on the GPU and CPU.

However, there is one caveat you must be aware of when laying out such arrays. The width value of the array must always be a multiple of the warp size. If it is not, pad the array to the next largest multiple of the warp size. Padding to the next multiple of the warp size should introduce only a very modest increase in the size of the dataset. Be aware, however, you'll need to deal with the padded boundary, or halo cells, differently than the rest of the cells. You can do this using divergence in the execution flow (e.g., using an if statement) or you can simply calculate the padded cells and discard the result. We'll cover divergence and the problems it causes later.

X and Y thread indexes

Having a 2D array in terms of blocks means you get two thread indexes, as you will be accessing the data in a 2D way:

```
const unsigned int idx = (blockIdx.x * blockDim.x) + threadIdx.x;
const unsigned int idy = (blockIdx.y * blockDim.y) + threadIdx.y;

some_array[idy][idx] += 1.0;
```

Notice the use of blockDim.x and blockDim.y, which the CUDA runtime completes for you, specifying the dimension on the X and Y axis. So let's modify the existing program to work on a 32 × 16 array. As you want to schedule four blocks, you can schedule them as stripes across the array, or as squares within the array, as shown in Figure 5.11.

You could also rotate the striped version 90 degrees and have a column per thread block. Never do this, as it will result in completely noncoalesced memory accesses that will drop the performance of your application by an order of magnitude or more. Be careful when parallelizing loops so that the access pattern always runs sequentially through memory in rows and never columns. This applies equally to CPU and GPU code.

Now why might you choose the square layout over the rectangle layout? Well, two reasons. The first is that threads within *the same block* can communicate using shared memory, a very quick way to cooperate with one another. The second consideration is you get marginally quicker memory access with single 128-byte transaction instead of two, 64-byte transactions, due to accessing within a warp being coalesced and 128 bytes being the size of a cache line in the Fermi/Kepler hardware. In the square layout notice you have threads 0 to 15 mapped to one block and the next memory location belongs to another block. As a consequence you get two transactions instead of one, as with the rectangular layout. However, if the array was slightly larger, say 64 × 16, then you would not see this issue, as you'd have 32 threads accessing contiguous memory, and thus a single 128-byte fetch from memory issued.

Use the following to modify the program to use either of the two layouts:

```
dim3 threads_rect(32,4);
dim3 blocks_rect(1,4);
```

Thread 0-15, Block 0	Thread 16-31, Block 0	Thread 0-15, Block 0	Thread 0-15, Block 1
Thread 32-47, Block 0	Thread 48-63, Block 0	Thread 16-31, Block 0	Thread 16-31, Block 1
Thread 64-79, Block 0	Thread 80-95, Block 0	Thread 32-47, Block 0	Thread 32-47, Block 1
Thread 96-111, Block 0	Thread 112-127, Block 0	Thread 48-63, Block 0	Thread 48-63, Block 1
Thread 0-15, Block 1	Thread 16-31, Block 1	Thread 64-79, Block 0	Thread 64-79, Block 1
Thread 32-47, Block 1	Thread 48-63, Block 1	Thread 80-95, Block 0	Thread 80-95, Block 1
Thread 64-79, Block 1	Thread 80-95, Block 1	Thread 96-111, Block 0	Thread 96-111, Block 1
Thread 96-111, Block 1	Thread 112-127, Block 1	Thread 112-127, Block 0	Thread 112-127, Block 1
Thread 0-15, Block 2	Thread 16-31, Block 2	Thread 0-15, Block 2	Thread 0-15, Block 4
Thread 32-47, Block 2	Thread 48-63, Block 3	Thread 16-31, Block 2	Thread 16-31, Block 4
Thread 64-79, Block 3	Thread 80-95, Block 3	Thread 32-47, Block 2	Thread 32-47, Block 4
Thread 96-111, Block 3	Thread 112-127, Block 3	Thread 48-63, Block 3	Thread 48-63, Block 4
Thread 0-15, Block 4	Thread 16-31, Block 4	Thread 64-79, Block 3	Thread 64-79, Block 4
Thread 32-47, Block 4	Thread 48-63, Block 4	Thread 80-95, Block 3	Thread 80-95, Block 4
Thread 64-79, Block 4	Thread 80-95, Block 4	Thread 96-111, Block 3	Thread 96-111, Block 4
Thread 96-111, Block 4	Thread 112-127, Block 4	Thread 112-127, Block 3	Thread 112-127, Block 4

OR

FIGURE 5.11

Alternative thread block layouts.

or
```
dim3 threads_square(16,8);
dim3 blocks_square(2,2);
```

In either arrangement you have the same total number of threads ($32 \times 4 = 128$, $16 \times 8 = 128$). It's simply the layout of the threads that is different.

The dim3 type is simply a special CUDA type that you have to use to create a 2D layout of threads. In the rectangle example, you're saying you want 32 threads along the X axis by 4 threads along the Y axis, within a single block. You're then saying you want the blocks to be laid out as one block wide by four blocks high.

You'll need to invoke the kernel with

```
some_kernel_func<<< blocks_rect, threads_rect >>>(a, b, c);
```

or

```
some_kernel_func<<< blocks_square, threads_square >>>(a, b, c);
```

As we no longer want just a single thread ID, but an X and Y position, we'll need to update the kernel to reflect this. However, we also need to linearize the thread ID because there are situations where you may want an absolute thread index. For this we need to introduce a couple of new concepts, shown in Figure 5.12.

You can see a number of new parameters, which are:

```
gridDim.x-The size in blocks of the X dimension of the grid.
gridDim.y-The size in blocks of the Y dimension of the grid.

blockDim.x-The size in threads of the X dimension of a single block.
blockDim.y-The size in threads of the Y dimension of a single block.
```

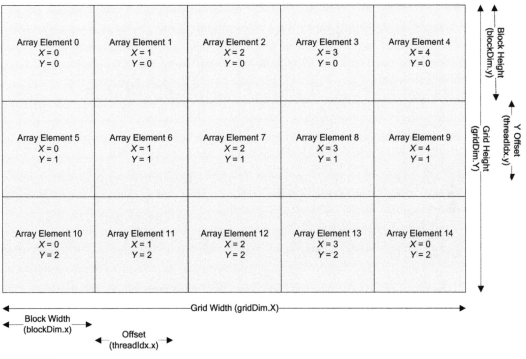

FIGURE 5.12

Grid, block, and thread dimensions.

```
theadIdx.x—The offset within a block of the X thread index.
theadIdx.y—The offset within a block of the Y thread index.
```

You can work out the absolute thread index by working out the *Y* position and multiplying this by number of threads in a row. You then simply add in the *X* offset from the start of the row. Thus, the thread index calculation is

```
thread_idx = ((gridDim.x * blockDim.x) * idy) + idx;
```

So we need to modify the kernel to additionally return the *X* and *Y* positions plus some other useful bits of information, as follows:

```
__global__ void what_is_my_id_2d_A(
unsigned int * const block_x,
unsigned int * const block_y,
unsigned int * const thread,
unsigned int * const calc_thread,
unsigned int * const x_thread,
unsigned int * const y_thread,
unsigned int * const grid_dimx,
```

```
unsigned int * const block_dimx,
unsigned int * const grid_dimy,
unsigned int * const block_dimy)
{
   const unsigned int idx        = (blockIdx.x * blockDim.x) + threadIdx.x;
   const unsigned int idy        = (blockIdx.y * blockDim.y) + threadIdx.y;
   const unsigned int thread_idx = ((gridDim.x * blockDim.x) * idy) + idx;

   block_x[thread_idx]     = blockIdx.x;
   block_y[thread_idx]     = blockIdx.y;
   thread[thread_idx]      = threadIdx.x;
   calc_thread[thread_idx] = thread_idx;
   x_thread[thread_idx]    = idx;
   y_thread[thread_idx]    = idy;
   grid_dimx[thread_idx]   = gridDim.x;
   block_dimx[thread_idx]  = blockDim.x;
   grid_dimy[thread_idx]   = gridDim.y;
   block_dimy[thread_idx]  = blockDim.y;
}
```

We'll call the kernel twice to demonstrate how you can arrange array blocks and threads.

As we're now passing an additional dataset to compute, we need an additional cudaMalloc, cudaFree, and cudaMemcpy to copy the data from the device. As we're using two dimensions, we will also need to modify the array size to allocate and transfer the correct size of data.

```
#define ARRAY_SIZE_X 32
#define ARRAY_SIZE_Y 16

#define ARRAY_SIZE_IN_BYTES ((ARRAY_SIZE_X) * (ARRAY_SIZE_Y) * (sizeof(unsigned int)))

/* Declare statically six arrays of ARRAY_SIZE each */
unsigned int cpu_block_x[ARRAY_SIZE_Y][ARRAY_SIZE_X];
unsigned int cpu_block_y[ARRAY_SIZE_Y][ARRAY_SIZE_X];
unsigned int cpu_thread[ARRAY_SIZE_Y][ARRAY_SIZE_X];
unsigned int cpu_warp[ARRAY_SIZE_Y][ARRAY_SIZE_X];
unsigned int cpu_calc_thread[ARRAY_SIZE_Y][ARRAY_SIZE_X];
unsigned int cpu_xthread[ARRAY_SIZE_Y][ARRAY_SIZE_X];
unsigned int cpu_ythread[ARRAY_SIZE_Y][ARRAY_SIZE_X];
unsigned int cpu_grid_dimx[ARRAY_SIZE_Y][ARRAY_SIZE_X];
unsigned int cpu_block_dimx[ARRAY_SIZE_Y][ARRAY_SIZE_X];
unsigned int cpu_grid_dimy[ARRAY_SIZE_Y][ARRAY_SIZE_X];
unsigned int cpu_block_dimy[ARRAY_SIZE_Y][ARRAY_SIZE_X];

int main(void)
{
   /* Total thread count = 32 * 4 = 128 */
   const dim3 threads_rect(32, 4); /* 32 * 4 */
   const dim3 blocks_rect(1,4);
```

```
/* Total thread count = 16 * 8 = 128 */
const dim3 threads_square(16, 8); /* 16 * 8 */
const dim3 blocks_square(2,2);

/* Needed to wait for a character at exit */
char ch;

/* Declare pointers for GPU based params */
unsigned int * gpu_block_x;
unsigned int * gpu_block_y;
unsigned int * gpu_thread;
unsigned int * gpu_warp;
unsigned int * gpu_calc_thread;
unsigned int * gpu_xthread;
unsigned int * gpu_ythread;
unsigned int * gpu_grid_dimx;
unsigned int * gpu_block_dimx;
unsigned int * gpu_grid_dimy;
unsigned int * gpu_block_dimy;

/* Allocate four arrays on the GPU */
cudaMalloc((void **)&gpu_block_x, ARRAY_SIZE_IN_BYTES);
cudaMalloc((void **)&gpu_block_y, ARRAY_SIZE_IN_BYTES);
cudaMalloc((void **)&gpu_thread, ARRAY_SIZE_IN_BYTES);
cudaMalloc((void **)&gpu_calc_thread, ARRAY_SIZE_IN_BYTES);
cudaMalloc((void **)&gpu_xthread, ARRAY_SIZE_IN_BYTES);
cudaMalloc((void **)&gpu_ythread, ARRAY_SIZE_IN_BYTES);
cudaMalloc((void **)&gpu_grid_dimx, ARRAY_SIZE_IN_BYTES);
cudaMalloc((void **)&gpu_block_dimx, ARRAY_SIZE_IN_BYTES);
cudaMalloc((void **)&gpu_grid_dimy, ARRAY_SIZE_IN_BYTES);
cudaMalloc((void **)&gpu_block_dimy, ARRAY_SIZE_IN_BYTES);

for (int kernel=0; kernel < 2; kernel++)
{
  switch (kernel)
  {
    case 0:
    {
      /* Execute our kernel */
      what_is_my_id_2d_A<<<blocks_rect, threads_rect>>>(gpu_block_x, gpu_block_y,
gpu_thread, gpu_calc_thread, gpu_xthread, gpu_ythread, gpu_grid_dimx, gpu_block_dimx,
gpu_grid_dimy, gpu_block_dimy);
    } break;

    case 1:
    {
```

```
        /* Execute our kernel */
        what_is_my_id_2d_A<<<blocks_square, threads_square>>>(gpu_block_x, gpu_block_y,
gpu_thread, gpu_calc_thread, gpu_xthread, gpu_ythread, gpu_grid_dimx, gpu_block_dimx,
gpu_grid_dimy, gpu_block_dimy);
    } break;

    default: exit(1); break;
  }

  /* Copy back the gpu results to the CPU */
  cudaMemcpy(cpu_block_x, gpu_block_x, ARRAY_SIZE_IN_BYTES,
            cudaMemcpyDeviceToHost);
  cudaMemcpy(cpu_block_y, gpu_block_y, ARRAY_SIZE_IN_BYTES,
            cudaMemcpyDeviceToHost);
  cudaMemcpy(cpu_thread, gpu_thread, ARRAY_SIZE_IN_BYTES,
            cudaMemcpyDeviceToHost);
  cudaMemcpy(cpu_calc_thread, gpu_calc_thread, ARRAY_SIZE_IN_BYTES,
            cudaMemcpyDeviceToHost);
  cudaMemcpy(cpu_xthread, gpu_xthread, ARRAY_SIZE_IN_BYTES,
            cudaMemcpyDeviceToHost);
  cudaMemcpy(cpu_ythread, gpu_ythread, ARRAY_SIZE_IN_BYTES,
            cudaMemcpyDeviceToHost);
  cudaMemcpy(cpu_grid_dimx, gpu_grid_dimx, ARRAY_SIZE_IN_BYTES,
            cudaMemcpyDeviceToHost);
  cudaMemcpy(cpu_block_dimx,gpu_block_dimx, ARRAY_SIZE_IN_BYTES,
            cudaMemcpyDeviceToHost);
  cudaMemcpy(cpu_grid_dimy, gpu_grid_dimy, ARRAY_SIZE_IN_BYTES,
            cudaMemcpyDeviceToHost);
  cudaMemcpy(cpu_block_dimy, gpu_block_dimy, ARRAY_SIZE_IN_BYTES,
            cudaMemcpyDeviceToHost);

  printf("\nKernel %d\n", kernel);
  /* Iterate through the arrays and print */
  for (int y=0; y < ARRAY_SIZE_Y; y++)
  {
      for (int x=0; x < ARRAY_SIZE_X; x++)
      {
          printf("CT: %2u BKX: %1u BKY: %1u TID: %2u YTID: %2u XTID: %2u GDX: %1u BDX: %
1u GDY %1u BDY %1u\n", cpu_calc_thread[y][x], cpu_block_x[y][x], cpu_block_y[y][x],
cpu_thread[y][x], cpu_ythread[y][x], cpu_xthread[y][x], cpu_grid_dimx[y][x],
cpu_block_dimx[y][x], cpu_grid_dimy[y][x], cpu_block_dimy[y][x]);

          /* Wait for any key so we can see the console window */
          ch = getch();
      }
  }
  /* Wait for any key so we can see the console window */
  printf("Press any key to continue\n");
```

```
    ch = getch();
}

/* Free the arrays on the GPU as now we're done with them */
cudaFree(gpu_block_x);
cudaFree(gpu_block_y);
cudaFree(gpu_thread);
cudaFree(gpu_calc_thread);
cudaFree(gpu_xthread);
cudaFree(gpu_ythread);
cudaFree(gpu_grid_dimx);
cudaFree(gpu_block_dimx);
cudaFree(gpu_grid_dimy);
cudaFree(gpu_block_dimy);
}
```

The output is too large to list here. If you run the program in the downloadable source code section, you'll see you iterate through the threads and blocks as illustrated in Figure 5.12.

WARPS

We touched a little on warp scheduling when talking about threads. Warps are the basic unit of execution on the GPU. The GPU is effectively a collection of SIMD vector processors. Each group of threads, or warps, is executed together. This means, in the ideal case, only one fetch from memory for the current instruction and a broadcast of that instruction to the entire set of SPs in the warp. This is much more efficient than the CPU model, which fetches independent execution streams to support task-level parallelism. In the CPU model, for every core you have running an independent task, you can conceptually divide the memory bandwidth, and thus the effective instruction throughput, by the number of cores. In practice, on CPUs, the multilevel, on-chip caches hide a lot of this providing the program fits within the cache.

You find vector-type instructions on conventional CPUs, in the form of SSE, MMX, and AVX instructions. These execute the same single instruction on multiple data operands. Thus, you can say, for N values, increment all values by one. With SSE, you get 128-bit registers, so you can operate on four parameters at any given time. AVX extends this to 256 bits. This is quite powerful, but until recently, unless you were using the Intel compiler, there was little native support for this type of optimization. AVX is now supported by the current GNU gcc compiler. Microsoft Visual Studio 2010 supports it through the use of a "/arch:AVX" compiler switch. Given this lack of support until relatively recently, vector-type instructions are not as widely used as they could be, although this is likely to change significantly now that support is no longer restricted to the Intel compiler.

With GPU programming, you have no choice: It's vector architecture and expects you to write code that runs on thousands of threads. You can actually write a single-thread GPU program with a simple if statement checking if the thread ID is zero, but this will get you terrible performance compared with the CPU. It can, however, be useful just to get an initial serial CPU implementation working. This approach allows you to check things, such as whether memory copying to/from the GPU is working correctly, before introducing parallelism into the application.

Warps on the GPU are currently 32 elements, although nVidia reserves the right to change this in the future. Therefore, they provide an intrinsic variable, warpSize, for you to use to obtain the warp size on the current hardware. As with any magic number, you should not hard code an assumed warp size of 32. Many SSE-optimized programs were hard coded to assume an SSE size of 128 bits. When AVX was released, simply recompiling the code was not sufficient. Don't make the same mistake and hard code such details into your programs.

So why should you be interested in the size of a warp? The reasons are many, so we'll look briefly at each.

Branching

The first reason to be interested in the size of a warp is because of branching. Because a warp is a single unit of execution, branching (e.g., if, else, for, while, do, switch, etc.) causes a divergence in the flow of execution. On a CPU there is complex hardware to do branch prediction, predicting from past execution which path a given piece of code will take. The instruction flow is then prefetched and pumped into the CPU instruction pipeline ahead of time. Assuming the prediction is correct, the CPU avoids a "stall event." Stall events are very bad, as the CPU then has to undo any speculative instruction execution, fetch instructions from the other branch path, and refill the pipeline.

The GPU is a much simpler device and has none of this complexity. It simply executes one path of the branch and then the other. Those threads that take the branch are executed and those that do not are marked as inactive. Once the taken branch is resolved, the other side of the branch is executed, until the threads converge once more. Take the following code:

```
__global__ some_func(void)
{
  if (some_condition)
  {
    action_a();
  }
  else
  {
    action_b();
  }
}
```

As soon as you evaluate some_condition, you will have divergence in at least one block or there is no point in having the test in the program. Let's say all the even thread numbers take the true path and all the odd threads take the false path. The warp scoreboard then looks as shown in Figure 5.13.

0	1	2	3	4	5	6	7	8	9	10	11	12	13	14	15	16
+	-	+	-	+	-	+	-	+	-	+	-	+	-	+	-	+

FIGURE 5.13

Predicate thread/branch selection.

For simplicity, I've drawn only 16 of the 32 threads, and you'll see why in a minute. All those threads marked + take the true or positive path and all those marked − take the false or negative path.

As the hardware can only fetch a single instruction stream per warp, half of the threads stall and half progress down one path. This is really bad news as you now have only 50% utilization of the hardware. This is a bit like having a dual-core CPU and only using one core. Many lazy programmers get away with it, but the performance is terrible compared to what it could be.

Now as it happens, there is a trick here that can avoid this issue. The actual scheduler in terms of instruction execution is half-warp based, not warp based. This means if you can arrange the divergence to fall on a half warp (16-thread) boundary, you can actually execute both sides of the branch condition, the if-else construct in the example program. You can achieve 100% utilization of the device in this way.

If you have two types of processing of the data, interleaving the data on a 16-word boundary can result in quite good performance. The code would simply branch on the thread ID, as follows:

```
if ((thread_idx % 32) < 16)
{
  action_a();
}
else
{
  action_b();
}
```

The modulus operator in C (%) returns the remainder of the integer division of the operand. In effect, you count from 0 to 31 and then loop back to 0 again. Ideally, the function action_a() has each of its 16 threads access a single float or integer value. This causes a single 64-byte memory fetch. The following half warp does the same and thus you issue a single 128-byte memory fetch, which it just so happens is the size of the cache line and therefore the optimal memory fetch size for a warp.

GPU utilization

So why else might you be interested in warps? To avoid underutilizing the GPU. The CUDA model uses huge numbers of threads to hide memory latency (the time it takes for a memory request to come back). Typically, latency to the global memory (DRAM) is around 400–600 cycles. During this time the GPU is busy doing other tasks, rather than idly waiting for the memory fetch to complete.

When you allocate a kernel to a GPU, the maximum number of threads you can put onto an SM is currently 768 to 2048, depending on the compute level. This is implementation dependent, so it may change with future hardware revisions. Take a quick look at utilization with different numbers of threads in Table 5.1.

Compute 1.0 and 1.2 devices are the G80/G92 series devices. Compute 1.3 devices are the GT200 series. Compute 2.0/2.1 devices are the Fermi range. Compute 3.0 is Kepler.

Notice that the only consistent value that gets you 100% utilization across all levels of the hardware is 256 threads. Thus, for maximum compatibility, you should aim for either 192 or 256 threads. The dataset should, however, match the thread layout to achieve certain optimizations. You should, therefore, also consider the 192-thread layout where you have a three-point data layout.

Table 5.1 Utilization %

Threads per Block/ Compute Capability	1.0	1.1	1.2	1.3	2.0	2.1	3.0
64	67	67	50	50	33	33	50
96	100	100	75	75	50	50	75
128	100	100	100	100	67	67	100
192	100	100	94	94	100	100	94
256	100	100	100	100	100	100	100
384	100	100	75	75	100	100	94
512	67	67	100	100	100	100	100
768	N/A	N/A	N/A	N/A	100	100	75
1024	N/A	N/A	N/A	N/A	67	67	100

Another alternative to having a fixed number of threads is to simply look up the compute level from the device and select a the smallest number of threads, that gives the highest device utilization.

Now you might want to also consider the number of blocks that can be scheduled into a given SM. This really only makes a difference when you have synchronization points in the kernel. These are points where every thread must wait on every other thread to reach the same point, for example, when you're doing a staged read and all threads must do the read. Due to the nature of the execution, some warps may make good progress and some may make poor progress to the synchronization point.

The time, or latency, to execute a given block is undefined. This is not good from a load balancing point of view. You want lots of threads available to be run. With 256 threads, 32 threads per warp give you 8 warps on compute 2.x hardware. You can schedule up to 24 warps ($32 \times 24 = 768$ threads) at any one time into a given SM for compute 1.x devices and 48 ($32 \times 48 = 1536$ threads) for compute 2.x devices. A block cannot be retired from an SM until it's completed its *entire* execution. With compute 2.0x devices or higher that support 1024 threads per block, you can be waiting for that single warp to complete while all other warps are idle, effectively making the SM also idle.

Thus, the larger the thread block, the more potential you have to wait for a slow warp to catch up, because the GPU can't continue until all threads have passed the checkpoint. Therefore, you might have chosen a smaller number of threads, say 128 threads in the past, to reduce this potential waiting time. However, this hurts the performance on Fermi-level hardware as the device utilization drops to two-thirds. As you can see from Table 5.1, on compute 2.0 devices (Fermi), you need to have at least 192 threads per block to make good use of the SM.

However, you should not get too tied up concerning the number of warps, as they are really just a measure of the overall number of threads present on the SMs. Table 5.3 shows the total number of threads running, and it's this total number that is really the interesting part, along with the percentage utilization shown in Table 5.1.

Notice with 128 or less threads per block, as you move from the compute 1.3 hardware (the GT200 series) to the compute 2.x hardware (Fermi), you see no difference in the total number of threads running. This is because there are limits to the number of blocks an SM can schedule. The number of

Table 5.2 Blocks per SM

Threads per Block/ Compute Capability	1.0	1.1	1.2	1.3	2.0	2.1	3.0
64	8	8	8	8	8	8	16
96	8	8	8	8	8	8	12
128	6	6	8	8	8	8	16
192	4	4	5	5	8	8	10
256	3	3	4	4	6	6	8
384	2	2	2	2	4	4	5
512	1	1	2	2	3	3	4
768	N/A	N/A	1	1	2	2	2
1024	N/A	N/A	1	1	1	1	2

Table 5.3 Total Threads per SM

Threads per Block/ Compute Capability	1.0	1.1	1.2	1.3	2.0	2.1	3.0
64	512	512	512	512	512	512	1024
96	768	768	768	768	768	768	1536
128	768	768	1024	1024	1024	1024	2048
192	768	768	960	960	1536	1536	1920
256	768	768	1024	1024	1536	1536	2048
384	768	768	768	768	1536	1536	1920
512	512	512	1024	1024	1536	1536	2048
768	N/A	N/A	N/A	N/A	1536	1536	1536
1024	N/A	N/A	N/A	N/A	1024	1024	2048

threads an SM could support was increased, but not the number of blocks. Thus, to achieve better scaling you need to ensure you have at least 192 threads and preferably considerably more.

BLOCK SCHEDULING

Suppose you have 1024 blocks to schedule, and eight SMs to schedule these onto. With the Fermi hardware, each SM can accept up to 8 blocks, but only if there is a low thread count per block. With a reasonable thread count, you typically see 6 to 8 blocks per SM.

Now 1024 blocks divided between six SMs is 170 complete blocks each, plus 4 blocks left over. We'll look at the leftover blocks in a minute, because it causes an interesting problem.

With the 1020 blocks that can be allocated to the SMs, how should they be allocated? The hardware could allocate 6 blocks to the first SM, 6 to the second, and so on. Alternatively, it could distribute 1 block to each SM in turn, so SM 0 gets block 0, SM 1 gets block 1, SM 2 gets block 2, etc. NVIDIA doesn't specify what method it uses, but it's fairly likely to be the latter to achieve a reasonable load balance across the SMs.

If you have 19 blocks and four SMs, allocating blocks to an SM until it's full is not a good idea. The first three SMs would get 6 blocks each, and the last SM, a single block. The last SM would likely finish quickly and sit idle waiting for the other SMs. The utilization of the available hardware is poor.

If you allocate blocks to alternate SMs on a rotating basis, each SM gets 4 blocks (4 SMs × 4 blocks = 16 total) and three SMs get an additional block each. Assuming each block takes the same time to execute you have reduced the execution time by 17%, simply by balancing the blocks among the SMs, rather than overloading some SMs while underloading others.

Now in practice you will usually have thousands or tens of thousands of blocks to get through in a typical application. Having done the initial allocation of blocks to an SM, the block dispatcher is then idle until one block finishes on any of the SMs. At this point the block is retired and the resources used by that block become free. As all the blocks are the same size, *any* block in the list of waiting blocks can be scheduled. The order of execution of blocks is deliberately undefined and there should be no implicit assumption that blocks will execute in any order when programming a solution to a problem.

This can have serious problems if there is some associative operation being performed, such as floating-point addition, which is not in practice associative. The order of execution of adds through an array in floating-point math will affect the result. This is due to the rounding errors and the way in which floating-point math works. The result is correct in all cases. It's not a parallel execution problem, but an ordering problem. You see exactly the same issue with single-thread CPU code. If you add a set of random numbers from bottom to top, or top to bottom, in a floating-point array on a CPU or GPU, you will get different answers. Perhaps worse still is that on a GPU, due to the undefined block scheduling, multiple runs on the same data can result in different but correct answers. There are methods to deal with this and it is something we cover later in the book. So for now, just be aware that because the result is different than before, it doesn't necessarily make the result incorrect.

Coming back to the problem of having leftover blocks, you will have this scenario anytime the number of blocks is not a multiple of the number of SMs. Typically you see CUDA devices ship with an odd number of SMs, due to it being difficult to make large, complex processors. As the physical amount of silicon used in creating a processor increases, the likelihood there is a failure in some section increases considerably. NVIDIA, like many processor manufacturers, simply disables faulty SMs and ships devices as lower-specification units. This increases yields and provides some economic value to otherwise faulty devices. However, for the programmer, this means the total number of SMs is not always even a multiple of two. The Fermi 480 series cards, and also the Tesla S2050/S2070/C2050/C2070 series, have a 16 SM device with 1 SM disabled, thus making 15 SMs. This was resolved in the 580 series, but this problem is likely to be repeated as we see future GPU generations released.

Having a few leftover blocks is really only an issue if you have a very long kernel and need to wait for each kernel to complete. You might see this, for example, in a finite time step simulation. If you had 16 blocks, assuming a Fermi 480 series card, 15 blocks would be allocated to each of the SMs. The remaining block will be scheduled only after one of the other 15 blocks has completed. If each kernel took 10 minutes to execute, it's likely all the blocks would finish at approximately the same time. The

GPU would then schedule one additional block and the complete kernel invocation would wait for an additional 10 minutes for this single block to execute. At the same time, the other 14 available SMs would be idle. The solution to this problem is to provide better granularity to break down the small number of blocks into a much larger number.

In a server environment you may not have just 15 SMs, but actually multiple nodes each having multiple GPUs. If their only task is this kernel, then they will likely sit idle toward the end of the kernel invocation. In this instance it might prove better to redesign the kernel in some way to ensure the number of blocks is an exact multiple of the number of SMs on each node.

From a load balancing perspective, this problem is clearly not good. As a consequence, in the later CUDA runtime, you have support for overlapping kernels and running multiple, separate kernels on the same CUDA device. Using this method, you can maintain the throughput if you have more than one source of jobs to schedule onto the cluster of GPUs. As the CUDA devices start to idle, they instead pick up another kernel from a stream of available kernels.

A PRACTICAL EXAMPLE—HISTOGRAMS

Histograms are commonly found in programming problems. They work by counting the distribution of data over a number of "bins." Where the data point contains a value that is associated with a given bin, the value in that bin is incremented.

In the simplest example, you have 256 bins and data that range from 0 to 255. You iterate through an array of bytes. If the value of the element in the array is 0, you increment bin 0. If the value of the element is 10, you increment bin 10, etc.

The algorithm from a serial perspective is quite simple:

```
for (unsigned int i=0; i< max; i++)
{
  bin[array[i]]++;
}
```

Here you extract the value from the array, indexed by i. You then increment the appropriate bin using the ++ operator.

The serial implementation suffers from a problem when you convert it to a parallel problem. If you execute this with 256 threads, you get more than one thread *simultaneously* incrementing the value in the *same* bin.

If you look at how the C language gets converted to an assembler, you see it can take a series of assembler instructions to execute this code. These would break down into

1. Read the value from the array into a register.
2. Work out the base address and offset to the correct bin element.
3. Fetch the existing bin value.
4. Increment the bin value by one.
5. Write the new bin value back to the bin in memory.

The problem is steps three, four, and five are not atomic. An atomic operation is one that cannot be interrupted prior to completion. If you execute this pseudocode in a lockstep manner, as CUDA does with its thread model, you hit a problem. Two or more threads fetch the same value at step three. They all increment it and write it back. The last thread to do the write wins. The value should have been incremented N times, but it's incremented only once. All threads read the same value to apply the increment to, thus you lose N increments to the value.

The problem here is that you have a data dependency you do not see on the serial execution version. Each increment of the bin value must complete before the read and increment by the next thread. You have a shared resource between threads.

This is not an uncommon problem and CUDA provides a primitive for this called

```
atomicAdd(&value);
```

This operation guarantees the addition operation is serialized among all threads.

Having now solved this problem, you come to the real choice here—how to structure the tasks you have to cover into threads, blocks, and grids. There are two approaches: the task decomposition model or the data decomposition model. Both generally need to be considered.

With the task decomposition model, you simply allocate one thread to every element in input array and have it do an atomic add. This is the simplest solution to program, but has some major disadvantages. You must remember that the bins are actually a shared resource. If you have 256 bins and an array of 1024 elements, assuming an equal distribution, you have 4 elements contending for each bin. With large arrays (there is no point in processing small arrays with CUDA) this problem becomes the dominant factor determining the total execution time.

If you assume an equal distribution of values in the histogram, which is often not the case, the number of elements contending for any single bin is simply the array size in elements divided by the number of bins. With a 512 MB array (524,288 elements) you would have 131,072 elements contending for each bin. In the worst case, all elements write to the same bin, so you have, in effect, a serial program due to the serialization of the atomic memory writes.

In either example, the execution time is limited by the hardware's ability to handle this contention and the read/write memory bandwidth.

Let's see how this works in reality. Here is the GPU program to do this.

```
/* Each thread writes to one block of 256 elements of global memory and contends for
write access */

__global__ void myhistogram256Kernel_01(
  const unsigned char const * d_hist_data,
  unsigned int * const d_bin_data)
{
  /* Work out our thread id */
  const unsigned int idx = (blockIdx.x * blockDim.x) + threadIdx.x;

  const unsigned int idy = (blockIdx.y * blockDim.y) + threadIdx.y;

  const unsigned int tid = idx + idy * blockDim.x * gridDim.x;

  /* Fetch the data value */
```

```
  const unsigned char value = d_hist_data[tid];

  atomicAdd(&(d_bin_data[value]),1);
}
```

With a GTX460 card, we measured 1025 MB/s with this approach. What is interesting is that it does not scale with the number of elements in the array. You get a consistently poor performance, regardless of the array size. Note that the GPU used for this test, a 1 GB GTX460, has a memory bandwidth of 115 GB/s, so this shows just how terrible a performance you can achieve by implementing the naive solution.

This figure, although bad, simply tells you that you are limited by some factor and it's your job as a programmer to figure out which factor and eliminate it. The most likely factor affecting performance in this type of program is memory bandwidth and/or atomic operations. You are fetching N values from the input array and compressing those down to N writes to a small, 1 K (256 elements × 4 bytes per integer counter) memory section.

If you look at the memory reads first, you will see each thread reads one *byte* element of the array. Reads are combined together (coalesced) at the half-warp level (16 threads). The minimum transfer size is 32 bytes, so wasting read memory bandwidth by about 50%, which is pretty poor. The optimal memory fetch for a warp is the maximum supported size, which is 128 bytes. For this, each thread has to fetch bytes of memory. You can do this by having each thread process four histogram entries instead of one.

We can issue a 4-byte read, by reading a single integer, and then extracting the component parts of that integer as shown in Figure 5.14. This should provide better read coalescing and therefore better performance. The modified kernel is as follows:

```
/* Each read is 4 bytes, not one, 32 x 4 = 128 byte reads */
__global__ void myhistogram256Kernel_02(
const unsigned int const * d_hist_data,
unsigned int * const d_bin_data)
{
  /* Work out our thread id */
  const unsigned int idx = (blockIdx.x * blockDim.x) + threadIdx.x;
```

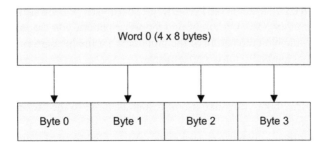

FIGURE 5.14

Word-to-byte mapping.

```
 const unsigned int idy = (blockIdx.y * blockDim.y) + threadIdx.y;

 const unsigned int tid = idx + idy * blockDim.x * gridDim.x;

 /* Fetch the data value as 32 bit */
 const unsigned int value_u32 = d_hist_data[tid];

 atomicAdd(&(d_bin_data[ ((value_u32 & 0x000000FF) ) ]),1);

 atomicAdd(&(d_bin_data[ ((value_u32 & 0x0000FF00) >> 8 ) ]),1);

 atomicAdd(&(d_bin_data[ ((value_u32 & 0x00FF0000) >> 16 ) ]),1);

 atomicAdd(&(d_bin_data[ ((value_u32 & 0xFF000000) >> 24 ) ]),1);
}
```

When running the kernel we notice we have achieved for all our effort zero speedup. This is, in fact, quite common when trying to optimize programs. It's a pretty strong indicator you did not understand the cause of the bottleneck.

One issue to note here is that in compute 2.x, hardware does not suffer with only being able to coalesce data from a half warp and can do full-warp coalescing. Thus, on the test device, a GTX460 (compute 2.1 hardware), the 32 single byte fetches issued by a single warp were coalesced into a 32-byte read.

The other obvious candidate is the atomic write operation, rather than the usual memory bandwidth culprit. For this you need to look at the alternative approach given by the data decomposition model. Here you look at the data flow side of the equation, looking for data reuse and optimizing the data size into that which works effectively with shared resources, such as a cache or shared memory.

You can see that the contention for the 256 bins is a problem. With multiple blocks writing to memory from multiple SMs, the hardware needs to sync the value of the bin array across the caches in all processors. To do this it needs to fetch the current value from memory, increment it, and then write it back. There is some potential for this to be held permanently in the L2 cache, which is shared between the SMs in the Fermi generation of hardware. With compute 1.x hardware, you are reading and writing to the global memory, so this approach is an order of magnitude slower.

Even if you can use the L2 cache on the Fermi/Kepler hardware, you are still having to go out of the SM to sync with all the other SMs. On top of this the write pattern you are generating is a scattered pattern, dependent very much on the nature of the input data for the histogram. This means no or very little coalescing, which again badly hurts performance.

An alternative approach is to build the histogram within each SM and then write out the histogram to the main memory at the end. This is the approach you must always try to achieve, whether for CPU or GPU programming. The more you make use of resources close to the processor (SM in this case), the faster the program runs.

We mentioned earlier that we can use shared memory, a special form of memory that is on chip and thus very fast. You can create a 256-bin histogram in the shared memory and then do the atomic add at the end to the global memory. Assuming you process only one histogram per block, you do not decrease the number of global memory reads or writes, but you do coalesce all the writes to memory. The kernel for this approach is as follows:

```
__shared__ unsigned int d_bin_data_shared[256];

/* Each read is 4 bytes, not one, 32 x 4 = 128 byte reads */
__global__ void myhistogram256Kernel_03(
const unsigned int const * d_hist_data,
unsigned int * const d_bin_data)
{
  /* Work out our thread id */
  const unsigned int idx = (blockIdx.x * blockDim.x) + threadIdx.x;
  const unsigned int idy = (blockIdx.y * blockDim.y) + threadIdx.y;
  const unsigned int tid = idx + idy * blockDim.x * gridDim.x;

  /* Clear shared memory */
  d_bin_data_shared[threadIdx.x] = 0;

  /* Fetch the data value as 32 bit */
  const unsigned int value_u32 = d_hist_data[tid];

  /* Wait for all threads to update shared memory */
  __syncthreads();

  atomicAdd(&(d_bin_data_shared[ ((value_u32 & 0x000000FF) ) ]),1);
  atomicAdd(&(d_bin_data_shared[ ((value_u32 & 0x0000FF00) >> 8 ) ]),1);
  atomicAdd(&(d_bin_data_shared[ ((value_u32 & 0x00FF0000) >> 16 ) ]),1);
  atomicAdd(&(d_bin_data_shared[ ((value_u32 & 0xFF000000) >> 24 ) ]),1);

  /* Wait for all threads to update shared memory */
  __syncthreads();

  /* The write the accumulated data back to global memory in blocks, not scattered */
  atomicAdd(&(d_bin_data[threadIdx.x]), d_bin_data_shared[threadIdx.x]);
}
```

The kernel must do an additional clear operation on the shared memory, as you otherwise have random data left there from other kernels. Notice also you need to wait (__syncthreads) until all the threads in a block have managed to clear their memory cell in the shared memory before you start allowing threads to update any of the shared memory cells. You need to do the same sync operation at the end, to ensure every thread has completed before you write the result back to the global memory.

You should see that, suddenly, there is get a huge *six* times jump in performance, simply by virtue of arranging the writes in order so they can be coalesced. We can now achieve 6800 MB/s processing speed. Note, however, you can only do this with compute 1.2 or higher devices as only these support shared memory atomic operations.

Now that we have the ordering correct, you need to look at reducing the global memory traffic. You have to read every value from the source data, and we only read each value once. We're already using the optimal transfer size for read accesses, so let's look at the data being written. If we process N histograms per block instead of one histogram per block we reduce the write bandwidth by a factor of N.

Table 5.4 shows the value achieved on the 512 MB histogram based on processing different values of N with a Fermi 460 card (which contains seven SMs). You can see a peak of 7886 MB/s at an N value of 64. The kernel is as follows:

```
/* Each read is 4 bytes, not one, 32 x 4 = 128 byte reads */
/* Accumulate into shared memory N times */
__global__ void myhistogram256Kernel_07(const unsigned int const * d_hist_data,
                                         unsigned int * const d_bin_data,
                                         unsigned int N)
{
  /* Work out our thread id */
  const unsigned int idx = (blockIdx.x * (blockDim.x*N) ) + threadIdx.x;
  const unsigned int idy = (blockIdx.y * blockDim.y ) + threadIdx.y;
  const unsigned int tid = idx + idy * (blockDim.x*N) * (gridDim.x);

  /* Clear shared memory */
  d_bin_data_shared[threadIdx.x] = 0;

  /* Wait for all threads to update shared memory */
  __syncthreads();

  for (unsigned int i=0, tid_offset=0; i< N; i++, tid_offset+=256)
  {
    const unsigned int value_u32 = d_hist_data[tid+tid_offset];

    atomicAdd(&(d_bin_data_shared[ ((value_u32 & 0x000000FF) ) ]),1);
    atomicAdd(&(d_bin_data_shared[ ((value_u32 & 0x0000FF00) >> 8 ) ]),1);
    atomicAdd(&(d_bin_data_shared[ ((value_u32 & 0x00FF0000) >> 16 ) ]),1);
    atomicAdd(&(d_bin_data_shared[ ((value_u32 & 0xFF000000) >> 24 ) ]),1);
  }
  /* Wait for all threads to update shared memory */
  __syncthreads();

  /* The write the accumulated data back to global memory in blocks, not scattered */
  atomicAdd(&(d_bin_data[threadIdx.x]), d_bin_data_shared[threadIdx.x]);
}
```

Let's examine this a little, because it's important to understand what you are doing here. You have a loop i that runs for N iterations. This is the number of times you will process 256 bytes of data into the shared memory histogram. There are 256 threads invoked for the kernel, one for each bin. As such, the only loop you need is a loop over the number of histograms to process. When you've done one iteration, you move 256 bytes on in memory to process the next histogram (tid_offset += 256).

Notice also that as you're using atomic operations throughout, you need sync points only at the start and end of the kernel. Adding unnecessary synchronization points typically slows down the program, but can lead to a more uniform access pattern in memory.

Table 5.4 Histogram Results

Factor	MB/s	Total Blocks	Blocks per SM	Remainder Blocks
1	6766	524,288	74,898	3
2	7304	262,144	37,449	1
4	7614	131,072	18,724	6
8	7769	65,536	9362	3
16	7835	32,768	4681	1
32	7870	16,384	2340	6
64	7886	8192	1170	3
128	7884	4096	585	1
256	7868	2048	292	6
512	7809	1024	146	3
1024	7737	512	73	1
2048	7621	256	36	6
4096	7093	128	18	3
8192	6485	64	9	1
16,384	6435	32	4	6
32,768	5152	16	2	3
65,536	2756	8	1	1

Now what is interesting here is that, after you start to process 64 or more histograms per block, you see no effective increase in throughput. The global memory bandwidth is dropping by a factor of two every time you increase that value of N. If global memory bandwidth is indeed the problem, you should see a linear speed up here for every factor of N you add. So what is going on?

The main problem is the atomic operations. Every thread must content for access to the shared data area, along with other threads. The data pattern has a huge influence on the execution time, which is not a good design.

We'll return to this issue later when we look at how you can write such algorithms without having to use atomic operations.

CONCLUSION

We covered a lot in this chapter and you should now be familiar with how CUDA breaks tasks into grids, blocks, and threads. We covered the scheduling of blocks and warps on the hardware and the need to ensure you always have enough threads on the hardware.

The threading model used in CUDA is fundamental to understanding how to program GPUs efficiently. You should understand how CPUs and GPUs are fundamentally different beasts to program, but at the same time how they are related to one another.

You have seen how arrangement of threads relative to the data you are going to process is important and impacts performance. You have also seen, in particular with applications that need to share data, it is not always an easy task to parallelize a particular problem. You should note that often taking time to consider the correct approach is somewhat more important than diving in with the first solution that seems to fit.

We also covered the use of atomics and some of the problems of serialization these cause. We touched on the problems branching can cause. You should have in the back of your mind the need to ensure all threads follow the same control path. We look at atomics and branching in more detail later in the book.

You have had some exposure to the extended C syntax used within CUDA and should feel comfortable in writing a CUDA program with a clear understanding of what will happen.

By reading this chapter you have gained a great deal of knowledge and hopefully should no longer feel that CUDA or parallel programming is a bit like a black art.

Questions

1. Identify the best and worst data pattern for the histogram algorithm developed in this chapter. Is there a common usage case that is problematic? How might you overcome this?
2. Without running the algorithm, what do you think is the likely impact of running this code on older hardware based on the G80 design?
3. When processing an array in memory on a CPU, is it best to transverse in row-column order or column-row order? Does this change when you move the code to a GPU?
4. Consider a section of code that uses four blocks of 256 threads and the same code that uses one block of 1024 threads. Which is likely to complete first and why? Each block uses four `syncthreads()` calls at various points through the code. The blocks require no interblock cooperation.
5. What are the advantages and disadvantages of an SIMD-based implementation that we find in GPUs versus the MIMD implementation we find in multicore CPUs?

Answers

1. The best case is uniform distribution of data. This is because this loads the buckets equally and you therefore get an equal distribution of atomic operations on the available shared memory banks.

The worst case is identical data values. This causes all threads to continuously hit the same shared memory bucket, causing serialization of the entire program through both the atomic operations and bank conflicts in the shared memory.

Unfortunately, one very common usage is with sorted data. This provides a variation on the worst-case usage. Here one bank after another gets continuously hit with atomic writes, effectively serializing the problem.

One solution is to step through the dataset such that each iteration writes to a new bin. This requires knowledge of the data distribution. For example, consider the case of 256 data points modeling a linear function using 32 bins. Let's assume data points 0 to 31 fall into the first bin and this is replicated for every bin. By processing one value for each bin, you can distribute writes to the bin and avoid contention. In this example, you would read data points 0, 32, 64, 96, 1, 33, 65, 97, 2, 34, 66, 98, etc.

2. The G80 devices (compute 1.0, compute 1.1) don't support shared memory atomics, so the code will not compile. Assuming you modified it to use global memory atomics, we saw a seven-fold decrease in performance in the example provided earlier in the chapter.

3. The row-column ordering is best because the CPU will likely use a prefetch technique, ensuring the subsequent data to be accessed will be in the cache. At the very least, an entire cache line will be fetched from memory. Thus, when the CPU comes to the second iteration of the row-based access, `a[0]` will have fetched `a[1]` into the cache.

The column transversal will result in much slower code because the fetch of a single cache line on the CPU is unlikely to fetch data used in the subsequent loop iteration unless the row size is very small. On the GPU each thread fetches one or more elements of the row, so the loop transversal, at a high level, is usually by column, with an entire row being made up of individual threads. As with the CPU the entire cache line will be fetched on compute 2.x hardware. However, unlike the CPU, this cache line will likely be immediately consumed by the multiple threads.

4. During a `syncthreads()` operation, the entire block stalls until every one of the threads meets the `syncthreads()` checkpoint. At this point they all become available for scheduling again. Having a very large number of threads per block can mean the SM runs out of available warps to schedule while waiting for the threads in a single block to meet the checkpoint. The execution flow as to which thread gets to execute when is undefined. This means some threads can make much better progress than others to the `syncthreads()` checkpoint. This is the result of a design decision in favor of throughput over latency at the hardware level. A very high thread count per block is generally only useful where the threads in the block need to communicate with one another, without having to do interblock communication via the global memory.

5. The SIMD model amortizes the instruction fetch time over many execution units where the instruction stream is identical. However, where the instruction stream diverges, execution must be serialized. The MIMD model is designed for divergent execution flow and doesn't need to stall threads when the flow diverges. However, the multiple fetch and decoding units require more silicon and higher instruction bandwidth requirements to maintain multiple independent execution paths.

A mixture of SIMD and MIMD is often the best way of dealing with both control flow and identical operations of large datasets. You see this in CPUs in terms of SSE/MMX/AVX support. You see this in GPUs in terms of warps and blocks allowing for divergence at a higher granularity.

Memory Handling with CUDA

6

INTRODUCTION

In the conventional CPU model we have what is called a linear or flat memory model. This is where any CPU core can access any memory location without restriction. In practice, for CPU hardware, you typically see a level one (L1), level two (L2), and level three (L3) cache. Those people who have optimized CPU code or come from a high-performance computing (HPC) background will be all too familiar with this. For most programmers, however, it's something they can easily abstract away.

Abstraction has been a trend in modern programming language, where the programmer is further and further removed from the underlying hardware. While this can lead to higher levels of productivity, as problems can be specified at a very high level, it relies hugely on clever compilers to implement these abstractions into a level understood by the hardware. While this is great in theory, the reality can be somewhat less than the marketing dream. I'm sure in the decades to come we'll see huge improvements in compilers and languages such that they will take advantage of parallel hardware automatically. However, until this point, and certainly until we get there, the need to understand how the hardware functions will be key to extracting the best performance from any platform.

For real performance on a CPU-based system, you need to understand how the cache works. We'll look at this on the CPU side and then look at the similarities with the GPU. The idea of a cache is that most programs execute in a serial fashion, with various looping constructs, in terms of their execution flow. If the program calls a function, the chances are the program will call it again soon. If the program accesses a particular memory location, the chances are most programs will access that same location again within a short time period. This is the principle of *temporal locality*, that it is highly likely that you will reuse data and reexecute the same code having used/executed it once already.

Fetching data from DRAM, the main memory of a computer system is very slow. DRAM has historically always been very slow compared to processor clock speeds. As processor clock speeds have increased, DRAM speeds have fallen further and further behind.

DDR-3 DRAM in today's processors runs up to 1.6 Ghz as standard, although this can be pushed to up to 2.8 Ghz with certain high speed modules and the correct processor. However, each of the CPU cores is typically running at around 3 GHz. Without a cache to provide quick access to areas of memory, the bandwidth of the DRAM will be insufficient for the CPU. As both code and data exist in the DRAM space, the CPU is effectively instruction throughput limited (how many instructions it executes in a given timeframe) if it cannot fetch either the program or data from the DRAM fast enough.

This is the concept of *memory bandwidth*, the amount of data we can read or store to DRAM in a given period of time. However, there is another important concept, *latency*. Latency is the amount of time it takes to respond to a fetch request. This can be hundreds of processor cycles. If the program wants four elements from memory it makes sense therefore to issue all requests together and then wait for them to arrive, rather than issue one request, wait until it arrives, issue the next request, wait, and so on. Without a cache, a processor would be very much memory bandwidth *and* latency limited.

To think of bandwidth and latency in everyday terms, imagine a supermarket checkout process. There are N checkouts available in a given store, not all of which may be staffed. With only two checkouts active (staffed), a big queue will form behind them as the customers back up, having to wait to pay for their shopping. The throughput or bandwidth is the number of customers processed in a given time period (e.g., one minute). The time the customer has to wait in the queue is a measure of the latency, that is, how long after joining the queue did the customer wait to pay for his or her shopping and leave.

As the queue becomes large, the store owner may open more checkout points and the queue disperses between the new checkout points and the old ones. With two new checkout points opened, the bandwidth of the checkout area is doubled, because now twice as many people can be served in the same time period. The latency is also halved, because, on average, the queue is only half as big and everyone therefore waits only half the time.

However, this does not come for free. It costs money to employ more checkout assistants and more of the retail space has to be allocated to checkout points rather than shelf space for products. The same tradeoff occurs in processor design, in terms of the memory bus width and the clock rate of the memory devices. There is only so much silicon space on the device and often the width of the external memory bus is limited by the number of physical pins on the processor.

One other concept we also need to think about is *transaction overhead*. There is a certain overhead in processing the payment for every customer. Some may have two or three items in a basket while others may have overflowing shopping carts. The shop owners love the shopping cart shoppers because they can be processed efficiently, that is, more of the checkout person's time is spent checking out groceries, rather than in the overhead of processing the payment.

We see the same in GPUs. Some memory transactions are lightweight compared to the fixed overhead to process them. The number of memory cells fetched relative to the overhead time is low, or, in other words, the percentage of peak efficiency is poor. Others are large and take a bunch of time to serve, but can be serviced efficiently and achieve near peak memory transfer rates. These translate to byte-based memory transactions at the inefficient end of the spectrum and to long word-based transactions at the other end. To achieve peak memory efficiency, we need lots of large transactions and very few, if any, small ones.

CACHES

A cache is a high-speed memory bank that is physically close to the processor core. Caches are expensive in terms of silicon real estate, which in turn translates into bigger chips, lower yields, and more expensive processors. Thus, the Intel Xeon chips with the huge L3 caches found in a lot of server machines are far more expensive to manufacture than the desktop version that has less cache on the processor die.

The maximum speed of a cache is proportional to the size of the cache. The L1 cache is the fastest, but is limited in size to usually around 16 K, 32 K, or 64 K. It is usually allocated to a single CPU core. The L2 cache is slower, but much larger, typically 256 K to 512 K. The L3 cache may or may not be present and is often several megabytes in size. The L2 and/or L3 cache may be shared between processor cores or maintained as separate caches linked directly to given processor cores. Generally, at least the L3 cache is a shared cache between processor cores on a conventional CPU. This allows for fast intercore communication via this shared memory within the device.

The G80 and GT200 series GPUs have no equivalent CPU-like cache to speak of. They do, however, have a hardware-managed cache that behaves largely like a read-only CPU cache in terms of constant and texture memory. The GPU relies instead primarily on a programmer-managed cache, or shared memory section.

The Fermi GPU implementation was the first to introduce the concept of a nonprogrammer-managed data cache. The architecture additionally has, per SM, an L1 cache that is both programmer managed and hardware managed. It also has a shared L2 cache across all SMs.

So does it matter if the cache is shared across processor cores or SMs? Why is this arrangement relevant? This has an interesting implication for communicating with other devices using the same shared cache. It allows interprocessor communication, without having to go all the way out to global memory. This is particularly useful for atomic operations where, because the L2 cache is unified, all SMs see a consistent version of the value at a given memory location. The processor does not have to write to the slow global memory, to read it back again, just to ensure consistency between processor cores. On G80/GT200 series hardware, where there is no unified cache, we see exactly this deficiency and consequently quite slow atomic operations compared with Fermi and later hardware.

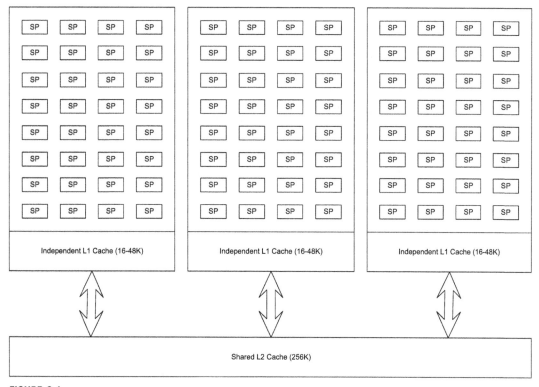

FIGURE 6.1

SM L1/L2 data path.

Caches are useful for most programs. Significant numbers of programmers either care little for or have a limited understanding of how to achieve good performance in software. Introducing a cache means most programs work reasonably well and the programmer does not have to care too much about how the hardware works. This ease of programming is useful for initial development, but in most cases you can do somewhat better.

The difference between a novice CUDA programmer and someone who is an expert can be up to an order of magnitude. I hope that through reading this book, you'll be able to get several times speedup from your existing code and move toward being routinely able to write CUDA code, which significantly outperforms the equivalent serial code.

Types of data storage

On a GPU, we have a number of levels of areas where you can place data, each defined by its potential bandwidth and latency, as shown in Table 6.1.

At the highest and most preferred level are registers inside the device. Then we have shared memory, effectively a programmer-managed L1 cache, constant memory, texture memory, regular device memory, and finally host memory. Notice how the order of magnitude changes between the slowest and fastest type of storage. We will now look at the usage of each of these in turn and how you can maximize the gain from using each type.

Traditionally, most texts would start off by looking at global memory, as this often plays a key role in performance. If you get the global memory pattern wrong then you can forget anything else until you get the correct pattern. We take a different approach here, in that we look first at how to use the device efficiently internally, and from there move out toward global and host memory. Thus, you will understand efficiency at each level and have an idea of how to extract it.

Most CUDA programs are developed progressively, using global memory exclusively at least initially. Once there is an initial implementation, then the use of other memory types such as zero copy and shared, constant, and ultimately registers is considered. For an optimal program, you need to be thinking about these issues while you are developing a program. Thus, instead of the faster memory types being an afterthought, they are considered at the outset and you know exactly where and how to improve the program. You should be continuously thinking about not only how to access global memory efficiently, but also how those accesses, especially for data that is reused in some way, can be eliminated.

Table 6.1 Access Time by Memory Type

Storage Type	Registers	Shared Memory/ L1 Cache	Texture/Read Only Cache	Constant Memory Cache	Global Memory
Bandwidth	~8 TB/s	~1.4 TB/s to ~2 TB/s	~200 GB/s	32 GB/s to 64 GB/s	~200 GB/s
Latency	1 clock	1 to 32 clocks depending on bank conflicts	~400 to 800 on miss	~400 to 800 on miss	~400 to 800
Use for Access Pattern	Any	One address per thread or broadcast	Scattered or 2D Spartial Locality	Same address for each thread	128 byte Aligned. Sequential.

REGISTER USAGE

The GPU, unlike its CPU cousin, has thousands of registers per SM (streaming multiprocessor). An SM can be thought of like a multithreaded CPU core. On a typical CPU we have two, four, six, or eight cores. On a GPU we have N SM cores. On a Fermi GF100 series, there are 16 SMs on the top-end device. The GT200 series has up to 30 SMs per device. The G80 series has up to 16 SMs per device.

It may seem strange that Fermi/Kepler has less SMs than their predecessors. This is until you realize that each Fermi/Kepler SM contains more SPs (streaming processors) and that it is these that do the "grunt" work. Due to the different number of SPs per core, you see a major difference in the number of threads per core. A typical CPU will support one or two hardware threads per core. A GPU by contrast has between 8 and 192 SPs per core, meaning each SM can at any time be executing this number of concurrent hardware threads.

In practice on GPUs, application threads are pipelined, context switched, and dispatched to multiple SMs, meaning the number of active threads across all SMs in a GPU device is usually in the tens of thousands range.

One major difference we see between CPU and GPU architectures is how CPUs and GPUs map registers. The CPU runs lots of threads by using register renaming and the stack. To run a new task the CPU needs to do a context switch, which involves storing the state of all registers onto the stack (the system memory) and then restoring the state from the last run of the new thread. This can take several hundred CPU cycles. If you load too many threads onto a CPU it will spend all of the time simply swapping out and in registers as it context switches. The effective throughput of *useful* work rapidly drops off as soon as you load too many threads onto a CPU.

The GPU by contrast is the exact opposite. It uses threads to hide memory fetch and instruction execution latency, so too few threads on the GPU means the GPU will become idle, usually waiting on memory transactions. The GPU also does not use register renaming, but instead dedicates real registers to each and every thread. Thus, when a context switch is required, it has near zero overhead. All that happens on a context switch is the selector (or pointer) to the current register set is updated to point to the register set of the next warp that will execute.

Notice I used the concept of warps here, which was covered in detail in the Chapter 5 on threading. A warp is simply a grouping of threads that are scheduled together. In the current hardware, this is 32 threads. Thus, we swap in or swap out, and schedule, groups of 32 threads within a single SM.

Each SM can schedule a number of blocks. Blocks at the SM level are simply logical groups of independent warps. The number of registers per kernel thread is calculated at compile time. All blocks are of the same size and have a known number of threads, and the register usage per block is known and fixed. Consequently, the GPU can allocate a fixed set of registers for each block scheduled onto the hardware.

At a thread level, this is transparent to the programmer. However, a kernel that requests too many registers per thread can limit the number of blocks the GPU can schedule on an SM, and thus the total number of threads that will be run. Too few threads and you start underutilizing the hardware and the performance starts to rapidly drop off. Too many threads can mean you run short of resources and whole blocks of threads are dropped from being scheduled to the SM.

Be careful of this effect, as it can cause sudden performance drops in the application. If previously the application was using four blocks and now it uses more registers, causing only three blocks to be available, you may well see a one-quarter drop in GPU throughput. You can see this type of problem with various profiling tools available, covered in Chapter 7 in the profiling section.

Depending on the particular hardware you are using, there is 8 K, 16 K, 32 K or 64 K of register space per SM for *all threads* within an SM. You need to remember that one register is required *per thread*. Thus, a simple local float variable in C results in N registers usage, where N is the number of threads that are scheduled. With the Fermi-level hardware, you get 32 K of register space per SM. With 256 threads per block, you would have ((32,768/4 bytes per register)/256 threads) = 32 registers per thread available. To achieve the maximum number of registers available on Fermi, 64 (128 on G80/GT200), you'd need to half the thread count to just 128 threads. You could have a single block per SM, with the maximum permitted number of registers in that block. Equally, you could have eight blocks of 32 threads ($8 \times 32 = 256$ threads in total), each using the maximum number of registers.

If you can make use of the maximum number of registers, for example, using them to work on a section of an array, then this approach can work quite well. It works because such a set of values is usually N elements from a dataset. If each element is independent, you can create instruction-level parallelism (ILP) within a single thread. This is exploited by the hardware in terms of pipelining many independent instructions. You'll see later an example of this working in practice.

However, for most kernels, the number of registers required is somewhat lower. If you drop your register requirements from 128 to 64, you can schedule another block into the same SM. For example, with 32 registers, you can schedule four blocks. In doing so, you are increasing the total thread count. On Fermi, you can have up to 1536 threads per SM and, for the general case, the higher the level of occupancy you can achieve, the faster your program will execute. You will reach a point where you have enough thread-level parallelism (TLP) to hide the memory latency. To continue to increase performance further, you either need to move to larger memory transactions or introduce ILP, that is, process more than one element of the dataset within a single thread.

There is, however, a limit on the number of warps that can be scheduled to an SM. Thus, dropping the number of registers from 32 to 16 does not get eight blocks. For that we are limited to 192 threads, as shown in Table 6.2.

Table 6.2 refers to the Fermi architecture. For the Kepler architecture, simply double the number of registers and blocks shown here. We've used 192 and 256 threads here as they provide good utilization of the hardware. Notice that the kernel usage of 16 versus 20 registers does not introduce any additional blocks to the SM. This is due to the limit on the number of warps that can be allocated to an SM. So in this case, you can easily increase register usage without impacting the total number of threads that are running on a given SM.

Table 6.2 Register Availability by Thread Usage on Fermi

No. of Threads	Maximum Register Usage					
192	16	20	24	28	32	64
Blocks Scheduled	8	8	7	6	5	2
No. of Threads	**Maximum Register Usage**					
256	16	20	24	28	32	64
Blocks Scheduled	6	6	5	4	4	2

You want to use registers to avoid usage of the slower memory types, but you have to be careful that you use them effectively. For example, suppose we had a loop that set each bit in turn, depending on the value of some Boolean variable. Effectively, we'd be packing and unpacking 32 Booleans into 32 bits of a word. We could write this as a loop, each time modifying the memory location by the new Boolean, shifted to the correct position within the word, as shown in the following:

```
for (i=0; i<31; i++)
{
 packed_result |= (pack_array[i] << i);
}
```

Here we are reading array element i from an array of elements to pack into an integer, packed_result. We're left shifting the Boolean by the necessary number of bits and then using a bitwise or operation with the previous result.

If the parameter packed_result exists in memory, you'd be doing 32 memory read and writes. We could equally place the parameter packed_result in a local variable, which in turn the compiler would place into a register. As we accumulate into the register instead of in main memory, and later write only the *result* to main memory, we save 31 of the 32 memory reads and writes.

Looking back at Table 6.1, you can see it takes several hundred cycles to do a global memory operation. Let's assume 500 cycles for one global memory read or write operation. For every value you'd need to read, apply the or operation, and write the result back. Therefore, you'd have 32 × read + 32 × write = 64 × 500 cycles = 32,000 cycles. The register version would eliminate 31 read and 32 write operations, replacing the 500-cycle operations with single-cycle operations. Thus, you'd have

$$(1 \times \text{memory read}) + (1 \times \text{memory write}) + (31 \times \text{register read}) + (31 \times \text{register write}) \text{ or}$$

$$(1 \times 500) + (1 \times 500) + (31 \times 1) + (31 \times 1) = 1062 \text{ cycles versus } 32,000 \text{ cycles}$$

Clearly, this is a huge reduction in the number of cycles. We have a 31 times improvement to perform a relatively common operation in certain problem domains.

We see similar relationships with common reduction operations like sum, min, max, etc. A reduction operation is where a dataset is reduced by some function to a smaller set, typically a single item. Thus, max (10, 12, 1, 4, 5) would return a single value, 12, the maximum of the given dataset.

Accumulating into a register saves huge numbers of memory writes. In our bit packing example, we reduce our memory writes by a factor of 31. Whether you are using a CPU or GPU, this type of register optimization will make a huge difference in the speed of execution of your programs.

However, this burdens the programmer with having to think about which parameters are in registers and which are in memory, which registers need to be copied back to memory, etc. This might seem like quite a bit of trouble to go to, and for the average programmer, often it is. Therefore, we see a proliferation of code that works directly on memory. For the most part, cache memory you find on CPUs significantly masks this problem. The accumulated value is typically held in the L1 cache. If a write-back policy is used on the cache, where the values do not need to be written out to main memory until later, the performance is not too bad. Note that the L1 cache is still slower than registers, so the solution will be suboptimal and may be several times slower than it could be.

Some compilers may detect such inefficiencies and implement a load into a register during the optimizer phase. Others may not. Relying on the optimizer to fix poor programming puts you at the mercy of how good the compiler is, or is not. You may find that, as the optimization level is increased, errors creep into the program. This may not be the fault of the compiler. The C language definition is quite complex. As the optimization level is increased, subtle bugs may appear due to a missed volatile qualifier or the like. Automatic test scripts and back-to-back testing against a nonoptimized version are good solutions to ensure correctness.

You should also be aware that optimizing compiler vendors don't always choose to implement the best solution. If just 1% of programs fail when a certain optimization strategy is employed by the compiler vendor, then it's unlikely to be employed due to the support issues this may generate.

The GPU has a computation rate many times in excess of its memory bandwidth capacity. The Fermi hardware has around 190 GB/s peak bandwidth to memory, with a peak compute performance of over one teraflop. This is over five times the memory bandwidth. On the Kepler GTX680/Tesla K10 the compute power increases to 3 Teraflops, yet with a memory bandwidth almost identical to the GTX580. In the bit packing example, without register optimization and on a system with no cache, you would require one read and one write per loop iteration. Each integer or floating-point value is 4 bytes in length. The best possible performance we could, theoretically, achieve in this example, due to the need to read and write a total of 8 bytes, would be one-eighth of the memory bandwidth. Using the 190 GB/s figure, this would equate to around 25 billion operations per second.

In practice you'd never get near this, because there are loop indexes and iterations to take into account as well as simply the raw memory bandwidth. However, this sort of back-of-the-envelope calculation provides you with some idea of the upper bounds of your application before you start coding anything.

Applying our factor of 31 reductions to the number of memory operations allows you to achieve a theoretical peak of 31 times this figure, some 775 billion iterations per second. We'll in practice hit other limits, within the device. However, you can see we'd easily achieve many times better performance than a simple global memory version by simply accumulating to or making use of registers wherever possible.

To get some real figures here, we'll write a program to do this bit packing on global memory and then with registers. The results are as follows:

```
ID:0 GeForce GTX 470:Reg. version faster by: 2.22ms (Reg=0.26ms, GMEM=2.48ms)
ID:1 GeForce 9800 GT:Reg. version faster by: 52.87ms (Reg=9.27ms, GMEM=62.14ms)
ID:2 GeForce GTX 260:Reg. version faster by: 5.00ms (Reg=0.62ms, GMEM=5.63ms)
ID:3 GeForce GTX 460:Reg. version faster by: 1.56ms (Reg=0.34ms, GMEM=1.90ms)
```

The two kernels to generate these are as follows:

```
__global__ void test_gpu_register(u32 * const data, const u32 num_elements)
{
  const u32 tid = (blockIdx.x * blockDim.x) + threadIdx.x;
  if (tid < num_elements)
  {
    u32 d_tmp = 0;

    for (int i=0;i<KERNEL_LOOP;i++)
    {
      d_tmp |= (packed_array[i] << i);
    }
```

```
    data[tid] = d_tmp;
   }
}


__device__ static u32 d_tmp = 0;
__global__ void test_gpu_gmem(u32 * const data, const u32 num_elements)
{
 const u32 tid = (blockIdx.x * blockDim.x) + threadIdx.x;
 if (tid < num_elements)
 {
  for (int i=0;i<KERNEL_LOOP;i++)
  {
   d_tmp |= (packed_array[i] << i);
  }

  data[tid] = d_tmp;
 }
}
```

The only difference in the two kernels is that one uses a global variable, d_tmp, while the other uses a local register. Looking at the results you can see the speedups in Table 6.3. You see an average speedup of 7.7 times. Perhaps, most surprisingly, the fastest speedup comes from the devices that have the largest number of SMs, which points to a problem that I hope you may have spotted. In the global memory version of the kernel, every thread from every block reads and writes to d_tmp. There is no guarantee as to in which order this will happen, so the program's output is indeterminate. The kernel executes perfectly well, with no CUDA errors detected, yet the answer will always be nonsense. This type of error is a remarkably common type of mistake when converting serial code to parallel code.

Strange answers should always point you toward something being wrong. So how is this issue corrected? In the register version, each thread writes to a unique register. In the GMEM (Global Memory) version, it must do the same. Therefore, you simply replace the original definition of d_tmp:

```
__device__ static u32 d_tmp = 0;
```

With

Table 6.3 Speedup Using Registers over GMEM

Card	Register Version	GMEM (Global Memory) Version	Speedup
GTX470	0.26	2.48	9.5
9800GT	9.27	62.14	6.7
GTX260	0.62	5.63	9.1
GTX460	0.34	1.9	5.6
Average			7.7

```
__device__ static u32 d_tmp[NUM_ELEM];
```

The kernel needs to be updated as follows:

```
__global__ void test_gpu_register(u32 * const data, const u32 num_elements)
{
 const u32 tid = (blockIdx.x * blockDim.x) + threadIdx.x;
 if (tid < num_elements)
 {
  u32 d_tmp = 0;

  for (int i=0;i<KERNEL_LOOP;i++)
  {
   d_tmp |= (packed_array[i] << i);
  }

  data[tid] = d_tmp;
 }
}
```

Now each thread gets to read and write from an independent area of global memory. What of the speedup now?

As you can see from Table 6.4, the average speedup drops to just 1.7 times. If it were not for the 9800GT (a compute 1.1 device) you'd see the average almost hit two times speedup in this simple piece of code. Where possible, you always need to avoid global memory writes through some other means. Converging on a single memory address, as in the first example, forces the hardware to serialize the memory operations, leading to terrible performance.

Now it's quite easy to make this code even faster. Loops are typically very inefficient, in that they cause branching, which can cause pipeline stalls. More importantly, they consume instructions that don't contribute to the final result. The loop code will contain an increment for the loop counter, a test of the end loop condition, and a branch for every iteration. In comparison, the useful instructions per iteration will load the value from pack_array, shift it left N bits, and or it with the existing d_tmp value. Just looking at the operations, we see 50% or so of the operations are based around the loop. You can look directly at the following PTX (Parallel Thread eXecution) code to verify this. The instructions that perform the loop, to make reading the virtual assembly code easier, are highlighted in bold.

Table 6.4 Real Speedup from Using Registers over GMEM

Card	Register Version	GMEM Version	Speedup
GTX470	0.26	0.51	2
9800GT	9.27	10.31	1.1
GTX260	0.62	1.1	1.8
GTX460	0.34	0.62	1.8
Average			1.7

```
        .entry _Z18test_gpu_register1Pjj (
         .param .u64 __cudaparm__Z18test_gpu_register1Pjj_data,
         .param .u32 __cudaparm__Z18test_gpu_register1Pjj_num_elements)
        {
        .reg .u32 %r<27>;
        .reg .u64 %rd<9>;
        .reg .pred %p<5>;
        // __cuda_local_var_108903_15_non_const_tid = 0
        // __cuda_local_var_108906_13_non_const_d_tmp = 4
        // i = 8
        .loc 16 36 0
        $LDWbegin__Z18test_gpu_register1Pjj:
        $LDWbeginblock_180_1:
        .loc 16 38 0
        mov.u32   %r1, %tid.x;
        mov.u32   %r2, %ctaid.x;
        mov.u32   %r3, %ntid.x;
        mul.lo.u32   %r4, %r2, %r3;
        add.u32   %r5, %r1, %r4;
        mov.s32   %r6, %r5;
        .loc 16 39 0
        ld.param.u32   %r7, [__cudaparm__Z18test_gpu_register1Pjj_num_elements];
        mov.s32   %r8, %r6;
        setp.le.u32   %p1, %r7, %r8;
        @%p1 bra   $L_0_3074;
        $LDWbeginblock_180_3:
        .loc 16 41 0
        mov.u32   %r9, 0;
        mov.s32   %r10, %r9;
        $LDWbeginblock_180_5:
        .loc 16 43 0
        mov.s32   %r11, 0;
        mov.s32   %r12, %r11;
        mov.s32   %r13, %r12;
        mov.u32   %r14, 31;
        setp.gt.s32   %p2, %r13, %r14;
        @%p2 bra   $L_0_3586;
        $L_0_3330:
        .loc 16 45 0
        mov.s32   %r15, %r12;
        cvt.s64.s32   %rd1, %r15;
        cvta.global.u64   %rd2, packed_array;
        add.u64   %rd3, %rd1, %rd2;
        ld.s8   %r16, [%rd3+0];
        mov.s32   %r17, %r12;
        shl.b32   %r18, %r16, %r17;
        mov.s32   %r19, %r10;
        or.b32   %r20, %r18, %r19;
```

```
 mov.s32  %r10, %r20;
 .loc 16 43 0
 mov.s32  %r21, %r12;
 add.s32  %r22, %r21, 1;
 mov.s32  %r12, %r22;
$Lt_0_1794:
 mov.s32  %r23, %r12;
 mov.u32  %r24, 31;
 setp.le.s32  %p3, %r23, %r24;
 @%p3 bra  $L_0_3330;
$L_0_3586:
$LDWendblock_180_5:
 .loc 16 48 0
 mov.s32  %r25, %r10;
 ld.param.u64  %rd4, [__cudaparm__Z18test_gpu_register1Pjj_data];
 cvt.u64.u32  %rd5, %r6;
 mul.wide.u32  %rd6, %r6, 4;
 add.u64  %rd7, %rd4, %rd6;
 st.global.u32  [%rd7+0], %r25;
$LDWendblock_180_3:
$L_0_3074:
$LDWendblock_180_1:
 .loc 16 50 0
 exit;
$LDWend__Z18test_gpu_register1Pjj:
 }
```

Thus, the PTX code first tests if the for loop will actually enter the loop. This is done in the block labeled $LDWbeginblock_180_5. The code at the $Lt_0_1794 label then performs the loop operation, jumping back to label $L_0_3330 until such time as the loop has completed 32 iterations. The other code in the section labeled $L_0_3330 performs the operation:

```
 d_tmp |= (packed_array[i] << i);
```

Notice, in addition to the loop overhead, because packed_array is indexed by a variable the code has to work out the address on every iteration of the loop:

```
cvt.s64.s32  %rd1, %r15;
cvta.global.u64  %rd2, packed_array;
add.u64  %rd3, %rd1, %rd2;
```

This is rather inefficient. Compare this to a loop unrolled version and we see something quite interesting:

```
.entry _Z18test_gpu_register2Pjj (
 .param .u64 __cudaparm__Z18test_gpu_register2Pjj_data,
 .param .u32 __cudaparm__Z18test_gpu_register2Pjj_num_elements)
{
.reg .u32 %r<104>;
.reg .u64 %rd<6>;
```

```
 .reg .pred %p<3>;
 // __cuda_local_var_108919_15_non_const_tid = 0
 .loc 16 52 0
$LDWbegin__Z18test_gpu_register2Pjj:
$LDWbeginblock_181_1:
 .loc 16 54 0
 mov.u32   %r1, %tid.x;
 mov.u32   %r2, %ctaid.x;
 mov.u32   %r3, %ntid.x;
 mul.lo.u32  %r4, %r2, %r3;
 add.u32   %r5, %r1, %r4;
 mov.s32   %r6, %r5;
 .loc 16 55 0
 ld.param.u32  %r7, [__cudaparm__Z18test_gpu_register2Pjj_num_elements];
 mov.s32   %r8, %r6;
 setp.le.u32  %p1, %r7, %r8;
 @%p1 bra  $L_1_1282;
 .loc 16 57 0
 ld.global.s8  %r9, [packed_array+0];
 ld.global.s8  %r10, [packed_array+1];
 shl.b32   %r11, %r10, 1;
 or.b32    %r12, %r9, %r11;
 ld.global.s8  %r13, [packed_array+2];
 shl.b32   %r14, %r13, 2;
 or.b32    %r15, %r12, %r14;

[Repeated code for pack_array+3 to packed_array+29 removed for clarity]

 ld.global.s8  %r97, [packed_array+30];
 shl.b32   %r98, %r97, 30;
 or.b32    %r99, %r96, %r98;
 ld.global.s8  %r100, [packed_array+31];
 shl.b32   %r101, %r100, 31;
 or.b32    %r102, %r99, %r101;
 ld.param.u64  %rd1, [__cudaparm__Z18test_gpu_register2Pjj_data];
 cvt.u64.u32  %rd2, %r6;
 mul.wide.u32  %rd3, %r6, 4;
 add.u64   %rd4, %rd1, %rd3;
 st.global.u32  [%rd4+0], %r102;
$L_1_1282:
$LDWendblock_181_1:
 .loc 16 90 0
 exit;
$LDWend__Z18test_gpu_register2Pjj:
 }
```

Almost all the instructions now contribute to the result. The loop overhead is gone. The address calculation for packed_array is reduced to a compile time–resolved base plus offset type address.

Everything is much simpler, but much longer, both in the C code and also in the virtual PTX assembly code.

The point here is not to understand PTX, but to see the vast difference small changes in C code can have on the virtual assembly generated. It's to understand that techniques like loop unrolling can be hugely beneficial in many cases. We look at PTX and how it gets translated in the actual code that gets executed in more detail in Chapter 9 on optimization.

So what does this do in terms of speedup? You can see from Table 6.5 that on the 9800GT or the GTX260, there was no effect at all. However, on the more modern compute 2.x hardware, the GTX460 and GTX470, you see a 2.4× and 3.4× speedup, respectively. If you look back to the pure GMEM implementation, on the GTX470 this is a 6.4× speedup. To put this in perspective, if the original program took six and a half hours to run, then the optimized version would take just one hour.

Register optimization can have a huge impact on your code execution timing. Take the time to look at the PTX code being generated for the *inner loops* of your program. Can you unroll the loop to expand it into a single, or set, of expressions? Think about this with your code and you'll see a huge performance leap. It is better to register usage, such as eliminating memory accesses, or provide additional ILP as one of the best ways to speed up a GPU kernel.

Table 6.5 Effects of Loop Unrolling

Card	Register Version	Unrolled Version	Speedup
GTX470	0.27	0.08	3.4
9800GT	9.28	9.27	1
GTX260	0.62	0.62	1
GTX460	0.34	0.14	2.4
Average			2

SHARED MEMORY

Shared memory is effectively a user-controlled L1 cache. The L1 cache and shared memory share a 64 K memory segment per SM. In Kepler this can be configured in 16 K blocks in favor of the L1 or shared memory as you prefer for your application. In Fermi the choice is 16 K or 48K in favor of the L1 or shared memory. Pre-Fermi hardware (compute 1.×) has a fixed 16 K of shared memory and no L1 cache. The shared memory has in the order of 1.5 TB/s bandwidth with extremely low latency. Clearly, this is hugely superior to the up to 190 GB/s available from global memory, but around one-fifth of the speed of registers.

In practice, global memory speeds on low-end cards are as little as one-tenth that of the high-end cards. However, the shared memory speed is driven by the core clock rate, which remains much more consistent (around a 20% variation) across the entire range of GPUs. This means that to get the most from any card, not just the high-end cards, you must use shared memory effectively in addition to using registers.

In fact, just by looking at the bandwidth figures—1.5 TB/s for shared memory and 190 GB/s for the best global memory access—you can see that there is a 7:1 ratio. To put it another way, there is potential for a 7× speedup if you can make effective use of shared memory. Clearly, shared memory is a concept that every CUDA programmer who cares about performance needs to understand well.

However, the GPU operates a load-store model of memory, in that any operand must be loaded into a register prior to any operation. Thus, the loading of a value into shared memory, as opposed to just loading it into a register, must be justified by data reuse, coalescing global memory, or data sharing between threads. Otherwise, better performance is achieved by directly loading the global memory values into registers.

Shared memory is a bank-switched architecture. On Fermi it is 32 banks wide, and on G200 and G80 hardware it is 16 banks wide. Each bank of data is 4 bytes in size, enough for a single-precision floating-point data item or a standard 32-bit integer value. Kepler also introduces a special 64 bit wide mode so larger double precision values no longer span two banks. Each bank can service only a *single* operation per cycle, regardless of how many threads initiate this action. Thus, if every thread in a warp accesses a separate bank address, every thread's operation is processed in that single cycle. Note there is no need for a one-to-one sequential access, just that every thread accesses a separate bank in the shared memory. There is, effectively, a crossbar switch connecting any single bank to any single thread. This is very useful when you need to swap the words, for example, in a sorting algorithm, an example of which we'll look at later.

There is also one other very useful case with shared memory and that is where every thread in a warp reads the *same* bank address. As with constant memory, this triggers a broadcast mechanism to all threads within the warp. Usually thread zero writes the value to communicate a common value with the other threads in the warp. See Figure 6.2.

However, if we have *any other pattern*, we end up with bank conflicts of varying degrees. This means you stall the other threads in the warp that idle while the threads accessing the shared memory address queue up one after another. One important aspect of this is that it is *not* hidden by a switch to another warp, so we do in fact stall the SM. Thus, bank conflicts are to be avoided if at all possible as the SM will idle until all the bank requests have been fulfilled.

However, this is often not practical, such as in the histogram example we looked at in Chapter 5. Here the data is unknown, so which bank it falls into is entirely dependent on the data pattern.

The worst case is where every thread writes to the same bank, in which case we get 32 serial accesses to the same bank. We see this typically where the thread accesses a bank by a stride other than 32. Where the stride decreases by a power of two (e.g., in a parallel reduction), we can also see this, with each successive round causing more and more bank conflicts.

Sorting using shared memory

Let's introduce a practical example here, using sorting. A sorting algorithm works by taking a random dataset and generating a sorted dataset. We thus need N input data items and N output data items. The key aspect with sorting is to ensure you minimize the number of reads and writes to memory. Many sorting algorithms are actually multipass, meaning we read every element of N, M times, which is clearly inefficient.

The quicksort algorithm is the preferred algorithm for sorting in the serial world. Being a divide-and-conquer algorithm, it would appear to be a good choice for a parallel approach. However, by default it uses recursion, which is only supported in CUDA compute 2.x devices. Typical parallel implementations spawn a new thread for every split of the data. The current CUDA model (see also discussion on Kepler's Dynamic Parallelism in chapter 12) requires a specification of the total number of threads at kernel launch, or a series of kernel launches per level. The data causes significant branch

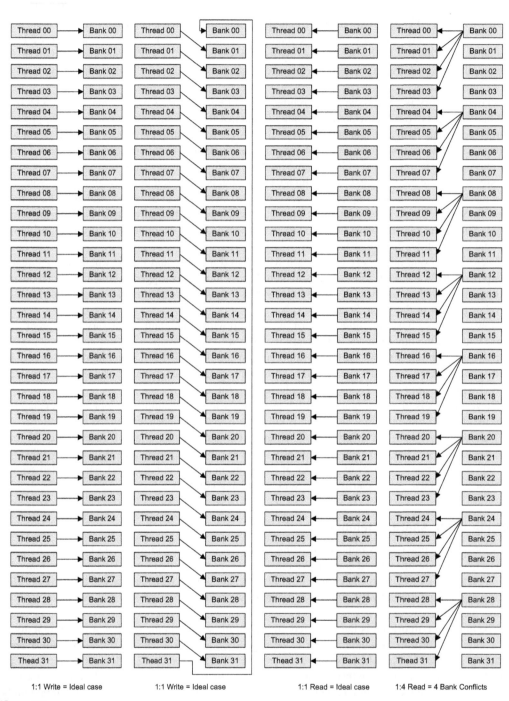

FIGURE 6.2

Shared memory patterns.

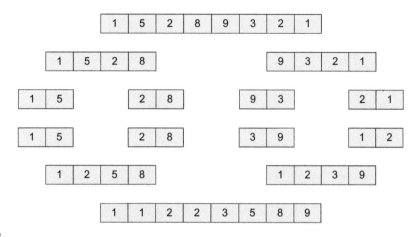

FIGURE 6.3

Simple merge sort example.

divergence, which again is not good for GPUs. There are ways to address some of these issues. However, these issues make quicksort not the best algorithm to use on a pre-Kepler GK110/ Tesla K20 GPU. In fact, you often find the best serial algorithm is not the best parallel algorithm and it is better to start off with an open mind about what will work best.

One common algorithm found in the parallel world is the merge sort (see Figure 6.3). It works by recursively partitioning the data into small and smaller packets, until eventually you have only two values to sort. Each sorted list is then merged together to produce an entire sorted list.

Recursion is not supported in CUDA prior to compute 2.×, so how can such an algorithm be performed? Any recursive algorithm will at some point have a dataset of size N. On GPUs the thread block size or the warp size is the ideal size for N. Thus, to implement a recursive algorithm all you have to do is break the data into blocks of 32 or larger elements as the smallest case of N.

With merge sort, if you take a set of elements such as {1,5,2,8,9,3,2,1} we can split the data at element four and obtain two datasets, {1,5,2,8} and {9,3,2,1}. You can now use two threads to apply a sorting algorithm to the two datasets. Instantly you have gone from $p = 1$ to $p = 2$, where p is the number of parallel execution paths.

Splitting the data from two sets into four sets gives you {1,5}, {2,8}, {9,3}, and {2,1}. It's now trivial to execute four threads, each of which compares the two numbers and swaps them if necessary. Thus, you end up with four sorted datasets: {1,5}, {2,8}, {3,9}, and {1,2}. The sorting phase is now complete. The maximum parallelism that can be expressed in this phase is $N/2$ independent threads. Thus, with a 512 MB dataset, you have 128K 32-bit elements, for which we can use a maximum of 64K threads ($N = 128K$, $N/2 = 64K$). Since a GTX580 GPU has 16 SMs, each of which can support up to 1536 threads, we get up to 24K threads supported per GPU. With around two and a half passes, you can therefore iterate through the 64K data pairs that need to be sorted with such a decomposition.

However, you now run into the classic problem with merge sort, the merge phase. Here the lists are combined by moving the smallest element of each list into the output list. This is then repeated until all members of the input lists are consumed. With the previous example, the sorted lists are {1,5}, {2,8}, {3,9}, and {1,2}. In a traditional merge sort, these get combined into {1,2,5,8} and {1,2,3,9}. These

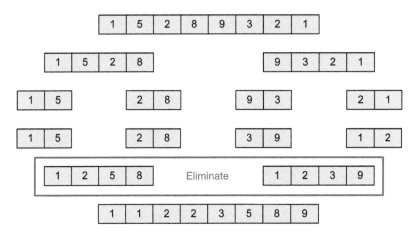

FIGURE 6.4

Merging *N* lists simultaneously.

two lists are then further combined in the same manner to produce one final sorted list, {1,1,2,2,3,5,8,9}.

Thus, as each merge stage is completed, the amount of available parallelism halves. As an alternative approach where *N* is small, you can simply scan *N* sets of lists and immediately place the value in the correct output list, skipping any intermediate merge stages as shown in Figure 6.4. The issue is that the sort performed at the stage highlighted for elimination in Figure 6.4 is typically done with two threads. As anything below 32 threads means we're using less than one warp, this is inefficient on a GPU.

The downside of this approach if that it means you would need to read the first element of the sorted list set from every set. With 64 K sets, this is 64 K reads, or 256 MB of data that has to be fetched from memory. Clearly, this is not a good solution when the number of lists is very large.

Thus the approach we will use here is to try to achieve a much better solution to the merge problem by limiting the amount of recursion applied to the original problem and stopping at the number of threads in a warp, 32, instead of two elements per sorted set, as with a traditional merge sort. This reduces the number of sets in the previous example from 64 K sorted sets to just 4 K sets. It also increases the maximum amount of parallelism available from *N*/2 to *N*/32. In the 128 K element example we looked at previously, this would mean we would need 4 K processing elements. This would distribute 256 processing elements (warps) to every SM on a GTX580. As each Fermi SM can execute a maximum of 48 warps, multiple blocks will need to be iterated through, which allows for smaller problem sizes and speedups on future hardware. See Figure 6.5.

Shared memory is bank switched. We have 32 threads within a single warp. However, if any of those threads access the same bank, there will be a bank conflict. If any of the threads diverge in execution flow, you could be running at up to 1/32 of the speed in the worst case. Threads can use registers that are private to a thread. They can only communicate with one another using shared memory.

By arranging a dataset in rows of 32 elements in the shared memory, and accessing it in columns by thread, you can achieve bank conflict–free access to the memory (Figure 6.6).

For coalesced access to global memory, something we'll cover in the next section, we'd need to fetch the data from global memory in rows of 32 elements. Then we can apply any sorting algorithm to

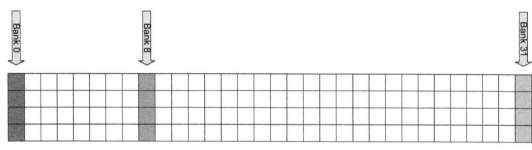

128 Elements
2 x 64 Elements
4 x 32 Elements

Set 0   Set 1   Set 2   Set 3

FIGURE 6.5

Shared memory–based decomposition.

Bank 0   Bank 8   Bank 31

FIGURE 6.6

Shared memory bank access.

the column without worrying about shared memory conflicts. The only thing you need to consider is branch divergence. You need to try to ensure that every thread follows the same execution flow, even though they are processing quite different data elements.

One side effect of this strategy is we will end up having to make a tradeoff. Assuming we have a single warp per SM, we will have no shared memory bank conflicts. However, a single warp per SM will not hide the latency of global memory reads and writes. At least for the memory fetch and write-back stage, we need lots of threads. However, during the sort phase, multiple warps may conflict with one another. A single warp would not have any bank conflicts, yet this would not hide the instruction execution latency. So in practice, we'll need multiple warps in all phases of the sort.

Radix sort

One algorithm that has a fixed number of iterations and a consistent execution flow is the radix sort. It works by sorting based on the least significant bit and then working up to the most significant bit. With a 32-bit integer, using a single radix bit, you will have 32 iterations of the sort, no matter how large the dataset. Let's consider an example with the following dataset:

{ 122, 10, 2, 1, 2, 22, 12, 9 }

The binary representation of each of these values is:

```
122 = 01111010
 10 = 00001010
  2 = 00000010
 22 = 00010010
 12 = 00001100
  9 = 00001001
```

In the first pass of the list, all elements with a 0 in the least significant bit (the right side) would form the first list. Those with a 1 as the least significant bit would form the second list. Thus, the two lists are

```
0 = { 122, 10, 2, 22, 12 }
1 = { 9 }
```

The two lists are appended in this order, becoming

```
{ 122, 10, 2, 22, 12, 9 }
```

The process is then repeated for bit one, generating the next two lists based on the ordering of the previous cycle:

```
0 = { 12, 9 }
1 = { 122, 10, 2, 22 }
```

The combined list is then

```
{ 12, 9, 122, 10, 2, 22 }
```

Scanning the list by bit two, we generate

```
0 = { 9, 122, 10, 2, 22 }
1 = { 12 }
  = { 9, 122, 10, 2, 22, 12 }
```

And so the program continues until it has processed all 32 bits of the list in 32 passes. To build the list you need $N + 2N$ memory cells, one for the source data, one of the 0 list, and one of the 1 list. We do not strictly need $2N$ additional cells, as we could, for example, count from the start of the memory for the 0 list and count backward from the end of the memory for the 1 list. However, to keep it simple, we'll use two separate lists.

The serial code for the radix sort is shown as follows:

```
__host__ void cpu_sort(u32 * const data,
                       const u32 num_elements)
{
 static u32 cpu_tmp_0[NUM_ELEM];
 static u32 cpu_tmp_1[NUM_ELEM];

 for (u32 bit=0;bit<32;bit++)
 {
  u32 base_cnt_0 = 0;
  u32 base_cnt_1 = 0;

  for (u32 i=0; i<num_elements; i++)
  {
   const u32 d = data[i];
   const u32 bit_mask = (1 << bit);

   if ( (d & bit_mask) > 0 )
   {
```

```
    cpu_tmp_1[base_cnt_1] = d;
    base_cnt_1++;
    }
    else
    {
    cpu_tmp_0[base_cnt_0] = d;
    base_cnt_0++;
    }
    }

    // Copy data back to source - first the zero list
    for (u32 i=0; i<base_cnt_0; i++)
    {
    data[i] = cpu_tmp_0[i];
    }

    // Copy data back to source - then the one list
    for (u32 i=0; i<base_cnt_1; i++)
    {
    data[base_cnt_0+i] = cpu_tmp_1[i];
    }
    }
}
```

The code works by being passed two values, a pointer to the data to sort and the number of elements in the dataset. It overwrites the unsorted data so the returned set is sorted. The outer loop iterates over all 32 bits in a 32-bit integer word and the inner loop iterates over all elements in the list. Thus, the algorithm requires $32N$ iterations in which the entire dataset will be read and written 32 times.

Where the size of the data is less than 32 bits (e.g., with 16- or 8-bit integer values), the sort runs two or four times faster due to having to do one-half and one-quarter of the work, respectively. An implementation of the radix sort is available in the Thrust library shipped with v4.0 onwards of the CUDA SDK so you don't have to implement your own radix sort.

Within the inner loop the data is split into two lists, the 0 list and the 1 list depending on which bit of the word is being processed. The data is then reconstructed from the two lists, the 0 list always being written before the 1 list. See Figure 6.7.

The GPU version is a little more complex, in that we need to take care of multiple threads.

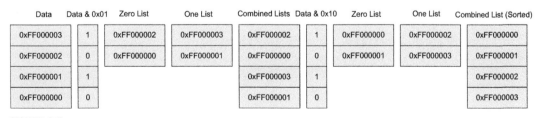

FIGURE 6.7

Simple radix sort.

```
__device__ void radix_sort(u32 * const sort_tmp,
                           const u32 num_lists,
                           const u32 num_elements,
                           const u32 tid,
                           u32 * const sort_tmp_0,
                           u32 * const sort_tmp_1)
{
  // Sort into num_list, lists
  // Apply radix sort on 32 bits of data
  for (u32 bit=0;bit<32;bit++)
  {
    u32 base_cnt_0 = 0;
    u32 base_cnt_1 = 0;

    for (u32 i=0; i<num_elements; i+=num_lists)
    {
      const u32 elem = sort_tmp[i+tid];
      const u32 bit_mask = (1 << bit);

      if ( (elem & bit_mask) > 0 )
      {
        sort_tmp_1[base_cnt_1+tid] = elem;
        base_cnt_1+=num_lists;
      }
      else
      {
        sort_tmp_0[base_cnt_0+tid] = elem;
        base_cnt_0+=num_lists;
      }
    }

    // Copy data back to source - first the zero list
    for (u32 i=0; i<base_cnt_0; i+=num_lists)
    {
      sort_tmp[i+tid] = sort_tmp_0[i+tid];
    }

    // Copy data back to source - then the one list
    for (u32 i=0; i<base_cnt_1; i+=num_lists)
    {
      sort_tmp[base_cnt_0+i+tid] = sort_tmp_1[i+tid];
    }
  }
  __syncthreads();
}
```

The GPU kernel is written here as a device function, a function only capable of being called within a GPU kernel. This is the equivalent of declaring a function as "static" in C or "private" in C++.

Table 6.6 Parallel Radix Sort Results (ms)

Device/Threads	1	2	4	8	16	32	64	128	256
GTX470	39.4	20.8	10.9	5.74	2.91	1.55	0.83	0.48	0.3
9800GT	67	35.5	18.6	9.53	4.88	2.66	1.44	0.82	0.56
GTX260	82.4	43.5	22.7	11.7	5.99	3.24	1.77	1.02	0.66
GTX460	31.9	16.9	8.83	4.56	2.38	1.27	0.69	0.4	0.26

Notice the inner loop has changed and instead of incrementing by one, the program increments by num_lists a value passed into the function. This is the number of independent lists of data the radix sort should produce. This value should equal the number of threads used to invoke the kernel block. The ideal value to avoid bank conflicts will be the warp size, 32. However, this is a less than ideal value in terms of hiding instruction and memory latency.

What this GPU version of this radix sort will produce is num_lists of independent sorted lists using num_lists threads. Since the SM in the GPU can run 32 threads at the same speed as just one thread and it has 32 shared memory banks, you might imagine the ideal value for num_lists would be 32. See Table 6.6 and Figure 6.8.

As you can see from the table and figure, the radix sort is actually very efficient. You see an approximate linear speedup, up to 128 threads. This is not too surprising because each doubling of the number of threads results in each thread processing half as much data as before. The point of interest is where this linear relationship stops because it shows us when we have hit some limit in the hardware. At 256 threads it starts to tail off with only a two-thirds speedup, so we know the ideal case is 128 threads. However, we also have to consider how using 128 threads might limit the usage in the SM, in particular in compute 2.x hardware. Therefore, we might select 256 threads depending on how

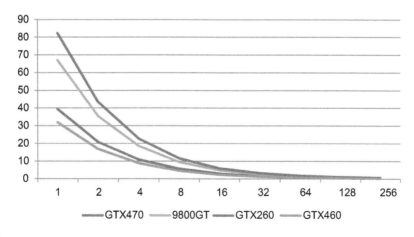

FIGURE 6.8

Parallel radix sort graph.

multiple blocks interact. As it happens, shared memory is the main factor we need to consider limiting the number of blocks we're likely to be able to put into each SM.

If you look at the initial radix sort function, it does not make very efficient use of the shared memory. How would you optimize this function? The most obvious change is that you do not need separate 0 and 1 lists. The 0 list can be created from reusing the space in the original list. This not only allows you to discard the 1 list, but also removes a copy back to the source list. This saves a lot of unnecessary work and frees up shared memory space.

Finally, did you notice that the bit mask is actually constant within a single iteration of the `bit` loop? It is thus an invariant within the `i` loop and can be moved out to the `bit` loop. This is a standard compiler optimization called invariant analysis. Most compilers would move this outside the `i` loop. Compiler optimization is notoriously badly documented and can change from one compiler to another and even between versions of compilers. Relying entirely on optimization steps of compilers is, generally, bad programming practice and best avoided. Therefore, we'll explicitly move the calculation to ensure it gets executed in the correct place. See Chapter 9 on optimization for coverage of typical compiler optimizations.

The slightly more optimal code we end up with is as follows:

```
__device__ void radix_sort2(u32 * const sort_tmp,
                            const u32 num_lists,
                            const u32 num_elements,
         const u32 tid,
         u32 * const sort_tmp_1)
{
 // Sort into num_list, lists
 // Apply radix sort on 32 bits of data
 for (u32 bit=0;bit<32;bit++)
 {
  const u32 bit_mask = (1 << bit);
  u32 base_cnt_0 = 0;
  u32 base_cnt_1 = 0;

  for (u32 i=0; i<num_elements; i+=num_lists)
  {
   const u32 elem = sort_tmp[i+tid];

   if ( (elem & bit_mask) > 0 )
   {
    sort_tmp_1[base_cnt_1+tid] = elem;
    base_cnt_1+=num_lists;
   }
   else
   {
    sort_tmp[base_cnt_0+tid] = elem;
    base_cnt_0+=num_lists;
   }
  }

 // Copy data back to source from the one's list
```

```
 for (u32 i=0; i<base_cnt_1; i+=num_lists)
 {
  sort_tmp[base_cnt_0+i+tid] = sort_tmp_1[i+tid];
 }
}
__syncthreads();
}
```

There are further optimizations that can be made, but the key issue here is that we're now using only one temporary storage area, which in turn allows the processing of more elements. This is important because, as we'll see later, the number of lists is an important factor. So how do these changes affect the performance of the radix sort?

If you look at Table 6.7, you'll see the worst case, using a single thread, has come down from 82 ms to 52 ms. The best case in the previous run, 0.26 ms, has come down to 0.21 ms, which is about a 20% improvement in execution speed.

Table 6.7 Optimized Radix Sort Results (ms)								
Device/Threads	**1**	**2**	**4**	**8**	**16**	**32**	**64**	**128**	**256**
GTX470	26.51	14.35	7.65	3.96	2.05	1.09	0.61	0.36	0.24
9800GT	42.8	23.22	12.37	6.41	3.3	1.78	0.98	0.63	0.4
GTX260	52.54	28.46	15.14	7.81	4.01	2.17	1.2	0.7	0.46
GTX460	21.62	11.81	6.34	3.24	1.69	0.91	0.51	0.31	0.21

Merging lists

Merge lists of sorted elements is an algorithm that is commonly used in parallel programming. However, let's start by looking at some serial code to merge an arbitrary number of sorted lists into a single sorted list, as this is the simplest case.

```
void merge_array(const u32 * const src_array,
                 u32 * const dest_array,
                 const u32 num_lists,
                 const u32 num_elements)
{
 const u32 num_elements_per_list = (num_elements / num_lists);

 u32 list_indexes[MAX_NUM_LISTS];

 for (u32 list=0; list < num_lists; list++)
 {
  list_indexes[list] = 0;
 }

 for (u32 i=0; i<num_elements;i++)
```

```
{
  dest_array[i] = find_min(src_array,
                           list_indexes,
                           num_lists,
                           num_elements_per_list);
}
}
```

Assuming there are num_lists lists to collect data from, you need some way to track where we are in the list. The program uses the array list_indexes for this. As the number of lists is likely to be small, you can use the stack and thus declare the array as a local variable. Note this would be a bad idea with a GPU kernel, as the stack allocation may get placed into slow global memory, depending on the particular GPU variant. Shared memory would likely be the optimal location on the GPU, depending on the number of lists needed.

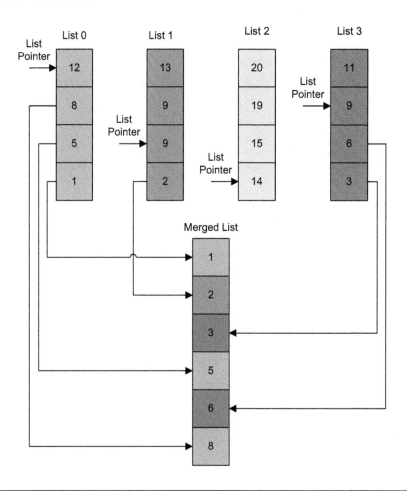

FIGURE 6.9

Multiple lists partially merged.

First, the index values are all set to zero. Then the program iterates over all elements and assigns the value in the sorted array from the result of a function, find_min. The find_min function identifies the smallest value from a set of num_lists values.

```
u32 find_min(const u32 * const src_array,
             u32 * const list_indexes,
             const u32 num_lists,
             const u32 num_elements_per_list)
{
 u32 min_val = 0xFFFFFFFF;
 u32 min_idx = 0;

 // Iterate over each of the lists
 for (u32 i=0; i<num_lists; i++)
 {
  // If the current list has already been emptied
  // then ignore it
  if (list_indexes[i] < num_elements_per_list)
  {
   const u32 src_idx = i + (list_indexes[i] * num_lists);

   const u32 data = src_array[src_idx];

   if (data <= min_val)
   {
     min_val = data;
     min_idx = i;
   }
  }
 }

 list_indexes[min_idx]++;
 return min_val;
}
```

The function works by iterating through the lists of sorted values and maintaining an index into where it is in each list. If it identifies a smaller value than min_val, it simply updates min_val to this new value. When it has scanned all the lists, it increments the relevant list index and returns the value it found.

Now let's look at the GPU implementation of this algorithm. First, the top-level function:

```
__global__ void gpu_sort_array_array(
u32 * const data,
const u32 num_lists,
const u32 num_elements)
{
 const u32 tid = (blockIdx.x * blockDim.x) + threadIdx.x;
```

```
__shared__ u32 sort_tmp[NUM_ELEM];
__shared__ u32 sort_tmp_1[NUM_ELEM];

copy_data_to_shared(data, sort_tmp, num_lists,
                    num_elements, tid);

radix_sort2(sort_tmp, num_lists, num_elements,
            tid, sort_tmp_1);

merge_array6(sort_tmp, data, num_lists,
             num_elements, tid);
}
```

This is quite a simple program for now. It will be invoked with a single block of N threads. We'll develop this as an example of how to use shared memory. Looking at the first function, we see the following:

```
__device__ void copy_data_to_shared(const u32 * const data,
                                     u32 * const sort_tmp,
                                     const u32 num_lists,
                                     const u32 num_elements,
                                     const u32 tid)
{
// Copy data into temp store
for (u32 i=0; i<num_elements; i+=num_lists)
 {
  sort_tmp[i+tid] = data[i+tid];
 }
__syncthreads();
}
```

Here the program reads data from global memory in rows and not columns into the shared memory. This step is important for two reasons. First, the program will repeatedly read and write from this memory. Therefore, you want the fastest memory possible, so we need to use shared memory instead of global memory. Second, global memory provides the best performance when accessed by rows. Column access produces a scattered memory pattern that the hardware is unable to coalesce, unless every thread accesses the same column value and these addresses are adjacent. Thus, in most cases the GPU has to issue far more memory fetch operations than are necessary and the speed of the program will drop by an order of magnitude.

When you compile this program, if you have the -v flag set on the nvcc compiler options, it will print an innocent looking message saying it created a stack frame. For example,

```
1>ptxas info : Function properties for _Z12merge_arrayPKjPjjjj
1> 40 bytes stack frame, 40 bytes spill stores, 40 bytes spill loads
```

When a function makes a call into a subfunction and passes parameters, those parameters must somehow be provided to the called function. The program makes just such a call:

```
dest_array[i] = find_min(src_array,
```

```
                        list_indexes,
                        num_lists,
                        num_elements_per_list);
```

There are two options that can be employed, to pass the necessary values through registers, or to create an area of memory called a stack frame. Most modern processors have a large register set (32 or more registers). Thus, for a single level of calls, often this is enough. Older architectures use stack frames and push the values onto the stack. The called function then pops the values off the stack. As you require memory to do this, on the GPU this would mean using "local" memory, which is local only in terms of which thread can access it. In fact, "local" memory can be held in global memory, so this is hugely inefficient, especially on the older architectures (1.x) where it's not cached. At this point we need to rewrite the merge routine to avoid the function call. The new routine is thus:

```
// Uses a single thread for merge
__device__ void merge_array1(const u32 * const src_array,
                             u32 * const dest_array,
                             const u32 num_lists,
                             const u32 num_elements,
                             const u32 tid)
{
 __shared__ u32 list_indexes[MAX_NUM_LISTS];

 // Multiple threads
 list_indexes[tid] = 0;
 __syncthreads();

 // Single threaded
 if (tid == 0)
 {
  const u32 num_elements_per_list = (num_elements / num_lists);

  for (u32 i=0; i<num_elements;i++)
  {
   u32 min_val = 0xFFFFFFFF;
   u32 min_idx = 0;

   // Iterate over each of the lists
   for (u32 list=0; list<num_lists; list++)
   {
    // If the current list has already been
    // emptied then ignore it
    if (list_indexes[list] < num_elements_per_list)
    {
     const u32 src_idx = list + (list_indexes[list] * num_lists);

     const u32 data = src_array[src_idx];
```

Table 6.8 Initial Single-Thread Merge Sort Results

Device/Threads	1	2	4	8	16	32	64	128	256
GTX470	27.9	16.91	12.19	12.31	17.82	31.46	59.42	113.3	212.7
9800GT	44.83	27.21	19.55	19.53	28.07	51.08	96.32	183.08	342.16
GTX260	55.03	33.38	24.05	24.15	34.88	62.9	118.71	225.73	422.55
GTX460	22.76	13.85	10.11	10.41	15.29	27.18	51.46	90.26	184.54

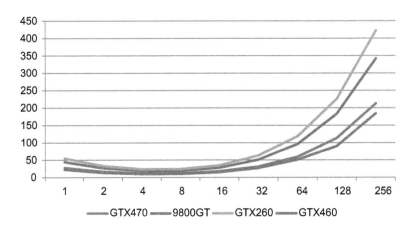

FIGURE 6.10

Initial single-thread merge sort graph.

```
        if (data <= min_val)
        {
          min_val = data;
          min_idx = list;
        }
      }
    }
  list_indexes[min_idx]++;
  dest_array[i] = min_val;
  }
 }
}
```

This function now combines the original merge_arrary function and its find_min function. Recompiling now results in no additional stack frame. Running the code, we find the results shown in Table 6.8. If you graph this, it's somewhat easier to see (Figure 6.10).

Table 6.9 Device Clock Rate and Bandwidth

Device	9800GT	GTX260	GTX460	GTX470
Core clock	650 Mz	625 MHz	726 MHz	608 MHz
Memory bandwidth	61 GB/s	123 GB/s	115 GB/s	134 GB/s

What is surprising from this graph is the worst performer is actually the GTX260, which is slower than the previous generation 9800GT. It's interesting to also note the GTX460 is faster than the GTX470 in this particular test. To understand this, you need to look at the specific devices used, as shown in Table 6.9.

You can see the 9800GT has a higher internal clock rate than the GTX260. The same is true of the GTX460 and GTX470. Since the program is using just a single SM, and memory access is dominated by shared memory access time, this is entirely to be expected.

However, perhaps the most interesting feature you can see from the graph is that increasing the number of threads beyond a certain point actually makes the calculation go slower. This initially seems counterintuitive if you have never seen this relationship before. What this type of result points to is that there is some conflict of resources meaning the problem does not scale in a linear manner when you increase the number of threads.

The problem is the latter. The merge step is single thread and must look at N lists for every element. As the number of lists are increased, the problem space becomes $2N$, $4N$, $8N$, etc. in line with the number of threads. The optimal point for this algorithm, based on the timings, is actually between four and eight lists of data. This is not good, as it considerably limits the potential amount of parallelism.

Parallel merging

For better performance, clearly more than one thread in the merge stage is required. However, this introduces a problem, in that we're writing to a single list. To do this, the threads need to cooperate in some manner. This makes the merge somewhat more complex.

```
// Uses multiple threads for merge
// Deals with multiple identical entries in the data
__device__ void merge_array6(const u32 * const src_array,
                             u32 * const dest_array,
                             const u32 num_lists,
                             const u32 num_elements,
                             const u32 tid)
{
 const u32 num_elements_per_list = (num_elements / num_lists);

 __shared__ u32 list_indexes[MAX_NUM_LISTS];
 list_indexes[tid] = 0;

 // Wait for list_indexes[tid] to be cleared
```

```
__syncthreads();

// Iterate over all elements
for (u32 i=0; i<num_elements;i++)
{
 // Create a value shared with the other threads
 __shared__ u32 min_val;
 __shared__ u32 min_tid;

 // Use a temp register for work purposes
 u32 data;

 // If the current list has not already been
 // emptied then read from it, else ignore it
 if (list_indexes[tid] < num_elements_per_list)
 {
  // Work out from the list_index, the index into
  // the linear array
  const u32 src_idx = tid + (list_indexes[tid] * num_lists);

  // Read the data from the list for the given
  // thread
  data = src_array[src_idx];
 }
 else
 {
  data = 0xFFFFFFFF;
 }

 // Have thread zero clear the min values
 if (tid == 0)
 {
  // Write a very large value so the first
  // thread thread wins the min
  min_val = 0xFFFFFFFF;
  min_tid = 0xFFFFFFFF;
 }

 // Wait for all threads
 __syncthreads();

 // Have every thread try to store it's value into
 // min_val. Only the thread with the lowest value
 // will win
 atomicMin(&min_val, data);

 // Make sure all threads have taken their turn.
 __syncthreads();
```

```
// If this thread was the one with the minimum
if (min_val == data)
{
  // Check for equal values
  // Lowest tid wins and does the write
  atomicMin(&min_tid, tid);
}

// Make sure all threads have taken their turn.
__syncthreads();

// If this thread has the lowest tid
if (tid == min_tid)
{
  // Incremene the list pointer for this thread
  list_indexes[tid]++;

  // Store the winning value
  dest_array[i] = data;
}
}
}
```

This version uses `num_lists` threads to do the merge operation. However, only a single thread writes to the output data list at a time, thus ensuring the single output list is correct at all times.

It makes use of the `atomicMin` function. Instead of one thread reading all the values from the lists and computing the minimum, each thread calls `atomicMin` with the value of its list entry. Once all threads have called the `atomicMin` function, each thread reads it back and compares this with the value it tried to write. If the values are the same, then the thread was the winning thread. However, there is one further problem in that there may be several winning threads, because the data item can be repeated in one or more lists. Thus, a second elimination step is required by only those threads with identical data. Most of the time, this second step will not be necessary. However, in the worst case of sorting a list of identical numbers, it would cause every thread to have to go through two elimination steps.

So how does this version perform? As you can see from Table 6.10 and Figure 6.11, we have reduced the total execution time using the larger number of threads (128 and 256 threads) by

Table 6.10 `atomicMin` Parallel Merge Sort Results (ms)

Device/Threads	1	2	4	8	16	32	64	128	256
GTX470	29.15	17.38	10.96	7.77	6.74	7.43	9.15	13.55	22.99
GTX260	55.97	32.67	19.87	13.22	10.51	10.86	13.96	19.97	36.68
GTX460	23.78	14.23	9.06	6.54	5.86	6.67	8.41	12.59	21.58

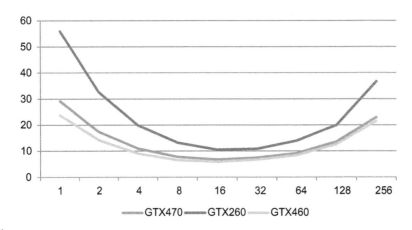

FIGURE 6.11

atomicMin parallel merge sort graph.

a factor of 10. However, single-thread timing is unchanged. More important, however, is the fastest time has moved from the 8- to the 16-thread version and has halved in terms of absolute time.

One thing I should mention here is that atomicMin on shared memory requires a compute 1.2 device or higher. The 9800GT is only a compute 1.1 device, so is not shown here as it cannot run the kernel.

If we look a little closer at the hardware counters with a tool like Parallel Nsight, we can see that beyond 32 threads the number of divergent branches and the number of shared memory accesses start to grow very rapidly. We currently have a good solution, but what alternative approaches are there and are they any quicker?

Parallel reduction

One common approach to this problem is parallel reduction. This can be applied for many problems, a min operation being just one of them. It works by using half the number of threads of the elements in the dataset. Every thread calculates the minimum of its own element and some other element. The resultant element is forwarded to the next round. The number of threads is then reduced by half and the process repeated until there is just a single element remaining, which is the result of the operation.

With CUDA you must remember that the execution unit for a given SM is a warp. Thus, any amount of threads less than one warp is underutilizing the hardware. Also, while divergent threads must all be executed, divergent warps do not have to be.

When selecting the "other element" for a given thread to work with, you can do so to do a reduction within the warp, thus causing significant branch divergence within it. This will hinder the performance, as each divergent branch doubles the work for the SM. A better approach is to drop whole warps by selecting the other element from the other half of the dataset.

In Figure 6.12 you see the item being compared with one from the other half of the dataset. Shaded cells show the active threads.

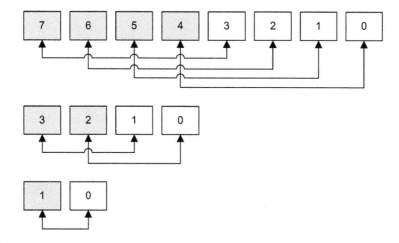

FIGURE 6.12

Final stages of GPU parallel reduction.

```
// Uses multiple threads for reduction type merge
__device__ void merge_array5(const u32 * const src_array,
                             u32 * const dest_array,
                             const u32 num_lists,
                             const u32 num_elements,
                             const u32 tid)
{
 const u32 num_elements_per_list = (num_elements / num_lists);

 __shared__ u32 list_indexes[MAX_NUM_LISTS];
 __shared__ u32 reduction_val[MAX_NUM_LISTS];
 __shared__ u32 reduction_idx[MAX_NUM_LISTS];

 // Clear the working sets
 list_indexes[tid] = 0;
 reduction_val[tid] = 0;
 reduction_idx[tid] = 0;
 __syncthreads();

 for (u32 i=0; i<num_elements;i++)
 {
  // We need (num_lists / 2) active threads
  u32 tid_max = num_lists >> 1;

  u32 data;

  // If the current list has already been
  // emptied then ignore it
```

```
if (list_indexes[tid] < num_elements_per_list)
{
 // Work out from the list_index, the index into
 // the linear array
 const u32 src_idx = tid + (list_indexes[tid] * num_lists);

 // Read the data from the list for the given
 // thread
 data = src_array[src_idx];
}
else
{
 data = 0xFFFFFFFF;
}

// Store the current data value and index
reduction_val[tid] = data;
reduction_idx[tid] = tid;

// Wait for all threads to copy
__syncthreads();

// Reduce from num_lists to one thread zero
while (tid_max != 0)
{
 // Gradually reduce tid_max from
 // num_lists to zero
 if (tid < tid_max)
 {
  // Calculate the index of the other half
  const u32 val2_idx = tid + tid_max;

  // Read in the other half
  const u32 val2 = reduction_val[val2_idx];

  // If this half is bigger
  if (reduction_val[tid] > val2)
  {
   // The store the smaller value
   reduction_val[tid] = val2;
   reduction_idx[tid] = reduction_idx[val2_idx];
  }
 }

 // Divide tid_max by two
 tid_max >>= 1;

 __syncthreads();
```

```
  }

  if (tid == 0)
  {
    // Incremenet the list pointer for this thread
    list_indexes[reduction_idx[0]]++;

    // Store the winning value
    dest_array[i] = reduction_val[0];
  }

  // Wait for tid zero
  __syncthreads();
 }
}
```

This code works by creating a temporary list of data in shared memory, which it populates with a dataset from each cycle from the num_list datasets. Where a list has already been emptied, the dataset is populated with 0xFFFFFFFF, which will exclude the value from the list. The while loop gradually reduces the number of active threads until there is only a single thread active, thread zero. This then copies the data and increments the list indexes to ensure the value is not processed twice.

Notice the use of the __syncthreads directive within the loop and at the end. The program needs to sync across warps when there are more than 32 threads (one warp) in use.

So how does this perform? As you can see from Table 6.11 and Figure 6.13, this approach is significantly slower than the atomicMin version, the fastest reduction being 8.4 ms versus the 5.86 ms atomicMin (GTX460, 16 threads). This is almost 50% slower than the atomicMin version. However, one thing to note is that it's a little under twice the speed of the atomicMin when using 256 threads (12.27 ms versus 21.58 ms). This is, however, still twice as slow as the 16-thread version.

Although this version is slower, it has the advantage of not requiring the use of the atomicMin function. This function is only available on compute 1.2 devices, which is generally only an issue if you need to consider the consumer market or you need to support *really* old Tesla systems. The main issue, however, is that atomicMin can only be used with integer values. A significant number of real-world problems are floating-point based. In such cases we need both algorithms.

However, what we can take from both the atomicMin and the parallel reduction method is that the traditional merge sort using two lists is not the ideal case on a GPU. You get increasing performance from

Table 6.11 Parallel Reduction Results (ms)

Device/Threads	1	2	4	8	16	32	64	128	256
GTX470	28.4	17.67	12.44	10.32	9.98	10.59	11.62	12.94	14.61
9800GT	45.66	28.35	19.82	16.25	15.61	17.03	19.03	21.45	25.33
GTX260	56.07	34.71	24.22	19.84	19.04	20.6	23.2	26.28	31.01
GTX460	23.22	14.52	10.3	8.63	8.4	8.94	9.82	10.96	12.27

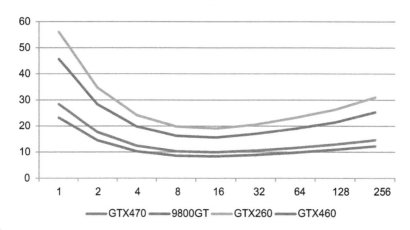

FIGURE 6.13

Parallel reduction graph.

the increasing parallelism in the radix sort as you increase the number of lists. However, you get decreasing performance from the merge stage as you increase the parallelism and move beyond 16 lists.

A hybrid approach

There is potential here to exploit the benefits of both algorithms by creating a hybrid approach. We can rewrite the merge sort as follows:

```
#define REDUCTION_SIZE 8
#define REDUCTION_SIZE_BIT_SHIFT 3
#define MAX_ACTIVE_REDUCTIONS ( (MAX_NUM_LISTS) / REDUCTION_SIZE )

// Uses multiple threads for merge
// Does reduction into a warp and then into a single value
__device__ void merge_array9(const u32 * const src_array,
                             u32 * const dest_array,
                             const u32 num_lists,
                             const u32 num_elements,
                             const u32 tid)
{
 // Read initial value from the list
 u32 data = src_array[tid];

 // Shared memory index
 const u32 s_idx = tid >> REDUCTION_SIZE_BIT_SHIFT;

 // Calcuate number of 1st stage reductions
 const u32 num_reductions = num_lists >> REDUCTION_SIZE_BIT_SHIFT;
```

```
const u32 num_elements_per_list = (num_elements / num_lists);

// Declare a number of list pointers and
// set to the start of the list
__shared__ u32 list_indexes[MAX_NUM_LISTS];
list_indexes[tid] = 0;

// Iterate over all elements
for (u32 i=0; i<num_elements;i++)
{
 // Create a value shared with the other threads
 __shared__ u32 min_val[MAX_ACTIVE_REDUCTIONS];
 __shared__ u32 min_tid;

 // Have one thread from warp zero clear the
 // min value
 if (tid < num_lists)
 {
  // Write a very large value so the first
  // thread thread wins the min
  min_val[s_idx] = 0xFFFFFFFF;
  min_tid = 0xFFFFFFFF;
 }

 // Wait for warp zero to clear min vals
 __syncthreads();

 // Have every thread try to store it's value into
 // min_val for it's own reduction elements. Only
 // the thread with the lowest value will win.
 atomicMin(&min_val[s_idx], data);

 // If we have more than one reduction then
 // do an additional reduction step
 if (num_reductions > 0)
 {
  // Wait for all threads
  __syncthreads();

  // Have each thread in warp zero do an
  // additional min over all the partial
  // mins to date
  if ( (tid < num_reductions) )
  {
   atomicMin(&min_val[0], min_val[tid]);
  }
```

```
    // Make sure all threads have taken their turn.
    __syncthreads();
    }

    // If this thread was the one with the minimum
    if (min_val[0] == data)
    {
    // Check for equal values
    // Lowest tid wins and does the write
    atomicMin(&min_tid, tid);
    }

    // Make sure all threads have taken their turn.
    __syncthreads();

    // If this thread has the lowest tid
    if (tid == min_tid)
    {
    // Incremenet the list pointer for this thread
    list_indexes[tid]++;

    // Store the winning value
    dest_array[i] = data;

    // If the current list has not already been
    // emptied then read from it, else ignore it
    if (list_indexes[tid] < num_elements_per_list)
     data = src_array[tid + (list_indexes[tid] * num_lists)];
    else
     data = 0xFFFFFFFF;
    }

    // Wait for min_tid thread
    __syncthreads();
    }
}
```

One of the main problems of the simple 1-to-N reduction is it becomes increasingly slower as the value of N increases. We can see from previous tests that the ideal value of N is around 16 elements. The kernel works by creating a partial reduction of N values and then a final reduction of those N values into a single value. In this way it's similar to the reduction example, but skips most of the iterations.

Notice that min_val has been extended from a single value into an array of shared values. This is necessary so each independent thread can minimize the values over its own dataset. Each min value is 32 bits wide so it exists in a separate shared memory bank, meaning there are no bank conflicts provided the maximum number of first-level reductions results in 32 or less elements.

The value of REDUCTION_SIZE has been set to eight, which means the program will do a min over groups of eight values prior to a final min. With the maximum of histogram bin 256 elements, we get

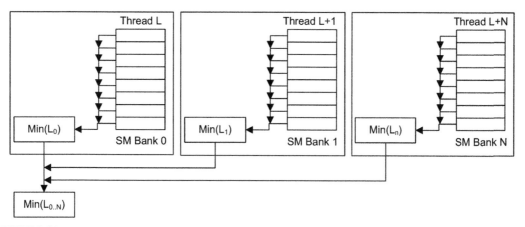

FIGURE 6.14

Hybrid parallel reduction.

Table 6.12 Hybrid Atomic and Parallel Reductions Results (ms)									
Device/Threads	**1**	**2**	**4**	**8**	**16**	**32**	**64**	**128**	**256**
GTX470	29.41	17.62	11.24	8.98	7.2	6.49	6.46	7.01	8.57
GTX260	56.85	33.54	20.83	15.29	11.87	10.5	10.36	11.34	14.65
GTX460	24.12	14.54	9.36	7.64	6.22	5.67	5.68	6.27	7.81

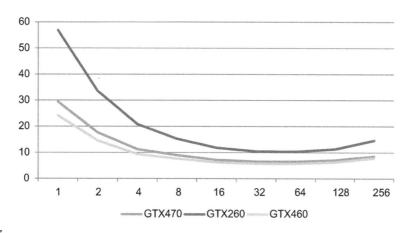

FIGURE 6.15

Hybrid atomic and parallel reduction graph.

exactly 32 seperate banks being used to do the reduction. In the 256 elements we have a 256:32:1 reduction. With a 128-element list we have a 128:16:1 reduction, etc.

The other major change is now only the thread that writes out the winning element reads a new value into data, a register-based value that is per thread. Previously, all threads re-read in the value from their respective lists. As only one thread won each round, only one list pointer changed. Thus, as N increased, this became increasingly ineffecient. However, this doesn't help as much as you might at first imagine.

So how does this version perform? Notice in Table 6.12 that the minimum time, 5.86 ms from the atomicMin example, has fallen to 5.67 ms. This is not spectacular, but what is interesting to note is the shape of the graph (Figure 6.15). No longer is the graph such an inclined U shape. Both the 32- and 64-thread versions beat the simple atomicMin based on 16 threads. We're starting to smooth out the upward incline introduced by the merge step as shown in table 6.12 and figure 6.15.

Shared memory on different GPUs

Not all GPUs are created equal. With the move to compute 2.x devices, the amount of shared memory became configurable. By default, compute 2.x (Fermi) devices are configured to provide 48K of shared memory instead of the 16 K of shared memory on compute 1.x devices.

The amount of shared memory can change between hardware releases. To write programs that scale in performance with new GPU releases, you have to write portable code. To support this, CUDA allows you to query the device for the amount of shared memory available with the following code:

```
struct cudaDeviceProp device_prop;
CUDA_CALL(cudaGetDeviceProperties(&device_prop, device_num));
printf("\nSharedMemory: %u", device_prop.sharedMemPerBlock);
```

Having more shared memory available allows us to select one of two strategies. We can either extend the amount of shared memory used from 16 K to 48 K or we can simply schedule more blocks into a single SM. The best choice will really depend on the application at hand. With our sorting example, 48 K of shared memory would allow the number of lists per SM to be reduced by a factor of three. As we saw earlier, the number of lists to merge has a significant impact on the overall execution time.

Shared memory summary

So far we have looked only at sorting within a single SM, in fact within a single block. Moving from a single-block version to a multiple-block version introduces another set of merges. Each block will produce an independent sorted list. These lists then have to be merged, but this time in global memory. The list size moves outside that which can be held in shared memory. The same then becomes true when using multiple GPUs—you generate N or more sorted lists where N equals the number of GPUs in the system.

We've looked primarily at interthread cooperation with shared memory in this section. The merging example was selected to demonstrate this in a manner that was not too complex and easy to follow. Parallel sorting has a large body of research behind it. More complex algorithms may well be more efficient, in terms of the memory usage and/or SM utilization. The point here was to use a practical example that could be easily followed and process lots of data that did not simply reduce to a single value.

We'll continue to look at sorting later and look at how interblock communication and coordination can be achieved in addition to thread-level communication.

Questions on shared memory

1. Looking at the `radix_sort` algorithm, how might the use of shared memory be reduced? Why would this be useful?
2. Are all the synchronization points necessary? In each instance a synchronization primitive is used. Discuss why. Are there conditions where they are not necessary?
3. What would be the effect of using C++ templates in terms of execution time?
4. How would you further optimize this sorting algorithm?

Answers for shared memory

1. There are a number of solutions. One is to use only the memory allocated to the sort. This can be done using an MSB radix sort and swapping the 1s with elements at the end of the list. The 0 list counts forward and the 1 list counts backward. When they meet, the next digit is sorted until the LSB is sorted. Reducing the memory usage is useful because it allows larger lists in the shared memory, reducing the total number of lists needed, which significantly impacts execution time.
2. The main concept to understand here is the synchronization points are necessary only when more than one warp is used. Within a warp all instructions execute synchronously. A branch causes the nonbranched threads to stall. At the point the branch converges, you are guaranteed all instructions are in sync, although the warps can then instantly diverge again. Note that memory must be declared as volatile or you must have syncthread points within the warp if you wish to guarantee visibility of writes between threads. See Chapter 12 on common problems for a discussion on the use of the volatile qualifier.
3. Templates would allow much of the runtime evaluation of the `num_lists` parameter to be replaced with compile time substitution. The parameter must always be a power of 2, and in practice will be limited to a maximum of 256. Thus, a number of templates can be created and the appropriate function called at runtime. Given a fixed number of iterations known at compiler time instead of runtime, the compiler can efficiently unroll loops and substitute variable reads with literals. Additionally, templates can be used to support multiple implementations for different data types, for example, using the `atomicMin` version for integer data while using a parallel reduction for floating-point data.
4. This is rather an open-ended question. There are many valid answers. As the number of sorted lists to merge increases, the problem becomes significantly larger. Elimination of the merge step would be a good solution. This could be achieved by partially sorting the original list into N sublists by value. Each sublist can then be sorted and the lists concatenated, rather than merged. This approach is the basis of another type of sort, sample sort, an algorithm we look at later in this chapter.

Consider also the size of the dataset in the example, 1024 elements. With 256 threads there are just four elements per list. A radix sort using a single bit is very inefficient for this number of elements, requiring 128 iterations. A comparison-based sort is much quicker for such small values of *N*.

In this example, we used a single bit for the radix sort. Multiple bits can be used, which reduces the number of passes over the dataset at the expense of more intermediate storage. We currently use an iterative method to sort elements into sequential lists. It's quite possible to work where the data will move to by counting the radix bits and using a `prefix sum` calculation to work out the index of where the data should be written. We look at `prefix sum` later in this chapter.

CONSTANT MEMORY

Constant memory is a form of virtual addressing of global memory. There is no special reserved constant memory block. Constant memory has two special properties you might be interested in. First, it is cached, and second, it supports broadcasting a single value to all the elements within a warp.

Constant memory, as its name suggests, is for read-only memory. This is memory that is either declared at compile time as read only or defined at runtime as read only by the host. It is, therefore, constant only in respect of the GPU's view onto memory and not the hosts. The size of constant memory is restricted to 64 K.

To declare a section of memory as constant at compile time, you simply use the __constant__ keyword. For example:

```
__constant__ float my_array[1024] = { 0.0F, 1.0F, 1.34F, ... };
```

To change the contents of the constant memory section at runtime, you simply use the `cudaCopyToSymbol` function call prior to invoking the GPU kernel. If you do not define the constant memory at either compile time or host runtime then the contents of the memory section are undefined.

Constant memory caching

Compute 1.x devices

On compute 1.x devices (pre-Fermi), constant memory has the property of being cached in a small 8K L1 cache, so *subsequent* accesses can be very fast. This is providing that there is some potential for data reuse in the memory pattern the application is using. It is also highly optimized for broadcast access such that threads accessing the same memory address can be serviced in a single cycle.

With a 64 K segment size and an 8 K cache size, you have an 8:1 ratio of memory size to cache, which is really very good. If you can contain or localize accesses to 8 K chunks within this constant section you'll achieve very good program performance. On certain devices you will find localizing the data to even smaller chunks will provide higher performance.

With a nonuniform access to constant memory a cache miss results in *N* fetches from global memory in addition to the fetch from the constant cache. Thus, a memory pattern that exhibits poor locality and/or poor data reuse should not be accessed as constant memory. Also, each divergence in the memory fetch pattern causes serialization in terms of having to wait for the constant memory. Thus, a warp with 32 separate fetches to the constant cache would take at least 32 times longer than an access to a single data item. This would grow significantly if it also included cache misses.

Single-cycle access is a huge improvement on the several hundred cycles required for a fetch from global memory. However, the several hundred–cycle access to global memory will likely be hidden by task switches to other warps, if there are enough available warps for the SM to execute. Thus, the benefit of using constant memory for its cache properties relies on the time taken to fetch data from global memory and the amount of data reuse the algorithm has. As with shared memory, the low-end devices have much less global memory bandwidth, so they benefit proportionally more from such techniques than the high-end devices.

Most algorithms can have their data broken down into "tiles" (i.e., smaller datasets) from a much larger problem. In fact, as soon as you have a problem that can't physically fit on one machine, you have to do tiling of the data. The same tiling can be done on a multicore CPU with each one of the N cores taking $1/N$ of the data. You can think of each SM on the GPU as being a core on a CPU that is able to support hundreds of threads.

Imagine overlaying a grid onto the data you are processing where the total number of cells, or blocks, in the grid equals the number of cores (SMs) you wish to split the data into. Take these SM-based blocks and further divide them into at least eight additional blocks. You've now decomposed your data area into N SMs, each of which is allocated M blocks.

In practice, this split is usually too large and would not allow for future generations of GPUs to increase the number of SMs or the number of available blocks and see any benefit. It also does not work well where the number of SMs is unknown, for example, when writing a commercial program that will be run on consumer hardware. The largest number of SMs per device to date has been 30 (GT200 series). The Kepler and Fermi range aimed at compyte have a maximum of 15 and 16 SMs respectively. The range designed primarily for gaming have up to 8 SMs.

One other important consideration is what interthread communication you need, if any. This can only reasonably be done using threads and these are limited to 1024 per block on Fermi and Kepler, less on earlier devices. You can, of course, process multiple items of data per thread, so this is not such a hard limit as it might first appear.

Finally, you need to consider load balancing. Many of the early card releases of GPU families had non power of two numbers of SMs (GTX460 = 7, GTX260 = 30, etc.). Therefore, using too few blocks leads to too little granularity and thus unoccupied SMs in the final stages of computation.

Tiling, in terms of constant memory, means splitting the data into blocks of no more than 64 K each. Ideally, the tiles should be 8 K or less. Sometimes tiling involves having to deal with halo or ghost cells that occupy the boundaries, so values have to be propagated between tiles. Where halos are required, larger block sizes work better than smaller cells because the area that needs to communicated between blocks is much smaller.

When using tiling there is actually quite a lot to think about. Often the best solution is simply to run through all combinations of number of threads, elements processed per thread, number of blocks, and tile widths, and search for the optimal solution for the given problem. We look at how to do this in Chapter 9 on optimization.

Compute 2.x devices

On Fermi (compute 2.x) hardware and later, there is a level two (L2) cache. Fermi uses an L2 cache shared between each SM. All memory accesses are cached automatically by the L2 cache. Additionally, the L1 cache size can be increased from 16 K to 48 K by sacrificing 32 K of the shared memory per SM. Because all memory is cached on Fermi, how constant memory is used needs some consideration.

Fermi, unlike compute 1.x devices, allows *any* constant section of data to be treated as constant memory, even if it is not explicitly declared as such. Constant memory on 1.x devices has to be explicitly managed with special-purpose calls like `cudaMemcpyToSymbol` or declared at compile time. With Fermi, any nonthread-based access to an area of memory declared as constant (simply with the standard `const` keyword) goes through the constant cache. By nonthread-based access, this is an access that does not include `threadIdx.x` in the array indexing calculation.

If you need access to constant data on a per-thread-based access, then you need to use the compile time (`__constant__`) or runtime function (`cudaMemcpyToSymbol`) as with compute 1.x devices.

However, be aware that the L2 cache will still be there and is much larger than the constant cache. If you are implementing a tiling algorithm that needs halo or ghost cells between blocks, the solution will often involve copying the halo cells into constant or shared memory. Due to Fermi's L2 cache, this strategy will usually be slower than simply copying the tiled cells to shared or constant memory and then accessing the halo cells from global memory. The L2 cache will have likely collected the halo cells from the prior block's access of the memory. Therefore, the halo cells are quickly available from the L2 cache and come into the device much quicker than you would on compute 1.x hardware where a global memory fetch would have to go all the way out to the global memory.

Constant memory broadcast

Constant memory has one very useful feature. It can be used for the purpose of distributing, or broadcasting, data to every thread in a warp. This broadcast takes place in just a *single* cycle, making this ability very useful. In comparison, a coalesced access to global memory on compute 1.x hardware would require a memory fetch taking hundreds of cycles of latency to complete. Once it has arrived from the memory subsystem, it would be distributed in the same manner to all threads, but only after a significant wait for the memory subsystem to provide the data. Unfortunately, this is an all too common problem, in that memory speeds have failed to keep pace with processor clock speeds.

Think of fetching data from global memory in the same terms as you might consider fetching data from disk. You would never write a program that fetched the data from disk multiple times, because it would be far too slow. You have to think about what data to fetch, and once you have it, how to reuse that data as much as possible, while some background process triggers the next block of data to be brought in from the disk.

By using the broadcast mechanism, which is also present on Fermi for L2 cache–based accesses, you can distribute data very quickly to multiple threads within a warp. This is particularly useful where you have some common transformation being performed by all threads. Each thread reads element N from constant memory, which triggers a broadcast to all threads in the warp. Some processing is performed on the value fetched from constant memory, perhaps in combination with a read/write to global memory. You then fetch element $N + 1$ from constant memory, again via a broadcast, and so on. As the constant memory area is providing almost L1 cache speeds, this type of algorithm works well.

However, be aware that if a constant is really a literal value, it is better to define it as a literal value using a `#define` statement, as this frees up constant memory. So don't place literals like PI into constant memory, rather define them as literal `#define` instead. In practice, it makes little difference in speed, only memory usage, as to which method is chosen. Let's look at an example program:

```
#include "const_common.h"
#include "stdio.h"
#include "conio.h"
#include "assert.h"

#define CUDA_CALL(x) {const cudaError_t a = (x); if (a != cudaSuccess) { printf("\nCUDA
Error: %s (err_num=%d) \n", cudaGetErrorString(a), a); cudaDeviceReset(); assert(0);} }
#define KERNEL_LOOP 65536

__constant__ static const u32 const_data_01 = 0x55555555;
__constant__ static const u32 const_data_02 = 0x77777777;
__constant__ static const u32 const_data_03 = 0x33333333;
__constant__ static const u32 const_data_04 = 0x11111111;

__global__ void const_test_gpu_literal(u32 * const data, const u32 num_elements)
{
 const u32 tid = (blockIdx.x * blockDim.x) + threadIdx.x;
 if (tid < num_elements)
 {
  u32 d = 0x55555555;

  for (int i=0;i<KERNEL_LOOP;i++)
  {
   d ^= 0x55555555;
   d |= 0x77777777;
   d &= 0x33333333;
   d |= 0x11111111;
  }

  data[tid] = d;
 }
}

__global__ void const_test_gpu_const(u32 * const data, const u32 num_elements)
{
 const u32 tid = (blockIdx.x * blockDim.x) + threadIdx.x;
 if (tid < num_elements)
 {
  u32 d = const_data_01;

  for (int i=0;i<KERNEL_LOOP;i++)
  {
   d ^= const_data_01;
   d |= const_data_02;
   d &= const_data_03;
   d |= const_data_04;
  }
```

```
  data[tid] = d;
 }
}


__host__ void wait_exit(void)
{
 char ch;

 printf("\nPress any key to exit");
 ch = getch();
}


__host__ void cuda_error_check(
 const char * prefix,
 const char * postfix)
{
 if (cudaPeekAtLastError() != cudaSuccess)
 {
  printf("\n%s%s%s", prefix, cudaGetErrorString(cudaGetLastError()), postfix);
  cudaDeviceReset();
  wait_exit();
  exit(1);
 }
}


__host__ void gpu_kernel(void)
{
 const u32 num_elements = (128*1024);
 const u32 num_threads = 256;
 const u32 num_blocks = (num_elements+(num_threads-1)) / num_threads;
 const u32 num_bytes = num_elements * sizeof(u32);
 int max_device_num;
 const int max_runs = 6;

 CUDA_CALL(cudaGetDeviceCount(&max_device_num));

 for (int device_num=0; device_num < max_device_num; device_num++)
 {
  CUDA_CALL(cudaSetDevice(device_num));

  for (int num_test=0;num_test < max_runs; num_test++)
  {
   u32 * data_gpu;
   cudaEvent_t kernel_start1, kernel_stop1;
   cudaEvent_t kernel_start2, kernel_stop2;
   float delta_time1 = 0.0F, delta_time2=0.0F;
   struct cudaDeviceProp device_prop;
   char device_prefix[261];
```

```
CUDA_CALL(cudaMalloc(&data_gpu, num_bytes));
CUDA_CALL(cudaEventCreate(&kernel_start1));
CUDA_CALL(cudaEventCreate(&kernel_start2));
CUDA_CALL(cudaEventCreateWithFlags(&kernel_stop1, cudaEventBlockingSync));
CUDA_CALL(cudaEventCreateWithFlags(&kernel_stop2, cudaEventBlockingSync));

// printf("\nLaunching %u blocks, %u threads", num_blocks, num_threads);
CUDA_CALL(cudaGetDeviceProperties(&device_prop, device_num));
sprintf(device_prefix, "ID:%d %s:", device_num, device_prop.name);

// Warm up run
// printf("\nLaunching literal kernel warm-up");
const_test_gpu_literal <<<num_blocks, num_threads>>>(data_gpu, num_elements);

cuda_error_check("Error ", " returned from literal startup kernel");

// Do the literal kernel
// printf("\nLaunching literal kernel");
CUDA_CALL(cudaEventRecord(kernel_start1,0));
const_test_gpu_literal <<<num_blocks, num_threads>>>(data_gpu, num_elements);

cuda_error_check("Error ", " returned from literal runtime kernel");

CUDA_CALL(cudaEventRecord(kernel_stop1,0));
CUDA_CALL(cudaEventSynchronize(kernel_stop1));
CUDA_CALL(cudaEventElapsedTime(&delta_time1, kernel_start1, kernel_stop1));
//  printf("\nLiteral Elapsed time: %.3fms", delta_time1);

// Warm up run
// printf("\nLaunching constant kernel warm-up");
const_test_gpu_const <<<num_blocks, num_threads>>>(data_gpu, num_elements);

cuda_error_check("Error ", " returned from constant startup kernel");

// Do the constant kernel
// printf("\nLaunching constant kernel");
CUDA_CALL(cudaEventRecord(kernel_start2,0));

const_test_gpu_const <<<num_blocks, num_threads>>>(data_gpu, num_elements);

cuda_error_check("Error ", " returned from constant runtime kernel");

CUDA_CALL(cudaEventRecord(kernel_stop2,0));
CUDA_CALL(cudaEventSynchronize(kernel_stop2));
CUDA_CALL(cudaEventElapsedTime(&delta_time2, kernel_start2, kernel_stop2));
// printf("\nConst Elapsed time: %.3fms", delta_time2);
```

```
    if (delta_time1 > delta_time2)
      printf("\n%sConstant version is faster by: %.2fms (Const=%.2fms vs. Literal=
%.2fms)", device_prefix, delta_time1-delta_time2, delta_time1, delta_time2);
    else
      printf("\n%sLiteral version is faster by: %.2fms (Const=%.2fms vs. Literal=
%.2fms)", device_prefix, delta_time2-delta_time1, delta_time1, delta_time2);

    CUDA_CALL(cudaEventDestroy(kernel_start1));
    CUDA_CALL(cudaEventDestroy(kernel_start2));
    CUDA_CALL(cudaEventDestroy(kernel_stop1));
    CUDA_CALL(cudaEventDestroy(kernel_stop2));
    CUDA_CALL(cudaFree(data_gpu));
  }

  CUDA_CALL(cudaDeviceReset());
  printf("\n");
  }

  wait_exit();
}
```

This program consists of two GPU kernels, const_test_gpu_literal and const_test_gpu_const. Notice how each is declared with the __global__ prefix to say this function has public scope. Each of these kernels fetches some data as either constant data or literal data within the for loop, and uses it to manipulate the local variable d. It then writes this manipulated value out to global memory. This is necessary only to avoid the compiler optimizing away the code.

The next section of code gets the number of CUDA devices present and iterates through the devices using the cudaSetDevice call. Note that this is possible because at the end of the loop the host code calls cudaDeviceReset to clear the current context.

Having set the device, the program allocates some global memory and creates two events, a start and a stop timer event. These events are fed into the execution stream, along with the kernel call. Thus, you end up with the stream containing a start event, a kernel call, and a stop event. These events would normally happen asynchronously with the CPU, that is, they do not block the execution of the CPU and execute in parallel. This causes some problems when trying to do timing, as a CPU timer would see no elapsed time. The program, therefore, calls cudaEventSynchronize to wait on the last event, the kernel stop event, to complete. It then calculates the delta time between the start and stop events and thus knows the execution time of the kernel.

This is repeated for the constant and literal kernels, including the execution of a warm-up call to avoid any initial effects of filling any caches. The results are shown as follows:

```
ID:0 GeForce GTX 470:Constant version is faster by: 0.00ms (C=345.23ms, L=345.23ms)
ID:0 GeForce GTX 470:Constant version is faster by: 0.01ms (C=330.95ms, L=330.94ms)
ID:0 GeForce GTX 470:Literal version is faster by: 0.01ms (C=336.60ms, L=336.60ms)
ID:0 GeForce GTX 470:Constant version is faster by: 5.67ms (C=336.60ms, L=330.93ms)
ID:0 GeForce GTX 470:Constant version is faster by: 5.59ms (C=336.60ms, L=331.01ms)
ID:0 GeForce GTX 470:Constant version is faster by: 14.30ms (C=345.23ms, L=330.94ms)
```

```
ID:1 GeForce 9800 GT:Literal version is faster by: 4.04ms (C=574.85ms, L=578.89ms)
ID:1 GeForce 9800 GT:Literal version is faster by: 3.55ms (C=578.18ms, L=581.73ms)
ID:1 GeForce 9800 GT:Literal version is faster by: 4.68ms (C=575.85ms, L=580.53ms)
ID:1 GeForce 9800 GT:Constant version is faster by: 5.25ms (C=581.06ms, L=575.81ms)
ID:1 GeForce 9800 GT:Literal version is faster by: 4.01ms (C=572.08ms, L=576.10ms)
ID:1 GeForce 9800 GT:Constant version is faster by: 8.47ms (C=578.40ms, L=569.93ms)

ID:2 GeForce GTX 260:Literal version is faster by: 0.27ms (C=348.74ms, L=349.00ms)
ID:2 GeForce GTX 260:Literal version is faster by: 0.26ms (C=348.72ms, L=348.98ms)
ID:2 GeForce GTX 260:Literal version is faster by: 0.26ms (C=348.74ms, L=349.00ms)
ID:2 GeForce GTX 260:Literal version is faster by: 0.26ms (C=348.74ms, L=349.00ms)
ID:2 GeForce GTX 260:Literal version is faster by: 0.13ms (C=348.83ms, L=348.97ms)
ID:2 GeForce GTX 260:Literal version is faster by: 0.27ms (C=348.73ms, L=348.99ms)

ID:3 GeForce GTX 460:Literal version is faster by: 0.59ms (C=541.43ms, L=542.02ms)
ID:3 GeForce GTX 460:Literal version is faster by: 0.17ms (C=541.20ms, L=541.37ms)
ID:3 GeForce GTX 460:Constant version is faster by: 0.45ms (C=542.29ms, L=541.83ms)
ID:3 GeForce GTX 460:Constant version is faster by: 0.27ms (C=542.17ms, L=541.89ms)
ID:3 GeForce GTX 460:Constant version is faster by: 1.17ms (C=543.55ms, L=542.38ms)
ID:3 GeForce GTX 460:Constant version is faster by: 0.24ms (C=542.92ms, L=542.68ms)
```

What is interesting to note is that there is very little, if any, difference in the execution time if you look at this as a percentage of the total execution time. Consequently we see a fairly random distribution as to which version, the constant or the literal, is faster. Now how does this compare with using global memory? To test this, we simply replace the literal kernel with one that uses global memory as shown in the following code:

```
__device__ static u32 data_01 = 0x55555555;
__device__ static u32 data_02 = 0x77777777;
__device__ static u32 data_03 = 0x33333333;
__device__ static u32 data_04 = 0x11111111;

__global__ void const_test_gpu_gmem(u32 * const data, const u32 num_elements)
{
 const u32 tid = (blockIdx.x * blockDim.x) + threadIdx.x;
 if (tid < num_elements)
 {
  u32 d = 0x55555555;

  for (int i=0;i<KERNEL_LOOP;i++)
  {
   d ^= data_01;
   d |= data_02;
   d &= data_03;
   d |= data_04;
  }

  data[tid] = d;
```

```
    }
}
```

Notice that to declare a global variable in the GPU memory space, you simply prefix it by a __device__ specifier. We have fairly much the same kernel as before, reading four values from memory *N* times. However, in this example, I've had to reduce KERNEL_LOOP from 64 K down to 4 K as otherwise the kernel takes a *very* long time to execute. So when comparing the timings, remember we're doing just one-sixteenth of the work. The results are interesting.

```
ID:0 GeForce GTX 470:Constant version is faster by: 16.68ms (G=37.38ms, C=20.70ms)
ID:0 GeForce GTX 470:Constant version is faster by: 16.45ms (G=37.50ms, C=21.06ms)
ID:0 GeForce GTX 470:Constant version is faster by: 15.71ms (G=37.30ms, C=21.59ms)
ID:0 GeForce GTX 470:Constant version is faster by: 16.66ms (G=37.36ms, C=20.70ms)
ID:0 GeForce GTX 470:Constant version is faster by: 15.84ms (G=36.55ms, C=20.71ms)
ID:0 GeForce GTX 470:Constant version is faster by: 16.33ms (G=37.39ms, C=21.06ms)

ID:1 GeForce 9800 GT:Constant version is faster by: 1427.19ms (G=1463.58ms, C=36.39ms)
ID:1 GeForce 9800 GT:Constant version is faster by: 1425.98ms (G=1462.05ms, C=36.07ms)
ID:1 GeForce 9800 GT:Constant version is faster by: 1426.95ms (G=1463.15ms, C=36.20ms)
ID:1 GeForce 9800 GT:Constant version is faster by: 1426.13ms (G=1462.56ms, C=36.44ms)
ID:1 GeForce 9800 GT:Constant version is faster by: 1427.25ms (G=1463.65ms, C=36.40ms)
ID:1 GeForce 9800 GT:Constant version is faster by: 1427.53ms (G=1463.70ms, C=36.17ms)

ID:2 GeForce GTX 260:Constant version is faster by: 54.33ms (G=76.13ms, C=21.81ms)
ID:2 GeForce GTX 260:Constant version is faster by: 54.31ms (G=76.11ms, C=21.80ms)
ID:2 GeForce GTX 260:Constant version is faster by: 54.30ms (G=76.10ms, C=21.80ms)
ID:2 GeForce GTX 260:Constant version is faster by: 54.29ms (G=76.12ms, C=21.83ms)
ID:2 GeForce GTX 260:Constant version is faster by: 54.31ms (G=76.12ms, C=21.81ms)
ID:2 GeForce GTX 260:Constant version is faster by: 54.32ms (G=76.13ms, C=21.80ms)

ID:3 GeForce GTX 460:Constant version is faster by: 20.87ms (G=54.85ms, C=33.98ms)
ID:3 GeForce GTX 460:Constant version is faster by: 19.64ms (G=53.57ms, C=33.93ms)
ID:3 GeForce GTX 460:Constant version is faster by: 20.87ms (G=54.86ms, C=33.99ms)
ID:3 GeForce GTX 460:Constant version is faster by: 20.81ms (G=54.77ms, C=33.95ms)
ID:3 GeForce GTX 460:Constant version is faster by: 20.99ms (G=54.87ms, C=33.89ms)
ID:3 GeForce GTX 460:Constant version is faster by: 21.02ms (G=54.93ms, C=33.91ms)
```

Notice that on every generation of hardware the constant cache performs better than the global memory access. On the compute 1.1 hardware (9800GT) you have a 40:1 speedup. On the compute 1.3 hardware (GTX260) you have a 3:1 speedup. On the compute 2.0 hardware (GTX470) you have a 1.8:1 speedup. On the compute 2.1 hardware (GTX460) you have a 1.6:1 speedup.

What is perhaps most interesting is that the Fermi devices (GTX460 and GTX470) would appear to show significant speedups using the constant cache, rather than the L1/L2 cache used for global memory access. Thus, even with Fermi, the use of constant cache appears to significantly improve throughput. However, is this really the case? It seems doubtful.

To examine this further, you need to look at the PTX (virtual assembly) code generated. To see this, you need to use the -keep option for the compiler. For the constant kernel, the PTX code for this single function is shown as follows:

```
.const .u32 const_data_01 = 1431655765;
.const .u32 const_data_02 = 2004318071;
.const .u32 const_data_03 = 858993459;
.const .u32 const_data_04 = 286331153;

.entry _Z20const_test_gpu_constPjj (
  .param .u64 __cudaparm__Z20const_test_gpu_constPjj_data,
  .param .u32 __cudaparm__Z20const_test_gpu_constPjj_num_elements)
{
.reg .u32 %r<29>;
.reg .u64 %rd<6>;
.reg .pred %p<5>;
// __cuda_local_var_108907_15_non_const_tid = 0
// __cuda_local_var_108910_13_non_const_d = 4
// i = 8
.loc 16 40 0
$LDWbegin__Z20const_test_gpu_constPjj:
$LDWbeginblock_181_1:
.loc 16 42 0
mov.u32  %r1, %tid.x;
mov.u32  %r2, %ctaid.x;
mov.u32  %r3, %ntid.x;
mul.lo.u32  %r4, %r2, %r3;
add.u32  %r5, %r1, %r4;
mov.s32  %r6, %r5;
.loc 16 43 0
ld.param.u32  %r7, [__cudaparm__Z20const_test_gpu_constPjj_num_elements];
mov.s32  %r8, %r6;
setp.le.u32  %p1, %r7, %r8;
@%p1 bra  $L_1_3074;
$LDWbeginblock_181_3:
.loc 16 45 0
mov.u32  %r9, 1431655765;
mov.s32  %r10, %r9;
$LDWbeginblock_181_5:
.loc 16 47 0
mov.s32  %r11, 0;
mov.s32  %r12, %r11;
mov.s32  %r13, %r12;
mov.u32  %r14, 4095;
setp.gt.s32  %p2, %r13, %r14;
@%p2 bra  $L_1_3586;
$L_1_3330:
.loc 16 49 0
mov.s32  %r15, %r10;
xor.b32  %r16, %r15, 1431655765;
mov.s32  %r10, %r16;
.loc 16 50 0
```

```
mov.s32   %r17, %r10;
or.b32    %r18, %r17, 2004318071;
mov.s32   %r10, %r18;
.loc 16 51 0
mov.s32   %r19, %r10;
and.b32   %r20, %r19, 858993459;
mov.s32   %r10, %r20;
.loc 16 52 0
mov.s32   %r21, %r10;
or.b32    %r22, %r21, 286331153;
mov.s32   %r10, %r22;
.loc 16 47 0
mov.s32   %r23, %r12;
add.s32   %r24, %r23, 1;
mov.s32   %r12, %r24;
$Lt_1_1794:
mov.s32   %r25, %r12;
mov.u32   %r26, 4095;
setp.le.s32  %p3, %r25, %r26;
@%p3 bra  $L_1_3330;
$L_1_3586:
$LDWendblock_181_5:
.loc 16 55 0
mov.s32   %r27, %r10;
ld.param.u64  %rd1, [__cudaparm__Z20const_test_gpu_constPjj_data];
cvt.u64.u32   %rd2, %r6;
mul.wide.u32  %rd3, %r6, 4;
add.u64   %rd4, %rd1, %rd3;
st.global.u32  [%rd4+0], %r27;
$LDWendblock_181_3:
$L_1_3074:
$LDWendblock_181_1:
.loc 16 57 0
exit;
$LDWend__Z20const_test_gpu_constPjj:
} // _Z20const_test_gpu_constPjj
```

Understanding the exact meaning of the assembly code is not necessary. We've shown the function in full to give you some idea of how a small section of C code actually expands to the assembly level. PTX code uses the format

<operator> <destination register> <source reg A> <source reg B>

Thus,

```
xor.b32   %r16, %r15, 1431655765;
```

takes the value in register 15 and does a 32-bit, bitwise xor operation with the literal value 1431655765. It then stores the result in register 16. Notice the numbers highlighted in bold within the previous PTX listing. The compiler has replaced the constant values used on the kernel with literals. This is why it's always worthwhile looking into what is going on if the results are not what are expected. An extract of the GMEM PTX code for comparison is as follows:

```
ld.global.u32  %r16, [data_01];
xor.b32  %r17, %r15, %r16;
```

The program is now loading a value from global memory. The constant version was not actually doing any memory reads at all. The compiler had done a substitution of the constant values for literal values when translating the C code into PTX assembly. This can be solved by declaring the constant version as an array, rather than a number of scalar variables. Thus, the new function becomes:

```
__constant__ static const u32 const_data[4] = { 0x55555555, 0x77777777, 0x33333333,
0x11111111 };

__global__ void const_test_gpu_const(u32 * const data, const u32 num_elements)
{
 const u32 tid = (blockIdx.x * blockDim.x) + threadIdx.x;
 if (tid < num_elements)
 {
  u32 d = const_data[0];

  for (int i=0;i<KERNEL_LOOP;i++)
  {
   d ^= const_data[0];
   d |= const_data[1];
   d &= const_data[2];
   d |= const_data[3];
  }

  data[tid] = d;
 }
}
```

In the generated PTX code you now see

```
ld.const.u32  %r15, [const_data+0];
mov.s32  %r16, %r10;
xor.b32  %r17, %r15, %r16;
mov.s32  %r10, %r17;
.loc 16 47 0
ld.const.u32  %r18, [const_data+4];
mov.s32  %r19, %r10;
or.b32  %r20, %r18, %r19;
mov.s32  %r10, %r20;
```

You now have an indexed address from the start of the constant array, which is what you'd expect to see. How does this affect the results?

```
ID:0 GeForce GTX 470:Constant version is faster by: 0.34ms (G=36.67ms, C=36.32ms)
ID:0 GeForce GTX 470:Constant version is faster by: 1.11ms (G=37.36ms, C=36.25ms)
ID:0 GeForce GTX 470:GMEM  version is faster by: 0.45ms (G=36.62ms, C=37.07ms)
ID:0 GeForce GTX 470:GMEM  version is faster by: 1.21ms (G=35.86ms, C=37.06ms)
ID:0 GeForce GTX 470:GMEM  version is faster by: 0.63ms (G=36.48ms, C=37.11ms)
ID:0 GeForce GTX 470:Constant version is faster by: 0.23ms (G=37.39ms, C=37.16ms)

ID:1 GeForce 9800 GT:Constant version is faster by: 1496.41ms (G=1565.96ms, C=69.55ms)
ID:1 GeForce 9800 GT:Constant version is faster by: 1496.72ms (G=1566.42ms, C=69.71ms)
ID:1 GeForce 9800 GT:Constant version is faster by: 1498.14ms (G=1567.78ms, C=69.64ms)
ID:1 GeForce 9800 GT:Constant version is faster by: 1496.12ms (G=1565.81ms, C=69.69ms)
ID:1 GeForce 9800 GT:Constant version is faster by: 1496.91ms (G=1566.61ms, C=69.70ms)
ID:1 GeForce 9800 GT:Constant version is faster by: 1495.76ms (G=1565.49ms, C=69.73ms)

ID:2 GeForce GTX 260:Constant version is faster by: 34.21ms (G=76.12ms, C=41.91ms)
ID:2 GeForce GTX 260:Constant version is faster by: 34.22ms (G=76.13ms, C=41.91ms)
ID:2 GeForce GTX 260:Constant version is faster by: 34.19ms (G=76.10ms, C=41.91ms)
ID:2 GeForce GTX 260:Constant version is faster by: 34.20ms (G=76.11ms, C=41.91ms)
ID:2 GeForce GTX 260:Constant version is faster by: 34.21ms (G=76.12ms, C=41.91ms)
ID:2 GeForce GTX 260:Constant version is faster by: 34.20ms (G=76.12ms, C=41.92ms)

ID:3 GeForce GTX 460:GMEM  version is faster by: 0.20ms (G=54.18ms, C=54.38ms)
ID:3 GeForce GTX 460:GMEM  version is faster by: 0.17ms (G=54.86ms, C=55.03ms)
ID:3 GeForce GTX 460:GMEM  version is faster by: 0.25ms (G=54.83ms, C=55.07ms)
ID:3 GeForce GTX 460:GMEM  version is faster by: 0.81ms (G=54.24ms, C=55.05ms)
ID:3 GeForce GTX 460:GMEM  version is faster by: 1.51ms (G=53.54ms, C=55.05ms)
ID:3 GeForce GTX 460:Constant version is faster by: 1.14ms (G=54.83ms, C=53.69ms)
```

Now we see the results we'd expect to see: On Fermi (compute 2.x hardware), global memory accesses that are within the L1 cache and constant memory accesses are the same speed. Constant memory, however, shows significant benefits on compute 1.x devices where the global memory is not cached.

Constant memory updates at runtime

Constant memory of the GPU is not really constant memory, in that there is no dedicated special area of memory set aside for constant memory. The 64 K limit is exactly a 16-bit offset, allowing very quick 16-bit addressing. This presents some opportunities and some problems. First, constant memory can be updated in chunks or tiles of up to 64 K at a time. This is done with the `cudaMemcpyToSymbol` API call. Revising our constant program somewhat, let's look at how this works.

```
#include "stdio.h"
#include "conio.h"
#include "assert.h"

typedef unsigned short int u16;
typedef unsigned int u32;

#define CUDA_CALL(x) {const cudaError_t a = (x); if (a != cudaSuccess) { printf("\nCUDA
Error: %s (err_num=%d) \n", cudaGetErrorString(a), a); cudaDeviceReset(); assert(0);} }
```

```
#define KERNEL_LOOP 4096

__constant__ static const u32 const_data_gpu[KERNEL_LOOP];
__device__ static  u32 gmem_data_gpu[KERNEL_LOOP];
static u32 const_data_host[KERNEL_LOOP];

__global__ void const_test_gpu_gmem(u32 * const data, const u32 num_elements)
{
 const u32 tid = (blockIdx.x * blockDim.x) + threadIdx.x;
 if (tid < num_elements)
 {
  u32 d = gmem_data_gpu[0];

  for (int i=0;i<KERNEL_LOOP;i++)
  {
   d ^= gmem_data_gpu[i];
   d |= gmem_data_gpu[i];
   d &= gmem_data_gpu[i];
   d |= gmem_data_gpu[i];
  }

  data[tid] = d;
 }
}

__global__ void const_test_gpu_const(u32 * const data, const u32 num_elements)
{
 const u32 tid = (blockIdx.x * blockDim.x) + threadIdx.x;
 if (tid < num_elements)
 {
  u32 d = const_data_gpu[0];

  for (int i=0;i<KERNEL_LOOP;i++)
  {
   d ^= const_data_gpu[i];
   d |= const_data_gpu[i];
   d &= const_data_gpu[i];
   d |= const_data_gpu[i];
  }

  data[tid] = d;
 }
}

__host__ void wait_exit(void)
{
 char ch;
```

```
 printf("\nPress any key to exit");
 ch = getch();
}


__host__ void cuda_error_check(const char * prefix, const char * postfix)
{
 if (cudaPeekAtLastError() != cudaSuccess)
 {
  printf("\n%s%s%s", prefix, cudaGetErrorString(cudaGetLastError()), postfix);
  cudaDeviceReset();
  wait_exit();
  exit(1);
 }
}


__host__ void generate_rand_data(u32 * host_data_ptr)
{
 for (u32 i=0; i < KERNEL_LOOP; i++)
 {
  host_data_ptr[i] = (u32) rand();
 }
}


__host__ void gpu_kernel(void)
{
 const u32 num_elements = (128*1024);
 const u32 num_threads = 256;
 const u32 num_blocks = (num_elements+(num_threads-1)) / num_threads;
 const u32 num_bytes = num_elements * sizeof(u32);
 int max_device_num;
 const int max_runs = 6;

 CUDA_CALL(cudaGetDeviceCount(&max_device_num));

 for (int device_num=0; device_num < max_device_num; device_num++)
 {
  CUDA_CALL(cudaSetDevice(device_num));

  u32 * data_gpu;
  cudaEvent_t kernel_start1, kernel_stop1;
  cudaEvent_t kernel_start2, kernel_stop2;
  float delta_time1 = 0.0F, delta_time2=0.0F;
  struct cudaDeviceProp device_prop;
  char device_prefix[261];

  CUDA_CALL(cudaMalloc(&data_gpu, num_bytes));
  CUDA_CALL(cudaEventCreate(&kernel_start1));
```

```
CUDA_CALL(cudaEventCreate(&kernel_start2));
CUDA_CALL(cudaEventCreateWithFlags(&kernel_stop1, cudaEventBlockingSync));
CUDA_CALL(cudaEventCreateWithFlags(&kernel_stop2, cudaEventBlockingSync));

// printf("\nLaunching %u blocks, %u threads", num_blocks, num_threads);
CUDA_CALL(cudaGetDeviceProperties(&device_prop, device_num));
sprintf(device_prefix, "ID:%d %s:", device_num, device_prop.name);

for (int num_test=0;num_test < max_runs; num_test++)
{
 // Generate some random data on the host side
 // Replace with function to obtain data block from disk, network or other
 // data source
 generate_rand_data(const_data_host);

 // Copy host memory to constant memory section in GPU
 CUDA_CALL(cudaMemcpyToSymbol(const_data_gpu, const_data_host,
         KERNEL_LOOP * sizeof(u32)));
 // Warm up run
 // printf("\nLaunching gmem kernel warm-up");
 const_test_gpu_gmem <<<num_blocks, num_threads>>>(data_gpu, num_elements);
 cuda_error_check("Error ", " returned from gmem startup kernel");

 // Do the gmem kernel
 // printf("\nLaunching gmem kernel");
 CUDA_CALL(cudaEventRecord(kernel_start1,0));

 const_test_gpu_gmem <<<num_blocks, num_threads>>>(data_gpu, num_elements);

 cuda_error_check("Error ", " returned from gmem runtime kernel");

 CUDA_CALL(cudaEventRecord(kernel_stop1,0));
 CUDA_CALL(cudaEventSynchronize(kernel_stop1));
 CUDA_CALL(cudaEventElapsedTime(&delta_time1, kernel_start1, kernel_stop1));
 // printf("\nGMEM Elapsed time: %.3fms", delta_time1);

 // Copy host memory to global memory section in GPU
 CUDA_CALL(cudaMemcpyToSymbol(gmem_data_gpu, const_data_host,
         KERNEL_LOOP * sizeof(u32)));
 // Warm up run
 // printf("\nLaunching constant kernel warm-up");
 const_test_gpu_const <<<num_blocks, num_threads>>>(data_gpu, num_elements);

 cuda_error_check("Error ", " returned from constant startup kernel");

 // Do the constant kernel
 // printf("\nLaunching constant kernel");
 CUDA_CALL(cudaEventRecord(kernel_start2,0));
```

```
    const_test_gpu_const <<<num_blocks, num_threads>>>(data_gpu, num_elements);

    cuda_error_check("Error ", " returned from constant runtime kernel");

    CUDA_CALL(cudaEventRecord(kernel_stop2,0));
    CUDA_CALL(cudaEventSynchronize(kernel_stop2));
    CUDA_CALL(cudaEventElapsedTime(&delta_time2, kernel_start2, kernel_stop2));
    // printf("\nConst Elapsed time: %.3fms", delta_time2);

    if (delta_time1 > delta_time2)
      printf("\n%sConstant version is faster by: %.2fms (G=%.2fms, C=%.2fms)",
  device_prefix, delta_time1-delta_time2, delta_time1, delta_time2);
    else
      printf("\n%sGMEM  version is faster by: %.2fms (G=%.2fms, C=%.2fms)",
  device_prefix, delta_time2-delta_time1, delta_time1, delta_time2);
    }

  CUDA_CALL(cudaEventDestroy(kernel_start1));
  CUDA_CALL(cudaEventDestroy(kernel_start2));
  CUDA_CALL(cudaEventDestroy(kernel_stop1));
  CUDA_CALL(cudaEventDestroy(kernel_stop2));
  CUDA_CALL(cudaFree(data_gpu));

  CUDA_CALL(cudaDeviceReset());
  printf("\n");
  }

 wait_exit();
 }
```

Notice how the `cudaMemcpyToSymbol` call works. You can copy to any named global symbol on the GPU, regardless of whether that symbol is in global memory or constant memory. Thus, if you chunk the data to 64 K chunks, you can access it from the constant cache. This is very useful if all threads are accessing the same data element, as you get the broadcast and cache effect from the constant memory section.

Notice also that the memory allocation, creation of events, destruction of the events and freeing of device memory is now done outside the main loop. CUDA API calls such as these are actually very costly in terms of CPU time. The CPU load of this program drops considerably with this simple change. Always try to set up everything at the start and destroy or free it at the end. Never do this in the loop body or it will greatly slow down the application.

Constant memory question

1. If you have a data structure that is 16 K in size and exhibits a random pattern of access per block but a unified access pattern per warp, would it be best to place it into registers, constant memory, or shared memory? Why?

Constant memory answer

1. Although it is a little tricky to get a large array into registers, tiling into blocks of registers per thread would allow for the fastest access, regardless of access pattern. However, you are limited to 32 K (compute < 1.2), 64 K (compute 1,2, 1.3), or 128 K (compute 2.x) or 256 K (compute 3.x) register space per SM. You have to allocate some of this to working registers on a per-thread basis. On Fermi you can have a maximum of 64 registers per thread, so with 32 allocated to data and 32 as the working set, you would have just 128 active threads, or four active warps. As soon as the program accessed off-chip memory (e.g., global memory) the latency may stall the SM. Therefore, the kernel would need a high ratio of operations on the register block to make this a good solution.

Placing it into shared memory would likely be the best case, although depending on the actual access pattern you may see shared memory bank conflicts. The uniform warp access would allow broadcast from the shared memory to all the threads in a single warp. It is only in the case where the warp from two blocks accessed the same bank that would you get a shared memory conflict.

However, 16 K of shared memory would consume entirely the shared memory in one SM on compute 1.x devices and limit you to three blocks maximum on compute 2.x/3.x hardware.

Constant memory would also be a reasonable choice on compute 1.x devices. Constant memory would have the benefit of broadcast to the threads. However, the 16 K of data may well swamp the cache memory. Also, and more importantly, the constant cache is optimized for linear access, that is, it fetches cache lines upon a single access. Thus, accesses near the original access are cached. Accesses to a noncached cache line result in a cache miss penalty that is larger than a fetch to global memory without a cache miss.

Global memory may well be faster on compute 2.x/3.x devices, as the unified access per warp should be translated by the compiler into the uniform warp-level global memory access. This provides the broadcast access constant memory would have provided on compute 1.x devices.

GLOBAL MEMORY

Global memory is perhaps the most interesting of the memory types in that it's the one you absolutely have to understand. GPU global memory is so termed because it's writable from both the GPU and the CPU. It can actually be accessed from any device on the PCI-E bus. GPU cards can transfer data to and from one another, directly, without needing the CPU. This peer-to-peer feature, introduced in the CUDA 4.x SDK, is not yet supported on all platforms. Currently, the Windows 7/Vista platforms are only supported on Tesla hardware, via the TCC driver model. Those using Linux or Windows XP can use this feature with both consumer and Tesla cards.

The memory from the GPU is accessible to the CPU host processor in one of three ways:

- Explicitly with a blocking transfer.
- Explicitly with a nonblocking transfer.
- Implicitly using zero memory copy.

The memory on the GPU device sits on the other side of the PCI-E bus. This is a bidirectional bus that, in theory, supports transfers of up to 8 GB/s (PCI-E 2.0) in each direction. In practice, the PCI-E bandwidth is typically 4–5 GB/s in each direction. Depending on the hardware you are using,

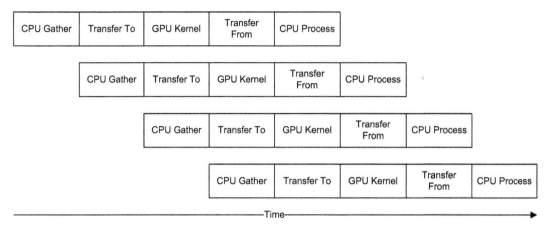

FIGURE 6.16

Overlapping kernel and memory transfers.

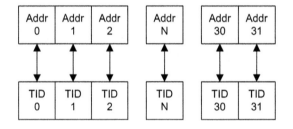

FIGURE 6.17

Addresses accessed by thread ID.

nonblocking and implicit memory transfers may not be supported. We'll look at these issues in more detail in Chapter 9.

The usual model of execution involves the CPU transferring a block of data to the GPU, the GPU kernel processing it, and then the CPU initiating a transfer of the data back to the host memory. A slightly more advanced model of this is where we use streams (covered later) to overlap transfers and kernels to ensure the GPU is always kept busy, as shown in Figure 6.16.

Once you have the data in the GPU, the question then becomes how do you access it efficiently on the GPU? Remember the GPU can be rated at over 3 teraflops in terms of compute power, but typically the main memory bandwidth is in the order of 190 GB/s down to as little as 25 GB/s. By comparison, a typical Intel I7 Nehalem or AMD Phenom CPU achieves in the order of 25–30 GB/s, depending on the particular device speed and width of the memory bus used.

Graphics cards use high-speed GDDR, or graphics dynamic memory, which achieves very high sustained bandwidth, but like all memory, has a high latency. Latency is the time taken to return the first byte of the data access. Therefore, in the same way that we can pipeline kernels, as is shown in

Figure 6.16, the memory accesses are pipelined. By creating a ratio of typically 10:1 of threads to number of memory accesses, you can hide memory latency, but only if you access global memory in a pattern that is coalesced.

So what is a coalescable pattern? This is where all the threads access a contiguous and aligned memory block, as shown in Figure 6.17. Here we have shown `Addr` as the logical address offset from the base location, assuming we are accessing byte-based data. TID represents the thread number. If we have a one-to-one sequential and aligned access to memory, the address accesses of each thread are combined together and a single memory transaction is issued. Assuming we're accessing a single precision float or integer value, each thread will be accessing 4 bytes of memory. Memory is coalesced on a warp basis (the older G80 hardware uses half warps), meaning we get $32 \times 4 = 128$ byte access to memory.

Coalescing sizes supported are 32, 64, and 128 bytes, meaning warp accesses to byte, 16- and 32-bit data will always be coalesced if the access is a sequential pattern and aligned to a 32-byte boundary.

The alignment is achieved by using a special malloc instruction, replacing the standard `cudaMalloc` with `cudaMallocPitch`, which has the following syntax:

```
extern __host__ cudaError_t CUDARTAPI cudaMallocPitch(void **devPtr, size_t *pitch,
size_t width, size_t height);
```

This translates to `cudaMallocPitch` (pointer to device memory pointer, pointer to pitch, desired width of the row in bytes, height of the array in bytes).

Thus, if you have an array of 100 rows of 60 float elements, using the conventional `cudaMalloc`, you would allocate $100 \times 60 \times$ sizeof(float) bytes, or $100 \times 60 \times 4 = 24,000$ bytes. Accessing array index [1][0] (i.e., row one, element zero) would result in noncoalesced access. This is because the length of a single row of 60 elements would be 240 bytes, which is of course not a power of two.

The first address in the series of addresses from each thread would not meet the alignment requirements for coalescing. Using the `cudaMallocPitch` function the size of each row is padded by an amount necessary for the alignment requirements of the given device (Figure 6.18). In our example, it would in most cases be extended to 64 elements per row, or 256 bytes. The pitch the device actually uses is returned in the pitch parameters passed to `cudaMallocPitch`.

Let's have a look at how this works in practice. Nonaligned accesses result in multiple memory fetches being issued. While waiting for a memory fetch, all threads in a warp are stalled until *all* memory fetches are returned from the hardware. Thus, to achieve the best throughput you need to issue a small number of large memory fetch requests, as a result of aligned and sequential coalesced accesses.

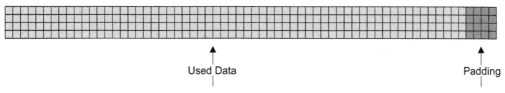

Used Data   Padding

FIGURE 6.18

Padding achieved with `cudaMallocPitch`.

So what happens if you have data that is interleaved in some way, for example, a structure?

```
typedef struct
{
 unsigned int a;
 unsigned int b;
 unsigned int c;
 unsigned int d;
} MY_TYPE_T;

MY_TYPE_T some_array[1024]; /* 1024 * 4 bytes = 4K */
```

Index 0 Element A	Index 0 Element B	Index 0 Element C	Index 0 Element D	Index 1 Element A	Index 1 Element B	Index 1 Element C	Index 1 Element D	Index N Element A, B, C, D

FIGURE 6.19

Array elements in memory.

Figure 6.19 shows how C will lay this structure out in memory.

Elements are laid out in memory in the sequence in which they are defined within the structure. The access pattern for such a structure is shown in Figure 6.20. As you can see from the figure, the addresses of the structure elements are not contiguous in memory. This means you get no coalescing and the memory bandwidth suddenly drops off by an order of magnitude. Depending on the size of our data elements, it may be possible to have each thread read a larger value and then internally within the threads mask off the necessary bits. For example, if you have byte-based data you can do the following:

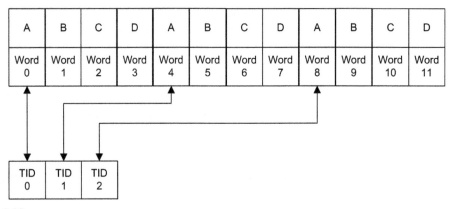

FIGURE 6.20

Words accessed by thread (no coalescing).

```
const unsigned int value_u32 = some_data[tid];
const unsigned char value_01 = (value_u32 & 0x000000FF)   );
const unsigned char value_02 = (value_u32 & 0x0000FF00) >> 8 );
const unsigned char value_03 = (value_u32 & 0x00FF0000) >> 16 );
const unsigned char value_04 = (value_u32 & 0xFF000000) >> 24 );
```

It's also possible to maintain the one thread to one data element mapping by simply treating the array of structure elements as an array of words. We can then allocate one thread to each element of the structure. This type of solution is, however, not suitable if there is some data flow relationship between the structure members, so thread 1 needs the x, y, and z coordinate of a structure, for example. In this case, it's best to reorder the data, perhaps in the loading or transfer phase on the CPU, into N discrete arrays. In this way, the arrays individually sit concurrently in memory. We can simply access array a, b, c, or d instead of the struct->a notation we'd use with a structure dereference. Instead of an interleaved and uncoalesced pattern, we get four coalesced accesses from each thread into different memory regions, maintaining optimal global memory bandwidth usage.

Let's look at an example of global memory reads. In this example, we'll sum the values of all the elements in the structure using the two methods. First, we'll add all the values from an array of structures and then from a structure of arrays.

```
// Define the number of elements we'll use
#define NUM_ELEMENTS 4096

// Define an interleaved type
// 16 bytes, 4 bytes per member
typedef struct
{
 u32 a;
 u32 b;
 u32 c;
 u32 d;
} INTERLEAVED_T;

// Define an array type based on the interleaved structure
typedef INTERLEAVED_T INTERLEAVED_ARRAY_T[NUM_ELEMENTS];

// Alternative - structure of arrays
typedef u32 ARRAY_MEMBER_T[NUM_ELEMENTS];

typedef struct
{
 ARRAY_MEMBER_T a;
 ARRAY_MEMBER_T b;
 ARRAY_MEMBER_T c;
 ARRAY_MEMBER_T d;
} NON_INTERLEAVED_T;
```

In this section of code, we declare two types; the first is INTERLEAVED_T, an array of structures of which the members are a to d. We then declare NON_INTERLEAVED_T as a structure that contains four arrays, a to d. As the types are named, with the first one we expect the data to be interleaved in memory. With the second one, we expect a number of contiguous memory areas.

Let's look first at the CPU code.

```
__host__ float add_test_non_interleaved_cpu(
 NON_INTERLEAVED_T * const host_dest_ptr,
 const NON_INTERLEAVED_T * const host_src_ptr,
 const u32 iter,
 const u32 num_elements)
{
 float start_time = get_time();

 for (u32 tid = 0; tid < num_elements; tid++)
 {
  for (u32 i=0; i<iter; i++)
  {
   host_dest_ptr->a[tid] += host_src_ptr->a[tid];
   host_dest_ptr->b[tid] += host_src_ptr->b[tid];
   host_dest_ptr->c[tid] += host_src_ptr->c[tid];
   host_dest_ptr->d[tid] += host_src_ptr->d[tid];
  }
 }

 const float delta = get_time() - start_time;

 return delta;
}


__host__ float add_test_interleaved_cpu(
 INTERLEAVED_T * const host_dest_ptr,
 const INTERLEAVED_T * const host_src_ptr,
 const u32 iter,
 const u32 num_elements)
{
 float start_time = get_time();

 for (u32 tid = 0; tid < num_elements; tid++)
 {
  for (u32 i=0; i<iter; i++)
  {
   host_dest_ptr[tid].a += host_src_ptr[tid].a;
   host_dest_ptr[tid].b += host_src_ptr[tid].b;
   host_dest_ptr[tid].c += host_src_ptr[tid].c;
   host_dest_ptr[tid].d += host_src_ptr[tid].d;
  }
 }

 const float delta = get_time() - start_time;
```

```
  return delta;
}
```

The two functions to add the data are broadly similar. Each function iterates over all elements in the list iter times and adds into the destination data structure a value from the source data structure. Each function also returns the time it takes to execute. As these will run on the CPU, we use the wall clock time on the CPU.

The GPU code is largely similar, with the outer loop, tid, replaced with *N* threads from invoking a kernel.

```
__global__ void add_kernel_interleaved(
 INTERLEAVED_T * const dest_ptr,
 const INTERLEAVED_T * const src_ptr,
 const u32 iter,
 const u32 num_elements)
{
 const u32 tid = (blockIdx.x * blockDim.x) + threadIdx.x;

 if (tid < num_elements)
 {
  for (u32 i=0; i<iter; i++)
  {
   dest_ptr[tid].a += src_ptr[tid].a;
   dest_ptr[tid].b += src_ptr[tid].b;
   dest_ptr[tid].c += src_ptr[tid].c;
   dest_ptr[tid].d += src_ptr[tid].d;
  }
 }
}


__global__ void add_kernel_non_interleaved(
 NON_INTERLEAVED_T * const dest_ptr,
 const NON_INTERLEAVED_T * const src_ptr,
 const u32 iter,
 const u32 num_elements)
{
 const u32 tid = (blockIdx.x * blockDim.x) + threadIdx.x;

 if (tid < num_elements)
 {
  for (u32 i=0; i<iter; i++)
  {
   dest_ptr->a[tid] += src_ptr->a[tid];
   dest_ptr->b[tid] += src_ptr->b[tid];
   dest_ptr->c[tid] += src_ptr->c[tid];
   dest_ptr->d[tid] += src_ptr->d[tid];
```

```
    }
  }
}
```

The caller of the GPU function is a fairly standard copy to device and time routine. I'll list here only the interleaved version, as the two functions are largely identical.

```
__host__ float add_test_interleaved(
 INTERLEAVED_T * const host_dest_ptr,
 const INTERLEAVED_T * const host_src_ptr,
 const u32 iter,
 const u32 num_elements)
{
 // Set launch params
 const u32 num_threads = 256;
 const u32 num_blocks = (num_elements + (num_threads-1)) / num_threads;

 // Allocate memory on the device
 const size_t num_bytes = (sizeof(INTERLEAVED_T) * num_elements);
 INTERLEAVED_T * device_dest_ptr;
 INTERLEAVED_T * device_src_ptr;

 CUDA_CALL(cudaMalloc((void **) &device_src_ptr, num_bytes));

 CUDA_CALL(cudaMalloc((void **) &device_dest_ptr, num_bytes));

 // Create a stop and stop event for timing
 cudaEvent_t kernel_start, kernel_stop;
 cudaEventCreate(&kernel_start, 0);
 cudaEventCreate(&kernel_stop, 0);

 // Create a non zero stream
 cudaStream_t test_stream;
 CUDA_CALL(cudaStreamCreate(&test_stream));

 // Copy src data to GPU
 CUDA_CALL(cudaMemcpy(device_src_ptr, host_src_ptr, num_bytes,
cudaMemcpyHostToDevice));

 // Push start event ahread of kernel call
 CUDA_CALL(cudaEventRecord(kernel_start, 0));

 // Call the GPU kernel
 add_kernel_interleaved<<<num_blocks, num_threads>>>(device_dest_ptr, device_src_ptr,
iter, num_elements);

 // Push stop event after of kernel call
 CUDA_CALL(cudaEventRecord(kernel_stop, 0));
```

```
// Wait for stop event
CUDA_CALL(cudaEventSynchronize(kernel_stop));

// Get delta between start and stop,
// i.e. the kernel execution time
float delta = 0.0F;
CUDA_CALL(cudaEventElapsedTime(&delta, kernel_start, kernel_stop));

// Clean up
CUDA_CALL(cudaFree(device_src_ptr));
CUDA_CALL(cudaFree(device_dest_ptr));
CUDA_CALL(cudaEventDestroy(kernel_start));
CUDA_CALL(cudaEventDestroy(kernel_stop));
CUDA_CALL(cudaStreamDestroy(test_stream));

 return delta;
}
```

When we run this code, we achive the following results:

```
Running Interleaved /  Non Interleaved memory test using 65536 bytes (4096 elements)
ID:0 GeForce GTX 470:  Interleaved time: 181.83ms
ID:0 GeForce GTX 470:  Non Interleaved time: 45.13ms

ID:1 GeForce 9800 GT:  Interleaved time: 2689.15ms
ID:1 GeForce 9800 GT:  Non Interleaved time: 234.98ms

ID:2 GeForce GTX 260:  Interleaved time: 444.16ms
ID:2 GeForce GTX 260:  Non Interleaved time: 139.35ms

ID:3 GeForce GTX 460:  Interleaved time: 199.15ms
ID:3 GeForce GTX 460:  Non Interleaved time: 63.49ms

      CPU (serial):  Interleaved time: 1216.00ms
      CPU (serial):  Non Interleaved time: 13640.00ms
```

What we see is quite interesting, and largely to be expected. The interleaved memory access pattern has an execution time three to four times longer than the noninterleaved pattern on compute 2.x hardware. The compute 1.3 GTX260 demonstrates a $3\times$ slow down when using the interleaved memory pattern. The compute 1.1 9800GT, however, exhibits an $11\times$ slow down, due to the more stringent coalescing requirements for these older devices.

We can look a bit deeper into the memory access pattern between the slow interleaved pattern and the much faster noninterleaved pattern with a tool such as Parallel Nsight. We can see that the number of memory transactions (CUDA Memory Statistics experiment) used in the noninterleaved version is approximately one-quarter that of the interleaved version, resulting in the noninterleaved version shifting one-quarter of the data to/from memory than the interleaved version does.

One other interesting thing to note is the CPU shows exactly the opposite effect. This may seem strange, until you think about the access pattern and the cache reuse. A CPU accessing element a in the interleaved example will have brought structure elements b, c, and d into the cache on the access to a since they will likely be in the same cache line. However, the noninterleaved version will be accessing memory in four seperate and physically dispersed areas. There would be four times the number of memory bus transactions and thus any read-ahead policy the CPU might be using would not be as effective.

Thus, if your existing CPU application uses an interleaved arrangement of structure elements, simply copying it to a GPU will work, but at a considerable cost due to poor memory coalescing. Simply reordering the declarations and access mechanism, as we've done in this example, could allow you to achieve a significant speedup for very little effort.

Score boarding

One other interesting property of global memory is that it works with a scoreboard. If we initiate a load from global memory (e.g., a=some_array[0]), then all that happens is that the memory fetch is initiated and local variable a is listed as having a pending memory transaction. Unlike traditional CPU code, we do not see a stall or even a context switch to another warp until such time as the variable a is later used in an expression. Only at this time do we actually need the contents of variable a. Thus, the GPU follows a lazy evaluation model.

You can think of this a bit like ordering a taxi and then getting ready to leave. It may take only five minutes to get ready, but the taxi may take up to 15 minutes to arrive. By ordering it before we actually need it, it starts its journey while we are busy on the task of getting ready to leave. If we wait until we are ready before ordering the taxi, we serialize the task of getting ready to leave with waiting for the taxi.

The same is true of the memory transactions. By comparison, they are like the slow taxi, taking forever in terms of GPU cycles to arrive. Until such time as we actually need the memory transaction to have arrived, the GPU can be busy calculating other aspects of the algorithm. This is achieved very simply by placing the memory fetches at the start of the kernel, and then using them much later during the kernel. We, in effect, overlap the memory fetch latency with useful GPU computations, reducing the effect of memory latency on our kernel.

Global memory sorting

Picking up from where we left off with shared memory sorting, how do you think the same algorithm would work for global memory–based sorting? What needs to be considered? First and foremost, you need to think about memory coalescing. Our sorting algorithm was specifically developed to run with the 32 banks of shared memory and accesses the shared memory in columns. If you look again at Figure 6.8, you'll see this also achieves coalesced access to global memory if all threads were to read at once.

The coalesced access occurs during the radix sort, as each thread marches through its own list. Every thread's access is coalesced (combined) together by the hardware. Writes are noncoalesced as the 1 list can vary in size. However, the zeros are both read and written to the same address range, thus providing coalesced access.

In the merge phase, during the startup condition one value from each list is read from global into shared memory. In every iteration of the merge, a single value is written out to global memory, and a single value is read into shared memory to replace the value written out. There is a reasonable amount of work being done for every memory access. Thus, despite the poor coalescing, the memory latency should be largely hidden. Let's look at how this works in practice.

Table 6.13 Single SM GMEM Sort (1K Elements)

Threads	GTX470	GTX260	GTX460
1	33.27	66.32	27.47
2	19.21	37.53	15.87
4	11.82	22.29	9.83
8	9.31	16.24	7.88
16	7.41	12.52	6.36
32	6.63	10.95	5.75
64	6.52	10.72	5.71
128	7.06	11.63	6.29
256	8.61	14.88	7.82

What you can see from Table 6.13 and Figure 6.21 is that 32 threads work quite well, but this is marginally beaten by 64 threads on all the tested devices. It's likely that having another warp to execute is hiding a small amount of the latency and will also improve slightly the memory bandwidth utilization.

Moving beyond 64 threads slows things down, so if we now fix the number of threads at 64 and increase the dataset size what do we see? See Table 6.14 and Figure 6.22 for the results. In fact we see an almost perfect linear relationship when using a single SM, as we are currently doing.

As Table 6.14 shows, 1024 KB (1 MB) of data takes 1486 ms to sort on the GTX460. This means we can sort 1 MB of data in around 1.5 seconds (1521 ms exactly) and around 40 MB per minute, regardless of the size of the data.

A 1 GB dataset would therefore take around 25–26 minutes to sort, which is not very impressive. So what is the issue? Well currently we're using just a single block, which in turn limits us to a single SM. The test GPUs consists of 14 SMs on the GTX470, 27 SMs on the GTX260, and 7 SMs on the

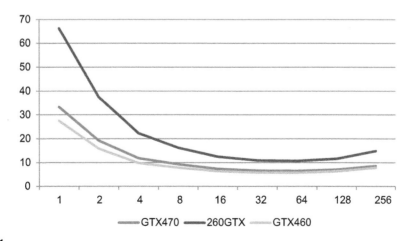

FIGURE 6.21

Graph of single SM GMEM sort (1K elements).

Table 6.14 GMEM Sort by Size

Size (Kb)	Absolute Time (ms)			Time per KB (ms)		
	GTX470	GTX260	GTX460	GTX470	GTX260	GTX460
1	1.67	2.69	1.47	1.67	2.69	1.47
2	3.28	5.36	2.89	1.64	2.68	1.45
4	6.51	10.73	5.73	1.63	2.68	1.43
8	12.99	21.43	11.4	1.62	2.68	1.43
16	25.92	42.89	22.75	1.62	2.68	1.42
32	51.81	85.82	45.47	1.62	2.68	1.42
64	103.6	171.78	90.94	1.62	2.68	1.42
128	207.24	343.74	181.89	1.62	2.69	1.42
256	414.74	688.04	364.09	1.62	2.69	1.42
512	838.25	1377.23	737.85	1.64	2.69	1.44
1024	1692.07	2756.87	1485.94	1.65	2.69	1.45

GTX460. Clearly, we're using a small fraction of the real potential of the card. This has been done largely to simplify the solution, so let's look now at using multiple blocks.

The output of one SM is a single linear sorted list. The output of two SMs is therefore two linear sorted lists, which is not what we want. Consider the following dump of output from a two-block version of the sort. The original values were in reverse sorting order from 0x01 to 0x100. The first value shown is the array index, followed by the value at that array index.

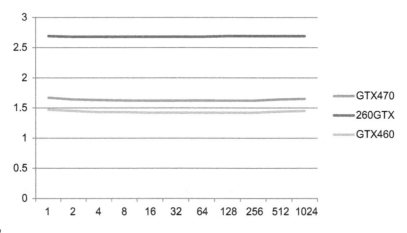

FIGURE 6.22

GMEM graph sorted by size.

```
000:00000041 001:00000042 002:00000043 003:00000044 004:00000045 005:00000046
006:00000047 007:00000048
008:00000049 009:0000004a 010:0000004b 011:0000004c 012:0000004d 013:0000004e
014:0000004f 015:00000050
016:00000051 017:00000052 018:00000053 019:00000054 020:00000055 021:00000056
022:00000057 023:00000058
024:00000059 025:0000005a 026:0000005b 027:0000005c 028:0000005d 029:0000005e
030:0000005f 031:00000060
032:00000061 033:00000062 034:00000063 035:00000064 036:00000065 037:00000066
038:00000067 039:00000068
040:00000069 041:0000006a 042:0000006b 043:0000006c 044:0000006d 045:0000006e
046:0000006f 047:00000070
048:00000071 049:00000072 050:00000073 051:00000074 052:00000075 053:00000076
054:00000077 055:00000078
056:00000079 057:0000007a 058:0000007b 059:0000007c 060:0000007d 061:0000007e
062:0000007f 063:00000080

064:00000001 065:00000002 066:00000003 067:00000004 068:00000005 069:00000006
070:00000007 071:00000008
072:00000009 073:0000000a 074:0000000b 075:0000000c 076:0000000d 077:0000000e
078:0000000f 079:00000010
080:00000011 081:00000012 082:00000013 083:00000014 084:00000015 085:00000016
086:00000017 087:00000018
088:00000019 089:0000001a 090:0000001b 091:0000001c 092:0000001d 093:0000001e
094:0000001f 095:00000020
096:00000021 097:00000022 098:00000023 099:00000024 100:00000025 101:00000026
102:00000027 103:00000028
104:00000029 105:0000002a 106:0000002b 107:0000002c 108:0000002d 109:0000002e
110:0000002f 111:00000030
112:00000031 113:00000032 114:00000033 115:00000034 116:00000035 117:00000036
118:00000037 119:00000038
120:00000039 121:0000003a 122:0000003b 123:0000003c 124:0000003d 125:0000003e
126:0000003f 127:00000040
```

We can see there are two sorted lists here, one from 0x41 to 0x80 and the other from 0x01 to 0x40. You might say that's not a great problem, and we just need to merge the list again. This is where we hit the second issue; think about the memory access on a per-thread basis.

Assume we use just two threads, one per list. Thread 0 accesses element 0. Thread 1 accesses element 64. It's not possible for the hardware to coalesce the two accesses, so the hardware has to issue two independent memory fetches.

Even if we were to do the merge in zero time, assuming we have a maximum of 16 SMs and using all of them did not flood the bandwidth of the device, in the best case we'd get 16×40 MB/min = 640 MB/min or around 10.5 MB/s. Perhaps an alternative approach is required.

Sample sort

Sample sort tries to get around the problem of merge sort, that is, that you have to perform a merge step. It works on the principle of splitting the data into N independent blocks of data such that each block is partially sorted and we can guarantee the numbers in block N are less than those in block $N + 1$ and larger than those in block $N - 1$.

We'll look first at an example using three processors sorting 24 data items (see Figure 6.23). The first phase selects S equidistant samples from the dataset. S is chosen as a fraction of N, the total number of elements in the entire dataset. It is important that S is representative of the dataset. Equidistant points are best used where the data is reasonably uniformly distributed over the data range. If the data contains large peaks that are not very wide in terms of sample points, a higher number of samples may have to be used, or one where the samples concentrate around the known peaks. We'll chose equidistant points and assume the more common uniform distribution of points.

The samples are then sorted such that the lowest value is first in the list, assuming an ascending order sort. The sample data is then split into bins according to how many processors are available. The data is scanned to determine how many samples fit in each bin. The number of samples in each bin is then added to form a prefix sum that is used to index into an array.

A prefix sum is simply the sum of all elements prior to the current element. Looking at the example, we can see nine elements were allocated to bin 0. Therefore, the start of the second dataset is element 9. The next list size, as it happens from the dataset, was also nine. Nine plus the previous sum is 18, and thus we know the index of the next dataset and so on.

The data is then shuffled, so all the bin 0 elements are written to the first index of the prefix sum (zero), bin 1 written to the next, and so on. This achieves a partial sort of the data such that all the samples in bin $N - 1$ are less than those in bin N, which in turn are less than those in bin $N + 1$. The bins are then dispatched to P processors that sort the lists in parallel. If an in-place sort is used, then the list is sorted once the last block of data is sorted, without any merge step. Figure 6.24 is this same example using six processing elements.

Notice that when we used three processors based on six samples, the bin sizes were 9, 9, 6. With six processors the bin sizes are 6, 3, 5, 4, 1, 5. What we're actually interested in is the largest value, as on P processors the largest block will determine the total time taken. In this example, the maximum is

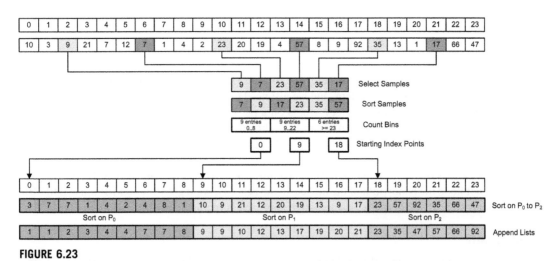

FIGURE 6.23

Sample sort using three processors.

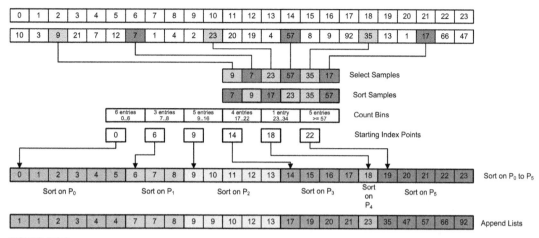

FIGURE 6.24

Sample sort using six processors.

reduced from nine elements to six elements, so a doubling of the number of processors has reduced the maximum number of data points by only one-third.

The actual distribution will depend very much on the dataset. The most common dataset is actually a mostly sorted list or one that is sorted with some new data items that must be added. This tends to give a fairly equal distribution for most datasets. For problem datasets it's possible to adjust the sampling policy accordingly.

With a GPU we don't just have six processors; we have N SMs, each of which we need to run a number of blocks on. Each block would ideally be around 256 threads based simply on ideal memory latency hiding, although we saw that 64 threads worked best with the radix sort we developed earlier in the chapter. With the GTX470 device, we have 14 SMs with a maximum of eight blocks per SM. Therefore, we need at least 112 blocks just to keep every SM busy. We'll find out in practice which is the best in due course. It is likely we will need substantially more blocks to load balance the work.

The first task, however, is to develop a CPU version of the sample sort algorithm and to understand it. We'll look at each operation in turn and how it could be converted to a parallel solution.

To follow the development of the code in the subsequent sections, it's important you understand the sample sort algorithm we just covered. It's one of the more complex sorting algorithms and was chosen both for performance reasons and also because it allows us to look at a real problem involving difficult issues in terms of GPU implementation. If you browsed over the algorithm, please re-read the last few pages until you are sure you understand how the algorithm works before proceeding.

Selecting samples

The first part of the sample sort is to select N samples from the source data. The CPU version works with a standard loop where the source data loop index is incremented by `sample_interval` elements. The sample index counter, however, is incremented only by one per iteration.

```
__host__ TIMER_T select_samples_cpu(
  u32 * const sample_data,
```

```
    const u32 sample_interval,
    const u32 num_elements,
    const u32 * const src_data)
{
    const TIMER_T start_time = get_time();
    u32 sample_idx = 0;

    for (u32 src_idx=0; src_idx<num_elements; src_idx+=sample_interval)
    {
        sample_data[sample_idx] = src_data[src_idx];
        sample_idx++;
    }

    const TIMER_T end_time = get_time();
    return end_time - start_time;
}
```

In the GPU version we can use a classic loop elimination method and simply create one thread per sample point, spread across as many blocks as necessary. Thus, the first statement

```
const u32 tid = (blockIdx.x * blockDim.x) + threadIdx.x;
```

simply takes the block index and multiplies it by the number of threads per block and then adds in the current thread to our combined thread index.

```
__global__ void select_samples_gpu_kernel(u32 * const sample_data,
    const u32 sample_interval, const u32 * const src_data)
{
    const u32 tid = (blockIdx.x * blockDim.x) + threadIdx.x;
    sample_data[tid] = src_data[tid*sample_interval];
}

__host__ TIMER_T select_samples_gpu(
    u32 * const sample_data,
    const u32 sample_interval,
    const u32 num_elements,
    const u32 num_samples,
    const u32 * const src_data,
    const u32 num_threads_per_block,
    const char * prefix)
{
    // Invoke one block of N threads per sample
    const u32 num_blocks = num_samples / num_threads_per_block;

    // Check for non equal block size
    assert((num_blocks * num_threads_per_block) == num_samples);

    start_device_timer();

    select_samples_gpu_kernel<<<num_blocks, num_threads_per_block>>>(sample_data,
    sample_interval, src_data);
    cuda_error_check(prefix, "Error invoking select_samples_gpu_kernel");
```

```
const TIMER_T func_time = stop_device_timer();

return func_time;
}
```

Finally, to work out the index into the source data we simply multiply our sample data index (tid) by the size of the sample interval. For the sake of simplicity we'll only look at the case where the dataset sizes are multiples of one another.

Notice both the CPU and GPU versions return the time taken for the operation, something we'll do in each section of the sort to know the various timings of each operation.

Sorting the samples

Next we need to sort the samples we've selected. On the CPU we can simply call the qsort (quicksort) routine from the standard C library.

```
__host__ TIMER_T sort_samples_cpu(
 u32 * const sample_data,
 const u32 num_samples)
{
 const TIMER_T start_time = get_time();

 qsort(sample_data, num_samples, sizeof(u32),
   &compare_func);

 const TIMER_T end_time = get_time();
 return end_time - start_time;
}
```

On the GPU, however, these standard libraries are not available, so we'll use the radix sort we developed earlier. Note, radix sort is also provided by the Thrust library, so you don't have to write it as we've done here. I won't replicate the code here since we've already looked at it in detail in the shared memory section.

One thing to note, however, is the version we developed before does a radix sort on a single SM in shared memory and then uses a shared memory reduction for the merge operation. This is not an optimal solution, but we'll use it for at least the initial tests.

Counting the sample bins

Next we need to know how many values exist in each sample bin. The CPU code for this is as follows:

```
__host__ TIMER_T count_bins_cpu(const u32 num_samples,
 const u32 num_elements,
 const u32 * const src_data,
 const u32 * const sample_data,
 u32 * const bin_count)
{
 const TIMER_T start_time = get_time();
 for (u32 src_idx=0; src_idx<num_elements; src_idx++)
```

```
{
  const u32 data_to_find = src_data[src_idx];
  const u32 idx = bin_search3(sample_data,
                              data_to_find,
                              num_samples);
  bin_count[idx]++;
}
const TIMER_T end_time = get_time();
return end_time - start_time;
}
```

To count the values in each bin we simply iterate over the source dataset, and for every element, call a search function that identifies in which bin a given data value will belong. We then increment the bin counter for that given index.

For the search we have two options: a binary search or a sequential search. A binary search takes advantage of the fact we have a sorted list of samples from the previous step. It works by dividing the list into two halves and asking whether the value it seeks is in the top or bottom half of the dataset. It then divides the list again and again until such time as it finds the value.

The worst case sort time for a binary search is $\log_2(N)$. We'll hit the worst case in many instances because most of the data is missing from the sample list. Therefore, we'll assume we'll hit the worst case in all cases when comparing the two approaches.

The sequential search worst case is N. That is, we start at the beginning of the list and do not find the item at all, having transversed the list from start to finish. However, with a sorted list and a uniform distribution of data the most likely case is $N/2$. Thus, for a sample set of 1024 elements, a binary search would take just 10 iterations compared with 512 iterations for the sequential search. Clearly, the binary search is the best approach in terms of the search space covered.

However, we have to consider that a binary search is not very good for a GPU from the perspective of coalesced memory accesses and branch divergence. As soon as one thread diverges in a warp, the hardware needs two control paths. We may well have the situation where the warps diverge such that we have entirely independent control for each thread. In this case we can multiply the time taken by the number of divergent threads. This will always be a maximum of the number of iterations, which is the $\log_2(N)$. Thus, our sample size needs to be huge before we see anything like the maximum amount of divergence—all threads in a warp.

Each thread is accessing potentially a different area of memory in the sample set, so there is no coalescing and therefore there is a drop of an order of magnitude in terms of global memory bandwidth. In practice, this should be largely hidden by the L1 and L2 cache on compute 2.x devices, depending on the size of the sample space. We could also store the sample space in shared memory, meaning we can discount the coalescing issues.

The standard C library again provides a bsearch function, which returns the value it finds in the array. However, we're not interested in the nearest value, but actually the array index. Therefore, we'll write a basic binary search function and use this on both the GPU and CPU. Notice the use of both __host__ and __device__ specifiers to run the identical source, but not binary, code on both the CPU and GPU.

```
__host__ __device__ u32 bin_search3(
  const u32 * const src_data,
  const u32 search_value,
```

```
const u32 num_elements)
{
// Take the middle of the two sections
u32 size = (num_elements >> 1);

u32 start_idx = 0;
bool found = false;

do
{
 const u32 src_idx = (start_idx+size);
 const u32 test_value = src_data[src_idx];

 if (test_value == search_value)
  found = true;
 else
  if (search_value > test_value)
   start_idx = (start_idx+size);

 if (found == false)
  size >>= 1;

} while ( (found == false) && (size != 0) );

return (start_idx + size);
}
```

The binary search routine works by reducing the size parameter to zero. It returns the index or the bin in which the search value should be placed.

```
// Single data point, atomic add to gmem
__global__ void count_bins_gpu_kernel5(
 const u32 num_samples,
 const u32 * const src_data,
 const u32 * const sample_data,
 u32 * const bin_count)
{
 const u32 tid = (blockIdx.x * blockDim.x) + threadIdx.x;

 // Read the sample point
 const u32 data_to_find = src_data[tid];

 // Obtain the index of the element in the search list
 const u32 idx = bin_search3(sample_data, data_to_find, num_samples);

 atomicAdd(&bin_count[idx],1);
}

__host__ TIMER_T count_bins_gpu(
```

```
const u32 num_samples,
const u32 num_elements,
const u32 * const src_data,
const u32 * const sample_data,
u32 * const bin_count,
const u32 num_threads,
const char * prefix)
{
const u32 num_blocks = num_elements / num_threads;

start_device_timer();

count_bins_gpu_kernel5<<<num_blocks, num_threads>>>(num_samples, src_data,
sample_data, bin_count);
cuda_error_check(prefix, "Error invoking count_bins_gpu_kernel");

const TIMER_T func_time = stop_device_timer();
return func_time;
}
```

Unlike the function to select samples where the maximum number of threads was limited by the number of samples, here we are limited only by the number of elements in the source array. Thus, the host function launches a kernel that contains one thread per element.

The kernel function works out its element, and reads it from the source dataset in a nice coalesced manner. Using more threads per block here allows for increased read bandwidth from the global memory.

Each thread of a warp will jump off into the binary search, and will, after not too many iterations, return. With a random list of elements you get some thread divergence. However, in the more common case of a mostly sorted list, all threads tend to follow the same route, thus causing very little thread divergence in practice.

When all the threads of a warp have returned from the binary search, they increment the values in one of N bins held in global memory via an atomic write. Atomic operations to global memory are operations that are guaranteed to complete, uninterrupted, regardless of which thread on which SM initiated the action. Thus, we can safely have many threads write to the same address. Obviously only one can physically write, so any clash of values results in serialization of the requests.

Unfortunately with a mostly sorted list we find that, because blocks are allocated in turn, most active blocks are in a similar area of memory. While this is very good for locality, it does mean all the threads are hitting the same memory area for the writes. With a sorted list we thus see a degradation of speed in this approach, but not a significant one, as we'll see later.

Prefix sum

A prefix sum is useful in that it can be used to create a table of values that index into an array that has variable-length records. The size of each bin in our case is a variable length and each bin is stored sequentially in memory one after another. Thus, we can calculate a prefix sum array and then use array element 0 to access the start of bin 0, array element one to access the start of bin one, etc.

The code for the prefix sum on the CPU is quite simple:

```
__host__ TIMER_T calc_bin_idx_cpu(const u32 num_samples,
        const u32 * const bin_count,
        u32 * const dest_bin_idx)
{
 const TIMER_T start_time = get_time();
 u32 prefix_sum = 0;

 for (u32 i=0; i<num_samples; i++)
 {
  dest_bin_idx[i] = prefix_sum;
  prefix_sum += bin_count[i];
 }

 const TIMER_T end_time = get_time();
 return end_time - start_time;
}
```

Here we simply iterate over the array `bin_count`, which contains how many elements there are in each bin. The prefix sum starts at zero and we store to the array `prefix_sum` the sum of the bin counts the loop has seen so far.

The main problem with this piece of code and with prefix sum in general is that at first it seems like an inherently serial problem. You cannot calculate the last value without its prior value. A loop iterating over all elements is actually a very efficient way to calculate this for a single-processor system. So how can a prefix sum be calculated in a parallel way so we can make use of more than just one SM?

It turns out that this simple implementation of prefix sum is actually quite fast for small numbers of elements. However, as the number of sample elements becomes larger, a somewhat faster and more complex approach is needed.

You can calculate prefix sum in parallel by splitting the array into a number of blocks and calculating the prefix sum on those blocks. The end point of each prefix sum block is then placed into another array. Another prefix sum is then done, in place, on this array. The result of this prefix sum is then added to each element in the original prefix sum calculation. This produces a parallel prefix sum that we can easily use on the GPU (Figure 6.25).

For the prefix sum blocks we'll use a single thread per block. As each thread processes the same number of elements and simply iterates around a loop, there is no thread divergence. However, the read memory access is poorly coalesced because thread 0 will be accessing addresses starting at a zero offset, while thread 1 will be accessing addresses starting at a (NUM_SAMPLES/NUM_BLOCKS) offset.

We want to run this on multiple SMs, which in turn means having to create multiple blocks. We need a synchronization point in the center where we do a prefix sum. This can't happen until all the blocks have completed. Therefore, we will need to launch a kernel to do the initial prefix sum, another to do the prefix sum over the results, and a final kernel to do the addition step.

This is actually quite beneficial as it gives us the opportunity to change the number of blocks and threads used. While we might use one thread per prefix sum block, the addition kernel parallelism is limited only by the number of sample points. Thus, we can run N blocks of M threads where $N \times M$ is the number of samples, maximizing the usage of the GPU.

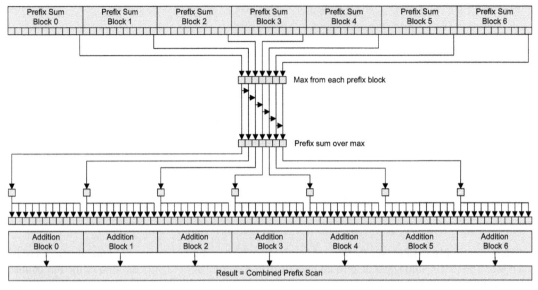

FIGURE 6.25

Parallel prefix sum.

As with most algorithms that are more complex, there is a tradeoff point where the simpler algorithm is faster. For the serial prefix sum versus the blocked prefix sum, this is around 4096 sample points. We could take this further and implement a more complex prefix sum in the first phase, but unless we have really large datasets, the prefix sum will not be a key factor in the sorting time.

Let's look at the GPU code in detail.

```
__global__ void calc_prefix_sum_kernel(
 const u32 num_samples_per_thread,
 const u32 * const bin_count,
 u32 * const prefix_idx,
 u32 * const block_sum)
{
 const u32 tid = (blockIdx.x * blockDim.x) + threadIdx.x;

 const u32 tid_offset = tid * num_samples_per_thread;
 u32 prefix_sum;

 if (tid == 0)
  prefix_sum = 0;
 else
  prefix_sum = bin_count[tid_offset-1];

 for (u32 i=0; i<num_samples_per_thread; i++)
 {
```

```
  prefix_idx[i+tid_offset] = prefix_sum;
  prefix_sum += bin_count[i+tid_offset];
 }

 // Store the block prefix sum as the value from the last element
 block_sum[tid] = prefix_idx[(num_samples_per_thread-1uL)+tid_offset];
}
```

First, we calculate our `tid` number based on the block and thread. Then we calculate the `tid_offset` based on the number of samples a thread will be calculating the prefix sum for.

Then for the first block the result must be zero. For the others, we include the first element of the bin count. We then simply implement the code we saw earlier, but add in `tid_offset` to read/write to the appropriate elements.

```
__global__ void add_prefix_sum_total_kernel(
u32 * const prefix_idx,
const u32 * const total_count)
{
 const u32 tid = (blockIdx.x * blockDim.x) + threadIdx.x;

 prefix_idx[tid] += total_count[blockIdx.x];
}
```

The addition kernel is very simple. The program simply calculates the threads individual `tid` and uses this to index into the destination array. The value to add is taken from the block count. Implicit in this implementation is the assumption the caller invokes N threads where N is the number of samples per thread used in the previous kernel. We do this explicitly because it allows the use of `blockIdx.x` (the block number) without the need to access a thread index. This allows the fetch to fall into the unified constant cache and cause a broadcast operation to all elements within the thread block.

In addition, we have the simple prefix sum kernel, called when there are a small number of elements to process. The parallel version, because it has to do an additional block prefix step, another addition, plus synchronization, takes longer in such cases. Only with larger block sizes where we can make better use of the hardware do we see a significant speedup with the more complex version.

```
__global__ void calc_prefix_sum_kernel_single(
 const u32 num_samples,
 const u32 * const bin_count,
 u32 * const dest_bin_idx)
{
 u32 prefix_sum = 0;

 for (u32 i=0; i<num_samples; i++)
 {
  dest_bin_idx[i] = prefix_sum;
  prefix_sum += bin_count[i];
 }
}
```

And finally the host function that sequences the kernels:

```
__host__ TIMER_T calc_bin_idx_gpu(
 const u32 num_elements,
 const u32 * const bin_count,
 u32 * const dest_bin_idx,
 const u32 num_threads_per_block,
 u32 num_blocks,
 const char * prefix,
 u32 * const block_sum,
 u32 * const block_sum_prefix)
{
 start_device_timer();

 if (num_elements >= 4096)
 {
  const u32 num_threads_total = num_threads_per_block
                                 * num_blocks;

  const u32 num_elements_per_thread = num_elements / num_threads_total;

  // Make sure the caller passed arguments which correctly divide the elements to blocks
and threads
  assert( (num_elements_per_thread *
          num_threads_total) == num_elements );

  // First calculate the prefix sum over a block
  calc_prefix_sum_kernel<<<num_blocks,
num_threads_per_block>>>(num_elements_per_thread, bin_count, dest_bin_idx, block_sum);

  cuda_error_check(prefix, "Error invoking calc_prefix_sum_kernel");

  // Calculate prefix for the block sums
  // Single threaded
  calc_prefix_sum_kernel_single<<<1,1>>>(num_threads_total, block_sum,
block_sum_prefix);
  cuda_error_check(prefix, "Error invoking calc_prefix_sum_kernel_single");

  // Add the prefix sums totals back into the original prefix blocks
  // Switch to N threads per block
  num_blocks = num_elements /
              num_elements_per_thread;
  add_prefix_sum_total_kernel<<<num_blocks, num_elements_per_thread>>>(dest_bin_idx,
block_sum_prefix);

  cuda_error_check(prefix, "add_prefix_sum_total_kernel");
 }
 else
 {
  // Calculate prefix for the block sums
```

```
   // Single threaded
   calc_prefix_sum_kernel_single<<<1,1>>>(num_elements, bin_count, dest_bin_idx);

   cuda_error_check(prefix, "Error invoking calc_prefix_sum_kernel_single");
   }
   const TIMER_T func_time = stop_device_timer();
   return func_time;
}
```

In this function we first check if it is best to use the simple prefix sum or the more complex prefix sum calculation. For the more complex solution, we work out how many elements each thread will initially process. We then call the three kernels in sequence. The function parameterized num_threads_per_block and num_blocks allow us to vary these parameters to allow for tuning.

At 4K sample points we see a transition between the two functions where the simpler version is around the same speed as the more complex version. As we get up to 16 K samples, the more complex version is already faster by a factor of four.

Sorting into bins

To avoid the merge operation, the samples must be pre-sorted into *N* bins. This involves at least one run through the entire array and a shuffle of data into the correct bins. The CPU code for this is as follows:

```
__host__ TIMER_T sort_to_bins_cpu(
 const u32 num_samples,
 const u32 num_elements,
 const u32 * const src_data,
 const u32 * const sample_data,
 const u32 * const bin_count,
 const u32 * const dest_bin_idx,
 u32 * const dest_data)
{
 const TIMER_T start_time = get_time();
 u32 dest_bin_idx_tmp[NUM_SAMPLES];

 // Copy the dest_bin_idx array to temp storage
 for (u32 bin=0;bin<NUM_SAMPLES;bin++)
 {
  dest_bin_idx_tmp[bin] = dest_bin_idx[bin];
 }

 // Iterate over all source data points
 for (u32 src_idx=0; src_idx<num_elements; src_idx++)
 {
  // Read the source data
  const u32 data = src_data[src_idx];

  // Identify the bin in which the source data
  // should reside
  const u32 bin = bin_search3(sample_data,
```

```
                              data,
                              num_samples);

 // Fetch the current index for that bin
 const u32 dest_idx = dest_bin_idx_tmp[bin];

 // Write the data using the current index
 // of the correct bin
 dest_data[dest_idx] = data;

 // Increment the bin index
 dest_bin_idx_tmp[bin]++;
 }

 const TIMER_T end_time = get_time();
 return end_time - start_time;
 }
```

Each data point in the source array needs to be placed into one of *N* bins that are linear in memory. The start and end of each bin has been calculated as an offset into the array. We need to preserve this data, but at the same time create *N* index pointers that track where we are in each bin. Thus, initially a copy of the `dest_bin_idx` array, the array storing the prefix indexes, must be made.

We then iterate over all the source points. For every source point a binary search is used to identify in which bin the data point should be placed. We then copy the data to the appropriate bin and increment the bin index pointer for that bin.

When trying to convert this algorithm to a parallel one, you hit the common problem of multiple threads trying to write to the same data item. There are two choices in this case. The first is to separate the data into *N* separate blocks and process each separately and then merge the final output. This was the approach used in the prefix sum kernel we looked at previously. There is, however, an alternative approach, which we'll use here.

```
__global__ void sort_to_bins_gpu_kernel(
 const u32 num_samples,
 const u32 * const src_data,
 const u32 * const sample_data,
 u32 * const dest_bin_idx_tmp,
 u32 * const dest_data)
{
 // Calculate the thread we're using
 const u32 tid = (blockIdx.x * blockDim.x) + threadIdx.x;

 // Read the sample point
 const u32 data = src_data[tid];

 // Identify the bin in which the
 // source data should reside
 const u32 bin = bin_search3(sample_data,
                             data,
```

```
                              num_samples);

    // Increment the current index for that bin
    const u32 dest_idx = atomicAdd(&dest_bin_idx_tmp[bin],1);

    // Write the data using the
    // current index of the correct bin
    dest_data[dest_idx] = data;
}
```

This is the approach of using atomics that in most cases allows for a much simpler implementation. However, this usually comes at the cost of performance. We can, of course, at a later date simply replace the atomic usage with an algorithm that splits and then merges the data. It's a tradeoff between programming effort in terms of higher complexity, which means longer development time and a higher number of errors, versus the sometimes very small gain in performance. If you have sufficient time, try both approaches. At the very least this provides a solution for older hardware where atomic support is somewhat limited.

The atomic `sort_to_bins_gpu_kernel` function simply unrolls the loop construct over the number of source elements from the CPU code into N parallel threads. These are then implemented as a combination of threads and blocks to invoke one thread per data element.

The thread reads the source element and does a binary search on the sample data space to find the appropriate bin for the element. We, however, then need single-thread access to increment the counter that stores the index into which the element must be written. You cannot simply increment the counter as shown in the CPU code,

```
// Increment the bin index
dest_bin_idx_tmp[bin]++;
```

Instead, we use an atomic call, `atomicAdd`:

```
// Increment the current index for that bin
const u32 dest_idx = atomicAdd(&dest_bin_idx_tmp[bin],1);
```

The `atomicAdd` function, when used on global memory, will add the second formal parameter, in this case 1, to the value at the address of the first parameter. If more than one thread calls this function, we're guaranteed that every addition will be completed. The `atomicAdd` function returns the value that it held prior to the addition. Thus, we can use the return value as a unique index into the array to write the new value to the bin.

However, be aware that this algorithm will change the ordering of the elements within the bins, as the blocks may run in any order. Thus, this is not a simple memory copy, due to the potential for more than one thread to try to write to the same bin at once. Also note that with a mostly sorted list, most threads will be hitting the same atomic address. This causes a slower execution, as you might expect, compared with that where the data is uniformly distributed.

Sorting the bins

Having sorted the data into bins, we then need to sort each individual bin in some parallel manner. On the CPU side we simply call `qsort` (quick sort) on each bin. On the GPU side we use the radix sort.

```
__host__ TIMER_T sort_bins_gpu(
```

```
 const u32 num_samples,
 const u32 num_elements,
 u32 * const data,
 const u32 * const sample_data,
 const u32 * const bin_count,
 const u32 * const dest_bin_idx,
 u32 * const sort_tmp,
 const u32 num_threads,
 const char * prefix)
{
 start_device_timer();

 const u32 num_blocks = num_samples / num_threads;


 sort_bins_gpu_kernel3<<<num_blocks, num_threads>>>(num_samples, num_elements, data,
sample_data, bin_count, dest_bin_idx, sort_tmp);


 cuda_error_check(prefix, "Error invoking sort_bins_gpu_kernel");

 const TIMER_T func_time = stop_device_timer();
 return func_time;
}
```

We use a host function to invoke num_samples threads that are split into blocks depending on the number of threads requested per block.

```
__global__ void sort_bins_gpu_kernel3(
 const u32 num_samples,
 const u32 num_elements,
 u32 * const data,
 const u32 * const sample_data,
 const u32 * const bin_count,
 const u32 * const dest_bin_idx,
 u32 * const sort_tmp)
{
 // Calculate the thread we're using
 const u32 tid = (blockIdx.x * blockDim.x) + threadIdx.x;

 if (tid != (num_samples-1))
  radix_sort(data, dest_bin_idx[tid], dest_bin_idx[tid+1], sort_tmp);
 else
  radix_sort(data, dest_bin_idx[tid], num_elements, sort_tmp);
}
```

The kernel is a two-level kernel, as the array dest_bin_idx holds only the start index. For the last element, accessing [tid+1] would cause an array overflow issue, so the very last thread needs to be handled slightly differently.

Sorting the multiple blocks is done with a modified version of the radix_sort kernel we developed in Chapter 5.

```
__device__ void radix_sort(
 u32 * const data,
 const u32 start_idx,
 const u32 end_idx,
 u32 * const sort_tmp_1)
{
 // Sort into num_list, lists
 // Apply radix sort on 32 bits of data
 for (u32 bit=0;bit<32;bit++)
 {
  // Mask off all but the bit we're interested in
  const u32 bit_mask = (1u << bit);

  // Set up the zero and one counter
  u32 base_cnt_0 = start_idx;
  u32 base_cnt_1 = start_idx;

  for (u32 i=start_idx; i<end_idx; i++)
  {
   // Fetch the test data element
   const u32 elem = data[i];

   // If the element is in the one list
   if ( (elem & bit_mask) > 0u )
   {
    // Copy to the one list
    sort_tmp_1[base_cnt_1++] = elem;
   }
   else
   {
    // Copy to the zero list (inplace)
    data[base_cnt_0++] = elem;
   }
  }

  // Copy data back to source from the one's list
  for (u32 i=start_idx; i<base_cnt_1; i++)
  {
   data[base_cnt_0++] = sort_tmp_1[i];
  }
 }
}
```

The radix sort simply iterates over the dataset it has been provided for a given block. For each bit it places the value into either the 0 or 1 list. The caller defines the start and end indexes of the array over which the sort will take place.

Analyzing the results

With a sample size of 16 K and a source dataset size of 1 MB we see the following results on a mostly sorted list:

```
ID:3 GeForce GTX 460: Test 32 - Selecting 16384 from 1048576 elements using 512 blocks
of 32 threads
Select Sample Time - CPU: 0.19 GPU:0.03
Sort Sample Time   - CPU: 2.13 GPU:125.57
Count Bins Time    - CPU: 157.59 GPU:17.00
Calc. Bin Idx Time - CPU: 0.03 GPU:0.58
Sort to Bins Time  - CPU: 163.81 GPU:16.94
Sort Bins Time     - CPU: 72.06 GPU:64.46
Total Time         - CPU: 395.81 GPU:224.59
Qsort Time         - CPU: 185.41 GPU:N/A


ID:3 GeForce GTX 460: Test 32 - Selecting 16384 from 1048576 elements using 256 blocks
of 64 threads
Select Sample Time - CPU: 0.53 GPU:0.03
Sort Sample Time   - CPU: 2.06 GPU:125.57
Count Bins Time    - CPU: 157.75 GPU:19.07
Calc. Bin Idx Time - CPU: 0.13 GPU:0.26
Sort to Bins Time  - CPU: 164.09 GPU:19.09
Sort Bins Time     - CPU: 72.31 GPU:62.11
Total Time         - CPU: 396.88 GPU:226.13
Qsort Time         - CPU: 184.50 GPU:N/A


ID:3 GeForce GTX 460: Test 32 - Selecting 16384 from 1048576 elements using 128 blocks
of 128 threads
Select Sample Time - CPU: 0.28 GPU:0.03
Sort Sample Time   - CPU: 2.09 GPU:125.57
Count Bins Time    - CPU: 157.91 GPU:13.96
Calc. Bin Idx Time - CPU: 0.09 GPU:0.26
Sort to Bins Time  - CPU: 164.22 GPU:14.00
Sort Bins Time     - CPU: 71.19 GPU:91.33
Total Time         - CPU: 395.78 GPU:245.16
Qsort Time         - CPU: 185.19 GPU:N/A


ID:3 GeForce GTX 460: Test 32 - Selecting 16384 from 1048576 elements using 64 blocks of
256 threads
Select Sample Time - CPU: 0.22 GPU:0.03
Sort Sample Time   - CPU: 2.00 GPU:125.57
Count Bins Time    - CPU: 158.78 GPU:12.43
Calc. Bin Idx Time - CPU: 0.13 GPU:0.49
Sort to Bins Time  - CPU: 164.38 GPU:12.39
Sort Bins Time     - CPU: 71.16 GPU:84.89
Total Time         - CPU: 396.66 GPU:235.80
Qsort Time         - CPU: 186.13 GPU:N/A
```

Notice how the entire sort process (224–245 ms) is dominated by the sorting of the sample dataset on the GPU (~125 ms). As the sample dataset becomes large the sort-and-merge approach used for this phase doesn't work well.

One solution to this problem would be to run the sample sort on the sample data; where the sample dataset is large, this is a good approach. However, for a 16 K sample set, it takes around 9 ms to run the sample sort compared with a 2 ms quick sort time from the CPU.

It always makes sense to use whatever device works best at a given solution. For small sample sizes, the CPU will usually be faster than the GPU. The GPU requires reasonably sized datasets, after which point it easily surpasses the CPU. Therefore, the optimal solution is simply to run quick sort on the sample set on the CPU and then transfer this to the GPU for the large-scale parallel "grunt" work of the sorting.

When we use this approach the timings drop significantly.

```
ID:3 GeForce GTX 460: Test 32 - Selecting 16384 from 1048576 elements using 512 blocks
of 32 threads
Select Sample Time  - CPU: 0.09 GPU:0.09
Sort Sample Time    - CPU: 2.09 GPU:2.09
Count Bins Time     - CPU: 157.69 GPU:17.02
Calc. Bin Idx Time  - CPU: 0.09 GPU:0.58
Sort to Bins Time   - CPU: 163.78 GPU:16.94
Sort Bins Time      - CPU: 71.97 GPU:64.47
Total Time          - CPU: 395.72 GPU:101.19
Qsort Time          - CPU: 184.78 GPU:N/A
```

You can see the total sample sort time is around 55% of the time of the quick sort on the CPU with a 16 K sample size (101 ms GPU, 185 ms CPU). If we vary the sample size, we increase the amount of available parallelism in the problem. See Table 6.15 and Figure 6.26.

What you can see from Table 6.15 and Figure 6.26 is that as the number of samples increases, the time drops dramatically. The best time is achieved for the GTX460 at 128K samples, or one-eighth of the number of the data to be sorted. The GTX470, with its much larger number of SMs, starts to rapidly outperform the GTX460 from 2048 sample points onward. The GTX260 by comparison (the previous generation of hardware) needs many more sample points to come close to the Fermi performance.

At 128K sample points the sorting of the samples again becomes significant (see Table 6.16) and our strategy of using quick sort on the CPU becomes the bottleneck. If we look in detail at the results from the GTX470, we see that at 256K sample points up to 50% of the time is spent sorting the sample data. At this point a sample sort of the sample data becomes a good option (Table 6.16).

Table 6.15 Sample Sort Results (ms)

Device/ Samples	256	512	1024	2048	4096	8K	16K	32K	64K	128K	256K
Qsort	184	184	184	184	184	184	184	184	184	184	184
GTX460	506	273	158	151	115	105	101	101	69	64	85
GTX470	546	290	161	94	91	72	62	60	43	46	68
GTX260	1082	768	635	485	370	286	215	190	179	111	88

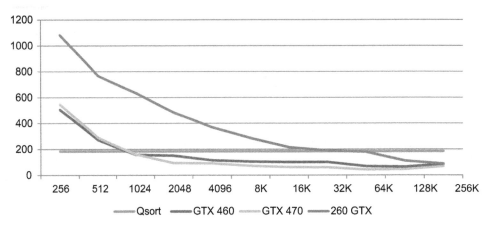

FIGURE 6.26

Graph of sample sort results.

Table 6.16 GTX470 Sample Sort Results (Mostly Sorted Data)											
Operation/ Samples	**256**	**512**	**1024**	**2048**	**4096**	**8 K**	**16 K**	**32 K**	**64 K**	**128 K**	**256 K**
Select samples	0	0.03	0	0.09	0.06	0.28	0.5	0.5	0.84	0.97	1.78
Sort samples	0	0.06	0.6	0.28	0.38	0.97	2.03	4.34	9.38	**19.72**	41.72
Count bins	14.6	14.2	13.62	12.38	10.66	9.34	9.26	8.38	6.03	5.35	5.38
Prefix sum	0.13	0.27	0.53	1.05	0.19	0.33	0.62	1.2	0.57	0.87	1.46
Sort to bins	14.6	14.2	13.65	12.4	10.7	9.37	9.33	8.45	6.09	5.41	5.46
Sort bins	517	261	133.5	68.29	69.86	52.5	40.9	37.2	20.2	13.94	12.15
Total	546	290	162	94	92	73	63	60	43	46	68

To give some comparison with almost sorted data versus entirely random data, we'll run the same test over a random dataset (Table 6.17). Various tests have shown the best performance was achieved with 128 threads per block.

As you can see from Table 6.17 the fastest run was the GTX470 at 67 ms. This is five times faster than the serial quick sort on the CPU host. Around 32 K samples with 128 threads per block would appear to be the optimal launch configuration for 1 MB of data. See Figure 6.27.

Questions on global memory

1. Discuss the reasons why sample sort is quicker when the list is mostly sorted?
2. How might you improve the sample sort algorithm presented here?
3. Do you foresee any problems using larger dataset sizes? What might you have to change to run larger datasets?

Table 6.17 Sample Sort on Random Data

Device/ Sample	256	512	1024	2048	4096	8192	16K	32K	64K	128K	256K
Qsort	337	337	337	337	337	337	337	337	337	337	337
GTX460	735	470	235	139	92	91	75	73	81	108	178
GTX470	831	535	263	156	97	70	77	68	67	90	155
GTX260	1311	919	463	255	170	124	106	100	106	123	160

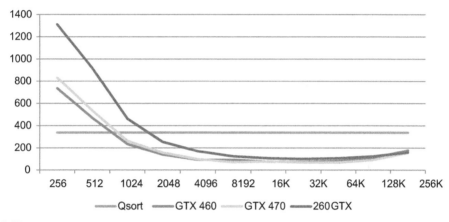

FIGURE 6.27

Chart of sample sort on random data.

Answers on global memory

1. Sample sort is quicker when using a mostly sorted list because the thread divergence is significantly less. Each bin has almost the same number of values. We end up with a near-optimal distribution of work to each of the SMs providing there are enough samples chosen from the dataset to generate a reasonable number of blocks.

2. One of the key issues with the algorithm is the noncoalesced access to global memory during the radix sort. This is caused by doing an in-place sort using the prefix calculation and the lower and upper bounds for each block. If you instead split each sample set so that it was interleaved by the number of threads, as was the radix sort in the shared memory example, we'd get coalesced access for most of the sort. The drawback of this is potentially wasted memory since some lists are a few entries long and others can be hundreds of entries long.

The other obvious solution is to improve the sorting of the samples. At 128 K samples, the sorting of sample data is contributing 43% of the total sort time. However, in practice, we'd never want to use so many samples, and the 32 K results are a more realistic use case. At this point sorting the samples contributes just 7% (see Table 6.16). The largest contributors are sorting the bins (62%), sorting to the bins (14%), and counting the bins (14%). The radix sort is clearly the place to start.

3. As the data size increases, you rapidly hit the maximum number of allowed blocks (65,535 on compute 2.x or lower platforms) using a single dimension. At this point you need to convert the `num_block` calculation in the various kernel invocations to a `dim3` type to include an `x` and `y` components in the block layout and possibly multiple grids, if the data size is really large. You then, of course, also need to modify the kernels to calculate correctly the block index based on block dimension and grid size.

TEXTURE MEMORY

Texture memory is not something we will cover in any detail in this text. However, we will mention it for some of the special uses it has in case it may be of some use in your applications. Texture memory can be used for two primary purposes:

- Caching on compute 1.x and 3.x hardware.
- Hardware-based manipulation of memory reads.

Texture caching

As compute 1.x hardware has no cache to speak of, the 6–8K of texture memory per SM provides the only method to truly cache data on such devices. However, with the advent of Fermi and its up to 48 K L1 cache and up to 768 K shared L2 cache, this made the usage of texture memory for its cache properties largely obsolete. The texture cache is still present on Fermi to ensure backward compatibility with previous generations of code.

The texture cache is optimized for locality, that is, it expects data to be provided to adjacent threads. This is largely the same cache policy as the L1 cache on Fermi. Unless you are using the other aspects of texture memory, texture memory brings you little benefit for the considerable programming effort required to use it on Fermi. However, on Kepler, the texture cache gets a special compute path, removing the complexity associated with programming it. See Kepler in chapter 12 for details. Note the constant memory cache is the only cache on compute 1.x hardware that is organized for broadcast access, that is, all threads accessing the same memory address.

On compute 1.x hardware, however, the texture cache can be of considerable use. If you consider a memory read that exhibits some locality, you can save a considerable number of memory fetches. Suppose we needed to perform a gather operation from memory, that is, to read an out-of-sequence set of memory addresses into N threads. Unless the thread pattern creates an aligned and sequential memory pattern, the coalescing hardware will issue multiple reads. If we instead load the data via the texture memory, most of the reads will hit the texture cache, resulting in a considerable performance benefit.

You can, of course, equally use shared memory for this purpose, reading in a coalesced way from memory and then performing a read from the shared memory. As the shared memory of a compute 1.x device is limited to 16 K, you may decide to allocate shared memory to a specific purpose and use texture memory where the memory pattern is not so deterministic.

Hardware manipulation of memory fetches

The second and perhaps more useful aspect of texture-based memory is that it allows some of the hardware aspects of GPUs to be automatically applied when accessing memory cells.

One useful feature is a low-resolution linear interpolation in hardware. Typically, linear interpolation is used to represent a function where the output is not easy or is computationally expensive to express mathematically. Thus, the input from a sensor might have a correction applied to its value at the low or high end of its range. Rather than model this you simply place a number of points in a table that represent discrete values across the range. For the points falling between the real points you use linear interpolation to work out the approximate value.

Consider an interpolation table of

```
P = 10, 20, 40, 50, 20
X =  0,  2,  4,  6,  8
```

If we have a new value, 5 for X, what is its interpolated value of P? The value 5 falls exactly halfway between the two points we have defined, 2 and 4. As the value for 2 is 20 and the value for 4 is 40 we can easily calculate the value for 5 as 30. See Figure 6.28.

With texture memory, you can set it up such that P is defined as an array normalized from the value 0 to 1 or -1 to $+1$. Fetches are then automatically interpolated in hardware. Combined with the cache properties, this can be a quick method of handling data that is not easily represented as a pure calculation. Bilinear and trilinear interpolation in hardware is also supported for two-dimensional and three-dimensional arrays, respectively.

One other nice feature of textures is the automatic handling of boundary conditions on array indexes. You can configure the handling of texture arrays to either wrap around or clamp at the array boundary. This can be useful, as it allows the normal case to be handled for all elements without having to embed special edge handling code. Special case code typically causes thread divergence and may not be necessary at all with the caching features of Fermi (see Chapter 9 on optimization).

Restrictions using textures

Textures come from the graphics world of the GPU and therefore are less flexible than the standard CUDA types. Textures must be declared as a fixed type, i.e. one of the various aligned vector types

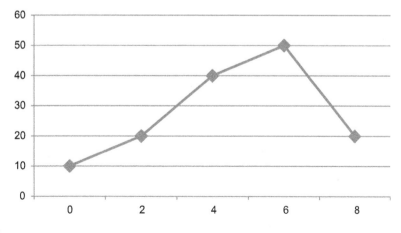

FIGURE 6.28

Interpolation.

(u8, u16, u32, s8, s16, s32) at compile time. How the values are interpreted is specified at runtime. Texture memory is read only to the GPU kernel and must be explicitly accessed via a special texture API (e.g., `tex1Dfetch()`, etc.) and arrays bound to textures.

Textures have their uses, especially on compute 1.x hardware. The uses for textures are quite specific and not always worth the trouble of learning yet another API. Thus, we have not covered the API side in this section, but simply stated some of the typical uses for textures. Concentrate on getting global/shared memory and register usage mastered and then look at texture memory, if it's applicable to your application.

For further information on textures, see the CUDA C Programming Guide.

CONCLUSION

We've looked at some of the aspects of using the different memory systems within the GPU. Program performance, both in the CPU and GPU domains, is generally dominated by memory throughput. You should have understood the principle of locality (i.e., the closer to the device the data is, the faster it can be accessed) and the cost of accessing off-chip resources.

Understanding the three major classes of storage available—registers, shared memory, and global memory—should allow you to write programs that use each type efficiently and correctly.

With global memory you need to think about generating patterns that provide for good coalescing of data and reduce the number of transactions the device needs to issue to the memory subsystem.

Consider using constant memory when you are going to be distributing the same value to many threads, or the same value to many blocks of thread.

With shared memory you need to think about data reuse. If there is no data reuse, then use registers and read directly from constant/global memory. Where there is potential for reuse or you need more register space, use shared memory.

Always use registers when possible, that is, declare data as local variables when possible. Think about each read to memory and if it will be reused. Avoid multiple writes to memory by writing to a register and writing back to memory later. Registers are the only way of achieving near full throughput of the device, but are a scarce and valuable resource. Be aware that excessive register usage can cause slowdowns due to spilling of registers to 'local' memory.

Now that you understand the principles of these memory types, we will, in subsequent chapters, look more at optimization and how these memory types can be used in practice.

Using CUDA in Practice

INTRODUCTION

In this chapter we'll look at a few examples of the not-so-common uses of GPUs to provide insight into how to solve a number of different types of computer problems. We'll look at the problems involved in using GPUs for such computations.

SERIAL AND PARALLEL CODE

Design goals of CPUs and GPUs

CPUs and GPUs, although both execute programs, are a world apart in their design goals. CPUs use an MIMD (multiple instruction, multiple data) approach, while GPUs use an SIMT (single instruction, multiple thread) instruction model.

The CPU approach to parallelism is to execute multiple independent instruction streams. Within those instruction streams it seeks to extract instruction level parallelism. That is, it fills a very long pipeline of instructions and looks for instructions that can be sent to independent execution units. These execution units usually consist of one or more floating-point units, one or more integer units, a branch prediction unit, and one or more load/store units.

Branch prediction is something computer architects have worked extensively on for over a decade or so. The problem with branching is that the single instruction stream turns into two streams, the branch taken path and the branch not taken path. Programming constructs such as `for`, `while` loops typically branch backwards to the start of the loop until the loop completes. Thus, in a lot of cases, the branch can be predicted statically. Some compilers help with this in setting a bit within the branch instruction to say if the branch is likely to be met or not. Thus, loops that branch backwards can be predicated as taken, whereas conditionals are usually predicated as not taken, thus avoiding the branch altogether. This has the added advantage that the next instructions have typically already been pre-fetched into the cache.

Branch prediction evolved from the simple but quite effective static model, to use a dynamic model that records previous branching history. Multiple levels of complex branch prediction are actually present in modern processors due to the very high cost of a mispredicted branch and the consequential refilling of the long execution pipeline.

Along with branch prediction, a technique called *speculative execution* is used. Given the CPU will likely have predicted a branch correctly, it makes sense to start executing the instruction stream at that branch address. However, this adds to the cost of branch misprediction, as now the instruction stream that has been executed has to be undone or discarded.

The optimal model for both branch prediction and speculative execution is simply to execute both paths of the branch and then commit the results when the actual branch is known. As branches are often nested, in practice such an approach requires multiple levels of hardware and is therefore rarely used.

Finally, we have the other major difference, seen until recently, which is the amount and number of cache memory levels. The CPU programming model works on the nice principle of abstraction, that is, the programmer doesn't have to care where the memory is because the hardware takes care of it. For most programs, except those that need to run fast, this works quite well. It used to be that instruction cycles were expensive, but with ever-increasing chip density, instruction cycles are now cheap. Accessing memory is now the bottleneck on modern processor design and this is addressed by the multiple levels of cache.

GPUs, until the introduction of Fermi, took an alternative approach to this design. Fermi designers believe the programmer is best placed to make use of the high-speed memory that can be placed close to the processor, in this case, the shared memory on each SM. This is the same as the L1 cache found on a conventional processor, a small area of low latency and higher bandwidth memory. If you think about most programs, this makes a lot of sense. A programmer knows the program better than anyone else and therefore should be able to identify which off-chip memory accesses can be prevented by using shared memory.

Fermi expanded the on-chip memory space to 64K, 16 K of which must be allocated to an L1 cache. So that there was always some shared memory present, they did not allow the entire space to be allocated to either cache or shared memory. By default, Fermi allocates 48 K to shared memory and 16 K to cache. However, you can switch this and have 48 K of cache and 16 K of shared memory. Kepler also introduces a 32K/32K split option. In programs that make no use of shared memory, setting this switch can significantly to prefer L1 cache instead of shared memory improve performance for memory-bound kernels. This is done with a call to

```
cudaFuncSetCacheConfig(cudaFuncCachePreferL1);
```

In the sample sort program we use to look at optimizing later in this chapter, this simple change reduced the overall execution time by 15%. This is a huge bonus for enabling a feature that is disabled by default.

With the inclusion of an L1 cache, GPUs and CPUs moved closer to one another in terms of the data fetched from memory. With previous GPU generations, memory accesses needed to be coalesced to achieve any sort of performance. Consider a noncoalesced memory fetch on the G80 and GT200 based hardware. If thread 0 reads from memory address 0x1000, thread 1 reads from 0x2000, thread 3 reads from 0x3000, etc., this results in one memory fetch per thread of 32 bytes. Not 32 bits, but 32 bytes, the minimum memory transaction size. The next access (0x1004, 0x2004, 0x3004, etc.) did exactly the same.

In Fermi, as with CPUs, a cache line of 128 bytes is fetched per memory access. Thus, subsequent access by an adjacent thread will usually hit the cache instead of having to go out to global memory on the device. This allows for a far more flexible programming model and is more akin to the CPU programming model most programmers are familiar with.

One of the aspects of GPU design that differs significantly from CPU design is the SIMT model of execution. In the MIMD model, there is separate hardware for each thread, allowing entirely separate instruction streams. In the case where the threads are processing the same instruction flow, but with different data, this approach is very wasteful of hardware resources. The GPU thus provides a single set of hardware to run N threads, where N is currently 32, the warp size.

This has a significant impact on GPU program design. SIMT implementation in the GPU is similar to the old vector architecture SIMD model. This was largely abandoned in the early 1970s when the ever-increasing speed of serial CPUs made the "hard" programming of SIMD machines less than appealing. SIMT solves one of the key issues of using vector processors, in that programmers are no longer forced to write code in which every thread must follow the same execution path. Threads can diverge and then converge at some later point. The downside of this flexibility is that there is only one set of hardware to follow multiple divergent program paths. Thus, each path must be executed in turn, or serialized, until the control flow converges once more. As a programmer you must be aware of this and think about it in the design of your kernels.

Finally, we'll come to one other significant difference between CPUs and GPUs. On the CPU model, there is serial control flow. Executing an instruction that requires a number of cycles to complete will stall the current thread. This is one of the reasons why Intel uses hyperthreading. The hardware internally switches to another thread when the current one stalls. GPUs have not just one other thread, but are designed to have thousands of other threads that they can potentially switch to. Such a stall happens as a result of both instruction latency and memory latency, that is, where the processor is waiting on the completion of an operation. The threading model is designed to hide both.

However, the GPU has one other benefit in that it uses lazy evaluation. That is, it will not stall the current thread until there is an access to the dependent register. Thus, you may read a value into a register early in the kernel, and the thread will not stall until such time as (sometime later) the register is actually used. The CPU model stalls at a memory load or long latency instruction. Consider the following program segments.

Segment 1:

```
int sum=0;
for (int i=0; i< 128; i++)
{
 sum += src_array[i];
}
```

If we look at the first segment, the program must calculate the address of `src_array[i]`, then load the data, and finally add it to the existing value of `sum`. Each operation is dependent on the previous operation.

Segment 2:

```
int sum=0;
int sum1=0, sum2=0, sum3=0, sum4=0;
for (int i=0; i< 128; i+=4)
{
 sum1 += src_array[i];
 sum2 += src_array[i+1];
 sum3 += src_array[i+2];
 sum4 += src_array[i+3];
}
sum = sum1 + sum2 + sum3 + sum4;
```

If we look at the second segment, we iterate in steps of four. Four independent `sum` values are used, allowing four independent summations to be computed in the hardware. How many operations are actually run in parallel depends on the number of execution units available on the processor. This could be execution units, in terms of processor cores (using threads), and/or execution units within a superscalar processor design.

Segment 3:

```
int sum=0;
int sum1=0, sum2=0, sum3=0, sum4=0;
for (int i=0; i< 128; i+=4)
{
  const int a1 = src_array[i];
  const int a2 = src_array[i+1];
  const int a3 = src_array[i+2];
  const int a4 = src_array[i+3];

  sum1 += a1;
  sum2 += a2;
  sum3 += a3;
  sum4 += a4;
}
sum = sum1 + sum2 + sum3 + sum4;
```

Finally, looking at the third segment, we move the load from memory operations out of the computation steps. Thus, the load operation for a1 has three further load operations after it, plus some array index calculations, prior to its usage in the sum1 calculation.

In the eager evaluation model used by CPUs the thread will stall on the first read into a1, and possibly on each subsequent read. With the lazy evaluation model used by GPUs we stall only on consumption of the data, the additions in the third code segment, if that data is not currently available. As most CPU and GPU designs are superscalar processors, using pipelined instructions, both benefit from such an approach within a single thread of execution.

Algorithms that work best on the CPU versus the GPU

There are many hundreds of computer science algorithms that for decades have been developed and optimized for serial CPUs. Not all of these can be applied easily to parallel problems. However, the vast majority of problems exhibit parallelism in one form or another. A significant number of problems can be broken down into operations on a dataset. In many cases, these operations are inherently parallel if viewed from either a data or task parallelism viewpoint.

One of the most important algorithms in parallel work is something called *scan*, otherwise known as prefix sum. In the world of serial computing this does not exist as it's not needed. Suppose we have a variable number of elements per output of some function. We could allocate a fixed amount of storage per output, such as an array, but this would mean there would be gaps in the memory. Output 0 might generate 10 entries, output 1, 5 entries, and output 3, 9 entries. We'd need an array with at least 10 entries, so we would have 6 wasted slots.

Prefix sum stores, in a separate array, the number of elements used for each output. The actual data is then compressed (i.e., all the blanks removed) to form a single linear array. The problem we have now is where does output for thread 2 write its values to? To calculate the output index for each output, we simply add up all the outputs prior to the current one. Thus, output 2 must write to array index 10 as output 1 wrote 10 elements (0...9). Output 2 will write 5 elements (10...14), so output 3 will start writing at element 15, and so on.

We covered in Chapter 6 an example of prefix sum using Sample Sort, so I will not repeat here how they can be calculated in parallel. The important point to understand is that through the use of prefix sum we can convert a great many algorithms to N independent outputs. It's important that we can write outputs independently and are not limited by atomics, potentially causing contention of resources. Such limits, depending on how overloaded they are, can severely slow a kernel execution.

Not all parallel architectures are created equal. Many parallel programs and parallel languages assume the MIMD model, that is, that threads are independent and do not need to execute in groups (or warps) as on the GPU. Thus, not even all parallel programs can work on GPUs unchanged. In fact, this has been one problem with parallel programs to date; optimization for a specific architecture often ties the application to that particular hardware.

Standards like MPI and OpenMP don't really fit well to the GPU model. OpenMP is perhaps the closest, in that it requires a shared view of memory. In OpenMP the compiler takes care of spawning threads that share a common data area. The programmer specifies which loop can be parallelized through various compiler pragmas and the compiler takes care of all that nasty "parallel stuff." MPI, on the other hand, considers all processes to be identical and is more suited to clusters of nodes than single-node machines.

You might take the approach of allocating one GPU thread per MPI process, or one block per MPI process. Neither would work particularly well on the GPU, unless you could identify that groups of MPI processes were, in fact, following the same execution flow and could combine them into warps on the GPU. Typically, MPI is implemented as shared CPU/GPU pairs with the CPU handling the network and disk input/output (I/O). Implementations using GPU Direct allow transfers to certain InfiniBand network cards via a common shared-memory host page. Direct peer-to-peer (P2P) transfers over the PCI-E bus without the use of host memory is preferable, and supported from the Fermi (compute 2.x) hardware onwards. The RDMA (remote DMA) is a feature of the new Kepler architecture that enables such features as GPU Direct and thus makes GPUs much more of a standalone peer on such networks.

With GPUs being included in an ever-higher number into data centers and supercomputer installations, both OpenMP and MPI will inevitably evolve to accommodate hardware designed to accelerate computations. In Chapter 10 we discuss the use of OpenACC, the directive-based approach to GPU computing. The OpenMP4ACC (OpenMP for accelerators) standard may well move such directives into the mainstream OpenMP standard.

With the GPU you have to consider that there are a limited number of threads that can easily work *together* on any given problem. Typically, we're looking at up to 1024 threads on Fermi and Kepler, less on older hardware. In practice, any reasonably complex kernel is limited to 256 or 512 threads due to register usage limitations. The interthread communication considerations dominate any decomposition of the problem. Interthread communication is performed via high-speed shared memory, so threads in the same block can communicate quickly and with little latency. By contrast, interblock communication can only be performed via separate kernel invocations, and global memory that is an order of magnitude slower. Kepler also extends this model to allow interwarp-based communication without the use of shared memory.

The other major consideration for GPU algorithms is the memory available on the device. The largest single GPU memory space available is 6 GB on the Tesla M2090 cards. Compared with typically 16 to 64 GB on the host, this may be problematic. However, this can be solved by using multiple GPU cards, with many high-end motherboards able to take up to four PCI-E cards, thus providing up to 24 GB per node of GPU memory.

Recursion is also problematic on GPUs, as it's only supported from compute 2.x GPUs onwards, but then only for `__device__` functions and not `__global__` functions. The upcoming dynamic parallelism feature found in the Kepler K20 design will help in many respects with recursive algorithms.

Many CPU algorithms make use of recursion. Often it's convenient to break down a problem into a smaller problem that is then broken down further and so on until it becomes a trivial problem. Binary search is a classic example of this. Binary search splits a sorted list of numbers in half and simply asks the question of whether the data we're looking for exists in the left or right set. It then repeats the split until either the item is found or the problem becomes just two items and is thus trivial to solve.

However, any recursive algorithm can also be represented as an iterative algorithm. The binary search problem just mentioned is shown as an iterative solution within the sample sort example (see Chapter 6). Quick sort is also a common example of an algorithm that is typically implemented recursively. The algorithm picks a pivot point and then sorts all items less than the pivot point to the left and less than or equal to the pivot point to the right. You now have 2 independent datasets that can be sorted by two independent threads. This then becomes 4 threads on the next iteration, then 8, then 16, and so on.

The GPU kernel invocation requires a *fixed* number of threads. It cannot currently exploit dynamic parallelism, although this will change with the Kepler K20 release. Dynamic parallelism is where the amount of parallelism in the problem changes over time. In the quick sort problem it grows by a factor of two at every level. In path finding–type problems, discovery of a new node may introduce 30,000 or more additional paths into a problem.

How do you replicate such algorithms on a GPU? There are a number of approaches. The easiest is when the parallelism scales in some known manner, as with quick sort. You can then simply invoke one kernel per level or one kernel per N levels of the algorithm back-to-back in a single stream. As one level finishes, it writes its state to global memory and the next kernel execution picks up on the next level. As the kernels are already pushed into a stream ready to execute, there is little CPU interaction needed to launch the next stream. See Figure 7.1.

Where the parallelism grows by some indeterminate amount per iteration, you can also store the state in global memory. You have to then communicate back to the host the number of the amount of

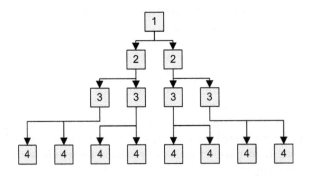

FIGURE 7.1

Kernel invocations for a recursive algorithm.

parallelism that the next iteration will explore. You can do this with an atomic write to shared memory within the block and then an atomic add to global memory prior to block completion. Then use a `memcpy` to copy the data back to the host that can use this to adjust the next kernel launch.

As an example with the first level of quick sort, you can use one block of data with a single thread. You then continue invoking single-thread block kernels until you reach some multiple of the number of SMs on the GPU. At the point where you would saturate the number of blocks on the SM, up to 16 blocks per SM, you extend the number of threads per block. At the point you reach 256 threads per block, you start again extending the number of blocks.

This approach, although relatively easy to implement, has some disadvantages. First, at least initially there is not enough work to saturate the GPU. With just one thread at the first level, the kernel overhead is significant. Even at level four, we're invoking just eight blocks, filling half the 16 SMs on a GTX580 device. Not until we reach level five would we have one block per SM. With 16 SMs, eight blocks per SM, and 256 threads per SM, we'd need 32 K points before all SMs were working at full efficiency. This would require 16 kernel invocations.

With compute 2.x devices this is not such an issue, as the initial few layers can simply be calculated using a recursive call, until you reach the desired depth into the structure to warrant relaunching the kernel with many more thread blocks. An alternative approach is to do some of the initial work on the CPU and only go to the GPU once there is enough parallelism in the problem. Don't think everything has to be done on the GPU. The CPU can be a very useful partner, especially for this type of less-parallel work.

One other solution to these types of problems is to use a special type of scan operation called a segmented scan. With a segmented scan you have a regular scan operation over a dataset (`min`, `max`, `sum`, etc.) plus an additional array that splits the source array into variable size blocks. A single thread or multiple threads are assigned per region to calculate the operation. As the additional array can also be updated at runtime, this can reduce the need to invoke multiple kernels if the segmented scan can be kept within a single block. Otherwise, you might just as well adopt the simpler solution, which in many cases works just as well and allows the flexibility of changing the number of threads/blocks as the problem grows and shrinks in parallelism.

All of these approaches try to deal with problems GPUs were not natively designed to deal with. As a programmer you should be aware of how well an algorithm does or does not fit the design model of the hardware. Recursive problems with today's GPUs are often best framed as iterative problems. Selecting an algorithm that is appropriate to the hardware and getting the data in the correct layout is often the key to good performance on the GPU.

PROCESSING DATASETS

With a typical data acquisition you will get data that is interesting, periods of data of no interest, and noise on the signal. One simple way of removing noise is to filter data above or below some threshold. With the dataset shown in Figure 7.2, we've placed a white line to show where the threshold level has been set. As you raise the threshold, you filter out low levels of noise. At the far right of the acquisition data you may wish to remove it altogether because you are only interested in the data peaks.

With a dataset that you expect to have a very small number of items being filtered you can easily append to the same data list, as the frequency of the append operation itself is very low. However, as

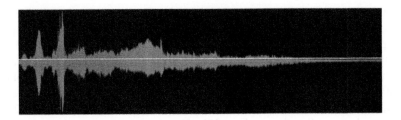

FIGURE 7.2

Sample data and threshold level.

the frequency of the filtered data becomes higher, the contention for the single list becomes a bottleneck. While this approach may work for a small number of parallel operations, say up to four that you might find on a quad-core CPU, the write to a single list, with locking approach does not scale.

A much better approach is to have a number of lists and then combine the lists together at a later stage. In fact, almost all parallel data processing algorithms use this approach in one way or another to avoid the serial bottleneck trying to update common data structure causes. This approach also maps very well to the model CUDA uses to decompose problems, the tiling approach.

We should also recognize that a filtering operation is actually a common parallel pattern, a split operation. A split operation takes a given dataset and splits it into N parts based on some primary key. In our filtering example we're using the threshold condition as the primary key and trying to extract the data that is above a given threshold. We may or may not be interested in keeping the data that is below the threshold. The split operation simply generates two lists, one matching some criteria and the other for the data that did not match.

When performing such an operation in parallel, we have a number of considerations. The first problem is we do not know how many data items will meet the matching criteria and how many would therefore be on the nonmatching list. The second is that we have many processing elements that need to cooperate in some way to build an output list. Finally, any ordering present in the original dataset must usually be maintained.

The scan primitive is incredibly powerful and can be used in a number of data processing scenarios. Suppose, for example, we have a list of students in a database in no particular order. We might want to extract, from that student list, all students who are in class CS-192. We thus end up with two datasets, those matching the criteria and those that do not.

Suppose we have a weather station near the equator that is collecting the temperature once per minute over several years. We might want to know how many sample points, or minutes, the temperature was in excess of 40 degrees centigrade over the sample period.

Equally, the data we are looking at may be financial data—for example, the value of transactions. You might wish to screen the data to know if there are transactions over a certain value, and how many. Certain high-value transactions may have a regulatory requirement to report or record, for example, to avoid money laundering. Your company policy may also dictate that transactions over a certain value require some additional checks. We want to extract from a vast set of data, easily and quickly, those that are of interest.

If the data is data from a scientific instrument, you may wish to screen the packet of data for "interesting" anomalies. Those packets that contain some anomaly are forwarded for further analysis, while the regular packets are sent elsewhere or discarded. How we define "interesting" varies according to the application, but the fundamental need to be able to scan and filter data is something we find in many domains.

Scanning one million data elements on a CPU can be time consuming. It's the standard "for *i* equals 0 to size of dataset" problem. Using a GPU we can scan the dataset in parallel. If the dataset is large, the only limit to this is the number of GPUs we can assign to the problem. As the largest GPU card to date, the Tesla M2090 can hold 6 GB of data, however, you are limited to a problem size of 18–24 GB per node before you need to use host or even disk-based storage.

Next we will look at using some of the less well-known features of CUDA to address data processing. This is, of course, applicable to any form of data as almost all problems involve processing input data in one form or another.

Using ballot and other intrinsic operations

As of compute 2.0 devices, NVIDIA introduced a very useful function:

```
unsigned int __ballot(int predicate);
```

This function evaluates the predicate value passed to it by a given thread. A predicate, in this context, is simply a true or false value. If the predicate value is nonzero, it returns a value with the *N*th bit set, where *N* is the value of the thread (`threadIdx.x`). This atomic operation can be implemented as C source code as follows:

```
__device__ unsigned int __ballot_non_atom(int predicate)
{
 if (predicate != 0)
  return (1 << (threadIdx.x % 32));
 else
  return 0;
}
```

The nonatomic version just shown is a similar speed to the intrinsic version, but will work on all compute versions. We'll use it later to provide backward compatibility with older hardware.

The usefulness of ballot may not be immediately obvious, unless you combine it with another atomic operation, `atomicOr`. The prototype for this is

```
int atomicOr(int * address, int val);
```

It reads the value pointed to by `address`, performs a bitwise `OR` operation (the | operator in C) with the contents of `val`, and writes the value back to the address. It also returns the old value. It can be used in conjunction with the `__ballot` function as follows:

```
volatile __shared__ u32 warp_shared_ballot[MAX_WARPS_PER_BLOCK];

// Current warp number - divide by 32
const u32 warp_num = threadIdx.x >> 5;

atomicOr( &warp_shared_ballot[warp_num],
                     __ballot(data[tid] > threshold) );
```

In this call we use an array that can be either in shared memory or global memory, but obviously shared memory is preferable due to it's speed. We write to an array index based on the warp number, which we implicitly assume here is 32. Thus, each thread of every warp contributes 1 bit to the result for that warp.

For the predicate condition, we asked if the value in data[tid], our source data, is greater than a given threshold. Each thread reads one element from this dataset. The results of each thread are combined to form a bitwise OR of the result where thread 0 sets (or not) bit 0, thread 1 sets (or not) bit 1, etc.

We can then make use of another compiler intrinsic, the __popc function. This returns the number of bits set within a 32-bit parameter. It can be used to accumulate a block-based sum for all warps in the block, as follows:

```
atomicAdd(&block_shared_accumulate,
          __popc(warp_shared_ballot[warp_num]));
```

Thus, we can accumulate for a given CUDA block the number of threads in every warp that had the condition we used for the predicate set. In this example, the condition is that the data value was larger than a threshold. A block-based sum is useful in many algorithms, but a CUDA kernel will consist of many blocks, typically thousands. If you'd like to know how many data items match the predicate across the whole dataset, you have to add up the sums from each block.

There are a number of choices for doing this. For a small number of blocks, we can simply ship the resultant block counts back to the CPU and have the CPU perform a summation. This may be a useful strategy if the CPU would otherwise be idle and there are other streams of GPU work that could be performed on the GPU (see Chapter 8 for a discussion of how to do this).

Another strategy is to write all the partial sums from the blocks to global memory on the GPU. However, to complete a summation of all the individual block components, all the blocks in all the SMs have to have completed the evaluation of the predicate. The only way to ensure this is to complete the current kernel and invoke another one. Then all global memory values previously written have to be re-read in some way, likely via a parallel reduction, and a final sum calculated. Although this might be the way taught in traditional CPU parallel programming, it's not the best way from a performance perspective on a GPU.

If we look at the number of blocks that are resident on a Fermi SM, up to eight blocks *can* be resident, although typically you see a maximum of six. Let's assume the maximum for now is eight blocks. There are 16 SMs in the largest Fermi device. Thus, there are a maximum of $8 \times 16 = 128$ blocks resident on the device at any one time. We can therefore simply accumulate to a *single value* in global memory using the atomicAdd function as we produce only one update per block.

Statistically, the probability of more than one block arriving at the atomic add instruction, at the same time, is quite small. Given that the memory transactions to read the source data will likely arrive in sequence, this in fact nicely sequences the execution flow within the SMs and consequently ensures the atomic add operations do not compete with one another.

Using this technique takes around 5 ms to scan one million elements, excluding the transfer time to and from the GPU. We exclude the transfer time because it's likely the data will remain entirely resident on the GPU. Consequently, we could process around two hundred million queries like this on the dataset per second. In practice, the predicates may be much more complex and we'll look at how this impacts the performance later.

For the moment, let's look at the complete function to do this in a little more detail:

```
__device__ int predicate_gt(const u32 a, const u32 b)
{
 return (a > b);
}


__global__ void kernel_gt_u32(const u32 * const data,
                              u32 * const block_results,
                              u32 * const acum,
                              const u32 num_elements,
                              const u32 threshold)
{
 kernel_ballot_u32_acum(data, block_results, acum,
                        num_elements, threshold,
                        &predicate_gt);
}
```

We declare a couple of functions: a device function that calculates the predicate condition and a global function that provides a wrapper to call the ballot function. To the ballot function we pass the dataset to search through an area of memory to place the block results into, an area of memory to place the accumulated result into, the number of elements to process, and finally a threshold for the comparison.

Notice with such a format we could easily implement other operations such as less than, equal to, etc. by writing a new predicate function and wrapper, as follows:

```
// Pad the SM array by 16 elements to ensure alignment
// on 32 element boundary to avoid bank conflicts
#define SM_PADDING 16

// Max threads is 1024 so therefore max warps
// is 1024 / 32 = 48
#define MAX_WARPS_PER_BLOCK (48 + (SM_PADDING))

#define WARP_SIZE 32

// SM output per warp
volatile __shared__ u32 warp_shared_ballot[MAX_WARPS_PER_BLOCK];

// SM output per block
volatile __shared__ u32 block_shared_accumulate;

// Ballot and accumulate if predicate function is non zero
__device__ void kernel_ballot_u32_acum(
 const u32 * const data,
 u32 * const block_results,
 u32 * const gmem_acum,
 const u32 num_elements,
 const u32 threshold,
```

```
int (*predicate_func)(const u32 a, const u32 b) )
{
// Calculate absolute thread number
const u32 tid = (blockIdx.x * blockDim.x) + threadIdx.x;

// Current warp number - divide by 32
const u32 warp_num = threadIdx.x >> 5;

// Total number of warp number - divide by 32
const u32 number_of_warps = blockDim.x >> 5;

// If not off the end of the array then contribute
if (tid < num_elements)
{
 // Have the first thread of every warp
 // clear the shared memory entry
 if ((threadIdx.x % WARP_SIZE) == 0)
 {
   warp_shared_ballot[warp_num] = 0;
 }

 // Call __ballot to set the N'th bit in the word
 // with a warp if the predicate is true

 // OR the bits from all threads in the warp into
 // one value per warp held in shared memory

 atomicOr( &warp_shared_ballot[warp_num],
          __ballot_non_atom( predicate_func(data[tid], threshold)) );
}

// Wait for all warps to complete
__syncthreads();

// From the first warp, activate up to 32 threads
// Actual number of threads needed is the number
// warps in the block
// All other warps drop out at this point
if (threadIdx.x < number_of_warps)
{
 // Have thread zero, zero the accumulator
 if (threadIdx.x == 0)
 {
  block_shared_accumulate = 0;
 }

 // Add to the single accumulator the number
 // of bits set from each warp.
```

```
// Max threads equals number of warps
// which is typically 8 (256 threads), but
// max 32 (1024 threads)

atomicAdd(&block_shared_accumulate,
          __popc(warp_shared_ballot[threadIdx.x]));

// No sync is required as only warp zero
// accumulates

// Have thread zero write out the result
if (threadIdx.x == 0)
{
 // Read from SMEM the result for the block
 const u32 block_result = block_shared_accumulate;

 // Store the value for the block
 block_results[blockIdx.x] = block_result;
 // Add the value into GMEM total for all blocks
 atomicAdd( gmem_acum, block_result );
 }
 }
}
```

The first part of the function calculates the absolute thread ID:

```
// Calculate absolute thread number
const u32 tid = (blockIdx.x * blockDim.x) + threadIdx.x;
```

This function is designed to work with a single dimension of threads. With large datasets (around 16 million elements plus), we'll need to make use of another dimension, as we would otherwise launch more than 64K blocks.

```
// Current warp number - divide by 32
const u32 warp_num = threadIdx.x >> 5;

// Total number of warp number - divide by 32
const u32 number_of_warps = blockDim.x >> 5;
```

We then calculate our current warp by simply dividing (right shifting) the current thread index by 32. We do the same with the block dimension to work out the number of warps in the current block.

```
// If not off the end of the array then contribute
if (tid < num_elements)
{
```

We then have to check if our absolute thread ID, tid, is within the dataset. In cases where the number of elements is not a power of two the tid calculation for the last block would end up after the end of the source data. We neither want to read or write out-of-bounds arrays, so this check is necessary.

Note that this also implicitly means we cannot perform a __syncthreads operation within this if block, as all threads, even those off the end of the array, must participate in such a synchronization operation.

```
// Have the first thread of every warp
// clear the shared memory entry
if ((threadIdx.x % WARP_SIZE) == 0)
{
warp_shared_ballot[warp_num] = 0;
}
```

Next we have to clear the value of the shared memory we're about to use. Shared memory can hold the value from the last kernel run and is not implicitly initialized to zero. As we need only a single writer, the first thread in each warp clears the value. Note we do not require any synchronization here because the first thread in every warp does the write. Branching within a warp in this way causes the other threads to implicitly wait at the end of the if statement.

```
// Call __ballot to set the N'th bit in the word
// with a warp if the predicate is true

// OR the bits from all threads in the warp into
// one value per warp held in shared memory

atomicOr( &warp_shared_ballot[warp_num],
          __ballot_non_atom( predicate_func(data[tid], threshold)) );
```

We can now have every thread in every active warp call the atomicOr function with the address of the shared memory element for this current warp. We pass to the OR operation the value returned from the __ballot call. We pass to __ballot the return value from calling the predicate_func function pointer, passing it the two data items to evaluate. This then jumps off and does the evaluation, in this case calling the predicate_gt function defined earlier.

```
// Wait for all warps to complete
__syncthreads();
```

Now we have to wait for all warps within the block to execute before we can do the second part, the block level accumulate.

```
// From the first warp, activate up to 32 threads
// Actual number of threads needed is the number
// warps in the block
// All other warps drop out at this point
if (threadIdx.x < number_of_warps)
{
```

As the maximum number of threads per block is 1024, the maximum number of warps per block is 32 ($1024 \div 32 = 32$). Thus, we can process the accumulate using just a single warp. We could have used thread 0 from each warp as we did before, but in this case we want the other warps to complete, not be left executing a single thread each.

```
// Have thread zero, zero the accumulator
if (threadIdx.x == 0)
{
 block_shared_accumulate = 0;
}
```

Again we have no idea of the existing value in the shared memory element we're about to use to accumulate into, so we need to zero it. Note that, as we now have only one warp running, no synchronization is required. Thread 0 will enter the condition while threads 1…31 will pass over it and implicitly wait for thread 0 to reconverge with them.

```
// Add to the single accumulator the number
// of bits set from each warp.

// Max threads equals number of warps
// which is typically 8 (256 threads), but
// max 32 (1024 threads)

atomicAdd(&block_shared_accumulate,
          __popc(warp_shared_ballot[threadIdx.x]));
```

We now add to the block-based shared memory accumulator the number of bits that were set in the result produced for the other warps in the block. These are in adjacent elements of shared memory, one element per warp. Thus, there are no read shared memory bank conflicts. However, the threads need to serialize the writes to the accumulator to ensure correctness. As you typically have 256 threads per block, this gives eight warps. This serialization does not really warrant a parallel-type reduction. However, with a larger number of warps a parallel reduction might work slightly faster.

```
// No sync is required as only warp zero
// accumulates

// Have thread zero write out the result
if (threadIdx.x == 0)
{
```

As we need only one writer, we select thread 0 to perform the next operation.

```
// Read from SMEM the result for the block
const u32 block_result = block_shared_accumulate;

// Store the value for the block
block_results[blockIdx.x] = block_result;

// Add the value into GMEM total for all blocks
atomicAdd( gmem_acum, block_result );
```

Finally, we read the block level accumulator from shared memory into a register, as we'll make use of it twice. We then write the block result to global memory, something we only have to do if we're interested in the block results in addition to the overall accumulated result.

We then call the `atomicAdd` function to add into the single global accumulator the overall result. Note that we cannot zero the result of the final accumulator in any of the blocks. It must be done by the host prior to the call to the function. The reason for this is simple. The blocks, and the warps within those blocks, may execute in any order. Thus, we cannot say something like `if (threadIdx.x == 0) && (blockIdx.x ==0)` then zero the accumulator. Doing this *may* work because it just so happens that warp 0 of block 0 executed first, but this is poor practice. CUDA's execution model is such that blocks can be, and are, executed out of order. You cannot assume any implicit order of block execution.

With a minor modification to supply the missing __ballot function for the GTX 260 (a compute 1.3 device), we can run this kernel on a range of devices. Note we can't use the 9800GT as it's a compute 1.1 device and therefore does not support shared memory based atomic operations.

```
Processing 48 MB of data, 12M elements
ID:0 GeForce GTX 470: GPU Reduction Passed. Time 8.34 ms
ID:2 GeForce GTX 260: GPU Reduction Passed. Time 12.49 ms
ID:3 GeForce GTX 460: GPU Reduction Passed. Time 17.35 ms
```

What is perhaps strange at first glance is that the GTX260 is 50% faster than the more modern GTX460. However, the GTX260 has approximately four times the number of SMs. Each SM has its own internal set of shared memory so the GTX260 has a much wider bandwidth to the shared memory than the GTX460.

We can also make one small modification. As we're using the `atomicOr` function we actually don't need the additional atomic functionality of __ballot, so we can in all cases use the nonatomic version. This revises the timing a little.

```
Processing 48 MB of data, 12M elements
ID:0 GeForce GTX 470: GPU Reduction Passed. Time 7.35 ms
ID:2 GeForce GTX 260: GPU Reduction Passed. Time 12.53 ms
ID:3 GeForce GTX 460: GPU Reduction Passed. Time 14.11 ms
Result: 8742545
```

You can see that this drops the time significantly on Fermi devices, as the GTX260 is already using the nonatomic version. The time for the GTX470 is reduced by 15% and the time for the GTX460 is reduced by 21%. This slightly improved time allows us to scan some 1632 million elements per second on a single GTX470. This will, however, be reduced if we use more complex predicates and/or a dataset requiring more than one block dimension.

To get a feel for this, what happens to the timing if we change the results to within a boundary, rather than simply larger than a threshold? For this we need to modify the predicate condition as follows:

```
__device__ int predicate_within(const u32 a,
                                 const u32 b,
                                 const u32 c)
{
  return ( (a > b) && (a < c) );
}
```

Thus, we have introduced another condition, potentially increasing significantly the overall timing. What is the effect in practice?

```
Processing 48 MB of data, 12M elements
ID:0 GeForce GTX 470: GPU Reduction Passed. Time 7.49 ms
ID:2 GeForce GTX 260: GPU Reduction Passed. Time 12.62 ms
ID:3 GeForce GTX 460: GPU Reduction Passed. Time 14.23 ms
Result: 7679870
```

You can see that the effect of adding another condition is marginal at best, with a 0.1 ms difference in execution time. This would imply the predicate could become reasonably complex without causing a significant slowdown.

The fact that we can use very complex predicate conditions allows for very complex operations to be coded efficiently on a GPU. Even codes where the data points must be gathered in some way can use such a set of primitives. All we need to do in such cases is adjust the predicate to take more data.

PROFILING

We'll pick up the example we looked at in Chapter 6, sample sort, and use it to look at how we can use profiling tools to identify problems in the implementation of a given algorithm.

The sample sort example already contains a number of timing elements, which we can use to adjust various parameters. Please re-read the sample sort example in Chapter 6 if you're not familiar with how sample sort works.

The major parameters are the number of samples and the number of threads. If we ask the program to explore the possible search space, doubling the number of samples per iterations and using 32, 64, 128, or 256 threads, we find the following promising cases.

```
ID:0 GeForce GTX 470: Test 16 - Selecting 16384 from 1048576 elements using 64 blocks of
256 threads
Num Threads:                          32    64    128    256
Select Sample Time- CPU:    0.56  GPU: 0.56  0.19  0.06  0.38
Sort Sample Time -  CPU:    5.06  GPU: 5.06  5.06  5.06  5.06
Count Bins Time  -  CPU: 196.88  GPU: 7.28  4.80  4.59  4.47
Calc. Bin Idx Time- CPU:    0.13  GPU: 1.05  0.71  0.70  0.98
Sort to Bins Time - CPU: 227.56  GPU: 7.63  4.85  4.62  4.49
Sort Bins Time -    CPU:   58.06  GPU:64.77 47.88 60.58 54.51
Total Time -        CPU: 488.25  GPU:86.34 63.49 75.61 69.88
QSORT Time -        CPU: 340.44

ID:0 GeForce GTX 470: Test 16 - Selecting 32768 from 1048576 elements using 128 blocks
of 256 threads
Num Threads:                          32    64    128    256
Select Sample Time- CPU:    0.63  GPU: 0.63  0.63  0.75  0.38
Sort Sample Time -  CPU:   10.88  GPU:10.88 11.06 10.63 10.69
Count Bins Time  -  CPU: 222.19  GPU: 7.85  5.51  5.39  5.22
Calc. Bin Idx Time- CPU:    0.19  GPU: 1.76  0.99  0.98  1.16
Sort to Bins Time - CPU: 266.06  GPU: 8.19  5.53  5.40  5.24
Sort Bins Time -    CPU:   37.38  GPU:57.57 39.40 44.81 41.66
```

```
Total Time -         CPU: 537.31  GPU:86.88 63.13 67.96 64.35
QSORT Time -         CPU: 340.44

ID:0 GeForce GTX 470: Test 16 - Selecting 65536 from 1048576 elements using 256 blocks
of 256 threads
Num Threads:                          32    64   128   256
Select Sample Time- CPU:   1.00  GPU: 1.00  0.88  0.81  0.94
Sort Sample Time -  CPU:  22.69  GPU:22.69 22.50 22.44 23.00
Count Bins Time -   CPU: 239.75  GPU: 8.32  5.90  5.79  5.62
Calc. Bin Idx Time- CPU:   0.25  GPU: 1.49  1.98  1.60  1.65
Sort to Bins Time - CPU: 300.88  GPU: 8.69  5.97  5.82  5.67
Sort Bins Time -    CPU:  24.38  GPU:52.32 33.55 30.85 32.21
Total Time -        CPU: 588.94  GPU:94.50 70.78 67.32 69.09
QSORT Time -        CPU: 340.44
```

If we view one example as a pie chart, it makes it easy to see where we're spending our time (Figure 7.3).

So it's clear from the chart that approximately three-quarters of the time is used for sorting and one-quarter for setting up the sample sort. However, as we increase the number of samples used, this changes (Figure 7.4).

As you can see from Figure 7.4, suddenly the time to sort the sample jumps to around one-third of the total time. We also see quite a lot of variability depending on the number of samples and the number of threads used. We'll concentrate on optimizing the middle case, 32 K samples using 64 threads per block.

Parallel Nsight provides a very useful feature listed under the "New Analysis Activity." Parallel Nsight is a free debugging and analysis tool that is incredibly useful for identifying bottlenecks.

The first option in Nsight to be sure is to select the "Profile" activity type (Figure 7.5). By default this will run a couple of experiments, "Achieved Occupancy" and "Instruction Statistics." Running these on the sample sort example produces a summary. At the top of the summary page is

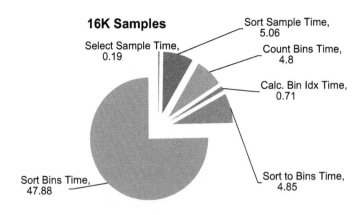

FIGURE 7.3

Sample sort time distribution, 16 K samples.

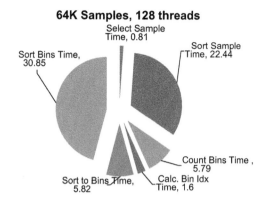

FIGURE 7.4

Sample sort time distribution, 64 K samples.

a dropdown box. Selecting "CUDA Launches" shows some useful information, as shown in Figure 7.6.

The first view is the "Occupancy View" (bottom left corner in Figure 7.6). What you should notice here is that there is a summary of the launch parameters for the kernel and what factors are limiting occupancy in red. In our case, the block limit per device, eight blocks, is limiting the maximum number of active warps on the device. Remember that warps are groups of threads from which the scheduler can select. The scheduler switches between warps to hide memory and instruction latency. If there are not enough warps resident, then this *may* limit performance if the GPU has no other warps to run.

We have launched around 16 warps, when the maximum per device is 48, achieving one-third of the maximum occupancy of the device. This would suggest that we should improve occupancy by increasing the number of warps per device, which in turn means increasing the number of threads. However, measured results show this produces the opposite effect, actually reducing performance.

The second screen that is interesting is the "Instruction Stats" (Figure 7.7). What is noticeable here (IPC section) is there is a large block of issued instructions that were never executed. The executed instructions are shown, on screen, in the pink section on the first bar chart on the bottom left where the lower line is drawn through the bars. The blue bars indicate that instructions are being reissued due to serialization. Serialization is where, for whatever reason, threads are not able to execute as a complete warp (set of 32 threads). This is usually associated with divergent control flow, uncoalesced memory accesses, or operations that have limited throughput because of conflicts (shared memory or atomics).

Also notice the distribution of work to the SMs is uneven (SM Activity block, Figure 7.7). We launched 512 blocks of 64 threads. Given 14 SMs on the GTX470 device being used, we'd expect just over 36 blocks (72 warps) per SM. In practice, some SMs got 68 warps while others got 78 warps (Warps Launched section, Figure 7.7). Also notice that, despite being given the same number of warps, some SMs take longer, implying all warps are not being given an equal amount of work in terms of execution time.

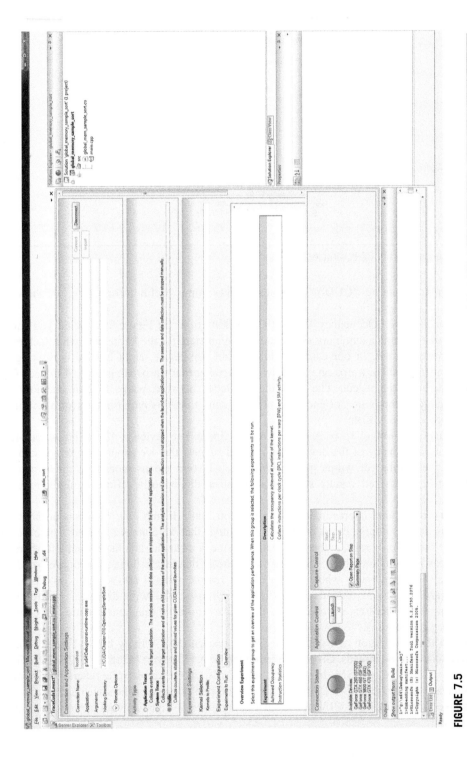

FIGURE 7.5

Parallel Nsight launch options.

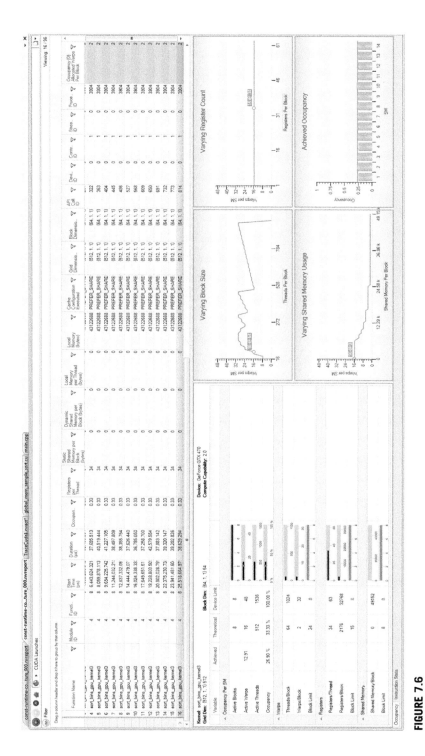

FIGURE 7.6

Parallel Nsight analysis.

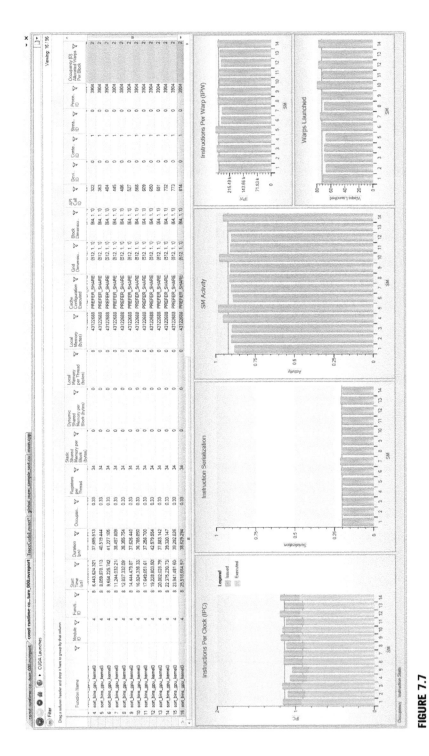

FIGURE 7.7

Parallel Nsight analysis.

When we move to 256 threads per block, the variability we see in issued versus executed instructions grows. The number of scheduled blocks drops from eight to just three due to the use of 34 registers per thread. Although not an issue with 64 threads per block, 256 threads per block limits the overall number of blocks that can be scheduled per SM. However, despite this, the number of warps scheduled climbs to 24 instead of 16, providing a 50% occupancy rate. Does further increasing occupancy help?

Simply asking the compiler to use a maximum of 32 registers (the `-maxregcount=32` compiler flag) proves to be a terrible optimization. The compiler then uses just 18 registers, allowing for six blocks to be scheduled, the maximum permitted. This increases the theoretical occupancy to 100%, but results in an increase in execution time from 63 ms to 86 ms.

This is due to the GPU having to push registers into "local" storage, which on Fermi is the L1 cache and global memory on the earlier-generation GPUs. On earlier-generation GPUs the time taken to use global memory would more than eliminate any gain due to better occupancy. On Fermi, pushing more data into the L1 cache reduces the available cache space for other purposes.

We can also go down the opposite path, to increase register usage. The original C code for the function that performs the sort bins time output shown earlier is as follows:

```
__device__ void radix_sort(
u32 * const data,
const u32 start_idx,
const u32 end_idx,
u32 * const sort_tmp_1)
{
// Sort into num_list, lists
// Apply radix sort on 32 bits of data
for (u32 bit=0;bit<32;bit++)
{
 // Mask off all but the bit we're interested in
 const u32 bit_mask = (1u << bit);

 // Set up the zero and one counter
 u32 base_cnt_0 = start_idx;
 u32 base_cnt_1 = start_idx;

 for (u32 i=start_idx; i<end_idx; i++)
 {
 // Fetch the test data element
 const u32 elem = data[i];

 // If the element is in the one list
 if ( (elem & bit_mask) > 0u )
 {
  // Copy to the one list
  sort_tmp_1[base_cnt_1++] = elem;
 }
 else
```

```
{
  // Copy to the zero list (inplace)
  data[base_cnt_0++] = elem;
 }
}

 // Copy data back to source from the one's list
 for (u32 i=start_idx; i<base_cnt_1; i++)
 {
  data[base_cnt_0++] = sort_tmp_1[i];
 }
 }
}
```

If we look at the PTX code generated for the kernel (see Chapter 9 for details on how to do this) we see the following code extract:

```
mov.s64 %rd5, %rd2;
cvt.u64.u32 %rd6, %r17;
mul.wide.u32 %rd7, %r17, 4;
add.u64 %rd8, %rd5, %rd7;
ld.u32 %r20, [%rd8+0];
mov.s32 %r21, %r20;
```

This equates to the C source code line for

```
// Fetch the test data element
const u32 elem = data[i];
```

There are a number of issues here. First, array indexing is causing the use of a multiply instruction. As elem is used immediately in the next C instruction to branch, the data load needs to have completed, so the thread stalls at this point. Multiply and divide instructions usually require many cycles to complete the instruction pipeline and there may be limited execution units that can perform such complex instructions.

We can replace all array indexes with a pointer to the array and then increment the pointer after each usage. Thus, the code extract we looked at earlier becomes

```
// Fetch the test data element
const u32 elem = (*data_in_ptr);
data_in_ptr++;
```

This means the compiler now translates this to the following PTX code:

```
; const u32 elem = (*data_in_ptr);
mov.s64   %rd20, %rd14;
ld.u32 %r18, [%rd20+0];
mov.s32   %r19, %r18;

; data_in_ptr++;
mov.s64   %rd21, %rd14;
add.u64   %rd22, %rd21, 4;
mov.s64   %rd14, %rd22;
```

We still have a total of six instructions, but now the first set does the load and the second set the increment of the pointer. The increment of the pointer is now a simple addition, much simpler than a multiply, and the result is not needed until the next iteration of the loop.

Applying the same strategy to the other array operations yields a reduction in execution time from 39.4 ms to 36.3 ms, a drop of 3 ms or around 10%. However, what about this variability in work done by each warp? Where does this come from?

Sample sort sorts data into blocks, or bins, which we independently sort using a single warp. If we do a dump of the values from single warp, we see something interesting.

```
Bin Usage - Max:331 Min:0 Avg:32 Zero:10275
0000:00000022 0001:00000000 0002:0000003e 0003:0000001d 0004:00000028 0005:00000000
0006:00000018 0007:0000003d
0008:00000052 0009:00000000 0010:0000001d 0011:00000000 0012:00000061 0013:00000000
0014:00000000 0015:00000000
0016:00000024 0017:0000009d 0018:00000021 0019:00000000 0020:0000002b 0021:00000021
0022:00000000 0023:00000000
0024:00000025 0025:00000000 0026:00000056 0027:00000050 0028:00000019 0029:00000000
0030:00000025 0031:0000001d
```

There are a significant number of bins where the entries are zero. There are others where the total number of entries is very large. As one thread processes each bin, to iterate over the entire dataset, we need to iterate for the maximum of the bins from a given warp. The first warp shown has a maximum value of 0x9d (157 decimals) and a minimum value of zero. By the time we're at iteration 157, only a single thread from the entire warp is active. We see this reflected in the large difference between issued and executed instructions we saw earlier (Instructions per clock, Figure 7.7). It's the bins with very large iteration counts that are taking the time.

We see a reduction in the execution time of the radix sort when we double the number of samples, because the peaks are pushed down and split out into more bins. However, sorting the samples then becomes the dominating issue. The problem is the distribution of samples to bins.

The large number of zero bins is actually caused by duplicates in the sample dataset. The source data array is filled with data via a simple call to rand(), which returns a not-so-random number. After a certain period these repeat. As the samples are selected at a uniform distance to one another, the sample set contains many duplicates. Removing this error in the random dataset removes almost all zeros from the bin count, but has an unintended effect that the execution time now climbs back up to the original 40 ms.

We can, however, apply another technique to this problem, that of loop unrolling and tail reduction, both of which we cover in Chapter 9. We replace the following code segment:

```
for (u32 i=start_idx; i<end_idx; i++)
{
// Fetch the test data element
const u32 elem = (*data_in_ptr);
data_in_ptr++;
```

with

```
// Unroll 4 times
u32 i=start_idx;
```

```
if ( (end_idx - start_idx) >= 4)
{
 for (; i< (end_idx-4); i+=4)
 {
  // Fetch the test first and second data element
  const u32 elem_1 = (*data_in_ptr);
  const u32 elem_2 = (*(data_in_ptr+1));
  const u32 elem_3 = (*(data_in_ptr+2));
  const u32 elem_4 = (*(data_in_ptr+3));
  data_in_ptr+=4;
```

Suppose the difference between start_idx and end_idx is 32, one of the common cases. The number of iterations in the first loop will be 32. However, by unrolling the loop by a factor of four, we reduce the number of operations by a factor of four, that is, eight iterations. There are a few other important effects of loop unrolling. Notice we need, in the case of a factor of four, three additional registers to store three additional data points. We also need to handle the end loop condition where we may still have zero to three elements to process.

Looking at the PTX code we see:

```
;const u32 elem_1 = (*data_in_ptr);
  mov.s64 %rd20, %rd14;
  ld.u32 %r23, [%rd20+0];
  mov.s32 %r24, %r23;

;const u32 elem_2 = (*(data_in_ptr+1));
  mov.s64 %rd21, %rd14;
  ld.u32 %r25, [%rd21+4];
  mov.s32 %r26, %r25;

;const u32 elem_3 = (*(data_in_ptr+2));
  mov.s64 %rd22, %rd14;
  ld.u32 %r27, [%rd22+8];
  mov.s32 %r28, %r27;

;const u32 elem_4 = (*(data_in_ptr+3));
  mov.s64 %rd23, %rd14;
  ld.u32 %r29, [%rd23+12];
  mov.s32 %r30, %r29;

;data_in_ptr+=4;
  mov.s64 %rd24, %rd14;
  add.u64 %rd25, %rd24, 16;
  mov.s64 %rd14, %rd25;
```

We're doing something quite important here, introducing instruction level parallelism through the use of independent elements per thread. Table 7.1 and Figure 7.8 show the effect loop unrolling has.

As you can see from Table 7.1 and Figure 7.8, introducing a small amount of thread level parallelism significantly drops the execution time of the radix sort. However, notice something else: The

Table 7.1 Unroll Level Versus Time and Register Usage

Unroll	0	2	4	6	8	10	12	14	16
Time	40	37.02	33.98	33.17	32.78	32.64	32.25	33.17	32.51
Registers	38	38	40	42	44	44	44	44	44

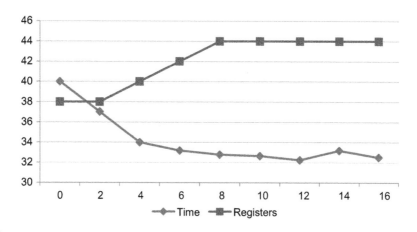

FIGURE 7.8

Unroll level versus time and register usage.

number of registers never climbs above 44, even though we can use up to 63 in Fermi. What is happening at this point is the compiler introduces a call stack and no longer grows the number of registers used.

We've applied a couple of optimization techniques to the source code, which you might reasonably expect a compiler to automatically apply. We'll not remove any of these, so any gain should come from the compiler adding additional optimizations. Let's see if this is the case by switching to the release mode, which enables all the compiler optimizations by default (Table 7.2 and Figure 7.9).

We see from Table 7.2 and Figure 7.9 a very similar pattern to the release or optimized version, indicating that the optimizations we have just applied are not themselves applied automatically by the compiler. What is also noticable is again we see the same pattern, that four elements per thread helps considerably, but beyond this the effect is marginal. Notice, even with optimizations enabled, the compiler does not automatically unroll the loop. Thus, we'll stick with manual unrolling by four, as the additional speed versus extra register usage is not a good tradeoff.

You might have expected the compiler to have pulled, or hoisted, out the read operations and placed them at the start of an unrolled loop. In many cases it will do this, except in the difficult cases, which are unfortunately all too often what we hit. Where you have a read followed by write followed by another read, the compiler cannot easily know if the write operation wrote to the same data area that is being read from. Thus, it must maintain the read-write-read sequence to ensure correctness. As

Table 7.2 Debug Versus Release Version Timing

Unroll	0	2	4	6	8	10	12	14	16
Debug	40	37.02	33.98	33.17	32.78	32.64	32.25	33.17	32.51
Release	32.34	26.25	25.07	24.7	24.36	24.26	24.1	24.13	24.24

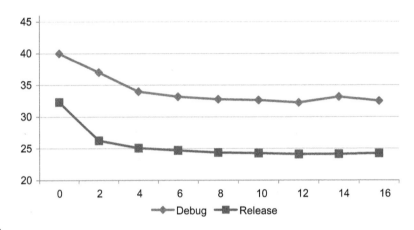

FIGURE 7.9

Debug versus release timing.

the programmer however, you know if the read operations are affected by the preceding write operations and can replace the read-write-read sequence with a much more efficient read-read-write sequence.

As we've now radically changed the timing on one aspect, dropping it from 40 ms to 25 ms, we should rerun the scan of the problem space to see if this now changes the optimum number of samples/threads.

One thing that becomes noticable is the release version of QSort is actually much faster, over twice the speed in fact. This makes it considerably harder to produce a faster sort. However, quick sort is now a large component of the sample sort, as we presort the samples on the CPU. Thus, this reduction in execution time helps considerably. The best timing is as follows:

```
ID:0 GeForce GTX 470: Test 16 - Selecting 32768 from 1048576 elements using 128 blocks
of 256 threads

Num Threads:                             32    64    128   256
Select Sample Time- CPU:    0.38  GPU: 0.38  0.19  0.50  0.31
Sort Sample Time -  CPU:    4.63  GPU: 4.63  4.69  4.31  4.31
Count Bins Time -   CPU:   64.50  GPU: 5.71  5.65  5.59  5.31
Calc. Bin Idx Time- CPU:    0.06  GPU: 1.55  0.79  0.86  0.79
Sort to Bins Time - CPU:   80.44  GPU: 6.25  6.08  5.96  5.71
Sort Bins Time -    CPU:   62.81  GPU:27.37 25.10 36.28 39.87
```

```
Total Time -          CPU: 212.81  GPU:45.89 42.49 53.50 56.31
QSORT Time -          CPU: 187.69
ID:0 GeForce GTX 470: Test 16 - Selecting 65536 from 1048576 elements using 256 blocks
of 256 threads

Num Threads:                          32    64   128    256
Select Sample Time- CPU:   0.50  GPU: 0.50  0.50  0.44  0.50
Sort Sample Time -  CPU:   9.56  GPU: 9.56  9.63  9.56  9.63
Count Bins Time -   CPU:  95.88  GPU: 6.70  6.67  6.60  6.34
Calc. Bin Idx Time- CPU:   0.06  GPU: 1.17  1.22  1.36  1.19
Sort to Bins Time - CPU: 119.88  GPU: 7.27  7.06  6.94  6.73
Sort Bins Time -    CPU:  52.94  GPU:24.23 16.84 25.22 29.95
Total Time -        CPU: 278.81  GPU:49.43 41.91 50.12 54.35
QSORT Time -        CPU: 187.69
```

So in fact both the 16 K and 32 K sample versions come out above even, with 0.6 ms between them. This is a 4.4× speedup over the CPU-based quick sort. Cache utilization is a key factor in play here. See the "Thread Memory Patterns" section in Chapter 9 where we look at the impact of this.

In summary, we used Parallel Nsight to show the impact of altering the number of and size of the blocks we used and saw how this could radically affect the overall performance. We then drilled down into this data and noticed there was, ultimately, a problem with the design of the sample sort. Serialization caused through the differing number of elements processed per thread was the cause of this. Despite this issue, we could optimize the implementation through thread level parallelism by using multiple elements per thread. Enabling additional compiler level optimization brought considerable additional benefits to both CPU and GPU code.

AN EXAMPLE USING AES

The AES (Advanced Encryption Standard) is an algorithm used to provide encryption in programs like WinZip, Bitlocker, TrueCrypt, etc. Depending on your industry, encryption may be something you already use or something that may seem irrelevant. Many companies make the mistake of thinking the data they create doesn't need to be kept securely on a local machine. All the nasty programs and hackers are outside the company firewall and therefore any data kept locally doesn't need security. This type of thinking is flawed, as very often a machine, employee, or contractor may create holes in such a firewall to enable working at home or outside the office, etc. Security needs to have a multi-layered approach.

The idea of encryption is that we take some data and apply an algorithm to it that obscures the data. Thus, the data, or the machine holding that data, such as a laptop, can be compromised, lost, or stolen, but the data itself is not accessible. Significant numbers of data breaches are a result of compromised machines. Moving the protection to the data means that to access it requires a "key." Applying that key and a given algorithm results in the data becoming unencrypted.

Encryption can also be used for secure connections between hosts on an insecure network such as the Internet. If you have a distributed application over a public network, how do you ensure that if you send a packet of data to another machine that packet is not intercepted and changed? Standards such as

OpenSSL (Open Secure Socket Layer) are used by browsers when logging into secure servers such as those for online banking to ensure no one listens in on the exchange of login data.

When you design software, you will need to consider the security aspects of it and how data is transmitted to and from various machines in any solution. The ITEF (Internet Engineering Task Force), the body that approves new Internet standards, requires all standard proposals to include a section on security. The fines levied against organizations for loss of consumer or corporate data are significant. It therefore pays to have a good understanding of at least some encryption standards if you are in any way networking computers or storing sensitive or personal data.

AES is mandated by many U.S. government organizations when storing data. As an algorithm in use today, we'll use this as a case study to see how you might approach AES-based encryption using a GPU. However, before we can dive into the implementation details, we first need to analyze the algorithm, understand it, and look for elements that can be computed in parallel. The AES algorithm contains many complexities, yet at the same time is understandable to someone with no cryptographic background. It is therefore a useful algorithm to look at to see how we can apply some of the techniques discussed to date.

The algorithm

AES is a block-based encryption algorithm. An encryption algorithm is often referred to as a *cipher*. Thus, the text to be encoded is referred to as plain text when not encoded and cipher text when encoded. To encode plain text into cipher text requires an algorithm and a key. The key is simply a series of numbers that acts very much like a mechanical key, the algorithm being the lock.

AES supports a number of modes of operation, the simplest being ECB (Electronic Cook Book), the one we'll look at here. AES splits up the data to be encoded into a number of blocks 128 bits in length (16 bytes). Each block in ECB mode is independently encoded based on a series of values derived from the encryption key. The encoding takes place in a series of "rounds," each of which uses a new derived key to further encrypt the data. See Figure 7.10.

The 128-bit key is independently adapted for each round and is independent of the text to be encoded or the previous round of encryption. Thus, the extraction of the keys for the various rounds can be done independently of the encoding round for the AES algorithm. Usually, as the key is constant for all blocks, this will be done before any encryption begins.

AES uses 128-, 192-, or 256-bit keys, although the block size (the size of the plain text) is always 128 bits. The number of rounds used changes according to the key length chosen: 10, 12, and 14 rounds, respectively.

The plain text is represented as a 4 × 4 matrix of byte data, known as the state space.

An encryption round itself consists of the following:

- Substitution—Bytes within the 4 × 4 matrix are swapped with other bytes from a lookup table.
- Row rotate left—Rows 1, 2, and 3 are rotated left by one, two, or three positions, respectively. Row 0 is unchanged.
- Mix columns—Each column has a step applied to diffuse the values.
- Round key—The data is XOR'd with the appropriate current round key extracted from the original key.

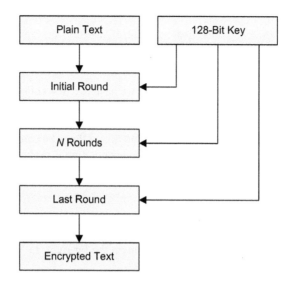

AES overview.

The initial round, also known as round zero, consists only of the round key operation. The final round drops the mix columns operation. Decryption is simply the inverse of the encryption process, starting at the last round and working backwards to the start.

Thus, to implement the algorithm, we need to look in detail at the five key aspects, those just shown plus the extraction of the round keys from the original 128 bit key.

Substitution

The substitution step swaps every byte in the 4×4 data block, the state space, with a value from a constant lookup table known as the Rijndael s-box.

```
unsigned char s_box[256] =
{
/*  0    1    2    3    4    5    6    7    8    9    A    B    C    D    E    F  */
0x63, 0x7C, 0x77, 0x7B, 0xF2, 0x6B, 0x6F, 0xC5, 0x30, 0x01, 0x67, 0x2B, 0xFE, 0xD7, 0xAB, 0x76, /* 0 */
0xCA, 0x82, 0xC9, 0x7D, 0xFA, 0x59, 0x47, 0xF0, 0xAD, 0xD4, 0xA2, 0xAF, 0x9C, 0xA4, 0x72, 0xC0, /* 1 */
0xB7, 0xFD, 0x93, 0x26, 0x36, 0x3F, 0xF7, 0xCC, 0x34, 0xA5, 0xE5, 0xF1, 0x71, 0xD8, 0x31, 0x15, /* 2 */
0x04, 0xC7, 0x23, 0xC3, 0x18, 0x96, 0x05, 0x9A, 0x07, 0x12, 0x80, 0xE2, 0xEB, 0x27, 0xB2, 0x75, /* 3 */
0x09, 0x83, 0x2C, 0x1A, 0x1B, 0x6E, 0x5A, 0xA0, 0x52, 0x3B, 0xD6, 0xB3, 0x29, 0xE3, 0x2F, 0x84, /* 4 */
0x53, 0xD1, 0x00, 0xED, 0x20, 0xFC, 0xB1, 0x5B, 0x6A, 0xCB, 0xBE, 0x39, 0x4A, 0x4C, 0x58, 0xCF, /* 5 */
0xD0, 0xEF, 0xAA, 0xFB, 0x43, 0x4D, 0x33, 0x85, 0x45, 0xF9, 0x02, 0x7F, 0x50, 0x3C, 0x9F, 0xA8, /* 6 */
0x51, 0xA3, 0x40, 0x8F, 0x92, 0x9D, 0x38, 0xF5, 0xBC, 0xB6, 0xDA, 0x21, 0x10, 0xFF, 0xF3, 0xD2, /* 7 */
0xCD, 0x0C, 0x13, 0xEC, 0x5F, 0x97, 0x44, 0x17, 0xC4, 0xA7, 0x7E, 0x3D, 0x64, 0x5D, 0x19, 0x73, /* 8 */
0x60, 0x81, 0x4F, 0xDC, 0x22, 0x2A, 0x90, 0x88, 0x46, 0xEE, 0xB8, 0x14, 0xDE, 0x5E, 0x0B, 0xDB, /* 9 */
0xE0, 0x32, 0x3A, 0x0A, 0x49, 0x06, 0x24, 0x5C, 0xC2, 0xD3, 0xAC, 0x62, 0x91, 0x95, 0xE4, 0x79, /* A */
0xE7, 0xC8, 0x37, 0x6D, 0x8D, 0xD5, 0x4E, 0xA9, 0x6C, 0x56, 0xF4, 0xEA, 0x65, 0x7A, 0xAE, 0x08, /* B */
```

```
0xBA, 0x78, 0x25, 0x2E, 0x1C, 0xA6, 0xB4, 0xC6, 0xE8, 0xDD, 0x74, 0x1F, 0x4B, 0xBD, 0x8B, 0x8A, /* C */
0x70, 0x3E, 0xB5, 0x66, 0x48, 0x03, 0xF6, 0x0E, 0x61, 0x35, 0x57, 0xB9, 0x86, 0xC1, 0x1D, 0x9E, /* D */
0xE1, 0xF8, 0x98, 0x11, 0x69, 0xD9, 0x8E, 0x94, 0x9B, 0x1E, 0x87, 0xE9, 0xCE, 0x55, 0x28, 0xDF, /* E */
0x8C, 0xA1, 0x89, 0x0D, 0xBF, 0xE6, 0x42, 0x68, 0x41, 0x99, 0x2D, 0x0F, 0xB0, 0x54, 0xBB, 0x16 /* F */
};
```

For each of the 16-byte elements in the state space we have to extract out a single hex digit. The first digit, or high nibble of the byte to encode, (0...F), is used as row reference. The second digit of the byte, or low nibble, is used as the column index. Thus, a value of 0x3E in the state space would result in a row value of 3 and a column value of E. If we look up this in the s_box table, we get 0xB2. Thus, the byte 0x3E in the state space is replaced by 0xB2. The same operation is performed for all the other bytes in the state space.

Row rotate left

In this step, rows 1, 2, and 3 are rotated left by one, two, or three positions, respectively. Row 0 is left unchanged. A rotate left operation takes the row and shuffles all bytes to the left by one position. The byte at the far left wraps around and becomes the byte on the far right. In Figure 7.11 I've pulled out each row to show how the rotation of the bytes works.

Mix columns

The Rijndael mix column step is a complex piece of code. It multiples the column r by a 4 × 4 matrix. The matrix is shown in Figure 7.12.

A one in the matrix means leave the value unchanged. A two indicates multiplication by 2. A three indicates a multiplication by 2 plus an XOR with the original value. In the three case, should the resultant value be larger than 0xFF, then an additional XOR with 0x1B needs to be performed. This is a simplification of Galois multiplication. A typical implementation in C code is shown here (Wikipedia, Jan. 31, 2012).

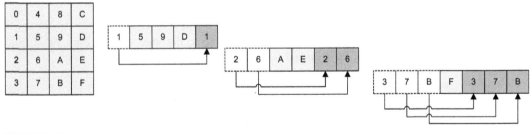

FIGURE 7.11

AES row rotate left.

```
2 3 1 1
1 2 3 1
1 1 2 3
3 1 1 2
```

FIGURE 7.12

Mix columns matrix.

```
void mix_column(unsigned char *r)
{
 unsigned char a[4];
 unsigned char b[4];
 unsigned char c;
 unsigned char h;

 for(c=0;c<4;c++)
 {
  a[c] = r[c];
  h = r[c] & 0x80; /* hi bit */
  b[c] = r[c] << 1;

  if(h == 0x80)
   b[c] ^= 0x1b; /* Rijndael's Galois field */
 }

 r[0] = b[0] ^ a[3] ^ a[2] ^ b[1] ^ a[1];
 r[1] = b[1] ^ a[0] ^ a[3] ^ b[2] ^ a[2];
 r[2] = b[2] ^ a[1] ^ a[0] ^ b[3] ^ a[3];
 r[3] = b[3] ^ a[2] ^ a[1] ^ b[0] ^ a[0];
}
```

This is not the most optimal, but the most likely example implementation you will find of this standard algorithm. In the preceding code, the input parameter r points to a 1×4 matrix that is a single column from the state space. It is copied to a temporary array a for use later. An array b is generated that holds the multiply by 2 (the <<1) operation. The multiply by 3 is actually a multiply by 2 followed by an XOR (^) operation. Thus, the final step becomes a series of XOR operations of the original data in a plus the result of the matrix multiplication in b. See Figure 7.13.

We'll look a little more at this step later, as it's one of the more time-consuming elements.

Add round key

The round key is the key extracted from the original cipher key for a given round or iteration of the encryption algorithm. It's in the form of a 4×4 matrix and is simply XOR'd with the current result.

Extracting the round keys

The AES algorithm uses a number of round keys, one for each round. Generating the keys is an iterative process where new keys depend on previous ones. The first part of the operation is to take the existing key and copy it as key 0, thus generating a 4×4 matrix providing the single starting round key.

The next N round keys must be constructed one at a time. The first column of any round key takes the last column of the previous round key as its starting point. The operation for the first column in the new key contains some addition operations over and above the standard column generation function.

For the first column of the key only, we need to do a column-based rotate such that the values move up the column. The value at the top of the column, row 0, moves to row 3. An identical operation is to rotate the row left on the cipher data, but instead of a row, the rotate is over a column. We then again use the substitution method and the Rijndael s-box to substitute values as we did for the cipher text.

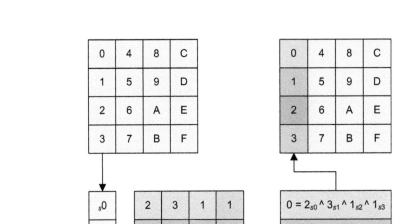

FIGURE 7.13

Mix columns with column 0 (repeated for columns 1, 2, and 3).

The operation for all elements is then the same. The newly calculated value must be XOR'd with the key value at index minus 4. For columns 1, 2, and 3 we're now done. However, column 0 has an addition operation. The first element of column zero is then XOR'd with 0x01, 0x02, 0x04, 0x08, 0x10, 0x20, 0x40, 0x80, 0x1b, or 0x36, the RCON value, depending on the current round (Figure 7.14).

Thus, the first column of round key 1 becomes the next extracted column. The calculation of columns 1, 2, and 3 is simpler (Figure 7.15). The column rotation and XOR with the RCON values is dropped. Thus, we simply have an XOR with the column at row minus 4. At column 4, the pattern repeats.

As the key generation always uses values from the previous key, this means the keys need to be generated in sequence. This in turn may form the bottleneck of any parallel implementation if many keys are needed. Thankfully for most uses, only a single set of keys is required. Thus, this step can be performed prior to any encoding or decoding and the keys simply stored in an array. As it's not time consuming for a single key, it can be done on either the CPU or GPU.

Serial implementations of AES

AES has been the subject of a lot of study. It was designed to run on 8-, 16-, or 32-bit machines without significant processing load. However, as we have seen from looking at the algorithm, it's not a simple algorithm to implement. Let's consider some of the design tradeoffs when thinking about optimizing such an algorithm for a GPU.

Access size

The first issue is that it is designed around byte-based access, to support 8-bit simple processors. All modern processors are at least 32-bit designs. Thus, if we use just single byte operations, 75% of the

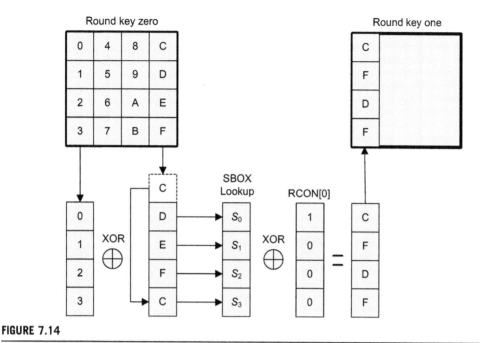

FIGURE 7.14

AES round key generation (first column).

space in the register work goes unused. Clearly with a 32-bit processor, an x86 or a Fermi GPU, we need to design a solution such that it uses 32 bits.

We can naturally combine a single row into one 32-bit word. We can also combine the entire 4×4 matrix into a 16-byte vector (128 bits). Such vectors are supported by the Intel AVX (Advanced Vector eXtension) instruction set. The GPU uint4 type would also allow for the GPU to fetch and store this data to/from memory in a single instruction. However, unlike Intel's AVX, the GPU has no per thread wide vector instructions other than storing to or from memory.

We have to consider that any encoding of the state or key matrix that is larger than a single byte would necessitate bit mask and shift operations if the operation needed to be individually applied to a single byte. Providing these were not considerable, the benefit of less memory reads/writes, though fetching the data in larger transactions, would easily outweigh register-based mask and shift operations.

Memory versus operations tradeoff

With most algorithms it's possible to trade an increased memory footprint for a decreased execution time. It depends significantly on the speed of memory versus the cost and number of arithmetic instructions being traded.

There are implementations of AES that simply expand the operations of the substitution, shift rows left, and mix columns operation to a series of lookups. With a 32-bit processor, this requires a 4 K constant table and a small number of lookup and bitwise operations. Providing the 4 K lookup table remains in the cache, the execution time is greatly reduced using such a method on most processors. We will, however, implement at least initially the full algorithm before we look to this type of optimization.

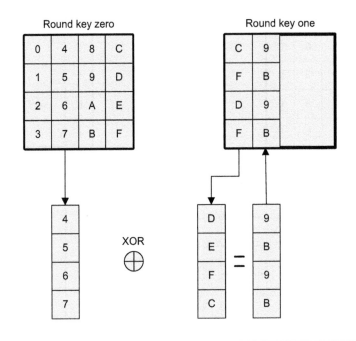

FIGURE 7.15

AES round key generation (columns 1, 2, and 3).

Hardware acceleration

The Intel AES-NI extension to the x86 processor instruction set is available on most Intel Sandybridge I5 and I7 processors as well as the Westmere-based I7 Xeon processors and their successors. The AES-NI instruction set consists of the following instructions:

- AESENC (cipher data, round key)—Standard round of encoding completely in hardware.
- AESENCLAST (cipher data, round key)—Last round of encoding completely in hardware.
- AESKEYGENASSIST (round key, cipher key, round number)—Assist in the generation of the round keys.
- ASDEC (cipher data, round key)—Standard round of decryption in hardware.
- ASDECLAST (cipher data, round key)—Last round of decryption in hardware.

Thus, the entire AES encryption and decryption process can be done entirely in hardware. Special 128-bit xmm1 and xmm2 registers are used to contain the operands in single registers. We see that in practice when such AES-NI is used with real applications, there is something in the order of a 2× or more performance improvement over a nonaccelerated processor (Toms Hardware, "AES-NI Benchmark Results: Bitlocker, Everest, And WinZip 14," http://www.tomshardware.co.uk/clarkdale-aes-ni-encryption,review-31801-7.html). Of course with handwritten assembler and optimal scheduling conditions over many cores, it's possible to get significantly more. This, however, gives us a feel for the likely benefit of coding such a solution and therefore it seems worth the effort.

An initial kernel

Let's look at an initial kernel for this algorithm.

```
__host__ __device__ void AES_encrypt_4x4_reg(uint4 * const cipher_block,
                                             KEY_T * const cipher_key,
                                             const u32 num_rounds)
{
```

First, we have the function prototype. Here we pass in a pointer to a cipher block as a `uint4` vector type. A single `uint4` vector (four integers) is sufficient to hold a single set of 16 bytes, the 128-bit cipher data. Next we have the cipher key, which is a set of 10 `uint4` keys. Finally, we have a specifier for the number of rounds, which we will replace with a fixed value at some point later. Note both the `__host__` and `__device__` qualifiers that allow the function to be called from both the CPU and GPU.

```
const u8 * const s_box_ptr = s_box;

// Read 4 x 32 bit values from data block
u32 w0 = cipher_block->w;
u32 w1 = cipher_block->x;
u32 w2 = cipher_block->y;
u32 w3 = cipher_block->z;
```

Next we extract from the `uint4` vector type the four unsigned integer component parts.

```
register u8 a0  = EXTRACT_D0(w0);
register u8 a1  = EXTRACT_D0(w1);
register u8 a2  = EXTRACT_D0(w2);
register u8 a3  = EXTRACT_D0(w3);
register u8 a4  = EXTRACT_D1(w0);
register u8 a5  = EXTRACT_D1(w1);
register u8 a6  = EXTRACT_D1(w2);
register u8 a7  = EXTRACT_D1(w3);
register u8 a8  = EXTRACT_D2(w0);
register u8 a9  = EXTRACT_D2(w1);
register u8 a10 = EXTRACT_D2(w2);
register u8 a11 = EXTRACT_D2(w3);
register u8 a12 = EXTRACT_D3(w0);
register u8 a13 = EXTRACT_D3(w1);
register u8 a14 = EXTRACT_D3(w2);
register u8 a15 = EXTRACT_D3(w3);
```

We next extract individual bytes from the four words into individual registers. Note the use of the `u8` type rather than the base C type, allowing an easy redefinition of this type. Note also the EXTRACT macro, which is used to allow support for both big-endian and little-endian representation of the bytes within the 32-bit words.

```
// Initial round - add key only
u32 round_num = 0;
// Fetch cipher key from memory
w0 = (*cipher_key)[round_num].w;
```

```
w1 = (*cipher_key)[round_num].x;
w2 = (*cipher_key)[round_num].y;
w3 = (*cipher_key)[round_num].z;
```

We then read a set of four values from the key, again from a `uint4` type into four 32-bit values.

```
a0  ^=  EXTRACT_D0(w0);
a4  ^=  EXTRACT_D1(w0);
a8  ^=  EXTRACT_D2(w0);
a12 ^=  EXTRACT_D3(w0);

a1  ^=  EXTRACT_D0(w1);
a5  ^=  EXTRACT_D1(w1);
a9  ^=  EXTRACT_D2(w1);
a13 ^=  EXTRACT_D3(w1);

a2  ^=  EXTRACT_D0(w2);
a6  ^=  EXTRACT_D1(w2);
a10 ^=  EXTRACT_D2(w2);
a14 ^=  EXTRACT_D3(w2);

a3  ^=  EXTRACT_D0(w3);
a7  ^=  EXTRACT_D1(w3);
a11 ^=  EXTRACT_D2(w3);
a15 ^=  EXTRACT_D3(w3);
round_num++;
```

The first round of the key encoding simply uses an XOR operation on the values in the columns.

```
while (round_num <= num_rounds)
{
// Fetch cipher key from memory
w0 = (*cipher_key)[round_num].w;
w1 = (*cipher_key)[round_num].x;
w2 = (*cipher_key)[round_num].y;
w3 = (*cipher_key)[round_num].z;

// Substitution step
a0 = s_box_ptr[a0];
a1 = s_box_ptr[a1];
a2 = s_box_ptr[a2];
a3 = s_box_ptr[a3];
a4 = s_box_ptr[a4];
a5 = s_box_ptr[a5];
a6 = s_box_ptr[a6];
a7 = s_box_ptr[a7];
a8 = s_box_ptr[a8];
a9 =  s_box_ptr[a9];
```

```
a10 = s_box_ptr[a10];
a11 = s_box_ptr[a11];
a12 = s_box_ptr[a12];
a13 = s_box_ptr[a13];
a14 = s_box_ptr[a14];
a15 = s_box_ptr[a15];
```

We then enter the main loop of the kernel. We run for num_rounds of iterations. As we later need the key and the key is to be fetched from memory, we initiate the read from memory as early as possible. Next we have the substitution step, which simply replaces the existing values with new ones from the s_box array shown earlier.

```
// Rotate Rows
u8 tmp0, tmp1, tmp2, tmp3;
// a0, a4, a8, a12 remains unchanged

// a1, a5, a9, a13 rotate 1
// a5, a9, a13, a1
tmp0 = a1;
a1 = a5;
a5 = a9;
a9 = a13;
a13 = tmp0;

// a2, a6, a10, a14 rotate 2
// a10, a14, a2, a6
tmp0 = a14;
tmp1 = a10;
a14 = a6;
a10 = a2;
a6 = tmp0;
a2 = tmp1;

// a3, a7, a11, a15 rotate 3
// a15, a3, a7, a11
tmp0 = a3;
tmp1 = a7;
tmp2 = a11;
tmp3 = a15;

a15 = tmp2;
a11 = tmp1;
a7 = tmp0;
a3 = tmp3;
```

The next step is to rotate rows 1, 2, and 3. As we have stored one byte per register, we cannot simply do a 32-bit rotate. As there is no native support in the GPU instruction set for such an operation, this is of little real relevance.

```
if (round_num != 10)
{
// Column Mix
const u8 b0 =  MIX_COL(a0);
const u8 b1 =  MIX_COL(a1);
const u8 b2 =  MIX_COL(a2);
const u8 b3 =  MIX_COL(a3);
const u8 b4 =  MIX_COL(a4);
const u8 b5  = MIX_COL(a5);
const u8 b6  = MIX_COL(a6);
const u8 b7  = MIX_COL(a7);
const u8 b8  = MIX_COL(a8);
const u8 b9  = MIX_COL(a9);
const u8 b10 = MIX_COL(a10);
const u8 b11 = MIX_COL(a11);
const u8 b12 = MIX_COL(a12);
const u8 b13 = MIX_COL(a13);
const u8 b14 = MIX_COL(a14);
const u8 b15 = MIX_COL(a15);

 tmp0 = XOR_5(b0, a3, a2, b1, a1 );
 tmp1 = XOR_5(b1, a0, a3, b2, a2 );
 tmp2 = XOR_5(b2, a1, a0, b3, a3 );
 tmp3 = XOR_5(b3, a2, a1, b0, a0 );

const u8 tmp4  = XOR_5(b4, a7, a6, b5, a5 );
const u8 tmp5  = XOR_5(b5, a4, a7, b6, a6 );
const u8 tmp6  = XOR_5(b6, a5, a4, b7, a7 );
const u8 tmp7  = XOR_5(b7, a6, a5, b4, a4 );
const u8 tmp8  = XOR_5(b8, a11, a10, b9, a9 );
const u8 tmp9  = XOR_5(b9, a8, a11, b10, a10 );
const u8 tmp10 = XOR_5(b10, a9, a8, b11, a11 );
const u8 tmp11 = XOR_5(b11, a10, a9, b8, a8 );
const u8 tmp12 = XOR_5(b12, a15, a14, b13, a13 );
const u8 tmp13 = XOR_5(b13, a12, a15, b14, a14 );
const u8 tmp14 = XOR_5(b14, a13, a12, b15, a15 );
const u8 tmp15 = XOR_5(b15, a14, a13, b12, a12 );

 a0 = tmp0;
 a1 = tmp1;
 a2 = tmp2;
 a3 = tmp3;
 a4 = tmp4;
 a5 = tmp5;
 a6 = tmp6;
 a7 = tmp7;
 a8 = tmp8;
 a9 = tmp9;
```

```
   a10 = tmp10;
   a11 = tmp11;
   a12 = tmp12;
   a13 = tmp13;
   a14 = tmp14;
   a15 = tmp15;
}
```

The next step is to mix the columns operation, which is done in every round except the last one. The previous mix column code shown earlier has had the c loop unrolled to form the MIX_COL macro. Additionally, to control the order of the XOR, we implement an XOR_5, which is a five-input XOR macro.

```
// Addkey
a0  ^= EXTRACT_D0(w0);
a4  ^= EXTRACT_D1(w0);
a8  ^= EXTRACT_D2(w0);
a12 ^= EXTRACT_D3(w0);

a1  ^= EXTRACT_D0(w1);
a5  ^= EXTRACT_D1(w1);
a9  ^= EXTRACT_D2(w1);
a13 ^= EXTRACT_D3(w1);

a2  ^= EXTRACT_D0(w2);
a6  ^= EXTRACT_D1(w2);
a10 ^= EXTRACT_D2(w2);
a14 ^= EXTRACT_D3(w2);

a3  ^= EXTRACT_D0(w3);
a7  ^= EXTRACT_D1(w3);
a11 ^= EXTRACT_D2(w3);
a15 ^= EXTRACT_D3(w3);

round_num++;
}
```

We then implement the XOR operation with the key fetched at the start of the loop.

```
cipher_block->w = (ENCODE_D0(a0) | ENCODE_D1(a4) | ENCODE_D2(a8)  | ENCODE_D3(a12));
cipher_block->x = (ENCODE_D0(a1) | ENCODE_D1(a5) | ENCODE_D2(a9)  | ENCODE_D3(a13));
cipher_block->y = (ENCODE_D0(a2) | ENCODE_D1(a6) | ENCODE_D2(a10) | ENCODE_D3(a14));
cipher_block->z = (ENCODE_D0(a3) | ENCODE_D1(a7) | ENCODE_D2(a11) | ENCODE_D3(a15));
}
```

Finally, the resultant key is combined into a 32-bit value and written back to the uint4 cipher word. At this point we've completed all 10 rounds and the cipher block is encoded based on the set of 10 round keys.

The macros used are defined as follows:

```
#define EXTRACT_D0(x) ( ( (x) >> 24uL ) )
#define EXTRACT_D1(x) ( ( (x) >> 16uL ) & 0xFFuL )
```

```
#define EXTRACT_D2(x) ( ( (x) >> 8uL ) & 0xFFuL )
#define EXTRACT_D3(x) ( ( (x)    ) & 0xFFuL )

#define ENCODE_D0(x) ( (x) << 24uL )
#define ENCODE_D1(x) ( (x) << 16uL )
#define ENCODE_D2(x) ( (x) << 8uL )
#define ENCODE_D3(x) ( (x)   )
#define MIX_COL(a) ( ((a) & 0x80uL) ? (((((a) << 1uL) & 0xFFuL) ^ 0x1Bu) : ((a) << 1uL) )
#define XOR_5(a,b,c,d,e) ( (((a)^(b)) ^ ((c)^(d))) ^ (e) )
```

Kernel performance

So how does such a kernel perform? How do we measure, understand, and predict performance? Initially, looking at the disassembled code for a compute 2.x target, we see something you might not expect. Declaring the registers as unsigned 8 bits results in sections of code to shift and mask data. The extract data macros are deliberately written to mask off the bits that are not used, so this is entirely unnecessary. In fact, we generate around four times the amount of code if we use a u8 type instead of a u32 type.

Changing the u8 definition to a u32 definition means we *potentially* waste a lot of register space, but it eliminates huge numbers of instructions. In practice, the GPU implements u8 registers as u32 registers, so this doesn't actually cost us anything in terms of register space.

Next we come to the number of registers used. Our initial kernel uses 43 registers, which is not altogether too surprising but is somewhat disappointing. If you load up the CUDA Occupancy Calculator, found in the "Tools" directory of the SDK, we can see that 43 registers will limit us to just a single block per SM of no more than 320 threads. This is just 10 active warps and nowhere near the maximum (24 on compute 1.3 devices, 48 on compute 2.x devices, 64 on compute 3.x devices). We need to have more blocks than this, so there is a greater mix of instructions for the warp scheduler to select from. There are limits on, for example, the number of XOR operations an SM can perform (see Chapter 9) and 10 warps will not hide the memory latency.

Thus, to achieve the best throughput, we don't want to execute just a series of the same instructions one after another. By having more than one block per SM there is a good probability that while one block is performing the XOR section, another block may be doing the s_box substitution operation. This involves a number of address calculations and memory lookups. We need to somehow decrease the register count.

The compiler provides a switch for this. How does this perform? We'll call the function with 16 blocks of 256 threads. Thus, we should see the improvement as and when we can schedule more blocks per SM. We'll run this test on a NVIDIA ION (compute 1.2)–based laptop, which has two SMs.

```
// Encodes multiple blocks based on different key sets
__global__ void AES_encrypt_gpu(uint4 * const cipher_blocks,
                                KEY_T * const cipher_keys,
                                const u32 num_cipher_blocks,
                                const u32 num_cipher_keys,
                                const u32 num_rounds)
{
  const int idx = (blockIdx.x * blockDim.x) + threadIdx.x;
```

```
if (idx < num_cipher_blocks)
{
 AES_encrypt_4x4_reg(&(cipher_blocks[idx]),
                     &(cipher_keys[0]),
                     num_rounds);
 }
}
```

As our `encrypt` function is a device function, we need a `global` function to call it. The `global` function extracts the appropriate block of cipher data and uses the same cipher key for all blocks. This represents what most encoding algorithms would do.

We see that for the original case, we get 6.91 ms to encode 512 keys simultaneously (two blocks of 256 threads each, one block per SM). Forcing the compiler to use just 32 registers should result in two blocks per SM, four blocks in total. Selecting 24 registers will result in three blocks per SM, six blocks in total. Indeed, we see a drop to 4.74 ms when using 32 registers, a huge improvement. However, when we try 24 registers, this time increases to 5.24 ms. Why is this?

Asking the compiler to use less registers does not cause them to magically disappear. The compiler has a number of strategies it can use. First, it can reload registers from memory. This may sound a bit counterintuitive, as we know global memory is very slow compared to registers. However, the additional block may bring in another set of warps that in turn may hide this memory latency. In the case of moving from 256 threads (1 block, 8 warps) to 512 threads (2 blocks, 16 warps), we gain significantly in terms of instruction mix and number of potential warps schedulable per SM.

The second strategy is to move registers into other memory types: shared, constant, or local memory. If you use the `-v` option during compilation, the compiler tells you what amount of each memory type it is using. Shared memory is slower than registers. Constant memory is cached, but again slower than registers. Local memory is the L1 cache on Fermi (compute 2.x) and global memory on compute 1.x devices.

Finally, the compiler can reuse registers if it can correctly identify the scope and usage of the registers within a section.

As we push the compiler to use ever fewer registers it eventually spills the registers into local memory. Although not too bad on Fermi, performance on our compute 1.2 test platform is thus terrible as, in fact, we're then using global memory. The additional gain of a third block is just simply not enough to overcome this rather huge penalty. Thus, we see the kernel slow down instead of speed up.

We achieved a 30% execution time reduction simply by setting a compiler switch, which is pretty impressive for five minutes of work. However, can we do any better by rewriting the C code? What is making the regular compilation take a massive 43 registers? What can we do to reduce this?

Taking the existing code, we can comment out certain sections. This tells us easily what *additional* registers that code section requires. Thus, we start by localizing all registers to individual blocks. We can create a new scope level in C by simply placing braces (the {} symbols) around a block of code. This should allow the scope of a variable or constant to be identified and localized to within a section.

It turns out the most expensive part of the code is the mix columns section. Looking at the code it's not too surprising. We calculate 16 `b<n>` values based on the 16 `a<n>` values, plus an additional 16 `tmp<n>` values. However, these are really just sets of four column parameters. The compiler should, when building the dependency tree, see it and rearrange the order of execution. Thus, instead of 32 additional registers, it needs only 8. However, it does not do this reordering, perhaps because it simply does not model such a large number of parameters efficiently. Whatever the cause, it's using far more registers than it needs to. We can therefore rewrite the mix column section:

```
// Column Mix
const u8 b0 = MIX_COL(a0);
const u8 b1 = MIX_COL(a1);
const u8 b2 = MIX_COL(a2);
const u8 b3 = MIX_COL(a3);
const u8 tmp0 = XOR_5(b0, a3, a2, b1, a1 );
const u8 tmp1 = XOR_5(b1, a0, a3, b2, a2 );
const u8 tmp2 = XOR_5(b2, a1, a0, b3, a3 );
const u8 tmp3 = XOR_5(b3, a2, a1, b0, a0 );
a0 = tmp0;
a1 = tmp1;
a2 = tmp2;
a3 = tmp3;
```

For simplicity, only the operation on a single column is shown here. This, however, moves the usage of the variables closer to the setting of the variable or constant. This improves the instruction mix and also reduces the scope of where a variable or constant needs to exist. In effect, we make it easier for the compiler to identify and reuse these registers.

We also change the reading of the key values. Previously we'd calculate the address calculation for each access:

```
w0 = (*cipher_key)[round_num].w;
```

Here the `cipher_key` pointer is being dereferenced, then indexed by `round_num`, with a zero-byte offset for the structure member w. This calculation would normally be made once and the offset part (w, x, y, or z) would then be added. To avoid creating a dependency on the next instruction the compiler actually repeats this instruction four times, once for each w<n> value. As the instruction latency is on the order of 20 cycles, this approach produces four answers in quick succession. However, it uses more registers than performing the calculation once and then adding the offset. As more blocks will bring us significantly more warps that in turn hide more latency, this is a good tradeoff. Thus, we replace this section of code with a new one:

```
// Fetch cipher key from memory
const uint4 * const key_ptr = &((*cipher_key)[0]);
w0 = key_ptr->w;
w1 = key_ptr->x;
w2 = key_ptr->y;
w3 = key_ptr->z;
```

Here we introduce a new pointer parameter that performs the base address calculation once. Accessing the members w, x, y, or z through the pointer just requires a simple addition of literal 0, 4, 8, or 12 to the base address when the compiler calculates the address offsets.

Note we also tried simply reading the `uint4` key into a `uint4` local constant. Unfortunately, this resulted in the compiler placing the `uint4` constant into local memory (`lmem`), which is exactly what we do not want, and perhaps something later versions of the compiler may resolve. The LLVM compiler (CUDA 4.1) seems to prefer to place vector types into local memory rather than registers.

Finally, we moved the definition of `round_num` from the start of the function to just before the `while` loop and replaced its usage in round zero with an explicit zero index.

These steps brought the kernel register usage down from 43 registers to just 25 registers and dropped the execution time to just 4.32 ms, somewhat faster than the forced register allocation version. Forcing this to just 24 again resulted in slower code due to the compiler's usage of local memory. Unfortunately, we really want a maximum of 24 registers, not 25, as this will increase the block count and bring in another set of warps, increasing the overall amount of parallelism.

Let's replace

```
while (round_num <= num_rounds)
```

with

```
while (round_num <= NUM_ROUNDS)
```

This will eliminate the need to hold the formal parameter `num_rounds` in a register and allow the compiler to instead use a literal value of 10, the value of the `#define` for `NUM_ROUNDS`. Using a literal value serves two purposes. First, it allows the comparison of the register holding `num_rounds` with an immediate value, rather than a comparison of two registers. Second, it means the bounds of the loop are known, which in turn allows the compiler to safely unroll the entire loop or sections of the loop as needed.

This indeed allows the compiler to use just 24 registers, the magic boundary number we need to potentially schedule another block. The savings are significant, although with 256 threads per block we do not bring in any additional blocks. Despite this the time for 16 blocks does drop. However, the timing becomes erratic and quite variable, with some runs now taking longer than before. We're now starting to see the warps compete with one another. With such a small sample size (16 cipher blocks) the results become highly variable from run to run. Therefore, we'll increase the number of cipher blocks to 2048 K and average the results.

The strategy CUDA adopts when allocating registers is to try for the smallest number of registers possible. With our transition from 25 to 24 registers, using 256 threads per block, we can still only schedule two blocks. However, if we halve the number of threads per block, we can squeeze in another block of 128 threads. Thus, we can run five blocks per SM at 128 threads, 24 registers (640 total). This is compared with four blocks at 25 registers per block (512 threads). Does this make a difference? Yes, it does (see Table 7.3).

If we use a 64-thread version as a baseline, we hit the maximum limit of eight blocks, which in turn limits us to a total of 512 threads. The 128-thread version is limited to five blocks, 640 threads in total. The 256-thread version is limited to two blocks, again 512 threads total.

Table 7.3 Effect of Using Different Numbers of Threads

64 Threads	128 Threads	256 Threads
1150 ms	1100 ms	1220 ms
100%	96%	111%

You might expect the 64-thread version and the 256-thread version, given they both run a total of 512 threads, to take the same time. The 64-thread version is faster because it provides a better instruction mix, with different blocks performing different parts of the algorithm. The 256-thread version tends to have its threads all doing the same thing at the same time. Remember in this compute 1.2 device there is no L1/L2 cache, so this is simply a comparison of instruction and memory throughput. It's also far easier for the CUDA runtime to get a better load balance between the two SMs due to the smaller scheduling unit.

Squeezing in that extra 64 threads by selecting a small number of threads per block gains us 120 ms, a 15% improvement over the 256-thread version on this compute 1.2 device. We can only do this because we are within the 24 register threshold.

With a small laptop ION-based GPU, we're encoding around 1.8 million cipher blocks per second, which is approximately 28 MB/s including transfer times. Excluding the transfer times, this approximately doubles. This is the next area to address.

Transfer performance

It's necessary to transfer data to the GPU over the PCI-E data bus. Compared to access to memory, this bus is very slow. Chapter 9 explores in detail PCI-E transfer sizes and the effects of using paged or pinned memory. Pinned memory is memory that cannot be paged (swapped) out to disk by the virtual memory management of the OS. PCI-E transfer can, in fact, only be done using pinned memory, and if the application does not allocate pinned memory, the CUDA driver does this in the background for you. Unfortunately, this results in a needless copy operation from the regular (paged) memory to or from pinned memory. We can of course eliminate this by allocating pinned memory ourselves.

In the application, we simply replace the following lines when allocating memory in the host application:

```
uint4 * cipher_data_host = (uint4 *) malloc(size_of_cipher_data_in_bytes);
KEY_T * cipher_key_host = (KEY_T *) malloc(size_of_cipher_key_size_in_bytes);
```

with

```
uint4 * cipher_data_host;
KEY_T * cipher_key_host;
CUDA_CALL(cudaMallocHost(&cipher_data_host, size_of_cipher_data_in_bytes));
CUDA_CALL(cudaMallocHost(&cipher_key_host, size_of_cipher_key_size_in_bytes));
```

And at the end, when cleaning up the memory allocation on the host, we replace

```
free(cipher_key_host);
free(cipher_data_host);
```

with

```
CUDA_CALL(cudaFreeHost(cipher_data_host));
CUDA_CALL(cudaFreeHost(cipher_key_host));
```

So how does this affect performance? It reduces our 1100 ms time down to 1070 ms, a drop of some 30 ms, just a 3% decrease in the execution time. The actual gain is *very* dependent on the processor and chipset being used. Typically you see anything up to 20% performance gain in transfer time using this method. However, the laptop we are using for this test is using an X1 PCI-E 2.0 link. The fact that we see a minor but consistent improvement would suggest removing the redundant copy is insignificant in comparison to the actual copy time over this rather slow link.

Despite the miserable gain pinned memory has brought us on this platform, we need to use pinned memory for the next step in the optimization of the transfers.

A single streaming version

We cover streams in detail in Chapter 8, as they are essential in using more than one GPU on a problem. We'll use them here on a single-GPU problem, as they allow us to both execute memory transfers and perform kernels at the same time. In effect, you want to overlap the kernel execution with the transfer time. If we're lucky the transfer time is less than or equal to the calculation time. Thus, the transfer time is effectively hidden behind the compute time of a different stream and becomes free.

Streams are simply virtual work queues that we'll use here in a relatively simple manner. Initially we'll create a single stream and move from a synchronous operation to an asynchronous operation with respect to the CPU. With this approach we will likely see a slight improvement due to the decreased synchronization needed for an asynchronous operation, but I'd expect this to be minor. Only once you introduce multiple streams can you really expect to see any significant speedup.

Stream 0 is the default stream; the stream used if you do not specify one. This is a synchronous stream that helps significantly when debugging an application but is not the most efficient use of the GPU. Thus, we must first create an alternative stream. We then need to push the memory copy, events, and kernel operations into the stream.

The first thing we need to do is to create an alternative stream. This is done with

```
cudaStream_t aes_async_stream;
CUDA_CALL(cudaStreamCreate(&aes_async_stream));
```

Conversely, we need to destroy the stream at the end of the host program once we're finished with it:

```
CUDA_CALL(cudaStreamDestroy(aes_async_stream));
```

Next the copy and event operations need to have the new stream added. Thus, we change

```
// Copy to GPU and then zero host cipher memory
CUDA_CALL(cudaEventRecord(start_round_timer));

CUDA_CALL(cudaMemcpyAsync(cipher_data_device, cipher_data_host,
size_of_cipher_data_in_bytes, cudaMemcpyHostToDevice));

CUDA_CALL(cudaMemcpyAsync(cipher_key_device, cipher_key_host,
size_of_cipher_key_size_in_bytes, cudaMemcpyHostToDevice));
```

to

```
// Copy to GPU and then zero host cipher memory
CUDA_CALL(cudaEventRecord(start_round_timer, aes_async_stream));
```

```
CUDA_CALL(cudaMemcpyAsync(cipher_data_device, cipher_data_host,
size_of_cipher_data_in_bytes, cudaMemcpyHostToDevice, aes_async_stream));

CUDA_CALL(cudaMemcpyAsync(cipher_key_device, cipher_key_host,
size_of_cipher_key_size_in_bytes, cudaMemcpyHostToDevice, aes_async_stream));
```

Notice how the newly created stream is used as the last parameter in each of the calls. The stream parameter is an optional parameter that defaults to stream zero unless otherwise specified. Then we need to launch the kernel into the correct stream, which we again do by specifying the stream. As the stream parameter is actually the fourth parameter, we need to use zero as parameter 3. Parameter 3 is the amount of dynamic shared memory the kernel will use. As we are using no dynamically allocated shared memory, we set this to zero. Thus,

```
AES_encrypt_gpu<<<num_blocks, num_threads>>> (cipher_data_device, cipher_key_device,
num_cipher_blocks, num_cipher_keys);
```

becomes

```
AES_encrypt_gpu<<<num_blocks, num_threads, 0, aes_async_stream>>> (cipher_data_device,
cipher_key_device, num_cipher_blocks, num_cipher_keys);
```

We do the same for the copy back and stop timer event. As the stop timer event is at the end of the kernel, we also need to ensure we wait for this event.

```
CUDA_CALL(cudaEventSynchronize(stop_round_timer));
```

As the kernel, copy, and event operations are now entirely asynchronous it is critical that the data returned from the kernel is not used until such time as the kernel is actually complete. Forgetting to add such a synchronize operation after the final memory copy back to the host is often a cause for failure when moving to an asynchronous operation.

How does this change help? Running the test program reveals the time drops from 1070 ms to just 940 ms, a drop of just over 12% in execution time. This is quite significant really, considering all we have done is to remove the implicit synchronization steps the CUDA driver was inserting when using stream 0.

AES in hardware

Intel provides a special extension to the AVX instruction set called AES-NI. This is based on a 128-bit-wide processing of the entire AES key state and key expansion. This equates to the u4 type we've been using so far for memory load/stores. AES-NI has hardware support for both encode/decode and the expand key operation. Therefore, let's look at how we can make use of this.

Intel provides a AES-NI sample library, which is available at *http://software.intel.com/en-us/articles/download-the-intel-aesni-sample-library/*. The library, once downloaded, needs to be built, as there are no precompiled binary libraries to link to. This is still via an old command line interface. Those running Microsoft Visual Studio need to run a command vcvars32.bat, which sets a number of command line environment variables for the command line version. This in practice maps to the vsvars32.bat file, which actually sets the environment variables.

Once the library is built, you need to add the library search path, and include the search path and library to the additional libraries in your Visual Studio project.

The Intel version of AES has one key difference to the GPU one we've developed to date. The original specification of AES lays out data in a column format, so A, B, C, and D are located in the same column. The Intel ASE-NI expects this to be transposed, so A, B, C, and D are all on the same row. AES-NI also, due to Intel's byte ordering, requires the bytes to be ordered in memory in the reverse order compared to the order we have now.

Thus, we have two choices: either restructure the code to match the Intel AES-NI ordering, or perform a transformation on the data to convert one to the other. To allow memory blocks to be directly compared on the host, we'll adapt our current solution to match the AES-NI format. As we also need AES-NI support, we'll move all future development onto our Sandybridge-E (Core i7 3930 K @ 3.2 Ghz) platform with GTX470 GPUs. Thus, any further timings will no longer be comparable with our atom-based ION system used to date for this development.

The other major issue we should note at this point is the `uint4` type is encoded on the GPU as x, y, z, w and not w, x, y, z. Both the GPU and CPU version gave the same wrong answer, as it was based on the same wrong code. This is easily corrected once you understood the rather strange ordering of the `uint4` type (this is usually a red, green, blue, alpha representation where w is the alpha channel). Clearly, we should have based the CPU version on either an existing library or used the AES-NI library sooner to have detected such issues. The AES-NI code is quite simple, as shown here:

```
void aes_encode_block_aes_ni(const u32 num_cipher_blocks,
                             const u32 num_cipher_keys,
                             const u8 * initial_keys,
                             u8 * src_data_blocks,
                             u8 * dest_data_blocks)
{
  // Encode the data blocks
  TIMER_T encode_key_time = get_time();

  // Encode using one or more blocks and single key
  intel_AES_enc128( (_AES_IN UCHAR *) src_data_blocks,
              (_AES_OUT UCHAR *) dest_data_blocks,
              (_AES_IN UCHAR *) initial_keys,
              (_AES_IN size_t) num_cipher_blocks );
  encode_key_time = (get_time() - encode_key_time);
  if (num_cipher_blocks > 1)
  {
   printf("\n\nEncrypting using AES-NI : %.u blocks", num_cipher_blocks);
   printf("\nEncrypt Encode : %.3fms", encode_key_time);
  }
}
```

The interface for the AES code needs to be a byte-based interface. Here is some sample code used to encode a single block of data `num_cipher_blocks` based on a single key. A similar set of code is used for the decode operation.

```
void aes_decode_block_aes_ni(const u32 num_src_cipher_blocks,
              const u32 num_cipher_keys,
              const u8 * key,
```

```
                    const u8 * src_data_blocks,
                    u8 * const dest_data_blocks)
{
  // Decode one or more blocks using a single key
  TIMER_T decode_key_time = get_time();
  intel_AES_dec128( (_AES_IN UCHAR *) src_data_blocks,
                    (_AES_OUT UCHAR *) dest_data_blocks,
                    (_AES_IN UCHAR * ) key,
                    (_AES_IN size_t) num_src_cipher_blocks );
  decode_key_time = (get_time() - decode_key_time);

  if (num_src_cipher_blocks > 1)
  {
   printf("\n\nDecrypting using AES-NI : %.u blocks", num_src_cipher_blocks);
   printf("\nDecrypt Decode   :%.3fms", decode_key_time);
  }
}
```

The key expansion operation is implicit in this operation as we pass an unexpanded key of just 16 bytes. However, it is done, internally, only once per encrypt/decrypt phase.

We'll develop a program that will generate a set of four million random data blocks (around 64 MB of data), and encode it using a single key. We'll then decode this data and check that the decoded data is the same as the original. We'll run AES-NI, Serial, and CUDA versions of these operations and cross-check the results from each to ensure all implementations agree.

Once the GPU and CPU versions matched the AES-NI library, we were able to see just how fast the AES-NI instruction set is. On our Sandybridge-E system, the software-based serial expand key and decode block operation took 3880 ms, whereas the hardware-enabled AES-NI version took just 20 ms. By comparison, the CUDA version took 103 ms excluding any transfer times to or from the device. In fact, the copy to and copy from device operations took 27 ms and 26 ms, respectively. Given we're using a GTX470 as our test device, a consumer GPU card, we'd not be able to overlap both the transfer in and the transfer out as there is only a single memory transfer engine enabled in this device. Therefore, the absolute best case we could possibly achieve would be to entirely hide the kernel execution time behind one of these transfers, effectively eliminating it. However, to do this we'd need a $5\times$ improvement in the kernel's execution time. Let's look therefore at the decode kernel in its revised form to be byte-for-byte compatible with the AES-NI output.

```
#define AES_U8_DECODE u32
__host__ __device__ void AES_decrypt_4x4_reg(const uint4 * const src_cipher_block,
                                             uint4 * const dest_cipher_block,
                                             KEY_T * const cipher_key)
{

  // Read 4 x 32 bit values from data block as 128 bit read
  uint4 key = *src_cipher_block;

  // Store into four 32 bit registers
  u32 w0 = key.x;
  u32 w1 = key.y;
```

```
 u32 w2 = key.z;
 u32 w3 = key.w;

 // Allocate room for sixteen 32 bit registers
 register AES_U8_DECODE a0, a4, a8, a12;
 register AES_U8_DECODE a1, a5, a9, a13;
 register AES_U8_DECODE a2, a6, a10, a14;
 register AES_U8_DECODE a3, a7, a11, a15;

 // Expand the 32 bit words into 16 registers
 EXTRACT_WORD(w0, a0, a1, a2, a3);
 EXTRACT_WORD(w1, a4, a5, a6, a7);
 EXTRACT_WORD(w2, a8, a9, a10, a11);
 EXTRACT_WORD(w3, a12, a13, a14, a15);

 // Always start at round ten
 u32 round_num = NUM_ROUNDS;

 // Setup some pointers to the lookup gmul tables
 const GMUL_U8 * const gmul_14_ptr = gmul_tab_14;
 const GMUL_U8 * const gmul_09_ptr = gmul_tab_09;
 const GMUL_U8 * const gmul_13_ptr = gmul_tab_13;
 const GMUL_U8 * const gmul_11_ptr = gmul_tab_11;

 // Define either a host or device point for the s_box function
#ifdef __CUDA_ARCH__
   const S_BOX_U8 * const s_box_ptr = s_box_inv_device;
#else
   const S_BOX_U8 * const s_box_ptr = s_box_inv_host;
#endif
 // Count down from round ten to round one
 while (round_num > 0)
 {
  // Add Round Key
  {
   // Fetch cipher key from memory as a 128 bit read
   key = ((*cipher_key)[round_num]);

   // Convert to four 32 bit values
   w0 = key.x;
   w1 = key.y;
   w2 = key.z;
   w3 = key.w;

   // Extract the key values, XOR'ing them with
   // the current values
   EXTRACT_WORD_XOR(w0, a0, a1, a2, a3);
   EXTRACT_WORD_XOR(w1, a4, a5, a6, a7);
```

```
    EXTRACT_WORD_XOR(w2, a8, a9, a10, a11);
    EXTRACT_WORD_XOR(w3, a12, a13, a14, a15);
}
// Invert Column Mix on every round except the first
if (round_num != 10)
{
  AES_U8_DECODE tmp0, tmp1, tmp2, tmp3;

  // Invert mix column operation on each column
  INV_MIX_COLUMN_PTR(a0, a1, a2, a3,
              tmp0, tmp1, tmp2, tmp3,
              gmul_14_ptr, gmul_09_ptr, gmul_13_ptr, gmul_11_ptr);

  INV_MIX_COLUMN_PTR(a4, a5, a6, a7,
              tmp0, tmp1, tmp2, tmp3,
              gmul_14_ptr, gmul_09_ptr, gmul_13_ptr, gmul_11_ptr);

  INV_MIX_COLUMN_PTR(a8, a9, a10, a11,
              tmp0, tmp1, tmp2, tmp3,
              gmul_14_ptr, gmul_09_ptr, gmul_13_ptr, gmul_11_ptr);
  INV_MIX_COLUMN_PTR(a12, a13, a14, a15,
              tmp0, tmp1, tmp2, tmp3,
              gmul_14_ptr, gmul_09_ptr, gmul_13_ptr, gmul_11_ptr);
}

// Invert Shift Rows
{
  // a0, a4, a8, a12 remains unchanged

  // a1, a5, a9, a13 rotate right 1
  AES_U8_DECODE tmp0;
  ROTR_1(a1, a5, a9, a13, tmp0);

  // a2, a6, a10, a14 rotate right 2
  AES_U8_DECODE tmp1;
  ROTR_2(a2, a6, a10, a14, tmp0, tmp1);

  // a3, a7, a11, a15 rotate right 3
  ROTR_3(a3, a7, a11, a15, tmp0);
}

// Invert Substitute bytes
{
  SBOX_SUB(s_box_ptr, a0, a4, a8, a12);
  SBOX_SUB(s_box_ptr, a1, a5, a9, a13);
  SBOX_SUB(s_box_ptr, a2, a6, a10, a14);
  SBOX_SUB(s_box_ptr, a3, a7, a11, a15);
}
```

```
  // Decrement the round counter
  round_num--;
}

// Execute round zero - only an XOR
// Read ahead of time, round zero of the cipher key
key = ((*cipher_key)[0]);

// Pack the values back into registers
w0 = ENCODE_WORD( a0, a1, a2, a3 );
w1 = ENCODE_WORD( a4, a5, a6, a7 );
w2 = ENCODE_WORD( a8, a9, a10, a11 );
w3 = ENCODE_WORD( a12, a13, a14, a15 );

// XOR the results with the last key
key.x ^= w0;
key.y ^= w1;
key.z ^= w2;
key.w ^= w3;
// Use a 128 bit memory write to store the decoded block
*dest_cipher_block = key;
}
```

The function first reads encrypted data and then decodes it into a set of 16 registers. The decode function is the inverse of the encode function. Therefore, we count the rounds down from 10 to 0.

The decode side is more complex than encode, mainly because of the Galois multiplication that is used. The multiplication is precalculated into a table. Thus, the simple series of XOR operations now needs to perform a number of data-dependent lookups into one of four tables, each of which is 1 K bytes in size. This, however, generates a poor scattered memory access pattern.

We then rotate the values in the rows and finally perform the s_box substitution as before. As with the inverted mix column operation, the s_box function generates a scattered memory read pattern. Finally, a single 128-byte write is used to write out the data to global memory.

Another significant problem with this initial implementation is that this to uses far too many registers, 44 in total. It's a complex kernel. We succeed in keeping the computation within registers until the very last moment. Forcing this (via the maxrregcount=42 compiler flag) to 42 registers allows the scheduling of one additional block into the SM. This in turn reduces the total execution time from 103 ms to 97 ms. Forcing register usage down means more spilling to global memory, and in this case, we see the memory bandwidth requirements jump by 25%. This suggests there is room to improve by reducing the register usage, but it needs to be done by other means.

We can achieve the desired effect of allowing more blocks to get scheduled by reducing the number of threads per block. Dropping down from 128 threads to 96 threads per block allows us to schedule the same number of warps as before, but with eight blocks instead of six. This drops the execution time to 96 ms. As the kernel uses no synchronization points, this is entirely down to the better instruction mix the additional blocks bring and also the effects of caching.

If we look at the memory view in Figure 7.16 from one of the experiments Parallel Nsight can run for use, we see that we have very high L1 cache usage, but nonetheless 281 MB is spilling out of this to

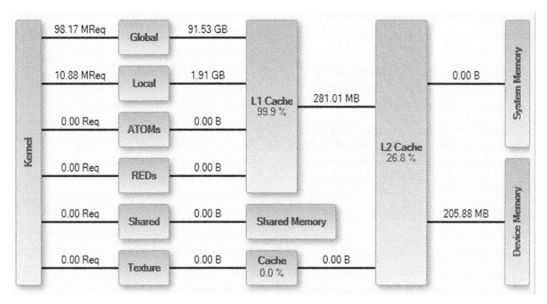

FIGURE 7.16

Initial memory bandwidth view.

the L2. Worse still, 205 MB of that is spilling into global memory. The kernel reads and writes to global memory so we will have some global memory traffic, but how much should we expect? We have 4,195,328 blocks with each block being 16 bytes in size. Therefore, we have 67,125,248 or exactly 64 MB of data to read. Equally, we write out a decrypted block, so we have 64 MB of data to write out. The statistics for global memory are shown for the device as a whole and shows we're reading/writing a total of 205MB. Therefore, we are generating 160% of the global memory traffic necessary, which in turn is limiting the performance.

Currently, the L1 cache is operating at peak efficiency, but there is 16 K of shared memory we're not using at all. It does not have the coalescing requirements global memory has, so it would be a good candidate for a small data region with a scattered memory pattern. However, unlike the L1 cache, the shared memory has a per-block visibility, which would mean having to duplicate the data for every resident block on the SM.

The constant memory cache is not shown in Figure 7.16, but it would also be large enough to hold the Galios multiplication (gmul) and/or s_box tables. However, the constant cache has only one 32-bit element bandwidth per clock and is designed for the same element being accessed by every thread. Thus, the shared memory is a better candidate.

However, let's first look at the two problem areas, s_box and the gmul tables. Both were declared as 32-bit unsigned types, to avoid huge numbers of instructions being added to shift and mask the 32-bit words. Given the memory traffic we're generating, this was probably not a good choice. Changing these to a u8 type, we see the off-chip memory accesses drop from 205 MB to 183 MB and the execution time drop from 96 ms to 63 ms. Clearly, this was causing a significant amount of overfetch from the global memory and reducing it helps considerably.

With a reduced memory footprint, each gmul table is now 256 bytes in size, so the four tables fit easily with 1 K. As we can place a maximum of eight blocks per SM, 8 K of shared memory is now sufficient to accommodate the gmul tables.

Performing this shared memory optimization, however, has a problem. Indeed we move 18 GB of memory bandwidth from the L1 cache to the shared memory, and the main memory bandwidth drops by 7 MB. However, we have to move 1 K of data at the start of each block, as the shared memory is not persistent or shared between blocks. The L1 cache, however, is shared between the blocks and is currently doing a very good job of dealing with this scattered memory pattern, as the tables are entirely resident within the cache. The net improvement of speed for our 8 K of shared memory usage is almost zero, so this optimization was removed, leaving the tables in the L1 cache instead. Note this would have brought considerable improvement on compute 1.x devices, compared to global memory accesses, where there are no L1/L2 caches.

Looking back at Figure 7.16, did you notice something interesting? Did you notice we were using 1.91 GB of local storage? Local storage is the compiler spilling registers to the memory system. Prior to compute 2.0 devices this would actually go to global memory space. From compute 2.0 onward it gets contained within the L1 cache if possible, but can still cause significant unwanted global memory traffic.

When compiling, the -v option will display a summary of the register usage from the kernel. Anytime you see the following message you have local memory being used:

```
nn bytes stack frame, nn bytes spill stores, nn bytes spill loads
```

The main issue here is the uint4 type being used. In combination with the high register usage elsewhere this uint4 load from global memory is immediately being spilled to local memory. A 128-bit uint4 load was deliberately chosen to minimize the number of load transactions to global memory. By spilling it to local memory instead of holding in registers, the compiler is unnecessarily polluting the caches and causing writes back to global memory.

We can explicitly move this data item into shared memory instead of local memory by simply declaring it as an array of __shared__ and indexing it by threadIdx.x. As shared memory is a per-block form of local memory, we can move the spilled register explicitly into the shared memory. Moving this parameter generates the memory view shown in Figure 7.17.

Notice how simply moving this data item to shared memory drops the local memory usage from 1.91 GB to just 256 MB, and the traffic to global memory from 183 MB to 133 MB. Our shared memory traffic is approximately double what it was before to the L1, which is largely due to the shared memory bank conflicts. These are caused by placing a 128-bit (16-byte) value into a 32-bit (4-byte) shared memory system. The compiler, however, still insists on creating a stack frame, much smaller than before, but it's still there. The overall execution time remains stubbornly stuck at 63 ms.

To see exactly what parameters are being spilled you have to look at the PTX code, the assembly code, generated within a given kernel. Any PTX instructions such as st.local or ld.local are operating on local data. Local data is also declared with local as a prefix. It turns out the remaining local data is actually the parameter data used between the __global__ caller and the __device__ function, that is,

```
__global__ void AES_decode_kernel_multi_block_single_key(uint4 * const src_block,
                                                          uint4 * const dest_blocks,
                                                          KEY_T * const expanded_key,
                                                          const u32 num_cipher_blocks)
{
  const u32 tid = (blockIdx.x * blockDim.x) + threadIdx.x;
```

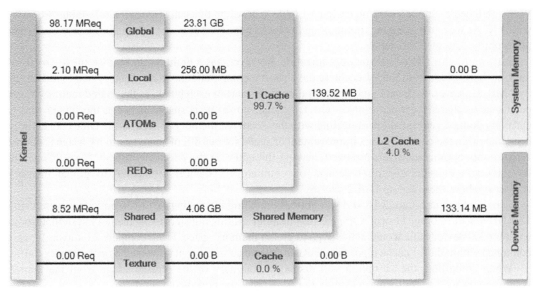

FIGURE 7.17

Memory transfers after using shared memory.

```
if (tid < num_cipher_blocks)
  AES_decrypt_4x4_reg( &(src_block[tid]), &(dest_blocks[tid]), &(expanded_key[0]) );
}


__host__ __device__ void AES_decrypt_4x4_reg(
 const uint4 * const src_cipher_block,
 uint4 * const dest_cipher_block,
 KEY_T * const cipher_key)
{
 ...
}
```

The fact that we have passed a number of parameters to the device function, which in turn allows it to be called by a number of global functions and the host function, causes the compiler to insert a stack frame. We rarely if ever want the compiler to call a stack and instead want it to inline the call to the device function, thereby eliminating any need to use a stack. We can do this using the __forceinline__ directive when declaring the function as shown here:

```
__host__ __device__ __forceinline__ void AES_decrypt_4x4_reg(
 const uint4 * const src_cipher_block,
 uint4 * const dest_cipher_block,
 KEY_T * const cipher_key)
{
 ...
}
```

Recompiling the code no longer produces the stack frame message. Due to the function now being a consolidated whole, the compiler can much better apply optimization techniques to it. The register usage drops to just 33 instead of the forced 42 registers we were using before to accommodate eight blocks. We can verify local memory is no longer being used by looking at the memory overview in Figure 7.18.

We can see in Figure 7.18 the local memory traffic now falls to zero. What little L2 cache usage there was is eliminated. The global memory usage falls by another 5 MB to 128 MB, the magic figure we were expecting the global memory bandwidth to be based on for the size of data we're processing. The execution time reduces marginally but still remains at 63 ms.

The kernel makes considerable use of the XOR operation, which is one of the instructions that is not available at full rate within the device. Thus, by ensuring we keep the maximum number of blocks in the SM, we ensure a good instruction mix and that everything doesn't start backing up behind the units performing the XOR operations.

At 96 threads per block with the previous high 42 register count we could schedule eight blocks using 24 warps. This is around 50% of the available capacity of the SM in terms of the number of warps it could run. However, we can see from looking at the Parallel Nsight "Issue Stalls" experiment how much of the SM capacity we're actually using. We stall just 0.01% of the time, which means the SM is already almost at peak capacity. Increasing the occupancy figure by increasing the list of possible warps, therefore, is unlikely to help significantly. Increasing the number of threads from 96 to 128 allows us to increase the number of warps available for scheduling from 24 to 28. This eliminates the remaining fractional stall issue and increases the fraction of the time that both warp scheduler have warps available, gaining us a 1.5 ms reduction in the timing. This brings the total execution time to 61.5 ms.

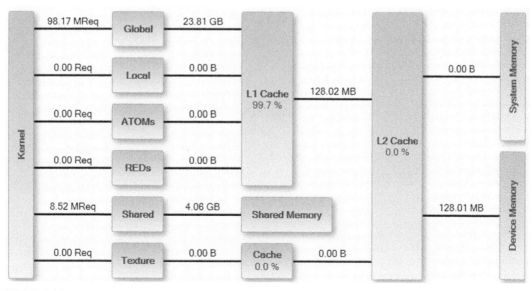

FIGURE 7.18

Memory usage after stack elimination.

Considerations for running on other GPUs

Having now developed a program for a single, modern GPU, how well does it work on other GPUs? Often, especially if you are writing commercial applications, your program will need to work well on each level of hardware in the marketplace. Although programs will run on most GPU generations, you should be aware of what adaptations may be required to achieve good performance on that hardware. We'll look at this with the AES program we've developed here.

Out first target is the GTX460 card, a compute 2.1 card based on Fermi. Major differences are the first revision of the compute 2.1 architecture (7 SMs × 48 CUDA cores vs. 14 SMs × 32 CUDA cores), reduced L2 cache size (512 K vs. 640 K), reduced L1 cache size per CUDA core (48 K L1 shared between 48 CUDA cores vs. 48K L1 shared between 32 CUDA cores), and the reduced memory bandwidth (115 GB/s vs. 134 GB/s).

Based purely on total CUDA core count (336 vs. 448), we'd expect around 75% of the performance. However, adjusting for clock speed differences, this gives us a little less than 10% performance difference between the two devices. Memory bandwidth is 15% less on the GTX460 compared to the GTX470.

For the decrypt function the time actually measured is 100 ms compared with 61.5ms, which is somewhat disappointing. Looking at the execution profile we see that the SMs on the GTX460 are able to clock through more instructions, so the ratio of when the data arrives to the compute has changed. We again see a tiny amount of stalling in the SMs. With 128 threads per block we manage to get seven blocks scheduled (28 warps). If we could just reduce the register usage slightly we could execute another block and make better use of the SM. We therefore apply the same technique we used in the encode operation and move the inverse mix columns operation closer to the decode operation. Thus,

```
// Add Round Key
{
 // Fetch cipher key from memory as a 128 bit read
 *key_ptr = ((*cipher_key)[round_num]);

 // Extract the key values, XOR'ing them with
 // the current values
 EXTRACT_WORD_XOR2((key_ptr->x), a0, a1, a2, a3);
 EXTRACT_WORD_XOR2((key_ptr->y), a4, a5, a6, a7);
 EXTRACT_WORD_XOR2((key_ptr->z), a8, a9, a10, a11);
 EXTRACT_WORD_XOR2((key_ptr->w), a12, a13, a14, a15);
}

// Invert Column Mix on every round except the first
if (round_num != 10)
{
 INV_MIX_COLUMN_PTR2(a0, a1, a2, a3,
             gmul_14_ptr, gmul_09_ptr, gmul_13_ptr, gmul_11_ptr);

 INV_MIX_COLUMN_PTR2(a4, a5, a6, a7,
             gmul_14_ptr, gmul_09_ptr, gmul_13_ptr, gmul_11_ptr);

 INV_MIX_COLUMN_PTR2(a8, a9, a10, a11,
             gmul_14_ptr, gmul_09_ptr, gmul_13_ptr, gmul_11_ptr);

 INV_MIX_COLUMN_PTR2(a12, a13, a14, a15,
```

```
                gmul_14_ptr, gmul_09_ptr, gmul_13_ptr, gmul_11_ptr);
}
```

becomes

```
// Add Round Key
{
 // Fetch cipher key from memory as a 128 bit read
 *key_ptr = ((*cipher_key)[round_num]);

 // Extract the key values, XOR'ing them with
 // the current values
 EXTRACT_WORD_XOR2((key_ptr->x), a0, a1, a2, a3);
 if (round_num != 10)
  INV_MIX_COLUMN_PTR2(a0, a1, a2, a3,
            gmul_14_ptr, gmul_09_ptr, gmul_13_ptr, gmul_11_ptr);

 EXTRACT_WORD_XOR2((key_ptr->y), a4, a5, a6, a7);
 if (round_num != 10)
  INV_MIX_COLUMN_PTR2(a4, a5, a6, a7,
            gmul_14_ptr, gmul_09_ptr, gmul_13_ptr, gmul_11_ptr);

 EXTRACT_WORD_XOR2((key_ptr->z), a8, a9, a10, a11);
 if (round_num != 10)
  INV_MIX_COLUMN_PTR2(a8, a9, a10, a11,
            gmul_14_ptr, gmul_09_ptr, gmul_13_ptr, gmul_11_ptr);

 EXTRACT_WORD_XOR2((key_ptr->w), a12, a13, a14, a15);
 if (round_num != 10)
  INV_MIX_COLUMN_PTR2(a12, a13, a14, a15,
            gmul_14_ptr, gmul_09_ptr, gmul_13_ptr, gmul_11_ptr);
}
```

This fusing of the operation allows the register usage to drop to the magic 31 registers, which in turn allows us to schedule another block, giving a total of 32 warps per SM. This compensates for the compute 2.1 devices having a higher ratio of compute to load/store units than compute 2.0 devices. We see a small drop from 100 ms to 98 ms. However, our compute 2.0 device (the GTX470) was already using its compute cores to full capacity. This change, which introduces a few more tests, costs us 0.5 ms, bringing us back up to 62 ms on the compute 2.0 device. You may sometimes find this, especially with compute 2.0/compute 2.1 devices where the balance of execution units within an SM is different.

The second target is the GTX260, a compute 1.3 device. The major difference here is the complete lack of L1 and L2 caches. SM architecture is different with 27 SMs versus 14 SMs, for a total of 216 CUDA cores versus 448 CUDA cores. Memory bandwidth is 112 GB/s versus 134 GB/s some 16% less and on par with the GTX460.

The initial run was 650 ms for the decode function, over 10 times slower than the GTX470. Why is this? One of the key reasons is the compute 1.x platform does not support a unified addressing mode. Thus, an explicit declaration of intended memory usage is needed. In the case of the gmul tables, they are generated on the device through a small compute kernel. As such, these tables exist in global memory. On compute 2.x platforms global memory is cached, whereas on compute 1.x platforms you have to explicitly make it cacheable. We can do this in a couple of ways.

First, we need to specify that the memory used for `gmul` is constant, which in turn means we can't write to it from the device. As we have a copy of the data on the host we can either copy it to the device via the `cudaMemcpyToSymbol` call or simply declare it on the device as constant memory and initialize it there statically. Thus, the code to calculate the `gmul` table was replaced with a simple expanded definition of the table lookup. This then resides in the constant cache. Rerunning the code we see a drop from 650 ms to 265 ms, a drop in execution time of nearly 60%. However, the GTX260 is still a factor of 4.2× slower than the GTX470 and 2.7× slower than the GTX460.

Finally, an older GT9800 card has approximately half the number of CUDA cores of the GTX260 and half the memory bandwidth. As might be expected, we see the 265 ms approximately double (1.8×) to 478 ms.

The issue with both GTX260 and GT9800 is the organization of the data. Having the data match the format used for AES-NI means the data for a single key value is laid out sequentially in memory. To achieve much better performance we need to organize the memory such that each successive 32-bit value from the key appears as a column in memory rather than a row. The typical sequential arrangement that is ideal for the CPU is far from ideal for the GPU.

The actual output of our AES encryption/decryption is shown here:

```
Intel AES NI support enabled.
Logical CUDA device 0 mapped to physical device 0. Device ID: GeForce GTX 470 on PCI-E 5
Logical CUDA device 1 mapped to physical device 1. Device ID: GeForce GTX 470 on PCI-E 4
Logical CUDA device 2 mapped to physical device 2. Device ID: GeForce GTX 470 on PCI-E 3
Logical CUDA device 3 mapped to physical device 3. Device ID: GeForce GTX 470 on PCI-E 2
Logical CUDA device 4 mapped to physical device 4. Device ID: GeForce GTX 470 on PCI-E 1


test_single_block_single_key_encode_decode
AES NI Key          : 2b, 7e, 15, 16, 28, ae, d2, a6, ab, f7, 15, 88, 09, cf, 4f, 3c,
AES NI Plaintext    : 6b, c1, be, e2, 2e, 40, 9f, 96, e9, 3d, 7e, 11, 73, 93, 17, 2a,
AES NI Ciphertext   : 3a, d7, 7b, b4, 0d, 7a, 36, 60, a8, 9e, ca, f3, 24, 66, ef, 97,
Expected Ciphertext : 3a, d7, 7b, b4, 0d, 7a, 36, 60, a8, 9e, ca, f3, 24, 66, ef, 97,
Single block single key AES-NI decode Passed
GPU Intial Key      : 16157e2b,  a6d2ae28,  8815f7ab,  3c4fcf09,
GPU Plaintext       : e2bec16b,  969f402e,  117e3de9,  2a179373,
CPU Ciphertext      : b47bd73a,  60367a0d,  f3ca9ea8,  97ef6624,
GPU Ciphertext      : b47bd73a,  60367a0d,  f3ca9ea8,  97ef6624,
Expected Ciphertext : b47bd73a,  60367a0d,  f3ca9ea8,  97ef6624,
Single block single key serial decode Passed
Single block single key parallel decode Passed
Single block single key parallel decode and AES-NI match Passed


Encrypting on GPU          : 4194304 blocks (32768 Blocks x 128 Threads)
Encrypt Copy To Device     : 28.469ms
Encrypt Expand Key Kernel  :  0.025ms
Encrypt Encode Key Kernel  : 45.581ms
Encrypt Copy From Device   : 25.428ms
```

```
Encrypt Total Time       :   99.503ms
Encrypting on CPU        :   4194304 blocks
Encrypt Encode           :   3900.000ms
Encrypting using AES-NI  :   4194304 blocks
Encrypt Encode           :   20.000ms
CPU and GPU encode result Passed.
CPU and GPU AES-NI encode result Passed.

Decrypting on GPU        :   4194304 blocks (32768 Blocks x 128 Threads)
Decrypt Copy To Device   :   27.531ms
Decrypt Expand Key Kernel :   0.028ms
Decrypt Decode Key Kernel :  62.027ms
Decrypt Copy From Device :   25.914ms
Decrypt Total Time       :  115.500ms

Decrypting on CPU  :   4194304 blocks
Decrypt Decode     :   2760.000ms

Decrypting using AES-NI  :   4194304 blocks
Decrypt Decode           :   20.000ms
CPU and GPU decode result Passed.
CPU and AES-NI decode result Passed.
```

Notice that with encrypt we've managed to get within approximately $2\times$ of the AES-NI hardware, and for decrypt approximately within $3\times$. We're using here a GTX470, which is hardware from the time of the regular Sandybridge CPU, rather than the more modern Sandybridge-E device. The regular Sandybridge device's AES-NI performance is approximately half of the Sandybridge-E, which puts us on similar timings. The Kepler-based GTX680 would be a representative device to pair with a Sandybridge-E CPU. This would bring us in the order of a $2\times$ performance improvement, bringing the GPU in line with the hardware-based AES-NI performance.

The issue of what GPUs to support is a tricky one. There are a lot of older GPUs in the consumer market, so applications have to work well on these if you have a consumer application. Yet in large installations, simply the power bill means it makes no sense at all to keep the old GPUs running if they can be replaced with newer ones. The introduction of Kepler will hugely accelerate the retirement of the older Tesla boards.

If you need to support older hardware, then the best approach is to develop on that hardware from day one. You will then have a baseline application that will work reasonably well on the later-generation cards. Many of the optimizations you'd need to do for these cards would show significantly less benefit on the later-generation cards. However, almost all would show *some* benefit, it's just a question of what return you get for the time you invest.

Using multiple streams

An example of multistream and multistream/multi-GPU programming is provided in Chapter 8. We'll therefore not cover how to implement a streamed version of this algorithm. However, we'll discuss some of the issues you'd need to think about to implement one, with this algorithm or a problem of your own.

Multiple streams are useful in that they allow some overlap of kernel execution with PCI-E transfers. Their usefulness, however, is seriously hampered by the fact that one PCI-E transfer engine is only ever enabled on consumer cards. Only the professional (Tesla) series cards have both PCI-E transfer engines enabled, allowing for simultaneous bidirectional transfers.

We typically want to transfer data to the card, process some data, and then transfer the data out of the card. With a single PCI-E transfer engine enabled, we have just a single queue for all the memory transfers in the hardware. Despite being in separate streams, memory transfer requests feed into a *single* queue on Fermi and earlier hardware. Thus, the typical workflow pattern of transfer from host to device, invoke kernel, and then transfer from device to host creates a stall in the workflow. The transfer out of the device blocks the transfer into the device from the next stream. Thus, all streams actually run in series.

The next issue we need to think about when using multiple streams is the resource usage. You need N sets of host and device memory, where N is the number of streams you wish to run. When you have multiple GPUs, this makes a lot of sense, as each GPU contributes significantly to the overall result. However, with a single-consumer GPU the gain is less easy to quantify. It works well only where either the input or output of the GPU workload is small in comparison to one another and the total transfer time is less than the kernel execution time.

In our application, we transfer in a set of blocks to be encoded in a single key set to use for the encoding. We transfer out the encoded blocks. The transfer in and transfer out are all but identical in size. The kernel execution time is around twice the size of the transfers. This means we have the opportunity to hide the input transfer time and only suffer the output transfer time.

A single GPU can support up to 16 hardware streams (32 in Kepler), so it would be possible to perform 16 inbound transfers, 16 kernels, and then 16 outbound transfers and still be within the bounds of the memory capacity on the device and the host. Transfers become more of an issue, as you will see in Chapter 9, where we introduce more than one GPU into the system. Due to contention for host resources, the transfer time itself may become longer the more concurrent transfers are in flight over the PCI-E bus.

AES summary

There were a number of issues we saw with AES that are worth summarizing here.

- The ideal memory pattern for the CPU and GPU versions are different. Optimizing the memory pattern for the GPU would have brought considerable benefits (typically at least $2\times$ on Fermi), especially on the earlier GPUs where this is far more critical.
- For compute 1.x devices read-only memory needs to be explicitly declared as constant memory, rather than auto-designated by the compiler as constant memory.
- It may be necessary to reorder or transform the kernel to allow the compiler to more easily see optimization opportunities.
- Efficient register usage and count were critical to achieving good performance.
- You can share read-only data between blocks using the L1 cache, whereas holding the same read-only data shared memory necessitates N copies where N is the number of resident blocks.
- Complex and thread-divergent algorithms, for example, the gmul function when decoding, can be replaced by nonthread-divergent memory lookups in the cache or shared memory. The cache was added specifically for such data-driven scattered memory patterns.
- Check the allocation of variables to registers and eliminate stack or local memory usage where possible.
- Always check correctness early in the solution, preferably with code developed independently.

- Always look at the *actual* timing of the program. Your mental model of how things work will not always be correct and often you will overlook something. Always look to the data for what effect each change has.

CONCLUSION

We've looked at a couple of applications of GPU technology, deliberately chosen for not being a simple matrix multiply shown in so many other examples of CUDA programming. We looked at using GPUs to filter data, which is useful from the perspective of searching data for interesting facts and also from a pure signal processing perspective. We've also looked how to implement AES, a standard encryption algorithm on GPUs. Even if you never have to implement this in CUDA, you should now understand and feel happy about implementing or using such algorithms.

You should also have picked up on some of the tradeoffs and design points when targeting multiple compute levels and how design decisions early on in project development can affect the outcome later. Thinking about the usage of registers, shared memory, cache, and access patterns to global memory are all key aspects of a design that should be understood and worked out before you write a single line of code.

One of the biggest issues programmers have today is growing up in a world where they are isolated from the hardware on which they are programming. To achieve great performance and not just average performance, it pays to understand, and understand thoroughly, the environment in which you are developing. Concepts such as various levels of memory hierarchy don't really exist in traditional programming languages. The C language was invented back in the early 1970s and only in the C11 (as in 2011) standard do we finally see thread and local thread storage start to appear. CUDA, and its native language C, follows the principle of trusting the programmer. It exposes aspects of the hardware to you, and you should therefore consider it your responsibility to understand those features and use them well.

With a few examples now covered, we'll move on to using multiple GPUs and optimizing applications, an area where we can extract massive speedups within a node simply by plugging more cards into the PCI-E bus and adapting our applications to be multi-GPU aware. The Kepler Tesla K10 product is the first Tesla dual-GPU solution, perhaps one of many we may see in the coming years. Multi-GPU programming, after CUDA 4.0, is actually not hard, as you'll see in the subsequent chapters.

Questions

1. What was the main reason why the AES application ran significantly slower on the GTX260 and GT9800 cards compared with the GTX460 and GTX470 cards? What would you do to address this?
2. In the AES application, why did changing the s_box and gmul tables from u32 to u8 improve performance?
3. What is thread level parallelism? Does it help, and if so why?
4. What problems are associated with using atomic operations?

Answers

1. The GTX260 and GT9800 cards are compute 1.3 and compute 1.1 cards, respectively. As such, they have no level one (L1) or level two (L2) caches as found on the compute 2.x cards. In the memory

figures shown we were using the L1 cache with a 99% hit rate. Going from L1 to global memory means we move from terabytes of bandwidth to just the low hundreds of megabytes of bandwidth. The memory coalescing also radically changes. The compute 2.x hardware fetches memory in 128-byte cache lines. If the thread fetches a single 128-byte value, uint4 for example, the hardware can service this. On compute 1.x hardware coalescing requirements are much stricter.

The uint4 type as currently compiled is hurting the algorithm. On compute 2.x hardware a four-word vector load from memory is used followed by a four-word vector to shared memory. On the compute 1.x hardware, the CUDA 4.1 compiler generates code to load each 32-bit word separately and thus generates four more times the traffic in each direction than is necessary. The encrypted cipher data needs to be placed into a suitable form for coalescing.

The constant cache is helpful. However, removing the uint4 type from the shared memory, replacing it with register-held u32 values, and then using the shared memory for the gmul and s_box tables would be more beneficial. You should also consider that on older devices, the texture cache can be a worthwhile additional resource worth the effort of exploiting.

2. The s_box and gmul tables are accessed with a data-dependent pattern. We have a total of four tables, each of which is 256 entries in size. Using a u8 type means we use 5 K of memory, which fits into both the L1 cache and the constant cache. Using u32 values removed a number of cvt (convert type) instructions, but shifts four times the data from the L1 or constant cache. The extra compute overhead is easily worth the cost of not moving so much data. As a u32 type, the caches need to store 20 K of data, easily exceeding the normal 16 K L1 cache allocation and the 8 K constant cache working set.

3. Thread level parallelism exploits the fact that most hardware is pipelined and thus able to accept nondependent instructions on successive clocks without blocking. A value of four independent items per thread is typically a good value to exploit to achieve thread level parallelism, something we look at in Chapter 9.

4. There are two main issues to consider. First, atomic operations, if oversubscribed, cause serialization. Thus, a warp of 32 values writing to the same memory address, be it shared or global memory, will serialize. Atomics, at least on Fermi, are warp-wide operations. Thus, having each thread in a warp perform an atomic operation to independent addressable locations will result in 32 atomic operations without serialization.

The second problem is ordering of atomic writes. If all values in a warp write to one address, the order of the operation is not defined. You can obviously observe the order and it's likely that this will remain consistent for a given device. Another device may, however, work differently. Thus, in using such knowledge, you'd be building a failure point into your application.

References

Wikipedia, Rijndael Mix Columns. Available at: *http://en.wikipedia.org/wiki/Rijndael_mix_columns*, accessed Jan. 31, 2012

Federal Information Processing Standards Publication 197, Advanced Encryption Standard (AES). Available at: *http://csrc.nist.gov/publications/fips/fips197/fips-197.pdf*, accessed Feb. 5, 2012.

Toms Hardware, AES-NI Benchmark Results: Bitlocker, Everest, and WinZip 14. Available at: *http://www.tomshardware.co.uk/clarkdale-aes-ni-encryption, review-31801–7.html*, accessed Apr. 26, 2012

Multi-CPU and Multi-GPU Solutions

INTRODUCTION

In modern computing systems it's common to have multiple devices, both CPUs and GPUs. In terms of CPUs we'll talk about sockets and cores. A socket is a physical socket on the motherboard into which a CPU is placed. A CPU may contain one or more cores. Each core is effectively a separate entity. A number of CPU and GPU sockets are located on a single node or computer system.

Knowing the physical arrangement of cores, sockets, and nodes allows for far more effective scheduling or distribution of tasks.

LOCALITY

The principle of locality is seen quite well in GPU and CPU design. Memory closer to the device (shared memory on the GPU, cache on the CPU) is quicker to access. Communication *within* a socket (i.e., between cores) is much quicker than communication to another core in a *different* socket. Communication to a core on another node is at least an order of magnitude slower than within the node.

Clearly, having software that is aware of this can make a huge difference to the overall performance of any system. Such socket-aware software can split data along the lines of the hardware layout, ensuring one core is working on a consistent dataset and cores that need to cooperate are within the same socket or node.

MULTI-CPU SYSTEMS

The most common multi-CPU system people will encounter is the single-socket, multicore desktop. Almost any PC you buy today will have a multicore CPU. Even in laptops and media PCs, you will find multicore CPUs. If we look at Steam's regular hardware (consumer/gaming) survey, it reveals that as of mid 2012 approximately 50% of users had dual-core systems and an additional 40% had quad-core or higher systems.

The second type of multi-CPU systems you encounter is in workstations and low-end servers. These are often dual-socket machines, typically powered by multicore Xeon or Opteron CPUs.

The final type of multi-CPU systems you come across are data center–based servers where you can have typically 4, 8, or 16 sockets, each with a multicore CPU. Such hardware is often used to create a virtualized set of machines, allowing companies to centrally support large numbers of virtual PCs from one large server.

One of the major problems you have with any multiprocessor system is memory coherency. Both CPUs and GPUs allocate memory to individual devices. In the case of GPUs, this is the global memory on each GPU card. In the CPU case, this is the system memory on the motherboard.

When you have independent programs using just a single core, you can scale quite well with this approach, as each program can be localized to a given core. The program then accesses its own data and makes good use of the CPU core's cache. However, as soon as you have two cores cooperating with one another, you have a problem.

To speed up access to memory locations, CPUs make extensive use of caches. When the value of a parameter is updated (e.g., x++), is x actually written to memory? Suppose two cores need to update x, because one core is assigned a debit processing task and the other a credit processing task. Both cores must have a consistent view of the memory location holding the parameter x.

This is the issue of cache coherency and it is what limits the maximum number of cores that can practically cooperate on a single node. In the hardware when core 1 writes to x, it informs all other cores that the value of x has now changed and then does a slow write out to the main memory instead of a quick write back cache access.

In a simple coherency model, the other cores then mark the entry for x in their caches as invalid. The next access to x then causes x to be reloaded from the slow main memory. As subsequent cores write to x, the process is repeated and the next core to access parameter x must again fetch it from memory and write it back again. In effect, the parameter x becomes noncached, which on a CPU means a huge performance hit.

In more complex coherency models, instead of invalidating x the invalidation request is replaced with an update request. Thus, every write has to be distributed to N caches. As the number of N grows, the time to synchronize the caches becomes impractical. This often limits the practical number of cores you can place into a symmetrical multiprocessor (SMP) system.

Now remember that caches are supposed to run at high speed. Within a single socket, this is not hard. However, as soon as you have to go outside of the socket, it's difficult to maintain the high clock rates and thus everything starts to slow down. The more sockets you have, the more difficult it becomes to keep everything synchronized.

The next major problem we have is memory access time. To make programming such machines easier, often the memory is logically arranged as a huge linear address space. However, as soon as a core from socket 1 tries to access a memory address from socket 2, it has to be serviced by socket 2, as only socket 2 can physically address that memory. This is called nonuniform memory access (NUMA). Although conceptually it makes a programmer's life easier by allowing an abstraction of the memory locality, in practice you need to think about memory locality or you write programs that perform very slowly.

MULTI-GPU SYSTEMS

Just like the CPU world, a lot of systems now have multiple GPUs inside them. From the enthusiast who has triple- or quad-SLI systems, or has dual cards like the 9800GX2, GTX295, GTX590 and

GTX690, down to the guy who upgraded his low-powered ION desktop with a dedicated GPU card, there are many people with multi-GPU systems. As a programmer you should always endeavor to produce the best experience possible on whatever hardware is available.

If the user has a dual-GPU system and you use only one GPU, you are being as lazy as those CPU programmers who can't be bothered to learn how to use more than one core. There are plenty of programs that monitor GPU load. The tech-savvy users or reviewers will slate your product for not going that extra mile.

If you are writing scientific applications or working with known hardware, rather than a consumer application, you should also be investigating multi-GPU solutions. Almost all PCs support at least two PCI-E slots, allowing at least two GPU cards to be put into almost any PC. CUDA does not use or require SLI (Scalable Link Interface), so not having an SLI-certified motherboard is no obstacle to using multiple GPUs in CUDA applications. Adding one additional GPU card, you will typically see a doubling in the level of performance, halving the current execution time. Rarely do you get such a speedup so easily.

ALGORITHMS ON MULTIPLE GPUS

The CUDA environment does not support, natively, a cooperative multi-GPU model. The model is based more on a single-core, single-GPU relationship. This works really well for tasks that are independent of one another, but is rather a pain if you wish to write a task that needs to have the GPUs cooperate in some way.

For example, an application like BOINC works well under this model. BOINC is an application which allows users to donate spare computing power to solving the world's problems. On a multi-GPU system it spawns N tasks, where N is equal to the number of GPUs in the system. Each task gets a separate data packet or job from a central server. As GPUs finish tasks, it simply requests additional tasks from the central server (task dispatcher).

Now if you look at a different example, where we need cooperation, the story is different. At the simplest level, encoding video is typically done by applying a JPEG-type algorithm to each individual frame and then looking for the motion vectors between frames. Thus, we have an operation within a frame that can be distributed to N GPUs, but then an operation that requires the GPUs to share data and has a dependency on the first task (JPEG compression) completing.

There are a couple of ways of dealing with this. The easiest is to use two passes, one kernel that simply does the JPEG compression on N independent frames, and a second kernel that does the motion vector analysis–based compression. We can do this because motion vector–based compression uses a finite window of frames, so frame 1 does not affect frame 1000. Thus, we can split the work into N independent jobs. The downside of this approach, as with any multipass algorithm, is we read the data more than once. As the dataset is typically quite large and will involve slow mass storage devices, this is generally a bad approach.

A single-pass method is more efficient, but more difficult to program. You can transform the problem, if you consider the set of frames on which you do motion vector compression to be the dataset. Each set of frames is independent and can be dispatched to a separate GPU card. The GPU kernel first does JPEG compression on all frames within the set it was provided. It then calculates, over those same frames, the motion aspects. By using this approach, you have managed to keep the data on the GPU card. This eliminates the major bottleneck with this type of problem—that of moving data around the system.

In this instance we managed to restructure the algorithm so it could be broken down into independent chunks of data. This may not always be possible and many types of problems require at least a small amount of data from the other GPUs. As soon as you require another GPU's data, you have to explicitly share that data and explicitly sequence the access to that data between the GPUs. Prior to the 4.0 SDK, there was no support for this in the CUDA environment. If it is at all possible to break down the problem into independent chunks, take this approach.

There are a couple of alternatives to this approach. You can use the GPU peer-to-peer communication model provided as of the 4.0 SDK version, or you can use CPU-level primitives to cooperate at the CPU level. The peer to peer approach does not work on all OSs, most noticeably Windows 7 with consumer hardware. The CPU solution requires OS-specific communication primitives, unless a common third-party solution is used.

WHICH GPU?

When there is more than one GPU on a system, are they the same or different? How does the programmer know? Does it matter?

Well it often matters, but it depends largely on the application. Embedded in the CUDA binary there are usually several binary images, one of each generation of GPUs. At a minimum a binary for the lowest compute–capability GPU should be present. However, additional binaries, optimized for higher-level compute devices, may also be present. The CUDA runtime will automatically select the highest level of binary based on the compute device when executing a kernel.

Certain functions, such as atomics, are only available on certain compute-level devices; running such code on a lower-level compute device results in the kernel failing to run. Therefore, for certain programs at least, we have to care which GPU is used. Other programs run much better or worse on newer hardware, due to the effects of caching and block size selection by the application. Others may have been written to use large numbers of registers on the G80/G200 series devices, something that was reduced on the Fermi architecture and then restored with Kepler.

Thus, some user or administration-level knowledge is required about which is the best platform on which to run a given kernel, or the programmer has to adapt the program so it runs well on all platforms. This can be done by either avoiding compute device–specific routines, which can often make things much harder to program, or by providing some alternative kernels that avoid the compute-level issue. However, the latter is often driven by commercial concerns. Programmer time costs money and you have to assess if the market segment you are targeting contains enough users with older hardware to justify the extra development and testing effort. In terms of the consumer market, as of August 2012, around one quarter of the market is still using pre-Fermi hardware. See Figure 8.1.

How does the programmer select a GPU device? We've seen a number of examples so far where we have used four devices and compared the results of each device. You should have seen from the various code examples that you need to set a device via a call to

```
cudaError_t cudaSetDevice(int device_num);
```

or the simplified version often used in this text,

```
CUDA_CALL(cudaSetDevice(0));
```

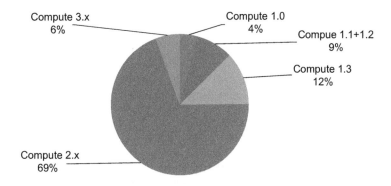

FIGURE 8.1

Consumer distribution of compute levels August 2012.

The parameter `device_num` is a number from zero (the default device) to the number of devices in the system. To query the number of devices, simply use the following call:

```
cudaError_t cudaGetDeviceCount(int * device_count);
```

or

```
CUDA_CALL(cudaGetDeviceCount(&num_devices));
```

Notice in both calls we make use of the `CUDA_CALL` macro we developed in Chapter 4. This simply takes the return value, checks it for an error, prints a suitable error message, and exits if there is a failure. See Chapter 4 on setting up CUDA for more information on exactly how this works.

Now that we know how many devices there are and how to select one, the question is which one to select. For this we need to know the details of a particular device. We can query this with the following call:

```
cudaError_t cudaGetDeviceProperties(struct cudaDeviceProp * properties, int device);
```

```
struct cudaDeviceProp device_0_prop;
CUDA_CALL(cudaGetDeviceProperties(&device_0_prop, 0));
```

The structure `properties` is made up of the structure members shown in Table 8.1.

Not all of these may be of interest, but certain ones will. The most important of these are the major and minor compute-level revisions. Note also that `warpSize` is present here, the implication being that warp size will change on different devices, although in practice it has remained at 32 for all devices released to date.

When selecting a device, it's not necessary to check each item to ensure it's what the particular user program needs. You can simply populate the same structure with the properties you would like (0 equates to don't care) and have the CUDA runtime select a suitable device for you. For example:

```
struct cudaDeviceProp device_prop;
int chosen_device;

memset(device_prop, 0, sizeof(cudaDeviceProp));
device_prop.major = 2;
device_prop.minor = 0;
```

Table 8.1 Device Properties Explained

Structure Member	Meaning	Tesla Only	Unit
char name[256];	Name of the device such as GTX460.		String
size_t totalGlobalMem;	The maximum amount of global memory present on the device.		Bytes
size_t sharedMemPerBlock;	The maximum amount of supported shared memory per block.		Bytes
int regsPerBlock;	The maximum number of allowed registers per block.		Registers
int warpSize;	The warp size of the device.		Threads
size_t memPitch;	Maximum supported pitch for memcpy operations using pitched allocated memory.		Bytes
int maxThreadsPerBlock;	The maximum number of threads supported per block.		Threads
int maxThreadsDim[3];	The maximum number of threads supported per dimension.		Threads
int maxGridSize[3];	The maximum number of blocks supported per grid dimension.		Blocks
int clockRate;	The clock rate of the GPU in KHz.		KHz
size_t totalConstMem;	The maximum amount of constant memory available on the device.		Bytes
int major;	The major compute revision.		Int
int minor;	The minor compute revision.		Int
size_t textureAlignment;	The minimum alignment required for textures.		Bytes
int deviceOverlap;	Set to 1 if the device supports overlapping memory transfers and kernels (deprecated).		Flag
int multiProcessorCount;	The number of SMs present on the device.		Int
int kernelExecTimeoutEnabled;	Set to 1 if the kernel timeout feature is enabled (enabled by default).		Flag
int integrated;	Set to 1 if the device is an integrated device, that is, a device that shares the CPU ram directly.		Flag
int canMapHostMemory;	Set to 1 if the device can map CPU host memory into the GPU virtual memory space.		Flag
int computeMode;	The current compute mode (cudaComputeModeDefault, cudaComputeModeExclusive, cudaComputeModeProhibited). Allows sharing of device, exclusive access to a device, or specifies if device access is prohibited.	x	Enum

Table 8.1 Device Properties Explained *(continued)*

Structure Member	Meaning	Tesla Only	Unit
int maxTexture1D;	The maximum 1D texture size supported.		Bytes
int maxTexture2D[2];	The maximum 2D texture size supported.		Bytes
int maxTexture3D[3];	The maximum 3D texture size supported.		Bytes
int maxTexture1DLayered[2];	The maximum 1D layered texture dimensions.		Bytes
int maxTexture2DLayered[3];	The maximum 2D layered texture dimensions.		Bytes
size_t surfaceAlignment;	Alignment requirements for surfaces.		Bytes
int concurrentKernels;	Set to 1 if concurrent kernels from the same context are supported.		Flag
int ECCEnabled;	Set to 1 if ECC memory is enabled.	x	Flag
int pciBusID;	PCI bus ID of the device.		Int
int pciDeviceID;	PCI device ID of the device.		Int
int pciDomainID;	PCI domain ID of the device.		Int
int tccDriver;	Set to 1 if TCC driver mode is enabled.	x	Flag
int asyncEngineCount;	Number of asynchronous copy engines present on the device.	x*	Int
int unifiedAddressing;	Set to 1 if the device and host share a unified address space.	x**	Flag
int memoryClockRate;	The maximum supported memory clock rate in KHz.		Khz
int memoryBusWidth;	Memory bus width in bits.		Bits
int l2CacheSize;	The size of the level two (L2) cache (0 = not present).		Bytes
int maxThreadsPerMultiProcessor;	The maximum number of threads supported on a single SM.		Threads

*Dual-copy engines are supported on Telsa devices only. Consumer-level devices are restricted to support only a single-copy engine.
**Unified address is supported only on 64-bit platforms. On Windows it requires the TCC driver, which in turn requires a Tesla card. On UNIX platforms this is not the case.

```
if (cudaChooseDevice(&chosen_device, device_prop) != cudaErrorInvalidValue)
{
CUDA_CALL(cudaSetDevice(chosen_device));
}
```

In this code we create a device properties' structure, clear it with a memset call, and then request a compute 2.0 device (any Fermi device). We then ask CUDA to set the context to the specified device.

SINGLE-NODE SYSTEMS

In versions of CUDA prior to the 4.0 SDK single-node systems were the only multi-GPU model available as shown in Figure 8.2. A single CPU-based task would be associated with a single-GPU context. A task in this context would be either a process or a thread. Behind the scenes the CUDA runtime would bind the CPU process/thread ID to the GPU context. Thus, all subsequent CUDA calls (e.g., cudaMalloc) would allocate memory on the device that was bound to this context.

This approach had a number of drawbacks but some advantages. From a programming perspective, the process/thread model on the host side is fragmented by the OS type. A process is a program that runs as an independent schedulable unit on a CPU and has its own data space. To conserve memory, multiple instances of the same process usually share the code space and the OS maintains a set of registers (or context) for each process.

A thread, by contrast, is a much more lightweight element of the CPU scheduling. It shares both the code *and* data space used by its parent process. However, as with a process, each thread requires the OS to maintain a state (instruction pointer, stack pointer, registers, etc.).

Threads may communicate and cooperate with other threads *within the same process*. Processes may communicate and cooperate with other processes through interprocess communication. Such communication between processes may be within a CPU core, within a CPU socket, within a CPU node, within a rack, within a computer system, or even between computer systems.

The actual API changes depending on the level of communication and OS. The API used on Windows is entirely different from that used on Linux. POSIX threads, or pthreads, is a commonly used threading model on Linux. This is not natively supported in Windows, although it is available as

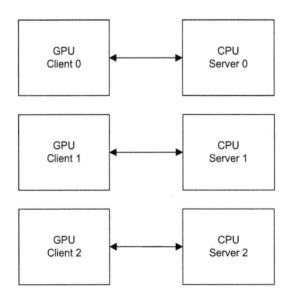

FIGURE 8.2

Multiple clients, multiple servers.

a port. The C++ Boost library supports a common threading package, `thread`, which provides support for both Linux and Windows.

CPU threads are similar to the GPU threads we've used when executing kernels, except that they don't execute in groups or warps as the GPU ones do. GPU threads communicate via shared memory and explicitly synchronize to ensure every thread has read/written to that memory. The shared memory is local to an SM, which means threads can only communicate with other threads within the same SM. However, because a block is the scheduling unit to an SM, thread communication is actually limited to a per-block basis.

Processes on the CPU can be thought of in the same way as blocks on the GPU. A process is scheduled to run on one of N CPU cores. A block is scheduled to run one of N SMs on the GPU. In this sense the SMs act like CPU cores.

CPU processes can communicate to one another via host memory on the same socket. However, due to processes using a separate memory space, this can only happen with the assistance of a third-party interprocess communications library, as neither process can physically see the address space of the other. The same is not true, however, for GPU blocks, as they access a common address space on the GPU global memory.

Systems with multiple CPUs using shared host memory can also communicate with one another via this shared host memory, but again with the help of a third-party interprocess communication library. Multiple GPUs can communicate to one another on the same host, using host memory, or, as of CUDA SDK 4.0, directly via the PCI-E bus peer-to-peer communication model. Note, however, peer-to-peer is only supported for 64-bit OSs using Fermi or later cards. For Windows this is only supported with the TCC (Tesla compute cluster) driver, which effectively means it's only supported for Tesla cards.

However, as soon as you no longer have the possibility to use shared host memory between CPU cores/sockets, you are forced to make use of some other network transport mechanism (TCP/IP, InfiniBand, etc.). The standard for this type of communication has become MPI (Message Passing Interface). There are also alternatives such as ZeroMQ (0MQ) that are less well known but equally effective.

Note that both of these make use of shared host memory transfers when communicating internally within a single host node. However, models that support threading (e.g., pthreads, ZeroMQ) perform interthread-based communication much quicker than those based on the process model such as MPI.

We'll focus here on the case where we have a single CPU socket, running a single-threaded CPU program with multiple GPUs present. This is the most common use case with consumer-level hardware and therefore the most useful case to cover. See Chapter 10 for more advanced topics such as peer to peer transfers between multiple GPUs.

STREAMS

Streams are virtual work queues on the GPU. They are used for asynchronous operation, that is, when you would like the GPU to operate separately from the CPU. Certain operations implicitly cause a synchronization point, for example, the default memory copies to and from the host or device. For the most part this is what the programmer wants, in that after copying the results back from the GPU they will instantly do something with those results on the CPU. If the results were to partially appear, then the application would work when debugged or single stepped, but fail when run at full speed—a debugging nightmare.

By creating a stream you can push work and events into the stream which will then execute the work in the order in which it is pushed into the stream. Streams and events are associated with the GPU context in which they were created. Thus, to show how to create a couple of streams and events on multiple GPUs we will setup a small program to demonstrate this.

```
void fill_array(u32 * data, const u32 num_elements)
{
 for (u32 i=0; i< num_elements; i++)
 {
  data[i] = i;
 }
}

void check_array(char * device_prefix,
                 u32 * data,
                 const u32 num_elements)
{
 bool error_found = false;

 for (u32 i=0; i< num_elements; i++)
 {
  if (data[i] != (i*2))
  {
   printf("%sError: %u %u",
          device_prefix,
          i,
          data[i]);

   error_found = true;
  }
 }

 if (error_found == false)
  printf("%sArray check passed", device_prefix);
}
```

In the first function we simply fill the array with a value from 0 to num_elements. The second function simply checks that the GPU result is what we'd expect. Obviously both functions would be replaced with real code to do something a little more useful, in practice.

```
__global__ void gpu_test_kernel(u32 * data)
{
 const int tid = (blockIdx.x * blockDim.x)
     + threadIdx.x;
 data[tid] *= 2;
}
```

Next we declare the kernel function itself. This does little more than multiply every data element by 2. Nothing very useful, but just something we can easily check to ensure every element of the array has been correctly processed.

```
// Define maximum number of supported devices
#define MAX_NUM_DEVICES (4)

// Define the number of elements to use in the array
#define NUM_ELEM (1024*1024*8)

// Define one stream per GPU
cudaStream_t stream[MAX_NUM_DEVICES];

// Define a string to prefix output messages with so
// we know which GPU generated it
char device_prefix[MAX_NUM_DEVICES][300];

// Define one working array per device, on the device
u32 * gpu_data[MAX_NUM_DEVICES];

// Define CPU source and destination arrays, one per GPU
u32 * cpu_src_data[MAX_NUM_DEVICES];
u32 * cpu_dest_data[MAX_NUM_DEVICES];
```

Finally, we come to the main part of the program. This function declares a number of values, each of which is indexed by device_num. This allows us to use the same code for every device and just increment the index.

```
// Host program to be called from main
__host__ void gpu_kernel(void)
{
 // No dynamic allocation of shared memory required
 const int shared_memory_usage = 0;

 // Define the size in bytes of a single GPU's worth
 // of data
 const size_t single_gpu_chunk_size = (sizeof(u32) *
         NUM_ELEM);

 // Define the number of threads and blocks to launch
 const int num_threads = 256;
 const int num_blocks = ((NUM_ELEM + (num_threads-1))
       / num_threads);

 // Identify how many devices and clip to the maximum
 // defined
 int num_devices;
 CUDA_CALL(cudaGetDeviceCount(&num_devices));
```

```
if (num_devices > MAX_NUM_DEVICES)
 num_devices = MAX_NUM_DEVICES;
```

The first task is to identify how many GPUs we have available with the cudaGetDeviceCount call. To ensure we don't have more than we planned, this number is clipped to the maximum supported, a simple #define. Allowing for four dual GPU cards, eight would be better maximum value than the four used here.

```
// Run one memcpy and kernel on each device
for (int device_num=0;
     device_num < num_devices;
     device_num++)
{
 // Select the correct device
 CUDA_CALL(cudaSetDevice(device_num));
```

The first section of each loop then sets the current device context to the device_num parameter to ensure all subsequent calls then work with that device.

```
// Generate a prefix for all screen messages
struct cudaDeviceProp device_prop;
CUDA_CALL(cudaGetDeviceProperties(&device_prop,
                                  device_num));
sprintf(&device_prefix[device_num][0], "\nID:%d %s:", device_num, device_prop.name);

// Create a new stream on that device
CUDA_CALL(cudaStreamCreate(&stream[device_num]));

// Allocate memory on the GPU
CUDA_CALL(cudaMalloc((void**)&gpu_data[device_num],
                     single_gpu_chunk_size));

// Allocate page locked memory on the CPU
CUDA_CALL(cudaMallocHost((void **)
                         &cpu_src_data[device_num],
                         single_gpu_chunk_size));

CUDA_CALL(cudaMallocHost((void **)
                         &cpu_dest_data[device_num],
                         single_gpu_chunk_size));

// Fill it with a known pattern
fill_array(cpu_src_data[device_num], NUM_ELEM);


// Copy a chunk of data from the CPU to the GPU
// asynchronous
```

```
CUDA_CALL(cudaMemcpyAsync(gpu_data[device_num],
        cpu_src_data[device_num],
        single_gpu_chunk_size,
        cudaMemcpyHostToDevice,
        stream[device_num]));

// Invoke the GPU kernel using the newly created
// stream - asynchronous invokation
gpu_test_kernel<<<num_blocks,
            num_threads,
            shared_memory_usage,
    stream[device_num]>>>(gpu_data[device_num]);

cuda_error_check(device_prefix[device_num],
            "Failed to invoke gpu_test_kernel");

// Now push memory copies to the host into
// the streams
// Copy a chunk of data from the GPU to the CPU
// asynchronous
CUDA_CALL(cudaMemcpyAsync(cpu_dest_data[device_num],
                gpu_data[device_num],
                single_gpu_chunk_size,
                cudaMemcpyDeviceToHost,
                stream[device_num]));
}
```

We create a stream, or work queue, for each GPU present in the system. Into this stream we place a copy from the host (CPU) memory to the GPU global memory followed by a kernel call and then a copy back to the CPU. They will execute in this order, so the kernel will not start executing until the preceding memory copy has completed.

Note the usage of page-locked memory on the host, allocated using cudaMallocHost instead of the regular C malloc function. Page-locked memory is memory that cannot be swapped out to disk. As the memory copy operations are being performed via a direct memory access (DMA) over the PCI-E bus, the memory at the CPU end must always physically be in memory. Memory allocated with malloc can be swapped out to disk, which would cause a failure if a DMA was attempted to or from it. As we used the cudaMallocHost function to allocate the memory, you must also use the cudaFreeHost function to deallocate the memory.

```
// Process the data as it comes back from the GPUs
// Overlaps CPU execution with GPU execution
for (int device_num=0;
  device_num < num_devices;
  device_num++)
{
  // Select the correct device
  CUDA_CALL(cudaSetDevice(device_num));
```

```
// Wait for all commands in the stream to complete
CUDA_CALL(cudaStreamSynchronize(stream[device_num]));
```

Finally, once the kernel streams have been filled, it's time to wait for the GPU kernels to complete. At this point the GPU may not have even started, as all we've done is to push commands into a stream or command queue.

```
// GPU data and stream are now used, so
// clear them up
CUDA_CALL(cudaStreamDestroy(stream[device_num]));
CUDA_CALL(cudaFree(gpu_data[device_num]));

// Data has now arrived in
// cpu_dest_data[device_num]
check_array( device_prefix[device_num],
             cpu_dest_data[device_num],
             NUM_ELEM);

// Clean up CPU allocations
CUDA_CALL(cudaFreeHost(cpu_src_data[device_num]));
CUDA_CALL(cudaFreeHost(cpu_dest_data[device_num]));

// Release the device context
CUDA_CALL(cudaDeviceReset());
  }
}
```

The CPU then waits for each device in turn to complete, and when this is done, it checks the contents and then frees the GPU and CPU resources associated with each stream. However, what happens if the GPU devices in the system are different and they take differing amounts of time to execute the kernel? First, we need to add some timing code to see how long each kernel takes in practice. To do this we have to add events to the work queue. Now events are special in that we can query an event regardless of the currently selected GPU. To do this we need to declare a start and stop event:

```
// Define a start and stop event per stream
cudaEvent_t kernel_start_event[MAX_NUM_DEVICES];
cudaEvent_t memcpy_to_start_event[MAX_NUM_DEVICES];
cudaEvent_t memcpy_from_start_event[MAX_NUM_DEVICES];
cudaEvent_t memcpy_from_stop_event[MAX_NUM_DEVICES];
```

Next, they need to be pushed into the stream or work queue:

```
// Push the start event into the stream
CUDA_CALL(cudaEventRecord(memcpy_to_start_event[device_num], stream[device_num]));
```

We push one start event at the start of the memory copy to the device, one prior to kernel invocation, one prior to the memory copy back to host, and, finally, one at the end of the memory copy. This allows us to see each stage of the GPU operations.

Finally, we need to get the elapsed time and print it to the screen:

```
// Wait for all commands in the stream to complete
CUDA_CALL(cudaStreamSynchronize(stream[device_num]));

// Get the elapsed time between the copy
// and kernel start
CUDA_CALL(cudaEventElapsedTime(&time_copy_to_ms,
 memcpy_to_start_event[device_num],
 kernel_start_event[device_num]));

// Get the elapsed time between the kernel start
// and copy back start
CUDA_CALL(cudaEventElapsedTime(&time_kernel_ms,
 kernel_start_event[device_num],
 memcpy_from_start_event[device_num]));

// Get the elapsed time between the copy back start
// and copy back start
CUDA_CALL(cudaEventElapsedTime(&time_copy_from_ms,
 memcpy_from_start_event[device_num],
 memcpy_from_stop_event[device_num]));

// Get the elapsed time between the overall start
// and stop events
CUDA_CALL(cudaEventElapsedTime(&time_exec_ms,
 memcpy_to_start_event[device_num],
 memcpy_from_stop_event[device_num]));

// Print the elapsed time
const float gpu_time = (time_copy_to_ms + time_kernel_ms + time_copy_from_ms);

printf("%sCopy To   : %.2f ms",
      device_prefix[device_num], time_copy_to_ms);

printf("%sKernel    : %.2f ms",
      device_prefix[device_num], time_kernel_ms);

printf("%sCopy Back : %.2f ms",
      device_prefix[device_num], time_copy_from_ms);

printf("%sComponent Time : %.2f ms",
      device_prefix[device_num], gpu_time);

printf("%sExecution Time : %.2f ms",
      device_prefix[device_num], time_exec_ms);

printf("\n");
```

We also need to redefine the kernel so it does considerably more work, so we can actually see some reasonable execution times on the kernel:

```
__global__ void gpu_test_kernel(u32 * data, const u32 iter)
{
 const int tid = (blockIdx.x * blockDim.x)
     + threadIdx.x;

 for (u32 i=0; i<iter; i++)
 {
  data[tid] *= 2;
  data[tid] /= 2;
 }
}
```

When we run the program we see the following result:

```
ID:0 GeForce GTX 470:Copy To        :   20.22 ms
ID:0 GeForce GTX 470:Kernel         : 4883.55 ms
ID:0 GeForce GTX 470:Copy Back      :   10.01 ms
ID:0 GeForce GTX 470:Component Time : 4913.78 ms
ID:0 GeForce GTX 470:Execution Time : 4913.78 ms
ID:0 GeForce GTX 470:Array check passed

ID:1 GeForce 9800 GT:Copy To        :    20.77 ms
ID:1 GeForce 9800 GT:Kernel         : 25279.57 ms
ID:1 GeForce 9800 GT:Copy Back      :    10.02 ms
ID:1 GeForce 9800 GT:Component Time : 25310.37 ms
ID:1 GeForce 9800 GT:Execution Time : 25310.37 ms
ID:1 GeForce 9800 GT:Array check passed

ID:2 GeForce GTX 260:Copy To        :    20.88 ms
ID:2 GeForce GTX 260:Kernel         : 14268.92 ms
ID:2 GeForce GTX 260:Copy Back      :    10.00 ms
ID:2 GeForce GTX 260:Component Time : 14299.80 ms
ID:2 GeForce GTX 260:Execution Time : 14299.80 ms
ID:2 GeForce GTX 260:Array check passed

ID:3 GeForce GTX 460:Copy To        :   20.11 ms
ID:3 GeForce GTX 460:Kernel         : 6652.78 ms
ID:3 GeForce GTX 460:Copy Back      :    9.94 ms
ID:3 GeForce GTX 460:Component Time : 6682.83 ms
ID:3 GeForce GTX 460:Execution Time : 6682.83 ms
ID:3 GeForce GTX 460:Array check passed
```

You can see from the results that the memory copy operations are within a small tolerance of one another. This is not too surprising as each device is running on an x8 PCI-E 2.0 link. The PCI link speed is considerably slower than even the slowest device's memory speed, so we are in fact limited by the PCI-E bus speed with regard to such transfers.

What is interesting, however, is the kernel execution speed varies quite dramatically, from 5 seconds to 25 seconds. Thus, if we provide data to each device strictly in turn such a cycle would take around 51 seconds (5s + 25s + 14s + 7s). However, at the time the program waits for device 1 9800GT, the slowest device, devices 2 (GTX260) and 3 (GTX460) are already complete. They could have been issued with more work in this time period.

We can solve this problem by querying the end event, rather than simply waiting on the end event. That is to say we look to see if the kernel has completed, and if not, move onto the next device and come back to the slow device later. This can be done using the following function:

```
cudaError_t cudaEventQuery (cudaEvent_t event);
```

This function takes a specified event and returns `cudaSuccess` if the event has already happened, or `cudaErrorNotReady` if the event has not yet occurred. Note, this means we can't use the regular `CUDA_CALL` macro, as the `cudaErrorNotReady` state is not really an error state, just status information.

We also need to specify how CUDA handles its tracking of pending GPU tasks via the following call:

```
// Give back control to CPU thread
CUDA_CALL(cudaSetDeviceFlags(cudaDeviceScheduleYield));
```

This call is done prior to any other CUDA calls and simply tells the driver that it should in all cases yield the CPU thread to other CPU threads when waiting for an operation. This can mean some additional latency in terms of the driver having to wait for its turn in the CPU work queue, but allows for other CPU tasks to progress. The alternative is that the driver spins the CPU thread (polls the device), which is certainly not what we want when there are other devices that could be ready.

To avoid polling the event queue ourselves and thus having the program behave poorly in relation to other CPU tasks, the program needs to put itself to sleep and then wake up sometime later and check the event queue again. The process to do this in Linux and Windows is slightly different, so we'll use a custom function, snooze, which works on both platforms.

```
// Give up control of CPU threads for some milliseconds
void snooze(const unsigned int ms)
{
#ifdef _WIN32
 Sleep(ms);
#else
 if ((ms/1000) <= 0)
  sleep(1);
 else
  sleep(ms/1000);
#endif
}
```

Finally, we will reorder the processing of the data to remove the `cudaStreamSynchronize` call and place this code into a function. We'll also remove the cleanup code and place this outside of the main loop. This particular action is important, as doing this within the loop, depending on the function, can cause serialization of the driver calls. Thus, the revised code for the querying of the event queue is as follows:

```
printf("\nWaiting");

u32 results_to_process = num_devices;
u32 sleep_count = 0;

// While there are results still to process
while(results_to_process != 0)
{
 // Process the data as it comes back from the GPUs
 // Overlaps CPU execution with GPU execution
 for (int device_num=0;
      device_num < num_devices;
      device_num++)
 {
  // If results are pending from this device
  if (processed_result[device_num] == false)
  {
   // Try to process the data from the device
   processed_result[device_num] =
        process_result(device_num);

   // If we were able to process the data
   if (processed_result[device_num] == true)
   {
    // Then decrease the number of pending
    // results
    results_to_process--;

    // print the time host waited
    printf("%sHost wait time : %u ms\n",
           device_prefix[device_num],
           sleep_count * 100);

    // If there are still more to process
    // print start of progress indicator
    if (results_to_process != 0)
     printf("\nWaiting");

    fflush(stdout);
   }
   else
   {
    printf(".");
    fflush(stdout);
   }
```

```
  }

  // Try again in 100ms
  sleep_count++;
  snooze(100);
 }
}

for (int device_num=0;
     device_num < num_devices;
     device_num++)
{
 cleanup(device_num);
}
```

The `while` loop simply runs until each device has provided results. We set up an array, `processed_results[num_devices]`, which holds false initially. As each GPU provides the results, the number of results pending is decremented and the array-processed results are marked to say this GPU has already provided the results. Where results are not yet available from any GPU, the CPU thread sleeps for 100 ms and then tries again. This results in the following output:

```
Waiting...................................
ID:0 GeForce GTX 470:Copy To   : 20.84 ms
ID:0 GeForce GTX 470:Kernel        : 4883.16 ms
ID:0 GeForce GTX 470:Copy Back     :   10.24 ms
ID:0 GeForce GTX 470:Component Time : 4914.24 ms
ID:0 GeForce GTX 470:Execution Time : 4914.24 ms
ID:0 GeForce GTX 470:Array check passed
ID:0 GeForce GTX 470:Host wait time : 5200 ms

Waiting............
ID:3 GeForce GTX 460:Copy To       :   20.58 ms
ID:3 GeForce GTX 460:Kernel        : 6937.48 ms
ID:3 GeForce GTX 460:Copy Back     :   10.21 ms
ID:3 GeForce GTX 460:Component Time : 6968.27 ms
ID:3 GeForce GTX 460:Execution Time : 6968.27 ms
ID:3 GeForce GTX 460:Array check passed
ID:3 GeForce GTX 460:Host wait time : 7100 ms

Waiting...................................
ID:2 GeForce GTX 260:Copy To       :   21.43 ms
ID:2 GeForce GTX 260:Kernel        : 14269.09 ms
ID:2 GeForce GTX 260:Copy Back     :   10.03 ms
ID:2 GeForce GTX 260:Component Time : 14300.55 ms
ID:2 GeForce GTX 260:Execution Time : 14300.55 ms
ID:2 GeForce GTX 260:Array check passed
ID:2 GeForce GTX 260:Host wait time : 14600 ms

Waiting........................
ID:1 GeForce 9800 GT:Copy To       :   21.19 ms
```

```
ID:1 GeForce 9800 GT:Kernel         : 25275.88 ms
ID:1 GeForce 9800 GT:Copy Back      :    11.01 ms
ID:1 GeForce 9800 GT:Component Time : 25308.08 ms
ID:1 GeForce 9800 GT:Execution Time : 25308.08 ms
ID:1 GeForce 9800 GT:Array check passed
ID:1 GeForce 9800 GT:Host wait time : 25300 ms
```

Notice how the order of the results now comes in as expected. The fastest device, the GTX470, takes just 5 seconds, while the slowest, the 9800 GT, takes 25 seconds. The CPU thread, for the most part, is idle during this time and could be doing something useful such as distributing more work to the GPUs when they finish. Let's look at how this would work in practice.

To start with, we need to abstract the task of pushing work into the stream or work queue. We can then use this for the initial stream filling, plus filling the stream when the work is complete.

```
__host__ void get_and_push_work(const int num_devices,
                                const size_t single_gpu_chunk_size,
                                const u32 new_work_blocks)
{
// Work out the total number to process
// Number already scheduled plus new work
u32 results_to_process = num_devices +
                         new_work_blocks;

// Keep track of the number of calculations in flow
u32 results_being_calculated = num_devices;

// Keep track of how long the CPU needs to sleep
u32 sleep_count = 0;

// While there are results still to process
while(results_to_process != 0)
{
 // Process the data as it comes back from the GPUs
 // Overlaps CPU execution with GPU execution
 for (int device_num=0;
      device_num < num_devices;
      device_num++)
 {
  // Assume will process nothing
  bool processed_a_result = false;

  // If results are pending from this device
  if (processed_result[device_num] == false)
  {
   // Try to process the data from the device
   processed_result[device_num] =
       process_result(device_num);
```

```
      // If we were able to process the data
      if (processed_result[device_num] == true)
      {
       // Then decrease the number of pending
       // results
       results_to_process--;

       // Increment the number this device
       // processed
       num_processed[device_num]++;

       // Decreate the number in flow
       results_being_calculated--;

       // Note we processed at least
       // one result
       processed_a_result = true;

       // print the time host waited
       printf("%sHost wait time : %u ms\n",
              device_prefix[device_num],
              sleep_count * 100);

       // If there are still more blocks
       // to process
       if (results_to_process >
           results_being_calculated)
       {
        // Give more work to the
        // finished GPU
        push_work_into_queue(device_num,
                             single_gpu_chunk_size);

        // Set flag to say GPU has work
        processed_result[device_num] =
              false;

        // Increment the number of
        // active tasks
        results_being_calculated++;

        // Format output
        printf("\n");
       }
       fflush(stdout);
      }
}
```

```
// If we processed no results then sleep
if (processed_a_result == false)
{
  sleep_count++;
  printf(".");
  fflush(stdout);

  // Try again in 100ms
  snooze(100);
  }
 }
 }
}
```

Here the program simply keeps track of the number of active GPU tasks and counts down the number of results still to process. This results in the allocation of work blocks shown in Figure 8.3 to GPUs when we allocate a total of 64 work units.

As you can see from the bar chart, the GTX470 can in the same time process 25+ units of work compared to the 9800 GT, which can process 5+ units, a ratio of 5:1. Simply cycling around and waiting on the stream sync operation would have caused an exactly equal work distribution when. You may find in many real-world systems, there is a mix of GPUs. Many gamers will have one card for gaming (GTX670) and then usually an older card dedicated to PhysX (GTX260), giving just such a scenario. In fact, the lesser cards if taken together contribute 37 work units, 10 more than the 27 contributed by the main card alone. This, in turn, more than doubles the available work throughput on the machine.

This is all very well, but we can actually do much better. We're actually not making the best use of each GPU in the system. Streams are designed to both provide an alternative to stream 0, the default stream, and provide multiple work queues for the GPU to work on. This is useful if the kernel is too small to exploit the full GPU, which is unlikely, or the more common case where the CPU may take

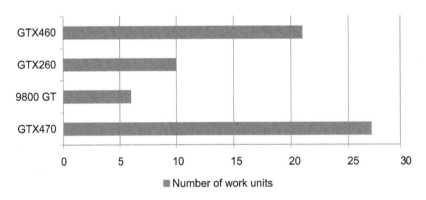

FIGURE 8.3

Distribution of work units to multiple GPUs.

some time to provide the GPU with additional work. In the example we have here, the CPU is simply checking the array against a set of expected values, but it could be doing a much slower operation such as loading the next work unit from disk. In this case we'd like the GPU to remain busy during this period also. For this we use a scheme called double buffering.

Double buffering works by having the GPU work with one buffer while the CPU is working with the other buffer. Thus, even while the CPU is processing one dataset, the GPU is still performing useful work, rather than waiting on the CPU. The CPU process may be something as simple as loading or saving data to disk. It might also include some additional processing and/or combination of data from multiple GPUs.

To do this we need to introduce another dimension to every array based on MAX_NUM_DEVICES. For example:

```
// Define N streams per GPU
cudaStream_t stream[MAX_NUM_DEVICES][MAX_NUM_STREAMS];
```

Then we have the option to support two or more streams per device. Using two streams per device has a small problem, in that if we allocate work units to GPUs with equal priority, they all get the same total number of work units. This, in practice, means we end up at the end of the work queue, still waiting on the slowest device. The solution to this is to allocate work units to the GPUs in proportion to their speed.

If you look back at Figure 8.3, you can see that the GT9800 is the slowest device. The GTX260 is approximately twice as fast, the GTX460 twice as fast again, and the GTX470 around 20% faster than the GTX460. Given that we want at least two streams to allow for double buffering, if we increase the number of streams allocated in proportion to the speed of the device, we get a work distribution that keeps all devices busy for about the same amount of time. We can do this with a simply array:

```
// Define the number of active streams per device
const u32 streams_per_device[MAX_NUM_DEVICES] =
{
 10, /* GTX470 */
 2, /* 9800 GT */
 4, /* GTX260 */
 8, /* 460 GTX */
};
```

Thus, initially we allocate 10 work units to device 0, the GTX470. However, we allocate only 2 work units to the GT9800, and so on. At the point we run out of work units each device has the queue length of approximately the value shown in the array. As this equates to approximately the same time, all devices finish within a short period of one another.

Here the list of the relative speeds of the various GPUs is constructed statically. If you always have the same hardware in the target machine, then this approach is fine. However, if you don't know what the target hardware is, you can do some initial timing runs and then complete such a table at runtime. The important point to remember is the minimum value in the list should always be at least 2 to achieve double buffering. The other values should be some multiple of 2, which reflects the relative timing to the slowest device.

One of the things that can be seen in the previous example, where we just used a single stream per GPU, is the GPU load varies. Sometimes it drops to 25% or less. In effect, we're seeing stalls in the GPU workload. Giving it multiple items to process without further CPU intervention increases the GPU load to an almost continuous 100% and all devices. This also has the benefit of reducing the sensitivity of the GPU kernel to CPU loading by other tasks, as it gives each GPU a large amount of work to do before the CPU *must* service it again.

In fact, if you run the single-stream kernel versus the multiple-stream kernel, we see a drop from 151 seconds to 139 seconds, an 8% decrease in execution time. The CPU side of the task is quite small, so it's able to relatively quickly fill the single entry queue. However, with a more complex CPU task, the overlapping of CPU time and GPU time becomes more important and you'll see this 8% value grow quite considerably.

As with any additional complexity you add to a program, it costs time to develop and can introduce additional errors. For most programs, using at least two streams per device will help improve the overall throughput enough to justify the additional programming effort.

MULTIPLE-NODE SYSTEMS

A single computer forms a single node on a network. Connect lots of single machines together and you have a cluster of machines. Typically, such a cluster will be composed of a set of rack-mounted nodes. The rack may then itself be interconnected with one or more additional racks.

The largest single GPU system in the world as of 2012, Tianhe-1A, consists of over 14,000 CPUs with over 7000 Tesla Fermi GPUs. These are split into 112 cabinets (racks), each of which contains 64 compute nodes. It runs a custom interconnect that supports up to 160 GB/s of communications bandwidth.

Now, in practice, most researchers and commercial organizations will never have access to something of this scale. However, what they typically will be able to purchase is a number networked nodes connected to a single 16 to 48 port gigabit Ethernet switch. This will typically take the form of a single 19-inch rack unit that is placed in an air conditioned computer room.

The ideal ratio of CPU cores to GPUs depends on the application and what percentage of the code is serial. If it is very little, then the simple one CPU core to multiple GPUs works well enough not to have to bother with any additional programming. However, if the CPU load is significant, it's likely this will limit the throughput. To overcome this we need to allocate less GPUs per CPU core, moving to a 1:2 or 1:1 ratio as the application demands. The simplest and most scalable method is via assigning one process to each set of CPU/GPUs on the node.

Once we move to this model it allows for much larger scaling, in that we can have two nodes, each of which have four GPUs and one or more CPU cores. If the problem can be further decomposed into eight blocks instead of four, then we should see a doubling of performance. In practice, as we have seen before, this will not happen due to the communications overhead. As the number of nodes grows, so does the impact of network communications on the problem. Therefore, you generally find a network of nodes with a higher number of GPUs per node will outperform a network with the same number of GPUs distributed to more nodes. Local node resources (disk, memory, CPU) can have a big impact on the best topology for a given problem.

To move to such a system, we need a communications mechanism that allows us to schedule work to a given CPU/GPUs set, regardless of where they are on the network. For this we'll use ZeroMQ, a very lightweight and fairly user-friendly communications library. Now we could use a sockets library, but this would be a lot more low level and for the most part harder to program correctly. We could also use MPI, which is a fairly standard protocol definition on Linux platforms, but generally needs a bit of setup and is more suited for very controlled environments. ZeroMQ handles errors well, allowing nodes to disappear and reappear without bringing the whole program down in a nasty mess.

ZeroMQ (or 0MQ) is a small, lightweight library that you simply link to. There are no compiler wrappers or the like, just a simple library. Once initialized, ZeroMQ runs in the background and allows the application to use synchronous or asynchronous communication without having to worry about buffer management. If you'd like to send a 10 MB file to another node, then send it, and ZeroMQ will internally handle any buffering. It makes a good interface for writing distributed applications. It is available free of charge from *http://www.zeromq.org/*.

ZeroMQ supports a number of transports between threads (INPROC), between processes (IPC), broadcast to many nodes (MULTICAST), and a network-based system (TCP). We'll make use of the latter, as it allows the most flexibility in terms of connecting multiple nodes anywhere on the network (or Internet).

The first task we need to cover with ZeroMQ is to set up a connection point. We'll be using the master/worker paradigm, as shown in Figure 8.4. This is where we have one master (server) that

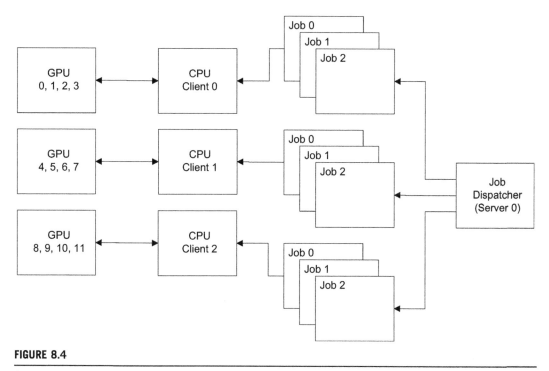

FIGURE 8.4

Single server, multiple clients.

distributes work packets to the worker (client) machines. Each client machine connects to a specific point on the network, provided by the server, and then waits for work to be given to it. Note that a client here is a CPU/GPUs set, not a physical node. Thus, a quad-core CPU with four GPUs attached with a 1:1 mapping of CPU cores to GPU devices would represent four clients. Equally, a quad-core CPU with a 1:4 mapping of CPU cores to GPU devices would appear as a single client.

In ZeroMQ terminology, the server will bind with a port, that is, it will create an access point. All clients will then connect to that known access point. At this point no application data has been transmitted. However, in the background, ZeroMQ will have set up an internal queue for each client that connects to the port.

The next step is to decide on a messaging pattern, the simplest being the request/reply pattern. This is similar to MPI in that we have a send and recv function, and that for every send, there must be a response. This is done as follows:

Client:

```
zmq::context_t context(1);
zmq::socket_t socket(context, ZMQ_REQ);
socket.connect("tcp://localhost:5555");
```

Server:

```
zmq::context_t context(1);
zmq::socket_t socket(context, ZMQ_REP);
socket.bind("tcp://*:5555");
```

The CPU client then maintains a work queue, usually at least two items to allow for GPU double buffering, plus at least one inbound and one outbound network message.

The protocol used in the application is that the CPU client connects to the server and asks the server for a batch of work. The server then responds with a range that it would like the client to work on. The client then does any work necessary on the CPU to generate data for that work packet. This might be, for example, generating all possible combinations for a given model value to test against some prediction.

```
// Host program to be called from main
__host__ void gpu_kernel_client(const u32 pid)
{
 printf("\nRunning as Client");

 // Init Network
 zmq::context_t context(1);
 zmq::socket_t socket(context, ZMQ_REQ);
 socket.connect("tcp://localhost:5555");

 // GPU params
 size_t chunk_size;
 u32 active_streams;
 u32 num_devices;
```

```
// Setup all available devices
setup_devices(&num_devices,
              &active_streams,
              &chunk_size);

u32 results_to_process;
get_work_range_from_server(pid,
                           &results_to_process,
                           &socket);

// Generate CPU data for input data
generate_cpu_data_range(0, results_to_process);

// Keep track of pending results
u32 pending_results = results_to_process;

// While there is still work to be completed
while (pending_results != 0)
{
 // Try to distribute work to each GPU
 u32 work_distributed = distribute_work(num_devices,
                                        chunk_size,
                                        pending_results);

 // Collect work from GPU
 u32 work_collected = collect_work(num_devices,
                                   chunk_size);

 // Decrement remaining count
 pending_results -= work_collected;

 // Post completed work units to server
 if (work_collected > 0)
 {
  send_completed_units_to_server(pid,
                                 chunk_size,
                                 &socket);
 }

 // If no work was distributed, or collected
 // and we've not finished yet then sleep
 if ( (work_distributed == 0) &&
      (work_collected == 0) &&
      (pending_results != 0) )
 {
  printf(".");
  fflush(stdout);
```

```
  snooze(100);
 }
}

// Print summary of how many each device processed
for (u32 device_num=0u;
     device_num < num_devices;
     device_num++)
{
 printf("%s processed: %u",
        device_prefix[device_num],
        num_processed[device_num]);
}

printf("\nTotal: src:%u dest:%u",
       unprocessed_idx, completed_idx);

cleanup_devices(num_devices);
}
```

The client code, after receiving the initial work from the server and generating the GPU work queue, runs over a loop until the work is complete. This loop distributes work to the available GPUs, processes work that is already complete, and posts any completed work to the server. Finally, if it was not able to do any of the above, it sleeps for 100 ms and then tries again. We then print a summary of how many work units each device processed when the program exits.

Notice the scheduling is different than it was in the previous example. We now need to have some additional buffer space to post out the completed units to the server and some time to push the data into the transmission queue. Thus, we no longer immediately reschedule work onto the GPU, but schedule additional work later. This allows for a simpler approach where we distribute work, collect any finished work, process it locally if necessary, and post it to the server.

```
__host__ u32 distribute_work(const int num_devices,
                             const size_t chunk_size,
                             u32 pending_results)
{
 u32 work_units_scheduled = 0;

 // Cycle through each device
 for (u32 device_num = 0;
      device_num < num_devices;
      device_num++)
 {
  u32 stream_num = 0;
  bool allocated_work = false;

  while ( (allocated_work == false) &&
          (stream_num < streams_per_device[device_num]) )
```

```
    {
      // If there is more work to schedule
      if (pending_results > 0)
      {
       // If the device is available
       if (processed_result[device_num][stream_num] == true)
       {
        // Allocate a job to the GPU
        push_work_into_queue(device_num,
                                chunk_size,
                                stream_num);

        // Set flag to say GPU has work pending
processed_result[device_num][stream_num] = false;

        // Keep track of how many new
        // units were issued
        work_units_scheduled++;

        // Move onto next device
        allocated_work = true;

        pending_results--;
       }
      }
      stream_num++;
     }
   }

   return work_units_scheduled;
}
```

Here we iterate over the `processed_results` array to see if any elements in the stream have been processed in the previous cycle and are now free again to be used. We then allocate the pending work such that one work unit it allocated per GPU device into an available stream slot.

```
__host__ void push_work_into_queue(const u32 device_num,
                                   const size_t chunk_size,
                                   const u32 stream_num)
{
 // No dynamic allocation of shared memory required
 const int shared_memory_usage = 0;

 // Define the number of threads and blocks to launch
 const int num_threads = 256;
 const int num_blocks = ((NUM_ELEM + (num_threads-1))
                            / num_threads);

 // Copy in the source data form the host queue
```

```
memcpy(cpu_src_data[device_num][stream_num],
       cpu_unprocessed_data[unprocessed_idx % MAX_IN_QUEUED_PACKETS],
       chunk_size);

// Processed this packet
unprocessed_idx++;

// Select the correct device
CUDA_CALL(cudaSetDevice(device_num));

// Push the start event into the stream
CUDA_CALL(cudaEventRecord(memcpy_to_start_event[device_num][stream_num], stream
[device_num][stream_num]));

// Copy a chunk of data from the CPU to the GPU
// asynchronous
CUDA_CALL(cudaMemcpyAsync(gpu_data[device_num][stream_num],
cpu_src_data[device_num][stream_num], chunk_size, cudaMemcpyHostToDevice, stream
[device_num][stream_num]));

// Push the start event into the stream
CUDA_CALL(cudaEventRecord(kernel_start_event[device_num][stream_num], stream
[device_num][stream_num]));

// Invoke the GPU kernel using the newly created
// stream - asynchronous invokation
gpu_test_kernel<<<num_blocks,
                  num_threads,
                  shared_memory_usage,
                  stream[device_num][stream_num]>>>
                  (gpu_data[device_num][stream_num],
                  kernel_iter);

 cuda_error_check(device_prefix[device_num],
                  "Failed to invoke gpu_test_kernel");

// Push the start event into the stream
CUDA_CALL(cudaEventRecord(memcpy_from_start_event[device_num][stream_num], stream
[device_num][stream_num]));

// Copy a chunk of data from the GPU to the CPU
// asynchronous
CUDA_CALL(cudaMemcpyAsync(cpu_dest_data[device_num][stream_num], gpu_data[device_num]
[stream_num], single_gpu_chunk_size, cudaMemcpyDeviceToHost, stream[device_num]
[stream_num]));

// Push the stop event into the stream
```

```
CUDA_CALL(cudaEventRecord(memcpy_from_stop_event[device_num][stream_num], stream
[device_num][stream_num]));

}
```

The `push_work_into_stream` function is much the same as before. However, it now accepts a `stream_num` parameter, allowing us to fill in any available slot in the stream. It also now copies data into CPU memory from `cpu_unprocessed_data`, an array of regular memory on the CPU host side. Note this is not the page-mapped host memory used by the GPU's aynchronous memory operations. The CPU host needs to be free to calculate/update this memory as needed without worrying about synchronizing it with the ongoing GPU kernels.

```
__host__ u32 collect_work(const int num_devices,
      const size_t chunk_size)
{
 // Keep track of the number of results processed
 u32 results_processed = 0;

 // Cycle through each device
 for (u32 device_num=0;
   device_num < num_devices;
   device_num++)
 {
 // Then cycle through streams
 for(u32 stream_num=0;
     stream_num < streams_per_device[device_num];
     stream_num++)
 {
  // If results are pending from this device
  if (processed_result[device_num][stream_num] == false)
  {
   // Try to process the data from the device
   processed_result[device_num][stream_num] = process_result(device_num, stream_num,
chunk_size);

   // If we were able to process the data
   if (processed_result[device_num][stream_num] == true)
   {
    // Increment the number this device
    // processed
    num_processed[device_num]++;

    // Increment this run's count
    results_processed++;
   }
  }
 }
 }
}
```

```
 return results_processed;
}
```

The `collect` result function simply iterates over all devices and each stream of every device and calls the `process_result` function to try to process any available results.

```
__host__ bool process_result(const u32 device_num,
                             const u32 stream_num,
                             const size_t chunk_size)
{
 bool result;

 bool stop_event_hit = (cudaEventQuery(memcpy_from_stop_event[device_num][stream_num])
== cudaSuccess);

 // Space is avaiable if network_out_idx is not
 // more than the total queue length behind
 bool output_space_avail = ((completed_idx - network_out_idx) <
MAX_OUT_QUEUED_PACKETS);

 // If the stop event has been hit AND
 // we have room in the output queue
 if (stop_event_hit && output_space_avail)
 {
  float time_copy_to_ms = 0.0F;
  float time_copy_from_ms = 0.0F;
  float time_kernel_ms = 0.0F;
  float time_exec_ms = 0.0F;

  // Select the correct device
  CUDA_CALL(cudaSetDevice(device_num));

  // Get the elapsed time between the copy
  // and kernel start
  CUDA_CALL(cudaEventElapsedTime(&time_copy_to_ms, memcpy_to_start_event[device_num]
[stream_num], kernel_start_event[device_num][stream_num]));

  // Get the elapsed time between the kernel start
  // and copy back start
  CUDA_CALL(cudaEventElapsedTime(&time_kernel_ms,
kernel_start_event[device_num][stream_num],
memcpy_from_start_event[device_num][stream_num]));

  // Get the elapsed time between the copy back start
  // and copy back start
  CUDA_CALL(cudaEventElapsedTime(&time_copy_from_ms,
memcpy_from_start_event[device_num][stream_num],
```

```
memcpy_from_stop_event[device_num][stream_num]));

  // Get the elapsed time between the overall start
  // and stop events
  CUDA_CALL(cudaEventElapsedTime(&time_exec_ms,
memcpy_to_start_event[device_num][stream_num],
memcpy_from_stop_event[device_num][stream_num]));

  // Print the elapsed time
  const float gpu_time = (time_copy_to_ms +
                          time_kernel_ms +
                          time_copy_from_ms);

  printf("%sCopy To  : %.2f ms",
        device_prefix[device_num], time_copy_to_ms);

  printf("%sKernel   : %.2f ms",
        device_prefix[device_num], time_kernel_ms);

  printf("%sCopy Back  : %.2f ms",
        device_prefix[device_num],
        time_copy_from_ms);

  printf("%sComponent Time : %.2f ms",
        device_prefix[device_num], gpu_time);

  printf("%sExecution Time : %.2f ms",
        device_prefix[device_num], time_exec_ms);
  fflush(stdout);

  // Data has now arrived in
  // cpu_dest_data[device_num]
  check_array( device_prefix[device_num],
              cpu_dest_data[device_num][stream_num],
              NUM_ELEM);

  // Copy results into completed work queue
  memcpy(cpu_completed_data[completed_idx % MAX_OUT_QUEUED_PACKETS],
    cpu_dest_data[device_num][stream_num],
    chunk_size);

  printf("\nProcessed work unit: %u", completed_idx);
  fflush(stdout);

  // Incremenet the destination idx
  // Single array per CPU
  completed_idx++;
```

```
   result = true;
  }
  else
  {
   result = false;
  }

  return result;
}
```

In the `process_results` function the two conditions for processing a stream are that the stream has completed, that is, that we have met the stop event on the stream, *and* that the output queue for transmission currently has a free slot. If both of these are not true, the function simply returns and does nothing.

Otherwise, the function collects some timing information and prints it. It then copies the received data to the output queue, thus freeing up the page-locked memory on the host and freeing up a stream slot on the GPU for subsequent use.

Finally, we look at what is necessary to send the data to the server.

```
__host__ void send_completed_units_to_server(
 const u32 pid,
 const size_t chunk_size,
 zmq::socket_t * socket)
{
 for (u32 packet=network_out_idx;
      packet < completed_idx;
      packet++)
 {
  // Define a client message
  CLIENT_MSG_T client_msg;
  client_msg.id.pid = pid;
  client_msg.id.ip = 0;
  client_msg.id.msg_type = 0;
  client_msg.id.msg_num = packet;
  memset(client_msg.data, 0, CLIENT_MSG_DATA_SIZE);

  SERVER_MSG_T server_msg;
  memset(&server_msg, 0, sizeof(SERVER_MSG_T) );

  // Create object to send to server
  zmq::message_t request(sizeof(CLIENT_MSG_T));
  zmq::message_t reply;

  // Copy in the output data
  memcpy(client_msg.data,
         cpu_completed_data[packet % MAX_OUT_QUEUED_PACKETS],
         chunk_size);

  // Copy the total message to ZEROMQ data area
```

```
memcpy( (void*) request.data(), &client_msg, sizeof(CLIENT_MSG_T) );

// Send to server
printf("\nSending data %u to server", packet);
socket->send(request);

// Free output buffer
network_out_idx++;

// Wait for a reply
socket->recv(&reply);

// Decode the reply
memcpy( &server_msg, (void*) reply.data(), sizeof(SERVER_MSG_T) );
printf("\nReceived acknowledge from server");
 }
}
```

To send a message with ZeroMQ we simply use the `zmq::message_t` constructor to create both a request and reply message. We then copy the associated element from the `cpu_completed_data` array into the payload area of the message, along with some header information, allowing the server to see who the sender was. We then post the message to the server and wait for an acknowledgment back from the server.

Now in terms of scheduling and workload, there are some caveats with this approach. The main issue is network loading and communication overhead. The amount of data we're sending on the network makes a huge difference regarding performance. The time to receive any inbound data, transform it on the CPU, and send it out again on the CPU must be smaller than the time taken for the GPU kernel to run. If not, then the application will be either CPU or network bound.

In the example, the server sends the client a range of data, the assumption being that the client knows how to process that data. This may be in terms of generating a dataset to work through, or loading some data from the local disk. What you need to avoid is simply sending the data itself to the client if at all possible. Make use of the local resources on the node, be it CPU, host memory, or local storage space, wherever possible.

Second, the output data is shipped in its entirety back to the server. The problem may be such that the output data is not a huge block of data, but simply a single value from, say, a reduction operation. Often it's then the input space that is large. However, if the input space can be partitioned and split out to N local disks, then the network traffic is really quite small and you really start to see scaling by using multiple GPU nodes.

CONCLUSION

We've looked at two examples of using multiple GPUs within a computer system. In the first one everything is contained in a single box or node. The second allows use of multiple nodes with multiple GPUs present on each node. We introduce the use of ZeroMQ as a simpler and more flexible alternative to the traditional MPI approach.

We use streams to implement a double-buffering system, meaning the GPU was always busy while the CPU was preparing the next data block and processing the previous one. We extended the use of streams from two streams to multiple streams to allow us to balance work between differing-speed GPU devices within a single node.

Using two or four GPUs per node opens up the possibility of doubling or even quadrupling the current throughput of a single application that is GPU bound. To grow this further you need to use multiple nodes and be crucially aware of the amount of data you are then communicating across the network. However, as systems like Tianhe-1A show us, you can scale to thousands of GPUs if your problem, and budget, allows.

Questions

1. The example given uses synchronous network communications, and specifically a send/acknowledge-based protocol. What are the advantages and disadvantages of this approach? How else might this be done and what benefit/cost would this bring?
2. What are some of the advantages and drawbacks of using threads versus processes when using multiple GPUs?
3. In converting the second example from ZeroMQ to MPI, what issues would you have to consider?

Answers

1. The synchronous model is the simplest one to work with and debug. However, in the same way that there are synchronous and asynchronous memory transfers to or from the GPU, we can operate in a synchronous or asynchronous model for communications. If the memory is pinned, a network controller can access it using DMA mode, which does not place any load onto the CPU. This has the advantage of freeing the CPU to do other tasks, but it adds the program complexity of managing another asynchronous device.

As for the send/acknowledge method, this is potentially very costly. You don't see it on a small local area network, but should the server get overloaded and take a long time to respond, the client work queue could stall. Simply increasing the number of streams per device would help, but there is an ultimate limit on the number of clients a *single* server can handle. There is also the latency of having to wait for the acknowledge message, which isn't really needed. The server could simply reissue work units that it did not receive. We can then use a post method at the client side. Combined with an asynchronous communication this lets the client get on with the client's work, offloading the communications work to the communications stack.

2. Threads are best used where there is a common data space between the threads, akin to using shared memory within an SM. Processes are best used where communication will be more formal, for example, using MPI. Processes allow easier scaling when using more than one node.

3. MPI is designed for closed systems, so a client that can drop out, reboot, and reappear can be problematic. MPI implementations typically have fixed size and limited buffers. Throwing too much data at a message will often crash the MPI stack. ZeroMQ is implicitly asynchronous, in that your message is copied to local storage and then pushed out to the network card by a background thread. It only blocks when its internal buffer reaches the high water mark. MPI

synchronous communication blocks immediately and its asynchronous communications requires the application data to remain persistent until MPI is done with it. This means less copying of data, but makes programming MPI somewhat more complex.

In terms of conversion, creating a ZeroMQ context is replaced with the `MPI_Init` call. Creating and binding to a socket in ZeroMQ is equivalent to the `MPI_Comm_size (MPI_COMM_WORLD)` call. Instead of using PIDs to identify a message (you need an IP plus a PID on multiple nodes) you have a simple `MPI_Comm_rank` call to get a unique ID across the whole system. The ZeroMQ `send` and `recv` calls are very similar to the `MPI_Send` and `MPI_Recv` calls. The only additional work you need to do on an MPI implementation is to remember to call `MPI_Finalize` at the end of the function, something that is not necessary with ZeroMQ.

For the more adventurous, the buffered, asynchronous communications inherent in ZeroMQ can be achieved using `MPI_Bsend` along with appropriate buffer management at the application level.

Note, as of the SDK 4.0, page-locked memory allocated by CUDA became accessible, by default, to other devices such as network cards. Thus, it's now possible to have the same page-locked memory used by both the network card and the GPU, eliminating unnecessary copies within host memory that were previously necessary.

Additionally, on Linux systems or with Fermi Tesla-based Windows systems, it's also possible to directly send data from the GPU to the network card or between GPUs without going via the host memory. This can greatly reduce the use of the limited PCI bus capacity to or from the host. This is not something we've covered here as it's not currently supported on all platforms. However, there is a peer-to-peer communication example in the SDK which we look at in detail in Chapter 10 for those wishing to make use of such functionality.

Optimizing Your Application

In this chapter we provide a detailed breakdown of the main areas that limit performance in CUDA. Each section contains small examples to illustrate the issues. They should be read in order. The previous chapters introduced you to CUDA and programming GPUs. The sections here assume you have read the previous chapters and are comfortable with the concepts introduced there, or are already familiar with CUDA and are specifically interested in techniques for improving execution speed of your programs.

This chapter is broken up into a number of strategies:

Strategy 1: Understanding the problem and breaking it down correctly into serial and parallel workloads.

Strategy 2: Understanding and optimizing for memory bandwidth, latency and cache usage.

Strategy 3: Understanding the implications of needing to transfer data to or from the host. A look at the effects of pinned and zero-copy memory and bandwidth limits on a selection of hardware.

Strategy 4: Understanding the threading and computational abilities in detail and how these impact performance.

Strategy 5: Where to look for algorithm implementations, with a couple of examples of optimization of some general-purpose algorithms.

Strategy 6: Focus on profiling and identifying where in your applications the bottlenecks are occurring and why.

Strategy 7: A look at how applications can tune themselves to the various hardware implementations out there.

STRATEGY 1: PARALLEL/SERIAL GPU/CPU PROBLEM BREAKDOWN

Analyzing the problem

This is the first step in considering if trying to parallelize a problem is really the correct solution. Let's look at some of the issues involved here.

Time

It's important to define what an "acceptable" time period is for the execution time of the algorithm you have in mind. Now acceptable does not have to mean the best time humanly possible. When considering optimization, you have to realize as a software professional, your time costs money, and if you work in the western world, your time is not cheap. The faster a program needs to execute, the more effort is involved in making this happen (Figure 9.1).

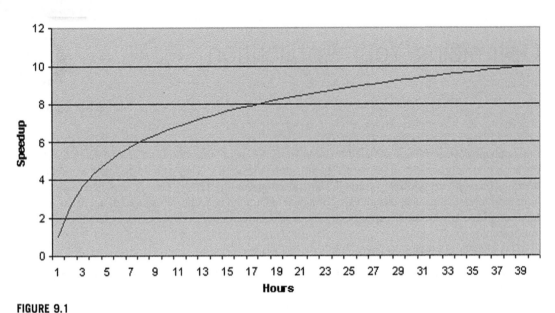

FIGURE 9.1

Programmer time versus speedup achieved.

You will usually find with any optimization activity there is a certain amount of so-called "low-hanging fruit." The changes required are easy and lead to a reasonable speedup. As these are removed, it becomes progressively harder to find optimizations and these require more complex restructuring, making them more costly in terms of time and the potential for errors they can introduce.

In most western countries, programming effort is quite expensive. Even if your programming time is free—for example, if you are student working on a project—time spent optimizing is still time that could be spent doing other activities. As engineers, we can sometimes get caught up in making things better than they need to be. Understand what is required and set a suitable goal.

In setting a suitable speedup goal, you have to be aware of what is reasonable, given a set of hardware. If you have 20 terabytes of data that needs to be processed in a few seconds, a single-GPU machine is just not going to be able to cope. You have exactly this sort of issue when you consider Internet search engines. They have to, within seconds, return a set of search results to the user. Yet at the same time, it used to be "acceptable" for their indexes to take several days to update—that is, the time taken for them to pick up new content. In this modern world, even this is considered slow. Thus, what is acceptable today may not be acceptable tomorrow, next month, or next year.

In considering what the acceptable time is, ask yourself how far away you currently are from this. If it's a factor of two or less, often it will be worth spending time optimizing the CPU implementation, rather than creating an entirely new, parallel approach to the problem. Multiple threads introduce all sorts of problems of dependencies, deadlock, synchronization, debugging, etc. If you can live with the serial CPU version, this may be a better solution in the short term.

Consider also the easy-fix solution to problems used for the past 30 or so years. Simply buy some faster hardware. Use profiling to identify where the application is spending it time to determine where it's bound. Is there an input/output (I/O) bottleneck, a memory bottleneck, or a processor bottleneck? Buy a high-speed PCI-E RAID card and use SATA 3/SAS SSD drives for I/O issues. Move to a socket 2011 system with a high clock rate on the memory, if memory bandwidth is an issue. If it's simply raw compute throughput, install an Extreme Edition or Black Edition processor with the highest clock rate you can buy. Purchase an out-of-the-box, liquid-cooled, Sandybridge K or X series overclocked processor solution. These solutions typically cost much less than $3,000–$6,000 USD, a budget you could easily spend on programming time to convert a program from a serial to a parallel program.

However, while this approach works well when you have a small amount of difference between where you are and where you want to be, it's not always a good approach. A high clock rate means high power consumption. The processor manufacturers have already abandoned that route in favor of multicore as the only long-term solution to providing more compute power. While the "buy new hardware" approach may work in the short term, it's not a long-term solution. Sometimes the hardware you have may not easily be changeable, because it's provided by a restrictive IT department, or because you have insufficient funds to purchase new hardware but lots of "free" programming time.

If you decide to go down the GPU route, which for many problems is a very good solution, then you should typically set your design goal to be around a 10× (ten times) improvement in execution time of the program. The actual amount you achieve depends on the knowledge of the programmers and the time available, plus a huge contribution from the next issue we'll talk about, how much parallelism there is in the application. At least a 2× or 3× speedup is a relatively easy goal, even for those new to CUDA.

Problem decomposition

The fundamental question here is simply this: Can the problem you have be broken down into chunks that can run in parallel; that is, is there an opportunity to exploit concurrency in the problem? If the answer is no, then the GPU is not the answer for you. You instead have to look at optimization techniques for the CPU, such as cache optimizations, memory optimizations, SIMD optimizations, etc. At least some of these we have covered on the GPU side in previous chapters and others are covered in this chapter. Many of these optimization techniques work very well on serial CPU code.

Assuming you are able to partition the problem into concurrent chunks, the question then is how many? One of the main limiting factors with CPU parallelization is that there is often just not enough large-granularity (or coarse-grained) parallel work to be done. GPUs run thousands of threads, so the problem needs to be decomposed into thousands of blocks, not just a handful of concurrent tasks as with the CPU.

The problem decomposition should always start with the data first and the tasks to be performed second. You should try to represent the problem in terms of the output dataset. Can you construct a formula that represents the value of a given output point in the dataset as a transformation of the input dataset *for that single point*? You may need more than one formula, for example, one for most data points and one for the data points around the edge of the problem space. If you can do this, then the transformation of a problem into the GPU space is relatively easy.

One of the issues with this type of approach is that you need to fully understand the problem for the best benefit. You can't simply peek at the highest CPU "hogs" and try to make them parallel. The real benefit of this approach comes from making the chain from the input data points to the output data points completely parallel. There may be parts of this chain where you could use 100,000 processors if you had the hardware and points where you are reduced to a few hundred processors. Rarely are any problems truly single threaded. It's just that as programmers, scientists, and engineers, this is the solution we may have learned many years ago at university. Thus, seeing the potential parallelism in a problem is often the first hurdle.

Now there are some problems where this single-output data point view is not practical—H264 video encoding, for example. In this particular problem, there are a number of stages defined, each of which defines a variable-length output data stream. However, there are aspects—filtering, in particular—within image encoding/processing that easily lend themselves to such approaches. Here the destination pixel is a function of N source pixels. This analogy works well in many scientific problems. The value of the forces of a given destination atom can be written as the sum of all the atoms that apply a force to the given destination atom. Where the input set is very large, simply apply a threshold or cutoff point such that those input data points that contribute very little are excluded from the dataset. This will contribute a small amount of error, but in some problems allows a huge section of the dataset to be eliminated from the calculation.

Optimization used to be about how to optimize the operations or functions being performed on the data. However, as compute capacity has increased hugely in comparison to memory bandwidth, it's now the data that is the primary consideration. Despite the fact GPUs have on the order of 5 to 10 times the memory bandwidth of CPUs, you have to decompose the problem such that this bandwidth can be used. This is something we'll talk about in the following section.

One final consideration here, if you plan to use multiple GPUs or multiple GPU nodes, is how to decompose the problem and the dataset over the processor elements. Communication between nodes will be *very* expensive in terms of computation cycles so it needs to be minimized and overlapped with computation. This is also something we'll touch on later.

Dependencies

A dependency is where some calculation requires the result of a previous calculation, be that some calculation in the problem domain or simply an array index calculation. In either case, the dependency causes a problem in terms of parallel execution.

Dependencies are seen in two main forms, where one element is dependent on one or more elements around it, or where there are multiple passes over a dataset and there exists a dependency from one pass to the next.

```
extern int a,c,d;
extern const int b;
extern const int e;

void some_func_with_dependencies(void)
{
  a = b * 100;
  c = b * 1000;
  d = (a + c) * e;
}
```

If you consider this example, you can see that both a and c have a dependency on b. You can also see that d has a dependency on both a and c. The calculation of a and c can be done in parallel, but the calculation of d requires the calculation of both a and c to have completed.

In a typical superscalar CPU, there are multiple independent pipelines. The independent calculations of a and c would likely be dispatched to separate execution units that would perform the multiply. However, the results of those calculations would be needed prior to being able to compute the addition operation for a and c. The result of this addition operation would also need to be available before the final multiplication operation could be applied.

This type of code arrangement allows for little parallelism and causes a number of stalls in the pipeline, as the results from one instruction must feed into the next. While stalled, the CPU and GPU would otherwise be idle. Clearly this is a waste, and both CPUs and GPUs use multiple threads to cover this problem.

On the CPU side, instruction streams from other virtual CPU cores fill in the gaps in the instruction pipeline (e.g., hyperthreading/Symmetrical Multi Threading or SMT). However, this requires that the CPU know from which thread the instruction in the pipeline belongs, which complicates the hardware. On the GPU, multiple threads are also used, but in a time-switching manner, so the latency of the arithmetic operations is hidden with little or no cost. In fact, on the GPU you need around 20 clocks to cover such latency. However, this latency need not come from another thread. Consider the following example:

```
extern int a,c,d,f,g,h,i,j;
extern const int b;
extern const int e;

void some_func_with_dependencies(void)
{
 a = b * 100;
 c = b * 1000;

 f = b * 101;
 g = b * 1001;

 d = (a + c) * e;
 h = (f + g) * e;

 i = d * 10;
 j = h * 10;
}
```

Here the code has been rearranged and some new terms introduced. Notice if you insert some independent instructions between the calculation of a and c and their use in d, you allow these calculations more time to complete before the result is obtained. The calculations of f, g, and h in the example are also overlapped with the d calculation. In effect, you are hiding the arithmetic execution latency through overlapping nondependent instructions.

One way of handling dependencies and introducing additional nondependent instructions is through a technique called loop fusion, as shown here.

```c
void loop_fusion_example_unfused(void)
{
 unsigned int i,j;

 a = 0;
 for (i=0; i<100; i++)  /* 100 iterations */
 {
  a + = b * c * i;
 }

 d = 0;
 for (j=0; j<200; j++)  /* 200 iterations */
 {
  d += e * f * j;
 }
}

void loop_fusion_example_fused_01(void)
{
 unsigned int i;   /* Notice j is eliminated */

 a = 0;
 d = 0;
 for (i=0; i<100; i++)  /* 100 iterations */
 {
  a += b * c * i;
  d += e * f * i;
 }

 for (i=100; i<200; i++) /* 100 iterations */
 {
  d += e * f * i;
 }
}

void loop_fusion_example_fused_02(void)
{
 unsigned int i;   /* Notice j is eliminated */

 a = 0;
 d = 0;
 for (i=0; i<100; i++)  /* 100 iterations */
 {
  a += b * c * i;
  d += e * f * i;
  d += e * f * (i*2);
 }
}
```

In this example, we have two independent calculations for results a and d. The number of iterations required in the second calculation is more than the first. However, the iteration space of the two calculations overlaps. You can, therefore, move part of the second calculation into the loop body of the first, as shown in function `loop_fusion_example_fused_01`. This has the effect of introducing additional, nondependent instructions, plus reducing the overall number of iterations, in this example, by one-third. Loop iterations are not free, as they need a loop iteration value and cause a branch. Thus, discarding a third of them brings us a significant benefit in terms of reducing the number of instructions executed.

In the `loop_fusion_example_fused_02` we can further fuse the two loops by eliminating the second loop and fusing the operation into the first, adjusting the loop index accordingly.

Now in the GPU it's likely these loops would be unrolled into threads and a single kernel would calculate the value of a and d. There are a number of solutions, but the most likely is one block of 100 threads calculating a with an additional block of 200 threads calculating d. By combining the two calculations, you eliminate the need for an additional block to calculate d.

However, there is one word of caution with this approach. By performing such operations, you are reducing the overall amount of parallelism available for thread/block-based scheduling. If this is already only a small amount, this will hurt the execution time. Also be aware that kernels, when fused, will usually consume more temporary registers. This may limit the amount of fusion you can practically achieve, as it will limit the number of blocks scheduled on an SM due to increased register usage.

Finally, you should consider algorithms where there are multiple passes. These are typically implemented with a number of sequential kernel calls, one for each pass over the data. As each pass reads and writes global data, this is typically very inefficient. Many of these algorithms can be written as kernels that represent a single or small set of destination data point(s). This provides the opportunity to hold data in shared memory or registers and considerably increases the amount of work done by a given kernel, compared with the number of global memory accesses. This will vastly improve the execution times of most kernels.

Dataset size

The size of the dataset makes a huge difference as to how a problem can be handled. These fall into a number of categories on a typical CPU implementation:

- Dataset within L1 cache (~16 KB to 32 KB)
- Dataset within L2 cache (~256 KB to 2 MB)
- Dataset within L3 cache (~512 K to 20 MB)
- Dataset within host memory on one machine (~1 GB to 128 GB)
- Dataset within host-persistent storage (~500 GB to ~20 TB)
- Dataset distributed among many machines (>20 TB)

With a GPU the list looks slightly different:

- Dataset within L1 cache (~16 KB to 48 KB)[1]
- Dataset within L2 cache (~512 KB to 1536 MB)[2]

---

[1]L1 cache is only available from the Fermi architecture onwards and is configurable between 16 KB and 48 KB. L1 cache on GT200/G80 is only via texture memory that is 24 KB in size.
[2]L2 cache is zero K on compute 1.x devices, up to 768 K on compute 2.x (Fermi) devices and up to 1536 K on compute 3.x (Kepler) devices.

- Dataset within GPU memory (~512 K to 6 GB)
- Dataset within host memory on one machine (~1 GB to 128 GB)
- Dataset within host-persistent storage (~500 GB to ~20 TB)
- Dataset distributed among many machines (>20 TB)

For very small problem sets, adding more CPU cores to a particular problem can result in a superscalar speedup. This is where you get more than a linear speedup by adding more CPU cores. What is happening in practice is that the dataset on each processor core is now smaller. With a 16-core CPU, the problem space is typically reduced by a factor of 16. If this now moves the problem from memory to the L3 cache or the L3 cache to the L2 cache, you see a very impressive speedup, not due to parallelism, but due instead to the much higher-memory bandwidth of the associated cache. Obviously the same applies when you transition from the L2 cache to holding the problem entirely in the L1 cache.

The major question for GPUs is not so much about cache, but about how much data can you hold on a single card. Transferring data to and from the host system is expensive in terms of compute time. To hide this, you overlap computation with data transfers. On the more advanced cards, you can do a transfer in and a transfer out at the same time. However, for this to work you need to use pinned memory on the host. As pinned memory can't be swapped out by the virtual memory management system, it has to be real DRAM memory on the host.

On a 6 GB Tesla system you might have allocated this as a 1 GB input buffer, a 1 GB output buffer, and 4 GB compute or working memory. On commodity hardware, you have up to 2 GB available, so much less to work with, although some commodity cards support up to 4 GB of global memory.

On the host side, you need at least as much memory as you pin for the input and output buffers. You typically have up to 24 GB available (6 DIMMs at 4 GB) on most I7 Nehalem platforms, 32 GB (8 DIMMs at 4 GBs) on Sandybridge–EP, and 16 GB on AMD platforms (4 DIMMs at 4 GB). As you'd typically pin only 2 GB maximum, you easily have room to support multiple GPUs. Most systems have support for at least two GPU cards. Four physical cards is the practical limit for a top-end system in one box.

When the problem size is much larger than the host memory size, you have to consider the practical limits of the storage capacity on a single host. Multiterabyte disks can allow node storage into the tens of terabytes. Most motherboards are equipped with six or more SATA connectors and 4 TB disks are readily available. Disks are easily transportable if the dataset is to be captured in some remote area. Next-day courier can often be the fastest way to transfer such data between sites.

Finally, when you cannot fit the dataset on a single machine, be it from compute, memory, storage, or power requirements, you have to look at multiple nodes. This brings you to the realm of internode communication. Internode communication is expensive in terms of time, at least an order of magnitude slower than any internal communication of data. You also have to learn another set of APIs, so this step is really best avoided if the problem can be contained to a single node.

Resolution

Consider the question of what can be done with 10 times or 50 times as much processing power. An existing problem that previously took one hour to resolve can be done in just over a minute. How does this change the questions that can be asked with a given dataset? What can now be done in real time or near real time that was impossible in the past? The previous batch submission problem is now an interactive problem.

Such a change allows for a step back from the problem, to consider how else it might be approached. Are there algorithms that were discarded in the past because they were too computationally expensive? Can you now process far more data points, or data points to a higher resolution, to produce a more accurate result? If you were previously happy with a runtime of a few hours or a day because that let you get on with other tasks, does increasing the resolution of the problem appeal more than the speedup? What does a more accurate result gain in your problem domain?

In finance applications, if your mathematical model of events is running ahead of the main market players, then you can react to changes faster than others, which can directly translate into making a better return on trading activities.

In medical applications, being able to present the doctor with the result of a test before the patient has finished getting dressed and left allows much more efficient use of both the doctor's and patient's time as it avoids repeat appointments.

In simulation applications, not having to wait a long time allows a much larger problem space to be explored within a given timeframe. It also allows for speculative execution. This is where you ask the system to explore all values of x between n and m in a given dataset. Equally, you might explore variables in the 2D or 3D space. With complex problems or a nonlinear system it's not always clear what the optimal solution is, especially when changing one parameter impacts many other parameters. It may be quicker to simply explore the problem space and observe the result than it is to have an expert try to sit down and work out the optimal solution. This brute-force approach is remarkably effective and will often come up with solutions the "experts" would not have considered.

As a student you can now kick off a problem between lectures on your personal desktop super-computer, rather than submit a job to the university machine and wait a day for it to run, only to find out it crashed halfway through the job. You can prototype solutions and come up with answers far quicker than your non-CUDA-literate peers. Think what you could cover if their batch jobs take a day and yours are done locally in an hour.

Identifying the bottlenecks

Amdahl's Law

Amdahl's Law is often quoted in work on parallel architecture. It's important because it tells us that, while serial elements of execution remain in the data flow, they will limit any speedup we can achieve.

Consider the simple case where we have 50% of the program's execution time spent on a section that could run in parallel and 50% that must be done serially. If you had an infinitely fast set of parallel processing units and you reduced the parallel aspect of the program down to zero time, you would still have the 50% serial code left to execute. The maximum possible speedup in this case is $2\times$, that is, the program executes in half the time period it did before. Not very impressive, really, given the huge amount of parallel processing power employed.

Even in the case where we have 90% of the program that could be parallelized, we still have the 10% serial code that remains. Thus, the maximum speedup is $9\times$, or nine times faster than the original, entirely serial, program.

The only way to scale a program infinitely is to eliminate all serial bottlenecks to program execution. Consider the diagram in Figure 9.2, where all the squares represent data items that need to be processed.

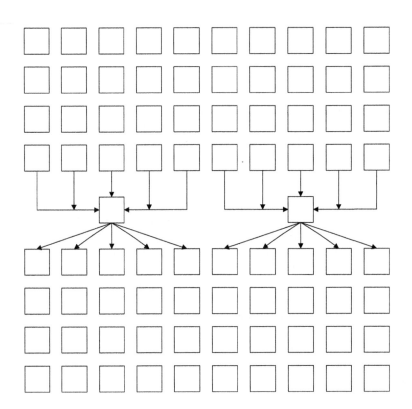

FIGURE 9.2

Data flow bottlenecks.

In this example, there are 10 threads, each processing one column of the data. In the center is a dependency, and thus all the threads must contribute their existing result to a single value before proceeding.

Imagine, for one moment, this is a field of crops, with each column a line of crops. Each thread is like a combine harvester, moving down the columns and collecting crops at each square. However, at the center of the field there is a wall with two gates.

With 1 or even 2 combine harvesters, the gates pose no problem and each combine harvester passes from one field to another. With 10 combine harvesters, one per column, getting each one through the gate takes time and slows down everyone in the process. This is one of the reasons why it's far more efficient to have large, open fields, rather than smaller, bounded ones.

So how is this relevant to software? Each gate is like a serial point in the code. The program is doing well, churning through the chunks of work, and then all of a sudden it hits a serial point or synchronization point and everything backs up. It's the same as everyone trying to leave the parking lot at the same time through a limited number of exits.

The solution to this type of problem is to parallelize up the bottlenecks. If we have 10 gates in the field or 10 exits from the parking lot, there would be no bottleneck, just an orderly queue that would complete in N cycles.

When you consider algorithms like histograms, you see that having all threads add to the same set of bins forms exactly this sort of bottleneck. This is often done with atomic operations, which effectively introduce serial execution to a set of parallel threads. If, instead, you give every thread a set of its own bins and then add these sets together later, you remove the serialization bottleneck.

Consider carefully in your code where you have such bottlenecks and how these might be eliminated. Often they will limit the maximum scaling available to your application. While this may not be an issue with two or even four CPU cores, with GPU code you need to think about tens of thousands of parallel threads.

Profiling

Profiling is one of the most useful tasks in identifying where you are today and knowing where you should spend your time. Often people think they know where the bottlenecks are, then go off and optimize that routine, only to find it makes 1% or 2% difference to the application's overall execution time.

In modern software development, there are usually many teams working on various aspects of a software package. It may not be possible to keep in contact with everyone who touches the software, especially in larger teams. Often what you may think is the bottleneck is not really that important.

Optimization should be based on hard numbers and facts, not speculation about what "might" be the best place to apply the software effort in terms of optimization. NVIDIA provides two good tools, CUDA Profiler and Parallel Nsight, that provide profiling information.

Profilers reveal, through looking at hardware counters, where the code spends it time, and also the occupancy level of the GPU. They provide useful counters such as the number of coalesced reads or writes, the cache hit/miss ratio, branch divergence, warp serialization, etc. The CUDA Memcheck tool is also very useful in identifying inefficient usage of memory bandwidth.

Having done an initial run using the profiler, you should first look at the routine in which the code spends the most *total* time. Typical unoptimized programs spend most of their time in a small section of the code. Optimizing the small section is the key to efficient use of your time and profiling is the key to identifying that code section.

Of course once this has been optimized as best as it can be, it's then progressively more and more time consuming to provide further speedups without a complete redesign. Measure the speedup and know when the time you're spending is no longer providing a good return on that effort.

Parallel Nsight is a very useful tool in this regard as it provides a number of default "experiments." That shed light on what your kernels are actually doing. Some off the more useful information you can take from the experiments is shown in Figure 9.3.

The first experiment is the CUDA Memory Statistics, which provides a nice graphical view of how the caches are laid out and the bandwidth being achieved in the different parts of the device. We used this in the AES example in chapter 7.

This particular example (see Figure 9.4) is taken from the odd/even sort we'll look at a little later. What is interesting to note are the cache ratios. As we're getting a 54% hit ratio in the L1 cache, we're achieving an average throughput of 310 GB/s to global memory, in the order of double the actual bandwidth available from global memory. It also lists the number of transactions, which is important. If we can lower the number of transactions needed, through better coalescing and/or issuing larger reads/writes, we can significantly boost memory throughput.

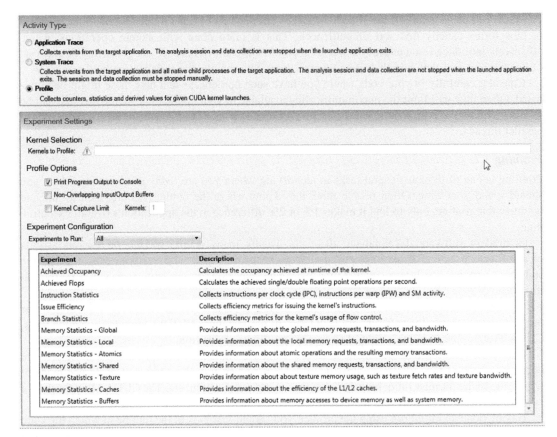

FIGURE 9.3

Parallel Nsight experiments.

The other important experiment is occupancy rates (see Figure 9.5). In this experiment, notice the Achieved occupancy column and in particular the number of Active Warps. As this is a compute 2.0 device, we can have up to 48 warps resident on a single SM. The achieved occupancy, as opposed to the theoretical occupancy, is the measured value of what was actually achieved. This will usually be significantly less than the theoretical maximum. Notice also that any limiting factor will be highlighted in red, in this case the number of blocks per SM at six. The "occupancy" graphs tab allows you to understand this in somewhat more detail. It's an extract from the occupancy calculation spreadsheet provided with the CUDA SDK.

The cause of this limit is actually the number of threads. Dropping this from 256 to 192 would allow the hardware to schedule eight blocks. As this kernel has synchronization points, having more blocks available may introduce a better instruction mix. There will also be more warps that are able to run due because they are not waiting at the synchronization point.

In practice, making this change helps quite significantly in terms of timing. It improves occupancy from 98.17% to 98.22%, which is marginal at best. However, the execution time drops significantly,

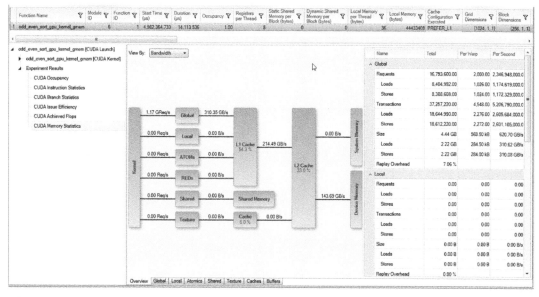

FIGURE 9.4

Parallel Nsight memory overview.

from 14 ms, to just 10 ms. The answer to this is in the reason this happens is memory usage. With 192 threads per block, we're accessing a smaller range of addresses which increases the locality of the accesses and consequently improves cache utilization. The total number of memory transactions needed by each SM drops by about one-quarter. Consequently, we see a proportional drop in execution time.

Grouping the tasks for CPU and GPU

Dr. M. Fatica from NVIDIA gave a great talk at GTC2010 concerning how Linpack had been optimized for GPUs. Linpack is a benchmark based on linear algebra. It is used in the Top500 supercomputer benchmark (*www.top500.org*) to benchmark the various supercomputers around the world. One interesting fact from this talk was the GPU used at that time, a Fermi Tesla C2050 card, produced around 350 gigaflops of DGEMM (double-precision matrix multiply) performance. The CPU used produced around 80 gigaflops. The contribution of 80 gigaflops is a little under one-quarter of the GPU contribution, so not something that can be ignored. A quarter or so extra performance goes a long way to reducing execution time.

In fact, the best applications tend to be those that play to the strengths of both the CPU *and* the GPU and split the data accordingly. The CPU must be considered in any GPU-based optimization, because it's the total application time that is important. If you have a four-, six-, or eight-core CPU and one core is busy handling a GPU application, why not use the other cores to also work on the problem? The more cores you have available, the higher the potential gain is by offloading some work to the CPU.

If we say a CPU core can handle work at one-tenth the rate of the GPU, then with just three CPU cores, you're gaining a 30% additional throughput. If you had an eight-core device, potentially this is a 70% gain in performance, which is almost the same as having two GPUs working in tandem. In

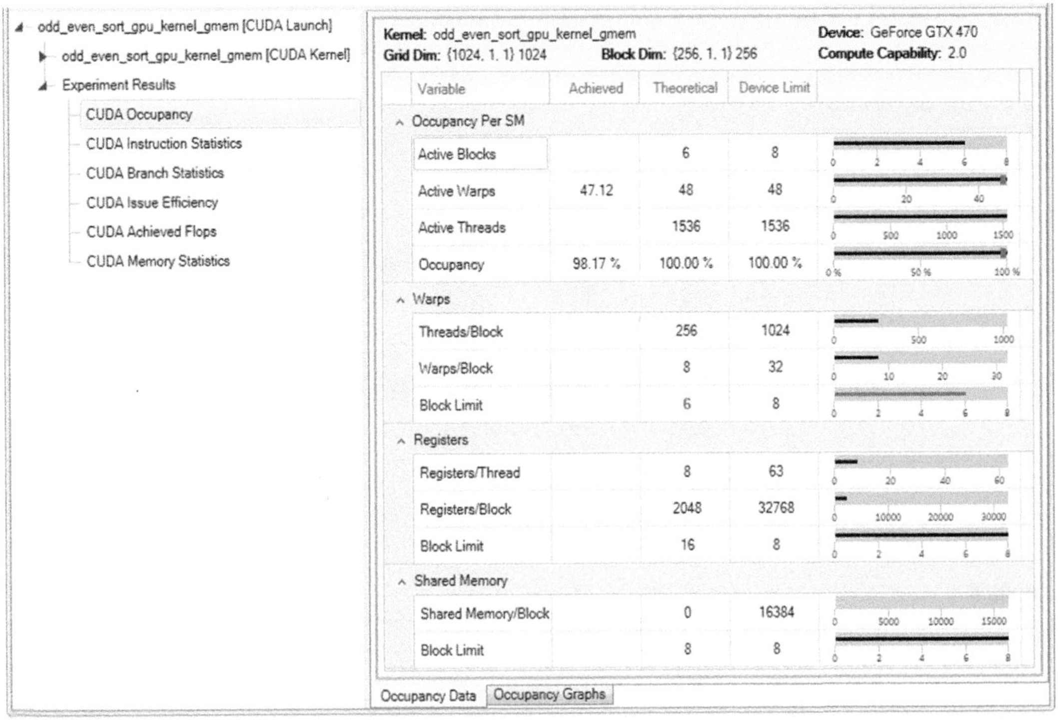

		odd_even_sort_gpu_kernel_gmem [CUDA Launch]
	▶	odd_even_sort_gpu_kernel_gmem [CUDA Kernel]
▲		Experiment Results
		CUDA Occupancy
		CUDA Instruction Statistics
		CUDA Branch Statistics
		CUDA Issue Efficiency
		CUDA Achieved Flops
		CUDA Memory Statistics

Kernel: odd_even_sort_gpu_kernel_gmem
Grid Dim: {1024, 1, 1} 1024   **Block Dim:** {256, 1, 1} 256
Device: GeForce GTX 470
Compute Capability: 2.0

Variable	Achieved	Theoretical	Device Limit	
▲ Occupancy Per SM				
Active Blocks		6	8	0 2 4 6 8
Active Warps	47.12	48	48	0 20 40
Active Threads		1536	1536	0 500 1000 1500
Occupancy	98.17 %	100.00 %	100.00 %	0% 50% 100%
▲ Warps				
Threads/Block		256	1024	0 500 1000
Warps/Block		8	32	0 10 20 30
Block Limit		6	8	0 2 4 6 8
▲ Registers				
Registers/Thread		8	63	0 20 40 60
Registers/Block		2048	32768	0 10000 20000 30000
Block Limit		16	8	0 2 4 6 8
▲ Shared Memory				
Shared Memory/Block		0	16384	0 5000 10000 15000
Block Limit		8	8	0 2 4 6 8

Occupancy Data | Occupancy Graphs

FIGURE 9.5

Parallel Nsight occupancy data.

practice, however, often other constraints might limit the overall speed, such as memory, network, or I/O bandwidth. However, even so, you're likely to see a significant speedup where the application is not already bound by one of these constraints on the host side.

Of these constraints, I/O is an interesting one, because introducing more CPU threads or processes can often significantly improve the overall I/O throughput. This may seem a strange statement, as surely the physical limits to and from an I/O device dictate the speed? On modern machines with large amounts of memory, most I/O is in fact cached. Therefore, I/O can be more about moving data in memory than it is about moving to or from devices. A decent RAID controller has its own processor to do the I/O operations. Multiple CPU cores allow for multiple independent memory transfers, which often provide a higher overall bandwidth than a single CPU core.

Separate CPU process or threads can create a separate GPU context and launch their own kernel onto the GPU. These additional kernels are then queued within the GPU for execution. When available resources become free the kernel is executed. If you look at the typical GPU usage you see that shown in Figure 9.6.

Notice there is significant idle time on both the GPU and the CPU. Idle time on the GPU is more expensive, as it's typically 10 times more useful than the CPU time. Tools such as Parallel Nsight allow you to display just such a timeline and you'll be amazed to see just how much idle time certain kernels can create.

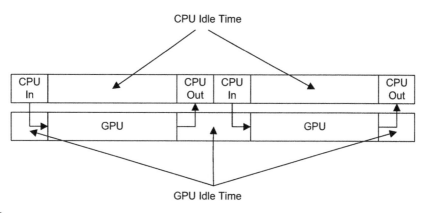

FIGURE 9.6

CPU and GPU idle time.

By placing multiple kernels onto a single GPU, these kernels then slot into the empty slots. This increases, marginally, the latency of the first set of kernels but greatly improves the overall throughput of the application. In a lot of applications, there can be as much as 30% idle time. Just consider what a typical application will do. First, fetch data from somewhere, typically a slow I/O device like a hard drive. Then transfer the data to the GPU and sit and wait until the GPU kernel is complete. When it's complete, the host transfers the data off the GPU. It then saves it somewhere, usually to slow I/O storage, fetches the next data block, and so on.

While the GPU is executing the kernel, why not fetch the next data block from the slow I/O device, so it's ready when the GPU kernel has completed? This is, in effect, what happens when you execute multiple processes. The I/O device blocks the second process, while fetching data for the first. When the first process is transferring data and invoking the kernel, the second process is accessing the I/O hardware. It then does a transfer, while process one is computing and the kernel invocation of the second process is queued. When the transfer back to the host for process one starts, the kernel from process two also starts executing. Thus, with the introduction of just a couple of processes, you have neatly overlapped the I/O, CPU, GPU, and transfer times, gaining a significant improvement in overall throughput. See the stream example in Chapter 8 for a detailed explanation of this.

Note that you can achieve the same results using threads or processes. Threads allow the application data to share a common data area and provide faster synchronization primitives. Processes allow for processor affinity, where you lock a process to a given CPU core, which can often improve performance because it allows for better core-specific cache reuse. The choice depends largely on how much, if any, synchronization is needed between the CPU tasks and if you want to have separate memory spaces or a single shared memory space.

The other aspect of the CPU/GPU decision is knowing how best to split the task. CPUs are great at serial problems, where the data is sparsely distributed, or where the dataset is small. However, with a typical 10:1 ratio of performance on the GPU to the CPU, you have to be careful that you will not be holding up the GPU. For this reason, many applications simply use the CPU to load and store data. This can sometimes fully load a single core on the CPU, depending on how much computation time is required on the GPU.

One usage you sometimes see a CPU being used for is the final stages of a reduction. A reduction operation typically reduces itself by a factor of two on every iteration of the reduction. If you start out with a million elements, within six iterations you are starting to hit the maximum number of schedulable threads on a GPU. Within a few more iterations, several of the SMs are idle. With the GT200 and prior generation of hardware, kernels were not overlapped, so the kernel had to continue to iterate down to the final elements before it freed up the idle SMs to do more work.

Thus, one optimization when a certain threshold is reached, is to forward the remaining part of the computation to the CPU to complete. If the CPU was in fact idle anyway, and the remaining data being transferred is not huge, this strategy can show significant gains over waiting for the GPU to complete the entire reduction. With Fermi, NVIDIA addressed this issue, allowing those idle SMs to start work on the next queued kernel. However, for the SM to become idle, it's necessary for all the thread blocks to have completed. Some nonoptimal kernels will have one or more active threads, even at the final levels of the reduction, which pins the kernel to the SM until the complete reduction is done. With algorithms like reduction, be sure you are reducing the number of active warps per iteration, not just the number of active threads.

Section summary

- Understand the problem and define your speedup goal in the context of the programming time and skills available to you.
- Identify the parallelism in the problem and think about how to best to allocate this between the CPU and one or more GPUs.
- Consider what is more important, a lower execution time or processing the data to a higher resolution.
- Understand the implication of any serial code sections and think about how these might best be handled.
- Profile your application to ensure your understanding reflects the actual reality. Repeat your earlier analysis if appropriate with your enhanced understanding.

STRATEGY 2: MEMORY CONSIDERATIONS

Memory bandwidth

Memory bandwidth and latency are key considerations in almost all applications, but especially so for GPU applications. Bandwidth refers to the amount of data that can be moved to or from a given destination. In the GPU case we're concerned primarily about the global memory bandwidth. Latency refers to the time the operation takes to complete.

Memory latency is designed to be hidden on GPUs by running threads from other warps. When a warp accesses a memory location that is not available, the hardware issues a read or write request to the memory. This request will be automatically combined or coalesced with requests from other threads in the same warp, provided the threads access adjacent memory locations and the start of the memory area is suitably aligned.

The size of memory transactions varies significantly between Fermi and the older versions. In compute 1.x devices (G80, GT200), the coalesced memory transaction size would start off at 128 bytes per memory access. This would then be reduced to 64 or 32 bytes if the total region being accessed by the coalesced threads was small enough and within the same 32-byte aligned block. This memory was not cached, so if threads did not access consecutive memory addresses, it led to a rapid drop off in memory bandwidth. Thus, if thread 0 reads addresses 0, 1, 2, 3, 4, ..., 31 and thread 1 reads addresses

32, 32, 34, ..., 63, they will not be coalesced. In fact, the hardware will issue one read request of at least 32 bytes for each thread. The bytes not used will be fetched from memory and simply be discarded. Thus, without careful consideration of how memory is used, you can easily receive a tiny fraction of the actual bandwidth available on the device.

The situation in Fermi and Kepler is much improved from this perspective. Fermi, unlike compute 1.x devices, fetches memory in transactions of either 32 or 128 bytes. A 64-byte fetch is not supported. By default every memory transaction is a 128-byte cache line fetch. Thus, one crucial difference is that access by a stride other than one, but within 128 bytes, now results in cached access instead of another memory fetch. This makes the GPU model from Fermi onwards considerably easier to program than previous generations.

One of the key areas to consider is in the number of memory transactions in flight. Each memory transaction feeds into a queue and is individually executed by the memory subsystem. There is a certain amount of overhead with this. It's less expensive for a thread to issue a read of four floats or four integers in one pass than to issue four individual reads. In fact, if you look at some of the graphs NVIDIA has produced, you see that to get anywhere near the peak bandwidth on Fermi and Kepler you need to adopt one of two approaches. First, fully load the processor with warps and achieve near 100% occupancy. Second, use the 64-/128-bit reads via the `float2`/`int2` or `float4`/`int4` vector types and your occupancy can be much less but still allow near 100% of peak memory bandwidth. In effect, by using the vector types you are issuing a smaller number of larger transactions that the hardware can more efficiently process. You also introduce a certain amount of instruction-level parallelism through processing more than one element per thread.

However, be aware that the vector types (`int2`, `int4`, etc.) introduce an implicit alignment of 8 and 16 bytes, respectively. The data must support this, so for example, you cannot cast a pointer to `int` from array element `int[5]` to `int2*` and expect it to work correctly. In such cases you're better off performing back-to-back 32-bit reads or adding some padding to the data structure to allow aligned access. As we saw when optimizing the sample sort example, a value of four elements per thread often provides the optimal balance between additional register usage, providing increased memory throughput and opportunity for the processor to exploit instruction-level parallelism.

Source of limit

Kernels are typically limited by two key factors, memory latency/bandwidth and instruction latency/ bandwidth. Optimizing for one when the other is the key limiter will result in a lot of effort and very little return on that effort. Therefore, being able to understand which of these two key factors is limiting performance is critical to knowing where to direct your efforts.

The simplest way in which you can see where the balance of the code lies is to simply comment out all the arithmetic instructions and replace them with a straight assignment to the result. Arithmetic instructions include any calculations, branches, loops, etc. If you have a one-to-one mapping of input values to calculated outputs, this is very simple and a one-to-one assignment works well. Where you have a reduction operation of one form or another, simply replace it with a sum operation. Be sure to include all the parameters read from memory into the final output or the compiler will remove the apparently redundant memory reads/writes. Retime the execution of the kernel and you will see the approximate percentage of time that was spent on the arithmetic or algorithmic part. If this percentage is very high, you are arithmetically bound. Conversely, if very little changed on the overall timing, you are memory bound.

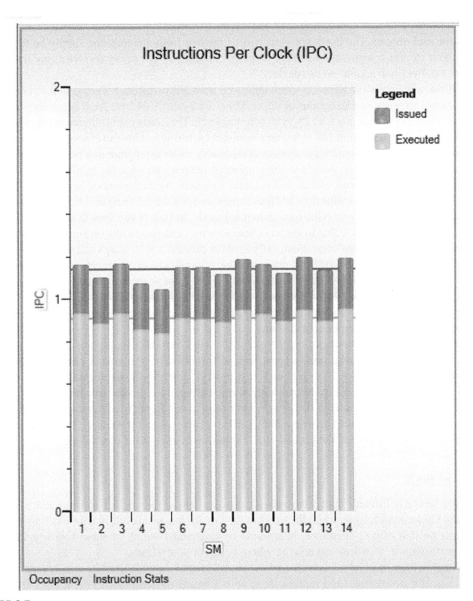

FIGURE 9.7

High instruction reissue rate.

With the arithmetic code still commented out, run the kernel using Parallel Nsight, using the Analysis function and the Profile setting. Examine the instruction statistics it produces (Figure 9.7). If the bar graph contains a significant amount of blue, then the kernel memory pattern is displaying poor coalescing and the GPU has to serialize the instruction stream to support scattered memory reads or writes.

If this is the case, is it possible to rearrange the memory pattern so the GPU can coalesce the memory access pattern by thread? Remember, to do this, thread 0 has to access address 0, thread 1 address 1, thread 2 address 2, and so on. Ideally, your data pattern should generate a column-based access pattern by thread, not a row-based access. If you can't easily rearrange the data pattern, can you rearrange the thread pattern such that you can use them to load the data into shared memory before accessing the data? If so, you don't have to worry about coalescing the reads when accessing them from shared memory.

Is it possible to expand the number of elements of the output dataset that are processed by a single thread? This will often help both memory- and arithmetic-bound kernels. If you do this, do it without introducing a loop into the thread, but by duplicating the code. If the code is nontrivial, this can also be done as a device function or a macro. Be sure to hoist the read operations up to the start of the kernel, so that the read operations have finished fetching data before they are needed. This will increase register usage, so be sure to monitor the number of warps being scheduled to see it does not suddenly drop off.

With arithmetic-bound kernels, look at the source code and think about how this would be translated into assembly (PTX) code. Don't be afraid to have a look at the actual PTX code being generated. Array indexes can often be replaced with pointer-based code, replacing slow multiplies with much faster additions. Divide or multiply instructions that use a power of 2 can be replaced with much faster right and left shift operations, respectively. Anything that is constant within a loop body, an invariant, should be moved outside the loop body. If the thread contains a loop, does unrolling the loop speed up things (it usually does)? What loop unrolling factor works best? We look at these optimization strategies in detail a little later in this chapter.

Are you using single- or double-precision floats in reality, and what did you want to use? Look out for floating-point constants without an F postfix, which the compiler will treat as double precision. Do you really need 32 bits of precision in all of the calculations? Try the `-use_fast_math` compiler switch and see if the results are still accurate enough for your needs. This switch enables 24-bit floating-point arithmetic, which can be significantly quicker than the standard IEEE 32-bit floating-point math logic.

Finally, are you testing speed with the "release" version of the code? As we saw in some of the examples earlier, this alone can increase performance by 15% or more due to compiler optimizations.

Memory organization

Getting the memory pattern correct for a GPU is often the key consideration in many applications. CPU programs typically arrange the data in rows within memory. While Fermi and Kepler will tolerate noncoalesced reads and writes, as we mentioned earlier, compute 1.x devices will not. You have to try and arrange the memory pattern such that access to it by consecutive threads will be in columns. This is true of both global memory and shared memory. This means for a given warp (32 threads) thread 0 should access address offset 0, thread 1 address offset 1, thread 2 address offset 2, etc. Think about the fetch to global memory.

However, assuming you have an aligned access, 128 bytes of data will come in from global memory at a time. With a single float or integer per thread, all 32 threads in the warp will be given exactly one element of data each.

Note the `cudaMalloc` function will allocate memory in 128-byte aligned blocks, so for the most part alignment is not an issue. However, if using a structure that would straddle such a boundary, then there are two approaches. First, you can either add padding bytes/words explicitly to the structure. Alternatively, you can use the `cudaMallocPitch` function we covered in Chapter 6.

Notice that alignment is a key criteria as to whether one or two memory transactions, or cache lines, need to be fetched. Suppose thread 0 accesses address offset 2 instead of 0. Perhaps you're accessing some data structure that has a header at the start, such as:

```
#define MSG_SIZE 4096
typedef struct
{
 u16 header;
 u32 msg_data[MSG_SIZE];
} MY_STRUCT_T;
```

If the kernel processes `msg_data`, then threads 30 and 31 of the warp cannot be served by the single memory fetch. In fact, they generate an additional 128-byte memory transaction as shown in Figure 9.8. Any subsequent warps suffer from the same issue. You are halving your memory bandwidth, just by having a 2-byte header at the start of the data structure.

You'll see this most acutely on compute 1.x devices where the additional fetch generated for threads 30/31 isn't even used to prefill the cache, but just discarded. Loading the header into a separate chunk of memory somewhere else allows for aligned access to the data block. If you are unable to do this, then manually insert padding bytes into the structure definition to ensure that `msg_data` is aligned to a 128-byte boundary. Note that simply reordering the structure elements to move 'header' after `msg_data` will also work, providing the structure is not subsequently used to create an array of structures. All of a sudden your threads match the memory organization and your memory throughput when working with the `msg_data` part of the structure will double.

Consider also the case where prefix sum is used. Prefix sum allows for multiple independent processes or threads to read or write to independent areas of memory without interfering with one another. Multiple reads from the same address are actually hugely beneficial, in that the GPU will simply forward the value to whatever additional threads within the warp need it without additional memory fetches. Multiple writes are of course an issue, in that they need to be sequenced.

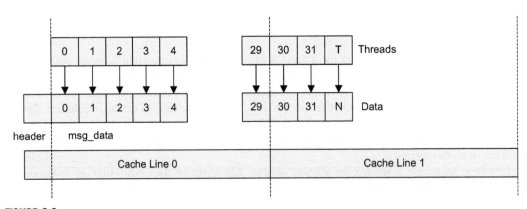

FIGURE 9.8

Cache line/memory transaction usage within structures.

If we assume integers or floats for now, the size of each entry in the data array is 4 bytes. If the distribution of the prefix array is exactly equal then we don't need prefix arrays to access the data anyway, as you could simply use a fixed offset per thread. Therefore, if you're using a prefix sum to calculate an offset into the dataset, it's highly likely there are a variable number of elements per bin. If you know the upper bounds of the number of elements per bin and you have a sufficient memory available, then just pad each bin to the alignment boundary. Use an additional array that holds the number of elements in the bin or calculate this value from the prefix sum index. In this way we can achieve aligned access to memory at the expense of unused cells at the end of most bins.

One very simple solution to the alignment problem is to use a padding value that has no effect on the calculated result. For example, if you're performing a sum over the values in each bin, padding with zero will mean no change to the end result, but will give a uniform memory pattern and execution path for all elements in the warp. For a `min` operation, you can use a padding value of 0xFFFFFFFF, and conversely 0 for a `max` operation. It is usually not hard to come up with a padding value that can be processed, yet contributes nothing to the result.

Once you move to fixed-sized bins, it's also relatively simple to ensure the dataset is generated and accessed in columns, rather than rows. It's often desirable to use shared memory as a staging buffer because of the lack of coalescing requirements. This can then be used to allow coalesced reads/writes to global memory.

Memory accesses to computation ratio

One question that you should often ask is what is the ratio of memory operations to arithmetic operations? You ideally want a ratio of at least 10:1. That is, for every memory fetch the kernel makes from global memory it does 10 or more other instructions. These can be array index calculations, loop calculations, branches, or conditional evaluations. Every instruction should contribute to useful output. Loops, in particular, especially when not unrolled, often simply contribute toward instruction overhead and not to any useful work.

If we look inside an SM, architecturally, we see that warps are dispatched to sets of CUDA cores based on even and odd instruction dispatchers. Compute 1.x devices have a single warp dispatcher and compute 2.x devices have two. In the GF100/GF110 chipset (Fermi GTX480/GTX580) there are 32 CUDA cores and four SFUs (special-function units) per SM (Figure 9.9). In the GF104/GF114-based devices (GTX460/GTX560) there are 48 CUDA cores and eight SFUs per SM (Figure 9.10). Each SM for both compute 2.0 and compute 2.1 devices has a single set of 16 LSUs (load store units) that are used to load values to and from memory (global, constant, shared, local, and cache).

Thus, in a single cycle, the warp dispatchers issue (or dispatch) a total of two (compute 2.0) or four (compute 2.1) instructions, one set from each dispatcher. As these come from different warps, the instructions are entirely independent of one another. These are then pushed into the pipeline of the execution units (CUDA cores, SFUs, and LSUs).

There are a few implications to this design. First, the absolute minimum number of warps that must be present is two for the GF100 series (compute 2.0) hardware and four for the GF104 series (compute 2.1) hardware. This in turn implies an absolute minimum of 64 or 128 threads per SM, respectively. Having less than this means that one or more of the instruction dispatch units will remain idle, causing up to a 50% loss in effective instruction throughput. Using a number of threads other than a multiple of 32 will mean some elements of the CUDA cores will idle, again undesirable.

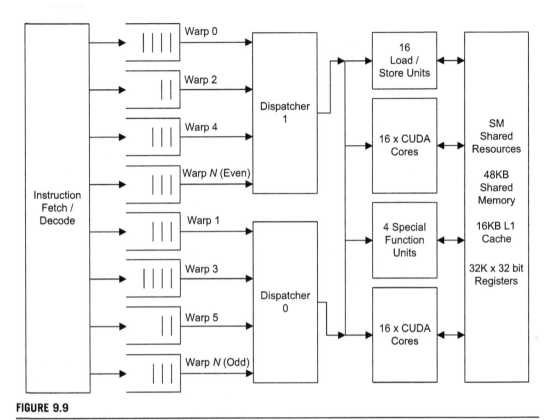

FIGURE 9.9

Dispatching of CUDA warps (GF100/GF110, compute 2.0).

Having this minimum number of resident warps provides absolutely no hiding of latency, either memory or instruction, based on the ability to switch to another warp. A stall in the instruction stream will actually stall the CUDA cores, which is highly undesirable. In practice, multiple blocks are allocated to an SM to try to ensure this problem never occurs and, to ensure a variable mix of instructions is generated.

The second implication is the shared resources limit the ability to continuously perform the same operation. Both the CUDA cores and the LSUs are pipelined, but are only 16 units wide. Thus, to dispatch an entire warp to either unit takes two cycles. On compute 2.0 hardware, only one instruction per dispatcher can be dispatched. Thus, to push an operation into the LSUs, one slot in the pipeline of one of the CUDA cores must be left empty. There are four possible receivers for the dispatch (CUDA, CUDA, SFUs and LSUs), yet only two suppliers per cycle.

The situation is drastically improved in compute 2.1 hardware, in that the two dispatchers dispatch two instructions each, for a total of four per clock. With three sets of CUDA cores it would be possible to supply three arithmetic instructions plus a load/save instruction without creating holes in the pipeline.

However, if all warps want to issue an instruction to the same execution unit, for example the LSU or SFU, there is a problem. Only a single warp can use the LSU per two clock cycles. As the SFU has just eight units, four on compute 2.0 hardware, a warp can take up to eight cycles to be fully consumed by the SFUs.

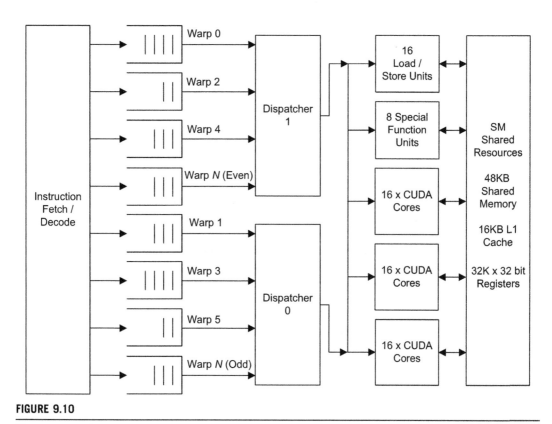

FIGURE 9.10

Dispatching of CUDA warps (GF104/GF114).

Thus, the bandwidth available to and from the LSUs on a compute 2.1 device is 50% less than a compute 2.0 device with the same number of CUDA cores. Consequently, the LSUs or SFUs can become a bottleneck. There needs to be other instructions in the stream such that the CUDA cores can do some useful work while the memory and transcendental instructions progress through the LSU or SFU pipeline.

The Kepler GK104 device (GTX680/Tesla K10) further extends the GF104/114 (GTX460/560) design by extending the number of CUDA cores from 48 to 96, and then putting two of these within an SM. Thus there are four warp schedulers, eight dispatch units, two LSUs and two SFUs per SM.

Let's expand a little on the example we looked at earlier. Consider the case of a typical kernel. At the start of the kernel, all threads in all warps fetch a 32-bit value from memory. The addresses are such that they can be coalesced. For example:

```
int tid = (blockIdx.x * blockDim.x) + threadIdx.x;
data[tid] = a[tid] * b[tid];
```

This would break down into a multiply and add (MADD) integer instruction, to calculate the value to put into the register for the variable tid. Variables data, b, and c are arrays somewhere in global memory. The variables data, a, and b are indexed by tid so the address to write to needs to be calculated by multiplying tid by the size of the elements making up the array. Let's assume they all are integer arrays, so the size is 4 bytes per entry.

We very quickly hit the first dependency in the calculation of tid (Figure 9.11). The warp dispatches the multiply of blockIdx.x and blockDim.x to the integer MADD units in the CUDA cores. Until the multiply and add instruction to calculate tid has completed we can continue no further, so the warp is marked as blocked and suspended.

At this point, the next warp is selected, which does the same operation and is again suspended at the calculation of tid. After all warps have progressed to this point, enough clocks have passed such that the value of tid in warp 0 is now known and can be fed into the multiply for the destination address calculations. Thus, three additional MADD instructions are dispatched to the CUDA cores, to calculate the address offsets. The next instruction would be a couple of loads, but for this we need the address of a and b from the multiply instructions. At this point we again suspend the warp and the other warps execute.

Once the address calculation of a is available, the load instruction can be dispatched. It's likely, due to the address calculation of b being issued back to back with that of a, that the address calculation of b will be retired by the time the load for a has been dispatched. Thus, we immediately issue the load for the 'b'. The next instruction in the stream would be a multiply of 'a' and 'b', neither of which will be available for some time yet as they have to be fetched from main memory to the SM. Thus, the warp is suspended and the subsequent warps execute to the same point.

As memory fetches take a long time, all warps dispatch the necessary load instructions to the LSU and are suspended. If there is no other work to do from other blocks, the SM will idle pending the memory transactions completing.

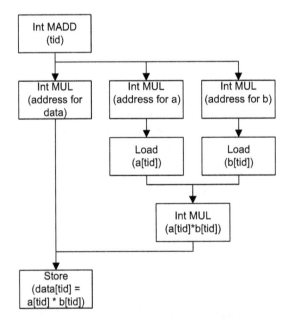

FIGURE 9.11

Data flow dependency.

Sometime later a finally arrives from the memory subsystem as a coalesced read of 128 bytes, a single cache line, or a memory transaction. The 16 LSUs distributes 64 of the 128 bytes to the registers used by the first half-warp of warp 0. In the next cycle, the 16 LSUs distribute the remaining 64 bytes to the register used by the other half-warp. However, warp 0 still can not progress as it has only one of the two operands it needs for the multiply. It thus does not execute and the subsequent bytes arriving from the coalesced read of a for the other warps are distributed to the relevant registers for those warps.

By the time all of the data from the coalesced read for a has been distributed to the registers of all the other warps, the data for b will likely have arrived in the L1 cache. Again, the 16 LSUs distribute the first 64 bytes to the registers of the first half-warp of warp 0. In the subsequent cycle they distribute the second 64 bytes to the second half-warp.

At the start of this second cycle, the first half-warp is able to progress the multiply instruction for a [tid] * b[tid]. In the third cycle the LSUs start providing data to the first half-warp of warp 0. Meanwhile, the second half-warp of warp 0 starts the execution of the multiply. As the next instruction in warp 0 would be a store and is dependent on the multiply, warp 0 is suspended.

Providing there are on the order of 18–22 warps resident, by the time the last warp has dispatched the final multiply, the multiply will have completed for warp 0. It can then dispatch the store instructions to the 16 LSUs and complete its execution. The other warps then do exactly the same and the kernel is complete.

Now consider the case of (see Figure 9.12).

```
int tid = (blockIdx.x * blockDim.x) + threadIdx.x;
data[tid] = a[tid] * b[tid];
data[tid+1] = a[tid+1] * b[tid+1];
```

By halving the number of blocks, we can process two elements per thread. Notice this introduces an independent execution stream into each thread of the warp. Thus, the arithmetic operations start to overlap with the load operations.

However, as the example C code is written, this will not help. This is because the code contains dependencies that are not immediately obvious. The write operation to the first element of data could affect the value in either the a or the b array. That is, the address space of data may overlap with a or b. Where you have a write in the data flow to global memory, you need to lift out the reads to the start of the kernel. Use the following code instead:

```
int tid = (blockIdx.x * blockDim.x) + threadIdx.x;
int a_0 = a[tid];
int b_0 = b[tid];
int a_1 = a[tid+1];
int b_1 = b[tid+1];
data[tid] = a_0 * b_0;
data[tid+1] = a_1 * b_1;
```

or

```
int tid = (blockIdx.x * blockDim.x) + threadIdx.x;
int2 a_vect = a[tid];
int2 b_vect = b[tid];
data[tid] = a_vect * b_vect;
```

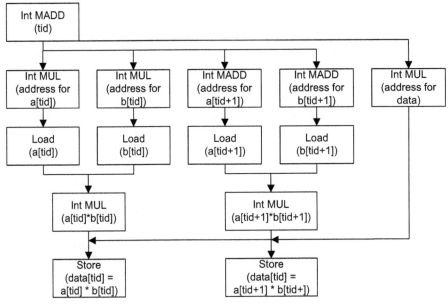

FIGURE 9.12

Dual data flow dependency.

We have two choices, a scalar approach or a vector approach. The GPU supports only vector loads and saves, not vector operations, in hardware. Thus, the multiplication is actually done as an overloaded operator in C++ and simply multiplies the two integers independently of one another. However, the vector loads and saves two 64-bit loads and a single 64-bit save, respectively, instead of the four separate 32-bit loads and a single 32-bit save with the nonvector version. Thus, 40% of the memory transactions are eliminated. The memory bandwidth usage is the same, but less memory transactions mean less memory latency, and therefore any stall time waiting for memory is reduced.

To use the vector types, simply declare all arrays as type `int2`, which is an in-built vector type of two integers. Supported types are `int2`, `int3`, `int4`, `float2`, `float3`, and `float4`. You can of course create your own types, such as `uchar4`, and define your own operators. Each vector type is actually just an aligned structure with *N* named member elements of the base type.

Thus, I hope you can actually see that a balance is therefore required between the different types of instructions. This becomes somewhat more critical with the compute 2.1 devices (GF104 series) where there are three sets of CUDA cores sharing the same resources within the SM. The change in compute 2.0 to compute 2.1 devices added significantly more arithmetic capacity within the SM without providing additional data transport capacity. The compute 2.0 devices have up to 512 CUDA cores on a bus of up to 384 bits wide, giving a ratio of 1:3 of cores to memory bandwidth. The compute 2.1 devices have up to 384 CUDA cores on a bus of up to 256 bits, giving a ratio of 1:5 cores to memory bandwidth. Thus, compute 2.0 devices are more suited to applications that are memory bound, whereas compute 2.1 devices are more suited to applications that are compute bound.

In practice, this is balanced in the compute 2.0 devices by having up to 33% more CUDA cores. The compute 2.1 devices, however, typically also run at somewhat higher clock rates, both in terms of the internal clock speed and also the external memory bus speed. This helps significantly in rebalancing the smaller memory bus width but is generally not sufficient to allow compute 2.1 devices to outperform their 2.0 counterparts.

What is important to realize, especially with compute 2.1 devices, is that there needs to be sufficient arithmetic density to the instruction stream to make good use of the CUDA cores present on the SMs. A kernel that simply does loads or stores and little else will not achieve anything like the peak performance available from these devices. Expand such kernels to also include independent instruction flow via processing two, four, or eight elements per thread. Use vector operations where possible.

Loop and kernel fusion

Another area where we can significantly save on memory bandwidth is a technique based on loop fusion we looked at in the last section. Loop fusion is where two apparently independent loops run over an intersecting range. For example, loop 1 runs from 0 to 100 and loop 2 from 0 to 200. The code for loop 2 can be fused with the code for loop 1, for at least the first 100 iterations. This increases the level of instruction-level parallelism, but also decreases the overall number of iterations by a third.

Kernel fusion is a variation on loop fusion. If you have a number of kernels that are run in sequence, one after the other, are there elements of these kernels that can be fused? Be careful doing this with kernels you did not write or do not fully understand. Invoking two kernels in series generates an implicit synchronization between them. This may have been intended by design and, as it's implicit, probably only the original designer is aware of it.

In developing kernels it's quite common to break down the operation into a number of phases or passes. For example, in the first pass you might calculate the results over the whole dataset. On the second pass you may filter data for certain criteria and perform some further processing on certain points. If the second pass can be localized to a block, the first and second pass can usually be combined into a single kernel. This eliminates the write to main memory of the first kernel and the subsequent read of the second, as well as the overhead of invoking an additional kernel. If the first kernel is able to write the results to shared memory, and you only need those results for the second pass, you eliminate the read/write to global memory entirely. Reduction operations often fall into this category and can benefit significantly from such an optimization, as the output of the second phase is usually many times smaller than the first phase, so it saves considerably on memory bandwidth.

Part of the reason why kernel fusion works so well is because of the data reuse it allows. Fetching data from global memory is slow, on the order of 400–600 clock cycles. Think of memory access like reading something from disk. If you've ever done any disk I/O, you'll know that reading a file by fetching one character at time is very slow and using `fread` to read large blocks is far more efficient than repeatedly calling read character functions like `fgetch`. Having read the data in, you keep it in memory. Apply the same approach to accessing global memory. Fetch data in chunks of up to 16 bytes per thread (`float4`, `int4`), not in single bytes or words. Once you have each thread successfully processing a single element, switch to `int2` or `float2` and process two. Moving to four may or may not help, but moving from one to two often does. Once you have the data, store it in shared memory, or keep it in the register set and reuse it as much as possible.

Use of shared memory and cache

Using shared memory can provide a 10:1 increase in speed over global memory, but is limited in size—48 K on Fermi/Kepler devices and 16 K on all the previous devices. This may not sound like a great deal of space, especially with multigigabyte memory systems found on the host, but this is actually per SM. Thus, a GTX580 or Tesla M2090 has 16 SMs active per GPU, each of which provides 48 K of shared memory, a total of 768 K. This is memory that runs at L1 cache speed. In addition, you have 768 K of L2 cache memory (on 16 SM devices) that is shared between all the SMs. This allows for an order of magnitude faster, global memory, atomic operations than in previous generation GPUs.

When you consider that a GTX580 comes with 1.5 GB of memory, 768 K means just a tiny fraction of that memory space can be held in cache at any one point in time. The equivalent Tesla card comes with 6 GB of memory but no increase in cache size. Thus, kernels that iterate over datasets need to be aware that they may be using either the cache or shared memory in an ineffective manner, if they are not reusing data.

Rather than a number of passes over a large dataset, techniques such as kernel fusion can be used to move through the data as opposed to passing over it multiple times. Think of the problem in terms of the output data and not the input data. Construct the problem such that you assign threads to output data items, not input data items. Create a fan in and not a fan out in terms of data flow. Have a preference for gather (collecting data) primitives, rather than scatter (distributing data) primitives. The GPU will broadcast data, both from global memory and the L2 cache, directly to each SM. This supports high-speed gather-type operations.

On Fermi and Kepler we have a very interesting choice, to configure the shared memory to either prefer L1 cache (48 K L1 cache, 16 K shared) or to prefer shared (48 K shared, 16 K cache). By default the device will prefer shared memory, and thus you'll have 48 K of shared memory available. This decision is not fixed, but set at runtime, and thus can be set per kernel call. Kernels that do not make use of shared memory, or keep to the 16 K limit to ensure compatibility with earlier GPUs, usually benefit significantly (10% to 20% performance gain) by enabling the additional 32 K of cache, disabled by default:

```
cudaFuncSetCacheConfig(cache_prefer, kernel_name);
```

where the `cache_prefer` parameter is `cudaFuncCachePreferShared` for 48 K of shared memory and 16 K of L1 cache, or `cudaFuncCachePreferL1` for 48 K of cache memory and 16 K of shared memory. Note, Kepler also allows a 32 K/32 K split.

There are, however, some areas where the cache causes Fermi and Kepler to operate slower than previous generation GPUs. On compute 1.x devices, memory transactions would be progressively reduced in size to as little as 32 bytes per access if the data item was small. Thus, a kernel that accesses one data element from a widely dispersed area in memory will perform poorly on any cache-based architecture, CPU, or GPU. The reason for this is that a single-element read will drag in 128 bytes of data. For most programs, the data brought into the cache will then allow a cache hit on the next loop iteration. This is because programs typically access data close in memory to where they previously accessed data. Thus, for most programs this is a significant benefit. However, for programs that only need one data element, the other 124 bytes are wasted. For such kernels, you have to configure the memory subsystem to fetch only the memory transactions it needs, not one that is cache line sized. You can do this only at compile time via the `-Xptxas -dlcm=cg` flag. This reduces all access to 32 bytes per transaction and disables the L1 cache. For read only data consider also using either texture or constant memory.

With G80/GT200, compute 1.x hardware, it's essential that you make use of shared memory as an integral part of the kernel design. Without cached accessed to data, be it explicitly via shared memory or implicitly via a hardware-managed cache, memory latency times are just huge. The arrival of cache on GPUs via the Fermi architecture has made it much, much easier to write at a program, or kernel, that performs at least reasonably well on the GPU.

Let's look at some of the obstacles to using shared memory. The first is the size available—16 K on compute 1.x hardware and up to 48 K on compute 2.x hardware. It can be allocated statically at compile time via the __shared__ prefix for variables. It is also one of the optional parameters in a kernel call, that is,

```
kernel<<<num_blocks, num_threads, smem_size>>>(a,b,c);
```

With runtime allocation, you additionally need a pointer to the start of the memory. For example,

```
extern volatile __shared__ int s_data[];

__global__ my_kernel(const int * a,
                     const int * b,
                     const int num_elem_a,
                     const int num_elem_b)
{
 const int tid = (blockIdx.x * blockDim.x) + threadIdx.x;

 // Copy arrays 'a' and 'b' to shared memory
 s_data[tid] = a[tid];
 s_data[num_elem_a + tid] = b[tid];

 // Wait for all threads
 __syncthreads();

 // Process s_data[0] to s_data[(num_elem_a-1)] - a
 // Process s_data[num_elem_a] to s_data[num_elem_a + (num_elem_b-1)] - array 'b'
}
```

Note that L2 cache size in Fermi is not always 768 K as stated in the CUDA C programmer guide. In fact, the L2 cache is based on the type of device being used and the number of SMs present. Compute 2.1 devices may have less L2 cache than compute 2.0 devices. Even compute 2.0 devices without all the SMs enabled (GTX470, GTX480, GTX570) have less than 768 K of L2 cache. The GTX460 device we're using for testing has 512 K of L2 cache and the GTX470 device has 640 K.

The size of the L2 cache is returned from a call to cudaGetDeviceProperties API as l2CacheSize member.

Section summary

- Think carefully about the data your kernel processes and how best to arrange this in memory.
- Optimize memory access patterns for coalesced 128-byte access, aligning with the 128-byte memory fetch and L1 cache line size.
- Consider the single-/double-precision tradeoff and how this impacts memory usage.
- Fuse multiple kernels to single kernels where appropriate.

- Make optimal use of shared memory and cache, ensuring you're making full use of the expanded size on later compute levels.

STRATEGY 3: TRANSFERS

Pinned memory

To work on a dataset you need to transfer the data from the host to the device, work on the dataset, and transfer the results back to the host. Performed in a purely serial manner, this causes periods where both the host and GPU are inactive, both in terms of unused transfer capacity and compute capacity.

We looked in detail in the chapter on multi-GPU usage at how to use streams to ensure the GPU always has some work to do. With a simple double-buffering technique, while the GPU is transferring back the results and acquiring a new work packet, the other buffer is being used by the compute engine to process the next data block.

The host processor supports a virtual memory system where a physical memory page can be marked as swapped out. It can then be paged to disk. Upon an access by the host processor to that page, the processor loads the page back in from disk. It allows the programmer to use a much larger virtual address space than is actually present on the hardware. Given that the programs typically exhibit quite good locality, this allows the total memory space to be much larger than the physical limits allow. However, if the program really does need 8 GB and the host only has 4 GB, the performance will typically be poor.

Arguably the use of virtual memory is a hangover from a time when memory capacities were very limited. Today you can purchase 16 GB of memory for a little over 100 euros/dollars/pounds, meaning the host's need to use virtual memory is almost eliminated for most applications.

Most programs, except for big data problems, will generally fit within the host memory space. If not, then there are special server solutions that can hold up to 128 GB of memory per node. Such solutions are often preferable, as they allow you to keep the data within one node rather than add the complexity of a multinode solution. Of course, loading the dataset in chunks is perfectly feasible, but then you are ultimately limited by the throughput of the I/O hardware.

You should always be using page-locked memory on a system that has a reasonable amount of host memory. Page-locked memory allows the DMA (direct memory access) controller on the GPU to request a transfer to and from host memory without the involvement of the CPU host processor. Thus, no load is placed onto the host processor in terms of managing a transfer or having to bring back from disk any pages that have been swapped out.

The PCI-E transfers in practice can only be performed using DMA-based transfer. The driver does this in the background when you don't use page-locked memory directly. Thus, the driver has to allocate (or malloc) a block of paged-locked memory, do a host copy from the regular memory to the page-locked memory, initiate the transfer, wait for the transfer to complete, and then free the page-locked memory. All of this takes time and consumes precious CPU cycles that could be used more productively.

Memory allocated on the GPU is by default allocated as page locked simply because the GPU does not support swapping memory to disk. It's the memory allocated on the host processor we're concerned with. To allocate page-locked memory we need to either allocate it using the special cudaHostMalloc function or allocate it with the regular malloc function and register it as page-locked memory.

Registering memory simply sets some internal flags to ensure the memory is never swapped out and also tells the CUDA driver that this memory is page-locked memory so it is able to use it directly rather than using a staging buffer.

As with malloc, if you use cudaHostAlloc you need to use the cudaFreeHost function to free this memory. Do not call the regular C free function with pointers allocated from cudaHostAlloc or you will likely get a crash, some undefined behavior, or a strange error later in your program.

The prototype for cudaHostAlloc is

```
cudaError_t cudaHostAlloc (void ** host_pointer, size_t size, unsigned int flags)
```

The flags consist of the following:

cudaHostAllocDefault—Use for most cases. Simply specifies the default behavior.
cudaHostAllocWriteCombined—Use for memory regions that will be transferred *to the device only.* Do not use this flag when the host will read from this memory area. This turns off the caching of the memory region on the host processor, which means it completely ignores the memory region during transfers. This speeds up transfer to the device with certain hardware configurations.
cudaHostAllocPortable—The page-locked memory becomes page locked and visible in all CUDA contexts. By default the allocation belongs to the context creating it. You must use this flag if you plan to pass the pointer between CUDA contexts or threads on the host processor.
cudaHostAllocMapped—We'll look at this shortly. It allocates host memory into device memory space, allowing the GPU kernel to directly read and write with all transfers being implicitly handled.

To demonstrate the effect of paged memory versus nonpaged memory, we have included here a short program. This simply does a number of transfers, varied by size to and from a device, and invokes a dummy kernel to ensure the transfers actually take place. The results are shown in Figure 9.13.

On the Y axis we have MB/second to or from the device and the transfer size in bytes along the X axis. What we can see from the chart is that there is a considerable difference between using paged memory and nonpaged memory, the page-locked (pinned) memory being 1.4× faster for writes and 1.8× faster for reads. It took 194 ms to send out 512 MB of data to the card using page-locked memory, as opposed to 278 ms to do this with nonpaged memory. Timings to transfer data from the device, for comparison, were 295 ms for paged memory versus 159 ms for pinned memory.

On the input side, we see a strange issue: With page-locked memory, the bandwidth *from* the device is 20% higher than *to* the device. Given that PCI-E provides for a full duplex connection of the same speed to and from the device, you'd expect to see a similar transfer speed for both reads and writes. This variation, as you will see in subsequent tests, is very hardware dependent. All the systems tested except the Intel Nehalem I7 system exhibiting it to varying degrees.

Transfer rates to and from the four test devices were almost identical, which is to be expected given the bandwidth of global memory on all of the cards is at least an order of magnitude greater than the PCI-E bandwidth.

What is also very noticable is that to get near-peak bandwidth, even with pinned memory, the transfer size needs to be on the order of 2 MB of data. In fact, we don't achieve the absolute peak until the transfer size is 16 MB or beyond.

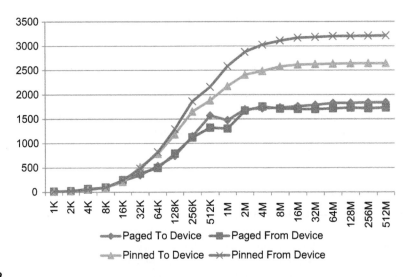

FIGURE 9.13

Transfer speed to and from the device (AMD Phenom II X4 905e, PCI-E 2.0 X8 link).

For comparison, the results are also shown in Figures 9.14, 9.15 and 9.16 for a number of systems we tested.

Figure 9.14 shows a small netbook based on Intel's low-power ATOM device, equipped with a dedicated GT218 NVIDIA ION graphics card. The peak PCI-E bandwidth you can typically see is up

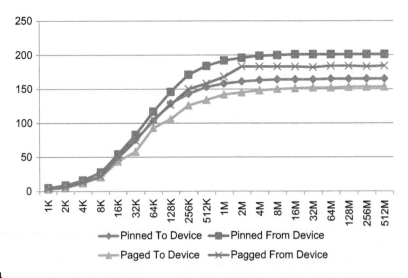

FIGURE 9.14

Transfer speed to and from the device (Intel Atom D525, PCI-E 2.0 X1 link).

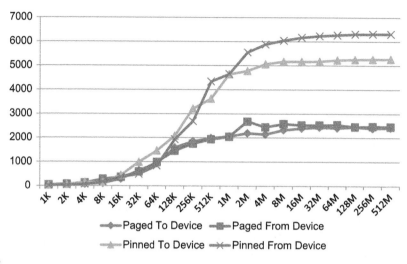

FIGURE 9.15

Transfer speed to and from the device (Intel I3 540, PCI-E X16 link).

to 5 GB/s when using a 2.0 X16 link. As this netbook uses an X1 link, we could expect a maximum of 320 MB/s and we see in the order of 200 MB/s.

However, we see a very similar pattern to the AMD system, in that we need around 2 MB plus transfer sizes before we start to achieve anything like the peak transfer rate. The only difference we see is there is a noticable difference between transfers to the device and transfers from the device.

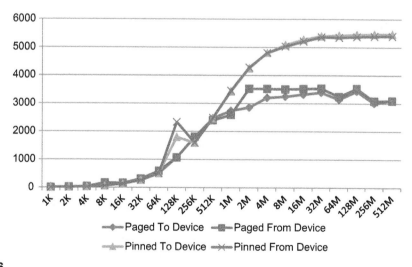

FIGURE 9.16

Transfer speed to and from the device (Intel I7 920, PCI-E X16 link).

A midrange system quite common in the consumer enviroment is the i3/i5 system from Intel. This particular one is the i3 540 running with a H55 chipset. As this device has a single GPU only, it's running at X16 the peak speed PCI-E 2.0 (Figure 9.15).

We can see the very large difference between pinned and nonpinned transfers, in excess of 2×. However, notice the absolute speed difference, approximately a 2× increase over the AMD system. This is largely due to the AMD system using an X8 PCI-E link, whereas the Intel system here uses an X16 PCI-E link.

The Intel I3 is a typical consumer processor. Anyone writing consumer-based applications should be very much aware by now that they need to be using pinned memory transfers, as we can see the huge difference it makes.

Finally, we look at one further system, this time from the server arena, using the Intel I7 920 Nehalem processor and the ASUS supercomputer socket 1366 motherboard. This is a common motherboard for high-end GPUs, as it allows up to four PCI-E slots. This particular one is equipped with 3× GTX290 GPUs each using an PCI-E 2.0 X16 connection.

What we see from the diagram is again interesting. Pinned and paged memory transfers are equal until transfer sizes larger than 512 KB, after which the pinned memory transfers lead by up to 1.8× over the paged memory–based transfers. Unlike the Nehalem I3 system, notice the Nehalem I7 system is more consistent and there is not a huge variation between inbound and outbound transfer speeds. However, also note the peak transfer speed, despite both devices being on a X16 PCI-E 2.0 link, is only 5400 MB/s as opposed to the I3, which achieved a peak of 6300 MB/s (Figures 9.15 and 9.16).

So in summary, we can say that across a selection of today's computing hardware, pinned memory transfers are approximately twice as fast as nonpinned transfers. Also we see there can be a considerable variance in performance between read and write speeds from and to the various devices. We can also see that we need to use larger, rather than smaller, block sizes, perhaps combining multiple transfers to increase the overall bandwidth utilization of the bus.

Zero-copy memory

Zero-copy memory is a special form of memory mapping that allows you to map host memory into the memory space of the GPU directly. Thus, when you dereference memory on the GPU, if it's GPU based, then you get high-speed (180 GB/s) bandwidth to global memory. If the GPU code reads a host-mapped variable it issues a PCI-E read transaction, and a (very) long time later the host will return the data over the PCI-E bus.

After looking at the PCI-E bus bandwidth in the previous section, this doesn't, at first glance, make a lot of sense. Big transfers are efficient and small transfers inefficient. If we rerun the test program we used for the previous examples, we see that the median transfer time is 0.06 ms on our sample AMD Phenom X4 platform. However, these are explicit, individual transfers, so it's possible the zero-copy implementation may be more efficient.

If you think about what happens with access to global memory, an entire cache line is brought in from memory on compute 2.x hardware. Even on compute 1.x hardware the same 128 bytes, potentially reduced to 64 or 32, is fetched from global memory.

NVIDIA does not publish the size of the PCI-E transfers it uses, or details on how zero copy is actually implemented. However, the coalescing approach used for global memory could be used with PCI-E transfer. The warp memory latency hiding model can equally be applied to PCI-E transfers, providing there is enough arithmetic density to hide the latency of the PCI-E transfers. This is, in fact, the key to getting this to work. If you do very little for each global memory fetch and your application is already memory bound, this approach is unlikely to help you.

However, if your application is arithmetically bound, zero-copy memory can be a very useful technique. It saves you the explicit transfer time to and from the device. In effect, you are overlapping computation with data transfers without having to do explicit stream management. The catch, of course, is that you have to be efficient with your data usage. If you fetch or write the same data point more than once, this will create multiple PCI-E transactions. As each and every one of these is expensive in terms of latency, the fewer there are the better.

This can also be used very effectively on systems where the host and GPU share the same memory space, such as on the low-end NVIDIA ION-based netbooks. Here a malloc of global memory on the GPU can actually result in a malloc of memory on the host. Clearly it doesn't make sense to copy from one memory area on the host to another memory area on the host if the host memory and GPU memory both reside in host memory. Zero-copy memory can eliminate the need to perform these copies in such systems, without the impact of a PCI-E bus transfer.

Zero-copy memory also has one very useful use case. This is during the phase where you are initially porting a CPU application to a GPU. During this development phase there will often be sections of code that exist on the host that have not yet been ported over to the GPU. By declaring such data references as zero-copy memory regions, it allows the code to be ported in sections and still have it work. The performance will be generally poor until all the intended parts are present on the GPU. It simply allows this to be done in smaller steps so it's not an "everything or nothing" problem.

Let's start by taking the existing memcpy program and expanding the kernel so it does the read of the data instead of relying on an explicit copy. For this we absolutely must coalesce accesses to memory, which when reading a simple one-dimensional array is easy. Thus, our kernel becomes

```
__global__ void kernel_copy(u32 * const gpu_data,
                            const u32 * const host_data,
                            const u32 num_elements)
{
 const u32 idx = (blockIdx.x * blockDim.x) + threadIdx.x;
 const u32 idy = (blockIdx.y * blockDim.y) + threadIdx.y;
 const u32 tid = ((gridDim.x * blockDim.x) * idy) + idx;

 if (tid < num_elements)
   gpu_data[tid] = host_data[tid];
}
```

In the kernel we simply make the x and y grid dimensions into a single linear array and assign one element from the source dataset to the destination dataset. Next we have to do three critical things to use zero-copy or host-mapped memory—that is, first to enable it, second to allocate memory using it, and finally to convert the regular host pointer to the device memory space.

Prior to any creation of a CUDA context, we need to make the following call:

```
// Enable host mapping to device memory
CUDA_CALL(cudaSetDeviceFlags(cudaDeviceMapHost));
```

When the CUDA context is created the driver will know it also has to support host-mapped memory. Without this the host-mapped (zero-copy) memory will not work. This will not work if it's done after the CUDA context has been created. Be aware that calls to functions like `cudaHostAlloc`, despite operating on host memory, still create a GPU context.

Although most devices support zero-copy memory, some earlier devices do not. It's not part of the compute level, so it has to be checked for explicitly as follows:

```
struct cudaDeviceProp device_prop;
CUDA_CALL(cudaGetDeviceProperties(&device_prop, device_num));
zero_copy_supported = device_prop.canMapHostMemory;
```

The next stage is to allocate memory on the host such that it can be mapped into device memory. This is done with an additional flag `cudaHostAllocMapped` to the `cudaHostAlloc` function.

```
// Allocate zero copy pinned memory
CUDA_CALL(cudaHostAlloc((void **) &host_data_to_device, size_in_bytes,
cudaHostAllocWriteCombined | cudaHostAllocMapped));
```

Finally, we need to convert the host pointer to a device pointer, which is done with the `cudaHostGetDevicePointer` function as follows:

```
// Convert to a GPU host pointer
CUDA_CALL(cudaHostGetDevicePointer( &dev_host_data_to_device, host_data_to_device, 0));
```

In this call we convert the `host_data_to_device` previously allocated in the host memory space to an equvalent pointer, but within the GPU memory space. Do not confuse the pointers. Use the converted pointer only with GPU kernels and the original pointer only in code that executes on the host. Thus, for example, to free the memory later, an operation performed on the host, the existing call remains the same:

```
// Free pinned memory
CUDA_CALL(cudaFreeHost(host_data_to_device));
```

As we're using memory blocks up to 512 MB in size, to access one element per thread no matter how many threads we allocate per block means the number of blocks will exceed 64 K. This is the hard limit on the number of blocks in any single dimension on devices up to compute level 2.1 (Fermi). Thus, we have to introduce another dimension. This introduces grids, which we covered in Chapter 5. We can do this relatively simply by fixing the number of grids at some value that will be large enough to allow sufficient flexibility in selecting the number of threads per block.

```
const int num_elements = (size_in_bytes / sizeof(u32));
const int num_threads = 256;
const int num_grid = 64;
const int num_blocks = (num_elements + (num_threads-1)) / num_threads;
int num_blocks_per_grid;

// Split blocks into grid
if (num_blocks > num_grid)
 num_blocks_per_grid = num_blocks / num_grid;
else
 num_blocks_per_grid = 1;

dim3 blocks(num_grid, num_blocks_per_grid);
```

The `dim3` operation simply assigns the regular scalar values we calculated to a structure type holding a triplet that can be used as a single parameter in the kernel launch. It causes the kernel to launch 64 grids of N blocks. This simply ensures that for a given block index we do not exceed the 64 K limit. Thus, on the kernel launch, we replace `num blocks`, a scalar type, with `blocks`, a `dim3` type:

```
// Run the kernel
kernel_copy<<<blocks, num_threads>>>(gpu_data, dev_host_data_to_device, num_elements);
```

What we see for transfers *to the device* is that the overall figures are identical to the transfers using explicit memory copies. This has significant implications. Most applications that do not already use the stream API simply copy memory to the GPU at the start and copy back once the kernel is complete. We can shrink that time drastically using pinned memory copies, but the time is still cumulative because it's a serial operation.

In effect, what happens with the zero-copy memory is we break both the transfer and the kernel operation into much smaller blocks, which execute them in a pipeline (Figure 9.17). The overall time is reduced quite significantly.

Notice we did not perform the same optimization with the copy from device. The reason for this is because consumer GPUs have only one copy engine enabled. Thus, they support only a single memory stream. When you do a read-kernel-write operation, if the write is pushed into the stream ahead of subsequent reads, it will block the read operations until the pending write has completed. Note this is not the case for Tesla devices, as both copy engines are enabled and thus Tesla cards are able to support independent to and from streams. Prior to Fermi, there was only ever one copy engine on any card.

However, with zero-copy memory the transfers are actually quite small. The PCI-E bus has the same bandwidth in both directions. Due to the high latency of the PCI-E-based memory reads, actually most of the reads should have been pushed into the read queue ahead of any writes. We may be able to achieve significant execution time savings over the explicit memory copy version.

Note the diagram in Figure 9.18 is simplified in that it lists a single "Pinned To & From Device" line, yet we show the zero device copy times explicitly for the devices. The pinned memory time was effectively the same for all devices, so it was not shown per device.

We have listed the entire execution time of a single memory copy to device, kernel execution, and memory copy from device. Thus, there is some overhead that is not present when purely measuring the

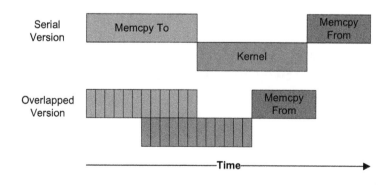

FIGURE 9.17

Serial versus overlapped transfer/kernel execution.

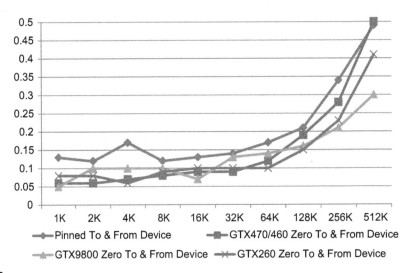

FIGURE 9.18

Zero-copy time versus explicit pinned copy time over different GPU generations.

transfer to/from the device. As we're using zero copy, the memory transactions and the kernel time cannot be pulled apart. However, as the kernel is doing very little, the overall execution time represents a fair comparison between the zero copy and explicit copy versions.

There is a considerable amount of variability. What we can see, however, is that for small transfer amounts, less than 512 KB, zero copy is faster than using explicit copies. Let's now look at sizes larger than 512 KB in Table 9.1 and Figure 9.19.

What is very interesting to see here is a considerable drop in execution time. On the Fermi hardware the overlapping of the kernel operation with the memory copies drops the execution time from 182 ms to 104 ms, a 1.75× speedup. The results are less impressive in the earlier devices, but still represent a significant speedup.

Table 9.1 Zero-Copy Results (execution time in ms)

Device	1M	2M	4M	8M	16M	32M	64M	128M	256M
Pinned to and from device	0.96	1.62	3	5.85	11.52	22.97	45.68	91.14	182.04
GTX470/460 zero to and from device	0.5	0.9	1.72	3.34	6.61	13.11	26.15	52.12	103.99
GT9800 zero to and from device	0.56	1.09	2	3.94	7.92	15.63	31.6	61.89	123.81
GTX260 zero to and from device	0.68	1.38	2.52	4.48	8.74	18.84	38.96	74.35	160.33

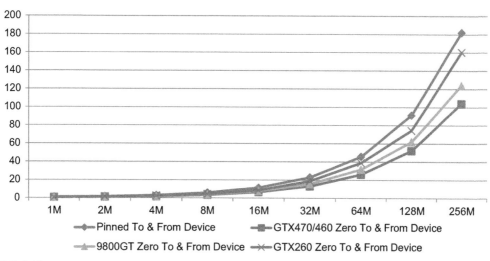

FIGURE 9.19

Zero-copy graph (time in ms versus transfer size).

You can of course achieve this using streams and asynchronous memory copies, as demonstrated in Chapter 8. Zero copy simply presents an alternative, and somewhat simpler, interface you can work with.

However, there are some caveats. Beware of exactly how many times the data is being fetched from memory. Re-reading data from global memory will usually exclude the use of zero-copy memory.

If we modify the program to read the value from host memory twice instead of once, then the performance drops by half on the 9800 GT and GTX260 platforms, the compute 1.x devices. This is because each and every fetch from global memory on these platforms is not cached. Thus, the number of PCI-E transactions issued is doubled, as we double the amount of times the GPU accesses the zero-copy memory area.

On Fermi the situation is somewhat different. It has an L1 and L2 cache and it's highly likely the data fetched earlier in the kernel will still be in the cache when the latter access hits the same memory address. To be sure, you have to explicitly copy the data you plan to reuse to the shared memory. So in Fermi, depending on the data pattern, you typically do not see the device issuing multiple PCI-E transactions, as many of these hit the internal caches and therefore never create a global memory transaction.

Thus, zero-copy memory presents a relatively easy way to speed up your existing serial code without having to explicitly learn the stream API, providing you are careful about data reuse and have a reasonable amount of work to do with each data item.

However, be aware that the bandwidth of the PCI-E bus is nowhere near the bandwidth available on a CPU. The latest Sandybridge I7 processor (Socket 2011) achieves some 37 GB/s of memory bandwidth, from a theoretical peak of 51 GB/s. We're achieving 5–6 GB/s from a theoretical peak of 8 GB/s on the PCI-E 2.0 bus. You must have enough work in your application to justify the cost of moving the data over the PCI-E bus. Consider that the CPU can be a better alternative in situations where very little work is being done per element.

The program used for these measurements is shown here for reference.

```
void memcpy_test_zero_to_from(const int device_num,
                             const size_t size_in_bytes,
                             TIMER_T * const kernel_time,
                             const u32 num_runs,
                             const bool pinned)
{
 char device_prefix[256];
 int major, minor;
 int zero_copy_supported;

 // Init

 // Enable host mapping to device memory
 CUDA_CALL(cudaSetDeviceFlags(cudaDeviceMapHost));

 // Get the device properties
 get_device_props(device_prefix, device_num, &major,
                  &minor, &zero_copy_supported);

 // Exit if zero copy not supported and is requested
 if (zero_copy_supported == 0)
 {
   printf("%s Error Zero Copy not supported", device_prefix);
   wait_exit(1);
 }

 // Select the specified device
 CUDA_CALL(cudaSetDevice(device_num));

 printf("%s Running Memcpy Test to device using",
        device_prefix);

 if (pinned)
    printf(" locked memory");
 else
   printf(" unlocked memory");

 printf(" %lu K", size_in_bytes / 1024);

 (*kernel_time) = 0;

 init_device_timer();

 // Allocate data space on GPU
 u32 * gpu_data;
 CUDA_CALL(cudaMalloc((void**)&gpu_data,
                      size_in_bytes));
```

```
u32 * dev_host_data_to_device;
u32 * dev_host_data_from_device;

// Allocate data space on host
u32 * host_data_to_device;
u32 * host_data_from_device;

if (pinned)
{
  // Allocate zero copy pinned memory
  CUDA_CALL(cudaHostAlloc((void **) &host_data_to_device, size_in_bytes,
cudaHostAllocWriteCombined | cudaHostAllocMapped));

  CUDA_CALL(cudaHostAlloc((void **) &host_data_from_device, size_in_bytes,
cudaHostAllocDefault | cudaHostAllocMapped));
}
else
{
  host_data_to_device = (u32 *) malloc(size_in_bytes);
  host_data_from_device = (u32 *) malloc(size_in_bytes);
}

// Convert to a GPU host pointer
CUDA_CALL(cudaHostGetDevicePointer(&dev_host_data_to_device, host_data_to_device, 0));

CUDA_CALL(cudaHostGetDevicePointer(&dev_host_data_from_device, host_data_from_device,
0));

// If the host allocation did not result in
// an out of memory error
if ( (host_data_to_device != NULL) &&
     (host_data_from_device != NULL) )
{
  const int num_elements = (size_in_bytes / sizeof(u32));
  const int num_threads = 256;
  const int num_grid = 64;
  const int num_blocks = (num_elements + (num_threads-1)) / num_threads;
  int num_blocks_per_grid;

  // Split blocks into grid
  if (num_blocks > num_grid)
      num_blocks_per_grid = num_blocks / num_grid;
  else
      num_blocks_per_grid = 1;

  dim3 blocks(num_grid, num_blocks_per_grid);

  for (u32 test=0; test < num_runs+1; test++)
  {
```

```
    // Add in all but first test run
    if (test != 0)
     start_device_timer();

    // Run the kernel
    kernel_copy<<<blocks, num_threads>>>(dev_host_data_to_device,
dev_host_data_to_device, num_elements);

    // Wait for device to complete all work
    CUDA_CALL(cudaDeviceSynchronize());

    // Check for kernel errors
    cuda_error_check(device_prefix, " calling kernel kernel_copy");

    // Add in all but first test run
    if (test != 0)
       (*kernel_time) += stop_device_timer();
    }

  // Average over number of test runs
  (*kernel_time) /= num_runs;

  if (pinned)
  {
   // Free pinned memory
   CUDA_CALL(cudaFreeHost(host_data_to_device));
   CUDA_CALL(cudaFreeHost(host_data_from_device));
  }
  else
  {
   // Free regular paged memory
   free(host_data_to_device);
   free(host_data_from_device);
  }
 }

CUDA_CALL(cudaFree(gpu_data));
destroy_device_timer();

// Free up the device
CUDA_CALL(cudaDeviceReset());

printf(" KERNEL:%.2f ms", (*kernel_time));

const float one_mb = (1024 * 1024);
const float kernel_time_for_one_mb = (*kernel_time) * (one_mb / size_in_bytes);

// Adjust for doing a copy to and back
```

```
const float MB_per_sec = ((1000.0F / kernel_time_for_one_mb) * 2.0F);

printf(" KERNEL:%.0f MB/s", MB_per_sec );
}
```

Bandwidth limitations

The ultimate bandwidth limitation of a significant number of applications is the I/O speed of whatever devices the input and output data have to be acquired from and written to. This is often the limitation on the speedup of any application. If your application takes 20 minutes to run on a serial CPU implementation and can express enough parallelism, it's quite feasible for that application to run on a GPU in less time than it takes to load and save the data from the storage device you are using.

The first problem we have in terms of bandwidth is simply getting the data in and out of the machine. If you are using network-attached storage, the limit to this will be the speed of the network link. The best solution to this problem is a high-speed SATA3 RAID controller using many high-speed SSD drives. However, this will not solve your bandwidth issues unless you are using the drive efficiently. Each drive will have a peak transfer rate into host memory, which is actually a function of the transfer rate of the drive, the controller, and the route to host memory.

Running a benchmark on a drive, such as the commonly used ATTO benchmark, can show you the effect of using different size blocks (see Figure 9.20). This benchmark simulates access to drives based on a certain size of reads and writes. Thus, it reads and writes a 2 GB file in blocks of 1 K, 2 K, 4 K, etc. to see the effect of changing the block size.

We can see from the results that only when we read data in 64 K chunks or more do we achieve the peak bandwidth from the single SSD drive. For the RAID 0 hard drive system we need at least 1 MB blocks to make use of the multiple disks. Thus, you need to make sure you're using the `fread` function

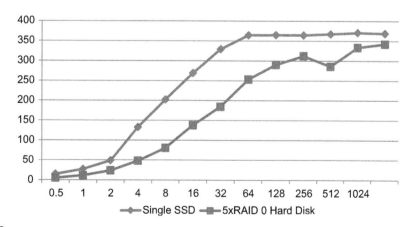

FIGURE 9.20

Bandwidth (MB/s) for a single SSD versus five hard disks in RAID 0.

in C to read suitable sized blocks of data from the disk subsystem. If we fetch data in 1 K chunks, we get just 24 MB/s from the drive, less than 10% of its peak read bandwidth. The more drives you add to a RAID system, the larger the minimum block size becomes. If you are processing compressed music or image files, the size of a single file may only be a few megabytes.

Note also that whether the data is compressible or not has a big impact on drive performance. The server level drives, such as the OCZ Vertex 3, provide both higher peak values and sustained bandwidth with uncompressible data. Thus, if your dataset is in an already compressed format (MP3, MP4, WMV, H.264, JPG, etc.), then you need to make sure you use server drives. The bandwidth on many consumer-level SSD drives can fall to half of quoted peak when using uncompressible data streams.

The reason for this is the use of synchronous NAND memory in the high-end server SSDs versus the cheaper and much lower-performing asynchronous NAND memory used in consumer SSDs. Even with noncompressed data, synchronous NAND-based drives still outperform their asynchronous cousins, especially once the drive starts to contain some data. OCZ also provides the RevoDrive R4 PCI-E-based product, which claims speeds in the order of 2 GB/s plus at the expense of a PCI-E slot.

The next bandwidth limit you hit is that of host memory speed. This is typically not an issue until you introduce multiple GPUs per node, if you consider that you can fetch data at 6 GB/s off the PCI-E bus from a very high-speed SSD RAID system. We then have to send out data at 6 GB/s to and from the host memory to the GPU. Potentially you could also write data again at 6 GB/s to the RAID controller. That's a potential 24 GB/s of pure data movement without the CPU actually doing anything useful except moving data. We're already hitting the bandwidth limits of most modern processor designs and have already surpassed that available from the older-generation CPUs. In fact, only the latest quad channel I7 Sandybridge-E CPU has anything like the bandwidth we could start moving around, if we were to solve the slow I/O device issue.

CUDA 4.0 SDK introduced Peer2Peer GPU communication. The CUDA 4.1 SDK also introduced Peer2Peer communication with non-NVIDIA hardware. Thus, with the correct hardware, GPUs can talk to any supported device. This is mostly limited to a small number of InfiniBand and other highspeed network cards. However, in principle, any PCI-E device can talk with the GPU. Thus, a RAID controller could send data directly to and from a GPU. There is a huge potential for such devices, as no host memory bandwidth, PCI-E, or memory is consumed. As data is not having to flow to a CPU and then back out again, latency is dropped considerably.

Once the data has been moved to the GPU, there is a bandwidth limit of up to 190 GB/s on GeForce cards and 177 GB for Tesla, to and from the global memory on the device. To achieve this you need to ensure coalescing of the data reads from the threads and ensure your application makes use of 100% of the data moved from memory to the GPU.

Finally, we have shared memory. Even if you partition data into tiles, move it into shared memory, and access it in a bank conflict–free manner, the bandwidth limit is on the order of 1.3 TB/s. For comparison the AMD Phenom II and Nehalem I7 CPUs have, for a 64 KB L1 cache block, the same capacity as the GPU L1 cache and shared memory, has around 330 GB/s bandwidth, some 25% of that of the GPU.

If we take a typical float or integer parameter, it's 4 bytes wide. Thus, the bandwidth to global memory is a maximum of 47.5 giga-elements per second (190 GB/s $\div$ 4). Assuming you read and write just one value, we can halve this figure to 23.75 giga-elements per second. Thus, with no data reuse, this is the maximum upper throughput of your application.

The Fermi device is rated in excess of 1 teraflop, that is, it can process on the order of 1000 giga floating-point operations per second. Kepler is rated at in excess of 3 teraflops. The actual available flops depend on how you measure flops. The fastest measure is the FMADD instruction (floating-point multiply and add) instruction. This multiplies two floating-point numbers together and adds another number to it. As such, this counts as two flops, not one. Real instruction streams intermix memory loads, integer calculations, loops, branches, etc. Thus, in practice, kernels never get near to this peak figure.

We can measure the real speed achievable by simply using the program we previously developed to visualize the PCI-E bandwidth. Simply performing a memory copy from global memory to global memory will show us the maximum possible read and write speed a kernel can achieve.

```
GTX 470: 8 bytes x 1 K (1x4x32)     0.060 ms, 489 MB/s
GTX 470: 8 bytes x 2 K (1x8x32)     0.059 ms, 988 MB/s
GTX 470: 8 bytes x 4 K (1x16x32)    0.060 ms, 1969 MB/s
GTX 470: 8 bytes x 8 K (1x32x32)    0.059 ms, 3948 MB/s
GTX 470: 8 bytes x 16 K (1x32x64)   0.059 ms, 7927 MB/s
GTX 470: 8 bytes x 32 K (1x64x64)   0.061 ms, 15444 MB/s
GTX 470: 8 bytes x 64 K (1x64x128)  0.065 ms, 28779 MB/s
GTX 470: 8 bytes x 128 K (1x64x256) 0.074 ms, 50468 MB/s
GTX 470: 8 bytes x 256 K (1x128x256) 0.090 ms, 83053 MB/s
GTX 470: 8 bytes x 512 K (1x256x256) 0.153 ms, 98147 MB/s
GTX 470: 8 bytes x 1 M (1x512x256) 0.30 ms, 98508 MB/s
GTX 470: 8 bytes x 2 M (1x1024x256) 0.56 ms, 105950 MB/s
GTX 470: 8 bytes x 4 M (1x2048x256) 1.10 ms, 108888 MB/s
GTX 470: 8 bytes x 8 M (1x4096x256) 2.19 ms, 112215 MB/s
GTX 470: 8 bytes x 16 M (1x8192x256) 4.26 ms, 112655 MB/s
GTX 470: 8 bytes x 32 M (1x16384x256) 8.48 ms, 113085 MB/s
GTX 470: 8 bytes x 64 M (1x32768x256) 16.9 ms, 113001 MB/s
GTX 470: 8 bytes x 128 M (2x32768x256) 33.9 ms, 112978 MB/s
GTX 470: 8 bytes x 256 M (4x32768x256) 67.7 ms, 113279 MB/s
```

Note the values in the parentheses shows grids × blocks × threads. The above figures are plotted in Figure 9.21.

These results are created by pushing 16 kernels into an asynchronous stream, with each call surrounded by a stop and start event. Each kernel performs a single-element copy from the source to the destination for every memory location. The execution time of the first kernel in each batch is ignored. The remaining kernels contribute to the total time, which is then averaged over the kernels. The quoted bandwidth for the GTX470 is 134 GB/s, so we're falling short of this, despite having a simple kernel and obviously hitting the peak at the larger transfer sizes.

What we see from this chart is that to achieve anywhere near the peak memory performance you need to have enough threads. We start off by using 32 threads per block until we launch a total of 64 blocks. This ensures that all the SMs are given work, rather than one SM getting a large number of threads and therefore most of the work. We then increase the thread count per block up to 256 threads once there is a reasonable distribution of blocks to the SMs.

Changing the element type from uint1 to uint2, uint3, and uint4 produces some interesting results. As you increase the size of a single element, the total number of transactions issued to the memory subsystem is reduced. On the GTX470, going from the 4-byte read (single-element integer or float) to an 8-byte read (dual-element integer, float, or single-element double) resulted in up to a peak

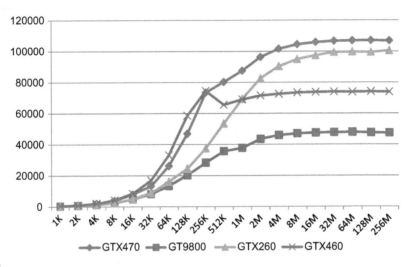

FIGURE 9.21

Global memory bandwidth across devices.

23% increase in measured bandwidth to and from global memory (Figure 9.22). The average improvement was somewhat lower at just 7%, but this still represents a reasonable improvement in execution time by simply switching from int/float to int2/float2 vector types. The GTX460 presents a similar, but more pronounced pattern (Figure 9.23).

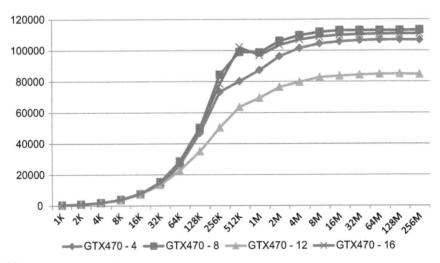

FIGURE 9.22

Global memory bandwidth GTX470/compute 2.0 (transaction size in bytes).

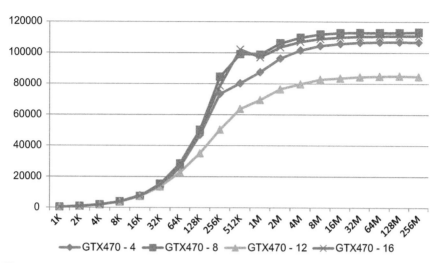

FIGURE 9.23

Global memory bandwidth GTX460/compute 2.1 (transaction size in bytes).

To achieve optimum bandwidth, the CUDA code was compiled specifically for compute 2.1 devices. We also found that thread blocks that were a multiple of 48 threads worked best. This is not surprising given that there are three sets of 16 cores per SM instead of the usual two. When moving from 4 bytes per element to 8 or 16 bytes per element, the bandwidth was increased by an average of 19%, but a best case of 38%.

A single warp transaction for 8 bytes per thread would result in a total of 256 bytes ($8 \times 32 \times 8$) moving over the memory bus. The GTX460 we are using has a 256-bit-wide bus to the global memory. This would clearly indicate that, regardless of any occupancy considerations, on such devices you should always be processing either 8 or 16 bytes (two or four elements) per thread. This is most likely due to the higher ratio of CUDA codes within the SM causing some contention for the single set of LSUs (load/store units).

The GTX260 for comparison, a compute 1.3 device similar to the Tesla C2050 device, gained, on average, 5% by moving from 4 to 8 bytes per element. However, its performance was drastically reduced when moving beyond this. The 9800 GT did not show any significant improvement, suggesting this device is already achieving the peak when using 4 bytes per element.

Finally, note that Fermi-based Tesla devices implement an ECC (error checking and correction) based memory protocol. Disabling this can boost transfer speeds by around 10% at the expense of the error detection and correction ability. In a single machine versus a server room, this may be an acceptable tradeoff.

GPU timing

Single GPU timing

Timing data on the GPU is not particularly straightforward. Using a timer that is CPU based is not a good solution, as the best way to use the GPU and CPU is to operate asynchronously. That is, both the

GPU and CPU are running at the same time. CPU timing is only semi-accurate when you force sequential operation of the GPU and CPU. As this is not what we want in practice, it's a poor solution.

The GPU, by default, operates in a synchronous mode in that the memcpy operations implicitly synchronize. The programmer expects to copy to the device, run the kernel, copy back from the device, and have the results in CPU memory to save to disk or for further processing. While this is an easy model to understand, it's also a slow model. It's one aimed at getting kernels to work, but not one aimed at performance.

We examined the use of streams, in detail, in Chapter 8. A stream is effectively a work queue. Stream 0 is used as the default work queue when you do not specify a stream to the CUDA API. However, stream 0 has many operations that implicitly synchronize with the host. You might be expecting an asynchronous operation, but in practice certain API calls have implicit synchronization when using stream 0.

To use asynchronous operations, we need to first create a stream such as

```
// Create a new stream on the device
cudaStream_t stream;
CUDA_CALL(cudaStreamCreate(&stream));
```

For the bandwidth test, we created an array of events.

```
#define MAX_NUM_TESTS 16
cudaEvent_t kernel_start[MAX_NUM_TESTS];
cudaEvent_t kernel_stop[MAX_NUM_TESTS];
```

The GPU provides events that can be time-stamped by the GPU hardware (Figure 9.24). Thus, to time a particular action on the GPU, you need to push a start event into the queue, then the action you wish to time, and finally a stop event. Streams are simply a FIFO (first in, first out) queue of operations for the GPU to perform. Each stream represents an independent queue of operations.

Having created a stream, you need to create one or more events.

```
for (u32 test=0; test < MAX_NUM_TESTS; test++)
{
 CUDA_CALL(cudaEventCreate(&kernel_start[test]));
 CUDA_CALL(cudaEventCreate(&kernel_stop[test]));
}
```

Here we have a simple loop creating MAX_NUM_TESTS events—a start event and a stop event. We then need to push the events into the stream on either side of the action to measure.

```
// Start event
CUDA_CALL(cudaEventRecord(kernel_start[test],stream));

// Run the kernel
```

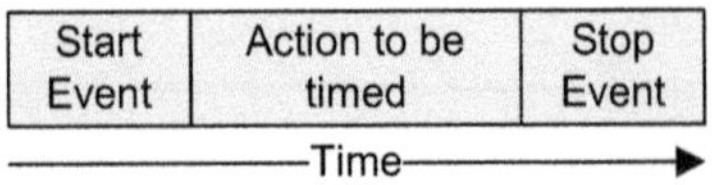

Start Event	Action to be timed	Stop Event

————————Time————————▶

FIGURE 9.24

Timing an action on the GPU.

```
kernel_copy_single<data_T><<<num_blocks, num_threads, dynamic_shared_memory_usage,
stream>>>(s_data_in, s_data_out, num_elements);

// Stop event
CUDA_CALL(cudaEventRecord(kernel_stop[test],stream));
```

To calculate the time, either per CUDA call or in total, call the CUDA function cudaEventElapsedTime to get the time difference between two time-stamped events.

```
// Extract the total time
for (u32 test=0; test < MAX_NUM_TESTS; test++)
{
 float delta;

 // Wait for the event to complete
 CUDA_CALL(cudaEventSynchronize(kernel_stop[test]));

 // Get the time difference
 CUDA_CALL(cudaEventElapsedTime(&delta, kernel_start[test], kernel_stop[test]));

 kernel_time += delta;
}
```

You should realize that in performing such a timed event, there is no guarantee of ordering of events between streams. The CUDA runtime could execute your start event in stream 0 and then switch to a previously suspended kernel execution in stream 5, sometime later come back to stream 0, kick off the kernel, jump to another stream to process a number of other start events, and finally come back to stream 0 and timestamp the stop event. The delta time is the time from the start period to the end period.

In this example, notice we have created only a single stream. We have multiple events, but they all execute from the same stream. With only a single stream the runtime can only execute events in order, so we guarantee achieving the correct timing.

Notice the call to the cudaEventSynchronize API. This call causes the CPU thread to block should it be called when the event has not completed. As we're doing nothing useful on the CPU, this is perfectly fine for our purposes.

At the end of the host program we must ensure that with any resources we allocated are freed up.

```
// Free up all events
for (u32 test=0; test < MAX_NUM_TESTS; test++)
{
 CUDA_CALL(cudaEventDestroy(kernel_start[test]));
 CUDA_CALL(cudaEventDestroy(kernel_stop[test]));
}
```

Destroying an event before it's actually been used will result in undefined runtime errors when executing the kernels.

Finally, you should be aware that events are not free. It takes some resources to handle the events at runtime. In this example we specifically wanted to time each kernel to ensure there was not significant variability. In most cases a single start and stop event at the start and end of the work queue will be entirely sufficient for the overall timing.

Multi GPU timing

Multi GPU timing is a little more complex, but based on the same principles. Again, we create a number of streams and push events into the streams.

Unfortunately, there is no function provided in the API to obtain the absolute timestamp from an event. You can only obtain the delta between two events. However, by pushing an event into the start of the stream, you can use this as time point zero and thus obtain the time relative to the start of the stream. However, asking for the delta time between events on different GPUs causes the API to return an error. This complicates creating a timeline when using multiple GPUs, as you may need to adjust the time based on when the start events actually happened. We can see in Figure 9.29 a copy to the device, a kernel execution, a copy from the device, a copy to the device, a second kernel invocation, and finally a copy from the device.

Notice that with different devices, the copy times are largely similar but the kernels' time will vary considerably. In the second-to-last copy from device operation for the GTX470 device (CFD 2), notice the bar is somewhat smaller (258 ms versus 290 ms). This is because the GTX470 starts its transfer first and only toward the tail end of the transfer do the other devices also initiate a transfer. The GT9800, being a much slower device, still has its kernel being executed while GTX470 has in fact completed its transfer. With different device generations, you will get such a pattern. The transfer rates are largely similar, but the kernel times cause shifts in the points where the transfers are initiated.

Figure 9.25 was generated using timers, but tools such as Parallel Nsight and the Visual Profiler will draw the timeline for you automatically, along with the CPU timeline so you can clearly see what has happened and when.

Note that it's possible with `cudaEventQuery` API to simply query if the event has completed without causing a blocking call as with `cudaEventSynchronize`. Thus, the CPU can continue to do useful work, or simply move onto the next stream to see if it has completed yet.

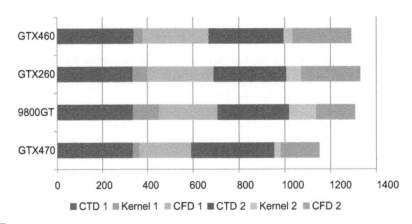

FIGURE 9.25

Multi-GPU timeline.

```
if ( cudaEventQuery( memcpy_to_stop[device_num][complete_count_in_stop[device_num]] )
== cudaSuccess)
{
 TIMER_T delta = 0.0F;

 CUDA_CALL( cudaEventElapsedTime( &delta, memcpy_to_start[device_num][0],
memcpy_to_stop[device_num][complete_count_in_stop[device_num]] ));

 printf("%sMemcpy to device test %d completed %.2f ms", device_prefix[device_num],
complete_count_in_stop[device_num], delta);

 complete_count_in_stop[device_num]++;
 event_completed = true;
}
```

In this particular example, taken from another program, we have an array of events, `memcpy_to_stop`, indexed by device number and test number. We check if the event has completed by a call to `cudaEventQuery`, which returns `cudaSuccess` if the event has already completed. If so, we get the delta time between this event and the start event `memcpy_to_start` from the same device, but for test 0, we get the start event for the whole kernel stream on that GPU. To obtain the delta time we simply call the `cudaEventElapsedTime` function.

Note, as this will generate an error if the event has not yet completed, it is guarded by the check with `cudaEventQuery`. We could equally call `cudaEventSynchronize` if we simply wanted a blocking call that would wait for the event to complete.

If we're particularly interested in the absolute time, the GPU does provide access to the low-level timers with the help of some embedded PTX code:

```
// Fetch the lower 32 bits of the clock (pre compute 2.x)
unsigned int clock;
asm("mov.u32 %0, %%clock ;" : "=r"(clock));

// Fetch the clock (req. compute 2.x)
unsigned long int clock64;
asm("mov.u64 %0, %%clock64 ;" : "=r"(clock64));
```

This section of code loads the raw clock value into a C variable that can then later be stored in a history buffer and transferred back to the host. The special `%clock` value is simply a 32-bit counter that wraps at max(u32). Compute 2.x hardware provides a 64-bit clock, thus allowing a wider time range over which values can be timed. Note, the CUDA API provides functions to access these register values through the use of the `clock` and `clock64` functions respectively.

You can use this to measure the times of device functions within kernel calls or sections of code. Such measurements are not shown with either the Visual Profiler or Parallel Nsight, as their resolution onto the timing stops at the global-level kernel functions. You can also use this to store the times warps arrive at a barrier point. Simply create a store on a per-warp basis prior to a call to a barrier primitive such as `syncthreads`. You can then see the distribution of the warps to the synchronization point.

However, one very important caveat here is you must understand that a given warp in a kernel will not be running all the time. Thus, as with timing multiple streams, a warp may store a start time, get suspended, sometime later get resumed, and meet the next timer store event. The delta is only the overall real time difference, not the time the SM spent executing code from the given warp.

You should also realize that instrumenting code in this way may well affect its timing and execution order relative to other warps. You will be making global memory stores to later transfer this data back to the host where it can be analyzed. Consequently, your instrumentation impacts not only execution flow, but memory accesses. The effect of this can be minimized by running a single block of 32 threads, that is, a single warp. However, this entirely discounts the quite necessary effects of running with other warps present on the SM and across multiple SMs within the GPU.

Overlapping GPU transfers

There are two strategies for trying to overlap transfer; first, to overlap transfer times with the compute time. We've look at this in detail in the last section, explicitly with the use of streams and implicitly with the use of zero-copy memory.

Streams are a very useful feature of GPU computing. By building independent work queues we can drive the GPU device in an asynchronous manner. That is, the CPU can push a number of work elements into a queue and then go off and do something else before having to service the GPU again.

To some extent, operating the GPU synchronously with stream 0 is like polling a serial device with a single character buffer. Such devices were used in the original serial port implementations for devices like modems that operated over the RS232 interface. These are now obsolete and have been replaced with USB1, USB2, and USB3 interfaces. The original serial controller, a UART, would raise an interrupt request to the processor to say it had received enough bits to decode one character and its single character buffer was full. Only once the CPU serviced the interrupt could the communications continue. One character at a time communication was never very fast, and highly CPU intensive. Such devices were rapidly replaced with UARTs that had a 16-character buffer in them. Thus, the frequency of the device raising an interrupt to the CPU was reduced by a factor of 16. It could process the incoming characters and accumulate them to create a reasonably sized transfer to the CPU's memory.

By creating a stream of work for the GPU we're effectively doing something similar. Instead of the GPU working in a synchronous manner with the CPU, and the CPU having to poll the GPU all the time to find out if it's ready, we just give it a chunk of work to be getting on with. We then only periodically have to check if it's now out of work, and if so, push some more work into the stream or work queue.

Through the CUDA stream interface we can also drive multiple GPU devices, providing you remember to switch the desired device before trying to access it. For asynchronous operation, pinned or page-locked memory is required for any transfers to and from the GPU.

On a single-processor system, all the GPUs will be connected to a single PCI-E switch. The purpose of a PCI-E switch is to connect the various high-speed components to the PCI-E bus. It also functions as a means for PCI-E cards to talk to one another without having to go to host memory.

Although we may have multiple PCI-E devices, in the case of our test machine, four GPUs on four separate X8 PCI-E 2.0 links, they are still connected to a *single* PCI-E controller. In addition, depending on the implementation, this controller may actually be on the CPU itself. Thus, if we perform a set of transfers to multiple GPUs at any one point in time, although the individual bandwidth to each device may be in the order of 5 GB/s in each direction, can the PCI-E switch, the CPU, the memory, and other components work at that speed if all devices become active?

With four GPUs present on a system, what scaling can be expected? With our I7 920 Nehalem system, we measured around 5 GB/s to a single card using a PCI-E 2.0 X16 link. With the AMD system, we have around 2.5–3 GB/s on the PCI-E 2.0 X8 link. As the number of PCI-E lanes are half that of the I7 system, these sorts of numbers are around what you might expect to achieve.

We modified the bandwidth test program we used earlier for measuring the PCI-E bandwidth to measure the bandwidth as we introduce more cards and more concurrent transfers. Any number of things can affect the transfers once we start introducing concurrent transfers to different GPUs. Anyone familiar with the multi-GPU scaling within the games industry will appreciate that simply inserting a second GPU does not guarantee twice the performance. Many benchmarks show that most commercial games benefit significantly from two GPU cards. Adding a third card often introduces some noticeable benefit, but nothing like the almost times two scaling that is often seen with a second card. Adding a fourth card will often cause the performance to drop.

Now this may not seem very intuitive, adding more hardware equals lower speed. However, it's the same issue we see on CPUs when the core count becomes too high for the surrounding components. A typical high-end motherboard/CPU solution will dedicate at most 32 PCI-E lands to the PCI-E bus. This means only two cards can run at full X16 PCI-E 2.0 speed. Anything more than this is achieved by the use of PCI-E switch chips, which multiplex (share) the PCI-E lines. This works well until the two cards on the PCI-E multiplexer both need to do a transfer at the same time.

The AMD system we've run most of these tests in this book on does not use a multiplexer, but drops the speed of each connected GPU to an X8 link when four GPUs are present. Thus, at 2.5–3 GB/s per device, we could achieve a theoretical maximum of 10–12.5 GB/s. In addition, being an AMD solution, the PCI-E controller is built into the processor, which also sits between the PCI-E system and main memory. The bandwidth to main memory is approximately 12.5 GB/s. Therefore, you can see this system would be unlikely to achieve the full potential of four GPUs. See Tables 9.2 and 9.3 and Figures 9.26 and 9.27.

What you can see from Tables 9.2 and 9.3 is that transfers scale quite nicely to three GPUs. We're seeing approximately linear scaling. However, when the four GPUs compete for the available resources (CPU, memory bandwidth, and PCI-E switch bandwidth) the overall rate is slower.

Table 9.2 Bandwidth Effects of Multiple PCI-E Transfers to the Device

	1 Device	2 Devices	3 Devices	4 Devices
470 to device	3151	3082	2495	1689
GT9800GT to device	0	3069	2490	1694
GTX260 to device	0	0	2930	1792
GTX460 to device	0	0	0	1822

Table 9.3 Bandwidth Effects of Multiple PCI-E Transfers from the Device

	1 Device	2 Devices	3 Devices	4 Devices
470 from device	2615	2617	2245	1599
GT9800 from device	0	2616	2230	1596
GTX260 from device	0	0	2595	1522
GTX460 from device	0	0	0	1493

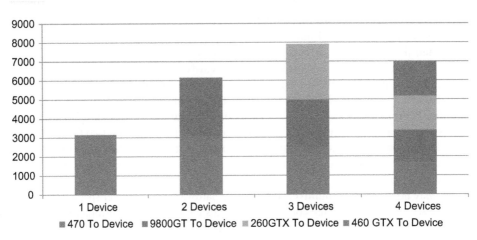

FIGURE 9.26

Multi-GPU PCI-E bandwidth to device AMD 905e Phenom II.

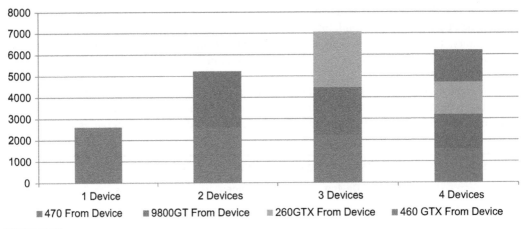

FIGURE 9.27

Multi-GPU PCI-E bandwidth from device AMD 905e Phenom II.

The other multi-GPU platform we have to work with is a six-GPU system based on the Nehalem I7 platform and the ASUS supercomputer motherboard (P6T7WS) with 3 GTX295 Dual GPU cards. This uses dual NF200 PCI-E switch chips allowing each PCI-E card to work with a full X16 link. While this might be useful for inter-GPU communication, the P2P (peer-to-peer) model supported in CUDA 4.x, it does not extend the bandwidth available to and from the host if both cards are simultaneously using the bus. Internally, each GPU has to share the X16 PCI-E 2.0 link. Table 9.4 and Figure 9.28 show what effect this has.

Table 9.4 I7 Bandwidth to Device						
	1 Device	**2 Devices**	**3 Devices**	**4 Devices**	**5 Devices**	**6 Devices**
To device 0	5026	3120	2846	2459	2136	2248
To device 1	0	3117	3328	2123	1876	1660
To device 2	0	0	2773	2277	2065	2021
To device 3	0	0	0	2095	1844	1588
To device 4	0	0	0	0	1803	1607
To device 5	0	0	0	0	0	1579
Overall	5026	6237	8947	8954	9724	10,703

As you can see from Table 9.4, we see an approximate linear increase in total bandwidth to the device. We achieve a peak of just over 10 GB/s, 20% or so higher than our AMD-based system.

We can see the bandwidth from the device is a different story (Table 9.5 and Figure 9.29). Bandwidth peaks with two devices, and is not significantly higher than our AMD system. This is not altogether unexpected if you consider the design in most GPU systems is based around gaming. In a game, most of the data is being sent *to* the GPU with very little if any coming back to the CPU host. Thus, we see a near linear scaling of up to three cards, which coincides with the top-end triple SLI (scalable link interface) gaming platforms. Vendors have little incentive to provide PCI-E bandwidth beyond this setup. As the GTX290 is actually a dual-GPU card, we may also be seeing that the internal

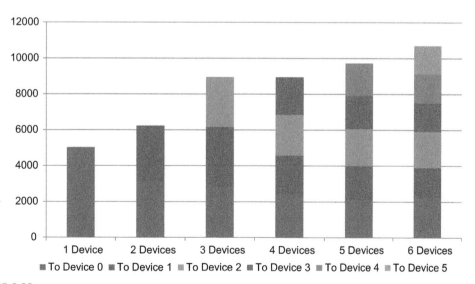

FIGURE 9.28

I7 bandwidth to device.

Table 9.5 I7 Bandwidth from Device

	1 Device	2 Devices	3 Devices	4 Devices	5 Devices	6 Devices
From device 0	4608	3997	2065	1582	1485	1546
From device 1	0	3976	3677	1704	1261	1024
From device 2	0	0	2085	1645	1498	1536
From device 3	0	0	0	1739	1410	1051
From device 4	0	0	0	0	1287	1035
From device 5	0	0	0	0	0	1049
Overall	4608	7973	7827	6670	6941	7241

SLI interface is not really able to push the limits of the card. We're clearly seeing some resource contention.

Section summary

- Understand and plan for the fact you will have limited PCI-E bandwidth capability.
- Always use pinned memory where possible.
- Use transfer sizes of at least 2 MB.
- Understand the use of zero-copy memory as an alternative to the stream API.
- Think about how to overlap transfer time with kernel execution time.
- Do not expect a linear scaling of bandwidth when using multiple GPUs.

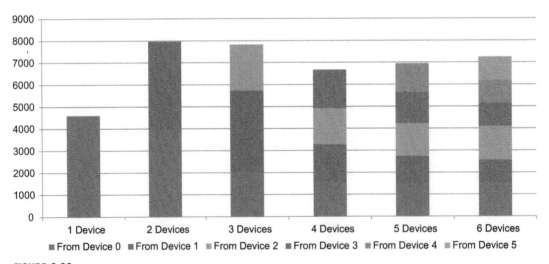

FIGURE 9.29

I7 bandwidth from device.

STRATEGY 4: THREAD USAGE, CALCULATIONS, AND DIVERGENCE
Thread memory patterns

Breaking down the application into *suitably* sized grids, blocks, and threads is often one of the key aspects of performance of CUDA kernels. Memory is the bottleneck in almost any computer design, the GPU included. A bad choice of thread layout typically also leads to a bad memory pattern, which will significantly harm performance.

Consider the first example, a 2×32 layout of threads (Figure 9.30) versus a 32×2 layout of threads. Think about how they would typically overlay memory if they were processing floating-point values. In the 2×32 example, thread 0 cannot be coalesced with any other thread than thread 1. In this case the hardware issues a total of 16 memory fetches. The warp cannot progress until at least the first half-warp has acquired all the data it needs. Therefore, at least eight of these very long memory transactions need to complete prior to any compute activity on the SM. As most warps will be following the same pattern, the SM will be swamped with issuing memory requests while the compute part of the SM is almost idle.

We saw from the bandwidth analysis in the previous section that there is a limit to the number of memory requests the SM can push out from the warps. The SM services the data request for any single warp over two clock cycles. In our example, the request has to be broken into 16×8 byte memory transactions.

Thread 0	Thread 1
Thread 2	Thread 3
Thread 4	Thread 5
Thread 6	Thread 7
Thread 8	Thread 9
Thread 10	Thread 11
Thread 12	Thread 13
Thread 14	Thread 15
Thread 16	Thread 17
Thread 18	Thread 19
Thread 20	Thread 21
Thread 22	Thread 23
Thread 24	Thread 25
Thread 26	Thread 27
Thread 28	Thread 29
Thread 30	Thread 31

FIGURE 9.30

2×32 thread grid layout.

On Fermi, the first of these would cause a read miss in the L1 cache. The L1 cache would request the minimum size of data possible, 128 bytes from the L2 cache, and some 16 times more data than the thread needs. Thus, when data is moved from the L2 cache to the L1 cache, just 3.125% of the data moved is consumed by thread 0. As thread 1 also wants the adjacent address, we can increase this to 6.25%, which is still terrible.

On the first run through the code the L2 cache is unlikely to contain the data. It issues a 128-byte fetch also to slow global memory. This latency-expensive operation is finally performed and 128 bytes arrive at the L2 cache.

The L2 cache is 768 K in size on a 16 SM device. Assuming we're using a GTX580, we have 16 SMs. That is just 48 KB per SM, the maximum size of the L1 cache. Using 128-byte cache lines we have just 384 entries in the cache per SM. If we assume the SM is fully loaded with 48 warps (Kepler supports 64), each warp will issue 16 separate reads, which is 768 reads in total. This means we'd need 768 cache lines, not the 384 we have, just to cache the data needed so each warp can hold a single block in memory.

The cache is effectively far too small to be used for temporal locality in this example. By temporal locality we mean we expect the data to remain in the cache from one read to the next. Halfway through processing the warps in each SM, the cache is full and the hardware starts filling it with new data. Consequently, there is absolutely no data reuse with the L2 cache, but a significant overhead in having to fetch entire cache lines. In fact, the only saving grace is that Fermi, unlike previous generations, will now forward the data it fetched to the other thread in our example.

The cache model is one that can cause problems in that it allows people to think the hardware will save them from poor programming. Let's assume for a moment we have to use this thread pattern and we would have processed the element we fetched from memory a number of times. The thread pattern for fetching data does not have to be the same thread pattern for using the data. We can fetch data into shared memory in a 32×2 pattern, synchronize the threads, and then switch to a 2×32 usage pattern if we wish. Despite the shared memory bank conflicts this would then incur, it would still be an order of magnitude faster than doing the global memory fetches. We can also simply add a padding element to the shared memory by declaring it as 33×2 to ensure when we access it, these bank conflicts are removed.

Consider for a moment the difference in handling of the memory system. We issue 1 coalesced read for 128 bytes instead of 16 separate reads. There's a factor of 16:1 improvement in both the number of memory transactions in flight and also bandwidth usage. Data can be moved from the L2 to the L1 cache in just one transaction, not 16.

The LSUs in the SM have to issue only a single fetch transaction instead of 16 separate fetches, taking just 2 clock cycles instead of 32 and freeing up the LSUs for other tasks from other warps.

Each warp consumes a single cache line, 48 maximum per SM in our compute 2.x device. Thus, of the 384 cache lines we have per SM in the L2 cache, we're using only 100, just 12.5% of the L2 cache instead of 200%. Thus, it's absolutely critical that to get anywhere near the full performance, even in Fermi with its multilevel caches, you have to fetch data in coalesced blocks of 128 bytes across a warp.

Now we could configure the L2 cache to fetch only 32 bytes instead of 128 bytes using the -Xptxas -dlcm=cg compiler flag. However, this also disables global memory storage in the L1 cache. It's an easy fix but a poor solution to the fact that you are not fetching data in large enough blocks from global memory. To get the best performance from a given device, you need to understand what's going on down inside or use libraries that are coded by someone who does.

We can see this quite clearly with the effects on memory bandwidth with Parallel Nsight if you select "Custom" experiment and then add in the L1 and L2 cache counters. The particular counters we

Table 9.6 Parallel Nsight Cache Counters

Nsight Counter	Usage
L1 global load hits	The number of global memory load requests met by the L1 cache.
L1 global load misses	The number of global memory load requests not met by the L1 cache.
L2 subpartition 0 read section misses	Half the number of L2 misses.
L2 subpartition 1 read section misses	The other half of the number of L2 misses.
L2 subpartition 0 read section queries	Half the number of L2 access attempts.
L2 subpartition 1 read section queries	The other half of the number of L2 access attempts.

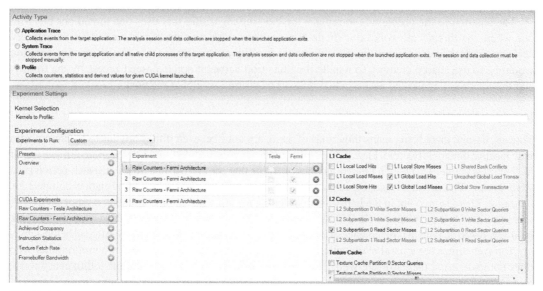

FIGURE 9.31

Setting up Parallel Nsight to capture cache statistics.

are interested in are shown in Table 9.6. These can be set up in Parallel Nsight using the "Custom" experiment, shown in Figure 9.31.

From these counters we can manually work out the L1 and L2 cache hit ratio. The hit ratio is the percentage of reads (or writes) that we cached. Every cached access saves us several hundreds of cycles of global memory latency.

Table 9.7 Cache Hit Ratio for Sample Sort

Function	Time	Occupancy	Active Warps	Blocks	Threads	L1 Hit %	L2 Hit %
sort_bins_gpu_kernel	28.8 ms	0.17	8	512	32	87	69
sort_bins_gpu_kernel	33.5 ms	0.33	16	256	64	86	60
sort_bins_gpu_kernel	44.4 ms	0.67	32	128	128	80	36
sort_bins_gpu_kernel	47 ms	0.83	40	64	256	78	32

When we look at the results for the sample sort algorithm in Table 9.7, we can instantly see the L2 cache hit ratio drops off sharply as soon as the kernel exceeds 64 threads. Occupancy increases, but performance drops off. This is not at all surprising given the usage of the L2 cache a prefix sum array will generate. If each thread is processing one bin, as we extend the number of threads, the size of the memory area being cached increases. As soon as it exceeds the L2 cache size the hit ratio rapidly drops off.

The solution to the problem is to replace the existing algorithm that uses one thread per bin with one where the threads all work on a single bin at a time. This way we'd achieve coalesced memory accesses on each iteration and significantly better locality of memory access. An alternative solution would be to use shared memory to handle the transition between noncoalesced access by the threads and the necessary coalesced access when reading or writing to global memory.

Inactive threads

Threads, despite there being many thousands of them, are not free, even if they are inactive. The problem with inactive threads is twofold. First, a warp will remain active, scheduled, and using resources if just one of its threads is active. There are a limited number of warps that can be dispatched in a dispatch period (two clock cycles). This is two on compute 2.0 hardware, four on compute 2.1 hardware and eight in compute 3.x hardware. There is no point in the hardware dispatching a warp with a single thread to a set of 16 CUDA cores and having it use just a single CUDA core while the other 15 idle. However, this is exactly what the hardware has to do if there is divergence of execution flow within a warp down to just one thread being active.

You sometimes see a parallel reduction–type operation that has been written by a programmer who does not understand the hardware well. They will perform the reduction operation within every warp, going from 32 to 16, to 8, to 4, to 2, and finally to 1 active thread. Regardless of whether you use 32 threads or 1 thread the hardware still allocates 32 and simply masks out the inactive ones. Because the warps are still active, even if they have only one thread active, they still need to be scheduled onto the hardware.

A much better approach to this is to have all 32 threads in every block compute a set of partial results. Let's use the sum operation, as it's easy to understand. With 32 threads per warp, you can compute 64 additions in one cycle. Now have each thread store its value into shared memory. Thus, the first warp stores to element 0..31, the second to 32..63, etc. Now divide N, the number of elements of the reduction, by 2. Repeat the reduction using the threshold if (threadIdx.x < (N/2)) until such time as N equals 2.

Threads 0..255 read values 0..511 (eight active warps).
Threads 0..127 read values 0..256 (four active warps).
Threads 0..63 read values 0..127 (two active warps).
Threads 0..31 read values 0..63 (one active warp).
Threads 0..15 read values 0..31 (half an active warp).
Etc.

Warps with thread numbers greater than the threshold simply no longer get scheduled. The warps with values less than N are fully populated with work, until such time as N equals some value less than 32. At this point we can simply do an addition of all remaining elements, or continue to iterate toward the final addition.

Inactive warps are not in themselves free either. Although the SM internally cares about warps, not blocks, the external scheduler can *only schedule blocks* into an SM, not warps. Thus, if each block contains only one active warp, we can have as little as 6 to 8 warps for the SM to select from for scheduling. Usually we'd have up to 64 warps active in an SM, depending on the compute version and resource usage. This is a problem because the thread-level parallelism (TLP) model relies on having lots of threads to hide memory and instruction latency. As the number of active warps drops, the ability of the SM to hide latency using TLP also dramatically drops. As some point this will hurt the performance, especially if the warp is still making global memory accesses.

Therefore, at the last levels of such a reduction-type operation, or any operation where progressively larger numbers of warps will drop out, we need to introduce some instruction level parallelism (ILP). We want to terminate the last warp as soon as possible so the entire block can be retired and replaced with another block that will likely have a fresh set of active warps.

We look at reduction in detail later in this chapter.

Arithmetic density

Arithmetic density is a term that measures the relative number of calculations per memory fetch. Thus, a kernel that fetches two values from memory, multiplies them, and stores the result back to memory has very low arithmetic density.

```
C[z] = A[y] * B[x];
```

The fetch and store operations may well involve some index calculations. The real work being done is the multiplication. However, with only one operation being performed per three memory transactions (two reads and one write), the kernel is very much memory bound.

The total execution time is

$$T = \text{read time}(A) + \text{reads time}(B) + \text{arithmetic time}(M) + \text{store time}(C)$$

or

$$T = A + B + M + C$$

Notice we use here $A + B$ as opposed to multiplying A, the single memory fetch time, by 2. The individual read times are not easy to predict. In fact neither A, B, or C have a constant execution time, as they are affected by the loads other SMs are making on the memory subsystem. Fetching of A may also bring into the cache B, so the access time for B may be considerably less than A. Writing C may evict from the cache *A* or *B*. Changes to the resident lines in the L2 cache may be the result of the activity of an entirely different SM. Thus, we can see caching makes timing very unpredictable.

When looking at the arithmetic density, our goal is to increase the ratio of useful work done relative to memory fetches and other overhead operations. However, we have to consider what we define as a memory fetch. Clearly, a fetch from global memory would qualify for this, but what about a shared memory, or cache fetch? As the processor must physically move data from shared memory to a register to operate on it, we must consider this also as a memory operation. If the data comes from the L1, L2, or constant cache, it too has to be moved to a register before we can operate on it.

However, in the case of a shared memory or L1 cache access, the cost of such operations is reduced by an order of magnitude compared to global memory accesses. Thus, a global memory fetch should be weighted at $10\times$ if a shared memory fetch equates to $1\times$.

So how do we increase the arithmetic density of such instruction flows? First, we have to understand the underlying instruction set. The maximum operand size of an instruction is 128 bytes, a four-element vector load/store operation. This tells us the ideal chunk size for our data is four elements, assuming we're using floats or integers, two if we're using doubles. Thus, our operation should be in the first instance:

```
C[idx_C].x = A[idx_A].x * B[idx_b].x;
C[idx_C].y = A[idx_A].y * B[idx_b].y;
C[idx_C].z = A[idx_A].z * B[idx_b].z;
C[idx_C].w = A[idx_A].w * B[idx_b].w;
```

I've written this in long-hand form to make the operations clear. If you extend the vector-type class yourself and provide a multiplication operator that performs this expanded code, you can simply write

```
C[idx_C] = A[idx_A] * B[idx_b];
```

Unfortunately, the GPU hardware currently doesn't support such vector manipulations, only loads, stores, moves, and pack/unpack from scalar types.

With such vector-based operations, we amortize the cost of the associated operations (load A, load B, write C, calculate idx_A, calculate idx_B, calculate idx_C) over four multiplies instead of one. The load and store operations take marginally longer as we have to introduce a pack and unpack operation that was not needed when accessing scalar parameters. We reduce the loop iterations by a factor of four with a consequential drop in the number of memory requests, issuing a much smaller number of larger requests to the memory system. This vastly improves performance (~20%), as we have seen with some examples in this book.

Transcendental operations

The GPU hardware is aimed at speeding up gaming environments. Often these require the manipulation of hundreds of thousands of polygons, modeling the real world in some way. There are certain accelerators built into the GPU hardware. These are dedicated sections of hardware designed for a single purpose. GPUs have the following such accelerators:

- Division
- Square root

- Reciprocal square root
- Sine
- Cosine
- Log^2
- Base 2 exponent Ex^2

These various instructions perform operations to 24-bit accuracy, in line with the typical 24-bit RGB setup used in many game environments. None of these operations are enabled by default. Compute 1.x devices take various shortcuts that make single-precision math not IEEE 754 compliant. These will not be relevant to many applications, but be aware they are there. Fermi (compute 2.x) hardware brings IEEE compliance with regard to floating-point operations by default.

If you'd like the faster but less precise operation, you have to enable them using either the compile switch (`-use_fast_math`) or explicitly using intrinsic operations. The first step is simply to enable the option in the compiler and check the outcome of your existing application. The answer will be different, but by how much and how important this is, are the key questions. In the gaming industry it doesn't matter if the flying globe projectile is one pixel off to the left or right of the target—no one will notice. In compute applications it can make a very real difference.

Individual operations can also be selectively enabled in 24-bit math using an explicit compiler intrinsic such as `__logf(x)`, etc. For a complete list of these and an explanation of the drawbacks of using them, see Appendix C.2 of the CUDA C programming guide. They can considerably speed up your kernels so it's worth investigating if this is an option for your particular code.

Approximation

Approximation is a useful technique in problems that explore a certain search space. Double-precision math is particularly expensive, in the order of at least twice as slow as floating-point math. Single-precision math uses 24 bits for the mantissa and 8 bits for the exponent. Thus, in the compute 1.x devices a fast 24-bit integer approximation could be used to provide an additional computation path to the single- and double-precision math. Note in Fermi, the 24-bit native integer support was replaced with 32-bit integer support, so an integer approximation in 24-bit math is actually slower than if the same approximation was made in 32-bit math.

In all compute hardware versions that natively support double precision (compute 1.3 onwards), approximation in single precision is at least twice the speed of double-precision math. Sometimes a much higher speedup can be achieved because the single-precision calculations require less registers and thus potentially more blocks can be loaded into the hardware. Memory fetches are also half the size, doubling the effective per-element memory bandwidth. Consumer-based GPUs also have less double-precision units enabled in the hardware than their Tesla counterparts, making single-precision approximation a far more attractive proposition for such hardware.

Clearly, with approximating you are performing a tradeoff between speed and accuracy and introducing additional complexity into the program. Often this is a tradeoff worth exploring, for it can bring a significant speedup.

Once we have done the approximation, the kernel can test the result to see if it is within a certain range or meets some criteria by which further analysis is warranted. For this subset of the dataset, the single- or double-precision calculation is performed as necessary.

The initial pass simply acts as a filter on the data. For every data point that falls outside the criteria of interest, you have saved the expensive double-precision calculations. For every point that falls into it, you have added an additional 24- or 32-bit filtering calculation. Thus, the benefit of this approach depends on the relative cost of the additional filtering calculation versus the cost of double-precision math required for the full calculation. If the filters remove 90% of the double-precision calculations, you have a huge speedup. However, if 90% of the calculations require a further double-precision calculation, then this strategy is not useful.

NVIDIA claims Tesla Fermi has in the order of $8\times$ faster double-precision math over the previous compute 1.3 implementations (GT200 series). However, consumer-level Fermi cards are artificially restricted to one-quarter the double-precision performance of Tesla cards. Therefore, if double precision is key to your application, clearly a Tesla is the easy-fix solution to the problem. However, some may prefer the alternative of using multiple consumer GPUs. Two 3 GB 580 GTXs would likely provide a faster solution than a single Fermi Tesla for considerably less money.

If double precision is secondary or you simply wish to prototype a solution on commonly available hardware, then single precision of 24-bit filtered may be an attractive solution to this issue. Alternatively, if you have a mixture of GPUs, with an older card that is still good for single-precision usage, you can use the older card to scan the problem space for interesting sections, and the second card to investigate problem space in detail based on the likely candidates from the first card's quick evaluation. Of course with a suitable Tesla card, you can perform both passes with just a single card.

Lookup tables

One common optimization technique used for complex algorithms is a lookup table. On CPUs where computation is quite expensive, these generally work reasonably well. The principle is that you calculate a number of representative points in the data space. You then apply an interpolation method between points based on the proportional distance to either edge point. This is typically used in modeling of the real world in that a linear interpolation method with a sufficient number of key sample points provides a good approximation of the actual signal.

A variation on this technique is used in brute-force attacks on ciphers. Passwords on most systems are stored as hashes, an apparently unintelligible series of digits. Hashes are designed so that it's difficult to calculate the password from the hash by reversing the calculation. Otherwise, it would be trivial to calculate the original password based on a compromised hash table.

One method of attack on this type of system involves a CPU spending a considerable time generating all possible permutations based on the use of common and/or short passwords. The attacker then simply matches the precomputer hash against the target hash until such time as a match is made.

In both cases, the lookup table method trades memory space for compute time. By simply storing the result, you have instant access to the answer. Many people will have learned multiplication tables in their heads as children. It's the same principle; instead of tediously calculating $a \times b$, for the most common set of values, we simply memorize the result.

This optimization technique works well on CPUs, especially older ones, where the compute time may be significant. However, as the compute resources have become faster and faster, it can be cheaper to calculate the results than to look them up from memory.

If you consider the average arithmetic GPU instruction latency is between 18 to 24 cycles and the average memory fetch in the order of 400 to 600 cycles, you can clearly see we can do a lot of calculation work in the time it takes for the memory fetch to come back from global memory. This, however, assumes we have to go out to global memory for the result and that it's not stored in shared memory or the cache. It also does not consider that the GPU, unlike the CPU, will not idle during this memory fetch time. In fact, the GPU will likely have switched to another thread and be performing some other operation. This, of course, depends on the number of available warps you have scheduled onto the device.

In many cases the lookup may win over the calculation, especially where you are achieving a high level of GPU utilization. Where you have low utilization, the calculation method often wins out, depending of course on how complex the calculation really is. Let's assume we have 20-cycle instruction latency for arithmetic operations and 600-cycle latency for memory operations. Clearly, if the calculation takes less than 30 operations it would be much faster than a lookup in memory when we have low GPU utilization. In this case the SM is behaving like a serial processor, in that it has to wait for the memory fetch. With a reasonable utilization the memory fetch effectively becomes free, as the SM is simply executing other warps.

It's often a case of trying this and seeing how well it works. Also be prepared to take it back out again should you suddenly manage to increase utilization of the GPU through other means.

Note, in the case of linear interpolation, a low-precision floating point–based linear interpolation is available in the GPU hardware. This is a feature of the texture memory hardware, something we do not cover in this text. Texture memory was useful for its cache features (24 K per SM) in compute 1.x hardware, but this use has largely been made redundant by the L1/L2 cache introduced in Fermi. However, the linear interpolation in hardware may still be useful for some problems. See the "Texture and Surface Memory" chapter of the CUDA programming guide if this is of interest to you.

Some common compiler optimizations

We'll take a quick look at some compiler optimizations and how they affect GPUs. We cover these here to highlight cases where the optimizer may struggle and also to give you some understanding of how optimizations may be applied at the source code level where the automatic optimizations fail.

Some compilers are well known for producing efficient code on certain targets. Not surprisingly, the Intel ICC compiler produces extremely efficient code for the Intel platform. New features of the processor are incorporated rapidly to showcase the technology. Mainstream compilers often come from a code base that supports many targets. This allows for more efficient development, but means the compiler may not be so easy to customize for a single target.

As of the 4.1 SDK CUDA moved from using an Open64-based compiler to a more modern LLVM-based compiler. The most significant benefit from the user perspective is significantly faster compile times. NVIDIA also claims a 10% improvement in code speed. We saw noticeable improvements in code generation with this move. However, as with any new technology, there is room for improvement and I'm sure this will happen over time.

The optimizations compilers apply are well documented. What we present here is a broad overview of some common ones. For most programmers, simply setting the optimization level is entirely sufficient. Others prefer to know what exactly is going on and check the output. This is of course a tradeoff of your programming time versus the potential gain and the relative costs of these.

Strength reduction

When accessing an array index, typically nonoptimized compiler code will use

```
array_element_address = index * element size
```

This can be more efficiently replaced by one of two techniques. First, we must load the array base address (element 0) into a base register. Then we have the option of accessing an index as base + offset. We can also simply add a fixed offset, the size of an array element in bytes, to the base register after each loop iteration.

In terms of C this is the same as writing

```
{
 int i;
 int a[4];

 for (i=0;i<4;i++)
   a[i]=i;
}
```

vs.

```
{
 int i;

 int a[4];
 int *_ptr = a;

 for (i=0; i<4; i++)
   *_ptr++ = i;
}
```

In terms of GPU usage, this optimization relies on the fact that certain instructions (multiply, divide) are computationally expensive and others (addition) are cheaper. It tries to replace the expensive operations with cheaper (or faster) ones. This technique works well on CPUs as well as on GPUs. This is especially the case with compute 2.1 devices where integer addition has three times the throughput of integer multiplication.

Notice also that the pointer version of the code creates a dependency between loop iterations. The value of ptr must be known to execute the assignment. The first example is much easier to parallelize because there is no dependency on the loop iteration and the address of a[i] can easily be statically calculated. In fact, simply adding the #pragma unroll directive would have caused the compiler to unroll the entire loop, as the boundaries in this simple example are literals.

It's a typical example of a CPU-based optimization that may have been applied and to parallelize the loop you need to reverse-engineer back to the original code. It's shown here because it helps you understand how C code may have been changed in the past to provide faster execution time for a given target. Like most optimizations at the C source code level, it can lead to the purpose of the source code being obscured.

Loop invariant analysis

Loop invariant analysis looks for expressions that are constant within the loop body and moves them outside the loop body. Thus, for example,

```
for (int j=0;j<100;j++)
{
  for (int i=0; i<100; i++)
  {
    const int b = j * 200;
    q[i]= b;
  }
}
```

In this example, the parameter j is constant within the loop body for parameter i. Thus, the compiler can easily detect this and will move the calculation of b outside the inner loop and generate the following code:

```
for (int j=0;j<100;j++)
{
  const int b = j * 200;

  for (int i=0; i<100; i++)
  {
    q[i]= b;
  }
}
```

This optimized code removes thousands of unnecessary calculations of b, where j, and thus b, are constant in the inner loop. However, consider the case where b is an external to the function, a global variable, instead of a local variable. For example:

```
int b;

void some_func(void)
{
  for (int j=0;j<100;j++)
  {
    for (int i=0; i<100; i++)
    {
      b = j * 200;
      q[i]= b;
    }
  }
}
```

The compiler cannot safely make this optimization because the write to q may affect b. That is, the memory space of q and b may intersect. It cannot even safely reuse the result of j * 200 in the assignment to q, but must reload it from memory, as the contents of b may have changed since the assignment in the prior line.

If you consider each line individually, then the issue becomes somewhat clearer. Any memory transaction, a read or write, will likely cause a switch to another warp, if that transaction involves accessing anything that is not immediately available. That area of global memory is accessible to any thread in any warp, on any active block in any SM. From one instruction to the next you get the very real possibility that any writable non register data could have changed.

You might say, well I've split up the application into N tiles and the tiles do not intersect, so this is not necessary. As the programmer you may know this, but it is very difficult for the compiler to figure that out. Consequently, it opts for the safe route and does not perform such optimizations. Many programmers do not understand what the optimization stage of a compiler does, and thus when it does something that breaks the code, they blame the compiler. Consequently, compilers tend to be rather conservative in how they optimize code.

As the programmer, understanding this allows you to make such optimization at the source level. Remember to think of global memory as you might a slow I/O device. Read from it once and reuse the data.

Loop unrolling

Loop unrolling is a technique that seeks to ensure you do a reasonable number of data operations for the overhead of running through a loop. Take the following code:

```
{
  for (i=0;i<100;i++)
    q[i]=i;
}
```

In terms of assembly code, this will generate:

* A load of a register with 0 for parameter i.
* A test of the register with 100.
* A branch to either exit or execute the loop.
* An increment of the register holding the loop counter.
* An address calculation of array q indexed by i.
* A store of i to the calculated address.

Only the last of these instructions actually does some *real* work. The rest of the instructions are overhead.

We can rewrite this C code as

```
{
  for (i=0;i<25;i+=4)
    q[i]=i;
    q[i+1]=i+1;
    q[i+2]=i+2;
    q[i+3]=i+3;
}
```

Thus, the ratio of useful work to overhead of using the loop is much increased. However, the size of the C source code is somewhat increased and it's now less obvious what exactly it was doing compared to the first loop.

In terms of PTX code, we see each C statement translated into PTX. For every branch test, there are now four memory copy operations. Thus, the GPU is executing more instructions than before, but a higher percentage of the memory copy operations are doing useful work.

In the CPU domain often there are limited registers, so the same registers will be reused in each step. This reduces register overhead, but means $q[i+1]$ cannot start processing until $q[i]$ has completed. We'd see the same overhead on the GPU with this approach. Each instruction has 20 cycles of latency. Therefore, the GPU assigns each address calculation to a separate register, so we have a set of four parallel instructions, rather than four sequential instructions executing. Each set is pushed into the pipelines and thus comes out one after another almost back to back.

With this approach the limit is the number of registers. As the GPU has 64 (compute 2.x,3.0) and 128 (compute 1.x) maximum, there is considerable scope for unrolling small loop bodies and achieving a good speedup.

The NVCC compiler supports the #pragma unroll directive, which will automatically unroll fully such loops when the iteration count is constant or silently do nothing when it's not. The latter is less than helpful, if the programmer has specified the loop should be unrolled. If the compiler is not able to, it should complain about this until the code is amended or the pragma removed.

You can also specify #pragma unroll 4 where four is replaced by any number the programmer wishes. Typically four or eight will work well, but beyond that too many registers will be used and this will result in register spilling. On compute 1.x hardware, this will cause a huge performance drop as registers are spilled to global memory. From compute 2.x hardware onwards, registers are spilled to the L1 cache and then to global memory if necessary. The best solution is to try it and see which value works best for each loop.

Loop peeling

Loop peeling is an enhancement to the loop unrolling, when the number of iterations is not an exact multiple of the loop unrolling size. Here the last few iterations are peeled away and done separately, and then the main body of the loop is unrolled.

For example, if we have 101 loop iterations and plan to use four levels of loop unrolling, the first 100 iterations of the loop are unrolled and the final iteration is peeled away to allow the bulk of the code to operate on the unrolled code. The final few iterations are then handled as either a loop or explicitly.

Loop peeling can be equally applied to the start of a loop as to the end. It can be used in such cases to allow a nonaligned structure to be accessed as an aligned structure. For example, copying a byte-aligned memory section to another byte-aligned memory is slow because it has to be done one byte at a time. The first few iterations can be peeled away such that a 32-, 64-, or 128-byte alignment is achieved. Then the loop can switch to much faster word, double-, or quad-word based copies. At the end of the loop the byte-based copies can be used again.

When using the #pragma loop unroll N directive, the compiler will unroll the loop such that the number of iterations does not exceed the loop boundaries and insert the end of loop peeling code automatically.

Peephole optimization

This optimization simple searches for combinations of instructions that can be replaced by more complex instructions with the same functionality. The classic example of this is multiply followed by an add instruction, as you might see in a gain and offset type calculation. This type of construct can be replaced with the more complex `madd` (multiply and add) instruction, reducing the number of instructions from two to one.

Other types of peephole optimizations include simplification of flow of control, algebraic simplifications, and removal of unreachable code.

Common subexpressions and folding

Many programmers write code that repeats some operation, for example,

```
const int a = b[base + i] * c[base + i];
```

or

```
const int a = b[NUM_ELEMENTS-1] * c[NUM_ELEMENTS-1];
```

In the first example, arrays `b` and `c` are indexed by the `base` and `i` parameters. Providing these parameters are within local scope, the compiler can simply calculate the index (`base + i`), and add this value to the start address of arrays `b` and `c` and to the work address for each parameter. However, if either of the index parameters are global variables, then the calculation must be repeated, since either could have changed once multiple threads are used. With a single thread it would be safe to eliminate the second calculation. With multiple threads it may also be safe to do so, but the compiler doesn't know for sure, so will typically perform two calculations.

In the second example, the term `NUM_ELEMENTS-1` is repeated. If we assume that `NUM_ELEMENTS` is a define, then the preprocessor will substitute the actual value, so we get `b[1024-1] * c[1024-1]`. Clearly, $1024 - 1$ can in both instances be replaced by 1023. However, if `NUM_ELEMENTS` was actually a formal parameter, as it is in many kernel calls, this type of optimization is not available. In this case we have to drop back to common subexpression optimization.

Therefore, be aware that in making such constants parameters of a function, or by having such parameters in global memory, you may be limiting the compiler's ability to optimize the code. You then have to ensure such common subexpressions are not present in the source code. Often eliminating the common subexpressions makes the code simpler to understand and improves the performance.

Divergence

GPUs execute code in blocks, or warps. A single instruction is decoded once and dispatched to a warp scheduler. There it remains in a queue until the warp dispatcher dispatches it to a set of 32 execution units, which execute that instruction.

This approach amortizes the instruction fetch and decoding time over *N* execution units. This in itself is very similar to the old vector machines. However, the main difference is that CUDA does not require that every instruction execute in this way. If there is a branch in the code and only some instructions follow this branch, those instructions diverge while the others wait at the point of divergence.

The single fetch/decode logic then fetches the instruction stream for the divergent threads and the other threads simply ignore it. In effect, each thread within the warp has a mask that enables its execution or not. Those threads not following the divergence have the mask cleared. Conversely, those following the branch have the bit set.

This type of arrangement is called predication. A predicate is created, which results in a single bit being set for those threads within a warp that follow the branch. Most PTX op-codes support an optional predicate allowing selective threads to execute an instruction.

Thus, for example, consider the following code:

```
if (threadIdx.x < 32)
{
 if (threadIdx.x < 16)
 {
   if (threadIdx.x < 8)
    func_a1();
   else
    func_a2();
 }
 else
 {
   func_b();
 }
}
```

In the first line of code the program eliminates all other warps in the current block except the first warp, the first 32 threads. This does not result in any divergence within the warp. The other warps in the block are simply not scheduled for this section of the code. They do not stall, but fall through the code and continue the execution of subsequent code.

The first warp then meets a test for `threadIdx.x < 16`, which splits the warp exactly in half. This is a special scenario where the warp does not actually diverge. Although the warp size is 32, the divergence criteria are actually a half-warp. If you noticed earlier, the CUDA cores are arranged in banks of 16 cores, not 32 cores. The scheduler issues instructions to two or more sets of 16 cores per cycle. Thus both the true and false path of the conditional are executed.

In the subsequent step, threads 16 to 31 call the function `func_b`. However, threads 0..15 hit another conditional. This time it's not half-warp based, but quarter-warp based. The minimum scheduling quantity is 16 threads. Thus, the first set of eight threads jump off to call function `func_a1` while the second set of eight threads (8..15) stall.

Functions `func_b` and `func_a1` will continue to independently fetch instructions and dispatch them to the two half-warps. This is somewhat less efficient than a single instruction fetch, but nonetheless better than sequential execution. Eventually `func_a1` will complete and `func_a2` will start, stalling the threads 0..7. In the meantime `func_b` may have also completed. We can write a short test program to demonstrate this.

```
// All threads follow the same path
__global__ void cuda_test_kernel(
 u32 * const a,
 const u32 * const b,
```

```
 const u32 * const c,
 const u32 num_elements)
{
 const u32 tid = (blockIdx.x * blockDim.x) + threadIdx.x;

 if (tid < num_elements)
 {
   for (u32 iter=0; iter<MAX_ITER; iter++)
   {
    a[tid] += b[tid] * c[tid];
   }
 }
}

// Thread diverge by half warps
__global__ void cuda_test_kernel_branched_half(
 u32 * const a,
 const u32 * const b,
 const u32 * const c,
 const u32 num_elements)
{
 const u32 tid = (blockIdx.x * blockDim.x) + threadIdx.x;

 if (tid < num_elements)
 {
   for (u32 iter=0; iter<MAX_ITER; iter++)
   {
    if (threadIdx.x < 16)
     a[tid] += b[tid] * c[tid];
    else
     a[tid] -= b[tid] * c[tid];
   }
 }
}

// Thread diverge into one quarter group
__global__ void cuda_test_kernel_branched_quarter(
 u32 * const a,
 const u32 * const b,
 const u32 * const c,
 const u32 num_elements)
{
 const u32 tid = (blockIdx.x * blockDim.x) + threadIdx.x;

 if (tid < num_elements)
 {
   for (u32 iter=0; iter<MAX_ITER; iter++)
   {
```

```
   if (threadIdx.x < 16)
   {
    if (threadIdx.x < 8)
    {
      a[tid] += b[tid] * c[tid];
    }
    else
    {
      a[tid] -= b[tid] * c[tid];
    }
   }
   else
   {
    a[tid] += b[tid] * c[tid];
   }
  }
 }
}

// Thread diverge into one eighth group
__global__ void cuda_test_kernel_branched_eighth(
 u32 * const a,
 const u32 * const b,
 const u32 * const c,
 const u32 num_elements)
{
 const u32 tid = (blockIdx.x * blockDim.x) + threadIdx.x;

 if (tid < num_elements)
 {
   for (u32 iter=0; iter<MAX_ITER; iter++)
   {
    if (threadIdx.x < 16)
    {
     if (threadIdx.x < 8)
     {
       if (threadIdx.x < 4)
        a[tid] += b[tid] * c[tid];
       else
        a[tid] -= b[tid] * c[tid];
     }
     else
     {
       if (threadIdx.x >= 8)
        a[tid] += b[tid] * c[tid];
       else
        a[tid] -= b[tid] * c[tid];
     }
```

```
  }
  else
  {
   a[tid] += b[tid] * c[tid];
  }
  }
 }
}
```

Here we have set up a number of kernels, each of which exhibit different levels of divergence. The first is the optimal with no divergence. The second diverges based on half-warps. These half-warps should execute in parallel. We then further subdivide the first half-warp into two groups. These should execute in series. We then subdivide again the first group into a total of four serial execution paths. The results we see are as follows:

```
ID:0 GeForce GTX 470:Running 32768 blocks of 32 threads to calculate 1048576 elements
ID:0 GeForce GTX 470:All threads : 27.05 ms (100%)
ID:0 GeForce GTX 470:Half warps : 32.59 ms (121%)
ID:0 GeForce GTX 470:Quarter warps: 72.14 ms (267%)
ID:0 GeForce GTX 470:Eighth warps : 108.06 ms (400%)

ID:1 GeForce 9800 GT:Running 32768 blocks of 32 threads to calculate 1048576 elements
ID:1 GeForce 9800 GT:All threads : 240.67 ms (100%)
ID:1 GeForce 9800 GT:Half warps : 241.33 ms (100%)
ID:1 GeForce 9800 GT:Quarter warps: 252.77 ms (105%)
ID:1 GeForce 9800 GT:Eighth warps : 285.49 ms (119%)

ID:2 GeForce GTX 260:Running 32768 blocks of 32 threads to calculate 1048576 elements
ID:2 GeForce GTX 260:All threads : 120.36 ms (100%)
ID:2 GeForce GTX 260:Half warps : 122.44 ms (102%)
ID:2 GeForce GTX 260:Quarter warps: 149.60 ms (124%)
ID:2 GeForce GTX 260:Eighth warps : 174.50 ms (145%)

ID:3 GeForce GTX 460:Running 32768 blocks of 32 threads to calculate 1048576 elements
ID:3 GeForce GTX 460:All threads : 43.16 ms (100%)
ID:3 GeForce GTX 460:Half warps : 57.49 ms (133%)
ID:3 GeForce GTX 460:Quarter warps: 127.68 ms (296%)
ID:3 GeForce GTX 460:Eighth warps : 190.85 ms (442%)
```

We can see this somewhat better in a graphical format in Figure 9.32.

Notice how the thread divergence is not such a significant problem on the compute 1.x devices (the 9800 GT and GTX260). It has an effect, but takes the maximum time to just 145% of the optimal time. By comparison, the Fermi compute 2.x cards (GTX460, GTX470) suffer over a 4× slowdown when diverging significantly within a warp. The GTX460 seems especially sensitive to warp divergence. Notice the GTX470 is almost 10× faster in absolute terms than the 9800 GT when there is no divergence, which is a massive improvement for just two generations of cards.

If you are curious to know how much a 32-way divergence costs, it leads to a 27× slowdown on the compute 1.x cards and a massive 125× to 134× slowdown on the compute 2.x cards. Note that the

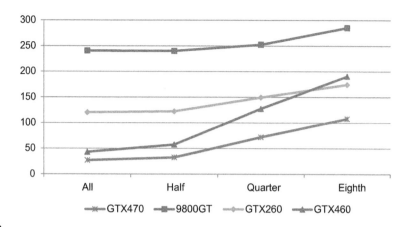

FIGURE 9.32

How thread divergence affects execution time.

code for this test was a simple switch statement based on the thread index, so it is not directly comparable to the code we're using here. However, clearly such divergence needs to be avoided at all costs.

The easiest method of avoiding divergence within a warp is to simply mask out the sections of the warp you don't wish to contribute to the result. How can you do this? Just perform the same calculation on every thread in the warp, but select a value that does not contribute for the threads you wish to mask out.

For example, for a `min` operation on 32-bit integers, select 0xFFFFFFFF as the value for threads that should not contribute. Conversely for `max`, `sum`, and many other arithmetic-type operations, just use 0 in the threads you do not wish to contribute. This will usually be much quicker than branching within a warp.

Understanding the low-level assembly code

The GPU compiles code into a virtual assembly system called PTX (Parallel Thread eXecution Instruction Set Architecture). This is a lot like Java byte-code in that it is a virtual assembly language. This can either be translated at compile time or runtime into the real code, which executes on the device. The compile time translation simply inserts a number of real binaries into the application, depending on which architectures you specify on the command line (the `-arch` switch).

To look at the virtual assembly generated, you simply add the `-keep` flag to the compiler command line. For Visual Studio users, the default NVIDIA projects contain an option to keep the PTX files (`-keep`) (Figure 9.33). You can also specify the place to store them if you prefer they do not clutter up the project directory using the `-keep-dir <directory>` option.

However, PTX is not what is really executed on the hardware, so it's useful only to a certain degree. You can also see the actual binary post translation using the `cuobjdump` utility as follows:

```
cuobjdump -sass global_mem_sample_sort.sm_20.cubin > out.txt
```

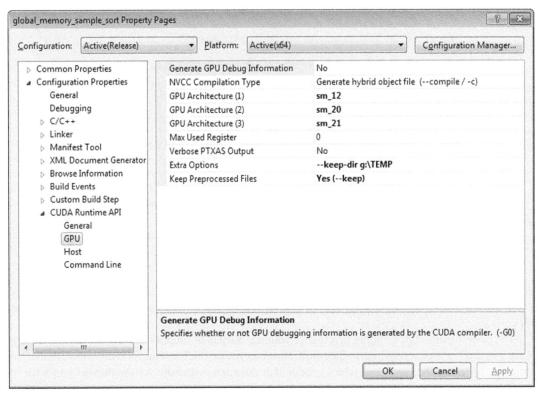

FIGURE 9.33

Visual C options—how to keep PTX files.

If we look at a small device function, this is what we see at the various levels:

```
__global__ void add_prefix_sum_total_kernel(
 u32 * const prefix_idx,
 const u32 * const total_count)
{
 const u32 tid = (blockIdx.x * blockDim.x) + threadIdx.x;

 prefix_idx[tid] += total_count[blockIdx.x];
}
```

In PTX:

```
.entry _Z27add_prefix_sum_total_kernelPjPKj(
 .param .u64 _Z27add_prefix_sum_total_kernelPjPKj_param_0,
 .param .u64 _Z27add_prefix_sum_total_kernelPjPKj_param_1
)
{
```

```
.reg .s32  %r<10>;
.reg .s64  %rl<9>;


ld.param.u64  %rl1, [_Z27add_prefix_sum_total_kernelPjPKj_param_0];
ld.param.u64  %rl2, [_Z27add_prefix_sum_total_kernelPjPKj_param_1];
cvta.to.global.u64  %rl3, %rl1;
.loc 2 923 1
mov.u32  %r1, %ntid.x;
mov.u32  %r2, %ctaid.x;
mov.u32  %r3, %tid.x;
mad.lo.s32  %r4, %r1, %r2, %r3;
cvta.to.global.u64  %rl4, %rl2;
.loc 2 925 1
mul.wide.u32  %rl5, %r2, 4;
add.s64  %rl6, %rl4, %rl5;
ldu.global.u32  %r5, [%rl6];
.loc 2 925 1
mul.wide.u32  %rl7, %r4, 4;
add.s64  %rl8, %rl3, %rl7;
ld.global.u32  %r6, [%rl8];
add.s32  %r8, %r6, %r5;
st.global.u32  [%rl8], %r8;
.loc 2 926 2
ret;
}
```

And the actual generated code for a compute 2.0 device:

```
Function : _Z27add_prefix_sum_total_kernelPjPKj

/*0000*/ MOV R1, c [0x1] [0x100];
/*0008*/ S2R R0, SR_CTAid_X;
/*0010*/ S2R R2, SR_Tid_X;
/*0018*/ MOV32I R6, 0x4;
/*0020*/ IMAD R2, R0, c [0x0] [0x8], R2;
/*0028*/ IMUL.U32.U32.HI R3, R2, 0x4;
/*0030*/ IMAD.U32.U32 R4.CC, R2, R6, c [0x0] [0x20];
/*0038*/ IADD.X R5, R3, c [0x0] [0x24];
/*0040*/ IMAD.U32.U32 R6.CC, R0, R6, c [0x0] [0x28];
/*0048*/ IMUL.U32.U32.HI R0, R0, 0x4;
/*0050*/ IADD.X R7, R0, c [0x0] [0x2c];
/*0058*/ LD_LDU.E.E.32.32 R2, R0, [R4], [R6+0x0];
/*0060*/ IADD R0, R2, R0;
/*0068*/ ST.E [R4], R0;
/*0070*/ EXIT;
```

I've removed from the final generated code the actual raw hex codes, as they are not useful. Both PTX and the target assembler code use the format

```
<instruction> <target_reg> <source_reg1> <source_reg2>
```

The PTX code is extensively documented in the PTX ISA found in the "doc" directory of the NVIDIA GPU Computing Toolkit as the "ptx_isa_3.0.pdf" file for the CUDA 4.1 SDK release. The binary instruction set is listed for GT200 and Fermi in the "cuobjdump.pdf" file found in the same directory. There is no detailed explanation of the actual instruction set as yet, as with the PTX, but it's fairly easy to see which instructions map back to the PTX ISA.

While NVIDIA supports forward compatibility with the PTX ISA between revisions of hardware, that is, PTX for compute 1.x will run on compute 2.x, the binaries are not compatible. This support of older versions of PTX will usually involve the CUDA driver recompiling the code for the actual target hardware on-the-fly.

You should read the PTX ISA document and understand it well. It refers to CTAs a lot, which are cooperative thread arrays. This is what is termed a "block" (of threads) at the CUDA runtime layer.

Changes in the C code will drastically affect the final assembly code generated. It's always good practice to look at the code being generated and ensure it is doing what is expected. If the compiler is reloading something from memory or doing something you would not expect, there is usually a good reason. You can usually then identify the cause in the C source code and eliminate the problem. In certain instances, you can also create inline PTX to get the exact functionality you require, although a lot of the very low-level instructions have equivalent compiler intrinsic functions that can be used.

One of the easiest ways to look at and understand the low-level assembly functions is to view the interleaved source and assembly listing via the "View Disassembly" option from within Parallel Nsight. Simply set a breakpoint within the CUDA code, run the code from the Nsight menu ("Start CUDA Debugging"), and wait for the breakpoint to be hit. Then right-click near the breakpoint and the context menu will show "View Disassembly." This brings up a new window showing the interleaved C, PTX, and SASS code. For example:

```
 // 0..127 (warps 0..3)
 if (threadIdx.x < 128)
0x0002caa0 [3393] mov.u32  %r30, %tid.x;
0x0002caa0      S2R R0, SR_Tid_X;
0x0002caa8      MOV R0, R0;
0x0002cab0 [3395] setp.lt.u32  %p7, %r30, 128;
0x0002cab0      ISETP.LT.U32.AND P0, pt, R0, 0x80, pt;
0x0002cab8 [3397] not.pred  %p8, %p7;
0x0002cab8      PSETP.AND.AND P0, pt, pt, pt, !P0;
0x0002cac0 [3399] @%p8 bra  BB16_13;
0x0002cac0      NOP CC.T;
0x0002cac8      SSY 0x858;
0x0002cad0      @P0 BRA 0x850; # Target=0x0002cb50
  {
  // Accumulate into a register and then write out
  local_result += *(smem_ptr+128);
0x0002cad8 [3403] ld.u64  %r128, [%r17+1024];
0x0002cad8      IADD R8.CC, R2, 0x400;
0x0002cae0      IADD.X R9, R3, RZ;
0x0002cae8      MOV R10, R8;
0x0002caf0      MOV R11, R9;
```

```
0x0002caf8    LD.E.64 R8, [R10];
0x0002cb00 [3405] add.s64  %rl42, %rl42, %rl28;
0x0002cb00    IADD R6.CC, R6, R8;
0x0002cb08    IADD.X R7, R7, R9;
```

Here you can easily see how the C source code, a test for threadIdx.x < 128, is translated into PTX and how each PTX instruction is itself translated into one or more SASS instructions.

Register usage

Registers are the fastest storage mechanism on the GPU. They are the only way of achieving anything like the peak performance of the device. However, they are limited in their availability.

To launch a block onto an SM, the CUDA runtime will look at the block's usage of registers and shared memory. Only if there are sufficient resources, the block will be launched. The number of blocks that are resident in an SM will vary, but typically you can achieve up to six blocks with reasonably complex kernels, and up to eight with simple ones (up to 16 on Kepler). The number of blocks is not really the main concern. It's the overall number of threads as a percentage of the maximum number supported, which is the key factor.

We listed a number of tables in Chapter 5 that gave an overview of how the number of registers per block affects the number of blocks that can be scheduled onto an SM, and consequentially the number of threads that the device will select from.

The compiler provides a -v option, which provides some more detailed output of what is currently allocated. An example of a typical kernel is:

```
ptxas info : Compiling entry function '_Z14functionTest' for 'sm_20'
ptxas info : Function properties for _Z14functionTest
40 bytes stack frame, 0 bytes spill stores, 0 bytes spill loads
ptxas info : Used 26 registers, 8+0 bytes lmem, 80 bytes cmem[0], 144 bytes cmem[2], 52
bytes cmem[16]
```

The output is useful, but only if you understand what the compiler is telling you. The first item of interest is the for sm_20 message, which tells you the code being created here is for the compute 2.x architecture (Fermi). If you're using exclusively Fermi devices for your target deployment, then make sure your target is set correctly. By default you will generate compute 1.0 code unless you specify otherwise, which will restrict the available operations and generate code that is not as efficient as it could be for Fermi.

The next interesting point is 40 bytes of stack frame, which generally means you have local variables you are taking the address of, or that you declared a local array. The term "local" in C refers to the scope of a variable, and in C++ was replaced with the keyword "private," which more accurately reflects what is meant.

In CUDA the term "local" refers to the scope of a variable for a given thread. Thus, the CUDA documentation also uses the term "local memory," meaning thread private data. Unfortunately, "local" implies near or close, which in memory terms might imply the data is held close to the processor. In fact, "local data" is stored in either global memory for compute 1.x devices or in the L1 cache on Fermi devices. Thus, only on Fermi is it really "local" to the processor, and even in this case, its size is limited.

The stack frame is something you typically see with compute 2.x device code, especially if using atomic operations. The stack frame will exist in the L1 cache unless it becomes too large. Where possible the CUDA compiler will simply inline calls to device functions, thereby removing the need to pass formal parameters to the called functions. If the stack frame is being created simply to pass values by reference (i.e., pointers) to the device function, it is often better to remove the call and manually inline the functions into the caller. This will eliminate the stack frame and generate a significant improvement in speed.

The next section lists `8+0 bytes lmem`. By "lmem" the compiler is referring to local memory. Thus, for 8 bytes, probably a couple of floats or integers have been placed into local memory. Again this is typically not a good indication as, especially in compute 1.x devices, there will be implicit memory fetches/writes to and from slow global memory. It's an indication you need to think about how you might rewrite the kernel, perhaps placing these values into shared memory or constant memory if possible.

Note the $a + b$ notation used here denotes the total amount of variables declared in those sections (the first number), and then the amount used by the system (the second number). Also smem (shared memory) usages will be listed in addition to lmem if shared memory is used by the kernel.

Next we see `80 bytes cmem[0]`. This says the compiler has used 80 bytes of constant memory. Constant memory is typically used for parameter passing, as most formal parameters do not change across calls. The value in the square brackets is the constant memory bank used and is not relevant. Simply add all the cmem figures to obtain the total constant memory usage.

Register usage can also be controlled, or forced, using the `-maxrregcount n` option in the compiler. You can use this to instruct the compiler to use more or less registers than it currently is. You may wish to have fewer registers to squeeze another block onto the SM. You may already be limited by some other criteria such as shared memory usage, so you may wish to allow the compiler to use more registers. By using more registers the compiler may be able to reuse more values in registers, rather than store/fetch them again. Conversely, asking for less registers usage will usually cause more memory accesses.

Asking for less registers to get an additional block is a tradeoff exercise as we saw in the AES example. The lower register count and the additional block may bring higher occupancy, but this does not necessarily make the code run faster. This is a concept most programmers starting with CUDA struggle with. The various analyzer tools try to get you to achieve higher occupancy rates. For the most part this is a good thing, as it allows the hardware scheduler to have a wider choice of warps to run. However, *only if* the scheduler actually runs out of warps at some point, and thus the SM stalls, does adding more available warps actually help. Fermi, due to its dual warp dispatcher and higher number of CUDA cores per SM, executes warps with a higher frequency than earlier models. The effect varies between applications, but generally asking for less register usage usually results in slower code. Try it for your particular application and see. We look at how you can see if the SMs are stalling in the later section on analysis tools.

A better approach to asking for less registers is to understand the register usage and allocation of variables. To do this, you need to look into the PTX code, using the `-keep` compiler flag. PTX, the virtual assembly language used by CUDA, defines a number of state spaces. A variable exists in one of these state spaces. These are shown in Table 9.8. Thus, you can always look into the PTX code to see where a variable has been placed.

Reducing register usage from say 26 to 25 per kernel will have little effect. However, transitioning over a register boundary (16, 20, 24, and 32) will usually allow for more blocks to be scheduled. This will bring a greater selection of warps and will usually improve performance. This is

Table 9.8 PTX State Space

Name	Description	Speed	Kernel Access	Host Access	Visibility
.reg	Registers (fastest)	Fastest	Read/write	None	Per thread
.const	Constant memory	Fast for uniform access	Read only	Read/ write	Per context
.global	Global memory	Slow (coalesced) to very slow (noncoalesced)	Read/write	Read/ write	Per context
.local	Private memory	Slow on compute 1.x devices; much faster on compute 2.x devices	Read/write	None	Per thread
.param (kernel call)	Formal parameters used in kernel call from host	As per constant memory	Read only	Read/ write	Per grid
.param (device call)	Formal parameters used in calls from global to device functions	As per registers; generally device functions are in-lined	Read/write	None	Per thread
.shared	Shared memory	Fast for bank conflict–free access	Read/write	None	Per block

not always the case. More blocks can mean more contention for shared resources (shared memory, L1/L2 caches).

Register usage can often be reduced simply be rearranging the C source code. By bringing the assignment and usage of a variable closer together you enable the compiler to reuse registers. Thus, at the start of the kernel you might assign a, b, and c. If in fact they are used only later in the kernel, you'll often find reduced register usage by moving the creation and assignment close to the usage. The compiler may then be able to use a single register for all three variables, as they exist in distinct and disjoint phases of the kernel.

Section summary

- Understand how thread layout impacts memory and cache access patterns.
- Use only multiples of 32 when specifying the thread count for kernel launch.
- Think about how to increase the amount of work performed per memory fetch.
- Understand at least a little of how compilers work when optimizing code and adapt your source code to aid the compiler.
- Consider how branching within a warp can be avoided.
- Look at the PTX and final target code to ensure the compiler is not generating inefficient code. If it is, understand why and make changes at the source level to address it.
- Be aware and understand where data is being placed and what the compiler is telling you.

STRATEGY 5: ALGORITHMS

Selecting an efficient algorithm on the GPU can be challenging. The best algorithm in the CPU domain is not necessarily the best for the GPU. The GPU has its own unique challenges. To get the best performance you need to understand the hardware. Thus, when considering algorithms, we need to think about:

- How to decompose the problem into blocks or tiles and then how to decompose those blocks into threads.
- How the threads will access the data and what sort of memory pattern this will generate.
- What data reuse opportunities are present and how these can be realized.
- How much work the algorithm will be performing in total and whether there is a significantly difference from a serial implementation.

There is an 800-plus-page book published by Morgan Kaufman entitled *GPU Computing Gems* that covers in detail implementation of various algorithms for the following areas:

- Scientific simulation
- Life sciences
- Statistical modeling
- Data-intensive applications
- Electronic design and automation
- Ray tracing and rendering
- Computer vision
- Video and image processing
- Medical imaging

The purpose of this section is not to look at algorithms that are specific to certain fields, as they are of limited general interest. Here we look at a few common algorithms that can be implemented, which in turn may form building blocks for more complex algorithms. This book is not about providing sets of examples you can copy and paste, but providing examples where you can learn the concepts of what makes good CUDA programs.

Sorting

There are many, many sorting algorithms available, some of which can easily and efficiently be implemented on the GPU and many of which are not well suited. We've looked already in previous chapters at merge sort, radix sort, and the more exotic sample sort. We'll look here at one more parallel sort that is useful in terms of looking at how algorithms are implemented in GPUs.

Odd/even sort

An odd/even sort works by selecting every even array index and comparing it with the higher adjacent odd array index (Figure 9.34). If the number at the even element is larger than the element at the odd index, the elements are swapped. The process is then repeated, starting with the odd indexes and

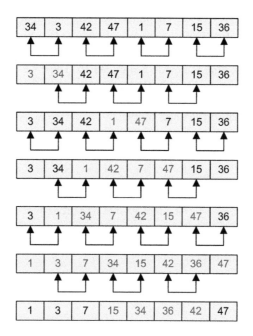

FIGURE 9.34

Odd/even sort.

comparing them with the higher adjacent even index. This is repeated until we make no swaps, at which point the list is sorted.

An odd/even sort is a variation of a bubble sort. A bubble sort works by selecting the number at the first index and comparing and swapping it with the index to the right until such time as it's no longer larger than the number to its right. The odd/even sort simply extends this to use P independent threads to do this, where P is half the number of elements in the list.

If we define the number of elements in an array as N, then the ability to deploy half of N threads may be appealing. The sort is also quite easy to conceptualize, but raises some interesting problems when trying to implement on the GPU, so it is a good example to look at.

The first issue is that odd/even sort is designed for parallel systems where individual processor elements can exchange data with their immediate neighbor. It requires a connection to the left and right neighbor only. A connection for our purposes will be via shared memory.

Having thread 0 access array elements zero *and* one and thread 1 access elements two *and* three causes a sequence issue for the coalescing hardware. It needs each thread to access a contiguous pattern for a coalesced access. Thus, on compute 1.x hardware this access pattern is terrible, resulting in multiple 32-byte fetches. However, on compute 2.x hardware, the accesses fetch at most two cache lines. The additional data fetched from the even cycle will likely be available for the odd cycle and vice versa. There is also a significant amount of data reuse with a high degree of locality, suggesting cache and/or shared memory would be a good choice. Shared memory would likely be the only choice for compute 1.x devices due to the poor coalescing.

If we consider shared memory, we need to think about bank conflicts. Thread 0 would need to read banks 0 and 1, plus write to bank 0. Thread 1 would need to reads banks 2 and 3 and write to bank 2. In a compute 1.x system with 16 banks, thread 8 would wrap around and start accessing banks 0 and 1. On compute 2.0 hardware, we'd see the same effect at thread 16. Thus, we'd have four bank conflicts per thread on compute 1.x hardware and two bank conflicts per thread on compute 2.x hardware with a shared memory implementation.

The CPU code for odd/even sort is quite simple:

```
void odd_even_sort_cpu(u32 * const data,
                       const u32 num_elem)
{
 u32 offset = 0; // Start off with even, then odd
 u32 num_swaps; // Keep track of the number of swaps
 u32 run = 0;   // Keep track of the number of iterations

 printf("\nSorting %u elements using odd/even sort on cpu\n", num_elem);
 print_array(run, data, num_elem);

 do
 {
  run++;
  num_swaps = 0; // Reset number of swaps each iteration

  // Iterate over 0..num_elements OR
  // 1..(num_elements-1) in steps of two
  for (u32 i=offset; i<(num_elem-offset); i+=2)
  {
   // Read values into registers
   const u32 d0 = data[i];
   const u32 d1 = data[i+1];

   // Compare registers
   if ( d0 > d1 )
   {
    // Swap values if needed
    data[i] = d1;
    data[i+1] = d0;

    // Keep track that we did a swap
    num_swaps++;
   }
  }

  // Switch from even to odd, or odd to even
  if (offset == 0)
   offset = 1;
  else
```

```
  offset = 0;

 // If something swapped then print the array
 if (num_swaps > 0)
   print_array(run, data, num_elem);

// While elements are still being swapped
} while (num_swaps != 0);
}
```

The code iterates over the dataset from array element 0 to `num_elem-1` and then from element 1 to `num_elem-2`. The two data elements are read into local variables and compared. They are swapped if necessary and a counter `num_swaps` is used to keep track of the number of swaps done. When no swaps are necessary, the list is sorted.

For a mostly sorted list, such algorithms work well. The reverse sorted list is the worst case, where we have to move elements all through the list to the end. The output of a reverse sorted list is shown here. We can see in each stage how the values move between the cells.

```
Run 000: 15 14 13 12 11 10 09 08 07 06 05 04 03 02 01 00
Run 001: 14 15 12 13 10 11 08 09 06 07 04 05 02 03 00 01
Run 002: 14 12 15 10 13 08 11 06 09 04 07 02 05 00 03 01
Run 003: 12 14 10 15 08 13 06 11 04 09 02 07 00 05 01 03
Run 004: 12 10 14 08 15 06 13 04 11 02 09 00 07 01 05 03
Run 005: 10 12 08 14 06 15 04 13 02 11 00 09 01 07 03 05
Run 006: 10 08 12 06 14 04 15 02 13 00 11 01 09 03 07 05
Run 007: 08 10 06 12 04 14 02 15 00 13 01 11 03 09 05 07
Run 008: 08 06 10 04 12 02 14 00 15 01 13 03 11 05 09 07
Run 009: 06 08 04 10 02 12 00 14 01 15 03 13 05 11 07 09
Run 010: 06 04 08 02 10 00 12 01 14 03 15 05 13 07 11 09
Run 011: 04 06 02 08 00 10 01 12 03 14 05 15 07 13 09 11
Run 012: 04 02 06 00 08 01 10 03 12 05 14 07 15 09 13 11
Run 013: 02 04 00 06 01 08 03 10 05 12 07 14 09 15 11 13
Run 014: 02 00 04 01 06 03 08 05 10 07 12 09 14 11 15 13
Run 015: 00 02 01 04 03 06 05 08 07 10 09 12 11 14 13 15
Run 016: 00 01 02 03 04 05 06 07 08 09 10 11 12 13 14 15
```

For the GPU implementation, we'll use global memory on a compute 2.x device. The GPU implementation is:

```
__global__ void odd_even_sort_gpu_kernel_gmem(
 u32 * const data,
 const u32 num_elem)
{
 const u32 tid = (blockIdx.x * blockDim.x) + threadIdx.x;

 u32 tid_idx;
 u32 offset = 0; // Start off with even, then odd
 u32 num_swaps;
```

```
// Calculation maximum index for a given block
// Last block it is number of elements minus one
// Other blocks to end of block minus one
const u32 tid_idx_max = min( (((blockIdx.x+1) * (blockDim.x*2))-1), (num_elem-1) );

do
{
  // Reset number of swaps
  num_swaps = 0;

  // Work out index of data
  tid_idx = (tid * 2) + offset;

  // If no array or block overrun
  if (tid_idx < tid_idx_max)
  {
   // Read values into registers
   const u32 d0 = data[tid_idx];
   const u32 d1 = data[tid_idx+1];

   // Compare registers
   if ( d0 > d1 )
   {
    // Swap values if needed
    data[tid_idx] = d1;
    data[tid_idx+1] = d0;

    // Keep track that we did a swap
    num_swaps++;
   }
  }

  // Switch from even to off, or odd to even
  if (offset == 0)
   offset = 1;
  else
   offset = 0;

} while (__syncthreads_count(num_swaps) != 0);
}
```

Instead of the traditional for loop construct, the CPU code uses a do..while construct. The obvious choice for parallelism from the algorithm is the compare and swap operation, meaning we need *N*/2 threads where *N* is the number of elements in the array. Given that most lists we'd bother sorting on the GPU will be large, this gives us potential to make use of the maximum number of threads on a given device (24,576 threads on GTX580).

As each thread processes two elements we cannot simply use `tid` as the array index, so create a new local parameter `tid_idx`, which is used to index into the array. We also create a parameter `tid_idx_max`, which is set to the last value in the array, or the last value in the current block where there is more than one block.

```
// Calculation maximum index for a given block
// Last block it is number of elements minus one
// Other blocks to end of block minus one
const u32 tid_idx_max = min( (((blockIdx.x+1) * (blockDim.x*2))-1), (num_elem-1) );
```

The end condition is somewhat problematic. The parameter `num_swaps` in the serial version is written to only once per iteration. In the parallel version we need to know if *any* thread did a swap. We could therefore use an atomic `add`, `increment`, `AND`, or `OR` operation for this, but this would represent a serial bottleneck, as every thread that did a write would have to be serialized.

We could mitigate the cost of the atomic operations somewhat by using a shared memory atomic operation. Note that shared memory atomics are supported only on compute 1.2 hardware or later (the GT200 series). For the older compute 1.1 hardware (the 9000 series) we'd need to use global memory atomics. The definition of the `num_swaps` variable would need to be changed accordingly.

For compute 2.x hardware, there is a much faster solution that we will use here. As we have to wait at the end of each round anyway, we can make use of the newly provided primitive, `__syncthreads_count`, to which we pass a predicate. If the predicate is nonzero in any of the threads, then the result to all threads is also nonzero. Thus, if just one thread does a swap, all threads again iterate around the loop.

```
} while (__syncthreads_count(num_swaps) != 0);
```

The host function to call the kernel is also shown here for completeness.

```
// Host function - copy to / from and invoke kernel
__host__ void odd_even_sort_gpu_gmem(
 u32 * const data_cpu,
 const u32 num_elem)
{
 const u32 size_in_bytes = (num_elem * sizeof(u32));
 u32 * data_gpu;

 // Allocate memory on the device
 CUDA_CALL(cudaMalloc((void **) &data_gpu,
                      size_in_bytes));

 // Copy data to GPU
 CUDA_CALL(cudaMemcpy(data_gpu, data_cpu, size_in_bytes, cudaMemcpyHostToDevice));

 // Use blocks of 256 threads
 const u32 num_threads = 256;
 const u32 num_blocks = (((num_elem/2) + (num_threads-1)) / num_threads);

 printf("\nInvoking Odd Even sort with %d blocks of
    %d threads (%u active)", num_blocks,
```

```
        num_threads, (num_elem / 2));

    // Invoke the kernel
    odd_even_sort_gpu_kernel_gmem<<<num_blocks, num_threads>>>(data_gpu, num_elem);

    cuda_error_check( "Error Invoking kernel",
            "odd_even_sort_gpu_kernel_gmem");

    // Copy back to CPU memory space
    CUDA_CALL(cudaMemcpy(data_cpu, data_gpu, size_in_bytes, cudaMemcpyDeviceToHost));

    // Free memory on the device
    CUDA_CALL(cudaFree(data_gpu));

    print_array(0, data_cpu, num_elem);
}
```

One question that should be in your mind about this code is what happens at the block boundaries. Let's look at the results with one and two blocks with a dataset small enough to print here:

```
Invoking Odd Even sort with 1 blocks of 8 threads (8 active)
Run 000: 00 01 02 03 04 05 06 07 08 09 10 11 12 13 14 15
Test passed
```

and

```
Invoking Odd Even sort with 2 blocks of 4 threads (8 active)
Run 000: 08 09 10 11 12 13 14 15 00 01 02 03 04 05 06 07
Test failed
```

Notice in the second output the sort occurred only within the block. The values on the right needed to propagate to the left and vice versa. However, as the blocks do not overlap, they are not able to do this. The obvious solution would be to overlap the blocks, but this would not be an ideal solution.

CUDA was designed to allow blocks to run in any order, without a means for cross-block synchronization within a single kernel run. It's possible by issuing multiple kernels to synchronize between blocks, but this mechanism works well only where you have a small number of synchronization steps. In this kernel we'd need to overlap the blocks on every iteration. This would lose all locality, as now two SMs need to share the same dataset. We also need a global memory atomic or a reduction operation to keep track of whether any blocks performed a swap and have to continue issuing kernels until no swaps had taken place in any block—a lot of host interaction. That would not be a good route to go down.

So we're left with the two choices found in most sorts that decompose into blocks. Either presort the input lists so the values in list N_{-1} are less than N_0, which are larger than N_1, the solution we used with the sample sort, or merge N separate lists, the merge sort problem we also looked at earlier.

Reduction

Reduction is used significantly in parallel programming. We'll look at some of the many ways we can perform a reduction to see which method produces the best results on the various compute platforms and to understand why.

We'll look first at computing the sum of N 32-bit integers, some 48 million to give a reasonable sized dataset. With such a large number of values one of the first issues we need to consider is overflow. If we add 0xFFFFFFFF and 0x00000001 then we have an overflow condition with a 32-bit number. Therefore, we need to accumulate into a 64-bit number. This presents some issues.

First, any atomic-based accumulation would require an atomic 64-bit integer add. Unfortunately, this is supported in shared memory only with compute 2.x hardware and in global memory only in compute 1.2 hardware onward.

Global atomic add

Let's look first at the simplest form of reduction:

```
// Every thread does atomic add to the same
// address in GMEM
__global__ void reduce_gmem(const u32 * const data,
                            u64 * const result,
                            const u32 num_elements)
{
 const u32 tid = (blockIdx.x * blockDim.x) + threadIdx.x;

 if (tid < num_elements)
  atomicAdd(result, (u64) data[tid]);
}
```

In this first example, each thread reads a single element from memory and adds it to a single result in global memory. This, although very simple, is probably one of the worst forms of a reduce operation. The interblock atomic operation means the value needs to be shared across all of the SMs.

In the older hardware this means physically writing to global memory. In the compute 2.x hardware this means maintaining an L2 cache entry, shared among all the SMs, and eventually writing this to global memory. The results we see are as follows:

```
Processing 48 MB of data, 12M elements
ID:0 GeForce GTX 470:GMEM   passed Time 197.84 ms
ID:3 GeForce GTX 460:GMEM   passed Time 164.28 ms
```

We'll look here at the compute 2.x devices, as these support 64-bit integer atomics.

The issue with the atomic writes, even to L2 cache, is they force a serialization of the threads. We have six blocks in each SM, 256 threads per block, generating 1536 threads per SM. On the GTX470 we have 14 SMs, so a total of 21, 504 active threads. On the GTX460 we have 7 SMs, so a total of 10,752 active threads. Performing an atomic operation on a single global memory cell means we create a lineup, or serialization, of 10 K to 21 K threads. Every thread has to queue, once for every single element it processes. Clearly a poor solution, even if it is a somewhat simple one.

Reduction within the threads

We can improve this situation by performing some of the reduction within the thread. We can do this very simply by changing the data type and adjusting the kernel to ensure we don't go out of bounds.

```
// Every thread does atomic add to the same
// address in GMEM
```

```
__global__ void reduce_gmem_ILP2(const uint2 * const data,
                                 u64 * const result,
                                 const u32 num_elements)
{
 const u32 tid = (blockIdx.x * blockDim.x) + threadIdx.x;

 if (tid < (num_elements>>1))
 {
  uint2 element = data[tid];

  const u64 add_value = ((u64)element.x) +
                        ((u64)element.y);

  atomicAdd(result, add_value);
 }
}

// Every thread does atomic add to the same
// address in GMEM
__global__ void reduce_gmem_ILP4(const uint4 * const data,
                                 u64 * const result,
                                 const u32 num_elements)
{
 const u32 tid = (blockIdx.x * blockDim.x) + threadIdx.x;

 if (tid < (num_elements>>2))
 {
  uint4 element = data[tid];

  const u64 add_value = ((u64)element.x) +
                        ((u64)element.y) +
                        ((u64)element.z) +
                        ((u64)element.w);

  atomicAdd(result, add_value);
 }
}
```

In the first example we process two elements per thread and four in the second using the built-in vector types uint2 and uint4. This produces the following timings:

```
ID:0 GeForce GTX 470:GMEM ILP2 passed Time 98.96 ms
ID:3 GeForce GTX 460:GMEM ILP2 passed Time 82.37 ms

ID:0 GeForce GTX 470:GMEM ILP4 passed Time 49.53 ms
ID:3 GeForce GTX 460:GMEM ILP4 passed Time 41.47 ms
```

Although, a dramatic reduction, we've not really solved the problem. All we have done is to half or quarter the number of times each thread has to queue by performing a local reduction. This drops the overall time to approximately one-half and one-quarter of the original. However, there is still a 5 K thread lineup trying to write to the global memory.

Note in performing the addition locally, we reduce the number of global writes by a factor equal to the level of ILP. However, we have to be careful about how the addition is performed. You could write:

```
const u64 add_value = ((u64)element.x) + element.y + element.z + element.w;
```

In C, an expression is typically evaluated from left to right. A promotion of the left operator generates an implicit promotion of the right operator. Thus, you might expect `element.x` to be promoted to an unsigned 64-bit type, and as `element.y` is to be added to it, it will also be promoted. As `element.z` and `element.w` will subsequently be added, you might also expect these to be promoted. You are, however, thinking like a serial programmer. The `z` and `w` elements can be calculated independently of `x` and `y`. This is exactly what the PTX code does. As neither `z` nor `w` has been promoted to a 64-bit value, the addition is done as a 32-bit addition, which may result in an overflow.

The problem lies in that C permits any order of evaluation where the operator is commutative. However, as you typically see a left to right evaluation, people assume this is how all compilers work. This is one of the portability issues between C compilers. When we move to a superscalar processor such as a GPU, it performs the two sets of additions independently to make the maximum use of the pipeline. We don't want it to wait 18–22 plus cycles for the first addition to complete then make the subsequent additions in series.

Thus, the correct way to write such additions is:

```
const u64 add_value = ((u64)element.x) + ((u64)element.y) + ((u64)element.z) + ((u64)
element.w);
```

Here every value is converted to a 64-bit number before the addition takes place. Then any ordering of the addition is fine for integer values. Note for floating-point values simply converting to doubles is not enough. Due to the way floating-point numbers work adding a very tiny number to a very large number will result in the small number being discarded, as the floating-point notation does not have the required resolution to hold such values. The best approach to this type of problem is to first sort the floating-point values and work from the smallest number to the largest.

We can take the ILP technique a little further by using multiple elements of `uint4` and adjusting the kernel accordingly.

```
// Every thread does atomic add to the same
// address in GMEM
__global__ void reduce_gmem_ILP8(const uint4 * const data,
                                 u64 * const result,
                                 const u32 num_elements)
{
 const u32 tid = (blockIdx.x * blockDim.x) + threadIdx.x;

 if (tid < (num_elements>>3))
 {
  const u32 idx = (tid * 2);

  uint4 element = data[idx];
  u64 value = ((u64)element.x) +
```

```
                    ((u64)element.y) +
                    ((u64)element.z) +
                    ((u64)element.w);

    element = data[idx+1];
    value += ((u64)element.x) +
                    ((u64)element.y) +
                    ((u64)element.z) +
                    ((u64)element.w);

    atomicAdd(result, value);
  }
}

// Every thread does atomic add to the same
// address in GMEM
__global__ void reduce_gmem_ILP16(const uint4 * const data,
                                  u64 * const result,
                                  const u32 num_elements)
{
  const u32 tid = (blockIdx.x * blockDim.x) + threadIdx.x;

  if (tid < (num_elements>>4))
  {
    const u32 idx = (tid * 4);

    uint4 element = data[idx];
    u64 value = ((u64)element.x) +
                    ((u64)element.y) +
                    ((u64)element.z) +
                    ((u64)element.w);

    element = data[idx+1];
    value += ((u64)element.x) +
                    ((u64)element.y) +
                    ((u64)element.z) +
                    ((u64)element.w);

    element = data[idx+2];
    value += ((u64)element.x) +
                    ((u64)element.y) +
                    ((u64)element.z) +
                    ((u64)element.w);

    element = data[idx+3];
    value += ((u64)element.x) +
                    ((u64)element.y) +
```

```
            ((u64)element.z) +
            ((u64)element.w);

  atomicAdd(result, value);
 }
}

// Every thread does atomic add to the same
// address in GMEM
__global__ void reduce_gmem_ILP32(const uint4 * const data,
                                  u64 * const result,
                                  const u32 num_elements)
{
 const u32 tid = (blockIdx.x * blockDim.x) + threadIdx.x;

 if (tid < (num_elements>>5))
 {
  const u32 idx = (tid * 8);

  uint4 element = data[idx];
  u64 value = ((u64)element.x) +
              ((u64)element.y) +
              ((u64)element.z) +
              ((u64)element.w);

  element = data[idx+1];
  value += ((u64)element.x) +
           ((u64)element.y) +
           ((u64)element.z) +
           ((u64)element.w);

  element = data[idx+2];
  value += ((u64)element.x) +
           ((u64)element.y) +
           ((u64)element.z) +
           ((u64)element.w);

  element = data[idx+3];
  value += ((u64)element.x) +
           ((u64)element.y) +
           ((u64)element.z) +
           ((u64)element.w);

  element = data[idx+4];
  value += ((u64)element.x) +
           ((u64)element.y) +
           ((u64)element.z) +
           ((u64)element.w);
```

```
element = data[idx+5];
value += ((u64)element.x) +
         ((u64)element.y) +
         ((u64)element.z) +
         ((u64)element.w);

element = data[idx+6];
value += ((u64)element.x) +
         ((u64)element.y) +
         ((u64)element.z) +
         ((u64)element.w);

element = data[idx+7];
value += ((u64)element.x) +
         ((u64)element.y) +
         ((u64)element.z) +
         ((u64)element.w);

  atomicAdd(result, value);
  }
}
```

Notice that we're mixing the loading of data with the addition. We could move all the loads to the start of the function. However, consider that each `uint4` type requires four registers. Thus, the `ILP32` example would require 32 registers just to hold the values from a single read iteration. In addition, some are needed for the addition and final write. If we use too many registers, the number of blocks that can be scheduled is reduced or the kernel spills registers to "local" memory. Such local memory is the L1 cache for compute 2.x devices and global memory for the compute 1.x devices. The results for these ILP kernels are shown here:

```
ID:0 GeForce GTX 470:GMEM ILP8 passed Time 24.83 ms
ID:3 GeForce GTX 460:GMEM ILP8 passed Time 20.97 ms

ID:0 GeForce GTX 470:GMEM ILP16 passed Time 12.49 ms
ID:3 GeForce GTX 460:GMEM ILP16 passed Time 10.75 ms

ID:0 GeForce GTX 470:GMEM ILP32 passed Time 13.18 ms
ID:3 GeForce GTX 460:GMEM ILP32 passed Time 15.94 ms
```

We can see that ILP significantly decreases the execution time, providing it's not taken too far. Note the `ILP32` solution actually takes longer. Despite achieving a $20\times$ speedup over the simplest version, we have still not solved the atomic write queuing problem, just reduced the overall number of elements. There are still too many active threads (10–21 K) all trying to write to the single accumulator.

Reduction of the number of blocks

Currently, we're invoking N blocks where N is the problem size, 12 million elements (48 MB) divided by the number of threads per block multiplied by the number of elements processed per block. We finally get *N* atomic writes, all of which are serialized and cause a bottleneck.

We can reduce the number of contentions if we create far, far less blocks and greatly increase the amount of work each block performs. However, we have to do this without increasing the register usage, something the ILP32 example did. This, in turn, caused a slowdown due to local memory reads and writes.

Currently, we launch 48 K blocks, but could reduce this to 16, 32, 64, 128, or 256 blocks. We can then have each thread march through memory, accumulating the result to a register, and only when the block is complete, write out the result. Depending on the number of blocks, this should generate quite good locality of memory references between the SMs, thus making good use of the memory bandwidth and L2 cache if present.

```
// Every thread does atomic add to the same
// address in GMEM after internal accumulation
__global__ void reduce_gmem_loop(const u32 * const data,
                                 u64 * const result,
                                 const u32 num_elements)
{
 // Divide the num. elements by the number of blocks launched
 // ( 4096 elements / 256 threads) / 16 blocks = 1 iter
 // ( 8192 elements / 256 threads) / 16 blocks = 2 iter
 // (16384 elements / 256 threads) / 16 blocks = 4 iter
 // (32768 elements / 256 threads) / 16 blocks = 8 iter
 const u32 num_elements_per_block = ((num_elements / blockDim.x) / gridDim.x);

 const u32 increment = (blockDim.x * gridDim.x);

 // Work out the initial index
 u32 idx = (blockIdx.x * blockDim.x) + threadIdx.x;

 // Accumulate into this register parameter
 u64 local_result = 0;

 // Loop N times depending on the number of
 // blocks launched
 for (u32 i=0; i<num_elements_per_block; i++)
 {
  // If still within bounds, add into result
  if (idx < num_elements)
   local_result += (data[idx]);

  // Move to the next element in the list
  idx += increment;
 }

 // Add the final result to the GMEM accumulator
 atomicAdd(result, local_result);
}
```

The first task is to work out how many iterations over the data each thread needs to make. The parameter gridDim.x holds the number of blocks launched. Each block consists of blockDim.x threads. Thus, we can work out how many elements of data each thread must accumulate. We then accumulate these in local_result, and only when the block is complete, do a single write to global memory.

This reduces the contention from a thread-level contention to a block-level contention. As we're only launching a few hundred blocks, the probability of them all requiring the write at the same time is reasonably low. Clearly as we increase the number of blocks, the potential contention increases. Once we have loaded all the SMs with the maximum number of permitted blocks, there is little reason to increase the number of blocks further, other than for work balancing.

The GTX460 is perhaps the worst example, as with only 7 SMs, each with 6 blocks, we should saturate the device at only 42 blocks. The GTX470 would need 90 blocks. We, therefore, try all number of blocks (49,152) down to 16 in powers of two, fewer blocks than would be necessary to fully populate the SMs. This generates the following results:

```
ID:0 GeForce GTX 470:GMEM loop1 49152 passed Time 197.82 ms
ID:0 GeForce GTX 470:GMEM loop1 24576 passed Time 98.96 ms
ID:0 GeForce GTX 470:GMEM loop1 12288 passed Time 49.56 ms
ID:0 GeForce GTX 470:GMEM loop1 6144 passed Time 24.83 ms
ID:0 GeForce GTX 470:GMEM loop1 3072 passed Time 12.48 ms
ID:0 GeForce GTX 470:GMEM loop1 1536 passed Time 6.33 ms
ID:0 GeForce GTX 470:GMEM loop1 768 passed Time 3.35 ms
ID:0 GeForce GTX 470:GMEM loop1 384 passed Time 2.26 ms
ID:0 GeForce GTX 470:GMEM loop1 192 passed Time 1.92 ms
ID:0 GeForce GTX 470:GMEM loop1 96 passed Time 1.87 ms
ID:0 GeForce GTX 470:GMEM loop1 64 passed Time 1.48 ms
ID:0 GeForce GTX 470:GMEM loop1 48 passed Time 1.50 ms
ID:0 GeForce GTX 470:GMEM loop1 32 passed Time 1.75 ms
ID:0 GeForce GTX 470:GMEM loop1 16 passed Time 2.98 ms

ID:3 GeForce GTX 460:GMEM loop1 49152 passed Time 164.25 ms
ID:3 GeForce GTX 460:GMEM loop1 24576 passed Time 82.45 ms
ID:3 GeForce GTX 460:GMEM loop1 12288 passed Time 41.52 ms
ID:3 GeForce GTX 460:GMEM loop1 6144 passed Time 21.01 ms
ID:3 GeForce GTX 460:GMEM loop1 3072 passed Time 10.77 ms
ID:3 GeForce GTX 460:GMEM loop1 1536 passed Time 5.60 ms
ID:3 GeForce GTX 460:GMEM loop1 768 passed Time 3.16 ms
ID:3 GeForce GTX 460:GMEM loop1 384 passed Time 2.51 ms
ID:3 GeForce GTX 460:GMEM loop1 192 passed Time 2.19 ms
ID:3 GeForce GTX 460:GMEM loop1 96 passed Time 2.12 ms
ID:3 GeForce GTX 460:GMEM loop1 64 passed Time 2.05 ms
ID:3 GeForce GTX 460:GMEM loop1 48 passed Time 2.41 ms
ID:3 GeForce GTX 460:GMEM loop1 32 passed Time 1.96 ms
ID:3 GeForce GTX 460:GMEM loop1 16 passed Time 2.70 ms
```

If we look at this first on the very large number of blocks we see a fairly linear drop as we halve the number of blocks for each run, for both the GTX470 and GTX460 cards. We're halving the number of

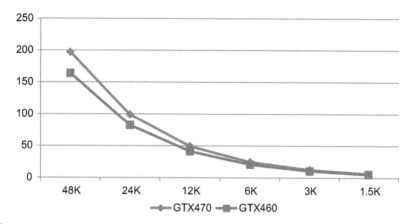

FIGURE 9.35

Time (ms) versus number of blocks (large number of blocks).

blocks each cycle by increasing the amount of work done per thread, but without increasing the ILP (indicated here with `loop1`).

Notice that the GTX460 has consistently outperformed the GTX470 in the previous examples. It does this until such time as we get down to a very small number of blocks (Figure 9.35). At 384 blocks we see the GTX470 outperform the GTX460. The GTX470's larger number of smaller SMs (32 CUDA cores versus 48 CUDA cores each) and larger cache starts to impact performance.

If you then look at the timing with a very small number of blocks, you can see that around 64 blocks is the minimum needed before the number of SM scheduling/occupancy issues come into play (Figure 9.36). In the figure, we've split the graphs into one with a large number of blocks and one with a smaller number, so we can see the time at small block numbers.

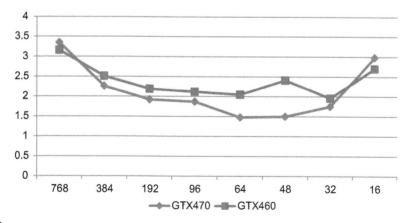

FIGURE 9.36

Time (ms) versus number of blocks (small number of blocks).

Note so far we've used no ILP (instruction-level parallelism). However, we know that introducing ILP allows us to achieve better timing. This is especially the case when we have a small number of blocks. The optimal timing is for 64 blocks. The GTX470 would have just over 4 blocks, 32 warps per SM. With 32-bit memory fetches we need a fully loaded SM, 48 warps, to achieve peak bandwidth from the global memory. We can achieve this only with ILP while maintaining this number of warps.

```
// Every thread does atomic add to the same
// address in GMEM after internal accumulation
__launch_bounds__(256)
__global__ void reduce_gmem_loop_ILP2(
 const uint2 * const data,
 u64 * const result,
 const u32 num_elements)
{
 const u32 num_elements_per_block = (( (num_elements / 2) / blockDim.x) / gridDim.x);
 const u32 increment = (blockDim.x * gridDim.x);

 // Work out the initial index
 u32 idx = (blockIdx.x * blockDim.x) + threadIdx.x;

 // Accumulate into this register parameter
 u64 local_result = 0;

 // Loop N times depending on the number
 // of blocks launched
 for (u32 i=0; i<num_elements_per_block; i++)
 {
  // If still within bounds, add into result
  if (idx < (num_elements>>1))
  {
   const uint2 elem = data[idx];

   local_result += ((u64)elem.x) + ((u64)elem.y);

   // Move to the next element in the list
   idx += increment;
  }
 }

 // Add the final result to the GMEM accumulator
 atomicAdd(result, local_result);
}

// Every thread does atomic add to the same
// address in GMEM after internal accumulation
__launch_bounds__(256)
__global__ void reduce_gmem_loop_ILP4(
 const uint4 * const data,
```

```
 u64 * const result,
 const u32 num_elements)
{
 const u32 num_elements_per_block = (( (num_elements/4) / blockDim.x) / gridDim.x);
 const u32 increment = (blockDim.x * gridDim.x);

 // Work out the initial index
 u32 idx = (blockIdx.x * blockDim.x) + threadIdx.x;

 // Accumulate into this register parameter
 u64 local_result = 0;

 // Loop N times depending on the number
 // of blocks launched
 for (u32 i=0; i<num_elements_per_block; i++)
 {
  // If still within bounds, add into result
  if (idx < (num_elements>>2))
  {
   const uint4 elem = data[idx];

   local_result += ((u64)elem.x) + ((u64)elem.y);
   local_result += ((u64)elem.z) + ((u64)elem.w);

   // Move to the next element in the list
   idx += increment;
  }
 }

 // Add the final result to the GMEM accumulator
 atomicAdd(result, local_result);
}
```

The effect on introducing ILP has one additional benefit: The time spent performing the loop (overhead) is amortized over more useful instructions (memory fetch, add). We therefore see the following results:

```
ID:0 GeForce GTX 470:GMEM loop1 64 passed Time 1.48 ms
ID:3 GeForce GTX 460:GMEM loop1 64 passed Time 2.05 ms
ID:0 GeForce GTX 470:GMEM loop2 64 passed Time 1.16 ms
ID:3 GeForce GTX 460:GMEM loop2 64 passed Time 1.49 ms
ID:0 GeForce GTX 470:GMEM loop4 64 passed Time 1.14 ms
ID:3 GeForce GTX 460:GMEM loop4 64 passed Time 1.38 ms
```

In loop1 we use a single 32-bit element, in loop2 we use two elements (uint2), and in loop4 we use four elements (uint4). In each case we use 64 blocks, the best result from the previous test. You can see that moving from 32-bit elements per thread to 64-bit elements per thread we gain on the order of 20–25%. Moving from 64-bit reads to 128-bit reads gains us almost nothing on the GTX470, but on the order of an 8% gain on the GTX460. This is entirely consistent with the bandwidth results we looked at earlier where the GTX460 (compute 2.1) device achieved a significantly higher bandwidth when using 128-bit reads instead of 64-bit reads.

Reduction using shared memory

If we look at the last instruction of the kernel to date, we still have one issue, using an atomic add to write out the result. With 256 threads per block and 64 blocks resident, we have 16 K threads all trying to write to this final accumulated value. What we actually need is a reduction across the threads within the block. This would drop the number of writes from 16 K to just 64, the number of blocks. This should reduce the overall timing considerably, as we're removing the serialization bottleneck.

However, going back to the first section in this chapter, know when fast is fast enough and appreciate the additional effort required to squeeze that last few percent out of the problem. Notice as the speed has improved, the kernels become more and more complex.

Shared memory is a bank-switched set of 32 banks (16 in compute 1.x). Providing each thread uses a unique bank index (0..31) the shared memory can process one element per clock, per thread. This is its peak performance, for a single warp. As we introduce more warps, if they too want to access shared memory, the ability of one warp to use the full bandwidth of shared memory is reduced as it must share the LSUs with other competing warps. Once the LSUs are running at 100% capacity, we're limited by the bandwidth from the combined 64 K of L1 cache/shared memory on the SM.

We could simply perform a block-level reduction into a single shared memory value for each SM. Thus, with 256 threads we'd have a 256:1 reduction ratio. However, this proves not to be particularly effective, as each of the 256 threads is serialized.

The execution units within an SM can execute a half-warp, a group of 16 threads. Therefore, it makes sense to perform a reduction across half-warps. We could then either perform an additional reduction across the set of 16 half-warps, or we could simply write out the set of values to shared memory. It turns out there is almost no difference in execution time between the two approaches.

The problem, however, with a subsequent intrablock reduction in shared memory is where to locate the shared memory parameter to perform the reduction. If you place it after the set of 64 bytes occupied by the intrawarp reduction parameters, it causes the next block of intrawarp not to be 64-byte aligned. The different blocks interact with one another to cause bank conflicts in the shared memory.

We opted for the direct write to global memory, as this was the simpler solution and shows marginal if any difference in performance. Thus, instead of reducing the 16 K conflicting writes to 64 potentially conflicting writes, we have 512 potentially conflicting writes, which is a factor of 32 reduction.

```
__global__ void reduce_gmem_loop_block(
 const uint4 * const data,
 u64 * const result,
 const u32 num_elements)
{
 const u32 num_elements_per_block = (( (num_elements/4) / blockDim.x) / gridDim.x);
 const u32 increment = (blockDim.x * gridDim.x);
 const u32 num_u4_elements = (num_elements>>2);
```

```
// Work out the initial index
u32 idx = (blockIdx.x * blockDim.x) + threadIdx.x;

// Accumulate into this register parameter
u64 local_result = 0;

// Loop N times depending on the
// number of blocks launched
for (u32 i=0; i<num_elements_per_block; i++)
{
 // If still within bounds, add into result
 if (idx < num_u4_elements)
 {
  const uint4 elem = data[idx];

  local_result += ((u64)elem.x) + ((u64)elem.y);
  local_result += ((u64)elem.z) + ((u64)elem.w);

  // Move to the next element in the list
  idx += increment;
 }
}

const u32 num_half_warps = blockDim.x >> 4;
const u32 half_warp = threadIdx.x >> 4;

// Have first N threads clear the half warps
if (threadIdx.x < num_half_warps)
 intra_half_warp_reduce[threadIdx.x] = 0;

// Wait for threads to zero SMEM
__syncthreads();


// Reduce first by half warp into SMEM
// 256 -> 16 (32 banks)
atomicAdd( &intra_half_warp_reduce[half_warp],
    local_result );

// Wait for all threads to complete
__syncthreads();

// Write up to 16 values out to GMEM
if (threadIdx.x < num_half_warps)
 atomicAdd(result,
    intra_half_warp_reduce[threadIdx.x]);
}
```

This results in the following:

```
ID:0 GeForce GTX 470:GMEM loopB 64 passed Time 0.93 ms
ID:0 GeForce GTX 470:GMEM loopC 64 passed Time 0.93 ms

ID:3 GeForce GTX 460:GMEM loopB 64 passed Time 1.34 ms
ID:3 GeForce GTX 460:GMEM loopC 64 passed Time 1.33 ms
```

In this example, `loopB` has 512 atomic writes to global memory. The second kernel, `loopC`, performs an additional intrablock reduction before making 64 atomic writes to global memory. As you can see, there is little if any difference in performance, demonstrating the additional reduction step gains us nothing and therefore was removed from the final solution. This is not really too surprising, as if the latency of the 512 memory writes is already hidden by the considerable computation workload, reducing this to just 64 writes would bring us nothing.

If we compare the best result from the previous section, using an accumulation into registers and then writing out the 16 K values we see on the GTX470 (compute 2.0), this took 1.14 ms. By adding this further reduction step in shared memory we've reduced this to just 0.93 ms, a 19% saving in execution time. As the GTX470 has 14 SMs, this intra-SM reduction step significantly reduces the number of final atomic global memory writes that must be coordinated between these SMs.

By contrast, the GTX460 device (compute 2.1) reduced from 1.38 ms to 1.33 ms, just 4%. The absolute difference is of course clear in that the GTX470 has a 320-bit memory bus compared with the 256-bit memory bus on the GTX460. It's the relative speedup difference that is interesting.

Such a small speedup would indicate that the multiple global memory atomic operations were not in fact the bottleneck as they were on the GTX470. It could also indicate that perhaps we were already using the LSUs to their full capacity. The ratio of LSUs to CUDA cores is much less on the compute 2.1 devices than on the compute 2.0 devices. Both global memory and shared memory accesses require the LSUs.

Thus, the shared memory–based reduction, based on half-warps, gains us a significant reduction over the purely atomic/global memory–based solution in the previous section.

An alternative approach

As with any implementation, you should always look to what previous work has been done and how this could be used to improve existing designs. Mark Harris wrote an excellent study of parallel reduction[3] back in the early GPU days based on the G80 device. Instead of performing a 512:16 reduction, it writes the entire set of values to shared memory and then uses shared memory to perform a series of partial reductions, always accumulating the result to shared memory.

The results are impressive. He used unsigned integer elements and achieved a total time of 0.268 ms on 4 million elements. Scaling this to the 12 million elements (48 MB data) we used in the example works out to 1.14 ms, a comparable number to the 0.93 ms we achieved on the GTX470.

The GTX470 has 448 CUDA cores, compared to the 128 CUDA cores of the G80, a factor of 3.5× improvement in arithmetic capacity. Memory bandwidth has increased from 86 GB/s to 134 GB/s, a factor of 1.5×. However, Mark's kernel accumulates into 32-bit integers, whereas we

---

[3]Mark Harris, NVIDIA Developer Technology, "Optimizing Parallel Reduction in CUDA," 2007.

accumulate into 64-bit integers to avoid the overflow problem. Therefore, the kernels are not directly comparable.

Nonetheless the method proposed may produce good results. Accumulation into a register will clearly be faster than accumulation into shared memory. As the hardware does not support operations that directly operate on shared memory, to perform any operation we need to move the data to and from shared memory. One of the reasons for selecting register-based accumulation was the elimination of this overhead. However, that is not to say we have an optimum set of code for this part of reduction yet.

Some time has passed since this chapter was originally written and this late addition comes after a transition from CUDA 4.0 to CUDA 4.1 SDK, which moved us from the Open64 compiler to an LLVM-based compiler. This should bring a performance boost, and indeed we find the more efficient compiler generates an execution time of 0.74 ms instead of our previous 0.93 ms, a huge improvement just from changing compilers.

However, of this time, how much is actually due to the reduction at the end of the code? We can find out simply by commenting out the final reduction. When we do this, the time drops to 0.58 ms, a drop of 0.16 ms or some 21%. Further investigation reveals that actually all but 0.1 ms of this time can be attributed to the atomic add operation.

Using the 2.1 version of Parallel Nsight we can extract a number of useful facts from the data:

- Of the 48 scheduled warps, on average we get only 32 active warps.
- The workload is unevenly distributed between the SMs.
- Most issue dependencies are the short class.
- There is very little divergent branching.
- Around 8% of the time the SMs stalled. This was due mostly to either instruction fetch or instruction dependencies.

This occupancy issue is a somewhat misleading one, in that it is caused by the uneven distribution rather than some runtime issue. The problem is the number of blocks launched. With 14 SMs, we can have 84 blocks resident with 6 blocks per SM. Unfortunately we only launch 64, so in fact some of the SMs are not fully loaded with blocks. This drops the average executed warps per SM and means some SMs idle at the end of the workload.

We ended up with a value of 64 due to it being identified as an ideal number from the earlier experiments. However, these were based on 16 K competing atomic writes to global memory. We've since reduced this to just 512 writes with most of the atomic writes being within the SM. Once we remove this global bottleneck, it would appear that 64 blocks in total is not the ideal number for the GTX460. Running a sample we see:

```
ID:0 GeForce GTX 470:GMEM loopC 6144 passed Time 2.42 ms
ID:0 GeForce GTX 470:GMEM loopC 3072 passed Time 1.54 ms
ID:0 GeForce GTX 470:GMEM loopC 1536 passed Time 1.11 ms
ID:0 GeForce GTX 470:GMEM loopC 768 passed Time 0.89 ms
ID:0 GeForce GTX 470:GMEM loopC 384 passed Time 0.80 ms
ID:0 GeForce GTX 470:GMEM loopC 192 passed Time 0.82 ms
ID:0 GeForce GTX 470:GMEM loopC 96 passed Time 0.83 ms
ID:0 GeForce GTX 470:GMEM loopC 64 passed Time 0.77 ms
ID:0 GeForce GTX 470:GMEM loopC 48 passed Time 0.82 ms
```

```
ID:0 GeForce GTX 470:GMEM loopC 32 passed Time 0.95 ms
ID:0 GeForce GTX 470:GMEM loopC 16 passed Time 1.40 ms
ID:3 GeForce GTX 460:GMEM loopC 6144 passed Time 3.53 ms
ID:3 GeForce GTX 460:GMEM loopC 3072 passed Time 2.04 ms
ID:3 GeForce GTX 460:GMEM loopC 1536 passed Time 1.41 ms
ID:3 GeForce GTX 460:GMEM loopC 768 passed Time 1.11 ms
ID:3 GeForce GTX 460:GMEM loopC 384 passed Time 0.97 ms
ID:3 GeForce GTX 460:GMEM loopC 192 passed Time 0.92 ms
ID:3 GeForce GTX 460:GMEM loopC 96 passed Time 0.91 ms
ID:3 GeForce GTX 460:GMEM loopC 64 passed Time 0.95 ms
ID:3 GeForce GTX 460:GMEM loopC 48 passed Time 1.00 ms
ID:3 GeForce GTX 460:GMEM loopC 32 passed Time 1.02 ms
ID:3 GeForce GTX 460:GMEM loopC 16 passed Time 1.29 ms
```

Notice the best number of blocks on the GTX470 is 64, while on the GTX460 it is 96. A value of 192 works well on both devices.

However, what about the last issue we noticed, that 8% of the time the SMs were idle? Well this improves to 7% when there are additional blocks, so this is helping. However, what is the cause of the problem? Looking to the kernel output gives us a clue to the issue:

```
1>ptxas info : Used 18 registers, 1032+0 bytes smem, 52 bytes cmem[0]
1>ptxas info : Compiling entry function '_Z27reduce_gmem_loop_block_256tPK5uint4Pyj'
for 'sm_20'
1>ptxas info : Function properties for _Z27reduce_gmem_loop_block_256tPK5uint4Pyj
1> 16 bytes stack frame, 0 bytes spill stores, 0 bytes spill loads
```

Notice, unlike the CUDA 4.0 SDK compiler, the 4.1 compiler places uint4 types into local memory. This local memory on Fermi is the L1 cache, so should you care? We can rewrite the uint4 access to use a uint4 pointer. As the uint4 types are 128-bit aligned (4 × 32 bit words), they are guaranteed to sit on a cache line and memory transaction boundary. Thus, an access to the first element of the uint4 by any thread will pull the remaining three elements into the L1 cache. Consequently, we have L1 local memory access versus L1 direct cache access. There should be no difference, in theory. Let's see:

```
ID:0 GeForce GTX 470:GMEM loopD 384 passed Time 0.68 ms
ID:0 GeForce GTX 470:GMEM loopD 192 passed Time 0.72 ms
ID:0 GeForce GTX 470:GMEM loopD 96 passed Time 0.73 ms

ID:3 GeForce GTX 460:GMEM loopD 384 passed Time 0.85 ms
ID:3 GeForce GTX 460:GMEM loopD 192 passed Time 0.81 ms
ID:3 GeForce GTX 460:GMEM loopD 96 passed Time 0.80 ms
```

Both the GTX470 and GTX460 devices show a significant drop in the execution time. Looking to the cache utilization statistics, we can see the L1 cache hit rate has jumped from 61.1% to 74.5% as we have moved from the local memory version (loopC) to the pointer version (loopD). We also see the percentage of stalls in the SMs drops to 5%. Actually for this statistic, the difference on the GTX460 is quite pronounced, as it started off at 9%, slightly higher than the GTX470. This is likely to be because we're now able to share the L1 cache data between threads as the data is no longer "thread private."

You may be wondering why we simply do not just use 84 blocks as we calculated earlier. The issue is one of rounding. The 12 million element dataset does not equally divide into 84 blocks. Thus, some blocks would need to process more than others. This means the logic would need to be more complex, but more complex for *every* block executed. Just running 84 blocks without solving this issue shows a time of 0.62 ms, a gain of 0.06 ms over the 384-block version. This demonstrates that the 384-block version introduces small enough blocks that the existing load-balancing mechanism handles it quite well. The value of making the code more complex significantly outweighs the benefits and is only necessary if we in fact do not know the size of the input dataset.

Coming back to the question of shared memory versus atomics, which is faster? We can replace the atomic-based reduction with the following code:

```
// Write initial result to smem - 256 threads
smem_data[threadIdx.x] = local_result;
__syncthreads();

// 0..127
if (threadIdx.x < 128)
 smem_data[threadIdx.x] += smem_data[(threadIdx.x)+128];
__syncthreads();

// 0..63
if (threadIdx.x < 64)
 smem_data[threadIdx.x] += smem_data[(threadIdx.x)+64];
__syncthreads();

// 0..31 - A single warp
if (threadIdx.x < 32)
{
 smem_data[threadIdx.x] += smem_data[(threadIdx.x)+32]; // 0..31
 smem_data[threadIdx.x] += smem_data[(threadIdx.x)+16]; // 0..15
 smem_data[threadIdx.x] += smem_data[(threadIdx.x)+8];  // 0..7
 smem_data[threadIdx.x] += smem_data[(threadIdx.x)+4];  // 0..3
 smem_data[threadIdx.x] += smem_data[(threadIdx.x)+2];  // 0..1

 // Have thread zero write out the result to GMEM
 if (threadIdx.x == 0)
  atomicAdd(result, smem_data[0] + smem_data[1]);
}
```

Notice how the code works. First, all 256 threads (warps 0..6) write out their current `local_result` to an array of 256 64-bit values in shared memory. Then those threads numbered 0 to 127 (warps 0..3) add to their result, the result from the upper set of warps. As the warps within a block are cooperating with one another, we need to ensure each warp runs to completion, so add the necessary `__syncthreads()`call.

We continue this reduction until the point at which we reach 32 threads, the size of a single warp. At this point all threads within the warp are synchronous. Thus, we no longer need to synchronize the threads, as the thread sync operation is really a warp sync operation within a single block.

We now have a couple of choices. We could continue the `if threadIdx.x < threshold` operation or we can simply ignore the fact that the redundant threads within the warp perform a useless operation. The additional test actually generates a considerable number of additional instructions, so we simply calculated all values within the warp. Note that this is different than running multiple warps, as in the case where we have the 128 and 64 test. Within a single warp, reducing the number of threads gains us nothing. By comparison, the prior tests eliminate entire warps.

So does this gain us anything compared to the atomic reduction?

```
ID:0 GeForce GTX 470:GMEM loopE 384 passed Time 0.64 ms
ID:3 GeForce GTX 460:GMEM loopE 192 passed Time 0.79 ms
```

Compared with the last version, we moved from 0.68 ms to 0.64 ms on the GTX470 and 0.8 ms to 0.79 ms on the GTX460. Not a significant gain, but nonetheless a gain in execution speed. We can provide one last optimization to this code before we move on.

Compilers typically generate less than optimal code for array indexing where the value of the array index is not a constant. The CUDA compiler is no exception. We can replace the array code with pointer code, which runs somewhat faster. We can also reduce the number of reads/writes to the shared memory area. However, as with most optimized solutions the code becomes more complex to understand and less easy to maintain and debug.

```
// Create a pointer to the smem data area
u64 * const smem_ptr = &smem_data[(threadIdx.x)];

// Store results - 128..255 (warps 4..7)
if (threadIdx.x >= 128)
{
 *(smem_ptr) = local_result;
}
__syncthreads();

// 0..127 (warps 0..3)
if (threadIdx.x < 128)
{
 // Accumulate into a register and then write out
 local_result += *(smem_ptr+128);

 if (threadIdx.x >= 64)    // Warps 2 and 3
  *smem_ptr = local_result;
}
__syncthreads();

// 0..63 (warps 0 and 1)
if (threadIdx.x < 64)
{
 // Accumulate into a register and then write out
 local_result += *(smem_ptr+64);
```

```
 *smem_ptr = local_result;

 if (threadIdx.x >= 32)    // Warp 1
  *smem_ptr = local_result;
}
__syncthreads();

// 0..31 - A single warp
if (threadIdx.x < 32)
{
 local_result += *(smem_ptr+32);
 *(smem_ptr) = local_result;

 local_result += *(smem_ptr+16);
 *(smem_ptr) = local_result;

 local_result += *(smem_ptr+8);
 *(smem_ptr) = local_result;

 local_result += *(smem_ptr+4);
 *(smem_ptr) = local_result;

 local_result += *(smem_ptr+2);
 *(smem_ptr) = local_result;

 local_result += *(smem_ptr+1);

 // Have thread zero write out the result to GMEM
 if (threadIdx.x == 0)
  atomicAdd(result, local_result );
}
```

The approach taken here is that, as we already have the current threads result stored in local_result, there is little point in accumulating into the shared memory. The only shared memory stores needed are those from the upper set of threads sending their data to the lower set. Thus, in each reduction step only the top set of threads write to shared memory. Once we get to a single warp, the code for this test takes longer than the reads/writes it saves from the shared memory, so we drop the test and write anyway. Also to avoid any address calculations, other than simple pointer addition, the address of the shared memory area is taken as a pointer at the start of the code section. The revised timings are:

```
ID:0 GeForce GTX 470:GMEM loopE 384 passed Time 0.62 ms
ID:3 GeForce GTX 460:GMEM loopE 192 passed Time 0.77 ms
```

Thus, we gained 0.02 ms on both the GTX470 and GTX460. We have also largely eliminated the shared memory based atomic reduction operations, which in turn allows for implementation on older hardware. To remove the final reduction to global memory, you'd need to write to an array indexed by blockIdx.x and then run a further kernel to add up the individual results.

An alternative CPU version

For reference, the CPU serial and parallel implementations are provided so we can see the same reduction on the CPU side.

```
u64 reduce_cpu_serial(const u32 * data,
                      const u32 num_elements)
{
 u64 result = 0;

 for (u32 i=0; i< num_elements; i++)
       result += data[i];

 return result;
}

u64 reduce_cpu_parallel(const u32 * data,
                        const int num_elements)
{
 u64 result = 0;
 int i=0;

#pragma omp paralle l for reduction(+:result)
 for (i=0; i< num_elements; i++)
    result += data[i];

 return result;
}
```

On an AMD Phenom II X4 processor (four cores) running at 2.5 MHz, this resulted in a timing of 10.65 ms for the serial version and 5.25 ms for the parallel version. The parallel version was created using OpenMP and the "reduction" primitive. To enable these quite useful pragma in the NVCC compiler simply use the `-Xcompiler -openmp` flag and you can use any of the OpenMP directives for CPU-level thread parallelism.

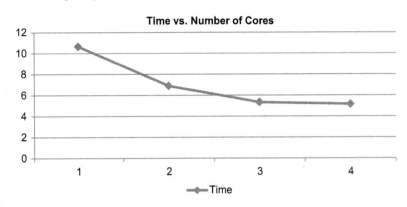

FIGURE 9.37

OpenMP scaling on four cores.

This code spawns N threads where N is the number of cores. The threads are then free to run on any available core. The work is split into N chunks and finally the results are combined.

As can often be the case with parallel programming on CPUs, we see sublinear scaling as the number of cores increases. We can see that the scaling works well from one core to two cores, with a 35% drop in time when using two cores and a 50% drop when using three. However, the addition of the fourth core drops the execution time by just an additional 2% so is effectively noncontributing (Figure 9.37). You typically see a U shape as the number of cores is further increased.

The reason for this is, while the compute performance is being scaled by the introduction of more cores, the memory bandwidth to the socket is shared between all cores. Taking our test system as an example, the AMD 905e processor has a typical memory bandwidth of 12.5 MB/s. Just to read the 48 MB of data from memory without any compute operations would therefore take 3.8 seconds, a considerable chunk of the 5.25 ms execution time. Thus, the issue here is not OpenMP versus CUDA but one of memory bandwidth available *per core* on a CPU versus that of a GPU.

Parallel reduction summary

The original, very simplistic GPU implementation took 197 ms and 164 ms (GTX470 and GTX460). Compared with the CPU parallel four-core result of 5.25 ms this is really terrible and an example of how an apparently fast device can be brought to its knees by poor programming practices.

The final GPU version uses atomic operations as little as possible outside of the SM. It achieves, in pure compute terms, a 6.8× (GTX460) or 8.4× (GTX470) speedup over a four-core CPU. However, 0.62 ms is very little compute time to hide any transfer time. At 5 GB/s to the device the PCI-E 2.0 bandwidth is around 40% of the bandwidth to main memory on our test platform (12 GB/s). A 5 GB per second transfer rate gives us around 5 MB per millisecond. Thus the transfer time of the 48 MB of data would be 9.6 ms alone. We'd be able to overlap less than 10% of compute time with this, which limits the overall execution to no faster than the PCI-E 2.0 transfer speed.

This is actually all too often a problem with GPUs in general. They need to have a sufficiently complex problem that the benefit of their huge compute power can be applied. In such cases, they can drastically outperform a CPU. A simple problem like performing a sum, min, max, or other simplistic task just doesn't provide enough of a problem to justify the time for the PCI-E transfer, unless we can discount the transfer time by ensuring the data is already resident on the device and stays there. This is one of the reasons why the 6 GB Teslas are more attractive than the much cheaper consumer cards that have a maximum capacity of 4 GB.

To increase the overall amount of data held in the GPU memory space, you can simply install multiple cards in a system, typically up to four per node, or more if you use exotic cooling methods. Thus, up to 24 GB in total data can be held on four Tesla class cards within a single node. The host memory space can be directly augmented with the GPU memory space using the UVA (universal virtual addressing) feature if this is available to you (requires a compute 2.x device onwards, a 64-bit OS, Linux or the TCC driver under Windows, CUDA 4.x runtime). Inter-GPU communication (peer-to-peer, P2P) can also be performed without routing the data through the CPU, saving hugely on PCI-E bandwidth.

As we move from PCI-E 2.0 (5 GB/s) to PCI-E 3.0 the bandwidth per PCI-E slot should effectively double, significantly alleviating this problem for GPU devices supporting the new PCI-E 3.0 standard. As of the start of 2012 we saw motherboards start to support PCI-E 3.0 standard with the

Ivybridge/Sandybridge-E processor. PCI-E graphics cards will start to appear through 2012 and beyond. In addition to increased PCI-E bandwidth came increased host memory bandwidth.

This also highlights another point that we've made throughout this book. The CPU can be a useful partner in dealing with all the simple problems in conjunction with a GPU. For example, where tiles of data need to communicate, it can process the halo cases where they need to share data while the GPU is processing the bulk of the data. Often such cases present a lot of branching, which is not efficient on the GPU and therefore can be better suited to a cooperative approach.

Section summary

- There are now well-documented sources that detail algorithms for specific fields. Many are available in the form of plug-in libraries.
- Be aware that not all parallel algorithms have obvious implementations on GPUs. Consider factors such as coalescing and communications when thinking about how to implement such algorithms.
- New functions such as `__syncthreads_count` may have been introduced to address certain types of problems as the API develops. Study carefully the various additions to the API and understand possible usage.
- Use multiple elements per thread wherever possible. However, using too many elements per thread may adversely affect performance.
- As our reduction example shows, the simplest kernel is often the slowest. To achieve the absolute best performance often takes significant programming time and a good understanding of the underlying hardware.
- A multicore CPU is more than a capable partner in calculating workloads, but will often be memory bandwidth constrained, which in turn may limit your ability to make effective use of all the cores.
- OpenMP can provide an easy-to-use multithreaded interface for threads on the CPU side and is included as part of the standard CUDA compiler SDK.

STRATEGY 6: RESOURCE CONTENTIONS

Identifying bottlenecks

It's often not clear to a programmer what, if anything, is wrong with a program. Most GPU programs, if they contain a reasonable amount of work for the GPU to do, show significant performance gains over their CPU counterparts. The question is how much is significant? The problem this question raises is that GPUs can be very good at some tasks, adequate at other tasks, and terrible with certain tasks. Anything that has a lot of arithmetic work and can be split into many independent problems works well.

Algorithms that have significant branching or are mostly sequential are not suited to GPU, or most parallel architectures for that matter. In going down the parallel route, you almost always see a tradeoff of single-thread performance versus multiple-thread performance. The GPUs are typically clocked at up to 1000 MHz, one-third or less than that of a typical CPU. They contain none of the fancy branch prediction logic that is necessary for large pipelines.

The CPU has had decades of development and we're pretty much at the end game of any significant single-thread performance gains. Consequently, largely serial code performs terribly on a GPU compared to a CPU. This may change with future hybrid architectures, especially if we see them include the dedicated CPU as it is proposed with NVIDIA's "Project Denver." This aims to embed an ARM-based CPU core into the GPU fabric. We already see the inclusion of GPU elements onto common CPU platforms, so it's fairly certain the future for both the CPU and GPU world is likely to be a hybrid, taking the most useful parts of each.

However, restricting ourselves to the data parallel problems that run well on current GPUs, what is a good baseline for your kernel? What should you compare it against? What is a realistic target?

There are many fields now where CUDA is used to accelerate problems. One of the best resources to provide both some idea of what you can achieve and to see if there is already a solution that you can just buy in is http://www.nvidia.com/object/cuda_app_tesla.html. Here they list the following types of applications:

- Government and Defense
- Molecular Dynamic, Computation Chemistry
- Life Sciences, Bio-Informatics
- Electrodynamics and Electromagnetic
- Medical Imagining, CR, MRI
- Oil and Gas
- Financial Computing and Options Pricing
- Matlab, Labview, Mathematica
- Electronic Design Automation
- Weather and Ocean Modeling
- Video, Imaging, and Vision Applications

Thus, if your field is options pricing, you can go to the relevant section, browse through a few of the sites, and see that the Monte Carlo pricing model is somewhere from a 30× to 50× speedup over a single-core CPU according to the particular vendor's analysis. Of course, you have to ask what CPU, what clock speed, how many cores were used, etc. to get a reasonable comparison. You also have to remember that any vendor-provided figures are trying to sell their product. Thus, any figures will be the best case and may well ignore certain difficult aspects of the problem to present a more compelling reason to purchase their product over their competitor's product. However, a few hours of research can tell you what would be a reasonable target figure for your particular field. You will also get an appreciation of what other people have done and more importantly what still needs to be developed.

However, don't be disappointed with your initial GPU results in comparison with many of these applications. Often these arise from years of effort, which can be a great advantage, but can also mean they have to carry a lot of legacy code. A new approach to the problem, or a long forgotten approach used in the time of vector machines, may be the best approach today.

Also remember that many of these projects are from startup companies, although as CUDA has become more mainstream, there are now more and more corporate offerings. Often startups come from talented PhD students who want to continue their field of research or thesis into the commercial world. Thus, they often contain a small number of individuals who understand a particular problem domain well, but who may not come from a computing background. Thus, as someone with a detailed understanding of CUDA *and* a detailed understanding of the application field, you may well be able to do much better than the existing commercial or research offerings.

Analysis tools

Visual profiler

One of the first places to start, at least with existing code, is the analysis tools provided with the SDK. The first of these is the NVIDIA Visual Profiler tool. This is a multiplatform tool. It has the very useful feature of pointing out what it thinks is wrong with your kernel, at least pointing you toward what you need to do.

To use this tool, you simply compile your CUDA kernel and then select File→New Session, selecting the executable you just created. You can also input any working directory and command line arguments if applicable. Finally, you have to tell the profiler how long the application run is, so it knows when the kernel has simply crashed and does not wait forever to start processing the results. Note with Windows, you need to disable the default Aero desktop and select the standard desktop theme.

You are probably unlikely to be able to see the detail on the timeline in Figure 9.38, but should be able to make out the major sections. The first thing that is striking about the timeline is how little compute is being performed (the green bar in the middle of the figure). This is a series of kernels using the default stream in sequence on a number of GPUs. We see that using the default stream causes implicit synchronization and the huge impact this has on overall timing.

Switching to a streaming example now, we get a different view. Here we can see a kernel pushed into a stream with a memcpy to and memcpy from device around it. Although we can see the two GPUs are being used together this time, the tool warns us that there is little kernel memory transfer overlap. This is entirely correct. It's caused by the fact that a typical kernel will have some input data *and* some output data. Although on all Fermi devices there are two memcpy engines in the physical hardware, only one is enabled in consumer devices such as the GTX470 and GTX460 used here. Thus, all transfers must go into the same memcpy stream and be executed in order. As the kernel does a "copy to" followed by a "copy from" on the first stream, the subsequent stream's "copy to" gets held up.

Thus, on Tesla devices where both copy engines are present, we do not see such an issue. For consumer-level hardware, we need to adopt a different approach. We simply do not issue any copy back transfers into the streams, until such time as all the memcpy to and kernel invocations have been issued. At this point we then push a set of "copy back" commands into the streams and do the transfers. There may be some kernel overlap with the last kernel and transfer back, but this will be minimal.

The other issue the analysis presents is the bandwidth to and from the device is being underutilized (the "Low Memcpy/Compute Overlap" message). In this example, we're using 32 MB chunks of data. If you look back to earlier sections of this chapter, you'll see this is plenty enough to achieve the peak bandwidth of the PCI-E bus. However, this issue here is the compute part is taking up most of the time. Even if we were to overlap the transfer and kernel execution, the benefit would be marginal. Therefore, it's important to understand the implications of what exactly the tools are telling you and if the associated effort will actually be worth the saving in execution time.

Overall it's a very useful tool and quite easy to set up and use. It produces reasonable results quite quickly and is supported on multiple platforms (Figure 9.39).

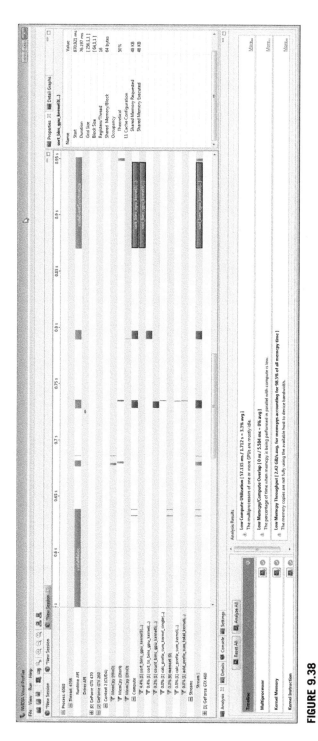

FIGURE 9.38

Visual Profiler timeline.

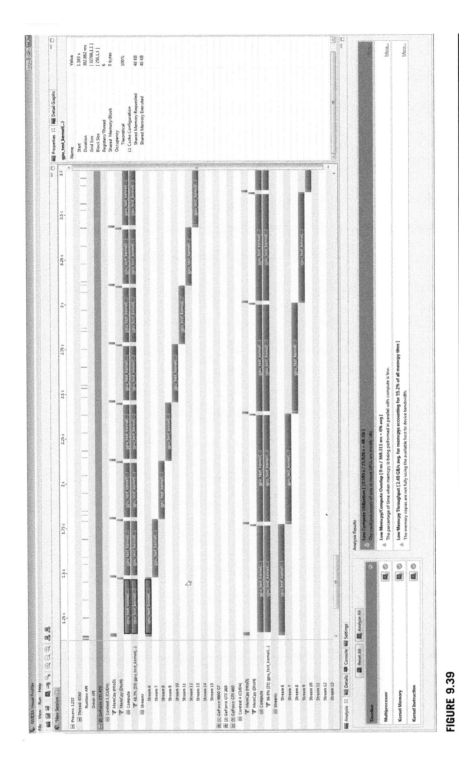

FIGURE 9.39

Visual Profiler, multi-GPU.

Parallel Nsight

Visual Profiler can, unfortunately, only tell you so much. A much better level of detail can be found with the Parallel Nsight tool, which is a Windows-only visual analyzer and debugger. Even if Windows is not your primary development environment, it's worth dedicating a spare PC to this tool for its analysis features alone.

Parallel Nsight is a far more in-depth tool than Visual Profiler. It will tell you a lot more about the kernels and what they are doing. However, as with any more complex tool, it takes a little time to learn how to use it well. The Visual Profiler tool is far simpler to set up and use. It's a beginner's tool, whereas Parallel Nsight is more of an intermediate to advanced tool.

Parallel Nsight is best set up with a single PC using one or more compute 2.x (Fermi) graphics cards. Parallel Nsight will also run remotely using two PCs, each of which has a NVIDIA graphics card. However, you'll find it much easier to have one PC, rather than wait whilst data is copied to/from a remote machine.

Parallel Nsight presents a number of options for debugging and profiling. The two main choices are "Application Trace" and "Profile." The "Application Trace" feature allows you to generate a timeline as with Visual Profiler. This is particularly useful for seeing how the CPU interacts with the GPU and shows the times taken for host/device interaction. You should also use the timeline to verify correct operation of streams and overlapping kernel/memory copy operations.

Multiple concurrent GPU timelines are also supported. For example, the timeline in Figure 9.40 shows we're failing to provide enough work to keep all GPUs busy. Only the computation parts are shown. The Fermi GPUs are shown in red as the first and last context, while the older GPUs are shown in green as the middle two bars. Each red square represents one kernel invocation on a given stream. You can see the first set of kernels end prior to the next set running. We have a huge time period where the first GPU is idle. It's only through using tools such as Parallel Nsight you can see issues such as this. It's difficult to see this using host/GPU timers alone.

The next useful feature is the "Profile" option under the Activity Type menu (Figure 9.41). This allows us to profile the CUDA kernels. However, as many of the experiments require multiple runs of the kernel, no timeline can be produced when selecting this option.

Selecting Experiments to Run as "All" from the dropdown box is the simplest option. As you can see from the list of experiments in Figure 9.42, they are quite extensive. To start acquiring data, simply press the "Launch" button in the application control panel (Figure 9.43). Note the green Connection Status circle. This tells you the Parallel Nsight monitor has successfully connected with the target devices. This needs to be green before any other options work. See the help options for details about setting up the monitor.

Once you press the "Launch" button your application will run until such time as it exits. You then will have a number of options in a dropdown box on the top of the screen, the last of which is "GPU Devices" (Figure 9.44). Select this and you will see an overview of the GPU devices in the system.

This is a useful dialog if you are not sure exactly what the properties of a particular device in your system are. Next, change the dropdown menu from "GPU Devices" to "CUDA Launches." You'll then see a list of kernels that were executed and various statistics. You'll also find "Experimental Results" in the panel below the expandable list.

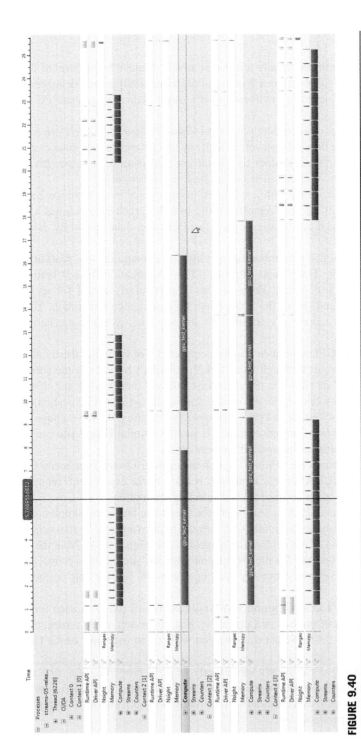

FIGURE 9.40

Parallel Nsight, multi-GPU timeline.

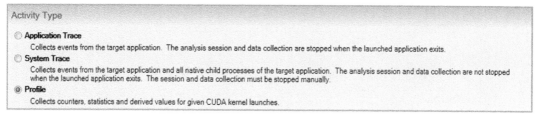

FIGURE 9.41

Parallel Nsight Activity Type selection.

In this particular example, we have six kernels. We can see from the results a number of issues. First, none of the kernels achieve a theoretical occupancy above 33% (Figure 9.45). In the case of the first kernel, this is caused by the block limit (8) being hit before we've achieved the maximum of 48 warps that can be resident on the device. Also note that the first kernel does not set the

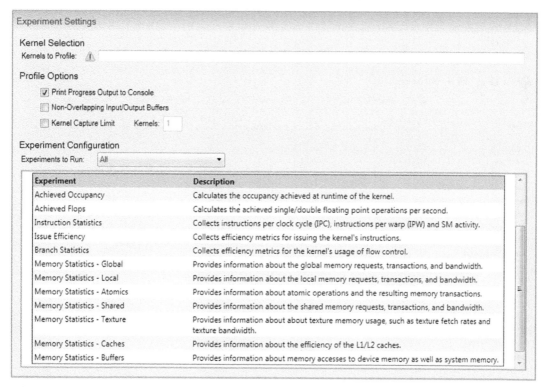

FIGURE 9.42

Parallel Nsight Experiments.

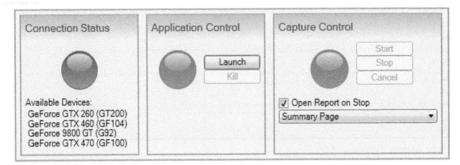

FIGURE 9.43

Parallel Nsight application Launch control.

cache configuration and the CUDA runtime uses the PREFER_SHARED option, allocating 48 K to shared memory instead of the cache. As the kernel does not use shared memory, this is pointless. We're missing a call in the host code to set to cache configuration to PREFER_L1 prior to the first kernel call.

Name	GPU 0 - GeForce GTX 470	GPU 1 - GeForce 9800 GT	GPU 2 - GeForce GTX 260	GPU 3 - GeForce GTX 460
Aliases	CUDA: Device 0, OddEven.exe [4716]	CUDA: Device 1, OddEven.exe [4716]	CUDA: Device 2, OddEven.exe [4716]	CUDA: Device 3, OddEven.exe [4716]
CUDA Cores	448	112	216	336
Driver Type	WDDM	WDDM	WDDM	WDDM
Driver Version	285.67	285.67	285.67	285.67
Frame Buffer Bandwidth (GB/s)	133.92	60.8	123.2	115.2
Frame Buffer Bus Width (bits)	320	256	448	256
Frame Buffer Location	Dedicated	Dedicated	Dedicated	Dedicated
Frame Buffer Physical Size (MB)	1280	1024	896	1024
GPU Family	GF100	G92	GT200	GF104
Graphics Clock (MHz)	607.5	650	625	725.5
Memory Clock (MHz)	1674	950	1100	1800
Name	GeForce GTX 470	GeForce 9800 GT	GeForce GTX 260	GeForce GTX 460
PCI Device ID	10DE.6CD	10DE.614	10DE.5E2	10DE.E22
PCI Ext Device ID	6CD	614	5E2	E22
PCI Revision ID	A3	A2	A1	A1
PCI Sub-System ID	19DA.1153	10B0.801	10B0.801	1462.2322
Processor Clock (MHz)	1215	1625	1348	1451
RAM Type	GDDR5	GDDR3	GDDR3	GDDR5
SM Count	14	14	27	7

FIGURE 9.44

Parallel Nsight, GPU devices present.

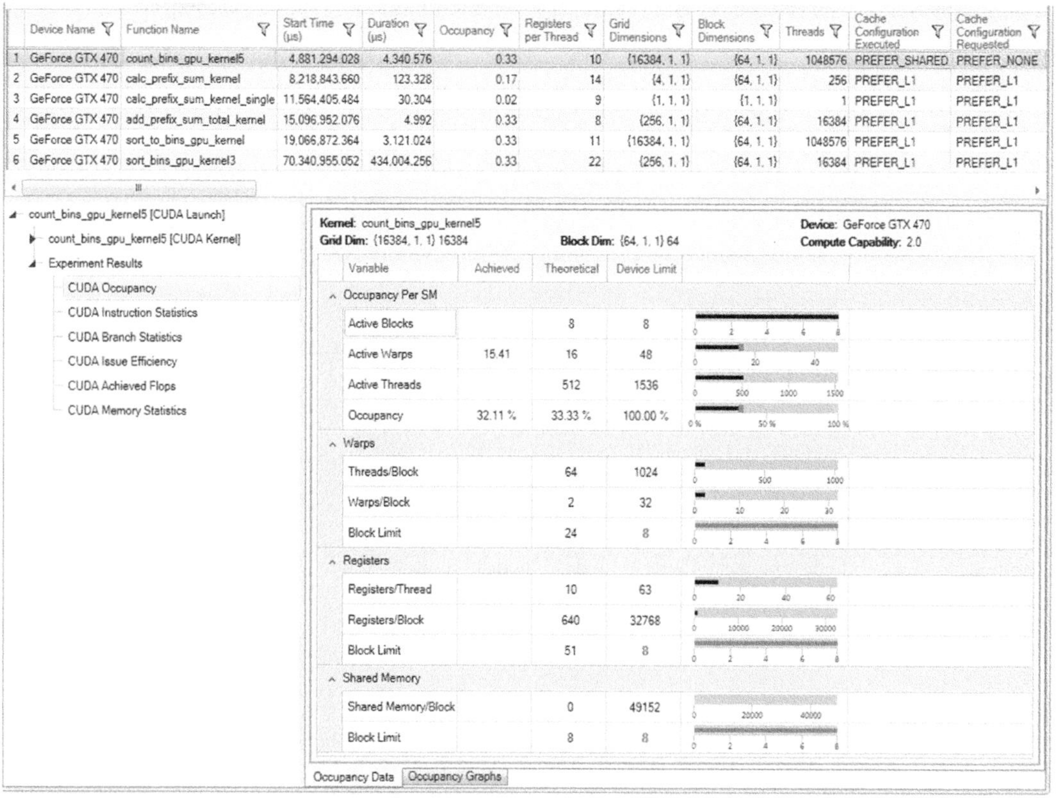

FIGURE 9.45

Parallel Nsight occupancy.

The next experiment to look at is the "Instruction Statistics" (Figure 9.46). Here we see a few issues. There is a very high level of instructions that are being issued but not executed. This is indicative of the SM having to serialize and thus reissue the same instructions. We also see a huge spike of activity on SM 2. This is in fact very bad, as it means one of the blocks that were allocated to this SM performed a huge amount of additional work compared with the other blocks. This indicates the blocks are not equally distributed in terms of work per block, and this is something we need to solve at the algorithm level. Some balancing of the work per block is needed.

The next experiment is the "Branch Statistics," which tells us how much the execution within a warp diverges (Figure 9.47). We ideally want a very small if not zero value for branch divergence. Here we see 16% of the branches diverge, which contributes to the reissuing of instructions we saw in the "Instruction Statistics" experiment. This too originates from the algorithm in that the amount of work per thread varies. It points to the need to balance the workload between the work blocks.

The next experiment looks at the ability of the SM to issue and execute instructions. We'd expect to see a roughly equal distribution in terms of the "Active Warps per Cycle" chart. It shows that despite

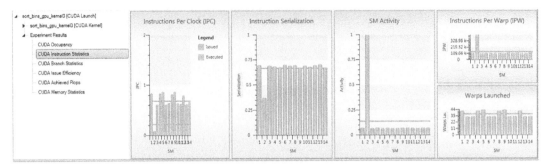

FIGURE 9.46

Parallel Nsight "Instruction Statistics."

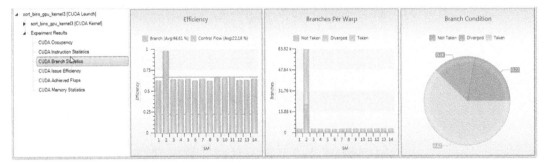

FIGURE 9.47

Parallel Nsight "Branch Statistics."

SM 2 taking a very long time to execute, it was actually only given a small number of warps to execute. This confirms that it was likely that one of the blocks given to it contained much more work than the other blocks. We also have a very low level of "Eligible Warps per Active Cycle," which may in turn suggest the SMs are stalling at some point (Figure 9.48).

Looking at the next tab we see the distribution of instruction dependencies (Figure 9.49). Instruction dependencies are caused by the output of one operation feeding into the input of the next. As the GPU uses a lazy evaluation model, the GPU operates best with long instruction dependencies.

The graph in Figure 9.49 shows there are too many immediate dependencies. The easiest method to solve this is by introducing some ILP at the thread level. As we in fact have very few blocks, we have a significant number of unused registers that could be used to introduce ILP. We could do this via the vector types or by expanding the loop to process N elements per iteration. We could also use one or more registers to prefetch the values from the next loop iteration.

The next tab confirms what we saw in the "Eligible Warps" tab, that the SMs are in fact hitting a stall condition. The first pie chart in Figure 9.50 shows that in 69% of the time, the SM has no eligible warp to execute, meaning it will stall or idle, which is of course not good. The second pie chart in Figure 9.50 shows the reason for the stall, which we can see is 85% of the time related to execution dependencies.

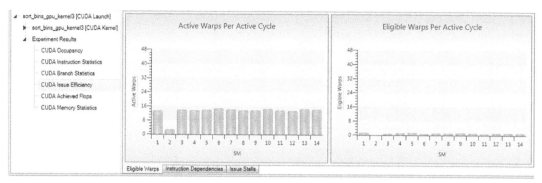

FIGURE 9.48

Parallel Nsight issue efficiency, eligible warps.

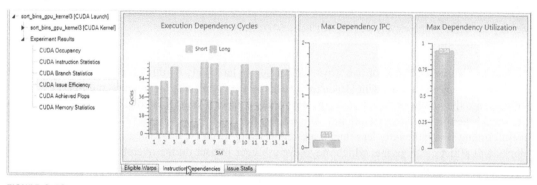

FIGURE 9.49

Parallel Nsight issue efficiency, instruction dependencies.

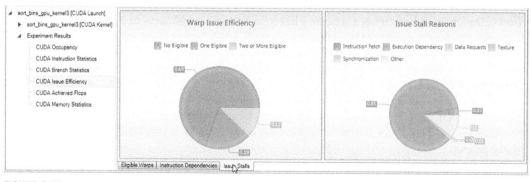

FIGURE 9.50

Parallel Nsight issue efficiency, issue stalls.

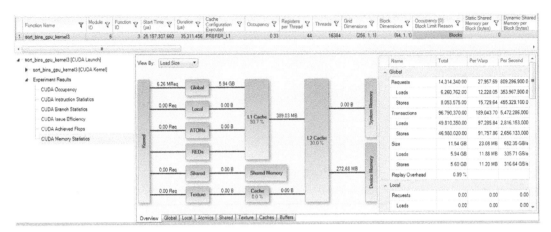

FIGURE 9.51

Memory statistics, memory overview (256 blocks × 64 threads).

This can be solved in one of two ways. Currently, we have only 64 threads per block, meaning we get too few warps that are resident (16 out of a possible 48). Increasing the number of threads per block will increase the number of resident warps. From this perspective only, we'd need to move from 64 to 192 threads per block. This in itself may well resolve the issue. However, the effect of this issue on the overall timing is significantly less than issues concerning memory. Increasing the number of resident blocks will affect cache usage, which may have a bigger impact on the overall timing.

We can see this in practice by looking at the total amount of data fetched from global memory by creating two versions, one that uses 128 threads per block and another that uses 64 threads per block. As we have registers to spare, we'll also fetch 16 elements in the 64-register version and 12 elements in the 128-register version. This maximizes the register usage while still maintaining eight blocks per SM.

Sure enough the "Warp Issue Efficiency" improves, reducing the "No Eligible" warps from 75% down to just 25%. The number of theoretical warps per SM also increases from 16 to 32 (13.25 versus 26.96 actual). The occupancy increases from 27% to 56%. These are all improvements, but they are secondary effects. The kernel is performing a sort, so is likely, as with almost all sorts, to be memory bound.

In fact, when we compare the two kernels with the "CUDA Memory Statistics" experiment, there is a difference. The increased number of blocks per SM means that the ratio of L1 cache to each block is reduced. This in turn results in a doubling of the number of global memory fetch operations that are not cached in the L1 or L2 cache.

In the first kernel, using 64 threads per block, we achieve a 93.7% cache hit rate, which is very good (Figure 9.51). Of the 6.3% of the transactions the L1 cache misses, the L2 cache picks up 30%, or around one-third. Thus, very few read transactions actually make it to global memory and we stay mostly on chip.

When we extend this to 128 threads per block, the overall number of blocks halves to 128 blocks in total (Figure 9.52). However, this is not an issue, as with 14 SMs on the device and a maximum of eight resident blocks, we can only accommodate a maximum of 112 blocks at any given time anyway. Thus, we can increase the number of resident warps without any SMs running out of blocks.

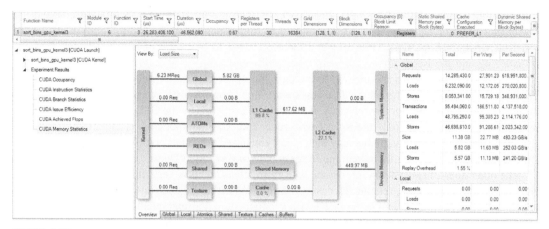

FIGURE 9.52

Memory statistics, memory overview (128 blocks × 128 threads).

Notice the problem with the cache hit ratio. Both the L1 and L2 caches achieve a lower hit ratio than before. The amount of memory fetched from global memory approximately doubles from 272 MB to 449 MB. This takes the execution time from 35 ms to 46 ms, despite the apparent improvements in utilization of the SMs. Note that due to the allocation of one thread to each sample block, these memory fetches are all uncoalesced, so they are in fact very expensive.

Note that a design in which the threads from a thread block cooperated on sorting a single sample block would be far less sensitive to this effect. This analysis shows us this dependency. Through using a different mapping of threads to work in the sort stage, or by balancing or adjusting the bin boundaries, we may well be able to significantly improve the throughput.

Resolving bottlenecks

It's all very well knowing what the code you are running is doing, but it's often another matter to both understand and fix the issue. The three types of bottlenecks you typically see, in order of importance, are:

- PCI-E transfer bottlenecks
- Memory bandwidth bottlenecks
- Compute bottlenecks

PCI-E transfer bottlenecks

PCI-E transfer bottlenecks are often a key consideration. As we saw from the earlier sections, PCI-E bus bandwidth is limited and you can expect to achieve a peak of around 5 GB/s on PCI-E 2.0 depending on the host hardware. However, to achieve this peak you need to be using pinned memory and an appropriately sized transfer. Adding more GPUs to a node typically reduces the overall bandwidth, but allows the overall amount of GPU to be increased. If you can keep everything in the

GPU memory space, be that a single Tesla GPU or multiple GPUs, then the transfer cost can be eliminated from the equation. The extent of the reduction in bandwidth by adding more cards is very much dependent on the host hardware. You therefore need to be aware of how much data you are transferring and its usage.

Compression techniques are one way to increase this apparently hard limit on PCI-E transfer rates. Do you really need to transfer all the data you are sending? For example, image data often contains an alpha channel that is used for transparency. If you are not using this on the GPU, then you can discard it and transfer from the host only the RGB (red, green, and blue) components, eliminating 25% of the data to be transferred. Although this may then mean you have 24 bits per pixel, the transfer time saving may significantly outweigh the nonaligned access pattern this might cause.

The other question is can you infer some data from others? This is very much problem dependent, but you may be able to compress the data using a simple algorithm such as run-length encoding. A long series of the same numbers can be replaced with a value, count pair and reconstructed at the GPU end in very little time. You may have lots of activity from a sensor and then no "interesting" activity for quite a period of time. Clearly, you can transfer the "interesting" data in full and either throw away the "uninteresting" data at the host end, or transfer it in some compressed form.

Interleaving transfer with computation using streams or zero-copy memory is another essential technique we have already covered. In the situation where your PCI-E transfer time is in excess of your kernel time, you effectively have the computation time for free. Without overlapping, the two times must be added and you end up with large gaps where no computation is taking place. See Chapter 8 for more information on using streams.

PCI-E is not the only transfer bottleneck you need to consider. The host will have a limit on the amount of memory bandwidth there is. Hosts such as the Intel Sandybridge-E processors use quad-banked memory, meaning they can achieve much higher host memory bandwidth than other solutions. Host memory bandwidth can also be saved by using P2P (Peer to Peer) transfers if your problem allows for this. Unfortunately, at the time of writing, to use the P2P function you need to use an OS other than Windows 7. With the exception of those using Tesla cards and thus the TCC (Tesla Compute Cluster) driver, Windows 7 is the only major OS not currently supported for this feature.

The speed at which the node can load and save data to storage devices, be they local devices or network devices, will also be a limiting factor. High-speed SSD drives connected in RAID 0 mode will help with this. These are all considerations for selecting host hardware. We look at a number of these in detail in Chapter 11.

Memory bottlenecks

Assuming you can get the data on and off the GPU, the next issue is memory bandwidth to or from global memory. Moving data is expensive in terms of time and power usage. Therefore, being able to efficiently fetch/store and reuse data are essential criteria for selecting an appropriate algorithm. The GPU has huge amounts of compute resources, so an inefficient algorithm with a memory pattern favorable to a GPU (coalesced, tiled, high locality) may outperform a more computationally intensive algorithm that exhibits less GPU-friendly memory pattern.

When considering memory, think also about thread cooperation and appreciate the cooperation is best limited to a single block of threads. Generic algorithms that assume any thread can talk to any other thread are less useful than those that value locality of threads to one another. Algorithms designed for use on older vector machines are often far more efficient than those designed around distributing work over N independent processing nodes, as commonly found in today's cluster machines.

On modern GPUs, the L1 and L2 caches can significantly affect the execution time of kernels in sometimes rather unpredictable ways. Shared memory should be used where you have data reuse, want a more predictable outcome, or are developing for compute 1.x hardware. Even with the full 48 K allocation to the L1 cache, there is still 16 K of local shared memory storage available on each SM.

A fully populated Fermi GPU has 16 SMs, so this amounts to a total of 256 K of high-speed memory in addition to the 768 K of L1 cache. This can be swapped, giving 768 K of programmer-managed shared memory and 256 K of L1 cache. Data reuse through either or both mechanisms is critical to achieving high throughput. This is typically achieved by ensuring locality of the calculation. Instead of multiple passes over large datasets, break the data into tiny tiles, use multiple passes over individual tiles, and then repeat for the other tiles. This allows the data to remain on chip throughout whatever transformation is being made on it, without multiple read/writes to and from global memory.

Memory coalescing is key to achieving high memory throughput, although a sufficiently high number of memory transactions is also required. On Fermi and Kepler devices, to achieve anything like the full bandwidth when using 32-bit values per thread (i.e., floats or integers), you need to have the GPU almost fully populated with threads (48 to 64 resident warps, 1536 to 2048 threads per SM). Increased transaction sizes through the use of the various vector types help improve both ILP and memory bandwidth. Having each thread process four values instead of one tends to work well for many applications.

Compute bottlenecks

Complexity

Surprisingly, despite the immense computing throughput of the GPU, there are still problems that are compute bound. These are usually problems where the overall amount of data is very large, such as the various forms of medical image scanning or data processing from devices that generate large amounts of sample data. These types of problems were previously processed on clusters. However, now due to the huge processing power available from a multi-GPU computer, many problems can be processed on a single standalone PC.

Algorithms that contain a lot of computations work really well on GPUs compared to their CPU counterparts. However, algorithms that also include a lot of control complexity do not. Take the example of boundary cells in a typical tiled algorithm. If the cells collect data from their immediate neighbors, then a cell at the corner of a tile needs to collect data from the corner points of three other tiles.

In Figure 9.53 you can see there is a large block of green cells in the centre that have no boundary condition. They can safely calculate some value from the surrounding cells within the current block. Unfortunately, some programmers write programs that deal with the problem cases first. Thus, their kernel goes along the lines

```
if (top left corner cell)
else if (top right corner cell)
else if (bottom right corner cell)
else if (bottom left corner cell)
else if (top row)
else if (right row)
```

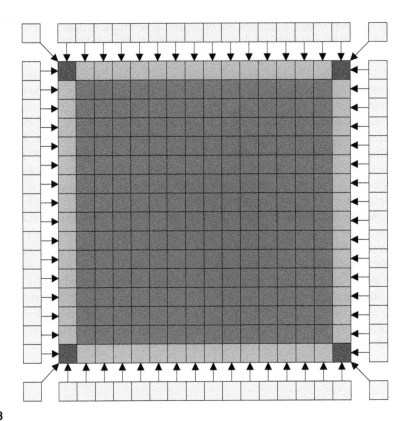

FIGURE 9.53

Halo cells needed.

```
else if (bottom row)
else if (left row)
else (must be centre element)
```

Particularly, control complex algorithms are not well suited to GPUs. If each thread runs the same kernel, the center elements have nine conditions to test before the thread does any work on them. Reversing the order of the tests, so the center elements are tested first, means we need four boundary tests. This would be an improvement, but is still far from optimal. The solution is to write customized kernels for each special case or let the CPU handle these complex conditionals.

The type of problem here is a stencil one, where cells N levels from the center contribute in some way to the result. In this simple example, N is 1, as the immediate neighbors are used. As N is increased, typically some factor is applied, as values that are a long way from the center often do not contribute as much to the result.

As each cell will need values from the surrounding cells, each cell value will be read multiple times. Thus, a common approach to such problems is to use many threads to read a tile of data into shared memory. This allows for high-performance coalesced access to global memory, both when reading the data and also when writing it back. However, shared memory is not visible between blocks and there is no mechanism to pass shared data directly between blocks. This is due to the design of CUDA where there is only ever a subset of the total number of blocks executing. Thus, shared memory is reused as old blocks are retired and new blocks scheduled.

Thus, to load the halo cells, the cells outside the boundary of our particular tile, you can either read them from global memory or also load these into shared memory. Reading the rows from global memory gives a nice coalesced memory pattern. However, the columns generate a number of separate memory transactions, one for each cell we load. As these cells may be read a number of times, reading the columns can be a memory-intensive operation that will limit performance. Thus, at least the columns are usually placed into shared memory.

Thus, writing multiple kernels is usually a good solution to the problem of eliminating the control flow complexity. We can have one kernel that handles corner elements, another for rows, another for columns, and another for the center elements. If appropriate, each of these can call a common routine that processes the data as a series of values, and now the complexity of where the data came from has been removed.

Note that for compute 1.x and compute 2.x different solutions are applicable. As compute 1.x hardware has no cache for global memory, each memory transaction would generate a considerable amount of latency. Thus, for these devices it can make sense to manually cache the necessary data from the surrounding tiles in shared memory or give the calculation to the CPU.

However, compute 2.x devices have both an L1 and L2 cache. As each tile will have to process its own elements, it's likely that the tiles above, above left, and left will have already been loaded into the cache by previous activity of other blocks. The tiles to the right, right bottom, and bottom will usually not be present unless there are multiple passes over quite a small dataset. Accessing these from global memory will bring them into the cache for the subsequent block. You can also explicitly request cache lines be brought into the cache using the prefetch PTX instruction (see PTX ISA).

As a consequence of the caching, we can eliminate a large amount of the control complexity necessary to manage shared memory by simply selecting a 48 K L1 cache and not using shared memory at all. Elimination of complexity is often useful in speeding up compute bound kernels.

Instruction throughput

As with many processors, not all instructions take the same amount of time to execute on every device. Selecting the correct instruction mix for a given processor is something the compiler should be able to perform quite well, but it's also something the programmer needs to be aware of.

First of all, you need to ensure you are targeting the correct binaries for your hardware. Ideally, you should have one compute level specification for each target hardware platform. In Visual Studio this is done in the project options and is something we've already covered. For those people using command line it's the `-arch` flag that specifies this.

In terms of single-precision floating-point operations, all compute levels achieve a throughput of one instruction per clock, per thread. Remember, however, as this is per thread. In absolute terms we need to consider this is warp wide times the number of simultaneous warps per SM times the number of SMs on the GPU. Thus on Kepler GTX680 we have a 32 wide warp x 8 warp dispatch x 8 SMs = 2048 instructions per clock. Now throughput is not the same as instruction latency. It may take up to the order of 20 clock cycles for the result to become available to feed into a subsequent operation. A series of floating-point operations fed into the instruction pipeline would therefore appear 20 cycles later, one each cycle. The throughput would be one instruction per cycle, per thread but the latency would be 20 cycles.

Double-precision floating-point hardware, however, does not achieve this. For compute 2.0 hardware, it's half the speed of single precision. For compute 2.1 hardware, it's actually only one-third of the speed. Compute 2.1 hardware (GTX460/560) and compute 3.0 hardware (GTX680) was aimed more toward the gaming market, so it lacks the same level of double-precision floating-point performance.

We see a similar issue with 32-bit integer values. Add and logical instructions only run at full speed. All other integer instructions (multiply, multiply-add, shift, compare, etc.) run at half speed on compute 2.0 hardware and one-third speed on compute 2.1 hardware. As usual, division and modulus operations are the exception. These are expensive on all compute levels, taking "tens of instructions" on compute 1.x hardware and "below 20 instructions" on compute 2.x hardware [NVIDIA CUDA C Programming Guide, v4.1, chapter 5].

Type conversion instructions operate at half speed on compute 2.0 devices and one-third speed on compute 2.1 devices. These are necessary when 8- or 16-bit integer types are used, as the hardware supports only native integer types (32-bit on compute 2.x, 24-bit on compute 1.x). Thus, the addition of two byte values results in promotion of these values to two integer values. The subsequent result then again needs to be demoted to a byte value. Similarly, conversions to and from single-/double-precision floating-point values cause additional type conversion instructions to be inserted.

In C all whole numbers are by default signed integers. All numbers containing a decimal place are treated as double-precision floating-point values unless an F postfix is placed immediately after the number. Thus,

```
#define PI (3.14)
```

creates a double-precision definition and

```
#define PI (3.14F)
```

creates a single-precision definition.

Using a non-postfixed constant in a floating-point expression causes an implicit conversion to double precision during the calculation. An implicit conversion to single precision is also performing when the result is assigned to a single-precision variable. Thus, forgetting to use the F postfix is a common cause of creating unnecessary conversion instructions.

Synchronization and atomics

Synchronization points are often necessary in many algorithms. Synchronization within a thread block is not costly, but does potentially impact performance. The CUDA scheduler will try to schedule up to sixteen blocks per SM, which it can do unless you start using larger numbers of threads (see Chapter 5). As the number of threads increases, the number of blocks that can be scheduled decreases. This in itself is not too bad, but when combined with synchronization points it can lead to the SM stalling.

When a block performs a synchronization, a number of warps out of the available set (24 on compute 1.x, 48 on compute 2.x, 64 on compute 3.x) effectively drop out of the scheduling availability, as all but the last warp hits the synchronization point. In the extreme case of 1024 threads per block (two blocks per SM), up to half of the resident warps would be at the synchronization barrier. Without any ILP, the ability of the SM to hide memory latency through running multiple threads then becomes insufficient. The SM stops running at peak efficiency. Clearly, we want maximum throughput from all the SMs for as much time as possible.

The solution to the synchronization issue is not to use large thread blocks. You should aim to fully populate the SM where possible, so 192 threads is an ideal number, which results in eight blocks per SM on compute 2.x hardware, 256 being better for compute 3.x hardware.

Unfortunately, if we're using interthread synchronization it is likely we'll also need interblock synchronization. It's more efficient to synchronize data between threads than between blocks. For block-based synchronization we need to use global memory, whereas interthread synchronization can be performed with shared memory. Thus, it's a tradeoff between the two scenarios best resolved by simply running both and seeing which is the fastest.

Atomic operations act very much like synchronization points in that all the threads in a warp have to line up one after another to perform the operation. It takes time for all the threads in a block to line up in groups of 32 to move through the atomic operation. However, unlike synchronization points, they are free to continue at full speed afterward. This helps in terms of increasing the availability of warps that can be run, but doesn't help the overall execution time of the block. The block cannot be retired from the SM until all the threads have completed. Thus, a single atomic operation effectively serializes and spreads out, in terms of execution time, the warps in a given block. The block can't finish until all the stragglers have completed.

The effect of synchronization and atomics on your kernel can be seen using the "CUDA Issue Efficiency" experiment within Parallel Nsight.

Control flow

As we saw earlier, branch divergence can have a serious impact on execution time as both paths have to be executed separately. The compiler is aware of this and thus uses something called predication.

Most of the PTX instructions can be predicated using the .p notation of the PTX ISA. For example,

```
setp.eq.s32 %p16, %r295, 1;
@%p16 bra  BB9_31;
```

Here we set up a predicate register in each thread, testing virtual register 295 for the value 1 and setting predicate register 16 accordingly. In the next instruction the predicate register 16 is used to predicate the bra (branch to) instruction. Thus, only those threads meeting the test condition of the earlier setp.eq.s32 instruction follow the branch. We could replace the branch with a mov or similar instruction. Typically, you see the compiler generate this for small if-else constructs. For example,

```
if (local_idx >= 12)
local_idx = 0;
```

will be translated to

```
setp.gt.u32 %p18, %r136, 11;
selp.b32 %r295, 0, %r136, %p18;
```

This works well in avoiding branches, as in fact all threads in the warp execute the predicate instruction, but those threads without the predicate bit set simply ignore it. The compiler has a strong preference for predication, even when other approaches would be better. The criteria is simply based on the size of the body of the `if` statement. Consider the following example:

```
// Fetch the test data element
switch(local_idx)
{
 case 0: elem = local_elem_00; break;
 case 1: elem = local_elem_01; break;
 case 2: elem = local_elem_02; break;
 case 3: elem = local_elem_03; break;

 case 4: elem = local_elem_04; break;
 case 5: elem = local_elem_05; break;
 case 6: elem = local_elem_06; break;
 case 7: elem = local_elem_07; break;

 case 8: elem = local_elem_08; break;
 case 9: elem = local_elem_09; break;
 case 10: elem = local_elem_10; break;
 case 11: elem = local_elem_11; break;

 case 12: elem = local_elem_12; break;
 case 13: elem = local_elem_13; break;
 case 14: elem = local_elem_14; break;
 case 15: elem = local_elem_15; break;
}
```

This code simply selects one of N local variables (registers) based on an index. The local variables are individually named, as creating an array causes the compiler to place this into local memory. Unfortunately, the compiler implements a series of `if-else-if` type statements, which means at element 16 we have to perform 15 prior tests. I'd have expected it to implement a jump table, creating an assignment at the target of each jump. This would be two instructions, load `local_idx` into a register and then an indirect jump to some base address plus the value in the register. The jump table itself is set up at compile time.

Thus, you need to ensure the control flow you expect is the control flow the compiler generates. You can do this relatively easily by inspecting the PTX code and/or the actual target code if you are still unsure. Predication works well in many but not all instances.

Section summary

- Use profiling tools to really see into what is happening as opposed to what you *think* is happening.
- Avoid overly complex kernels by generating a general case and exception case kernel, or by using the caching features to eliminate the complex kernel altogether.
- Understand how predication works in control flow.
- Don't assume the compiler will provide the same scope of optimizations found with more mature compilers. CUDA is still quite new and things will take time.

STRATEGY 7: SELF-TUNING APPLICATIONS

GPU optimization is not like CPU optimization. Many techniques overlap, while others have undesirable effects. I've tried to cover the major areas of optimization in the preceding sections. However, optimization is never an exact science, not when practiced by human programmers anyway. There are lots of factors that need to be considered when designing code for the GPU. Getting an optimal solution is not easy and it takes considerable time to become familiar with what works, try different solutions, and understand why one works when another doesn't.

Consider some of the major factors:

- Transfer to and from the host.
- Memory coalescing.
- Launch configuration.
- Theoretical and achieved occupancy.
- Cache utilization.
- Shared memory usage/conflicts.
- Branch divergence.
- Instruction-level parallelism.
- Device compute level.

For someone starting out with CUDA, there is a lot to think about and it will take time to become proficient with each of these areas. However, the most challenging aspect of this is that what works on one device many not work on another. Throughout this book we've used the whole range of available devices and a number of different host platforms where necessary to highlight differences.

In the same way as different CPUs provide different levels of performance and functionality, so do GPUs. The CPU world is largely stuck with an x86 architecture, which reflects design goals of a system designed to run serial programs. There have been many extensions to provide additional functionality, such as MMX, SSE, AVX, etc. The x86 instruction set is today translated within the hardware to micro-instructions, which can be really for any target hardware. Sandybridge is perhaps the best example of this, where the micro-instructions themselves are actually cached instead of the x86 assembly code instructions.

GPU hardware is also not fixed and has changed significantly since the first CUDA-enabled devices were released back in the GTX8800 times. CUDA compiles to PTX, a virtual assembly code, aimed at a parallel processor–like architecture. PTX can itself be compiled to many targets, including CPUs, as the cooperative thread array concept lends itself to implementation in most parallel hardware. However, as far as we're concerned, it's compiled to a specified compute level for various NVIDIA GPUs. Therefore, you need to be familiar with what a given compute level provides, that is you need to understand for what hardware you are writing code. This has always been the basis of good optimization. Trends toward abstraction, layering, and hiding the architecture are all aimed at programmer productivity, but often at the expense of performance.

Not every programmer is interested in the intricate workings of the hardware. Even with the previous list of issues to consider you're unlikely to get an optimal solution the first time, the second time, or the Nth time without considerable thought and a lot of trial and error. Thus, one approach to this issue that works well is simply to ask the program to work out the best use of the hardware for a given problem. This can either be done on a small set of the problem or the real problem itself.

Identifying the hardware

The first step in any optimization process is to know what hardware is available and what it is. To find out how many GPUs we have, you simply call

```
cudaError_t cudaGetDeviceCount(int * count);
```

This sets whatever parameter you pass as count to the number of devices available. If there is no CUDA hardware available the function returns cudaErrorNoDevice.

Then for each device found we need to know what its capabilities are. For this we call

```
cudaError_t cudaGetDeviceProperties (struct cudaDeviceProp * prop, int device);
```

We covered in detail the properties of a device in Chapter 8 so will not repeat this here. You should, however, be interested in at least the following:

- Members major and minor that, when combined, provide the compute level of the device.
- The integrated flag, especially when combined with the canMapHostMemory flag. This allows you to use zero-copy memory (covered in Strategy 3) and avoid memory copies to and from the device for devices of which the GPU memory is actually on the host.
- The totalGlobalMem value so you can maximize the use of GPU memory and ensure you don't try to allocate too much memory space on the GPU.
- The sharedMemPerBlock value so you know how much shared memory is available per SM.
- The multiProcessorCount, which is the number of SMs present in the device. Multiply this number by the number of blocks you are able to run on an SM. The occupancy calculator, the Visual Profiler, and Parallel Nsight will all tell you the number of blocks you can run for a given kernel. It's typically up to eight but can be as many as 16 on Kepler. This is the minimum number of blocks you need to schedule to this GPU.

This information gives us some bounds with which we can define the problem space. We then have two choices: either analyze offline the best solution or try to work it out at runtime. The offline approach generally leads to better results and can greatly increase your understanding of the issues involved and may cause you to redesign certain aspects of the program. The runtime approach is necessary for optimal performance, even after significant analysis has taken place.

Thus, the first part of the optimization takes place offline, during the development phase. If you are targeting multiple compute levels, you'll need a suitable card to test your application on. For consumer cards as a whole the most popular NVIDIA cards have always been the 9800 (compute 1.1), 8800 (compute 1.0), GTX260 (compute 1.3), and GTX460 (compute 2.1). For more modern DirectX 11 cards, the 460/560 cards dominate, with a smaller number of power users opting for the more expensive 470/570 cards. Our choice of hardware for this book pretty much reflects the market trends to make the figures presented as useful as possible for people developing mass-market applications.

As we've been working with CUDA since it release on the 8800 series of cards, we have a number of consumer cards at hand. Clearly, many of these are no longer available for sale but can easily be purchased on eBay or elsewhere. All you need is a motherboard with four dual-spaced PCI-E connectors all running at the same speed when fully populated. The primary board used in the development of this book was the (AMD) MSI 790FX-GD70, although this has now been replaced with the MSI 890FXX-G70. Note the newest 990FX board in the series no longer provides four double-spaced connectors.

Device utilization

Having identified what hardware we have, we then have to make use of it. If there are multiple GPUs in the system, as is often the case, then be sure to make use of them. Multi-GPU programming, as of the CUDA 4.x SDK, is now much easier than before, so be sure you are not leaving a 100% performance gain on the table because you're only using a single GPU. See Chapter 8 for more information on this.

All applications are different, so the same primary performance factors may not always be the same. However, many will be. Primary among these is the launch configuration. The first part of this is ensuring you have multiple targets set up in the build process, one target for each compute level you plan on supporting. The target code will automatically be selected based on which GPU you are running the kernel on. Make sure also before running any performance tests you have the "Release" version selected as the build target, something in itself that can provide up to a 2× performance improvement. You're not going to release the debug version, so don't select this as your build target, other than for testing.

Next we need some sort of check to ensure correctness. I suggest you run the GPU code back to back with the CPU code and then do a memory compare (memcmp) on the output of the two identical tests. Note this will detect any error, even if the error is not significant. This is especially the case with floating point, as the order in which the operations are combined will cause small rounding/precision errors. In such cases your check needs to iterate through both results and see if the answers differ by whatever you consider to be significant (0.01, 0.001, 0.0001, etc.) for your particular problem.

In terms of launch configuration we're trying to optimize for the following:

- Number of threads per block.
- Overall number of blocks.
- Work performed per thread (ILP).

The answer for each of these will vary between compute levels. A simple for loop is all that is needed to iterate through all possible combinations and record the timings for each. Then at the end simply print a summary of the results.

In terms of threads per block, start at 1 and increase in powers of two until you reach 16. Then increase the thread count in 16-step intervals until you reach 512 threads per block. Depending on the kernel resource usage (registers, shared memory) you may not be able to reach 512 threads on the earlier compute devices, so scale this back as necessary for these devices only.

Note that we chose 16 here as the increment value, rather than 32, the warp size. This is because warp divergence is half-warp based. Certain devices such as the GTX460s are actually based on three sets of 16 CUDA cores, rather than two as found in other compute levels. Thus, a number of threads that is a multiple of 48 may work better on such devices.

As a general rule, you'll find well-written kernels work best with 128, 192, or 256 threads per block. You should use a consistent scaling from one thread per block up to a peak point where the performance will level off and then fall away. The plateau is usually hit when you achieve the maximum number of resident warps per SM and thus the instruction and memory latency hiding is working at its peak.

Using a slightly smaller number of threads (e.g., 192 instead of 256) is often desirable if this increases the number of resident blocks per SM. This usually provides for a better instruction mix, as more blocks increases the chance they will not all hit the same resource contention at the same time.

If you are hitting the maximum performance at 16, 32, or 64 threads then this usually indicates there is a contention issue, or that your kernel is highly geared toward ILP and you are using a lot of registers per thread.

Once you have a baseline figure for the ideal number of threads per block, try increasing the amount of work done by each thread to two or four elements using the various vector_N types (e.g., int2, int4, float2, float4, etc.). You'll typically see this will improve performance further. The easiest way of doing this is to create additional functions with the same name and simply overload the kernel function. CUDA will call the appropriate kernel depending on the type passed to it at runtime.

Using the vector types will increase register usage, which in turn may decrease the number of resident blocks per SM. This in turn may improve cache utilization. Memory throughput will also likely be increased as the overall number of memory transactions falls. However, kernels with synchronization points may suffer as the number of resident blocks drops and the SM has less choice of which warps are available to execute.

As with many optimizations, the outcome is difficult to predict with any degree of certainty, as some factors play in your favor while others don't. The best solution is to try it and see. Then work backwards, to understand what factor(s) are the primary ones and which are secondary. Don't waste your time worrying about secondary factors unless the primary ones are already addressed.

Sampling performance

The final part of a self-tuning application is sampling. Although you can build a good performance model around compute level and number of SMs, there are many other factors. The same card model may be produced using GDD3 and GDD5 memory, the latter having significantly more global memory bandwidth. The same card may be clocked internally at 600 MHz yet also appear as a 900 MHz model. An optimization strategy that works well for a card with 16 SMs may not work well on one with half that number and vice versa. A mobile processor in a laptop may have been put on a PCI-E X1 link and may have dedicated or shared memory with the host.

It's impossible to collect every card and address every variation that your product might have to address. Even if you could do this, next week NVIDIA will release another card. This is of course mostly a problem for those people writing consumer applications, rather than the somewhat less diverse Tesla population of cards. Nonetheless, when a new card is released people first expect their existing applications to run on it, and second, if they have upgraded, to see a suitable performance boost.

Sampling is the answer to this issue. Each card will have a peak value in terms of a launch configuration that works best for its particular setup. As we've seen in some of the tests run throughout this book, different cards prefer different setups. The Fermi cards work well with 192 or 256 threads per block, yet the prior GPUs work well with 128 and 192 threads per block. The compute 2.1 cards perform best with 64- or 128-byte memory fetches, mixed with ILP, instead of 32-byte memory fetches and a single element per thread. The earlier cards are hugely sensitive to thread/memory ordering when coalescing. Global memory bandwidth on these cards is a fraction of the newer models, yet they can perform to a similar level with some problems if shared memory is used well. The cache in Fermi can play a big part to the extent that very low thread numbers (32 or 64) can outperform higher occupancy rates if the data is then entirely contained in the cache.

When the program is installed, run a short test suite as part of the installation procedure. Run a loop through all feasible numbers of threads. Try ILP values from one to four elements per thread. Enable and disable shared memory usage. Run a number of experiments, repeating each a number of times, and average the result. Store in a data file or program configuration file the ideal values and for which GPU these relate. If the user later upgrades the CPU or GPU, then rerun the experiments and update the configuration. As long as you don't do this on every startup, the user will be happy you are tuning the application to make the best possible use of their hardware.

Section summary

- There are too many factors to say with certainty the effect of a change without actually trying it.
- Some experimentation is often required during development to get the optimal solution.
- The optimal solution will be different on different hardware platforms.
- Write your applications to be aware of the different hardware out there and what works best on each platform, either statically or dynamically.

CONCLUSION

We've looked in detail at a number of strategies for trying to improve the throughput of your kernels with various examples throughout this chapter. You should be aware of the factors that affect performance and their relative importance (primary ones are transfers, memory/data patterns, and finally SM utilization).

Correctness is a key issue in optimizing code. You cannot reliably optimize code without automatic regression testing. This doesn't have to be hugely complex. A back-to-back run against a known working version with several known datasets is entirely sufficient. You should aim to spot 95% plus of the errors before any program leaves your desk. Testing is not the job of some test group, but your responsibility as a professional to produce reliable and working code. Optimization often breaks code and breaks it many times. The wrong answer in one minute instead of the correct answer in one hour is no use to anyone. Always test for correctness after every change and you'll see the errors there and then, as and when they are introduced.

You should also be aware that optimization is a time-consuming and iterative process that will grow your understanding of your code and how the hardware functions. This in turn will lead you to design and write better code from the outset as you become more familiar with what does and what does not work well on GPUs.

Questions on Optimization

1. Take an existing program that has one or more GPU kernels. Run the Visual Profiler and Parallel Nsight to analyze the kernels. What are the key indicators you need to look for? How would you optimize this program?
2. A colleague brings a printout of a GPU kernel to you and asks your advice about how to make it run faster. What would be your advice?
3. Another colleague proposes to implement a web server using CUDA. Do you think this is a good idea? What issues, if any, would you expect with such a program?
4. Implement a shared memory version of the odd–even sort, which produces a single sorted list. What issues might you expect to deal with?

Answers

1. You should be looking first to the execution time of each kernel. If one or more kernels dominate the timing, then, until these are optimized, trying to optimize the others is a waste of your time.

Second, you should be looking to the timeline, specifically concerning transfers. Are they overlapped with kernel operations and are they using pinned memory or not? Is the GPU busy all the time or only periodically given work by the host?

Of the two longest executing kernels, what is causing them to take this time? Is there a sufficient number of threads overall? Are there enough blocks to populate all the SMs? Are there any peaks on one SM, and if so, why? What is the thread to memory pattern and can this be coalesced by the hardware? Are there any serialization points, for example, shared memory bank conflicts, atomics, synchronization points?

2. First, you need to understand the problem before looking at specifics. The "look at the code" optimization strategy can be hit or miss. Sure you can probably optimize the code on the paper in some way, but you need much more information to provide a good answer to the question the person is really asking.

Probably the best answer would be to tell your colleague to profile the application, including the host timeline, and then come back with the results. In doing this they will likely see what the problems are and these may well not even be related to the original kernel printout.

3. Applications that are highly data parallel are well suited to GPUs. Applications that are highly task parallel with lots of divergence threads are not. The typical implementation of a web server on a CPU is to spawn one thread per N connections and to distribute connections dynamically over a cluster of servers to prevent overloading any single node.

GPUs execute code in groups of 32 warps, effectively a vector processor with the ability to follow single-thread control flow when necessary, but at a large performance penalty. Constructing in real time a dynamic web page is very expensive in terms of control flow, a significant amount of which will diverge on a per-user basis. PCI-E transfers would be small and not efficient.

A GPU would not be a good choice, with the CPU host being a much better choice. However, the GPU may be able to be used in the back-end operations of the server, performing some analytical work, churning through the user-generated data to make sense of it, etc.

4. This is a useful exercise to think about how to solve some open-ended problems. First, the question does not specify how to combine the output of N blocks.

The quickest solution for largest datasets should be the sample sort method as it completely eliminates the merge sort step. The framework for sample sort is provided in the text, but is nonetheless quite a complex sort. However, it suffers from a variable number of elements per bin. A prefix sum that padded the bins to 128-byte boundaries would help significantly.

Merge sort is much easier to implement, allows for fixed block sizes, and is what I'd expect most implementations to opt for.

In terms of the odd/even sort, the coalescing problems with global memory are largely hidden by the cache in Fermi due to the locality being extremely high. A compute 1.x implementation would need to use shared memory/registers for the sort. It would need to access the global memory in a coalesced manner in terms of loading and writing back.

Libraries and SDK

INTRODUCTION

Writing programs directly in CUDA is not the only option available to people wishing to speed up their work by making use of GPUs. There are three broad ways of developing applications for CUDA:

- Using libraries
- Directive-based programming
- Writing CUDA kernels directly

We'll look at each of these in turn and when you should apply them.

LIBRARIES

Libraries are useful components that can save you weeks or months of development effort. It makes perfect sense to use libraries where possible because, generally, they are developed by experts in their particular field and thus are both reliable and fast. Some of the more common, and free, libraries are as follows:

- Thrust—An implementation of the C++ STL (Standard Template Interface).
- NVPP—NVIDIA performance primitives (similar to Intel's MKK).
- CuBLAS—GPU version of BLAS (basic linear algebra) library.
- cuFFT—GPU-accelerated fast Fourier transformation library.
- cuSparse—Linear algebra and matrix manipulation for sparse matrix data.
- Magma—LAPACK and BLAS library.
- GPU AI—GPU-based path planning and collision avoidance.
- CUDA Math Lib—C99 standard math support and optimized functions.

There are also a number of commercial offerings, including the following, many of which offer either a limited functionality free or trial version:

- Jacket—An alternative GPU-based Matlab engine for M-code.
- ArrayFire—Matrix, signal, and image processing similar to IPP, MKL, and Eigen.
- CULA tools—Linear algebra.
- IMSL—Implementation of the Fortran IMSL numerical library.

There are, of course, many others that are not shown here. We maintain a list of CUDA libraries at *www.cudalibs.com*, including a number of our own libraries, provided free for personal or academic use, or licensed and supported for commercial use.

General library conventions

The NVIDIA-provided libraries, as a general principle, do no memory management for the caller. They instead expect the caller to provide pointers to the area of allocated memory *on the device*. This allows for a number of functions on the device to be run one after another without unnecessary device/host transfer operations between calls.

As they perform no memory operations, it is the caller's responsibility to both allocate and free memory after usage. This extends even to providing memory for any scratch space or buffer areas used by the library calls.

Although this may seem an overhead to place onto the programmer, it's actually a very good design principle and one you should follow when designing libraries. Memory allocation is a costly operation. Resources are limited. Having a library continuously allocating and freeing memory in the background is far less efficient than you performing these operations once at startup and then again at program exit.

NPP (Nvidia Performance Primitives)

The NPP library provides a set of functions for image and general signal processing. It supports all CUDA platforms. To include NPP into your project, simply include the relevant header files and link to the precompiled library.

For signal processing functions, the library expects one or more source pointers (pSrc1, pSrc2, etc.), one or more destination pointers (pDst1, pDst2, etc.), or one or more mixed pointers for in-place operations (pSrcDst1, pSrcDst2, etc). The library names the functions according to the data type processed. C++ function name overloading—that is, using a single name for a common function—is not supported.

The supported data types for signal processing are Npp8u, Npp8s, Npp16u, Npp16s, Npp32u, Npp32s, Npp64u, Npp64s, Npp32f, and Npp64f. These equate to unsigned and signed versions of 8, 16, 32, and 64 types plus the 32- and 64-bit single-precision and double-precision floating-point types.

The image part of the library follows a similar naming convention, in that the function names reflect intended usage and data type. Image data can be organized in a number of ways, so there are a few key letters that allow you to see the functionality and data type from the name. These are:

- A—Used where the image contains an alpha channel that should not be processed.
- Cn—Used where the data is laid out in a packed or interleaved format of *n* channels, for example {R, G, B}, {R, G, B}, {R, G, B}, etc. would be C3.
- Pn—Used where the color data is split into planes, such as all the data from one color is contiguous, so {R, R, R}, {G, G, G}, {B, B,.B}, etc. would be P3.

In addition to how the data is organized, the naming also tells you how the function will manipulate the data.

- I—Used where the image data is manipulated in-place. That is, the source image data will be overwritten by the operation being performed on it.

- M—Indicates that a nonzero mask will be used to determine which pixels meet the criteria. Only those pixels will be processed. Useful, for example, in overlaying one image onto another.
- R—Indicates that the function operates on a subsection of the image, via the caller specifying an ROI (region of interest).
- Sfs—Indicates the function performs a fixed scaling and saturation on the output data as part of the operation.

The use of such short function naming postfixes leads to function names that may appear somewhat obscure to the casual reader. However, once you memorize the meaning of each attribute of the function name and work with NPP a little bit, you'll quickly recognize what operation a given function is performing.

The image data functions take also an additional parameter of `pSrcStep` or `pDstStep`, which are pointers to the size of a given image line/row in bytes, including any padding bytes that are added to the line width to ensure alignment. Many image processing functions will add padding bytes to the end of a line to ensure the following lines starts on a suitable boundary. Thus, an image 460 pixels wide may be padded to 512 bytes per line. A line width value that is a multiple of 128 is a good choice, as this will allow entire cache lines to be brought in from the memory subsystem.

Let's look at a simple example from the signal manipulation library. We'll take two sets of random data and XOR them together. We'll do this both on the host and the device and then compare the result.

```c
#include <stdlib.h>
#include <stdio.h>
#include <iostream>

#include "cuda.h"
#include "cuda_helper.h"
#include "common_types.h"
#include "timer.h"

// NPP Library
#include "npp.h"
#include "nppcore.h"
#include "nppdefs.h"
#include "nppi.h"
#include "npps.h"
#include "nppversion.h"

#define NPP_CALL(x) {const NppStatus a = (x); if (a != NPP_SUCCESS) { printf("\nNPP
Error: (err_num=%d) \n", a); cudaDeviceReset(); ASSERT(0);} }

int main(int argc, char *argv[])
{
  const int num_bytes = (1024u * 255u) * sizeof(Npp8u);
```

```
// Declare and allocate memory on the host
Npp8u * host_src_ptr1 = (u8 *) malloc(num_bytes);
Npp8u * host_src_ptr2 = (u8 *) malloc(num_bytes);
Npp8u * host_dst_ptr1 = (u8 *) malloc(num_bytes);
Npp8u * host_dst_ptr2 = (u8 *) malloc(num_bytes);

// Check memory allocation worked
if ( (host_src_ptr1 == NULL) || (host_src_ptr2 == NULL) ||
     (host_dst_ptr1 == NULL) || (host_dst_ptr2 == NULL) )
{
 printf("\nError Allocating host memory");
 exit(0);
}

// Declare and allocate memory on the device
Npp8u * device_src_ptr1;
Npp8u * device_src_ptr2;
Npp8u * device_dst_ptr1;
Npp8u * device_dst_ptr2;
CUDA_CALL(cudaMalloc((void **) &device_src_ptr1, num_bytes));
CUDA_CALL(cudaMalloc((void **) &device_src_ptr2, num_bytes));
CUDA_CALL(cudaMalloc((void **) &device_dst_ptr1, num_bytes));
CUDA_CALL(cudaMalloc((void **) &device_dst_ptr2, num_bytes));

// Fill host src memory with random data
for (u32 i=0; i< num_bytes; i++)
{
 host_src_ptr1[i] = (rand() % 255);
 host_src_ptr2[i] = (rand() % 255);
}

// Copy the random data to the device
 CUDA_CALL(cudaMemcpy(device_src_ptr1, host_src_ptr1, num_bytes,
cudaMemcpyHostToDevice));
 CUDA_CALL(cudaMemcpy(device_src_ptr2, host_src_ptr2, num_bytes,
cudaMemcpyHostToDevice));

// Call NPP library to perform the XOR operation on the device
 TIMER_T start_time_device = get_time();
 NPP_CALL(nppsXor_8u(device_src_ptr1, device_src_ptr2, device_dst_ptr1, num_bytes));
 NPP_CALL(nppsAnd_8u(device_src_ptr1, device_dst_ptr1, device_dst_ptr2, num_bytes));
 TIMER_T delta_time_device = get_time() - start_time_device;

// Copy the XOR'd data on the device back to the host
 CUDA_CALL(cudaMemcpy(host_dst_ptr1, device_dst_ptr2, num_bytes,
cudaMemcpyDeviceToHost));
```

```
// Perform the same XOR followed by AND on the host
TIMER_T start_time_cpu = get_time();
for (u32 i=0; i< num_bytes; i++)
{
 host_dst_ptr2[i] = host_src_ptr1[i] ^ host_src_ptr2[i];
 host_dst_ptr2[i] &= host_src_ptr1[i];
}
TIMER_T delta_time_cpu = get_time() - start_time_cpu;

// Compare the device data with the host calculated version
printf("\nComparison between CPU and GPU processing: ");
if (memcmp(host_dst_ptr1, host_dst_ptr2, num_bytes) == 0)
{
 printf("Passed");
}
else
{
 printf("**** FAILED ****");
}
printf("\nCPU Time: %f, GPU Time: %f", delta_time_cpu, delta_time_device);

// Free host and device memory
CUDA_CALL(cudaFree(device_src_ptr1));
CUDA_CALL(cudaFree(device_src_ptr2));
CUDA_CALL(cudaFree(device_dst_ptr1));
CUDA_CALL(cudaFree(device_dst_ptr2));
free(host_src_ptr1);
free(host_src_ptr2);
free(host_dst_ptr1);
free(host_dst_ptr2);

// Reset the device so it's clear for next time
CUDA_CALL(cudaDeviceReset());
}
```

Notice in the code we have used an NPP_CALL macro around the call to the NPP library. This is similar to the CUDA_CALL macro we've used throughout this text. It checks that the return value from the caller is always equal to NPP_SUCESS (zero) and otherwise prints the error code associated with the returned value. Negative values are associated with errors and positive values with warnings. Unfortunately, there is no function to convert the error code to an error message, so you have to look up the error value in the NPP documentation (Section 7.2, "NPP Type Definitions and Constants," as of v4.1 of the library).

```
NPP_CALL(nppsXor_8u(device_src_ptr1, device_src_ptr2, device_dst_ptr1, num_bytes));
NPP_CALL(nppsAnd_8u(device_src_ptr1, device_dst_ptr1, device_dst_ptr2, num_bytes));
```

Each of the NPP calls is invoking a kernel on the device. By default, NPP operates in a synchronous mode using the default stream 0. However, often you will want to perform a number of operations one after another. You may then want to do some other work on the CPU, so you will come back later to check the progress of the GPU task.

To specify that NPP will use a given, already defined stream, use the following API call:

```
void nppSetStream (cudaStream_t hStream);
```

As we saw from some other examples in this text, if you have a number of sequential kernel calls, you can achieve much better overall performance by pushing them into the nondefault stream. This is largely because this permits asynchronous memory transfers and thus overlapping compute and transfer work. However, to achieve this, we need to change the program somewhat, as follows.

```
// Max for compute 2.x devices is 16
#define NUM_STREAMS 4

int main(int argc, char *argv[])
{
  // 64MB
  const int num_bytes = (1024u * 255u * 256) * sizeof(Npp8u);

  // Select the GTX470 in our test setup
  CUDA_CALL(cudaSetDevice(0));

  printf("\nXOR'ing with %d MB", (num_bytes / 1024) / 1024);

  // Declare and allocate pinned memory on the host
  Npp8u * host_src_ptr1;
  Npp8u * host_src_ptr2;
  Npp8u * host_dst_ptr1[NUM_STREAMS];
  Npp8u * host_dst_ptr2;

  CUDA_CALL(cudaMallocHost((void **) &host_src_ptr1, num_bytes));
  CUDA_CALL(cudaMallocHost((void **) &host_src_ptr2, num_bytes));
  CUDA_CALL(cudaMallocHost((void **) &host_dst_ptr2, num_bytes));
  for (u32 i=0; i< NUM_STREAMS; i++)
  {
    CUDA_CALL(cudaMallocHost((void **) &(host_dst_ptr1[i]), num_bytes));
  }

  // Declare and allocate memory on the device
  Npp8u * device_src_ptr1[NUM_STREAMS];
  Npp8u * device_src_ptr2[NUM_STREAMS];
  Npp8u * device_dst_ptr1[NUM_STREAMS];
  Npp8u * device_dst_ptr2[NUM_STREAMS];
  for (u32 i=0; i< NUM_STREAMS; i++)
  {
    CUDA_CALL(cudaMalloc((void **) &(device_src_ptr1[i]), num_bytes));
    CUDA_CALL(cudaMalloc((void **) &(device_src_ptr2[i]), num_bytes));
    CUDA_CALL(cudaMalloc((void **) &(device_dst_ptr1[i]), num_bytes));
```

```
  CUDA_CALL(cudaMalloc((void **) &(device_dst_ptr2[i]), num_bytes));
}

// Fill host src memory with random data
for (u32 i=0; i< num_bytes; i++)
{
 host_src_ptr1[i] = (rand() % 255);
 host_src_ptr2[i] = (rand() % 255);
}

TIMER_T start_time_device = get_time();

printf("\nRunning Device Synchronous version");

for (u32 i=0; i< NUM_STREAMS; i++)
{
 // Copy the random data to the device
 CUDA_CALL(cudaMemcpy(device_src_ptr1[i], host_src_ptr1,
                num_bytes, cudaMemcpyHostToDevice));
 CUDA_CALL(cudaMemcpy(device_src_ptr2[i], host_src_ptr2,
           num_bytes, cudaMemcpyHostToDevice));

 // Call NPP library to perform the XOR operation on the device
 NPP_CALL(nppsXor_8u(device_src_ptr1[i], device_src_ptr2[i],
         device_dst_ptr1[i], num_bytes));

 // Copy the XOR'd data on the device back to the host
 CUDA_CALL(cudaMemcpy(host_dst_ptr1[i], device_dst_ptr1[i],
           num_bytes, cudaMemcpyDeviceToHost));
}

// Grab the end time
// Last memcpy is synchronous, so CPU time is fine
TIMER_T delta_time_device = get_time() - start_time_device;

printf("\nRunning Host version");

// Perform the same XOR on the host
TIMER_T start_time_cpu = get_time();
for (u32 i=0; i< NUM_STREAMS; i++)
{
 for (u32 i=0; i< num_bytes; i++)
 {
  host_dst_ptr2[i] = host_src_ptr1[i] ^ host_src_ptr2[i];
 }
}
```

```
TIMER_T delta_time_cpu = get_time() - start_time_cpu;

// Compare the device data with the host calculated version
for (u32 i=0; i< NUM_STREAMS; i++)
{
 compare_results(host_dst_ptr1[i], host_dst_ptr2, num_bytes,
             "\nSingle Stream Comparison between CPU and GPU processing: ");
}

printf("\nRunning Device Asynchronous version");

// Now run and alternate streamed version
// Create a stream to work in

cudaStream_t async_stream[NUM_STREAMS];
for (u32 i=0; i< NUM_STREAMS; i++)
{
 CUDA_CALL(cudaStreamCreate(&async_stream[i]));
}

// Grab the CPU time again
start_time_device = get_time();

for (u32 i=0; i< NUM_STREAMS; i++)
{
 // Tell NPP to use the correct stream
 NPP_CALL(nppSetStream(async_stream[i]));

 // Copy the random data to the device using async transfers
 CUDA_CALL(cudaMemcpyAsync(device_src_ptr1[i], host_src_ptr1, num_bytes,
             cudaMemcpyHostToDevice, async_stream[i]));
 CUDA_CALL(cudaMemcpyAsync(device_src_ptr2[i], host_src_ptr2, num_bytes,
             cudaMemcpyHostToDevice, async_stream[i]));

 // Call NPP library to perform the XOR operation on the device
 NPP_CALL(nppsXor_8u(device_src_ptr1[i], device_src_ptr2[i],
             device_dst_ptr1[i], num_bytes));
}

for (u32 i=0; i< NUM_STREAMS; i++)
{
 // Tell NPP to use the correct stream
 NPP_CALL(nppSetStream(async_stream[i]));

 // Copy the XOR'd data on the device back to the host using async mode
 CUDA_CALL(cudaMemcpyAsync(host_dst_ptr1[i], device_dst_ptr1[i], num_bytes,
             cudaMemcpyDeviceToHost, async_stream[i]));
}
```

```
// Wait for everything to complete
for (u32 i=0; i< NUM_STREAMS; i++)
{
 CUDA_CALL(cudaStreamSynchronize(async_stream[i]));
}


// Grab the end time
TIMER_T delta_time_device_async = get_time() - start_time_device;

// Compare the device data with the host calculated version
for (u32 i=0; i< NUM_STREAMS; i++)
{
 compare_results(host_dst_ptr1[i], host_dst_ptr2, num_bytes, "\nMulti Stream
Comparison between CPU and GPU processing: ");
}

printf("\nCPU Time: %.1f, GPU Sync Time: %.1f, GPU Async Time: %.1f", delta_time_cpu,
delta_time_device, delta_time_device_async);

// Free host and device memory
for (u32 i=0; i< NUM_STREAMS; i++)
{
 CUDA_CALL(cudaFree(device_src_ptr1[i]));
 CUDA_CALL(cudaFree(device_src_ptr2[i]));
 CUDA_CALL(cudaFree(device_dst_ptr1[i]));
 CUDA_CALL(cudaFree(device_dst_ptr2[i]));
 CUDA_CALL(cudaFreeHost(host_dst_ptr1[i]));
 CUDA_CALL(cudaStreamDestroy(async_stream[i]));
}

CUDA_CALL(cudaFreeHost(host_src_ptr1));
CUDA_CALL(cudaFreeHost(host_src_ptr2));
CUDA_CALL(cudaFreeHost(host_dst_ptr2));

// Reset the device so it's clear for next time
CUDA_CALL(cudaDeviceReset());
}
```

The major difference we see with the streamed version is that we now need multiple output data blocks on the host as well as multiple copies on the device. Thus, all the device arrays are now indexed by [NUM_STREAMS], allowing the streams to operate entirely separately and independently of one another.

To use the asynchronous model we need to allocate host memory as pinned, so we have to use cudaHostMalloc instead of malloc, paired with cudaFreeHost instead of free. We also need to wait on the completion of the stream prior to processing its data. In this example we wait on all four streams, but in reality as one stream completes, it would be provided with more work. See Chapters 8 and 9 regarding multi-GPU programming and optimization, respectively, to see how this works.

If we look at a plot from Parallel Nsight we can actually see this happening with our new streamed version of the code (Figure 10.1). Notice on the output two large transfers to the device followed by a small series of kernel operations. Notice also that the transfer in stream 3 starts while the kernels in stream 2 are still running (Memory and Compute rows). Finally, notice all the transfers back to the host come one after another.

In this example the transfers, as can often be the case, dominate the overall timeframe. It depends largely on the amount of processing you are doing on the GPU and if, in fact, you need to transfer the data all the time. Leaving the data on the GPU is a good solution, especially if you later intend to visualize it or just simply do not need a host copy.

In this particular example, because the series of kernels is small in comparison to the transfer, the synchronous time was 300 ms whereas the asynchronous time was 280 ms. We have a very small kernel/transfer overlap, so we save only this time from the overall timeframe. To benefit significantly from parallel independent workloads we actually need multiple GPUs where the transfers and kernels can operate in parallel across N GPUs.

Depending on the mix of events, memory copies, and kernels, you can achieve a significant improvement by using the asynchronous mode. This is because the CUDA device can simply get on with the work set, rather than idle while the CPU organizes more work for it. By using multiple streams for independent work units you can define task level parallelism in addition to the regular data level parallelism. This is exploitable on Fermi-class GPUs (compute 2.x), to some extent, in that it's used to fill the GPU via back-to-back and concurrent kernels. As the SM devices within the GPUs become larger, as is the case for Kepler, this becomes more and more important.

Note that the setup here is for a single DMA transfer engine, as found on consumer cards. The Telsa devices have both DMA engines enabled, allowing transfer to and from the device to also be

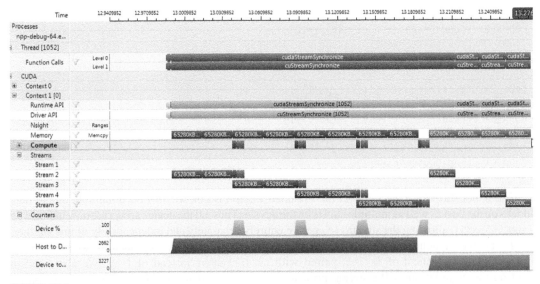

FIGURE 10.1

NPP streamed calls.

overlapped. In the previous timeline this would cause, with some program changes, the copy-back-to-host transfers to occur while the copy-to-device transfers were occurring. In effect, we'd eliminate the time of the copy-back-to-host transfers, a significant savings. Due to both DMA engines being enabled on Tesla devices, enabling streams can bring significant benefits for this platform.

Note also that for this test we are using a PCI-E 2.0 X8 link. Using a PCI-E 3.0 X16 link would reduce the transfer time to around a quarter of what is shown here, making transfers less of an issue.

Once you have your kernel working, and only once you have it working, switch to an asynchronous mode of operation. An Asynchronous operation, however, can make debugging somewhat more complex so this is best done only once everything works correctly.

SDK Samples: Grabcut, Histogram Equalization, BoxFilter, Image Segmentation, Interoperability with the FreeImage library.

Thrust

Those familiar with C++ may have used the C++ STL and specifically the BOOST library. For those not familiar with templates, they are actually a very useful feature of C++. In traditional C if you have a simple function that you wish to perform an operation, sum for example, you have to specify the operand type explicitly. Thus, you might have something like the following:

```
int sum(const int x, const int y)
{
   return x+y;
}
```

If I wish to call the function and pass a float then I need a new function. As C does not allow the same name for two functions, I need something like sum_i32, sum_u8, sum_u32, sum_f32, etc. It's somewhat tedious to provide and use a library that is type specific.

C++ tried to address this in the form of function overloading. This allows the same name to be used for many functions. Depending on the type of the parameters passed, the appropriate function is called. However, the library provider still needs to write one function body to handle int8, int16, f32, etc. even if he or she can now use a common name for the function.

The C++ template system addresses this. We have a generic function that changes only in terms of the type of its parameters. Thus, why does the programmer have to copy and paste the code a dozen times to support all the possible permutations he or she might imagine? Templates, as the name suggests, mean supplying a template of what you'd like to do in a type agnostic manner. The compiler then generates a version of the function at compile time if, and only if, it is actually called.

Thus, the STL was born, a type agnostic definition of some very common functions in C++. If you happen to use the int32 version, but not the f32 version, only the int32 version results in actual code within your application. The downside of templates, as opposed to libraries, is that they are compiled during every compilation run, so they can increase compile times.

The NVCC compiler is actually a C++ front end, rather than a C front end. The standard development package on Windows, Microsoft Visual Studio, also supports C++ language, as do the primary Linux and Mac development environments.

The Thrust library supports many of the STL containers for which it makes sense to support on a massively parallel processor. The simplest structures are often the best and thus arrays (or vectors as the STL calls them) are well supported in Thrust. Not all containers make sense, such as lists which have unknown access times and are of variable length.

One other C++ concept we need to cover before we look at Thrust is C++ namespaces. In C if you declare two functions with the same name you get an error at the link stage if it is not detected during compilation. In C++ this is perfectly valid providing the two functions belong to a different namespace. A namespace is a little like specifying a library prefix to differentiate which library the compiler should search for the function. The C++ namespace is actually a class selector. Classes in C++, at a very high level, are simply a way of grouping related functions and data together in one definition. Thus, we can have two calls to the same function, providing the namespace used is different. For example:

```
ClassNameA::my_func();
ClassNameB::my_func();
```

Because of the namespace prefix the compiler can identify which function is intended to be called. The `::` (double colon) is equivalent to the `->` operator if you think of the class definition as a structure definition that has a number of function pointers as well as data.

Finally, to use the Thrust library we need one more C++ concept, that of a *functor*. A functor can be thought of as a function pointer that can also store state or data. It is actually a pointer to an instance of an object that is based on a given class definition.

If you have ever used any functions like `qsort` (Quicksort) from the standard C libraries, you'll be familiar with the concept of a user-provided function. In the case of `qsort` you provide the comparison function to say whether one opaque data object is greater than or less than another opaque data object. You may have specific or multiple criteria to rank records by. The provider of the `qsort` library cannot hope to cover a significant number of these possibilities, so they provide a formal parameter where you must provide your own comparison function.

The Thrust library provides you with two vector containers. Vectors in the STL are simply resizable arrays that can hold elements of any type. Thrust provides both host and device vector classes that, reside in the global memory of the host and device, respectively.

Vectors can be read or modified using the array subscript notation (the `[` and `]` symbols). However, be aware that Thrust is in the background performing individual transfers over the PCI-E bus for each such access, if the vector is on the device. Therefore, putting such a construct within a loop is a *really* bad idea.

The first aspect of using Thrust is simply how to get the data you need into and out of thrust vectors. Thus, we first need to include the necessary include files. Thrust provides the following broad set of function types:

- Transformation
- Reduction
- Prefix sum
- Reordering
- Sorting

Thrust is not a library in the traditional sense, as all of its contents are contained within the header files you include into your source. Thus, you wish to avoid simply including everything and should include only the header files you need.

Thrust provides two vector objects, `host_vector` and `device_vector`, which are used with C++ terminology to create an instance of these objects. For example,

```
thrust::host_vector <float> my_host_float_vector(200);
thrust::device_vector <int> my_device_int_vector(500);
```

In this code we declare two objects, one that physically resides on the host and one that will physically reside on the device.

The `thrust::` part specifies a class namespace that you can largely think of as a library specifier in C. The `host_vector` and `device_vector` are functions (constructors) provided by the object. The `<int>` and `<float>` specifiers are passed to the constructor (the initialization function) for the object. The constructor then uses them along with the value passed into the function to allocate 200 elements of `sizeof(float)` and 500 elements of `sizeof(int)`, respectively. Internally there may be other data structures, but at a high level this is effectively what you are doing when using such a C++ constructor.

Objects in C++ also have a destructor, a function that is called when the object goes out of scope. This function is responsible for deallocating any resources allocated by the constructor or during the runtime of the object. Thus, unlike C, it's not necessary to call `free` or `cudaFree` for Thrust vectors.

Having defined a vector you now need to get data into and out of the vector. A Thrust vector is conceptually simply a resizable array. Thus, a vector object provides a `size()` function that returns the number of elements in the vector. This allows you to use standard loop constructs, for example,

```
for (int i=0; i < my_device_int_vector.size(); i++)
{
  int x = my_device_int_vector[i];
  ...
}
```

In this example the array `[]` operator is being supplied by the class definition. Thus, in every iteration, a function is being called to transform `i` into a physical piece of data. Because of this, if the data happens to be on the device, Thrust will generate a transfer from the device to the host, in the background, which is completely hidden from the programmer. The `size()` function means the number of iterations is only known at runtime. As this can change within the loop body, it must be called on each loop iteration. This in turn prevents the compiler from statically unrolling the loop.

Depending on your view of such things, you'll either love it or hate it. The love it camp loves abstractions because they make programming easier and you don't have to care about the hardware. This camp is primarily made up of inexperienced programmers and people who simply want to get a calculation done. The hate it camp wants to know what is happening and is very keen to maximize performance from the hardware it has. They don't want to have a "simple" array dereference initiate a hugely inefficient 4-byte PCI-E transfer. They'd much prefer a far more efficient several-megabyte transfer to or from the device/host when they schedule it.

Thrust actually makes both camps happy. Large transfers are simply done by initiating a host vector with a device vector or vice versa. For example:

```
thrust::host_vector <float> my_host_float_out_vector
(my_device_float_results_vector.begin(), my_device_float_results_vector.end() );
```

or

```
thrust::copy(my_host_float_out_vector.begin(), my_host_float_out_vector.end(),
my_device_float_results_vector.begin(), my_device_float_results_vector.begin() );
```

In the first example we are creating a new vector on the host side and initializing the host vector with the device vector. Notice we did not specify only one value for the constructor as we did previously when creating a host vector, but two. In such cases Thrust does a subtraction to work out the number of elements that need to be copied and allocates storage on the host accordingly.

In the second example we use the explicit copy method. This method (function) takes three parameters, the start and end of the destination region, plus the start of the source region. Because Thrust knows what type of vector you are using, the copy method works for both host and device vectors. There is no need to specify additional parameters such as cudaMemcpyDeviceToHost or cudaMemcpyHostToDevice, or to call different functions depending on the type passed. Thrust is simply using C++ templates to overload the namespace to invoke a number of functions depending on the parameters passed. As this is done at compile time, you have the benefit of strong type checking and no runtime overhead. Templates are one of the major benefits of C++ over C.

Using the functions provided by Thrust

Once the data is within a Thrust device vector or host vector container, there are a number of standard functions Thrust provides. Thrust provides a simple sort function that requires only the start and end of the vector. It distributes the work over the different blocks and performs any reduction and interblock communications for you. This is often code that people new to CUDA get wrong. Having something such as a sort function makes using the GPU as easy as using the common C qsort library routine.

```
thrust::sort(device_array.begin(), device_array.end());
```

We can see this in action with a short program.

```
#include <thrust/host_vector.h>
#include <thrust/device_vector.h>
#include <thrust/generate.h>
#include <thrust/sort.h>
#include <thrust/copy.h>
#include <cstdlib>

// 1M Elements = 4MB Data
#define NUM_ELEM (1024*1024)

int main(void)
{
 // Declare an array on the host
 printf("\nAllocating memory on host");
 thrust::host_vector<int> host_array(NUM_ELEM);

 // Populate this array with random numbers
 printf("\nGenerating random numbers on host");
 thrust::generate(host_array.begin(), host_array.end(), rand);
```

```
// Create a device array and populate it with the host values
// A PCI-E transfer to device happens here
printf("\nTransferring to device");
thrust::device_vector<int> device_array = host_array;

// Sort the array on the device
printf("\nSorting on device");
thrust::sort(device_array.begin(), device_array.end());

// Sort the array on the host
printf("\nSorting on host");
thrust::sort(host_array.begin(), host_array.end());

// Create a host array and populate it with the sorted device values
// A PCI-E transfer from the device happens here
printf("\nTransfering back to host");
thrust::host_vector<int> host_array_sorted = device_array;

printf("\nSorting Complete");

return 0;
}
```

Problems with Thrust

What is interesting to note here is that the GPU- and CPU-based sorts may or may not be performed at the same time, depending on how you arrange the transfers. Unfortunately, Thrust always uses the default stream and you cannot change this as with NPP library. There is no stream parameter to pass, or function to set the currently selected stream.

Using the default stream has some serious implications. The sort operation is actually just a series of kernels run in stream 0. Kernels, like regular kernels, launch asynchronously. However, memory transfers, unless explicitly done asynchronously, operate synchronously. Thus, any function you call from Thrust that returns a value, reduce for example, and any copy back to the host causes an implicit synchronization. In the example code, placing the sort host array call after the copy back from the device code would have serialized the GPU and CPU sorts.

Multi-CPU/GPU considerations

On the CPU side, Thrust automatically spawns N threads where N is the number of physical processor cores. Thrust is actually using OpenMP for the CPU side, and by default OpenMP will use the number of physical cores on the CPU.

It would be nice if the GPU version did this also, splitting the task over N GPUs. The host side implements a NUMA (nonuniform memory access)-based memory system. This means all memory addresses are accessible to any CPU socket and any CPU core. Thus, even on a dual-CPU system, 8, 12, or 16 CPU cores can work in parallel on a problem.

Multiple GPUs are more like a cluster of distributed memory machines all attached to the PCI-E bus. The GPUs can talk over the bus directly to one another using the peer-to-peer (P2P) functionality if you have the correct hardware and operating system (OS). To have multiple GPUs work together on a sort is a little more complicated.

However, just like regular multi-GPU programming, Thrust supports the single-thread/multiple-GPU and multiple-threads/multiple-GPU model. It does not implicitly make use of multiple GPUs. It's left to the programmer to either spawn multiple threads or use cudaSetDevice calls where appropriate to select the correct device to work on.

When sorting on multiple processors there are two basic approaches. The first is used by merge sort. Here the data is split into equal-size blocks with each block independently sorted and a final merge operation applied. The second, used by algorithms like the sample sort we looked at earlier, is to partially sort, or presort, the blocks. The resultant blocks can then be independently sorted, or can also simply be concatenated together to form the sorted output.

As memory access time is much slower than comparison time, algorithms that have the fewest passes over the data, both in terms of reading and writing, tend to be the fastest. Operations that create contention, such as merging, ultimately limit scaling compared with those algorithms that can maintain wide parallelism throughout the entire process.

For basic types (u8, u16, u32, s8, s16, s32, f32, f64) Thrust uses a very fast radix sort, something we looked at earlier with sample sort. For other types and user-defined types it uses a merge sort. Thrust automatically adjusts the number of bits used for the radix sort depending on the type and the range of the data. Thus, a 32-bit sort where the maximum range of the data is only 256 is significantly faster than one where the entire range is used.

Timing sort

To see some timings, let's add some timers to the Thrust example code and see what values we get.

```
#include <thrust/host_vector.h>
#include <thrust/device_vector.h>
#include <thrust/generate.h>
#include <thrust/sort.h>
#include <thrust/copy.h>
#include <cstdlib>

#include "cuda_helper.h"
#include "timer.h"

void display_gpu_name(void)
{
  int device_num;
  struct cudaDeviceProp prop;

  CUDA_CALL(cudaGetDevice(&device_num));

  // Get the device name
  CUDA_CALL( cudaGetDeviceProperties( &prop, device_num ) );
```

```
  // Print device name and logical to physical mapping
  printf("\n\nUsing CUDA Device %u. Device ID: %s on PCI-E %d",
   device_num, prop.name, prop.pciBusID);
 }

// 4M Elements = 16MB Data
#define NUM_ELEM (1024*1024*4)

int main(void)
{
 int num_devices;
 CUDA_CALL(cudaGetDeviceCount(&num_devices));
 for (int device_num = 0; device_num < num_devices; device_num++)
 {
  CUDA_CALL(cudaSetDevice(device_num));
  display_gpu_name();

  const size_t size_in_bytes = NUM_ELEM * sizeof(int);
  printf("\nSorting %lu data items (%lu MB)", NUM_ELEM, (size_in_bytes/1024/1024));

  // Allocate timer events to track time
  float c2d_t, sort_d_t, sort_h_t, c2h_t;
  cudaEvent_t c2d_start, c2d_stop;
  cudaEvent_t sort_d_start, sort_d_stop;
  cudaEvent_t c2h_start, c2h_stop;

  CUDA_CALL(cudaEventCreate(&c2d_start));
  CUDA_CALL(cudaEventCreate(&c2d_stop));
  CUDA_CALL(cudaEventCreate(&sort_d_start));
  CUDA_CALL(cudaEventCreate(&sort_d_stop));
  CUDA_CALL(cudaEventCreate(&c2h_start));
  CUDA_CALL(cudaEventCreate(&c2h_stop));

  // Declare an array on the host
  printf("\nAllocating memory on host");
  thrust::host_vector<int> host_array(NUM_ELEM);

  // Populate this array with random numbers
  printf("\nGenerating random numbers on host");
  thrust::generate(host_array.begin(), host_array.end(), rand);

  // Create a device array and populate it with the host values
  // A PCI-E transfer to device happens here
  printf("\nTransferring to device");
  CUDA_CALL(cudaEventRecord(c2d_start, 0));
  thrust::device_vector<int> device_array = host_array;
```

```
CUDA_CALL(cudaEventRecord(c2d_stop, 0));

// Sort the array on the device
printf("\nSorting on device");
CUDA_CALL(cudaEventRecord(sort_d_start, 0));
thrust::sort(device_array.begin(), device_array.end());
CUDA_CALL(cudaEventRecord(sort_d_stop, 0));
CUDA_CALL(cudaEventSynchronize(sort_d_stop));

// Sort the array on the host
printf("\nSorting on host");
sort_h_t = get_time();
thrust::sort(host_array.begin(), host_array.end());
sort_h_t = (get_time() - sort_h_t);

// Create a host array and populate it with the sorted device values
// A PCI-E transfer from the device happens here
printf("\nTransfering back to host");
CUDA_CALL(cudaEventRecord(c2h_start, 0));
thrust::host_vector<int> host_array_sorted = device_array;
CUDA_CALL(cudaEventRecord(c2h_stop, 0));

// Wait for last event to be recorded
CUDA_CALL(cudaEventSynchronize(c2h_stop));

printf("\nSorting Complete");

// Calculate time for each aspect
CUDA_CALL(cudaEventElapsedTime(&c2d_t, c2d_start, c2d_stop));
CUDA_CALL(cudaEventElapsedTime(&sort_d_t, sort_d_start, sort_d_stop));
CUDA_CALL(cudaEventElapsedTime(&c2h_t, c2h_start, c2h_stop));

printf("\nCopy To Device : %.2fms", c2d_t);
printf("\nSort On Device : %.2fms", sort_d_t);
printf("\nCopy From Device : %.2fms", c2h_t);
printf("\nTotal Device Time: %.2fms", c2d_t + sort_d_t + c2h_t);
printf("\n\nSort On Host : %.2fms", sort_h_t);

CUDA_CALL(cudaEventDestroy(c2d_start));
CUDA_CALL(cudaEventDestroy(c2d_stop));
CUDA_CALL(cudaEventDestroy(sort_d_start));
CUDA_CALL(cudaEventDestroy(sort_d_stop));
CUDA_CALL(cudaEventDestroy(c2h_start));
CUDA_CALL(cudaEventDestroy(c2h_stop));
}
return 0;
}
```

Table 10.1 Thrust Sort Timings on Various Devices

Device	Time
GTX470	67.45
GTX460	85.18
GTX260	109.02
9800 GT	234.83

As Thrust uses the default stream for all calls, to time device code we simply insert a number of events and then get the delta time between the various events. Notice, however, that we need to synchronize the stream after the sort and after the final event. The `cudaEventRecord` function, even if the device is not currently doing anything, returns immediately, without setting the event. Thus, leaving out the synchronize call after the device sort significantly reduces the actual time reported.

The timings we see across our four devices are shown in Table 10.1 and Figure 10.2 for sorting 16 MB of random data. As you can see from the table there is a fairly linear decline of speed as we move back the various GPU generations. As we hit the compute 1.1 9800 GT device we see a significant jump in execution time. The 9800 GT has less than half of the memory bandwidth and around two-thirds, at best, of the processing power of the GTX260.

Host times by comparison are pretty poor on our 2.5 Ghz AMD Phenom II X4. Sort time averages around 2400 ms, some 10× slower than even the 9800 GT. However, is this really a fair comparison? It depends on how efficiently Thrust implements the sort on the CPU, and on the particular CPU used and the host memory bandwidth. Both Parallel Nsight and the task manager indicate Thrust does not load the CPU on our test system by more than 25%. This would indicate it's far from making the best use of the CPU resources. Thus, to use it as a comparison is unfair to the CPU and artificially inflates the GPU performance figures.

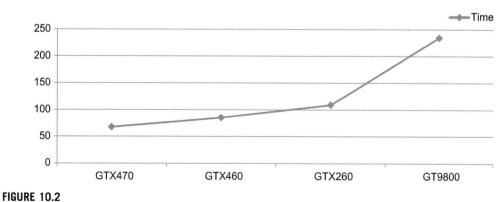

FIGURE 10.2

Thrust sort time by device (16 MB data).

```
Using CUDA Device 0. Device ID: GeForce GTX 470 on PCI-E 8
Sorting 4194304 data items (16 MB)
Allocating memory on host
Generating random numbers on host
Transferring to device
Sorting on device
Sorting on host
Transfering back to host
Extracting data from Thrust vector
Sorted arrays Match
Running single core qsort comparison
Sorting Complete
Copy To Device : 10.00ms
Sort On Device : 58.55ms
Copy From Device : 12.17ms
Total Device Time : 80.73ms


Thrust Sort On Host: 2398.00ms
QSort On Host : 949.00ms
```

As you can see a single-core qsort easily outperforms Thrust sorting on the CPU side and uses near 100% of a single core. If we assume a similar speedup for a parallel version as we saw on the OpenMP reduce we looked at earlier, a typical CPU figure would be half that shown here, let's say 475 ms. Even so, a GPU-based Thrust sort is outperforming the CPU by a factor of almost six times, even accounting for transfers to and from the PCI-E bus.

Thrust also has a number of other useful functions:

- Binary search
- Reductions
- Merging
- Reordering
- Prefix sum
- Set operations
- Transformations

Documentation on each of these is provided in the Thrust user guide. The usage of each is similar to the sort example we've used here.

We could obviously write a great deal on Thrust, but this chapter is about libraries in general, so we'll look at just one more example, that of reduction.

```
#include <thrust/host_vector.h>
#include <thrust/device_vector.h>
#include <thrust/sequence.h>
#include <thrust/sort.h>
#include <thrust/copy.h>
#include <cstdlib>
```

```c
#include "cuda_helper.h"
#include "timer.h"

void display_gpu_name(void)
{
 int device_num;
 struct cudaDeviceProp prop;

 CUDA_CALL(cudaGetDevice(&device_num));

 // Get the device name
 CUDA_CALL( cudaGetDeviceProperties( &prop, device_num ) );

 // Print device name and logical to physical mapping
 printf("\n\nUsing CUDA Device %u. Device ID: %s on PCI-E %d",
  device_num, prop.name, prop.pciBusID);
}

long int reduce_serial(const int * __restrict__ const host_raw_ptr,
                       const int num_elements)
{
 long int sum = 0;

 for (int i=0; i < num_elements; i++)
  sum += host_raw_ptr[i];

 return sum;
}

long int reduce_openmp(const int * __restrict__ const host_raw_ptr,
            const int num_elements)
{
 long int sum = 0;

#pragma omp parallel for reduction(+:sum) num_threads(4)
 for (int i=0; i < num_elements; i++)
  sum += host_raw_ptr[i];

 return sum;
}

// 1M Elements = 4MB Data
#define NUM_ELEM_START (1024*1024)
#define NUM_ELEM_END (1024*1024*256)
```

```
int main(void)
{
 int num_devices;
 CUDA_CALL(cudaGetDeviceCount(&num_devices));

 for (unsigned long num_elem = NUM_ELEM_START; num_elem < NUM_ELEM_END; num_elem *=2)
 {
  const size_t size_in_bytes = num_elem * sizeof(int);

  for (int device_num = 0; device_num < num_devices; device_num++)
  {
   CUDA_CALL(cudaSetDevice(device_num));
   display_gpu_name();

   printf("\nReducing %lu data items (%lu MB)", num_elem, (size_in_bytes/1024/1024));
   // Allocate timer events to track time
   float c2d_t, reduce_d_t, reduce_h_t, reduce_h_mp_t, reduce_h_serial_t;
   cudaEvent_t c2d_start, c2d_stop;
   cudaEvent_t sort_d_start, sort_d_stop;

   CUDA_CALL(cudaEventCreate(&c2d_start));
   CUDA_CALL(cudaEventCreate(&c2d_stop));
   CUDA_CALL(cudaEventCreate(&sort_d_start));
   CUDA_CALL(cudaEventCreate(&sort_d_stop));
   // Declare an array on the host
   thrust::host_vector<int> host_array(num_elem);

   // Populate this array with random numbers
   thrust::sequence(host_array.begin(), host_array.end());

   // Create a device array and populate it with the host values
   // A PCI-E transfer to device happens here
   CUDA_CALL(cudaEventRecord(c2d_start, 0));
   thrust::device_vector<int> device_array = host_array;
   CUDA_CALL(cudaEventRecord(c2d_stop, 0));

   // Sort the array on the device
   CUDA_CALL(cudaEventRecord(sort_d_start, 0));
   const long int sum_device = thrust::reduce(device_array.begin(),
device_array.end());
   CUDA_CALL(cudaEventRecord(sort_d_stop, 0));
   CUDA_CALL(cudaEventSynchronize(sort_d_stop));

   // Sort the array on the host
   reduce_h_t = get_time();
   const long int sum_host = thrust::reduce(host_array.begin(), host_array.end());
   reduce_h_t = (get_time() - reduce_h_t);
```

```
    // Allocate host memory
    int * const host_raw_ptr_2 = (int *) malloc(size_in_bytes);
    int *p2 = host_raw_ptr_2;

    if ( (host_raw_ptr_2 == NULL) )
    {
     printf("\nError allocating host memory for extraction of thrust data");
     exit(0);
    }

    // Extract data from Thrust vector to normal memory block
    for (int i=0; i<num_elem; i++)
    {
     *p2++ = host_array[i];
    }

    reduce_h_mp_t = get_time();
    const long int sum_host_openmp = reduce_openmp(host_raw_ptr_2, num_elem);
    reduce_h_mp_t = (get_time() - reduce_h_mp_t);

    reduce_h_serial_t = get_time();
    const long int sum_host_serial = reduce_serial(host_raw_ptr_2, num_elem);
    reduce_h_serial_t = (get_time() - reduce_h_serial_t);

    // Free memory
    free(host_raw_ptr_2);

    if ( (sum_host == sum_device) && (sum_host == sum_host_openmp) )
     printf("\nReduction Matched");
    else
     printf("\n**** FAILED ****");

    // Calculate time for each aspect
    CUDA_CALL(cudaEventElapsedTime(&c2d_t, c2d_start, c2d_stop));
    CUDA_CALL(cudaEventElapsedTime(&reduce_d_t, sort_d_start, sort_d_stop));

    printf("\nCopy To Device : %.2fms", c2d_t);
    printf("\nReduce On Device : %.2fms", reduce_d_t);
    printf("\nTotal Device Time : %.2fms", c2d_t + reduce_d_t);
    printf("\n\nThrust Reduce On Host: %.2fms", reduce_h_t);
    printf("\nSerial Reduce On Host: %.2fms", reduce_h_serial_t);
    printf("\nOpenMP Reduce On Host: %.2fms", reduce_h_mp_t);

    CUDA_CALL(cudaEventDestroy(c2d_start));
    CUDA_CALL(cudaEventDestroy(c2d_stop));
    CUDA_CALL(cudaEventDestroy(sort_d_start));
    CUDA_CALL(cudaEventDestroy(sort_d_stop));
  }
 }
 return 0;
}
```

Table 10.2 Reduce Timing for Multiple Sizes and GPUs (in ms)

Device	4 MB	8 MB	16 MB	32 MB	64 MB	128 MB	256 MB	512 MB
GTX470	1.21	2.14	4.12	7.71	15.29	30.17	59.87	119.56
GTX460	1.7	3.34	6.26	12.13	23.9	47.33	97.09	188.39
GTX260	2.38	1.85	3.53	6.8	13.46	26.64	55.02	106.28
9800 GT	1.75	3.24	6.4	12.59	26.18	51.39	110.82	202.98
Copy	2.97	6.51	9.34	17.69	38.15	68.55	134.96	278.63
Serial	6	11	22	43	91	174	348	696
OpenMP	1	4	5	9	33	37	91	164

Reduction is an interesting problem in that, as we saw earlier, it's difficult to write a reduction that is faster than an OpenMP version given the transfer time of the data to the GPU. We win considerably because there is only one significant transfer to the device, but this dominates the overall time. However, if the data is already on the GPU, then of course this transfer is not associated with the reduction step.

We will time a Thrust-based reduction, both on the host and device, against a standard single-core serial reduction, an OpenMP quad-core reduction, and the four GPU test devices with a range of data sizes. See Table 10.2 and Figure 10.3. The one item missing from the table is the Thrust reduce time on the CPU. It was excluded because it was significantly larger than any of the other figures. With consistency across all the block sizes, the CPU Thrust sort took approximately 10 times the execution time of the single-core serial version.

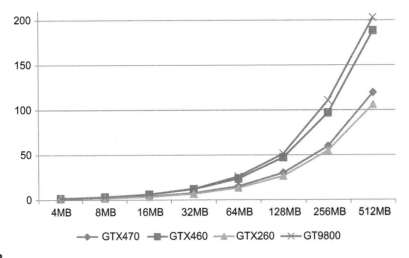

FIGURE 10.3

GPU reduce time (in ms) by size.

Notice in Figure 10.3, and also in Table 10.2, the *y* axis is time in milliseconds. Thus, a lower value is better. The GTX260, surprisingly, comes out with the best reduction times, marginally out-performing the later-generation GTX470.

This is all very well, but how does it compare with the CPU versions? All the cards are faster than the single-core serial implementation, by 3.5× to 7×. The GTX470 and GTX260 cards fare very well against the OpenMP version, coming in at around two-thirds of the time of the parallel CPU version. The GTX460 is about the same time as the CPU, with the 9800 GT being slower. However, if we take into account the (PCI-E 2.0 x8) transfer time, 278 ms for 512 MB of data, even the GTX260 at 106 ms (plus 278 ms transfer time) is slower than the OpenMP version at 164 ms.

With a CUDA-implemented reduction, or a Thrust asynchronous version that supported streams, we could have subtracted the kernel time as we overlapped successive transfers and kernels. This is, of course, assuming we have more than one reduction to perform or we broke the single reduction down into a series of reductions. Even with this, we're looking at a best case of 178 ms, which is still slower than the OpenMP version. The clear message here is make use of OpenMP and the CPU when appropriate. If the data is already on the GPU, then perform the reduction on the GPU. Otherwise, use the CPU for some useful purpose. See Figure 10.4.

Using Thrust and CUDA

Thus, we'd like to be able to use these features of the Thrust library with regular CUDA code. It may well be that you can write your application entirely using the provided Thrust operations. However, libraries never cover everything and always end up doing certain things well and others not so well. Therefore, we don't want to be forced into a particular way of thinking just to make use of a library.

Thrust does not provide a mechanism to copy data out of its `host_vector` structure in an easy manner. It provides only a read single element method. Thus, a copy can only be performed one element at a time, which is laboriously slow. However, with `device_vectors` we have an alternative method.

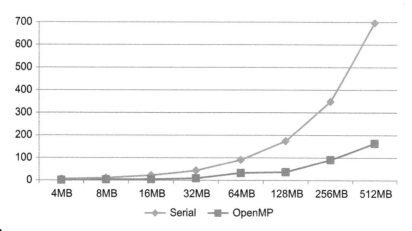

FIGURE 10.4

OpenMP and serial reduction timing (in ms).

First, you need to allocate the storage space on the device yourself, thus obtaining a pointer to the data and not a Thrust iterator. Then you need to cast the regular device pointer to a Thrust device pointer. This is done using the `device_ptr` constructor. You may then pass this Thrust device pointer to the various Thrust functions. Now Thrust works on the underlying data you have supplied and thus it is visible to you, rather than being hidden within the Thrust library.

We can adapt the sort example to make use of this.

```
#include <thrust/host_vector.h>
#include <thrust/device_vector.h>
#include <thrust/sort.h>
#include <cstdlib>

#include "cuda_helper.h"
#include "timer.h"
#include "common_types.h"

void display_gpu_name(void)
{
 int device_num;
 struct cudaDeviceProp prop;

 CUDA_CALL(cudaGetDevice(&device_num));

 // Get the device name
 CUDA_CALL( cudaGetDeviceProperties( &prop, device_num ) );

 // Print device name and logical to physical mapping
 printf("\n\nUsing CUDA Device %u. Device ID: %s on PCI-E %d",
  device_num, prop.name, prop.pciBusID);
}

__global__ void fill_memory(int * const __restrict__ data,
             const int num_elements)
{
 const int tid = (blockIdx.x * blockDim.x) + threadIdx.x;
 if (tid < num_elements)
  data[tid] = (num_elements - tid);
}

// 4M Elements = 16MB Data
#define NUM_ELEM (1024*1024*4)

int main(void)
{
 const size_t size_in_bytes = NUM_ELEM * sizeof(int);
 display_gpu_name();

 printf("\nSorting %lu data items (%lu MB)", NUM_ELEM, (size_in_bytes/1024/1024));
```

```
// Declare an array on the device
printf("\nAllocating memory on device");
int * device_mem_ptr;
CUDA_CALL(cudaMalloc((void **) &device_mem_ptr, size_in_bytes));

const u32 num_threads = 256;
const u32 num_blocks = (NUM_ELEM + (num_threads-1)) / num_threads;

printf("\nFilling memory with pattern");
fill_memory<<<num_threads, num_blocks>>>(device_mem_ptr, NUM_ELEM);

// Convert the array to
printf("\nConverting regular device pointer to thrust device pointer");
thrust::device_ptr<int> thrust_dev_ptr(device_mem_ptr);

// Sort the array on the device
printf("\nSorting on device");
thrust::sort(thrust_dev_ptr, thrust_dev_ptr + NUM_ELEM);

printf("\nFreeing memory on device");
CUDA_CALL(cudaFree(device_mem_ptr));

return 0;
}
```

Notice the constructor `thrust::device_ptr`, which creates the object `thrust_dev_ptr` that can then be passed into the `thrust::sort` function. Unlike the conventional iteration a Thrust device pointer does not have "begin" and "end" functions, so we simply use base plus length to obtain the last element for the sort.

This allows host-initiated Thrust calls to be implemented alongside simple device kernels. However, be aware there is (as of 4.2 SDK) no device level interface for Thrust, so you cannot call Thrust functions from within a device or global function. Functions like `sort`, for example, spawn multiple kernels themselves. As the GPU cannot, at least until Kepler K20 is released, spawn additional work itself, we're limited to host-based control.

SDK Samples: Line of Sight, Radix Sort, Particles, Marching Cubes, Smoke Particles.

CuRAND

The CuRAND library provides various types of random number generation on the GPU. In C you are probably used to calling the standard library function `rand()` on the host. Like many standard library functions `rand()` is not available to be called in device code. Thus, your only option is to create a block of random numbers on the host and copy this over to the device. This causes a number of problems:

- Increased startup time on the host.
- Increased PCI-E bandwidth.
- In practice, usually a poorly distributed random number set.

The standard library rand() function is not designed for true randomness. It works, like many random number generation algorithms, by creating a list of pseudo-random numbers and simply selecting the next element from the list. Thus, anyone who knows the seed used can use this knowledge to accurately predict the next random number in the given sequence.

This has some implications, not least of which is from the security field. Many algorithms use randomness, in one way or another, to make it difficult to impersonate a peer. Suppose two peers exchange a seed of a random number generator. Peer A encodes a random number into the message frame. Peer B using the same seed and same random number generator knows what data identifier it should expect from peer A. Given a captured sequence of identifiers from peers A and B, it's possible for an attacker, C, to work out the next number and spoof (pretend to be) either peer A or B.

This is possible because the random numbers are usually just a small, repeating sequence of pseudo-random numbers. If the set of random numbers is small, then an attack is easy. The seed is either never set by the programmer, set to some "secret" number, or set based on the current time. Startup times are not really very random and thus time-based seeds are actually within a very small window. Secrets rarely remain secrets.

Another example is password generation. If you have a few hundred users to set up on a system, they will usually be issued "random" passwords that are changed on first login. These passwords may be long character strings, leading to the belief that they are secure. However, if they are actually chosen from a random number generator with a small pseudo-random set of numbers, the actual search space for a brute-force attack is quite small.

Thus, for anything where predictability of the sequence is a problem, we need much better random numbers than most standard library implementations of rand() provide.

To use the CuRAND library, you need to include the following header file:

```
#include <curand_kernel.h>
```

Additionally, you need to ensure you link to the following library:

```
C:\Program Files\NVIDIA GPU Computing Toolkit\CUDA\v4.1\lib\x64\curand.lib
```

Obviously, replace the path with the current version of the CUDA toolkit you are using. Let's therefore look at an example of generating some random numbers:

```
#include <stdio.h>
#include <stdlib.h>
#include <curand_kernel.h>
#include "cuda_helper.h"
#include "cuda.h"

#define CURAND_CALL(x) {const curandStatus_t a = (x); if (a != CURAND_STATUS_SUCCESS) {
printf("\nCuRand Error: (err_num=%d) \n", a); cudaDeviceReset(); ASSERT(0);} }
__host__ void print_array(const float * __restrict__ const data, const int num_elem)
{
  for (int i=0; i<num_elem; i++)
  {
   if ( i% 4 == 0)
    printf("\n");
```

```
  printf("%2d: %f ", i, data[i]);
 }
}

__host__ int main(int argc, char *argv[])
{
 const int num_elem = 32;
 const size_t size_in_bytes = (num_elem * sizeof(float));

 curandGenerator_t rand_generator_device, rand_generator_host;
 const unsigned long int seed = 987654321;
 const curandRngType_t generator_type = CURAND_RNG_PSEUDO_DEFAULT;

 // Allocate memory on the device
 float * device_ptr;
 CUDA_CALL( cudaMalloc( (void **) &device_ptr, size_in_bytes ));

 // Allocate memory on the host for the device copy
 float * host_ptr;
 CUDA_CALL( cudaMallocHost( (void **) &host_ptr, size_in_bytes ));

 // Allocate memory on the host for the host version
 float * host_gen_ptr = (float *) malloc(size_in_bytes);
 if (host_gen_ptr == NULL)
 {
  printf("\nFailed to allocation memory on host");
  exit(0);
 }

 // Print library version number
 int version;
 CURAND_CALL(curandGetVersion(&version));
 printf("\nUsing CuRand Version: %d and generator: CURAND_RNG_PSEUDO_DEFAULT",
version);

 // Register the generator - note the different function calls
 CURAND_CALL(curandCreateGenerator(&rand_generator_device, generator_type));
 CURAND_CALL(curandCreateGeneratorHost(&rand_generator_host, generator_type));

 // Set the seed for the random number generators
 CURAND_CALL(curandSetPseudoRandomGeneratorSeed(rand_generator_device, seed));
 CURAND_CALL(curandSetPseudoRandomGeneratorSeed(rand_generator_host, seed));

 // Create a set of random numbers on the device and host
 CURAND_CALL(curandGenerateUniform(rand_generator_device, device_ptr, num_elem));
 CURAND_CALL(curandGenerateUniform(rand_generator_host, host_gen_ptr, num_elem));

 // Copy the set of device generated data to the host
 CUDA_CALL(cudaMemcpy(host_ptr, device_ptr, size_in_bytes, cudaMemcpyDeviceToHost));
```

```
printf("\n\nRandom numbers from GPU");
print_array(host_ptr, num_elem);

printf("\n\nRandom numbers from Host");
print_array(host_gen_ptr, num_elem);
printf("\n");

// Free device resources
CURAND_CALL(curandDestroyGenerator(rand_generator_device));
CUDA_CALL(cudaFree(device_ptr));
CUDA_CALL(cudaFreeHost(host_ptr));
CUDA_CALL(cudaDeviceReset());

// Free host resources
CURAND_CALL(curandDestroyGenerator(rand_generator_host));
free(host_gen_ptr);
}
```

This program generates num_elem number of random numbers on the device and the host using the CuRand API. It then prints both sets of random numbers. The output is shown here:

```
Using CuRand Version: 4010 and generator: CURAND_RNG_PSEUDO_DEFAULT

Random numbers from GPU
 0: 0.468090  1: 0.660579  2: 0.351722  3: 0.891716
 4: 0.624544  5: 0.861485  6: 0.662096  7: 0.007847
 8: 0.179364  9: 0.260115 10: 0.453508 11: 0.711956
12: 0.973453 13: 0.152303 14: 0.784318 15: 0.948965
16: 0.214159 17: 0.236516 18: 0.020540 19: 0.175973
20: 0.085989 21: 0.863053 22: 0.908001 23: 0.539129
24: 0.849580 25: 0.496193 26: 0.588651 27: 0.361609
28: 0.025815 29: 0.778294 30: 0.194206 31: 0.478006

Random numbers from Host
 0: 0.468090  1: 0.660579  2: 0.351722  3: 0.891716
 4: 0.624544  5: 0.861485  6: 0.662096  7: 0.007847
 8: 0.179364  9: 0.260115 10: 0.453508 11: 0.711956
12: 0.973453 13: 0.152303 14: 0.784318 15: 0.948965
16: 0.214159 17: 0.236516 18: 0.020540 19: 0.175973
20: 0.085989 21: 0.863053 22: 0.908001 23: 0.539129
24: 0.849580 25: 0.496193 26: 0.588651 27: 0.361609
28: 0.025815 29: 0.778294 30: 0.194206 31: 0.478006
```

One important issue to note from the example program is the API calls are the same for device and host functions, except for registering the generator. The device version must be used with curandCreateGenerator and the host version with curandCreateGeneratorHost. Additionally, note that the curandGenerateUniform function must be called with the associated host or device-based pointer.

Getting either of these mixed up will likely result in a CUDA "unknown error" issue or the program simply crashing. Unfortunately, as both host-side and device-side memory allocations are just regular C pointers, it's not possible for the library to tell if this pointer passed to it, is a host-side pointer, or device-side pointer.

Also be aware that CuRand, as with NPP, supports streams. Thus, a call to `curandSet Stream(generator, stream)` will switch the library to an asynchronous operation in that stream. By default the library will use stream 0, the default stream.

There are many types of generators you can use with the CuRand library, including one based on the Mersenne Twister algorithm used for Monte Carlo simulations.

SDK Samples: Monte Carlo, Random Fog, Mersenne Twister, Sobol.

CuBLAS (CUDA basic linear algebra) library

The last library we'll mention is the CuBLAS. The CuBLAS library aims to replicate the functionality of the Fortran BLAS library commonly used in Fortran scientific applications. To allow easy porting of existing Fortran BLAS code, the CuBLAS library maintains the Fortran column-major layout, the opposite of the standard C row-major layout. It also uses the 1..N as opposed to the C standard 0..(N-1) notation when accessing array elements.

Thus, for porting legacy Fortran code to CUDA, the CuBLAS library is ideal. There are many large codebases written over the past decades in Fortran. Allowing this existing legacy code to run on modern GPU-accelerated hardware without significant code changes is one of the great strengths of this library. However, it's also one of its weaknesses, as it will not appeal to anyone who learned to program in a modern computing language.

The CuBLAS library documentation provides some sample macros to convert the old-style Fortran array indexes into what most programmers would consider "regular" array indexing. However, even if implemented as macros or as an inline function, this adds execution time overhead to anyone attempting to work with non-Fortran indexing. This makes using the library rather a pain for C programmers. C programmers may have preferred to see a separate C style CuBLAS implementation that natively supported C array indexing.

As of version four of the library, it deprecated the older API. It now requires all callers to first create a handle via a call to the `cublasCreate` function call before any other calls are made. The handle is used in subsequent calls and allows CuBLAS to be both re-entrant and to support multiple GPUs using multiple asynchronous streams for maximum performance. Note although these features are provided, it's the programmers responsibility to handle multiple devices. Like so many of the other libraries provided, the CuBLAS library does not automatically distribute its load across multi-GPU devices.

The current API can be used by including the `cublas_v2.h` file instead of the older `cublas.h` include file. Any current usage of the older API should be replaced with the newer API. As with the NPP library, operations are expected to be performed on data already present on the GPU and the caller is therefore responsible for transferring the data to and from the device. A number of "helper" functions are provided for such purposes.

The new CuBLAS interface is entirely asynchronous in nature, meaning even functions that return values do it in such a way as the value may not be available unless the programmer specifically waits for the asynchronous GPU operation to complete. This is part of the move to asynchronous streams that will become important when the Kepler K20 is released.

We'll look at a simple example here, declaring a matrix on the host side, copying it to the device, performing some operations, copying the data back to the host, and printing the matrix.

```c
#include <stdio.h>
#include <stdlib.h>
#include <cublas_v2.h>
#include "cuda_helper.h"
#include "cuda.h"

#define CUBLAS_CALL(x) {const cublasStatus_t a = (x); if (a != CUBLAS_STATUS_SUCCESS) {
printf("\nCUBLAS Error: (err_num=%d) \n", a); cudaDeviceReset(); ASSERT(0);} }

__host__ void print_array(const float * __restrict__ const data1,
                          const float * __restrict__ const data2,
                          const float * __restrict__ const data3,
                          const int num_elem,
                          const char * const prefix)

{
 printf("\n%s", prefix);
 for (int i=0; i<num_elem; i++)
 {
  printf("\n%2d: %2.4f %2.4f %2.4f ", i+1, data1[i], data2[i], data3[i]);
 }
}


__host__ int main(int argc, char *argv[])
{
 const int num_elem = 8;
 const size_t size_in_bytes = (num_elem * sizeof(float));

 // Allocate memory on the device
 float * device_src_ptr_A;
 CUDA_CALL( cudaMalloc( (void **) &device_src_ptr_A, size_in_bytes ));
 float * device_src_ptr_B;
 CUDA_CALL( cudaMalloc( (void **) &device_src_ptr_B, size_in_bytes ));
 float * device_dest_ptr;
 CUDA_CALL( cudaMalloc( (void **) &device_dest_ptr, size_in_bytes ));

 // Allocate memory on the host for the device copy
 float * host_src_ptr_A;
 CUDA_CALL( cudaMallocHost( (void **) &host_src_ptr_A, size_in_bytes ));
 float * host_dest_ptr;
 CUDA_CALL( cudaMallocHost( (void **) &host_dest_ptr, size_in_bytes ));
 float * host_dest_ptr_A;
 CUDA_CALL( cudaMallocHost( (void **) &host_dest_ptr_A, size_in_bytes ));
 float * host_dest_ptr_B;
 CUDA_CALL( cudaMallocHost( (void **) &host_dest_ptr_B, size_in_bytes ));
```

```
// Clear destination memory
memset(host_dest_ptr_A, 0, size_in_bytes);
memset(host_dest_ptr_B, 0, size_in_bytes);
memset(host_dest_ptr, 0, size_in_bytes);

// Init the CUBLAS library
cublasHandle_t cublas_handle;
CUBLAS_CALL(cublasCreate(&cublas_handle));

// Print library version number
int version;
CUBLAS_CALL(cublasGetVersion(cublas_handle, &version));
printf("\nUsing CUBLAS Version: %d", version);

// Fill the first host array with known values
for (int i=0; i < num_elem; i++)
{
 host_src_ptr_A[i] = (float) i;
}
print_array(host_src_ptr_A, host_dest_ptr_B, host_dest_ptr, num_elem, "Before Set");

const int num_rows = num_elem;
const int num_cols = 1;
const size_t elem_size = sizeof(float);

// Copy a matrix one cell wide by num_elem rows from the CPU to the device
CUBLAS_CALL(cublasSetMatrix(num_rows, num_cols, elem_size, host_src_ptr_A,
          num_rows, device_src_ptr_A, num_rows));

// Clear the memory in the other two
CUDA_CALL(cudaMemset(device_src_ptr_B, 0, size_in_bytes));
CUDA_CALL(cudaMemset(device_dest_ptr, 0, size_in_bytes));

// SAXPY on device based on copied matrix and alpha
const int stride = 1;
float alpha = 2.0F;
CUBLAS_CALL(cublasSaxpy(cublas_handle, num_elem, &alpha, device_src_ptr_A,
          stride, device_src_ptr_B, stride));

alpha = 3.0F;
CUBLAS_CALL(cublasSaxpy(cublas_handle, num_elem, &alpha, device_src_ptr_A,
          stride, device_dest_ptr, stride));

// Calculate the index of the max of each maxtrix, writing the result
// directly to host memory
int host_max_idx_A, host_max_idx_B, host_max_idx_dest;
```

```
CUBLAS_CALL(cublasIsamax(cublas_handle, num_elem, device_src_ptr_A,
        stride, &host_max_idx_A));
CUBLAS_CALL(cublasIsamax(cublas_handle, num_elem, device_src_ptr_B,
        stride, &host_max_idx_B));
CUBLAS_CALL(cublasIsamax(cublas_handle, num_elem, device_dest_ptr,
        stride, &host_max_idx_dest));

// Calculate the sum of each maxtrix, writing the result directly to host memory
float host_sum_A, host_sum_B, host_sum_dest;
CUBLAS_CALL(cublasSasum(cublas_handle, num_elem, device_src_ptr_A,
        stride, &host_sum_A));
CUBLAS_CALL(cublasSasum(cublas_handle, num_elem, device_src_ptr_B,
        stride, &host_sum_B));
CUBLAS_CALL(cublasSasum(cublas_handle, num_elem, device_dest_ptr,
        stride, &host_sum_dest));

// Copy device versions back to host to print out
CUBLAS_CALL(cublasGetMatrix(num_rows, num_cols, elem_size, device_src_ptr_A,
        num_rows, host_dest_ptr_A, num_rows));
CUBLAS_CALL(cublasGetMatrix(num_rows, num_cols, elem_size, device_src_ptr_B,
        num_rows, host_dest_ptr_B, num_rows));
CUBLAS_CALL(cublasGetMatrix(num_rows, num_cols, elem_size, device_dest_ptr,
        num_rows, host_dest_ptr, num_rows));

// Make sure any async calls above are complete before we use the host data
const int default_stream = 0;
CUDA_CALL(cudaStreamSynchronize(default_stream));

// Print out the arrays
print_array(host_dest_ptr_A, host_dest_ptr_B, host_dest_ptr, num_elem, "After Set");

// Print some stats from the arrays
printf("\nIDX of max values : %d, %d, %d", host_max_idx_A,
 host_max_idx_B, host_max_idx_dest);
printf("\nSUM of values : %2.2f, %2.2f, %2.2f", host_sum_A,
 host_sum_B, host_sum_dest);

// Free device resources
CUBLAS_CALL(cublasDestroy(cublas_handle));
CUDA_CALL(cudaFree(device_src_ptr_A));
CUDA_CALL(cudaFree(device_src_ptr_B));
CUDA_CALL(cudaFree(device_dest_ptr));

// Free host resources
CUDA_CALL(cudaFreeHost(host_src_ptr_A));
CUDA_CALL(cudaFreeHost(host_dest_ptr_A));
CUDA_CALL(cudaFreeHost(host_dest_ptr_B));
```

```
CUDA_CALL(cudaFreeHost(host_dest_ptr));

// Reset ready for next GPU program
CUDA_CALL(cudaDeviceReset());
}
```

The basic steps of the program are as follows:

- Create a CuBLAS handle using the `cublasCreate` function.
- Allocate resources on the device and host.
- Set a matrix on the device directly from a matrix on the host.
- Run Saxpy on the device.
- Run `max` and `sum` functions on the device.
- Copy the resultant matrix back to the host and display it.
- Free any allocated resources.

In practice, real programs will be significantly more complex. We've attempted to show here the basic template necessary to get some simple CuBLAS functions working on the GPU.

SDK Samples: Matrix Multiplication.

CUDA COMPUTING SDK

The CUDA SDK is a separate download from regular toolkits and drivers, although it is now bundled with the CUDA 5 release candidate for Windows users, so it may become a single download in the future. It contains lots of sample code and a nice interface to find all the provided CUDA documentation.

There are almost 200 samples, so we'll select a few sample applications to look at in detail. We'll look at some general-purpose applications since these are easier to understand for the wider audience this text is aimed at than some of the more domain-specific examples in the toolkit.

The computing samples are incredibly useful for someone starting out with GPU programming, as well as more advanced programmers who want examples of how something should be done. Unfortunately, a lot of the underlying CUDA API is hidden from you. When you are learning a new API the last thing you need is yet another API layer on top of the one you wish to learn, so this rather complicates understanding.

Many of the SDK examples use the `cutil` or other packages that are *not* part of the standard CUDA release. Thus, when you see the line

```
cutilSafeCall(cudaGetDeviceProperties(&deviceProps, devID));
```

you might expect it to work in your own code. However, to do this it's also necessary to include the relevant `cutil` source headers from the SDK. NVIDIA makes no guarantee about the version-to-version compatibility of these libraries. They are not part of the official CUDA release and therefore are not supported.

The CUDA APIs always start `cuda`.... Therefore, if you see anything other than this, you should realize that you will need to bring in additional code from the SDK samples, should you wish to use such calls.

So what does `cutilSafeCall` do? Fairly much the same as the `CUDA_CALL` macro we've used throughout this text. If there is an error returned from the caller, it prints the file and line number and then exits. So why not use the `cutil` package directly? Largely because there are many functions in this library and you only need a small number of them in reality.

There are, however, many useful functions within this package, for example, the `gpuGetMaxGflopsDeviceId` function that identifies the fastest GPU device in the system. You should browse through the libraries provided with the SDK to help you understand some of the samples before jumping into the samples themselves.

Device Query

Device query is an interesting application in that it's quite simple and allows you to see what your GPU is capable of. It is run from the command line rather than the Windows interface and can be found in "C:\ProgramData\NVIDIA Corporation\NVIDIA GPU Computing SDK 4.1\C\bin\win64\Release."

Obviously it is the Windows 64-bit version we're using here from the 4.1 toolkit, which may be different on your system. The output is shown here:

```
Found 4 CUDA Capable device(s)

Device 0: "GeForce GTX 470"
  CUDA Driver Version / Runtime Version          4.1 / 4.1
  CUDA Capability Major/Minor version number:    2.0
  Total amount of global memory:                 1280 MBytes (1342177280 bytes)
  (14) Multiprocessors x (32) CUDA Cores/MP:     448 CUDA Cores
  GPU Clock Speed:                               1.22 GHz
  Memory Clock rate:                             1674.00 Mhz
  Memory Bus Width:                              320-bit
  L2 Cache Size:                                 655360 bytes
  Max Texture Dimension Size (x,y,z)             1D=(65536), 2D=(65536,65535),
                                                 3D=(2048,2048,2048)
  Max Layered Texture Size (dim) x layers        1D=(16384) x 2048, 2D=(16384,16384) x
                                                 2048
  Total amount of constant memory:               65536 bytes
  Total amount of shared memory per block:       49152 bytes
  Total number of registers available per block: 32768
  Warp size:                                     32
  Maximum number of threads per block:           1024
  Maximum sizes of each dimension of a block:    1024 x 1024 x 64
  Maximum sizes of each dimension of a grid:     65535 x 65535 x 65535
  Maximum memory pitch:                          2147483647 bytes
  Texture alignment:                             512 bytes
  Concurrent copy and execution:                 Yes with 1 copy engine(s)
  Run time limit on kernels:                     No
  Integrated GPU sharing Host Memory:            No
  Support host page-locked memory mapping:       Yes
  Concurrent kernel execution:                   Yes
  Alignment requirement for Surfaces:            Yes
  Device has ECC support enabled:                No
```

```
Device is using TCC driver mode:              No
Device supports Unified Addressing (UVA):     No
Device PCI Bus ID / PCI location ID:          8 / 0
Compute Mode:
  < Default (multiple host threads can use ::cudaSetDevice() with device simultaneously) >

Device 1: "GeForce 9800 GT"
CUDA Capability Major/Minor version number:   1.1
Total amount of global memory:                1024 MBytes (1073741824 bytes)
(14) Multiprocessors x ( 8) CUDA Cores/MP:    112 CUDA Cores
GPU Clock Speed:                              1.63 GHz
Memory Clock rate:                            950.00 Mhz
Memory Bus Width:                             256-bit
Total amount of shared memory per block:      16384 bytes
Total number of registers available per block: 8192
Maximum number of threads per block:          512
Device PCI Bus ID / PCI location ID:          7 / 0


Device 2: "GeForce GTX 260"
CUDA Capability Major/Minor version number:   1.3
Total amount of global memory:                896 MBytes (939524096 bytes)
(27) Multiprocessors x ( 8) CUDA Cores/MP:    216 CUDA Cores
GPU Clock Speed:                              1.35 GHz
Memory Clock rate:                            1100.00 Mhz
Memory Bus Width:                             448-bit
Total amount of shared memory per block:      16384 bytes
Total number of registers available per block: 16384
Maximum number of threads per block:          512
Device PCI Bus ID / PCI location ID:          1 / 0


Device 3: "GeForce GTX 460"
CUDA Capability Major/Minor version number:   2.1
Total amount of global memory:                1024 MBytes (1073741824 bytes)
( 7) Multiprocessors x (48) CUDA Cores/MP:    336 CUDA Cores
GPU Clock Speed:                              1.45 GHz
Memory Clock rate:                            1800.00 Mhz
Memory Bus Width:                             256-bit
L2 Cache Size:                                524288 bytes
Total amount of shared memory per block:      49152 bytes
Total number of registers available per block: 32768
Maximum number of threads per block:          1024
Device PCI Bus ID / PCI location ID:          2 / 0
```

The program will iterate through all GPUs to find and list the various details of each device. For brevity, we have listed only one of the four devices completely and extracted the interesting parts from the other devices. For those interested in Kepler GK104, the relevant details are as follows:

```
Device 0: "GeForce GTX 680"
CUDA Capability Major/Minor version number:   3.0
```

```
Total amount of global memory:                        2048 MBytes (2146762752 bytes)
( 8) Multiprocessors x (192) CUDA Cores/MP:           1536 CUDA Cores
GPU Clock Speed:                                      1006 MHz
Memory Clock rate:                                    3004.00 Mhz
Memory Bus Width:                                     256-bit
L2 Cache Size:                                        524288 bytes
Total amount of shared memory per block:              49152 bytes
Total number of registers available per block:        65536
Warp size: 32
Maximum number of threads per block:                  1024
Concurrent copy and execution:                        Yes with 1 copy engine(s)
```

Items reported of note are the current driver and runtime version, which should be the same. Compute capability defines what type of device we have for a given device number. Also detailed is the number of cores/SMs per device, speed of the device, along with memory speed and width. Thus, it's possible to calculate the peak bandwidth on a given device. Talking of bandwidth, this brings us to the next useful application in the SDK.

Bandwidth test

The bandwidth example provided by the SDK provides the following useful statistics about your particular device/host setup:

- Host-to-device bandwidth (paged and pinned memory)
- Device-to-host bandwidth (paged and pinned memory)
- Device-to-device bandwidth

The actual output is shown here for a GTX470 on an x8 PCI-E 2.0 link:

```
>> bandwidthtest --device=0 --memory=pageable
Device 0: GeForce GTX 470
 Quick Mode

 Host to Device Bandwidth, 1 Device(s), Paged memory
  Transfer Size (Bytes) Bandwidth(MB/s)
  33554432 1833.6

 Device to Host Bandwidth, 1 Device(s), Paged memory
  Transfer Size (Bytes) Bandwidth(MB/s)
  33554432 1700.5

 Device to Device Bandwidth, 1 Device(s)
  Transfer Size (Bytes) Bandwidth(MB/s)
  33554432 113259.3

>> bandwidthtest --device=0 --memory=pinned
Host to Device Bandwidth, 1 Device(s), Pinned memory
  Transfer Size (Bytes) Bandwidth(MB/s)
```

```
33554432 2663.6

Device to Host Bandwidth, 1 Device(s), Pinned memory
 Transfer Size (Bytes) Bandwidth(MB/s)
 33554432 3225.8

Device to Device Bandwidth, 1 Device(s)
 Transfer Size (Bytes) Bandwidth(MB/s)
 33554432 113232.3
```

One of the things you'll see when using this example program is just how much benefit using pinned memory on your system brings. We looked at this in Chapter 9, but there is nothing like seeing it on your own system to drive home the point that pinned memory can be much faster for memory transfers. Even a modern Sandybridge-E processor achieves 3 GB/s versus 2.3 GB/s when using pinned versus paged memory on a similar PCI-E 2.0 x8 link.

Typical memory on a consumer GPU card is anything from 512 MB (88/9800 series) to 2 GB (GTX680). There is really no reason why you should not pin system memory to do the transfers to or from the GPU. Even in a 32-bit system with a 4 GB memory limit, CUDA will still be using pinned transfers in the background. Therefore, you may just as well pin the memory yourself and avoid the implicit pageable to pinned memory copy within the driver.

As memory is now very cheap there is no reason why you should not fully load the machine. This is especially the case if you have more than one GPU card or are using Tesla cards. You can purchase 16 GB of host memory for less than 100 euros/dollars/pounds.

If we take the memory clock from the GTX470, there is 1674 MHz with a bus width of 320 bits. Thus, we take the bus width and divide by 8 to get bytes (40 bytes). Next we multiply this by the clock rate (66,960 MB/s). Then we multiply by 2 for GDDR5 (133,920 MB/s). Then we divide by 1000 to get listed memory bandwidth (133.9 GB/s) or 1024 (130.8 GB/s) to get actual bandwidth.

So why do we get device-to-device bandwidth of 113,232 MB/s instead of 133,920 MB/s? Where did the missing 20 MB/s or 15% of the memory bandwidth go? The GPU never achieves this theoretical peak bandwidth. This is why it's useful to run the bandwidth test as opposed to calculating the theoretical peak. You then have a very good idea of what bandwidth you will get in *your* system, with your PCI-E arrangement, your host CPU, your CPU chipset, your host memory, etc. By knowing this you know what your application should be able to achieve on a given target and can therefore see how much potential you have yet to exploit.

Note with Tesla-based Fermi devices you can gain a significant boost in bandwidth by disabling the ECC memory option using the nvidia-smi tool. Error checking and correction (ECC) distributes the bit patterns using Hamming codes. This, in effect, means you need a larger memory space to store the same data block. This additional storage requirement means you trade both space and speed for the extra redundancy ECC brings. NVIDIA claims to have addressed this issue in Kepler K20 (GK110), where the impact of using ECC is claimed to be around one-third of that of Fermi.

SimpleP2P

The SimpleP2P example shows how to use the P2P memory transfer capabilities introduced in compute 2.x devices (Fermi). The principle of P2P transfers to avoid having to go through host

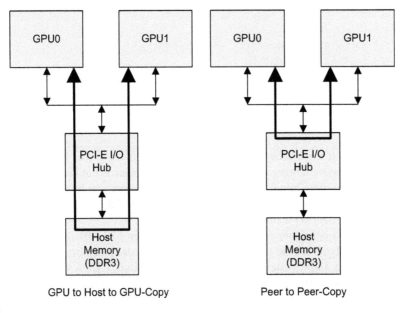

GPU to Host to GPU-Copy   Peer to Peer-Copy

FIGURE 10.5

P2P transfers.

memory (see Figure 10.5). Host memory may be directly accessible to the PCI-E I/O hub (Northbridge), as is often the case with Intel's QPI-based system. It may also be to the other side of the processor, as with Intel's DMI and AMD's hypertransport-based systems.

Depending on the number of GPUs in the system, the host memory may represent a bottleneck for the transfer in terms of its own speed. The maximum PCI-E transfer speed approaches 6 GB/s on a PCI-E 2.0 link. With PCI-E 3.0 (GTX680, GTX690, Tesla K10) the actual bandwidth almost doubles to just under 12 GB/s in each direction. To maximize bandwidth, you typically define two pinned memory areas and use a double buffer scheme to transfer into one block and out of the other. Especially with the older processors, you can rapidly consume the entire host memory bandwidth simply by performing transfers between GPUs through host memory. This will severely hamper any attempt to use the CPU for additional processing capabilities, as it will be competing for host memory bandwidth with the GPU transfers.

The idea of P2P is to keep the data out of the host memory space and to do a transfer directly between the GPUs. While this is an extremely useful feature, support for this in the mainstream Windows 7 systems has been noticeably lacking. Thus it is not something we've looked at yet in this text, so we will cover it here as there are a number of uses for this technology. Requirements to use the P2P functionality are:

- A 64-bit OS, and thus UVA (unified virtual addressing) enabled, a requirement for P2P to be available.
- Two or more compute 2.x devices that support this feature.
- GPU Devices that are on the same PCI-E I/O hub.
- Appropriate driver level support.

To use this feature under Windows 7 you need the 64-bit OS plus the TCC (Tesla compute cluster) drivers active. As the TCC driver will only activate with Tesla cards, effectively there is no mainstream consumer support for this in Windows 7. Thus, this should be considered as a feature suitable for clusters, high-performance computing (HPC), and other compute-centered applications. It's not something you can exploit with, say, a video transcoding application for consumer PCs.

To support P2P first you should check UVA is enabled:

```
struct cudaDevice device_prop;
CUDA_CALL(cudaGetDeviceProperties(&device_prop));
if (device_prop.unifiedAddressing == 1) // If unified addressing is enabled
```

Next you need to check if device A can talk to device B. Note, just because this test passes, it does not imply that device B can talk to device A. Resources are consumed in enabling P2P access in a given direction. This test can be performed with the following code:

```
int peer_access_avail;
int src_device = 0;
int peer_device = 1;

CUDA_CALL(cudaDeviceCanAccessPeer( &peer_access_avail, src_device, peer_device));

if (peer_access_avail == 1) // If peer access from device 0 to device 1 is available
{
  int flags = 0;
  CUDA_CALL(cudaSetDevice(peer_device));
  CUDA_CALL(cudaEnablePeerAccess(peer_device, flags);
}
```

Once peer access has been enabled, memory can be accessed, in the direction of the peer access, either in device kernels or as host-initiated memory copies. Thus, device 0 can enable peer access to device 1, as in the previous example. You can then call a kernel on device 1, passing it a pointer to the global memory space from device 0. The kernel will then dereference this pointer in the same way as it would a zero-copy device pointer to host memory. Every time there is an access through that pointer device 1 will initiate a fetch over the PCI-E bus from device 0. Of course, the same caveats apply as with zero-copy memory usage, specifically that you should avoid re-reading such memory and try to achieve coalesced access patterns for performance reasons.

You can of course use such features for device-initiated memory copies. To do this from the device, have a device kernel fetch the data via a device pointer, and simply store it to the local device's global memory. Equally you can push as well as pull data from one device to another. However, if you want bidirectional access, you will need to remember to enable P2P access in both directions.

The second approach is an explicit memory copy, something we must initiate from the host. There are the two standard forms of this, the synchronous version and the asynchronous streamed version:

```
cudaMemcpyPeer(dest_device_ptr, dst_device_num, src_device_ptr,
src_device_num,num_bytes);
```

and

```
cudaMemcpyPeerAsync( dest_device_ptr, dst_device_num, src_device_ptr, src_device_num,
num_bytes, stream );
```

Finally, once we're done, we need to disable the provisioning of the resources for the P2P access by calling

```
cudaDeviceDisablePeerAccess(device_num);
```

Performance wise the SimpleP2P application reports 2.4 GB/s, which is quite close to the peak 3 GB/s available on this particular (PCI-E 2.0 x8) test system.

The SimpleP2P example program in the SDK provides some simple template code as to how to do this in practice. It does a series of GPU transfers between two GPUs and then computes the transfer speed. With the background we've covered here you should be able to read and follow the example code.

asyncAPI and cudaOpenMP

The `asyncAPI` SDK sample provides an example of using the asynchronous API, but is not actually very simple for someone new to CUDA to understand. We've covered streams and asynchronous operation already in the text. These are important for getting multi-GPU setups to work alongside CPU usage. Therefore, we'll look at this example and see what exactly it does.

The basic premise of the `asyncAPI` example is that it creates an asynchronous stream, into which it puts a memory copy to the device, a kernel, and finally a memory copy back to the host. During this time it runs some code on the CPU that simply counts up while the GPU is running the asynchronous kernel.

The `cudaOpenMP` example shows how to use OpenMP with CUDA. It identifies the number of CPU threads, and the number and name of each attached CUDA device. It then tries to spawn one thread per GPU device and work-share the different devices.

We'll provide a similar example here that fuses the two SDK examples, but simplifies them somewhat and is potentially more useful as template code for your own work.

```
#include <stdio.h>
#include <omp.h>

#include "cuda_helper.h"
#include "cuda.h"

__global__ void increment_kernel(int * __restrict__ const data,
                                  const int inc_value,
                                  const int num_elem)
{
  const int idx = blockIdx.x * blockDim.x + threadIdx.x;

  // Check array index does not overflow the array
  if (idx < num_elem)
```

```
 {
  // Repeat N times - just to make the kernel take some time
  const int repeat = 512;

  for (int i=0; i < repeat; i++)
   data[idx] += inc_value;
 }
}

// Max number of devices on any single node is, usually at most, eight
#define MAX_NUM_DEVICES 8

__host__ int main(int argc, char *argv[])
{
 const int num_elem = 1024 * 1024 * 16;
 const int size_in_bytes = num_elem * sizeof(int);
 const int increment_value = 1;
 const int loop_iteration_check = 1000000;
 const int shared_mem = 0;

 // Define the number of threads/blocks needed
 const int num_threads = 512;
 const int num_blocks = ((num_elem + (num_threads-1)) / num_threads);

 // One array element per CPU thread
 int host_counter[MAX_NUM_DEVICES];
 float delta_device_time[MAX_NUM_DEVICES];
 cudaDeviceProp device_prop[MAX_NUM_DEVICES];

 int num_devices;
 CUDA_CALL(cudaGetDeviceCount(&num_devices));
 printf("\nIdentified %d devices. Spawning %d threads to calculate %d MB using (%dx%d)",
num_devices, num_devices, ((size_in_bytes/1024)/1024), num_blocks, num_threads );

 // Declare thread private, per thread variables
 int * device_ptr[MAX_NUM_DEVICES];
 int * host_ptr[MAX_NUM_DEVICES];
 cudaEvent_t start_event[MAX_NUM_DEVICES], stop_event[MAX_NUM_DEVICES];
 cudaStream_t async_stream[MAX_NUM_DEVICES];

 // Create all allocations outside of OpenMP in series
 for (int device_num=0; device_num < num_devices; device_num++)
 {
  // Set the device to a unique device per CPU thread
  CUDA_CALL(cudaSetDevice(device_num));

  // Get the current device properties
  CUDA_CALL(cudaGetDeviceProperties(&device_prop[device_num], device_num));
```

```
    // Allocate the resources necessary
    CUDA_CALL(cudaMalloc((void **) &device_ptr[device_num], size_in_bytes));
    CUDA_CALL(cudaMallocHost((void **) &host_ptr[device_num], size_in_bytes));
    CUDA_CALL(cudaEventCreate(&start_event[device_num]));
    CUDA_CALL(cudaEventCreate(&stop_event[device_num]));
    CUDA_CALL(cudaStreamCreate(&async_stream[device_num]));
  }

  // Spawn one CPU thread for each device
#pragma omp parallel num_threads(num_devices)
  {
    // Variables declared within the OpenMP block are thread private and per thread
    // Variables outside OpenMP block exist once in memory and are shared between
    // threads.

    // Get our current thread number and use this as the device number
    const int device_num = omp_get_thread_num();

    // Set the device to a unique device per CPU thread
    CUDA_CALL(cudaSetDevice(device_num));

    // Push start timer, memset, kernel, copy back and stop timer into device queue
    CUDA_CALL(cudaEventRecord(start_event[device_num], async_stream[device_num]));

    // Copy the data to the device
    CUDA_CALL(cudaMemsetAsync(device_ptr[device_num], 0, size_in_bytes,
             async_stream[device_num]));

    // Invoke the kernel
    increment_kernel<<<num_blocks, num_threads, shared_mem, async_stream[device_num]
>>>(device_ptr[device_num], increment_value, num_elem);

    // Copy data back from the device
    CUDA_CALL(cudaMemcpyAsync(host_ptr[device_num], device_ptr[device_num],
             size_in_bytes, cudaMemcpyDeviceToHost,
             async_stream[device_num]));

    // Record the end of the GPU work
    CUDA_CALL(cudaEventRecord(stop_event[device_num], async_stream[device_num]));

    // Device work has now been sent to the GPU, so do some CPU work
    // whilst we're waiting for the device to complete its work queue

    // Reset host counter
    int host_counter_local = 0;
    int complete = 0;
```

```
// Do some work on the CPU until all the device kernels complete
do
{
 // Insert useful CPU work here
 host_counter_local++;

 // Check device completion status every loop_iteration_check iterations
 if ( (host_counter_local % loop_iteration_check) == 0 )
 {
  // Assume everything is now complete
  complete = 1;

  // Check if all GPU streams have completed. Continue to do more CPU
  // work if one of more devices have pending work.
  for ( int device_check_num=0; device_check_num < num_devices;
   device_check_num++)
 {
   if ( cudaEventQuery(stop_event[device_check_num]) == cudaErrorNotReady )
    complete = 0;
  }
 }

} while( complete == 0 );

// Write out final result
host_counter[device_num] = host_counter_local;

// Calculate elapsed GPU time
CUDA_CALL(cudaEventElapsedTime(&delta_device_time[device_num],
         start_event[device_num],
         stop_event[device_num]));
} // End parallel region

// Now running as a single CPU thread again

// Free allocated resources
// Create all allocations outside of OpenMP in series
for (int device_num=0; device_num < num_devices; device_num++)
{
 // Set the device to a unique device per CPU thread
 CUDA_CALL(cudaSetDevice(device_num));

 CUDA_CALL(cudaStreamDestroy(async_stream[device_num]));
 CUDA_CALL(cudaEventDestroy(stop_event[device_num]));
 CUDA_CALL(cudaEventDestroy(start_event[device_num]));
 CUDA_CALL(cudaFreeHost(host_ptr[device_num]));
```

```
CUDA_CALL(cudaFree(device_ptr[device_num]));

// Reset the device for later use
CUDA_CALL(cudaDeviceReset());
}

// Print a summary of the results
for (int device=0; device < num_devices; device++)
{
 printf("\n\nKernel Time for device %s id:%d: %.2fms",
        device_prop[device].name, device, delta_device_time[device]);
 printf("\nCPU count for thread %d: %d", device, host_counter[device]);
 }
}
```

There are a few points in the SDK examples that need further discussion. First, with the `asyncAPI` example, stream 0, the default stream, is used. Unfortunately, there are many instances where the default stream causes implicit synchronization between streams. You will almost certainly end up using a double- or triple-buffered method and this implicit synchronization will catch you out. When using asynchronous operations, always create your own streams.

```
cudaStream_t async_stream[MAX_NUM_DEVICES];
CUDA_CALL(cudaSetDevice(device_num));
CUDA_CALL(cudaStreamCreate(&async_stream[device_num]));
```

The second point from the `asyncAPI` stream example that you may not have noticed is that it takes the number of elements, *N*, and divides it directly by the number of threads to get the number of blocks for the grid. As it happens *N* is a multiple of the number of threads, but what if it is not? What happens is, the last elements in the array are not processed by the GPU kernel. This may not be at all obvious for anyone starting out with CUDA. Always use the following formula for generating the number of blocks if you plan on allowing *N* not to be a multiple of the number of threads:

```
const int num_elem = 1024 * 1024 * 16;
const int num_threads = 512;
const int num_blocks = ((num_elem + (num_threads-1)) / num_threads);
```

And in the kernel, add a check for array overrun:

```
// Check array index does not overflow the array
if (idx < num_elem)
```

Now this creates the overhead of passing `num_elem` to the kernel and checking it within the kernel. If you can *guarantee* you will always use a multiple of the number of threads, then you can avoid the need for this code and stick with the much simpler `num_blocks = num_elem / num_threads` approach. Most of the time we can say as programmers this holds true, as we often control the data block sizes.

If we look at the `cudaOpenMP` example now, how are multiple CPU threads launched? It uses a call to `omp_set_num_threads`:

```
omp_set_num_threads(num_gpus);
//omp_set_num_threads(2*num_gpus);
#pragma omp parallel
{
}
```

There are two approaches here: to set one thread per GPU or multiple threads per GPU (Figure 10.6). The later approach is more useful where you have many more CPU cores than GPUs. A simpler form of this OpenMP directive that often works more reliably is the one we've used in the sample program:

```
// Spawn one CPU thread for each device
#pragma omp parallel num_threads(num_devices)
{
}
```

With this approach it does not matter how OpenMP may or may not have been configured, what environment variables are set or not; it spawns the specified number of threads. Note that the current thread is one of the threads used to execute work.

```
Identified 4 devices. Spawning 4 threads to calculate 64 MB using (32768x512)

Kernel Time for device GeForce GTX 470 id:0: 427.74ms
CPU count for thread 0: 1239000000

Kernel Time for device GeForce 9800 GT id:1: 3300.55ms
CPU count for thread 1: 1180000000

Kernel Time for device GeForce GTX 285 id:2: 1693.63ms
CPU count for thread 2: 1229000000

Kernel Time for device GeForce GTX 460 id:3: 662.61ms
CPU count for thread 3: 1254000000
```

You can see from the program output that, by using different GPUs, the threads finish at different times. You can see from Figure 10.6 that there are four threads running, including the originating thread. If viewed on screen you would see dark green bars along the top showing the threads are mostly running (~95%) with occasional stalls that would be shown in light green. Below are the four GPU tasks each of which is performing a memset, a kernel launch, and then a copy back to host. The bottom row of bars shows the CPU utilization for this timeframe. You can see the CPU is busy almost the entire time.

As the four GPUs finish, the CPU threads continue to work until all GPUs in the set have completed. We could of course, and you would in practice, allocate more GPU work to these GPUs if we really had such different performance characteristics with our GPUs. However, most GPU systems will have all of the same GPUs present and thus we'd not have to care about reissuing work until they had all completed. As they are all the same, given a similar job, they would all complete around the same time.

The next issue we should address with using OpenMP is where to put resource allocations and deallocations. Allocation of memory and creation of resources on a given device is a time-consuming process. Often there needs to be a common understanding of the allocation across threads and thus common data structures. To share common data structures across threads requires locking and this in

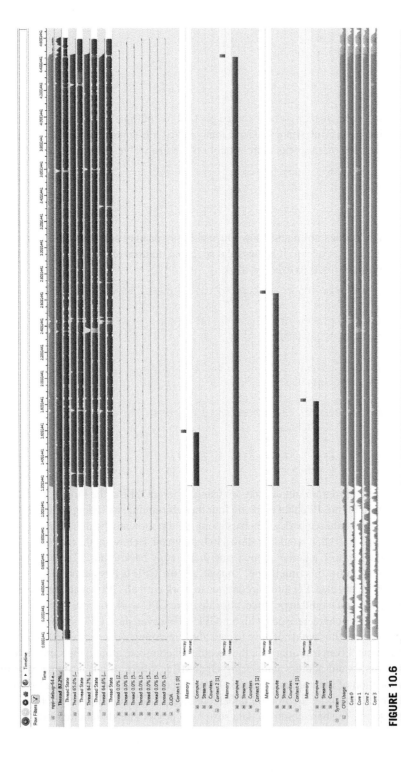

FIGURE 10.6

Multiple GPUs with OpenMP.

turn often causes serialization. We see exactly this when we place the resource allocation/deallocation within the OpenMP parallel region. Therefore, allocation/deallocation prior to and after the OpenMP parallel region achieves the best CPU utilization within that region.

In connection with this is the use of calls into the CUDA API, in particular the `cudaEventQuery` call, to check if the device has completed. Such calls should in no way be considered as low overhead. If we change the value of `loop_iteration_check` constant from one million to just one, we see the CPU count drop from 1,239,000,000 to just 16,136. In effect, every thread is then asking, in every loop iteration, for the status of the device. Thus, the CPU spends more time in the driver than doing anything else. Unfortunately, this is exactly how the `asyncAPI` is coded and one of the reasons for highlighting it here. Be sensible about any API call you make within a loop. It will take time, so don't just have the CPU poll the device every cycle. Do something useful with the CPU between device queries.

Aligned types

The aligned types example seeks to show the effect of using the `__align__(n)` directive. For example:

```
typedef struct __align__(8)
{
  unsigned int l, a;
} LA32;
```

Here the 8 part is the number of bytes the start of any element shall be aligned to. The example explains, in the associated text, that the `align` directive allows the compiler to use larger reads per thread than it would otherwise use. In the `LA32` case, the compiler can use a 64-bit read instead of two 32-bit reads. As we saw in Chapter 9, less memory transactions equate to more bandwidth. We used the vector types in the examples there, which also used the `align` directive within their definitions.

One of the things we saw in the earlier examples was that to achieve anything like peak bandwidth you had to generate a sufficient number of memory transactions in flight. Unfortunately, this SDK sample is not written with this in mind. It uses 64 blocks of 256 threads, a total of 32 warps. To load a compute 2.x device fully we need 48 warps, (64 for Kepler) so the example uses too few blocks. We therefore extended this to 1024 blocks and chose a figure of 192 threads, a figure that works well across the entire set of compute levels.

We also added the basic type output to the test so we can see baseline figures. Additionally each run was compiled specifically generating code for that device compute level. Note that this SDK example, even with the changes, only reaches about 50% of the peak memory transfer capacity. However, the relative memory bandwidth is actually the figure we're interested in here.

Initially we see the baseline figures shown in Table 10.3 and Figure 10.7 from the various devices. We can use this baseline performance table to assess how well aligned and nonaligned types perform.

As you can see from Figure 10.7, they all hit the maximum coalesced memory size at u32, or four bytes. This would equate to 32 threads, multiplied by 4 bytes, or 128 bytes in total. On Fermi, this is the size of a single cache line, so we flatline at this point on compute 2.x devices.

The GTX285 device (compute 1.3) is executing 16-thread coalesced memory reads instead of 32 as in compute 2.x devices. Thus, it benefits from back-to-back reads and can make use of the 64-bit (8-byte) reads per thread. Additionally, with twice the number of SMs than the Fermi generation cards, and a wider memory bus than the GTX470, in this particular kernel it's able to outperform the GTX470.

Table 10.3 Table of Baseline Performance across Devices

Type	GT9800	GTX285	GTX460	GTX470	Size in Bytes
u8	0.6	18	20	32	1
u16	1	36	22	48	2
u32	19	48	42	49	4
u64	23	59	43	51	8

In the 9800 GT (compute 1.1) we see a similar pattern to the GTX285. However, the major difference here is the physical memory bandwidth is only around half of that of the GTX285. Thus, we see a minor gain between 32- to 64-bit accesses per thread, much less than we see with the GTX285. See Table 10.4. We can see from running the example the percentage change in the aligned versus the nonaligned access. In Table 10.5, 100% would represent no change.

Thus, we can see that as we move back through the compute levels, especially for the early compute levels, aligned access gains greatly. In the best case we see a 31× speed improvement when adding such a directive to the data structure. Even moving to the modern GPUs we can see a 2× performance gain. Clearly, adding such a directive is very beneficial in all cases except where it causes more memory to be moved from main memory to the GPU.

Note the `RGB32` case. This is actually a 96-bit structure (three `u32`s), effectively an `int3` or `float3` type. Adding the `align` directive inserts 4 bytes of padding at the end of the structure. Although this allows coalesced accesses, 25% of the data being transferred from the memory system is being

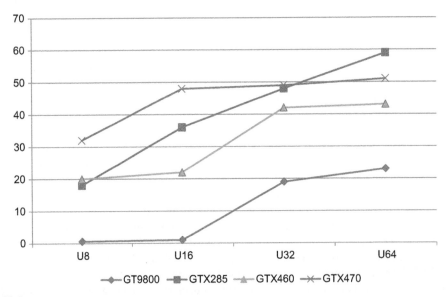

FIGURE 10.7

Graph of baseline performance across the devices (MB/s vs. transfer size).

Table 10.4 MB/s Aligned/Nonaligned for Various Devices

Type	GT9800 Nonaligned	9800 Aligned	GTX285 Nonaligned	GTX285 Aligned	GTX460 Nonaligned	GTX460 Aligned	GTX470 Nonaligned	GTX470 Aligned
RBGA8	0.6	18.7	11	48	21	41	40	49
LA32	2.4	23.3	30	59	42	42	47	51
RGB32	2.6	2	20	9	33	30	32	29
RGBA32	2.7	23.6	15	51	25	43	24	51
RGBA32_2	10.7	10.6	25	25	34	34	32	32

Table 10.5 Percentage Change for Aligned versus Nonaligned Access Patterns

Type	GTX470	GTX460	GTX285	GT9800
RBGA8	123	195	436	3117
LA32	109	100	197	971
RGB32	91	91	45	77
RGBA32	213	172	340	874
RGBA32_2	100	100	100	99

discarded. In the nonaligned case, the overfetch from the previous cache line on Fermi devices saves 33% of the subsequent memory fetch.

The conclusion we can draw from this example is that, if you are using structures, you need to think about the coalescing impact of this and, at a minimum, use the `align` directive. A better solution entirely is to create structures of arrays, rather than arrays of structures. For example, have separate red, green, and blue (RGB) color planes instead of interleaved RGB values.

DIRECTIVE-BASED PROGRAMMING

This book has largely focused on writing CUDA directly. This is good if you enjoy writing programs and are maybe from a CS (computer science) background like myself. However, very many people who find themselves writing CUDA today are not in this category. Many people's primary concern is their own problem space, not CUDA or elegant solutions from a CS perspective.

One of the great successes of OpenMP is that it's relatively easy to learn and pick up. It involves decorating the C source code with directives that tell the compiler various things about the parallel nature of the code it's currently compiling. Thus, it requires the programmer to explicitly identify parallelism within the code. The compiler takes care of the somewhat harder task of exploiting that parallelism. On the whole, it does this reasonably well.

Thus, the obvious solution to making GPU programming easier is to extend the OpenMP model to GPUs. There are, unfortunately, two standards that have/will come about for this: the OpenMP4ACC and OpenACC standards. We'll concentrate here on the OpenACC standard, as this is the one NVIDIA

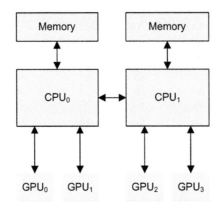

FIGURE 10.8

Multi-GPU data pathways.

is clearly supporting. Generally, you find the size of a backer and the take up among programmers will largely dictate the success or failure of a given software programming initiative. Most standards, regardless of who develops them, largely cover the same space, so in most cases learning one makes it much easier to learn another.

If you are interested in writing GPU code using directives, you will likely already have a reasonable understanding of the OpenMP directives for CPUs. The major difference we find with standards such as OpenACC is that they, and thus the programmer, also have to deal with the location of data. In an OpenMP system where there is more than a single physical socket for the CPU we have what is called a NUMA (nonuniform memory access) system.

As we can see from Figure 10.8, memory in a system with more than one CPU is attached directly to a given CPU. Thus, a process that resides on CPU_0 takes considerably longer to access memory that resides on CPU_1 than if that memory was local to CPU_0. Let's assume we have eight processes running over two CPU sockets, each CPU with four cores. To perform an exchange of data that requires many-to-many communications means we're limited to the throughput of the slowest communication link. This will be the QPI/Hypertransport link between processors over which the memory traffic to the other processor's memory bus must go. The OpenMP model simply ignores this effect and lacks many of the data concepts accelerator-based solutions require.

OpenACC

OpenACC is a move toward directive programming and very much follows in the footsteps of OpenMP, which has been very successful in providing a easy to use interface for parallelism within a single machine.

OpenACC is aimed at:

- Independent loop-based parallelism.
- Programmers who have not yet been exposed to CUDA or found it too complex.

- Programmers who have no wish to learn CUDA and are happy to abstract the details of the particular target architecture to the compiler.
- Programmers who would like rapidly to prototype an existing serial application on the GPU.
- Those who do not wish to be tied to a single vendor.

OpenACC, as with OpenMP, tries to abstract the hardware and let the programmer write standard serial code that the compiler then transforms into code that runs on the accelerator. As with OpenMP it involves adding a series of pragma statements around loops to instruct the compiler to run particular loops in parallel.

Advantages:

- Looks similar to OpenMP so it is easy to learn for anyone who has used OpenMP.
- Existing serial source code remains unchanged and is simply decorated with directives.
- Single set of source for both CPU and GPU accelerated versions.
- Accelerator vendor agnostic. The potential, as with OpenCL, to target multiple hardware platforms including CPU-based AVX acceleration.
- Takes care of many of the "details", such as moving data to and from shared memory for data the user specifies shall be cached.
- Vendor-cited studies show easy learning curve for non-CUDA programmers.
- Supports Fortran in addition to C. Allows many existing Fortran programs to benefit from acceleration without a massive rewrite.

Disadvantages:

- Not currently supported, as of 2012, under Visual Studio, so is effectively a Linux-only solution.
- Commercial product currently supported by PGI, CAPS, and Cray, so it is not part of the free CUDA SDK product suite.
- To achieve a comparable or better level of performance to OpenMP with nontrivial programs, the user must additionally specify various simple data clauses to minimize PCI-E-based transfers.
- Is targeted at single-CPU/single-GPU solutions. Does not autoscale when additional GPUs are added. Multiple GPU usage requires the use of multiple CPU threads/processes. This may change in the future.
- New features of the CUDA toolkit or the hardware may require explicit support from the compiler vendor. Currently OpenACC compiler support can take several months to switch over to a CUDA SDK release or to support a new hardware release.

The main issue with regard to OpenACC versus OpenMP is that OpenMP has no concept of various levels of memory hierarchy and locality because these concepts do not exist in the traditional CPU programming models. In OpenMP data is either thread private or global (shared).

By contrast the GPU system is much more complex. You have:

- Host memory
- GPU global memory
- GPU constant memory
- GPU block private memory (shared memory in CUDA)
- GPU thread private memory (local memory in CUDA)

The OpenACC model, for simplicity, works on the basis that the data resides on the host and is shipped to the accelerator memory space at the start of the parallel region and shipped back at the end of the parallel region. Thus, every parallel region is, by default, bounded by these implicit memory copies over the PCI-E bus.

Although a simplistic way to think of this, conceptually it's an easy way to ensure correctness at the potential expense of performance. If you had only one calculation and would not reuse the data, then this is effectively what you'd do in CUDA anyway. If, however, you plan to make a number of transformations on the data, then you need to explicitly specify what data is to remain on the device by adding data qualifiers to the directives.

So let's look at a simple program to give some idea of how it might be converted to OpenMP/OpenACC. If we take the classic reduction, you typically see the following:

```
long int reduce_serial(const int * __restrict__ const host_ptr,
                       const int num_elements)
{
 long int sum = 0;

 for (int i=0; i < num_elements; i++)
      sum += host_ptr[i];

 return sum;
}


long int reduce_openmp(const int * __restrict__ const host_ptr,
                       const int num_elements)
{
 long int sum = 0;

#pragma omp parallel for reduction(+:sum)
  for (int i=0; i < num_elements; i++)
  {
   sum += host_ptr[i];
  }

 return sum;
}

long int reduce_openacc(const int * __restrict__ const host_ptr,
                        const int num_elements)
{
  long int sum = 0;

#pragma acc kernels
  for (int i=0; i < num_elements; i++)
  {
   sum += host_ptr[i];
  }

 return sum;
}
```

As you can see all we do is replace the OpenMP directive with an OpenACC directive. We then compile with the vendor-supplied OpenACC compiler. This may generate anything from high-level CUDA code to raw PTX code. It will then usually invoke the NVCC compiler to generate the target GPU code. Some vendors support additional targets other than simply NVIDIA GPUs.

During the compilation stage most vendors' compilers provide statistics about how they are transforming the serial code to device code. However, this is a little like the -v option in NCC, in that you need to be able to understand what the compiler is telling you. We look here at an example of the PGI compiler output.

```
Accelerator kernel generated
60, #pragma acc loop gang, vector /* blockIdx.x threadIdx.x */
CC 1.3 : 21 registers; 1024 shared, 20 constant, 0 local memory bytes; 100% occupancy
CC 2.0 : 23 registers; 1048 shared, 40 constant, 0 local memory bytes; 100% occupancy
```

To understand this output, you need to understand how the OpenACC terminology maps onto CUDA terminology (Table 10.6).

The first line states that the kernel occupied 60 gangs (blocks in CUDA terminology). It then states it generated output for "CC 1.3 and CC 2.0," compute capacity 1.3 and 2.0 devices, respectively. It also tells you the number of registers used, the amount of shared memory per block used, the number of bytes of constant memory per block, and any registers spilled to local memory.

Finally, it calculates the ideal number of threads (OpenACC calls these vectors) to achieve near 100% occupancy as possible based on the number of registers and shared memory the kernel is using. It may, however, not always select the best values for a given kernel/data pattern. Specifying this allows us to override or partially override such choices.

It will look at your data and decide on the best launch parameters (number of threads, number of blocks, number of grids, etc.). It will also automatically try to allocate data to constant and/or global memory. You are free to override these selections if you wish.

To override the default behavior of mirroring global data on the host (automatic background update commands), you need to specify how the data must be managed. This can be done as follows:

```
#pragma acc data <directives>
```

where <directives> can be one of the following plus some additional more complex ones not shown here:

copy (data1, data2, …)—Maintain an identical CPU version by copying in at the start of the kernel and out at the end (the default behavior).
copyin (data1, data2, …)—Only copy data to the GPU and do not copy it back, that is, discard the GPU data. This is useful for read-only data the GPU will process.

Table 10.6 OpenACC and CUDA Terminology

OpenACC	CUDA
Gangs	Blocks
Workers	Warps
Vectors	Threads

copyout (data1, data2, ...)—Only copy data from the GPU back to the CPU. Useful for declaring output data on the GPU.

create (data1, data2, ...)—Allocates temporary storage on the GPU with no copy operation in either direction.

present (data1, data2, ...)—Data is already present on the GPU so does not need to be copied or allocated anew.

Be aware that the OpenACC model expects you to use the C99 standard and in particular the __restrict__ keyword in C to specify that any pointers used do not alias with one another. Failure to do this will likely result in your code failing to vectorize.

You can tell if adding data directives helps (it almost always will) by using the PGI_ACC_TIME=1 (vendor-specific) option. This, in the case of the PGI compiler, will enable profiling. It will then tell you how often the kernel was called, the block dimensions of the kernel and how long it took, and finally how much time was spent transferring data. It's this later part that is often the most critical and where the data clauses help out. You can also use the standard profiling tools available in Linux, such as the Visual Profiler, to see into what the OpenACC compiler is doing in reality. In doing so you may spot issues you would otherwise be unaware of.

In being able to see the block size chosen you can also then perform certain optimizations to it. For example, you can specify less blocks and threads than you have data elements. By default, OpenACC compilers tend to select one thread per element, although there is nothing in the standard to say they have to. Thus, if you'd like to process four elements per thread, something we have seen tends to work well, you can do it by specifying a smaller number of blocks and threads:

```
#define NUM_ELEM 32768
#pragma acc kernels loop gang(64), vector(128)
for( int i = 0; i < NUM_ELEM; i++ )
{
 x[i] += y[i];
}
```

Here we've specified the loop should use 64 blocks (gangs) of 128 threads (vectors) each. Thus, we have 8192 active threads on the device. Assuming a 16 SM device such as the GTX580, this would be four blocks per SM, each of 128 threads. This equates to 16 warps per SM, which is too few for ideal occupancy on the GTX580. To solve the issue, we'd need to increase the block (gang) or thread (vector) count.

Depending on the particular algorithm, you may wish to process more than one element per thread, rather than increase the block or thread count. As long as the number of elements is known to the compiler, as in the previous example, it will process multiple elements per thread, in this case four.

Remember also, as with regular CUDA, threads in reality run as warps, groups of 32 threads. Allocating 33 threads allocates 64 threads in the hardware, 31 of which do nothing but consume space resources on the device. Always allocate thread blocks (vectors in OpenACC) in blocks of 32.

Also as with CUDA, if you specify gangs or vectors (blocks or threads), which you don't have to, then the usual kernel launch rules apply. Thus, there is a limit on the number of threads a block can support, which will change depending on the compute level of the hardware you are targeting. Generally, you'll find 64, 128, 192, and 256 vales work well with compute 1.x devices. Values of 128,

192, 256, 384, and 512 work well with compute 2.x devices. The 256 value is usually the best for the compute 3.x platform.

However, when considering adding any specifiers here, consider the likely impact of future hardware and how this might limit the use of other accelerator targets. By specifying nothing you are letting the compiler select what it thinks is the best value. When a new GPU comes out with more threads per block and more blocks per SM, once the vendors update the compiler to accommodate it, it all works. If you do specify these parameters, you should be specifying some multiple of the current maximum to allow for your code to run on future devices without running out of blocks.

By default the OpenACC model uses synchronous kernel calls. That is, the host processor will wait for the GPU to complete and then continue execution once the GPU kernel call returns. This is akin to making a function call in C as opposed to spawning a worker thread and later converging.

You should be aware by now that this approach, although nice to develop the initial application on, should be replaced with an asynchronous model as soon as the application is running well. You probably have a reasonable multicore CPU in the machine and could make good use of it while the GPU is off calculating something. On the top of the list of things to allocate to the CPU should be those operations requiring few compute actions compared to loads and stores to and from memory.

One of the reasons why we see the reduction operation perform better, or at least the at same speed as the GPU, is the amount of work done per memory read/write. To calculate data on the GPU we need to either generate it there or send it over the PCI-E bus. If you are shipping two data items over the bus just to perform a simple operation such as addition, forget it and do it on the CPU instead. The cost of the PCI-E transfer greatly outweighs any other consideration in such a scenario. The best candidates for the GPU are those computationally intensive areas, or where the additional memory bandwidth on the GPU can make a difference.

Thus, OpenACC provides the `async` clause for kernels and data to allow them to run asynchronously to the host and perform asynchronous transfers with the host.

```
#pragma acc kernels loop async
for (i=0; i< num_elem; i++)
{
...
}
```

Asynchronous transfers require the use of pinned memory, that is, memory that cannot be swapped to disk. You do not need to explicitly care about this in OpenACC as you do with CUDA. Specifying the `async` clause will cause the OpenACC compiler to use pinned memory under the hood for transfers. Of course, one thing to remember when using an asynchronous operation is that you cannot change the data that is being transferred or operated on by the kernel until the asynchronous operation has completed.

Once people have mastered asynchronous communication and achieved the best performance they are able to on a single-core/GPU pair, the obvious question is: Can I speed up my application by using multiple GPUs? The answer is of course yes, and very often you'll see near linear scaling if you can stay within a single node.

The OpenACC standard supports only a "one CPU thread per GPU" view of multiple GPUs on a single node. If you plan on performing some work on the CPU, this makes perfect sense, as it allows you to exploit the full potential of a multicore CPU. Thus, with OpenMP you simply launch a number of threads using the OpenMP directive

```
#pragma omp parallel num_thread(4)
```

Assuming you have a quad-core CPU and four GPU cards attached, then you would specify to OpenACC that you wish the current thread to use a given GPU.

```
#pragma omp parallel num_thread(4)
{
    const int cpu_thread_id = omp_get_thread_num();
    acc_set_device_num( cpu_thread_id, acc_device_nvidia );
}
```

If you have only two GPUs in the system then you might be better off specifying two threads for OpenMP. If you wished to make use of four threads, but only have two for GPU usage, you could do the following:

```
const int num_gpus = acc_get_num_devices( acc_device_nvidia );

#pragma omp parallel num_thread(4)
{
  const int cpu_thread_id = omp_get_thread_num();
  if (cpu_thread_id < num_gpus)
  {
   // Do CPU and GPU work
   acc_set_device_num( cpu_thread_id, acc_device_nvidia );
  }
  else
  {
      // Do CPU only work
  }
}
```

We can do the same in MPI by using

```
const int num_gpus = acc_get_num_devices( acc_device_nvidia );

// Get my MPI virtual process id (rank)
int my_rank;
MPI_Comm_rank( MPI_COMM_WORLD, &my_rank );

if ( my_rank < num_gpus)
{
// Do CPU and GPU work e.g. workers
   acc_set_device_num( my_rank, acc_device_nvidia );
}
else
{
  // Do CPU only work, e.g. master
}
```

One issue to be careful of here is that the `acc_set_device_num` API call is a one-time event only per host thread. This is very much the way the `cudaSetDevice` call used to work prior to the CUDA 4.x SDK. You cannot select a context from a single host thread and thus control multiple GPUs from that single thread. The only model supported is one where there is a single host thread per GPU context.

Note that a dedicated 1:1 ratio of CPU cores to GPUs is the ideal for heavily used systems. However, oversubscribing GPUs to CPU cores can be useful, as rarely will GPU programs actually saturate the GPU. Thus, there may be points where the GPUs are underutilized, typically at synchronization points or between kernel invocations. In cases where you have a master/worker arrangement, which is typical in MPI, it can be beneficial to dedicate a non-GPU, CPU core to be the master.

One aspect I should touch on here is memory patterns. OpenACC, when implemented on an accelerator that does coalescing of global memory, will be just as badly affected by a poor memory layout as a CUDA program will. There is no automatic transpose. You need to think about your memory layout and create one that is optimal for a GPU (data in columns of 32 elements, rather than sequential rows).

Overall OpenACC represents a very interesting development in GPU programming and potentially opens up the GPU programming arena to many non-GPU programmers. Many of these people will progress to use learn CUDA, as it's perfectly possible to mix OpenACC and CUDA. Thus, you can start with OpenACC, and if you find specific areas where you need that extra control, switch over to CUDA, while leaving most of the application untouched.

WRITING YOUR OWN KERNELS

We've presented a number of other options in this chapter that range from specifying the parallelism at a high level and having the compiler do the heavy lifting, to using libraries developed by those far better at exploiting the hardware than you are. You will never, and in fact probably should not try to, be the best in everything. Tools such as compiler directives and libraries allow you to leverage the effort of others to achieve your goals. Your knowledge resides primarily within your own field of interest.

As a professional developer, or even as a student, you should be conscious of the time you take to develop a solution. It may be technically challenging to develop the most efficient parallel quick sort, but probably some bright computer science graduate has already written a paper on it. If you are hiring, then the obvious thing to do is bring this person on board. Buying in knowledge, in terms of people or software, is something that can give you a huge head start on whomever your competition may be.

It also makes a lot of sense to select libraries where they cover something that is not your area of expertise. If you are developing an image blur algorithm, for example, loading/saving the images from the disk is not really what you are interested in. There are a number of open-source, or commercial, libraries that may cover this aspect of your development.

One common problem you may encounter using libraries is memory allocation. Most CPU-based solutions, if they allocate memory, do not allocate pinned memory. Thus, an image library that returns a pointer to the loaded image will cause a slowdown in your application when you transfer that image data to the GPU. Therefore, look for libraries that allow the user to control the memory management, or are GPU aware and support pinned memory.

The next issue we hit with the directive and library approach is they are, generally, not multi-GPU aware unless written as such. As you can usually get up to four GPU cards into a workstation, this approach is a bit like using only one of the cores in a standard quad-core CPU. The programming required to support multi-GPU configurations is not trivial, but neither is it rocket science. The libraries we use internally at CudaDeveloper support multiple GPU setups. It complicates the handling of the data and requires a lot more thought, but is certainly doable.

The issue of how much you need to write yourself often is a question of performance. In using directives you trade a certain percentage of performance for quicker program development. Libraries, by comparison, may bring a significant speedup along with a reduction in development effort, but at the potential cost of flexibility and license issues. Many are restricted in terms of commercial usage, which simply reflects that if you intend to avoid your own development costs by using libraries, you should be prepared to pay for that privilege. For academic usage, simply acknowledging the contribution is usually sufficient.

Thus, there are a number of reasons why you might chose to develop your own kernels in CUDA. This text provides good insight to the issues of developing kernels using CUDA. The basic principles (coalesced memory access, fully utilizing the hardware, avoiding contention of resources, understanding the hardware limitations, data locality) apply regardless of whether you write the kernels yourself or abstract them to someone else's problem.

We've covered in this section some of the NVIDIA-provided libraries. If you are working in a field that these cover, why would you not chose to use such libraries? They are developed by the manufacturer to run well on their hardware. They are designed to be used as the basic building blocks of more complex algorithms. NVIDIA's licensing terms are very generous in that they want people to use the libraries and to build CUDA applications. This is hardly surprising when you consider wider acceptance of CUDA means more GPUs get sold, and of course the more valuable your knowledge of CUDA becomes.

The question is really does this bring you sufficient level of performance? Most people program in a high-level language because it's much more productive than something like Assembler. The better programmers out there understand both C and Assembler in great detail. They know when they should use C for the productivity gains and know when a small number of functions need to be hand-coded in Assembler. The question of using libraries/directives is largely a similar one. You could write everything yourself, but unless you have to, why make your life so hard?

When developing applications for GPUs, a good approach is to first get a prototype working on the CPU side. Consider how you'd like to make that CPU version multicore aware and if it would benefit the application. What will be the CPU/GPU work balance? How will you create threads on the CPU side if you need them? However, at least initially, stick with a single CPU thread and a single GPU, but think at the start about what you want to achieve in the end.

Now think about the host/device transfers. The transfer-compute-transfer model will usually (depending on the ratios) underutilize the GPU. To some extent we can overlap transfer/compute depending on the hardware you have to support.

Next think about the memory hierarchy within the GPU. What locality (registers, shared, cache, constant, texture) are you going to exploit on the GPU? What data layout do you need for these various types of data stores?

Now think about the kernel design. The decomposition into threads and blocks has implications in terms of the amount of interthread/interblock communication and resource usage. What serialization or contention issues are you likely to have?

Once you have a working CPU/GPU application, profile it and get it working as efficiently as you can. At this stage keep a very close eye on correctness, preferably through some back-to-back automated tests.

This brings us then to the issue of efficiency of the kernel implementation and where you need to consider the CUDA/libraries/directives choice. Given the plan of how you'd like to use the GPU, how does your choice here affect your ability to do that? Is your choice to use our CUDA/libraries/ directives positively or negatively impacting performance, and by what percentage?

Consider shared memory as an example. OpenACC has a `cache` qualifier that instructs the compiler to place and hold this data in shared memory, a resource it may otherwise ignore or use depending on the compiler vendor. Libraries rarely expose shared memory, but often use it very efficiently internally and will usually document this fact. Newer hardware may have different implementations. For example, Kepler can configure shared memory as 32- or 64-bit wide, meaning many financial and other applications could benefit significantly from this optimization.

Can you make use of such significant optimizations? If you are reliant on the directive vendor or library developer to do this, what level of support will they provide and how long might this take? If the library was written by a student as part of his or her thesis work, unless you or someone else is willing to maintain it or you pay someone to do so, it won't get updated. If you require a feature the directive vendor doesn't think there is a widespread need for, it's unlikely they will develop it just for your application.

When you have an efficient single-CPU/single-GPU implementation, move it to a multicore/ multi-GPU solution as appropriate for your workload. For GPU-dominated workflow where the CPU is underutilized, the simple single-CPU core controls and all-GPU asynchronous model works fine. Where the CPU core is also loaded, how might using multiple threads and thus one GPU per thread help? With the underutilized CPU load case, is there not something useful the multicore CPU can be doing? Optimal design is about using the resources you have most effectively to solve a given problem.

Moving to a multithread/multi-GPU approach may be a painless or very painful experience. Your GPU global memory data is now split over multiple GPUs' memory spaces. What inter-GPU communication is now needed? The P2P model, if supported, is usually the best method for such communication. Alternatively, the coordination or transfers need to be done by the host. Having a single CPU coordinate N GPUs may be simpler that having multiple CPU threads coordinate those same GPUs.

How well do your directives or libraries support a multi-GPU approach? Are they thread safe, or do they maintain an internal state assuming there will only be one instance or CPU thread? What support is there for exchanging data and concurrent operations? Are you forced to serially send or receive data to or from each GPU in turn, or can you perform N simultaneous transfers?

When selecting tools or libraries, consider how mature they are and for what purpose they were written. How do you debug the code when it goes wrong, as it inevitably will? Are you left on your own to figure out the issue or is there support provided for bug fixes, feature requests, etc.? When were they written and for which GPU do they work best? Are they optimized for, or aware of, different GPU generations?

By thinking about your design in advance and realizing where you'd like to end up, you can decide what sort of software/tools you will need at the outset. You may be able to prototype a solution with one approach, but may ultimately have to use CUDA to get the performance and efficiency you'd like.

There is no mystical "silver bullet" in software development. You have to think about the design, plan how you will achieve it, and understand how far certain approaches can take you.

CONCLUSION

We have looked at a number of approaches to development of code for the GPU in this chapter. What appeals to you will largely depend on your background and how comfortable and experienced you currently are with CUDA. I specifically encourage you to look at the NVIDA-provided libraries as they provide very large coverage of many common problems.

We have looked at a number of the nondomain-specific examples in the SDK, specifically because everyone can follow and benefit from looking at these. There are many domain-specific examples in the SDK. I encourage you to explore these as, with now a good understanding of CUDA, you will be able to get a lot more out of looking at these examples.

I hope you have seen from this chapter that writing everything yourself in CUDA is not the *only* option. Significant productivity gains can be made by the use of libraries. Directives also allow a much higher level of programming that many people may prefer to the more low-level CUDA approach. People make different choices for various reasons. Understand what the key criteria are for you, and select accordingly.

Designing GPU-Based Systems

11

INTRODUCTION

Server environments are typically large, specially air conditioned rooms, often sealed against the excessive noise they generate. They consume hundreds of kilowatts to many megawatts of power. Typically, the computers are arranged by 1U, 2U, or 4U nodes, which slot into a large rack unit. These racks are often interconnected using a high-speed interconnect, such as InfiniBand, as shown in Figure 11.1.

Each node is connected to every other node within a given server by a high-speed switch. This can be something as simple as gigabit Ethernet. Most motherboards ship with two gigabit Ethernet ports, allowing one internal and one external connection per node. All the external connections go to a common switch, which itself sits on a high-speed backbone network such as InfiniBand.

This arrangement has one very interesting property: Communication from one node to another within the server rack may be considerably faster than communication with a node in another server rack. This type of arrangement leads to a nonuniform memory access (NUMA) architecture. As a programmer, you have to deal with this transition. You can simply choose to ignore the problem, but this leads to poor performance. You need to think about where the data resides and what data sharing is needed between nodes.

If you look at a multi-GPU system, you will see it's actually quite similar to a single-server box shown in Figure 11.1. Instead of a gigabit Ethernet connection between nodes, each node is a GPU card that is connected to a central PCI-E bus. Each group of GPU cards make up a much more powerful node, which is connected via a high-speed link to other such nodes, as shown in Figure 11.2.

Notice in the figure a total of seven GPUs within a single node. In practice, this is only possible using specialist racks or liquid-cooled GPU systems. One such example we built at CudaDeveloper is shown in Figure 11.3.

Most GPU cards are dual-slot cards, with the exception of some of the older G80-based systems. Most motherboards support only up to a maximum of four PCI-E slots, meaning for any air-cooled system you are limited to four GPUs per node if you have a desktop form factor. Given that each Kepler series card is on the order of 3 teraflops of processing power, that's 12 teraflops on the desktop, not in a remote server room.

One of the main issues limiting the use of high-speed computing these days is power and heat. As the clock rate increases, so does the heat generated. As the heat goes up, the power consumed for the same clock rate also rises. The thermal envelope is exceeded at just over 212°F (100°C) for Fermi devices. A system with more than two GPUs next to one another can easily start to rapidly climb toward this threshold if there is poor airflow.

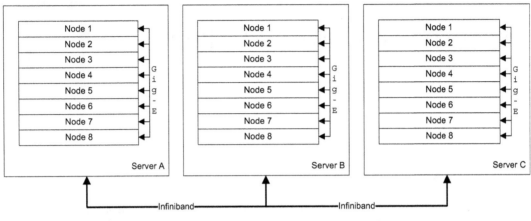

FIGURE 11.1

Typical high-performance computing (HPC) setup.

Hold your hand behind the exhaust of a modern GPU and it's somewhat like putting your hand near a hair dryer. Multiply this four times and very rapidly most small offices find they have a nice heating system included with their teraflop workstation free of charge.

The 580 series Fermi cards (GF110) introduced a much better vapor chamber cooling system later dropped on the GTX680 due to the lower heat output. With this, hollow copper pipes contain a liquid that quickly takes the heat away to the cooling fins and fans. This is very similar to liquid-cooled systems, except the heat still has to be dissipated from the fins using fans inside the small area of the GPU card. Keeping the GPUs cooler means less power consumption and less heat generation. However, there are limits to how far you can go with air-based cooling and ultimately this will limit the ability of GPUs to

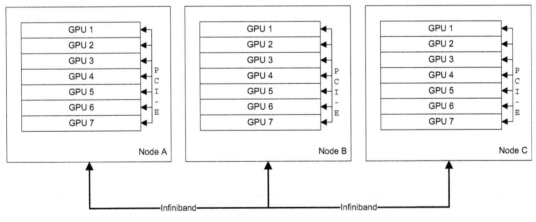

FIGURE 11.2

GPU HPC setup.

FIGURE 11.3

3x GTX290 (6 GPUs) liquid-cooled machine built at CudaDeveloper.

grow significantly from where they currently are. A typical 480/580 series card can draw up to 250 W per card. Thus, a four-card system is easily exceeding 1 kW per node. The Kepler GTX680 comes in at just under 200 W per card with the dual GTX690 managing to come in at under 300 W.

However, the GPU is not the only component in a typical high-speed workstation or server. We'll look at each one of these in turn and see how they impact the system design. The key aspect to remember in designing any system is the slowest component will limit the overall throughput no matter what speed GPUs you have.

CPU PROCESSOR

The choice of processor is primarily one between Intel and AMD. Ignoring obsolete processors, you have a choice today of the Intel I7 series or the AMD Phenom/FX series. Note, the Sandybride socket 1156/1155 designs are not considered here due to the limited PCI-E lanes provided. Looking at these options, we have:

Intel I7 Nehalem (Socket 1366; Figure 11.4):
- 4 to 6 Cores
- QPI-based DDR-3 triple-bank memory interface
- 125 W thermal design
- 36 PCI-E 2.0 Lanes

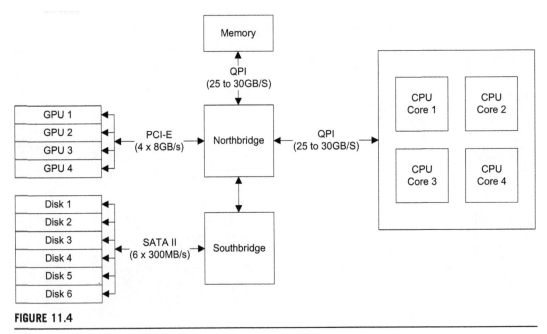

FIGURE 11.4

Typical I7 Nehalem layout.

Intel I7 Sandybridge-E (Socket 2011)
- 4 to 6 Cores (up to 8 on the Xeon variant)
- QPI-based DDR-3 quad-bank memory interface
- 130 W thermal design
- 40 PCI-E 2.0 Lanes

AMD Phenom II / FX
- Hypertransport-based DDR-2/DDR-3 memory interface
- 125 W thermal design
- 42 PCI-E 2.0 Lanes

Performance wise, the Intel parts are typically faster than the AMD parts for a similar number of cores and clock speed. Price wise, the AMD part is usually significantly cheaper. Low Power versions are also available and are certainly attractive for machines in constant operation. However, the choice of motherboards supporting four or more PCI-E slots is limited, meaning you might have to settle for less GPUs per node, which may be an issue. The Sandybridge-E platform is significantly faster than either of the other solutions, but brings a significant price premium both in terms of processor and motherboard.

You typically allocate one thread core per GPU in applications that require significant CPU involvement. This gives the opportunity to fix a thread or process to a physical core. Unless you have more than four GPUs, or you have significant extra workload for a CPU core, the additional two cores in the hex core device may be under utilized. The I7 in this instance is a clear winner on the performance side. However, with six GPUs, slotting in a six-core device may well prove advantageous.

One other alternative is the recently released IvyBridge based Intel processor line. This supports PCI-E 3.0 standard. With the socket 2011 Ivybridge-E scheduled for release late 2013 this will finally bring a PCI-E 3.0 solution with enough PCI-E lanes for GPU based computing.

GPU DEVICE

The GPU in a GPU machine is obviously the most important consideration in any design. GPUs change generations about every 12–24 months, a slightly faster rate than the CPU side. So far we've seen an approximate doubling of GPU performance every 18–24 months, exactly following Moore's law, for now anyway. The CPUs did this for many years, but there are limits to just how fast you can make a single core go. As long as there is sufficient parallelism in the problem domain, GPUs should continue this scaling for quite a few years to come, mirroring the multicore growth seen in CPUs.

So what are the major considerations of a GPU? First, there is no point in not having the last generation of hardware. With a doubling of performance in every major hardware generation for approximately the same power budget, there is little point in keeping old hardware around unless you already have acceptable performance. Going from 2 minutes to 1 minute is no big deal, but from 10 hours to 5 hours, or 10 days to 5 days can make a huge difference, both in terms of usability, power and space budget.

The GPU market is driven by the gamers—thank them, for they have brought parallel hardware to the masses at commodity prices. GPU hardware is split into two major areas, the gaming GPUs and the server GPUs. NVIDIA provides the Tesla range of GPUs for the server and workstation market with a number of key advantages over their desktop cousins:

- Large memory support
- ECC memory support (Fermi onward)
- Tesla compute cluster driver
- Higher double-precision math
- Large memory bus width
- SMI (system management interrupt)
- Status LEDs

Let's look at what these are and why they are important for the server market.

Large memory support

Shipping data onto and off of a GPU is slow. You have, at best, a 5 GB/s bidirectional PCI-E 2.0 bus (10 GB/s total) bandwidth to the main CPU memory. The larger the memory on the GPU, the more data you can leave on the GPU. This avoids the need to transfer data to or from the GPU. Tesla cards typically come with 4 GB to 6 GB of memory. With the introduction of Fermi, we finally moved away from the 32-bit limit on memory space, allowing GPUs to have up to 6 GB of memory. Given a maximum 4 GPUs per CPU, that is a total of 24 GB of RAM, easily within the limit on memory size you'll find on most server boards.

ECC memory support

ECC memory is a special type of memory used in server environments, or where the memory may be subject to corruption. With large amounts of electromagnetic interference, it's possible that memory cells may be changed to some random value with non ECC memory. The higher the density of electronics around the device, the more electromagnetic radiation is generated and the higher the error rate. Placing lots of GPUs into a rack and then placing that rack next to several other racks generates a significant amount of electronic noise. For years now, servers on the CPU side have used ECC. ECC can both detect and correct errors found within the memory, making it ideal for this type of environment.

Memory corruption of the data on the GPU doesn't generally matter for gamers and would usually go entirely unnoticed. It may result in an odd pixel, or a strangely appearing object. However, as the frame buffer is typically redrawn 50 to 60 times a second, completely from scratch, it's very hard to see any single pixel getting corrupted.

When you shift this to the compute world, however, corruption of the data memory means the wrong answer for one or more elements in the output dataset, which is clearly not acceptable. You can tackle this in a number of ways, either using ECC or running every calculation twice to check the result. The latter choice requires you to double up on the hardware, which effectively means twice the initial investment and twice the operating costs—a less-than-optimal solution.

Tesla compute cluster driver (TCC)

This is a Tesla-only supported driver. The Tesla cards have no graphics output and are designed for compute only. There is a considerable overhead and latency on the kernel calls due to the need to support the graphics interface. By removing this, the TCC drivers produce a significant increase in performance over the standard GeForce driver. There are also certain parts of the hardware that are enabled only on Tesla devices, such as ECC and dual PCI-E copy engines.

The TCC driver is included in the standard NVIDIA driver download package, but can only be enabled on Tesla-based hardware.

Higher double-precision math

As most games have very little, if any, double-precision math present, the Fermi range of cards comes with one of the two double-precision units within each SM disabled. Thus, the standard GeForce Fermi cards have around half of the double-precision performance of the equivalent Tesla cards. Single-float performance is comparable, and in many cases faster on the GeForce cards due to the higher clock rates. However, if double precision is important in your application, as it is in many financial applications, it makes sense to install only Telsa-based GPUs.

Larger memory bus width

The Tesla cards, being the top-end cards, are usually the ones with all the SMs enabled. NVIDIA charges much more for the server-level cards, so they can afford to "bin" the GPUs according to how many SMs are functional. Those with nonfunctional SMs can be sold as cheaper GeForce cards where having one or two SM units disabled make little difference to overall game performance.

Having all the SMs enabled usually also means the full bus width is available for transfers to or from the global memory on the card. As memory bandwidth is often the single limiting factor in a lot of algorithms, having 512 bits as opposed to 448 bits can make a significant difference. In the older G200 series cards, you often saw a reasonable performance increase at a considerable cost increase, by using a 285 card over a 275 card, due to this additional bus bandwidth. The GeForce 480 and 580 cards have the same issue, with 320 bits versus 384 bits, a 20% improvement on memory bus bandwidth alone, not to mention the additional SM unit. The Kepler targeted for compute, the Tesla K20 model, also has a 384 bit bus as compared with the 256 bit bus found on the GTX680.

SMI

SMI is a useful feature for remotely querying devices over a network. In a large data center you may have thousands of GPUs installed. There are already existing centrally managed solutions for CPU nodes and adding SMI support simply extends this to GPUs as well. Thus, the GPU has the capability to respond to a request and report a number of useful pieces of information to the central management system.

Status LEDs

The Tesla cards have a number of LEDs on the back of the card that show the card's status. With the exception of the GeForce 295 cards, these LEDs are not present on any standard GeForce card. They allow a technician to walk around an installation of GPUs and identify the GPU that is failing. In a data center with a thousand GPUs, being able to quickly see if any node has a problem is a huge benefit to the IT people looking at the system.

PCI-E BUS

The Intel system uses the Northbridge/Southbridge chipset design. The Northbridge is basically a fast switch, connecting all the high-speed peripherals. The slower Southbridge handles all the mundane requests, like USB, mouse, keyboards, etc. On AMD-based systems, and also the later Intel designs, some aspects of the PCI-E bus controller are integrated into the CPU, rather than being a completely separate device.

On the Intel I7 Nehalem systems, you get a total of 36 (40 on Sandybridge-E) lines of PCI-E bus bandwidth available. These are combined into groups of 16 lines to form a single PCI-E 2.0 X16 link. This is what the GPU will utilize, giving a total of 5 GB/s in either direction. A single I7 or AMD processor supports up to two GPUs in full X16 mode. As you add more GPUs, the number of lanes, and thus the bandwidth allocated to each GPU, is reduced. With four GPUs, you're running an X8 link, or 2.5 GB/s in either direction.

Most motherboards do not support more than 4 PCI-E slots. However, some do, using a special NVIDIA multiplexer device (NF200) to multiplex up the number of lanes. Motherboards such as the ASUS supercomputer are an example. This board supports seven PCI-E slots.

When designing a system, remember that other devices may also need to sit on the PCI-E bus. The six GPU workstations shown in Figure 11.3 also has a 24-channel PCI-E raid card in the last PCI-E slot. Other systems may use InfiniBand or gigabit Ethernet network cards in the spare PCI-E slots, so it's not just GPUs that need to be considered.

PCI-E 3.0 is also now available on many motherboards. This will significantly boost the current bus bandwidth available to each GPU because the same number of lanes on PCI-E 3.0 equates to double that of PCI-E 2.0. However, PCI-E 3.0 is only supported on the Kepler line of graphics cards.

GEFORCE CARDS

An alternative to the Tesla cards are the GeForce cards. The Tesla cards are aimed at the server and corporate market. If you are a student or an engineer learning CUDA on your own and do not have access to these cards through your company or university, a GeForce card is entirely suitable for developing CUDA code. If you are developing for the consumer market, clearly these are what you need to develop on.

The consumer cards vary primarily in terms of compute level. Currently, almost any card you purchase from the 400 or 500 series will contain a Fermi-class GPU. The 600 series cards are mostly Kepler based designs. If you specifically want an older card, the previous generations (compute 1.3) are numbered in the 200 series. The compute 1.1/1.2 cards are typically numbered in the 9000 series. Finally, the 8000 series are usually compute 1.0 cards, which are actually pretty difficult to program well compared with the more modern designs.

Within a generation of the cards, the cards vary by the number of SMs and the global memory present. You should purchase a card with at least 1 GB of memory. Currently, the largest memory capacity of a GeForce card is 4 GB. Be aware that most GPU cards are noisy compared with a typically quiet PC. If this is an issue for you, select one of the less powerful cards, or opt for a card with a customized cooler such as the MSI Frozr series. Note the later 500 series cards are typically quieter than the 400 series cards as they are based on a revision of the silicon that reduced both power consumption and heat. The Kepler based cards tend to be marginally quieter than the 500 series cards due to generating less heat. However, as with anything, you get what you pay for. Thus, a card near the top end of the price scale for a given series (560, 570, 580, etc.) will typically be quieter than one at the very low end.

In terms of card design, almost all the cards produced are based on the standard NVIDIA layout. Thus, they are largely identical and vary in terms of brand, accessories, and software provided. The exceptions to this are the very high-end cards where the manufacturers have actually innovated. The Gigabyte SOC (Super OverClock) brand is perhaps the best example of this. The typical stock single-fan cooler is replaced by a three-fan cooler. The GPUs have been speed-binned to select those that work reliably at a higher speed, typically a 10% overclock. Power circuitry has been redesigned to provide additional power to reliably drive the GPU to this specification.

In terms of a low-end card, the GTX520/GTX610 is one of the cheapest cards at less than $50 USD, or around £30 or 35 Euros. It doesn't require any special power connectors and will fit in just about any PC. It's an ideal low-budget card to do some CUDA development on.

On the liquid cooling side, the Zoltac Infinity Edition card is perhaps the most useful in that it comes with a sealed and self-contained liquid cooling system, similar to some systems available for the CPU. As such, all you need to do is replace the existing exhaust fan with the provided radiator and fan. It is ideal for a single-card solution, but not a good choice for a multi-GPU system. The Point of View (POV) TGT Beast GTX580 Liquid cooled edition comes with 3 GB of RAM and a prefitted water block that can be easily connected to additional blocks. Pre-fitted liquid cooled cards are also available from EVGA, MSI and PNY.

CPU MEMORY

CPU memory may not seem like such a consideration. However, any transfer of data must come from somewhere and eventually return to the sender. At the maximum 5 GB/s of PCI-E 2.0 bandwidth in both directions, each GPU card can use up to 10 GB/s of memory bandwidth.

The amount of bandwidth you need depends a lot on your data structures and how much you can keep on the GPU cards. You may have a large input dataset but a tiny output dataset, or vice versa.

Assuming a balanced dataset, having three GPU cards (total 30 GB/s peak bandwidth) can saturate the CPU memory bandwidth without the CPU itself actually doing any work. Four or more cards means you may need the server edition of the I7 Nehalem or the Sandybridge-E processor with the 6 GT/s QPI bus connector just to keep the cards supplied with data if your application has large input and output bandwidth requirements.

Standard 1066/1333 MHz memory clocks will be a bottleneck on multi-GPU systems if there is a lot of data needing to be transferred. For applications that are primarily compute bound, it will make little difference. DDR-3 memory can be safely clocked up to 2 GHz on the I7 platform, but rarely this high on the AMD platform. Officially neither device supports memory clocks beyond 1333 MHz. Memory also comes with certain timing information, sometimes abbreviated to CL7, CL8, or CL9. This broadly measures the response time to requests for data. Thus, the same CL7 memory at 1066 MHz may also be sold as CL9 memory at 1333 MHz. As with most computer hardware, the higher the clock rate and the lower the response time, the more expensive the memory becomes.

Special memory DIMMs containing embedded information (Intel XMP) are available. With the appropriate motherboard support, they can automatically be used to safely clock the memory to an optimum rate. Of course, this certified memory, due to the licensing costs associated with such a brand, is more expensive than the noncertified memory that may in all other respects be identical.

Be aware, however, the higher the clock rate, the more heat and power is consumed. Memory devices are the same in this respect. Typically, you should budget for around 1 W of power per gigabyte of DDR-3 present on the motherboard.

As well as the speed of the memory, you need to consider the total capacity of memory you will likely need. The fastest transfers are achieved using page-locked memory, which is where a dedicated block of memory is allocated to each card in the system. Using the Tesla cards, you may wish to transfer up to 6 GB to the card, the full memory capacity of the card. As Tesla cards are headless (have no monitor) a typical desktop configuration will use three Tesla cards and one dedicated graphics card. Thus, in terms of page-locked memory alone, you could need up to 18 GB of memory.

The OS also needs around 1–2 gigabytes of memory for its own purposes. Around another 2 GB or so should be allocated to a disk cache. Thus, for a three-card Tesla system, you can see we need around 20 GB of memory.

However, the DDR3 memory system is typically a triple or quad bank on the Intel system and dual bank on the AMD system. Most Intel systems have between four and eight DIMMs, and most AMD systems have four DIMM sockets. You generally have to use the same size memory in each slot: 4 GB DIMMs are fairly standard now, with 8 GB DIMMS also being available at around twice the cost per gigabyte of the 4 GB DIMMs. Thus, with four slots you typically find up to 16 GB/32 GB AMD systems and up to 16 GB/24 GB/32 GB/64 GB Intel systems. Note that 4 GB 32-bit systems are still the most common consumer-level platform.

With non-Tesla cards, we typically have up to 2 GB memory capacity on the card, meaning the total footprint of memory we need to allocate to page-locked memory is much less. With four cards, we need just 8 GB. With the maximum of seven cards, we need 14 GB, well within the capacity you'd find on a typical high-end motherboard.

AIR COOLING

Heat and power are the bane of any system designer. As you increase the clock speed, the power needed increases, which in turn generates more heat. The hotter the device, the more power is required to drive the gates. The higher the clock speed, the more of a problem it becomes.

CPU designers gave up pushing the 4 GHz limit some time ago and went down the parallel core route. Hardened overclockers will tell you they can run systems reliably at 4 GHz and beyond. However, the amount of heat generated and the power consumption is huge compared to the standard clock and power footprint of the device.

GPUs have always drawn a lot of power and generated a lot of heat. This is not because they are inefficient, but because they contain so many cores on one device. A CPU has four cores typically, but up to 16 in some high-end server devices. When you start to consider that the top-end GPUs have >2500 CUDA cores to keep cool, you start to understand the problem. It's arguable whether a fair comparison with CPU cores is at the SM level or at the CUDA core level. Whichever measure is used, the GPU devices end up with many times more cores than a CPU.

A retail CPU typically comes with a fairly basic heat sink and fan unit. They are low-cost, mass-produced units. Replace the standard heat sink and fan with an advanced one and the CPU temperature can easily drop by 20 degrees or more.

GPUs come typically as a dual-height board (two PCI-E slots) with the top part being an air cooler. When taken apart, you can usually see quite a substantial cooler (Figure 11.5).

The GeForce 580 design even features vapor chamber cooler, where the copper surface next to the GPU is filled with a liquid to aid transfer of heat from the GPU to the set of cooling fins. This is highly advanced technology just to cool a GPU. However, one of the problems you find is the GPUs' coolers work well *only* when surrounded by cool air, but if you put one next to another and you will suffocate their air supply.

Put four GPU cards in a standard PC case and it sounds like a hovercraft and does a good job replacing a storage heater. Unfortunately, it will most likely start to overheat after as little as

FIGURE 11.5

Heat sink from a GTX295 (dual-GPU) board.

FIGURE 11.6

Four GPU air-cooled system (various consumer GPU cards).

10 minutes once you start loading the GPUs. Overheating will eventually translate into errors in the calculations and operators who have to come to work in t-shirts and shorts.

The only way to run four GPUs with air cooling is either to feed in air conditioned air (costly) or to purchase special cards with custom coolers (Figure 11.6). Most server environments do the former and the servers are kept in specially air conditioned server rooms. The custom cooler solution is more suitable for office workstation usage. This, however, means you can't use the Tesla cards, or can use at most two of them with a gap between them if you'd like a machine next to your desk and expect the machine to be silent. With larger cases, motherboards such as the ASRock X58 Extreme6 work well due to the three-slot spacing of the PCI-E sockets, making a three-card air-cooled system a real possibility.

There are many review sites on the Internet that review the GeForce cards and almost all of them will measure the noise output of the cards. MSI, Gigabyte, and Gainward produce some very interesting cooling solutions for air-cooled GPUs. The regular stock cooler that comes with most solutions (GPU or CPU) should generally be avoided at all costs, as they are often far too noisy for usage next to a desk. Spending $20 USD more on a custom cooling solution will often make your life far quieter and keep the GPU far cooler, saving on running costs.

LIQUID COOLING

Liquid has two interesting properties over air when considered for cooling. It is both thermally more conductive and has a higher thermal mass. This means it both more easily absorbs heat and can carry more of it away.

FIGURE 11.7

Single CPU and GPU water cooling loop.

Liquid cooling may sound like an exotic solution to the heat problem, but it's actually quite a practical one. One of the major breakthroughs in cooling in the early days of supercomputers was the use of nonconductive liquids. The Cray-II, for example, used a special nonconductive liquid made by 3M called Fluorinert into which the entire circuit boards were immersed. The liquid was pumped through the system and then to an external cooling unit where the heat was dispersed.

For GPU computing, we've moved on a little. Although immersing an entire motherboard and GPU in a nonconductive liquid such as commonly available oils works, it's not a good solution. The liquid can eventually penetrate sensitive components, which ultimately results in system failure.

Liquid cooling enthusiasts came up with the idea of liquid cooling blocks. These are hollow blocks of copper through which liquid runs and never makes physical contact with anything electrical (Figure 11.7). You can buy nonconductive liquids, which we use in our liquid-cooled systems, minimizing the risk of any damage to components should some spillage occur.

A modern liquid-cooled system consists of a number of heat collectors, a CPU block, one or more GPU blocks, and, optionally, memory and chipset blocks. The hollow copper blocks have liquid pumped through them, which is fed from a reservoir. The output of the heated liquid is then fed into a cooling system, usually one or more radiators or a heat exchanger. The typical layout is shown in Figure 11.8.

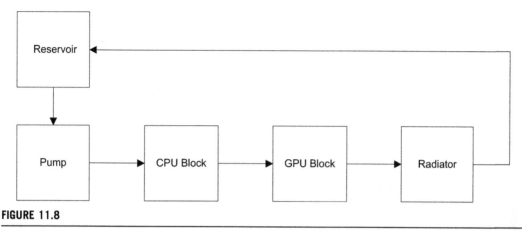

FIGURE 11.8

Typical liquid-cooled loop.

There are many variations on this type of layout. The more units there are in a serial run like the one shown in Figure 11.8, the higher the resistance to the flow of the liquid. There are parallel flow solutions that overcome this, but it's actually quite hard to ensure exactly the same flow goes through each parallel route, as the liquid will always pick the route of least resistance.

The main issue with liquid cooling is that it doesn't really solve the heat generation issue. It only allows you to move the heat to somewhere it can be dispersed more easily. Thus, the radiator may be a large external one, or even mounted internally within the workstation if only a small amount of cooling is required.

The key aspect of any water cooling system is actually the radiator and more importantly the size and the amount and temperature of the airflow. One of the best radiators is the external Watercool MO-RA3, available in a 9 × 120 mm or 4 × 180 mm form factor. Internal radiators should be the largest size (height, width, depth) that can fit within the case and should exhaust the air out of the case. Always try to ensure you consider the laws of physics, specifically that heat rises. A top-mount radiator is often the best solution, but will require some method to purge the residual air when initially filling the system. Place the pump as low as possible and the reservoir as high as possible to ensure the pump is always pumping liquid and never air. Think about how you will fill and empty such a system and where any air may accumulate. Often included are a drain point and an air purge point.

Liquid cooling connectors come in many sizes. Most liquid cooling systems use G1/4-threaded connectors. These have a 10 mm intertube diameter (ID). Thus, 13 mm/10 mm (3/8 inch ID) tubing is commonly used. The first size is the outertube diameter (OD) followed by the ID. The connectors may be a barb, push fit, or compression-type fitting. Compression and barb fittings use a system that requires a reasonable force to remove the connector even if it is not sealed. The compression seal slides over the barb and screws into place, ensuring it's pretty much impossible to remove without unscrewing the top. The barb fitting instead uses a hose clip that is not so tight, but is often easier to maneuver into place in smaller cases. Compression fittings are the least likely to leak or work free of the connector and are highly recommended. See Figure 11.9.

FIGURE 11.9

CPU liquid cooling block with barb and compression fitting side by side.

As for liquids, many people use various premixed fluids. These often contain the necessary anti-bacterial agents to prevent algae growth. Some are nonconductive, although most are at least somewhat electrically conductive. Alternatively, distilled or deionized water may be used, but never tap water as it contains all sorts of things you'd not want in a liquid cooling loop.

Multiple GPUs in the system have to be connected together. This is done with a dedicated connector block, such as the AquaComputer twin connect and other similar systems. These consist of a solid plastic connector to which all the cards sit at a 90-degree angle. These are far preferable to the metal bar–type SLI connectors as they provide a nice grip for the cards and ensure the correct spacing. See Figure 11.10.

The main advantage of liquid cooling is that it allows you to create an almost silent workstation, but also to cool components far better than an air-cooled system. This in turn means lower power consumption. It also allows the increase in the clock speed beyond the original clock specification, so-called overclocking. Such overclocked GeForce cards can, on single-precision tasks, easily outperform Tesla cards found in workstations and server environments by around 20% or more. You can even purchase liquid-cooled versions of many cards out of the box, either as components or self-contained sealed systems.

The downside is twofold. First, there is the additional cost and effort required to plumb in all the components. Second, there is a risk of a leak of coolant, which is generally only a major issue when the system is first put together. Maintenance is also higher in that most liquids must be replaced on an annual basis.

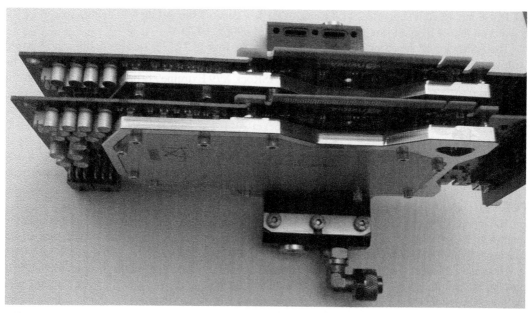

FIGURE 11.10

Twin liquid-cooled GPU cards fitted in solid connector block.

DESKTOP CASES AND MOTHERBOARDS

People interested in building their own GPU system will need to house it in a case of some description. A case has to be something that is a suitable size. The main criteria will be how many GPUs you wish to fit into the case and also the form factor of the motherboard. Most motherboards are ATX or E-ATX designs, meaning they will fit most desktop cases. Some smaller cases, however, do not support E-ATX.

A number of motherboards that support four PCI-E or more connectors are larger than the E-ATX specification, EVGA being a typical example. EVGA sells the only dual-X58 motherboard, the EVGA Classified SR-2, which accepts two Xeon-based Nehalem I7 processors and up to 48 GB of RAM. However, selecting such a motherboard limits the case choice to just a few models (see EVGA's website at *http://www.evga.com* for an up-to-date list).

ASUS was among the first to produce a dedicated compute platform motherboard aimed at CUDA with its P6T7 WS supercomputer motherboard. This is an X58 platform (Nehalem I7) supporting four double-spaced PCI-E 2.0 sockets at full x16 PCI-E 2.0 speed. Note this board is a CEB form factor, which generally means it will fit most E-ATX cases. It's one of the few boards that supports the x16 speed on all four slots.

The ASUS Rampage III Extreme is also a good E-ATX design, although it only supports x8 PCI-E speeds with four cards. The ASUS Extreme V board is one of the few Ivybridge compatible PCI-E 3.0 boards supporting 4 PCI-E connectors.

MSI produce the BigBang series of motherboards aimed at power users, sporting seven physical PCI-E sockets. However, when populated with four cards, as is the case for most motherboards, only

X8 PCI-E bus speed is supported. MSI is one of the few vendors supporting four double-spaced PCI-E sockets on the AMD platform, for example, the MSI 890FXA-GD70.

The ASRock X58 supercomputer design provides for four PCI-E 2.0 sockets running at x8 speed with up to 24 GB of RAM. Its designs since this have improved tremendously, especially with its latest socket 2011 (Sandybridge-E) design. The ASRock X79 Extreme9 is one of the best designs for the Sandybridge-E platform we've seen to date (see Figure 11.9). It supports five PCI-E x8 sockets, eight SATA-3 ports, the PCI-E 3.0 standard, and up to 64 GB of RAM while still being an ATX form factor design. ASROCK recently released the socket 2011, Extreme 11 board which boasts 7 PCI-E 3.0 x16 slots.

Gigabyte is also a well-respected manufacturer. Its UD9-X58 platform, as with the ASUS super-computer, has dual NF200 chips, meaning it supports four full-speed x16 PCI-E 2.0 slots. Its GA-990FXA-UD7 AMD platform supports the latest 990 chipset, providing SATA-3 support and four PCI-E 2.0 sockets up to x8 speed.

Having decided on the motherboard, you need a case that supports the form factor, but also the number of PCI-E slots you plan to use. Standard PC cases only come with seven PCI-E slots, which causes an issue if you in fact have four double-height PCI-E cards.

Heat and airflow should be big considerations in selecting a case, especially with multiple GPUs present. Silverstone produces a number of cases that rotate the motherboard 90 degrees and thus vent the hot air from the CPU and GPUs directly up and out of the case. Figure 11.3 shows a design used with Raven's RV02 case. We've found this design to be the most effective in terms of cooling. The upward-flowing air design drops the internal case temperature by several degrees. Raven's Fortress FT02 and Temjin TJ11 cases follow similar designs. The Raven cases have an aesthetic you either love or hate. The Fortress and Temjin designs are much more traditional, although all three cases are quite large. Note, the newer edition Raven (the RV02-evolution) and Fortress cases support only seven PCI-E slots, whereas the Temjin supports nine slots.

As an alternative, the Coolermaster HAF and Antec 1200 series cases also have very good airflow. However, both support only seven PCI-E slots. The Raven RV03 is a much more compact version of Raven RV02. It supports a full set of eight PCI-E slots and is one of the cheapest cases on the market.

In terms of liquid-cooled cases, most are aimed at single CPU–based cooling, so there is a lack of necessary space for a multi-GPU liquid-cooled configuration. With four GPUs and an I7 CPU you are burning in excess of 1 kW of power, a significant amount of which is heat. Such systems are best cooled externally. As an approximate guide, you'll need one 120 mm radiator capacity to cool each device (CPU or GPU). The Silverstone Temjin TJ11 allows you to remove the internal hard drive section at the bottom of the case and replace it with a 4 × 140 mm radiator and pump assembly. This is perhaps one of the best, but most expensive, cases currently on the market.

MASS STORAGE

Motherboard-based I/O

The mass storage subsystem is something that is quite important. You need to be able to easily import and export data from a system. If you consider that each GPU has a maximum of 5 GB/s input bandwidth and 5 GB/s output bandwidth, you will have a problem supplying such a large amount of data from a mass storage device.

A typical hard disk has a transfer rate of around 160 MB/s maximum. Due to the construction of hard disks, the density of the data is diminished as you approach the center of the disk. As such, the data rate drops off to around half of the maximum rate at the outside of the disk as it becomes full and starts to use the inner part of the drive.

Most Intel I7 motherboards come with an built-in controller that supports up to six SATA-based hard disks. This is part of the Southbridge chipset, which controls the slow devices such as keyboards and mice. It also handles the SATA hard disks and network interfaces.

The SATA-2 standard defines a speed of up to 300 MB/s per SATA channel. The SATA-3 standard supports twice this. The built-in controller supports up to six hard drives, meaning you could theoretically achieve a transfer capability of 1.8 GB/s from the SATA ports to the main memory. With SATA-2 SSD disks exceeding 250 MB/s read speeds, you might expect to be able to simply connect up to six disks and get a reasonable input data rate, but even this is only half the bandwidth of a *single* PCI-E X16 graphics card.

However, life is never that easy. In practice, Southbridge-based built-in controllers will peak out at about 600 MB/s to 700 MB/s, which is nowhere near close to the 1.8 GB/s you'd need to support all hard drives at the full data rate. For 160 MB/s physical hard disks, this may work, but for SSD drives that can match or exceed the SATA-2 interface speeds, the standard motherboard SATA controller will not be of much use. With just four SSD drives present, the controller is already a bottleneck in the system.

The more modern boards have now entirely moved to SATA-3 on the AMD platforms and a mixture of SATA-2 and SATA-3 on the Intel platforms. SATA-3 doubles the SATA-2 speed, meaning an SSD drive can peak at up to 550 MB/s (SATA-3 speed is 600 MB/s). With six of these, peak speeds are rapidly approaching the speeds we need for a single GPU. However, as with the SATA-2 controllers, most on-board SATA3 controllers peak at around 1GB/s transfer rates and thus cannot support large numbers of SSDs.

Dedicated RAID controllers

For faster input of data you need to turn to a dedicated hard disk controller, which sits on the PCI-E bus. However, this approach conflicts with our need to have the graphics compute cards on exactly this same bus. With air based cooling, all the GPUs are double-slot cards. You may have to remove a GPU card to be able to insert a dedicated hard disk controller card and/or a high-speed network card.

With liquid-cooled systems it's a little easier, because each card is single slot. However, you are still limited by the overall power consumption of a PC, typically up to 1.5 kW. This in effect means, at least with the high-end cards, there will be spare PCI-E slots.

Assuming you have a 550 MB/s SATA-3 SSD drive subsystem, to achieve the 5 GB/s input capacity for a single GPU card, you need 10 SSD drives. If the RAID card you are using supports simultaneous transfers to and from the PCI-E bus, then you'd need a total of 20 SATA-3 SSD drives to support the full bandwidth of a single PCI-E X16 RAID controller.

So to be able to supply and store in real time the full bandwidth of a *single* GPU card, even using SSDs, it will take 20 SSDs. Even with four 6 SSDs per drive bay, you'd need 4 drive bays to support this.

If you look at a high-end GPU setup, the solution is a four GPU liquid-cooled solution based on a motherboard that supports seven PCI-E bus connectors. With no additional cards, all GPUs run at the X8 speed (2.5 GB/s in, 2.5 GB/s out) with four GPU cards and X16 with two GPU cards.

With a liquid-cooled system, you have spare slots between the cards, as most liquid-cooled solutions are single slot. As soon as you add a RAID controller card, the associated slot drops to X8 or X4 for both the GPU and RAID card. This is unless you dedicate an X16 slot to the RAID controller, something we'd recommend.

There is a physical limit on the number of drive bays that can be included in a workstation format. Even a motherboard with seven PCI-E slots, often dubbed supercomputer motherboards, have only three slots left available once four liquid-cooled GPUs are present. This may allow for two RAID controllers and a single high-speed network card to be squeezed into such systems.

RAID, however, is not simply about speed, although the RAID-0 mode is used for this. RAID-1 supports mirroring, where the data is completely duplicated onto another disk. Failure of one disk then means the system falls back to the remaining disk without significant impact on the operation of the system. Clearly, however, the faulty disk needs to be replaced as soon as possible. It saves you the case where several weeks of compute time could be lost due to a faulty hard drive.

With a small cluster, hard drives fail rarely enough that it's not that much of a problem. However, in a larger setup, with thousands of active drives, you will be changing drives regularly.

RAID-5 is a system that balances storage usage with redundancy, allowing data to be split over multiple drives in a safe manner. One of the drives in a set is a dedicated parity drive that, if one drive fails, can be used to recover the RAID array. RAID is something you definitely need to consider if restarting your job on another machine and losing the computations to date is not acceptable.

Check pointing is a system that is often used to avoid the effects of failure. After a certain period, the entire results to data are check-pointed or dumped to permanent storage. Thus, the job can be moved to another node by simply moving the check-pointed data and the associated program code. In designing applications that run for some period of time, you should always consider building a check pointing system into the application.

HDSL

HDSL is a standard from a company called OCZ that has developed a number of innovative products in the SSD market. Most notable of these is the RevoDrive range, a product that is basically a number of SSD drives on a PCI-E card with a built-in hard disk controller. This original card achieved on the order of 500 MB/s, which is quite reasonable; the high-end cards (the R4 C series) claim 2800 MB/s. You would need a SATA-3 controller and at least five top-end SSDs to achieve the same sort of bandwidth.

The HDSL drive offered by OCZ is also an interesting product and an insight into where storage is likely to go. It embeds four older-style SSD drives into a standard 3.5 inch hard disk, with an embedded RAID-0 controller. A special controller card is used that basically extends four lanes of the PCI-E bus through a cable directly to the drive interface. Four PCI-E 2.0 lanes equates to around 1 GB/s in both directions, vastly superior to the unidirectional SATA-3 interface.

Being a new technology, it has some way to go before the drives themselves match this bandwidth. Currently, the drive peaks at around 750 MB/s, which is somewhat shy of the 1000 MB/s capacity of the link. The drive ships with a single-port X4 HDSL controller, but dual- and quad-port X8 and X16 controllers are planned. Assuming the drive picks up a little in speed to the full bandwidth of the interface, which is almost certain given the march of technology, this will be a very interesting technology to see evolve.

As the drives themselves are a 3.5 inch format, this means more drives can be put in the same physical space. Allocating two X8 slots would support four HDSL drives, giving a read/write capacity of around 3 GB/s.

Mass storage requirements

As well as speed of input from the mass storage devices, we have the total storage capacity. Take one of the largest users of data in the world, Google. In 2008 they were processing 20 petabytes of data *per day*. A petabyte is 1000 terabytes, which is itself 1000 gigabytes. Given that the largest single mass storage drive available today is around 4 terabytes, just to store that amount of data would require $(20 \times 1000) \div 4 = 5000$ hard disk drives!

So clearly one consideration in designing any node is mass storage needs. In practice, most large installations use dedicated storage nodes that do not have any compute functionality. Thus, the compute nodes need only the storage capacity necessary for a single compute run. They can download data over a high-speed interconnect from a central data cluster, meaning you can design them with high-speed, small-capacity SSD drives, which we've done with some of our test machines at CudaDeveloper.

Networking

Networking is one of the key issues when you consider a system that contains more than a single node. Clusters of nodes have become very common in universities and commercial organizations as the availability of cheap commodity hardware has become commonplace. It is relatively straightforward to configure a small network of machines and have them work together on a problem.

You typically see two types of networks: those based on gigabit Ethernet and those using somewhat faster, but considerably more expensive, InfiniBand networks. Gigabit Ethernet is cheap, usually comes as free on the motherboard, and can be connected to a multi-port switch with relative ease. Some motherboards offer dual-gigabit Ethernet connections, which often include a feature called Link Aggregation. This, when supported by the switch, allows for the two physical links to be used as one, doubling the amount of bandwidth available to and from that node.

How critical networking is to your problem depends greatly on the amount of data that needs to be shared. If you can stay within a single node and go down the multiple-GPU route, this will be far, far more effective than going down the multiple-node route in most cases.

Systems like Google's MapReduce is one example where, due to the huge amount of data being used, you are forced to split the data between multiple nodes. MapReduce works on the principle of a shared and distributed file system, making the file system appear as one very large disk. The data itself is located in chunks on the local storage of each node. Instead of bringing the data to the program, MapReduce sends the program to where the data is physically located. Hadoop is an open-source implementation of MapReduce, allowing you to set up a very similar framework for distributing and scheduling such jobs. Typically the dataset is very large and the program very small, so this type of approach works really well in greatly reducing network traffic.

Dedicated communication with something like MPI is also typically how such a system is set up. However, as soon as network communication becomes the dominant feature of the program, in terms of time, you need to move to a faster network architecture such as InfiniBand. This obviously incurs cost, which you may be able to avoid through clever programming, such as asynchronous communication, compressing data packets, etc.

Peer-to-peer communication within a node between the GPUs is now supported with the CUDA 4.0 SDK. In addition, the GPUs can talk directly to certain InfiniBand cards in the same way, without the interaction of the host CPU. Thus, for larger-scale GPU installations, InfiniBand and other higher-speed interconnects can become a necessity if network traffic plays a significant role.

POWER CONSIDERATIONS

Power usage is a big consideration when designing machines that run constantly. Often the operating costs of running a supercomputer over just a few years can equate to the cost of installing it in the first place. Certainly, the cost of running such a machine over its lifetime will easily exceed the original installation costs.

Power usage comes from the components themselves, but also from the cooling necessary to allow such computers to operate. Even one high-end workstation with four GPUs requires some planning on how to keep it cool. Unless you live in a cold climate and can banish the computer to somewhere cold, it will do a nice job of heating up the office for you. Put a number of such machines into one room, and very rapidly the air temperature in that room will start to rise to quite unacceptable levels.

A significant amount of power is therefore expended on installing air conditioning systems to ensure computers remain cool and can operate without producing errors. This is especially so where summer temperatures can reach 85°F/ 30°C or higher. Air conditioning is expensive to run. Significant thought should be given to how best to cool such a system and if the heat energy can in some way be reused. Liquid-cooled systems are very efficient in this way in that the liquid can be circulated through a heat exchanger and into a conventional heating system without any chance of the two liquids ever mixing. I'm always amazed by the lack of thought that goes into how to reuse waste heat in computer installations. With the ever-increasing costs of natural resources, and the increasing pressures on companies to be seen as green, simply pumping the heat out the window is no longer economically or socially acceptable.

If you look at the top-end GPU cards, they typically come in around the 250 W mark in terms of power consumption. A typical CPU is around 125 W by comparison. A typical power budget for a four-GPU system might therefore be as shown in Table 11.1.

Table 11.1 Typical Power Usage

Component	Number	Power per Unit	Total Power
GPU	4	250	1000
CPU	1	125	125
Memory	16	1	16
Motherboard	1	50	50
Boot drive	2	5	10
Data drive	8	5	40
Peripherals	1	10	10
Total			**1251**

Table 11.2 Gigaflops per Core

Card	CUDA Cores	Clock (MHz)	Power Usage (W)	Gigaflops	Gigaflops per Core	Gigaflops per Watt
430	96	700	49	269	2.8	5.5
450	192	790	106	455	2.37	4.3
460	336	675	160	907	2.7	5.7
470	448	607	215	1089	2.43	5.1
480	480	700	250	1345	2.8	5.4
560 Ti (GF114)	384	822	170	1260	3.28	7.4
560 (GF110)	448	732	210	1312	2.93	6.2
570	480	732	219	1405	2.93	6.4
580	512	772	244	1581	3.09	6.5
590	1024	607	365	2488	2.43	6.8
680	1536	1006	195	3090	2.01	15.8
690	3072	915	300	5620	1.83	18.7

As you can see from the table, you can be drawing up 1250 W (1.3 kW) of power per node with such a configuration. Off-the-shelf power supplies top out at around the 1.5 kW mark, after which you're looking at a very expensive, custom solution.

Selection of the GPU can make a huge difference to overall power consumption. If you look at watts per core and gigaflops per core we see something interesting (Table 11.2). Notice how the architectural improvements in the 500 series Fermi cards produce much better performance, both in terms of watts and gigaflops. Fermi devices also automatically clock down much lower than the older G80 or G200 series cards, using a lot less power when idle. In fact, one of the best performing cards in terms of gigaflops per watt is the GF114-based 560 Ti range. The 560 Ti is aimed squarely at the game market and comes with a high internal clock speed, producing some 1.2 gigaflops versus the almost 1.6 gigaflops of the 580. However, it does this at just 170 W compared with the 240 W of the 580, giving it by far the best performance per watt. Note the 560 Ti was relaunched at the end of 2011 as a 448-core device based on the 570 design. The GTX680 is based on the 560 design. The dual GPU 690 contains two of these devices, specially binned and clocked to achieve 300 W, giving this card the best overall GFlops per watt ratio.

One important consideration when selecting a power supply is to realize that not all power supplies are made equal. A lot of the cheaper power supplies claim a certain power rating, but fail to provide this on the 12v rails, which is where the primary power draw is in such a system (from the graphics cards). Also, others do not provide enough PCI-E connectors to support more than a small number of cards.

However, one of the most important issues to be concerned about is the efficiency of a power supply. This can be as low as <80% or as high as 96%. That difference of 16% is effectively a cost of $0.16 cents on every dollar (Euro/pound/franc) spent on electricity.

Power supplies are rated according to an efficiency rating. Those meeting the 80-plus standard guarantee a minimum of 80% efficiency across the entire power range. More efficient models are rated bronze (82%), silver (85%), gold (87%), platinum (89%), and titanium (91%) in terms of efficiency at 100% usage. Efficiency is typically a few percent higher at 50% load and slightly higher with the European 240v power supplies than the U.S. 115v standard. See the website *http://www.80plus.org* for a list of certified power supplies.

Table 11.3 Typical Costs per Year by Power Consumption

Power	Usage (Hours/ Day)	Unit Cost (Euros/ kW)	Per Day (kW)	Per Week (kW)	Per Year (kW)	Per Day (Euro)	Per Week (Euro)	Per Year (Euro)
CPU								
65	24	0.2	1.56	10.92	568	0.31	2.18	114
95	24	0.2	2.28	15.96	830	0.46	3.19	166
125	24	0.2	3	21	1092	0.6	4.2	218
GPU								
50	24	0.2	1.2	8.4	437	0.24	1.68	87
100	24	0.2	2.4	16.8	874	0.48	3.36	175
150	24	0.2	3.6	25.2	1310	0.72	5.04	262
200	24	0.2	4.8	33.6	1747	0.96	6.72	349
250	24	0.2	6	42	2184	1.2	8.4	437
300	24	0.2	7.2	50.4	2621	1.44	10.08	524
600	24	0.2	14.4	100.8	5242	2.88	20.16	1048
900	24	0.2	21.6	151.2	7862	4.32	30.24	1572
1200	24	0.2	28.8	201.6	10,483	5.76	40.32	2097
1500	24	0.2	36	252	13,104	7.2	50.4	2621

If you take the typical European cost of electricity at, say, 0.20 Euros per kilowatt hour, a 1.3 kW machine costs $0.20 \times 1.3 = 0.26$ per hour to run. That is 6.24 Euros per day, 43.48 Euros a week, or 2271 Euros a year to constantly run in terms of electricity cost alone. This assumes you have a 100% efficient power supply, something that just doesn't exist. See Table 11.3.

With an 80% efficient power supply, for 1.3 kW output, you'd need to put in 1.625 kW of power, an additional 325 W, which is wasted. This increases the annual bill from 2271 Euros to 2847 Euros, some 216 Euros. With a 92% efficient power supply, you'd need just 1.413 kW (212 W less), which costs you 2475 Euros per year. This is a savings of around 400 Euros a year, which easily covers the additional costs of a high-efficiency power supply.

In terms of the U.S. market, electricity is somewhat cheaper at around $0.12 cents per kW. Thus, a 1.3 kW machine with an 80% efficient power supply (1.625 kW input power) would cost around $0.19 per hour to run. With a 92% efficient supply (1.413 kW input power) it would cost $0.17 per hour. That little $0.02 cents per hour translates into $175 per year when the machine is constantly run. Multiply that by N nodes and you can soon see why efficiency is a key criterion for many companies purchasing computer systems.

Certainly in our own machines we always use the most efficient power supply available at the time any development machine is built. Companies such as Google follow similar policies, using highly efficient power supplies, targeting 90% plus efficiency. Energy prices are unlikely to do anything other than increase over time, so this makes perfect sense.

Liquid-cooled systems provide an interesting option in terms of recycling the waste heat energy. While an air-cooled system can only be used to heat the immediate area it is located in, heat from liquid-based coolants can be pumped elsewhere. By using a heat exchanger, the coolant can be cooled using conventional water. This can then be pumped into a heating system or even used to heat an outdoor swimming pool or other large body of water. Where a number of such systems are installed, such as in a company or university computer center, it can really make sense to use this waste heat energy to reduce the heating bill elsewhere in the organization.

Many supercomputer installations site themselves next to a major river precisely because they need a ready supply of cold water. Others use large cooling towers to dissipate the waste heat energy. Neither solution is particularly green. Having paid for the energy already it makes little sense to simply throw it away when it could so easily be used for heating.

When considering power usage, we must also remember that program design actually plays a very big role in power consumption. The most expensive operation, power wise, is moving data on and off chip. Thus, simply making efficient use of the registers and shared memory within the device vastly reduces power usage. If you also consider that the total execution time for well-written programs is much smaller than for poorly written ones, you can see that rewriting old programs to make use of new features such as larger shared memory can even reduce operating costs in a large data center.

OPERATING SYSTEMS

Windows

The CUDA development environment is officially supported by Windows XP, Windows Vista, and Windows 7/8 in both the 32- and 64-bit variants. It is also supported by the Windows HPC (high-performance computing) Server edition.

Support for certain features related to rendering on DirectX versions later than version 9 are not supported on XP due to the lack of support for DirectX 10 and 11. Support for more than four GPUs can be problematic, both from an OS (Operating Systems) perspective and also from the BIOS (Basic Input Output System) of the motherboard. Support may vary from one CUDA driver release to another, but for the most part it now works.

GPU support when using Windows remote desktop is nonexistent, as the exported desktop does not contain any CUDA devices. There are other packages that provide SSH (Secure Shell) type connections that do support this, UltraVNC being a very common one.

Ease of installation of the drivers on the Windows platform and the availability of debugging tools, notably Parallel NSight, is excellent. For multi-GPU solutions, a 64-bit version is essential, as the CPU memory space is otherwise limited to a total of 4 GB.

Linux

CUDA is supported for most major Linux distributions. However, one of the key differences between the Linux distribution and the Windows distribution is the expected level of the installer's knowledge. The CUDA drivers need to be explicitly installed for most distributions. This varies by distribution. Refer to Chapter 4 where we covered installation procedures for each of the major distributions.

Support for multiple GPUs is much better in Linux than under Windows. It's also possible with a custom BIOS to get around some of the BIOS issues found when booting a system containing more than four GPUs. The problem encountered is that most older BIOS designs are 32 bit and thus cannot map such a large amount of memory into the memory space that is presented by very large numbers of GPUs. If you'd like to try this approach, then have a look at the Fastra II project (*http://fastra2.ua.ac.be/*), where they used a BIOS with 13 GPUs in a single desktop.

The primary Linux-supported debugger is the GDB package from GNU. This is not as comprehensive as the Parallel NSight package that is now also available on Linux, but is steadily improving. Other common parallel debuggers for the most part already support or are in the process of having support added for CUDA.

As with the Windows versions, for multi-GPU solutions a 64-bit version is essential because the CPU memory space is otherwise limited to a total of 4 GB. However, unlike Windows, the OS footprint is significantly smaller, so more memory is made available to the application.

CONCLUSION

In this chapter we looked at some of the aspects of building GPU-based machines, both from the perspective of using GPUs in a data center and considerations for building your own GPU machines. If you're a researcher and you want a superfast machine, building one yourself is a very useful experience in setting everything up. For those wishing for an out-of-the-box solution, NVIDIA provides prebuilt desktop and server systems, tested and certified to work reliably. Whether you decide to build your own or buy, by reading this chapter you will be far more informed about the key decisions and issues you need to consider before committing to the purchase of any hardware.

Common Problems, Causes, and Solutions

12

INTRODUCTION

In this chapter we look at some of the issues that plague CUDA developers and how you can avoid or at least mitigate these issues with some relatively simple practices. Issues with CUDA programs often fall into one the following categories:

- Errors of usage of various CUDA directives.
- General parallel programming errors.
- Algorithmic errors.

Finally, we finish this last chapter with a discussion of where to continue your learning. There are many other texts on the subject of CUDA and GPU programming in general, as well as a lot of online material. We provide some pointers for what to read and where to find it. We also briefly discuss NVIDIA's professional certification program for CUDA developers.

ERRORS WITH CUDA DIRECTIVES

Errors using the CUDA API are by far the most common issue we see with people learning CUDA. It is a new API for many, and therefore mistakes in its usage should be expected and planned for.

CUDA error handling

In Chapter 4, we introduced the CUDA_CALL macro. All of the CUDA API functions return an error code. Anything other than cudaSuccess generally indicates you did something wrong in calling the API. There are, however, a few exceptions, such as cudaEventQuery, which returns the event status as opposed to an error status.

The CUDA API is by nature asynchronous, meaning the error code returned at the point of the query, may have happened at some distant point in the past. In practice, it will usually be as a result of the call immediately prior to the error being detected. You can, of course, force this by synchronizing (i.e., calling the cudaDeviceSynchronize function) after every API call. While this strategy might be a good one for debugging, it's not something that should be in any release version of the code.

Each error code can be turned into a semi-useful error string, rather than a number you have to look up in the API documentation. The error string is a somewhat helpful first attempt to identify the potential cause of the problem. However, it relies on the programmer explicitly checking the return code in the host program. It would be better if the CUDA runtime could trap such exceptions and perform some error indication, as we do explicitly with the CUDA_CALL macro, when running the debug version. This would help tremendously in pointing out errors in the user's program, as and when they are introduced. We see some move toward this in the CUDA v4.1 SDK.

The CUDA error handling can be somewhat rudimentary. Most of the time, you'll get a useful error message. However, often you will get a not-so-useful message such as unknown error, usually after a kernel invocation. This basically means your kernel did something it should not have, for example, writing over the end of the array in global or shared memory. There are debugging tools and methods we cover later in this chapter that help identify this type of problem.

Kernel launching and bounds checking

One of the most common failings in CUDA is an array overrun. You should ensure all your kernel invocations start with a check to ensure the data they will access, both for read and write purposes, is guarded by a conditional. For example,

```
if (tid < num_elements)
{
... array[tid] = ....
}
```

This conditional takes a marginal amount of time, but will save you a lot of debugging effort. You typically see such a problem where you have a number of data elements that are not multiples of the thread block size.

Suppose we have 256 threads per block and 1024 data elements. This would invoke four blocks of 256 threads. Each thread would contribute to the result. Now suppose we had 1025 data elements. You would typically have two types of errors here. The first is to not invoke a sufficient number of threads, due to using an integer division. This will usually truncate the number of blocks needed. Typically people write

```
const int num_blocks = num_elements / num_threads;
```

This will work, but only where the number of elements is an exact multiple of the number of threads. In the 1025 elements case we launch 4 × 256 threads, some 1024 threads in total. The last element remains unprocessed. I've also seen, as well as other variations, attempts to "get around" this issue. For example,

```
const int num_blocks = ((float) num_elements / num_threads);
```

This does not solve the problem. You cannot have 4.1 blocks. The assignment to integer truncates the number to four blocks. The solution is a simple one. You write the following instead:

```
const int num_blocks = (num_elements + (num_threads-1)) / num_threads;
```

This will ensure you always allocate enough blocks.

The second issue we commonly see then follows. We now invoke five blocks for a total of 1280 threads. Without such guarded access to the array within the kernel, all but the first thread in block 5 would be accessing an out-of-bounds memory location. The CUDA runtime performs little if any runtime checks, such as array bounds. You will never see it halt the kernel and display a message such as `array overrun in line 252 file kernel.cu`. However, rather than silently fail, which is the worst case, it does at least trap the error in some way and then returns a message such as `unknown error`.

Invalid device handles

The other type of errors you typically see are incorrect mixing of handles, most often pointers. When you allocate memory on the device or on the host, you receive a pointer to that memory. However, that pointer comes with an implicit requirement that *only the host* may access host pointers and *only the device* may access device pointers. There are a few exceptions, such as zero-copy memory, where a host pointer can be converted to a device pointer to host memory, but even in this case you have a separation.

As the pointers are not interchangeable, one might have hoped that device pointers would be declared using a different type. This would allow for type-based checks on calls to the API to flag such issues at compile time. Unfortunately, a device pointer and a host pointer are the same basic type, which means there is no static-type checking performed by the compiler.

There is, of course, no reason why you could not define such a type. You could then develop your own wrapper functions around the API functions that performed type checking. Certainly for those who are starting out writing CUDA, this would be a tremendous help and perhaps something we'll see as CUDA develops. The Thrust library we looked at in Chapter 10 has the concept of a host vector and a device vector. It uses C++ function overloading to ensure that the correct function is always called for the given data type.

The standard CUDA runtime checks for this type of incorrect mixing of device and host pointers, in terms of passing a host pointer to a device function are reasonable. The CUDA API checks the pointer's origin and will generate a runtime error if you pass a host pointer to a kernel function without first converting it to a device pointer to host memory. However, the same cannot be said for the standard C/C++ system libraries. If you call the standard `free` function as opposed to the `cudaFree` function with a device pointer, the system libraries will try to free that memory on the host, and then will likely crash. The host libraries have no concept of a memory space they can't access.

The other type of invalid handle comes from the usage of a type before it's been initialized. This is akin to using a variable before assigning it a value. For example,

```
cudaStream_t my_stream;
my_kernel<<<num_blocks, num_threads, dynamic_shared, my_stream>>>(a, b, c);
```

In this example we're missing the call to `cudaStreamCreate` and subsequent `cudaStreamDestroy` functions. The create call performs some initialization to register the event in the CUDA API. The destroy call releases those resources. The correct code is as follows:

```
cudaStream_t my_stream;
cudaStreamCreate(&my_stream);
my_kernel<<<num_blocks, num_threads, dynamic_shared, my_stream>>>(a, b, c);
cudaStreamSynchronize(my_stream);
cudaStreamDestroy(my_stream);
```

Unfortunately, the CUDA multiple-device model is based on selecting a device context prior to performing an operation. A somewhat cleaner interface would have been to specify an optional device_num parameter in each call, which would default to device 0 if not specified. This would then allow the following:

```
{
cudaStream_t my_stream(device_num); // constructor for stream
my_kernel<<<num_blocks, num_threads, dynamic_shared, my_stream, device_num>>>(a, b, c);
cudaStreamSynchronize(my_stream);
} // destructor for stream
```

Although this is moving from C to C++, it provides a somewhat cleaner interface, as resources would be automatically created with a constructor and destroyed with a destructor. You can, of course, easily write such a C++ class.

Invalid device handles, however, are not simply caused by forgetting to create them. They can also be caused by destroying them prior to the device finishing usage of them. Try deleting the cudaStreamSynchronize call from the original code. This will cause the stream in use by the asynchronous kernel to be destroyed while the kernel is potentially still running on the device.

Due to the asynchronous nature of streams, the cudaStreamDestroy function will not fail. It will return cudaSuccess, so it will not even be detected by the CUDA_CALL macro. In fact, you will not get an error until sometime later, from an entirely unrelated call into the CUDA API. One solution to this is to embed the cudaSynchronizeDevice call into the CUDA_CALL macro. This can help in identifying the exact cause of the problem. However, be careful not to leave this in production code.

Volatile qualifiers

The C "volatile" keyword specifies to the compiler that all references to this variable, read or write, must result in a memory reference, and those references must be in the order specified in the program. Consider the following sequential code segment:

```
static unsigned int a = 0;
void some_func(void)
{
 unsigned int i;
 for (i=0; i<= 1000; i++)
 {
   a += i;
 }
}
```

Here we declare a global variable a starting at 0. Every time we call the function it iterates i from 0 to 1000 and adds each value to the variable a. In the nonoptimized version of this code, it's likely each write of a will result in a physical memory write. However, this is highly unlikely in the optimized code version.

The optimizer can apply two approaches here. First, and the most common, would be to load the value of a into a register at the start of the loop, run the loop to the end, and then write the resulting register back to memory as a *single* store operation. This is simply an example of the programmer being unaware, or not caring, about the cost of memory access. The C code could have been written as follows:

```
static unsigned int a = 0;
void some_func(void)
{
 unsigned int register reg_a = a;
 unsigned int i;
 for (i=0; i<1000; i++)
 {
   reg_a += i;
 }
 a = reg_a;
}
```

This is effectively what the compiler will likely replace it with. A somewhat more advanced optimizer may be able to unroll the loop, as if it had constant boundaries, to a single expression. As that expression would contain a plus a series of constants, the constants could be reduced to a single constant at compile time, eliminating the loop altogether. For example,

```
static unsigned int a = 0;
void some_func(void)
{
 a += (1 + 2 + 3 + 4 + 5 + 6 + 7 .......);
}
```

or

```
static unsigned int a = 0;
void some_func(void)
{
 a += 500500;
}
```

While many compilers will unroll loops, I'd not expect many, if any, compilers to produce the later, simplified code. However, in theory there is no reason why this could not be the case.

Either approach potentially causes problems if some other thread needs to share the value of parameter a during any intermediate loop iteration. On the GPU this shared parameter can be either in shared or global memory. For the most part these types of problems are largely hidden from the GPU programmer in that the call to __syncthreads() causes an implicit flush of any writes to memory in both shared and global memory for the *current block*. As most shared memory code typically does some action, writes the result, and then synchronizes, the synchronization operation also serves to automatically distribute the data between threads.

Problems occur when the programmer takes account of the fact that threads within a warp operate in a synchronous manner and thus omits the synchronization primitive. You typically see such optimizations when a reduction operation is in use and the last 32 values don't need a synchronization primitive. This is true only in the case in which the shared memory is additionally declared as volatile. Otherwise, the compiler does not have to write any values at all to shared memory.

Shared memory has two purposes: first, to act as a block of local, high-speed, per-thread memory, and second, to facilitate interthread communication within a block. Only in the latter case does shared memory need to be declared as volatile. Thus, the __shared__ directive does not implicitly declare the parameter as volatile since the programmer may not always wish to enforce reads and writes when the compiler is able to use a register to optimize out some of these. It is perfectly valid practice not to use a syncthread call when the threads are cooperating within a warp, but you must realize that the shared memory may longer been made coherent between every thread in the warp unless the shared memory is also declared as volatile.

When you have interblock communication via global memory, the view each block sees of global memory is again not consistent between blocks without explicit synchronization. We have the same issue as with shared memory, in that the compiler may optimize away intermediate global writes and write only the last one out to memory. This can be overcome by using the volatile keyword for access within a block. However, CUDA does not specify block execution order, so this does not deal with interblock-based dependencies. These are handled in two ways. First, and the most common, is the termination and invocation of another kernel. Implicit in this is a completion of all pending global memory transactions and a flush of all caches. The second method is used where you wish to perform some operation within the same kernel invocation. In this instance you need to call the __threadfence primitive, which simply causes, and waits for, any writes from the calling thread to be visible to all affected threads. For shared memory, this equates to the threads within the same block, as only these threads can see the shared memory allocated to a given block. For global memory, this equates to all threads within the device.

Compute level–dependent functions

The compute 2.x hardware supports many additional functions not present in the earlier hardware. The same is true of compute 1.3 devices. If you search through the CUDA programming guide it will list various functions as available only on certain compute levels. For example, __syncthreads_count is a compute 2.0 function.

Unfortunately, as of the CUDA 4.1 release, the default CUDA project (e.g., the New Project wizard in Visual Studio) has CUDA 1.0 support. Thus, when you have a Fermi card installed (a compute 2.x device) and compile the project using a compute 2.0 directive, the compiler rather unhelpfully states the following:

```
Error 1 error: identifier "__syncthreads_count" is undefined j:\CUDA\Chapter-009-
OddEvenSort\OddEven\kernel.cu 145 OddEven
```

It doesn't say this function is supported only under the compute 2.0 architecture. This would be at least helpful in helping you identify the problem. It just says it's undefined, which makes most programmers assume they have missed an include statement or have done something wrong. Thus, they are sent off in the wrong direction searching for a solution.

The issue is simply resolved by setting the GPU architecture level by changing the properties of the GPU option of the CUDA runtime, as shown in Figure 12.1. This results in the following command line option being added to the compiler invocation command:

```
-gencode=arch=compute_20,code=\"sm_20,compute_20\"
```

Note that you can set, by default, up to three architectures in the standard project created by Visual Studio for CUDA projects. Code can be written for various compute levels using the compiler preprocessor. In fact, this is what is being used to make higher compute level functions visible.

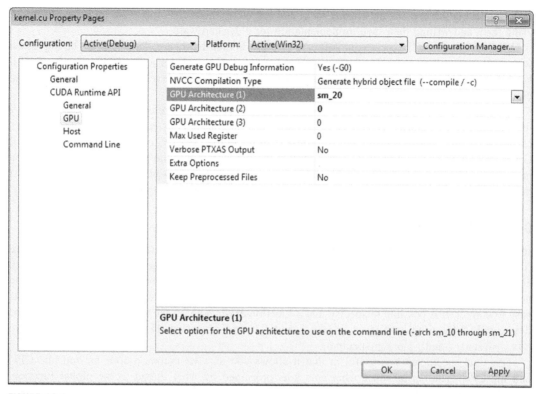

FIGURE 12.1

Setting the correct architecture.

CUDA defines a preprocessor symbol __CUDA_ARCH__, which currently holds the value 100, 110, 120, 130, 200, 210, or 300. Clearly, as future architectures are defined these will increase. Thus, you can write

```
#if (__CUDA_ARCH__ >= 200)
 my_compute_2x_function();
#else
 my_compute_1x_function();
#endif
```

Alternatively, you can write a single function that uses conditional compilation only where necessary to either make use of the later compute level functions or provide an alternative solution for lower compute level devices.

Many of the compute 2.x functions simplify the programming necessary and therefore make development easier. However, most of these later functions can also be implemented by lower compute level devices in a slower manner or with slightly more programming. By not providing any implementation to provide for backward compatibility, CUDA forces programmers to make a choice of either not using the new features, using them and excluding those customers with older hardware, or using them and writing their own implementation for older hardware.

Most consumers will expect your software to work on their hardware. They will not be impressed with a message telling them to swap out their 9800 GT or GTX260 for a 400/500/600 series Fermi/Kepler card. Most consumers will have no clue what the compute level is anyway and will have purchased the card to play the latest version of a particular game.

If you work in the research or commercial fields, then your hardware is largely defined for you by the institution or company. If you have an input into this, absolutely choose at least compute 2.x hardware or later, as it is much easier to program. You can then largely forget about the evolution of GPUs to date and work with a cache-based system far more familiar to most CPU programmers. If you have a mix of hardware, as do many of our clients, then you need to think about how to achieve the best performance on each generation of hardware and write your program accordingly.

Device, global, and host functions

In CUDA you have to specify if a function or data item exists on the host (the CPU side) or the device (the GPU side) of the PCI-E data bus. Thus, there are three specifiers that can be used, as shown in Table 12.1. If you omit the specifier, then the CUDA compiler will assume the function exists on the host and will only allow you to call it from there. This is an error detected at compile time and thus easy to correct. It is possible to specify that a function exists both on the host (CPU) and also on the device (GPU) by using both the __device__ and __host__ specifiers. However, it's not possible to mix __global__ and __host__ specifiers.

This dual specification is useful in that it allows you to write common code on both the GPU and the CPU. You can abstract what data gets processed by what thread to the global function. The global function then calls the device function, passing it a pointer to the data it should perform the task on. The host function can simply call the device function in a loop to achieve the same functionality.

In terms of how device and global functions get translated, device functions are similar to static functions in C. That is, the CUDA compiler expects to be able to see the entire scope of a device function at compile time, not link time. This is because device functions, by default, get in-lined into the global function.

In-lining is a process where the formal parameters and the call overhead are eliminated and every call to the function is expanded as if the body of the called function was included at the point of the call. This might lead you to think the compiler is wasting code space, as you will have potentially two copies of the same device function in the program memory space. However, usually the context of the

Table 12.1 GPU and Host Functions

Specifier	Code Is Located on	May Be Called by
__device__	GPU	A global or device function
__global__	GPU	A host function using a kernel invocation
__host__	Host	A regular C function call

call will allow additional optimization strategies to be used, so although the device function is largely duplicated, it may be slightly different in each usage.

The problem this causes for you, the programmer, is that the compiler expects one source file. If you want to have two kernel source files (.cu files) that share a common device function, then you need to #include the .cu source file into each caller instead of declaring the usual header file approach and having the linker resolve the call. Note that in the CUDA 5.0 release of the SDK, its new GPU Library Object Linking feature allows for standard object code generation of the device code kernel and even placing this code into static linkable libraries. This allows for much better reuse of existing code and somewhat quicker compile times.

Kernels within streams

Getting an asynchronous operation to work as you intend is actually quite tricky since the stream model is not reflected in the actual hardware, at least up to compute 2.1 devices. Thus, you might create two streams and fill stream A with a number of memory copies and then stream B with a number of memory copies. You might expect that as streams A and B are different, the hardware would interleave copies from each stream. What happens in practice is the hardware has only a single queue and executes commands based on the order in which they were issued. Thus, two streams that implement a copy to device, execute kernel, and copy from device operation will be run in sequence rather than being overlapped with one another.

In consumer hardware up to and including compute 3.0 devices there are just two queues—one for the memory copies and one for the kernels. In the memory queue, any preceding operation must complete prior to a new operation being issued. This makes perfect sense, as a single DMA (direct-memory access) engine can do a single transfer at a time. However, this means filling the queues, depth first by stream has the effect of serializing the stream operations, which defeats the object of using streams, to achieve an enhanced level of concurrent kernel/memory transfers.

The solution is still to fill the queue depth first, but to exclude the copy back memory operations from the queue. Thus, the copy to and kernel operations will overlap execution with one another. In a situation where the input data is larger than the output data, this works quite well. Once the last kernel in the batch has been pushed into the queue, all of the copy back operations are then pushed into the transfer queue.

In Fermi devices based on the GF100/GF110 devices (i.e., GTX470, GTX480, GTX570, GTX580, Tesla C2050, C2070, C2075, Tesla M2050/2070) there are two DMA engines. However, only the Tesla devices enable this second transfer engine, known as "async engine count," in the driver. Thus, on Fermi Tesla devices, the depth-first approach mentioned previously can be improved upon. As we no longer have a single transfer queue, we in fact should issue commands to the stream breadth first. This vastly simplifies stream handling, as we can effectively forget about the hardware handling internally and expect it to work as the logical stream model predicts.

However, do be aware of one optimization in the hardware that can cause issues. The hardware will tie successive transfers together in terms of when they complete. Thus, launching two memory copies followed by two kernel calls results in both the memory copies having to complete before either kernel gets launched. You can break this behavior by inserting an event into the stream in between the memory copies. Then each copy is handled independently of the ones after it.

PARALLEL PROGRAMMING ISSUES

Having gotten over the usage of the API issues, the next pitfalls most CUDA developers fall into are some of the more general problems that plague all parallel software development. We look in this section at some of these issues and how they affect GPU development.

Race hazards

In a single-thread application, the problem of producer/consumer is quite easy to handle. It's simply a case of looking at the data flow and seeing if a variable was read before anything wrote to it. Many of the better compilers highlight such issues. However, even with this assistance, complex code can suffer from this issue.

As soon as you introduce threads into the equation, producer/consumer problems become a real headache if not thought about carefully in advance. The threading mechanism in most operating systems—and CUDA is no exception—tries to operate to achieve the best overall throughput. This usually means threads can run in any order and the program must not be sensitive to this ordering.

Consider a loop where iteration i depends on loop iteration i-1. If we simply assign a thread to each element of the array and do nothing else, the program will work only when the processor executes one thread at a time according to the thread ID from low to high thread numbers. Reverse this order or execute more than one thread in parallel and the program breaks. However, this is a rather simple example and not all programs break. Many run and produce the answer correctly sometimes. If you ever find you have a correct answer on some runs, but the wrong answer on others, it is likely you have a producer/consumer or race hazard issue.

A race hazard, as its name implies, occurs when sections of the program "race" toward a critical point, such as a memory read/write. Sometimes warp 0 may win the race and the result is correct. Other times warp 1 might get delayed and warp 3 hits the critical section first, producing the wrong answer.

The major problem with race hazards is they do not always occur. This makes debugging them and trying to place a breakpoint on the error difficult. The second feature of race hazards is they are extremely sensitive to timing disturbances. Thus, adding a breakpoint and single-stepping the code always delays the thread being observed. This delay often changes the scheduling pattern of other warps, meaning the particular conditions of the wrong answer may never occur.

The first question in such a situation is not where in the code is this happening, but requires you to take a step backward and look at the larger picture. Consider under what circumstances the answer can change. If there is some assumption about the ordering of thread or block execution in the design, then we already have the cause of the problem. As CUDA does not provide any guarantee of block ordering or warp execution ordering, any such assumption means the design is flawed. For instance, take a simple sum-based reduction to add all the numbers in a large array. If each run produces a different answer, then this is likely because the blocks are running in a different order, *which is to be expected*. The order should not and must not affect the outcome of the result.

In such an example we can fix the ordering issues by sorting the array and combining values from low to high in a defined order. We can and should define an order for such problems. However, the actual execution order in the hardware should be considered as undefined with known synchronization points.

Synchronization

Synchronization in CUDA is the term used for sharing of information between threads within a block, or between blocks within a grid. A thread can access register space or local memory space, both of which are private to the thread. For threads to work together on a problem they will often use the on-chip shared memory. We saw some examples of this in the reduction problem we looked at earlier.

Threads are grouped into warps of 32 threads. Each warp is an independent schedulable unit for the hardware. The SMs themselves have 8, 16, 32, 48, or more CUDA cores within them. Thus, they can schedule at any single point in time a number of warps and will switch warps to maintain the throughput of the device. This causes us some issues in terms of synchronization. Suppose we have 256 threads in a single block. This equates to eight warps. On a compute 2.0 device, with 32 CUDA cores, two warps will be running at any single time. There are two warps running and not one warp because the hardware actually runs two independent halfwarps per shader clock (two full warps per GPU clock). Thus, two warps may make some progress in the program while others remain idle.

Let's assume warps 0 and 1 are the ones that are initially selected by the hardware to run. The SMs do not use a conventional time-slicing method, but run until the warp is blocked or hits a maximum run period. In principle this is all that is needed of the scheduler. As soon as warp 0 issues an operation, arithmetic or memory, it will stall and the warp will switch. If all warps follow the same path this has the effect of pipelining the operations within a block, one warp at a time. This in turn allows for extremely efficient execution of the instruction stream across N warps.

However, this arrangement rarely remains for long, as one or more external dependencies will cause one warp to get delayed. For example, let's assume every warp in the block reads from global memory. All but the last warp hit the L1 cache. The last warp was unlucky and its data is now being fetched from global memory. If we assume a 20-clock-cycle instruction latency and a 600-cycle memory latency, the other warps will have progressed 30 instructions by the time the memory request is satisfied. If the kernel has a loop, then warps 0..6 could be several iterations ahead of warp 7.

Let's look at an example of this from Chapter 9, adding a dataset. To do this we add the following sections of code to the start of the loop:

```
#define MAX_WARPS_PER_SM 8
__shared__ u64 smem_start_clock_times[MAX_WARPS_PER_SM];
__shared__ u64 smem_sync_clock_times[MAX_WARPS_PER_SM];
__global__ void reduce_gmem_loop_block_256t_smem(const uint4 * const data,
                                                 u64 * const result,
                                                 const u32 num_elements)
{
 // Calculate the current warp id
 const u32 log_warp_id = threadIdx.x >> 5;

 // For the first SM only, store the start clock times
 if (blockIdx.x == 0)
    smem_start_clock_times[log_warp_id] = clock64();

 // Shared memory per block
 // Divide the number of elements by the number of blocks launched
 // ( 4096 elements / 256 threads) / 16 blocks = 1 iteration
 // ( 8192 elements / 256 threads) / 16 blocks = 2 iterations
```

```
// (16384 elements / 256 threads) / 16 blocks = 4 iterations
// (32768 elements / 256 threads) / 16 blocks = 8 iterations
const u32 num_elements_per_block = (( (num_elements/4) / 256) / gridDim.x);
const u32 increment = (gridDim.x * 256);
const u32 num_elem_per_iter = (num_elements>>2);

// Work out the initial index
u32 idx = (blockIdx.x * 256) + threadIdx.x;

// Accumulate into this register parameter
u64 local_result = 0;

// Loop N times depending on the number of blocks launched
for (u32 i=0; i<num_elements_per_block; i++)
{
 // If still within bounds, add into result
 if (idx < num_elem_per_iter)
 {
  const uint4 * const elem = &data[idx];

  local_result += ((u64)(elem->x)) + ((u64)(elem->y)) + ((u64)(elem->z)) +
((u64)(elem->w));
  // Move to the next element in the list
  idx += increment;
 }
}

// Create a pointer to the smem data area
u64 * const smem_ptr = &smem_data[(threadIdx.x)];

// Store results - 128..255 (warps 4..7)
if (threadIdx.x >= 128)
{
 *(smem_ptr) = local_result;
}

// For the first SM only, store the clock times before the sync
if (blockIdx.x == 0)
    smem_sync_clock_times[log_warp_id] = clock64();

__syncthreads();
...
}
```

What we've done here is to store into shared memory the internal GPU clock at the start of the accumulation, and then again just prior to the synchronization operation. The raw data results are shown in Table 12.2. Notice a few things from this data. First, the first run through the data takes more

Table 12.2 Clock Data from Reduction Example

```
Processing 48 MB of data, 12M elements
CPU Serial Time: 10.33 ms Parallel Time: 4.79 ms

ID:0 GeForce GTX 470:GMEM loop E 384 passed Time 0.77 ms
Warp:  0          1          2          3          4          5          6          7
Start: 3989317792 3989317764 3989317798 3989317768 3989317802 3989317772 3989317806 3989317776
Sync : 3989402014 3989401760 3989403480 3989401716 3989402022 3989402188 3989401620 3989401960
Delta: 84222      83996      85682      83948      84220      84416      83814      84184
Start: 3990392804 3990392798 3990392806 3990392802 3990392812 3990392806 3990392816 3990392810
Sync : 3990468116 3990471366 3990471466 3990470474 3990472008 3990468490 3990472060 3990470096
Delta: 75312      78568      78660      77672      79196      75684      79244      77286
Start: 3991404250 3991404244 3991404252 3991404252 3991404248 3991404258 3991404252 3991404256
Sync : 3991479140 3991478900 3991481020 3991479272 3991480994 3991481338 3991479262 3991481158
Delta: 74890      74656      76768      75024      76736      77086      75000      76902

ID:3 GeForce GTX 460:GMEM loop E 192 passed Time 0.89 ms
Warp:  0          1          2          3          4          5          6          7
Start: 3854029986 3854029982 3854029988 3854029992 3854029994 3854029996 3854029998 3854030000
Sync : 3854182306 3854181636 3854181640 3854181850 3854181916 3854182082 3854181956 3854182702
Delta: 152320     151654     151652     151858     152088     151920     151958     152702
Start: 3855394420 3855394406 3855394424 3855394408 3855394428 3855394502 3855394432 3855394418
Sync : 3855543696 3855543430 3855541802 3855543036 3855542248 3855543322 3855541356 3855541446
Delta: 149276     149024     147378     148628     147820     148820     146924     147028
Start: 3856767160 3856767224 3856767164 3856767310 3856767168 3856767314 3856767172 3856767318
Sync : 3856914982 3856915592 3856915748 3856913948 3856918534 3856914904 3856915896 3856916670
Delta: 147822     148368     148584     146638     151366     147590     148724     149352
```

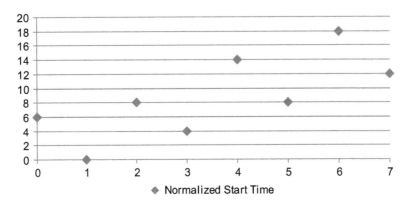

FIGURE 12.2

Normalized warp start time distribution (Fermi).

time. This is because the data is being fetched from memory rather than the cache. Second, notice the actual start time varies between the warps. We can see the even and odd warps being scheduled within a few clocks of one another, as you might expect.

However, even so, there is still quite some variation in the start time at this very early stage. Figure 12.2 shows a scatter plot of start times for a normalized version. Warps are shown along the X axis and cycles on the Y axis. Notice how we see the alternate warp schedulers issue warps into the SM.

As we might expect, given the warps are executed out of order, the timing variation by the time we hit the synchronization operation is on the order of 4000 clocks. Even though warp 1 started after warp 0, it hits the synchronization point just over 3000 cycles later (Figure 12.3).

Clearly, we can see that it is impossible to rely on *any* execution order to achieve correct operation. Synchronization points are needed at any point where the threads within different warps need to exchange data.

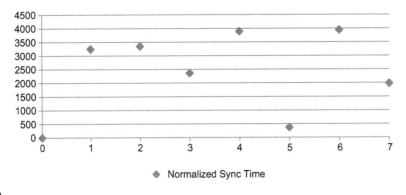

FIGURE 12.3

Normalized warp sync time distribution.

We see the same issue when we try to exchange data from different blocks:

```
Block  Id: 16 SM: 0 Start: 10420984500 End: 10421078132 Delta: 93632
Block  Id: 22 SM: 0 Start: 10420984504 End: 10421079614 Delta: 95110
Block  Id: 36 SM: 0 Start: 10420984508 End: 10421086198 Delta: 101690
Block  Id: 50 SM: 0 Start: 10420984512 End: 10421105046 Delta: 120534
Block  Id: 64 SM: 0 Start: 10420984592 End: 10421137178 Delta: 152586
Block Id: 171 SM: 0 Start: 10421223384 End: 10421308772 Delta: 85388
Block Id: 172 SM: 0 Start: 10421223406 End: 10421311256 Delta: 87850
Block Id: 176 SM: 0 Start: 10421223424 End: 10421322372 Delta: 98948
Block Id: 177 SM: 0 Start: 10421223518 End: 10421350178 Delta: 126660
Block Id: 178 SM: 0 Start: 10421233178 End: 10421381276 Delta: 148098
Block Id: 303 SM: 0 Start: 10421449580 End: 10421535186 Delta: 85606
Block Id: 304 SM: 0 Start: 10421449618 End: 10421538246 Delta: 88628
Block Id: 305 SM: 0 Start: 10421449800 End: 10421546884 Delta: 97084
Block Id: 306 SM: 0 Start: 10421449822 End: 10421577204 Delta: 127382
Block Id: 313 SM: 0 Start: 10421469888 End: 10421606770 Delta: 136882
```

Here we have dumped the start time and completion time from thread 0 for those blocks running on SM 0. You can see that initially SM 0 gets wide distribution of block IDs as the blocks are distributed to many SMs in turn. We'd expect to see that pattern continue, as individual blocks are retired from the SM and new blocks introduced.

In practice, we see the scheduler add large sets of near linear block IDs to each SM. This would suggest the block scheduler is allocating new blocks only once a certain threshold of free block slots, or free resources, is reached with a given SM. This would be beneficial in terms of localizing the cache accesses, which may in turn improve the L1 cache hit rate. However, it comes at the cost of potentially reducing the number of available warps for scheduling. Thus, we can see that both warps and blocks are distributed in time, and therefore it is essential that any thread- or block-based cooperation allows for all elements of the calculation to complete.

For thread synchronization you need to use the __syncthreads primitive and can make use of on-chip shared memory. For block-based synchronization you write the data to global memory and launch a further kernel.

One final point that often trips up people with synchronization is that you need to remember that *all* threads in a thread block must reach any barrier synchronization primitive such as __syncthreads or else your kernel will hang. Therefore, be careful of using such primitives within an if statement or looping construct, as such usage may cause the GPU to hang.

Atomic operations

As you can see in the previous section, you cannot rely on, or make any assumption about, ordering to ensure an output is correct. However, neither can you assume a read/modify/write operation will be completed synchronously with the other SMs within the device. Consider the scenario of SM 0 and SM 1 both performing a read/modify/write. They must perform it in series to ensure the correct answer is reached. If SM 0 and SM 1 both read 10 from a memory address, add 1 to it, and both write 11 back, one of the increments to the counter has been lost. As the L1 cache is not coherent, this is a very real possibility if more than one block writes to the same output address within a single kernel call.

Atomic operations are used where we have many threads that need to write to a common output. They guarantee that the read/write/modify operation will be performed as an entire serial operation. They, however, do not guarantee any ordering of the read/write/modify operation. Thus, if both SM 0 and SM 1 ask to perform an atomic operation on the same address, which SM goes first is not defined.

Let's consider the classic parallel reduction algorithm. It can be viewed as a simple tree as shown in Figure 12.4. We have a number of ways to view this operation. We could allocate A, B, C, and D to a single thread and have those threads do an atomic add to an output storing (A,B) and (C,D). We then drop down to two threads, each of which would add the partial result to the final result.

Alternatively, we could start with the second line and use two threads. Thread 0 would read the contents of A and B and write it as the designated output address. Thread 1 would handle the inputs from C and D. Thread 1 would then drop out, leaving thread 0 to add the two partial results. Equally, we could reduce the problem to a single thread by simply having thread 0 calculate A + B + C + D.

The first approach works by considering the destination data writing to a common output, a scatter operation. The other approaches work by considering the source data and gathering it for use in the next stage. The scatter operation, because more than one contributor is writing to the output, requires the use of atomic operations. The gather approach completely eliminates the use of atomic operations and is therefore usually the preferable solution.

Atomic operations introduce serialization if, in fact, there is more than a single thread trying to perform a write at exactly the same time. If the writes are distributed in time such that there is no conflicting write, then an atomic operation has no significant cost. However, you cannot say with any certainty in a complex system that there will be absolutely no two writes happening at any single point in time. Therefore, even if the writes are expected to be sparsely distributed in time, we need to use atomics to *ensure* this is always the case.

Given we can replace an atomic write with a gather operation, which does not need any form of data locking, does it makes sense to use atomics at all? The answer in most cases is the gather approach will be quicker. However, this comes at a cost.

In our reduction example the addition of two numbers is trivial. Given just four numbers, we could easily eliminate all threads and have a single thread add the four numbers sequentially. This clearly

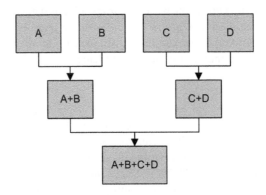

FIGURE 12.4

Classic reduction.

Table 12.3 OpenMP Scaling on Sandybridge-E

Number of Threads	Execution Time	% Time	Expected %	Overhead %
1	5.78	100	100	0
2	3.05	53	50	3
3	2.12	37	33	4
4	1.71	30	25	5
5	1.52	26	20	6
6	1.46	25	17	8

works for trivial amounts of values, but what if we have 32 million values that we have to process in some form of reduction?

We saw in the reduction example from Chapter 9 that using a single thread on a CPU was slower than two threads, which itself was slower than three. There is a clear tradeoff here between the amount of work done by a given thread and the overall number of threads running. In the CPU case the maximum throughput on our AMD Phenom II 905e system was effectively limited to three threads due to memory bandwidth issues on the host.

A more modern processor, such as the Sandybridge-E, has higher host memory bandwidth, but at the same time, two additional processor cores (six instead of four). Running the same OpenMP reduction on a Sandybridge-E I7 3930 K system produces the results shown in Table 12.3 and Figure 12.5. Thus, even if we hugely increase the memory bandwidth and increase the core count, we see the same issue as before. Using more threads on CPU-based architecture produces progressively lower returns as we add more and more cores.

Running only two threads would not make use of the hardware. Running 16 million threads and killing half of them every reduction round would also not be a good approach on a CPU. On a GPU we could adopt this approach since the GPU creates a thread pool that gradually moves through the 32 million threads the programmer requested. We can, of course, manually create a similar thread pool on the CPU, although we have far fewer cores with which we can run threads.

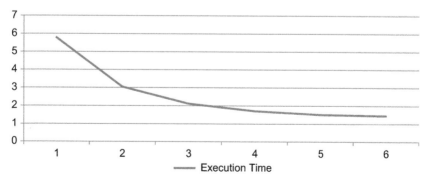

FIGURE 12.5

OpenMP scaling on Sandybridge-E.

Our approach with the reduction example from Chapter 9 is a gather operation mixed with the scatter operation. We schedule a number of blocks based on a multiple of the number of SMs physically present on the device. We then divide the data set into N blocks and have each thread gather the necessary data from memory to perform a local, on-chip accumulation.

Each thread is doing a significant amount of work. We can see from the Chapter 9 timing example that the wider data bus and double the number of SMs on the GTX470 allow it to complete this operation much quicker than the GTX460. We want to ensure we're using the parallelism present in the device, be it a GPU or CPU, to the maximum.

Having calculated the partial sums on a per-thread basis, the issue then is how to combine the partial sums. This is where atomic operations become necessary because the accumulated data is private to the thread. Thus, it's not possible to gather this data from another thread without the source thread writing its data somewhere.

A typical compute 2.0 GPU has up to 16 SMs, each of which can run up to 48 warps of 32 threads each. Thus, we have up to 24.5 K threads active at any point in time. Atomic operations can be performed in shared memory (from compute 1.2 devices and later) or in global memory. Shared memory atomics are, not surprisingly, significantly faster than having to go all the way out of the SM to global memory for global memory–based atomics. As we have up to 16 SMs, the shared memory–based atomics are 16 times wider than an atomic write to global memory. Therefore, we want to use shared memory atomics wherever possible.

Atomic functions as a whole are only available on compute 1.1 devices, which is basically any device except the early GTX8800 series cards. 32-bit integer atomic operations on shared memory became available in compute 1.2 (the 9800 series and later). 64-bit integer atomic operations became available in global memory from compute 1.2 devices and in shared memory from compute 2.0 devices (the GTX400 series).

Single-precision, floating point–based atomic operations are available only in compute 2.0 and later. Double-precision atomics are not natively supported in any current hardware. However, you can implement them via software. The CUDA programming guide provides an example of how to do this using the atomic CAS (compare and swap) operation.

Understanding when to use gather operations and when to use scatter operations are often key to achieving both correctness and performance. Think about how best to structure the design to minimize the use of atomics (scatters) and maximize the use of gather operations instead.

ALGORITHMIC ISSUES

The final type of problem programmers hit is a tricky one. The program runs and doesn't produce any errors, but the answer is wrong.

Back-to-back testing

Testing is something that is key to a programmer being perceived as either someone who writes "good code" or someone who throws together something that occasionally works. As a professional programmer you should strive to deliver the best-quality software you are able to in the timeframe available. How can you achieve this?

Back-to-back testing is a technique that acknowledges that it is much harder to write code that executes in parallel than a functionally equivalent set of code for a serial processor. With this in mind you always develop, in parallel to or prior to the CUDA application, a serial implementation of the problem. You then run the identical dataset through both sets of code and compare the output. Any difference tells you that you may have an issue.

Now why do I only say "may" have an issue? The answer is largely down to if you are using floating-point (single- or double-precision) numbers or not. The issue with floating-point numbers is rounding and precision. Adding a large series of random floating-point numbers on a serial CPU from the lowest array value to the highest array value will result in a different value than if you were to add the same numbers from the highest array index to the lowest array index. Try it and see.

Now why is this? Single-precision, floating-point numbers use 24 bits to hold the mantissa value and 8 bits to hold the exponent. If we add $1.1e+38$ to $0.1e-38$ what do you think the result will be? The answer is $1.1e+38$. The tiny value represented by $0.1e-38$ is too small to be represented in the mantissa part. Over a large set of numbers there will be many of these types of issues. Therefore, the order in which the numbers are processed becomes important. To preserve accuracy often the best way to solve this issue is to sort the set of numbers and add from the lowest number to the largest. However, this introduces potentially a significant amount of work, in the terms of the sort, for this enhanced precision.

There are also other issues concerning the handling of floating-point values in compute 1.x devices, especially with very small numbers around 0, which may cause them to handle floating-point numbers in different ways than the same code running on the CPU. Thus, it's often best to compromise and allow a certain threshold of error when dealing with floating-point equivalence tests.

If you have an existing CPU solution, then it is relatively simple to compare the results. With integer-based problems the standard C library function `memcmp` (memory compare) is quite sufficient to see if there is a difference between two sets of outputs. Usually when there is a programming error on the GPU side, the results are not just a little different, but greatly different, so it's easy to say this code does or does not work and at which point in the output the difference occurs.

More difficult are aspects where the results match up until a certain point. Typically this might be the first 256 values. As 256 is often used as a thread count, this points to an error in the block index calculation. Only the first 32 values being correct points to an error in the thread index calculation.

Without an already existing CPU implementation, you'll need to write one or use someone else's implementation that you know works. However, actually writing your own serial implementation allows you to formulate the problem and understand it much better before attempting a parallel implementation. You have to, of course, ensure the serial version produces the expected answer before you start the parallel work.

It also provides a useful benchmark to see if using the GPU is providing a good speedup. In this evaluation always consider any transfer times for the PCI-E bus. As with the reduction example, we could write a reduction algorithm on the GPU that runs much faster than its CPU OpenMP equivalent. However, just sending the data to the GPU swamped any execution time saving. Be aware the GPU is not always the best solution. Having a CPU counterpart can let you evaluate this decision easily. The solution should be about maximizing the use of whatever resources are available, CPU and GPU.

Once the back-to-back test is set up, and there are many such examples where we do this in the various examples in this book, you can instantly see if you introduce an error. As you see this *at the point* you introduce it, it makes finding and identifying the error far easier. Combining this with a version control system, or simply always making a new backup after every major step, allows you to eliminate a lot of hard debugging effort later in the development cycle.

Memory leaks

Memory leaks are a common problem and something that is not just restricted to the CPU domain. A memory leak, as its name suggests, is available memory space simply leaking away as the program runs. The most common cause of this is where a program allocates, or mallocs, memory space but does not free that space later.

If you have ever left a computer on for weeks at a time, sooner or later it will start to slow down. Sometime afterwards it will start to display out of memory warnings. This is caused by badly written programs that don't clean up after themselves.

Explicit memory management is something you are responsible for within CUDA. If you allocate memory, you are responsible for deallocating that memory when the program completes its task. You are also responsible for not using a device handle or pointer that you previously released back to the CUDA runtime.

Several of the CUDA operations, in particular streams and events, require you to create an instance of that stream. During that initial creation the CUDA runtime may allocate memory internally. Failing to call `cudaStreamDestroy` or `cudaEventDestory` means that memory, which may be both on the host and on the GPU, stays allocated. Your program may exit, but without the explicit release of this data by the programmer, the runtime does not know it should be released.

A nice catchall for this type of problem is the `cudaResetDevice` call, which completely clears all allocations on the device. This should be the last call you make before exiting the host program. Even if you have released all the resources you think you have allocated, with a program of a reasonable size, you or a colleague on the team may have forgotten one or more allocations. It's a simple and easy way to ensure everything is cleaned up.

Finally, a very useful tool available for developers, supported on Linux, Windows, and Mac, is the `cuda-memcheck` tool. This can be integrated into `cuda-gdb` for Linux and Mac users. For Windows users it's simply run from the command line

```
cuda-memcheck my_cuda_program
```

The program will execute your kernel and print appropriate error messages should your kernel contain any of the following issues:

- Unspecified launch failures.
- Out-of-bounds global memory access.
- Misaligned global memory access.
- Certain hardware-detected exceptions on compute 2.x GPUs.
- Errors detected by the `cudaGetLastError` API call.

It will run on both debug and release versions of the kernels. In the debug mode, due to the additional information present in the executable, the source line causing the issue in the source can also be identified.

Long kernels

Kernels that take a long time to execute can cause a number of problems. One of the most noticeable is slow screen updates when the kernel is executing in the background on a device also used to display the screen. To run a CUDA kernel and at the same time support a display, the GPU must context switch between the display updates and the kernel. When the kernels take a short time, the user has little perception of this. However, when they become longer, it can become quite annoying to the point of the user not using the program.

Fermi attempted to address this issue, and users with compute 2.x hardware or better suffer far less from this than those with earlier hardware. However, it is still noticeable. Thus, if your application is something like BOINC, which uses "spare" GPU cycles, then it will likely get switched off by the user—clearly not good.

The solution to this issue is to ensure you have small kernels in the first instance. If you consider the display needs to be updated every 60 ms, this means each screen update takes place at approximately 16 ms intervals. You could break up your kernel into sections that would fit within this time period. However, that would likely mean your overall problem execution time would increase considerably, as the GPU would need to continuously switch between the graphics context and the CUDA context.

There is no easy solution to this particular issue. Lower-powered machines and older (compute 1.x) cards suffer badly from trying to execute CUDA and graphics workloads if the CUDA workload becomes significant. Just be aware of this and test your program on older hardware to ensure it behaves well. Users often prefer slightly slower programs if it means they can still use the machine for other tasks.

FINDING AND AVOIDING ERRORS
How many errors does your GPU program have?

One of the most beneficial development changes we ever made at CudaDeveloper was to move to encapsulating all CUDA API calls in the CUDA_CALL macro. We looked at this in Chapter 4 on setting up CUDA. This is an incredibly useful way to free yourself of laboriously checking return values, yet see the point in a CUDA program where you introduced an error.

If you are not using such a detection mechanism, the number of errors your kernels generates is shown in tools such as Parallel Nsight. Unfortunately, they do not pinpoint the error for you. They simply tell you the number of errors returned from the execution run. Obviously any value other than zero is not good. Trying to track down those errors is then troublesome. It's usually a case of you not checking a return value, which is of course bad programming practice. Either the function should handle all errors internally or, if it does not, the caller must handle them.

The errors detected by the runtime are the easy issues to fix. Simply using the CUDA_CALL macro in every CUDA API, along with cudaGetLastError() after the kernel has completed, will pick up most problems. The back-to-back testing against the CPU code will pick up the vast majority of the functional/algorithmic errors in any kernel.

Tools such as Memcheck and the Memory Checker tool within Parallel Nsight are also extremely useful (Figure 12.6). One of the most common mistakes that often leads to "Unknown Error" being returned after a kernel call is out-of-bounds memory access. The Memcheck utility we have already covered. However, the Parallel Nsight Debugger can also check for out-of-bounds memory access.

Selecting the Nsight→Options menu allows you to enable the memory checker during sessions where Nsight is running as a debugger. If your kernel then writes out of bounds, be it in global memory or shared memory, the debugger will break on the out-of-bounds access.

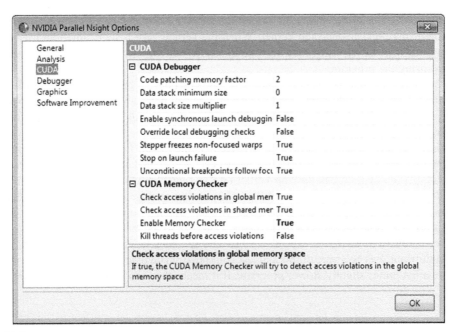

FIGURE 12.6

Enabling CUDA Memory Checker tool by default.

Note, however, this does not work where the out-of-bounds memory access occurs on thread local variables, and enabling this feature slows down the overall execution time of the kernel. As it's only enabled when debugging with Parallel Nsight, this is usually not an issue.

Enabling this option will also provide some useful information about misaligned accesses to memory. Misaligned accesses are not errors in the strictest sense, but simply point where, if you could make the access aligned, you may considerably improve the kernel's speed. These messages are written to the Nsight Output window, which is one of the many output windows selectable by a dropdown box in Microsoft Visual Studio. This is the same output window that the compile error messages are written to, usually the bottom pane of the three standard windows that open in a Visual Studio project.

Divide and conquer

The divide-and-conquer approach is a common approach for debugging and is not GPU specific. However, it's quite effective, which is why we mention it here. It is useful where your kernel is causing some exception that is not handled by the runtime. This usually means you get an error message and the program stops running or, in the worst case, the machine simply hangs.

The first approach in this sort of problem should be to run through with the debugger, stepping over each line at a high level. Sooner or later you will hit the call that triggers the crash. Start with the host debugger, ensuring you are using the CUDA_CALL macro, and see at which point the error occurs. It's most likely it will be the kernel invocation or the first call into the CUDA API after the kernel invocation.

If you identify the issue as within the kernel, switch to a GPU debugger such as Parallel Nsight or CUDA-GDB. Then simply repeat the process following a single thread through the kernel execution process. This should allow you to see the top-level call that triggers the fault. If not, the cause may be a thread other than the one you are tracking. Typically the "interesting" threads are threads 0 and 32 within any given block. Most CUDA kernel errors that are not otherwise detected are either to do with interwarp or interblock behavior not working as the programmer imagined they would work.

Single step through the code and check that the answer for every calculation is what it is expected to be. As soon as you have one wrong answer, you simply have to understand why it's wrong and often the solution is then clear. What you are attempting to do is a very high level binary search. By stepping over the code until you hit the failure point, you are eliminating a single level of functionality. You can then very quickly identify the problem function/code line.

You can also use this approach without a debugger if for whatever reason you have no access to such a debugger within your environment or the debugger is in some way interfering with the visibility of the problem. Simply place #if 0 and #endif preprocessor directives around the code you wish to remove for this run. Compile and run the kernel and check the results. When the code runs error free, the error is likely to be somewhere within the section that is removed. Gradually reduce the size of this section until it breaks again. The point it breaks is a clear indicator of the likely source of the issue.

You may also wish to try the approach of seeing if the program runs with the following:

- One block of 1 thread.
- One block of 32 threads.
- One block of 64 threads.
- Two blocks of 1 thread.
- Two blocks of 32 threads.
- Two blocks of 64 threads.
- Sixteen blocks of 1 thread.
- Sixteen blocks of 32 threads.
- Sixteen blocks of 64 threads.

If one or more of these tests fail, it tells you there is some interaction of either the threads within a warp, threads within a block, or blocks within a kernel launch that is causing the issue. It provides a pointer as to what to look for in the code.

Assertions and defensive programming

Defensive programming is programming that assumes the caller will do something wrong. For example, what is wrong with the following code?

```
char * ptr = malloc(1024);
free(ptr);
```

The code assumes that `malloc` will return a valid pointer to 1024 bytes of memory. Given the small amount of memory we're requesting, it's unlikely in reality to fail. If it fails, `malloc` returns a null pointer. For the code to work correctly, the `free()` function also needs to handle null pointers. Thus, the start of the free function might be

```
if (ptr != NULL)
{
... search list of allocated memory areas for ptr and de-allocate memory.
}
```

The `free()` function needs to consider both receiving a null pointer and also an apparently valid pointer. The `NULL` pointer, however, doesn't point to a valid area of allocated memory. Typically, if you call `free()` with a null or an invalid pointer, a function that is written defensively will not corrupt the heap storage, but will instead do nothing. Defensive programming is about doing nothing erroneous in the case of bad inputs to a function.

However, this has a rather nasty side effect. While the user no longer sees the program crash, neither does the test or quality assurance department, or the author for that matter. In fact, the program now silently fails, despite the programming errors in the caller. If a function has implicit requirements on the bounds or range of an input, this should be checked. For example, if a parameter is an index into an array, you should absolutely check this value to ensure the array access does not generate an out-of-bounds access. This is a question that is often addressed incorrectly.

C provides a very useful construct that is rarely used, except by those programmers familiar with good software engineering practices—the `assert` directive. When a program fails, to have it fail silently is bad practice. It allows bugs to remain in the code and go undetected. The idea behind `assert` is the opposite. If there is an error with the parameters passed by the caller, there is a programming error. The called function should scream about the issue until it's fixed. Thus, if a null pointer is not allowed as one of the input parameters to the function, then replace the `if ptr =! NULL` check with the following:

```
// Null pointers not supported
assert(ptr_param != NULL);
```

This means we no longer require an additional indent, plus we document in the code the precondition for entry into the function. Always make sure you place a comment above the assertion explaining why the assertion is necessary. It will likely fail at some point in the future and you want the caller of that function to understand as quickly as possible why their call to the function is invalid. That caller may very often be yourself, so it's in your own best interests to ensure it is commented.

Six months from now you'll have forgotten why this precondition was necessary. You will then have to search around trying to remember why it was needed. It also helps prevent future programmers from removing the "incorrect" assertion and therefore making the problem "go away" before the upcoming release. Never do this without entirely understanding why the assertion was put there in the first place. In almost all cases, removing the `assert` check will simply mask an error later in the program.

When using assertions, be careful not to mix handling of programming errors with valid failure conditions. For example, this following code is incorrect:

```
char * ptr = malloc(1024);
assert(ptr != NULL);
```

It is a valid condition for `malloc` to return a `NULL` pointer. It does so when the heap space is exhausted. This is something the programmer should have a valid error handling case for, as it's something that will always happen eventually. Assertions should be reserved for handling an invalid condition, such as index out of bounds, default switch case when processing enumerations, etc.

One of the concerns with using defensive programming and assertions is that the processor spends time checking conditions that for the most part will always be valid. It can do this on each and every function call, loop iteration, etc., depending on how widespread the use of assertions are. The solution to this issue is a simple one—to generate two sets of software, a debug version and a release version. If you're already using a package such as Visual Studio this is inherent in the default project setup. Older systems, especially non-IDE-based systems, may need this to be set up.

Once done, you can simply generate a version of the `assert` macro, `ASSERT`.

```
#ifdef DEBUG
#define ASSERT(x) (assert(x))
#else
#define ASSERT(x)
#endif
```

This simple macro will include the assertion checks only into the debug code, the version you and the quality assurance people test alongside the release version.

As of the CUDA 4.1 release, it's now also possible to place assertions into device code for compute 2.x devices. This was not something that was previously possible due to the inability of the GPU to raise such an exception.

Debug level and printing

As well as having a single release and debug version, it's often useful to have a debug level that is easily changeable, for example, by setting the value of a global variable, #define, or other constant. You may also wish to allow for setting such a parameter via the command line, for example `-debug=5` to set debug level five, etc.

During development, you can add useful information messages to the code, for example:

```
#ifdef DEBUG
#ifndef DEBUG_MSG
// Set to 0..4 to print errors
// 0 = Critical (program abort)
// 1 = Serious
// 2 = Problem
// 3 = Warning
// 4 = Information
#define DEBUG_ERR_LVL_CRITICAL (0u)
#define DEBUG_ERR_LVL_SERIOUS (1u)
#define DEBUG_ERR_LVL_PROBLEM (2u)
#define DEBUG_ERR_LVL_WARNING (3u)
#define DEBUG_ERR_LVL_INFO (4u)

// Define the global used to set the error indication level
extern unsigned int GLOBAL_ERROR_LEVEL;
```

```
void debug_msg(char * str, const unsigned int error_level)
{
 if (error_level <= GLOBAL_ERROR_LEVEL)
 {
  if (error_level == 0)
   printf("\n***********%s%s", str, "*************\n");
  else
   printf("\n%s", str);

  fflush(stdout);

  if (error_level == 0)
   exit(0);
 }

}
#define DEBUG_MSG(x, level) debug_msg(x, level)
#else
#define DEBUG_MSG(x, level)
#endif
#endif
```

In this example, we've created five levels of debug messages. Where the debug version of the software is not used, these messages are stripped from the executable in a way that does not cause compilation errors.

```
#define DEBUG
#include "debug_msg.h"
unsigned int GLOBAL_ERROR_LEVEL = DEBUG_ERR_LVL_WARNING;

int main(int argc, char *argv[])
{
 DEBUG_MSG("Error from level four", DEBUG_ERR_LVL_INFO);
 DEBUG_MSG("Error from level three", DEBUG_ERR_LVL_WARNING);
 DEBUG_MSG("Error from level two", DEBUG_ERR_LVL_PROBLEM);
 DEBUG_MSG("Error from level one", DEBUG_ERR_LVL_SERIOUS);
 DEBUG_MSG("Error from level zero", DEBUG_ERR_LVL_CRITICAL);

 return 0;
}
```

To call the function, you simply place the macro into the code as shown in the previous example. This will work fine in host code, but will not work on device code without some minor modifications.

First, you have to be aware of some issues when printing a message within a kernel. Kernel level printf is only supported for compute 2.x capability. If you try to use printf in a kernel that is being compiled for compute 1.x devices, you will get an error saying you cannot call printf from a global or device function. This is not strictly true—it's simply that it's not supported for compute 1.x devices and the target architecture must be compute 2.x.

Let's assume you have a Fermi-level device so the `printf` call is supported. Unless you take care not to, the message will be printed from every thread in groups of 32, the warp size. Clearly, as you should be launching tens of thousands of threads, simply printing a single message may result in 10,000 plus lines scrolling off the top of the terminal window. As the `printf` buffer is of a fixed size, and wraps, you will lose the earlier output.

As the lines can also be printed in any order, we cannot take the order of printing to represent the order of execution without also some reference to the time to confirm exactly when the message originated. Consequently, we need to identify the source of each message and timestamp it.

The first issue is easily handled, by having one thread in a block or warp print the message. By convention this is usually thread 0. We might also wish to print a message from every warp, so again we select only the first thread from each warp to print the message. You may also have some other criteria, such as the threads that calculate halo regions, etc. A sample set of code is shown here.

```
if ( (blockIdx.x == some_block_id) && ((threadIdx.x %32) == 0) )
{
// Fetch raw clock value
unsigned int clock32 = 0;
asm("mov.u32 %0, %%clock ;" : "=r"(clock32));

// Fetch the SM id
unsigned int sm = 0;
asm("mov.u32 %0, %%smid ;" : "=r"(sm));

printf("\nB:%05d, W:%02d, SM:%02u, CLK:%u", blockIdx.x, (threadIdx.x>>5), sm,
clock32);
}
```

This simply looks for a specified block ID and prints the block ID, warp number, SM we're executing on, and the raw clock value.

```
B:00007, W:05, SM:13, CLK:1844396538
B:00001, W:04, SM:05, CLK:1844387468
B:00002, W:09, SM:09, CLK:1844387438
B:00007, W:10, SM:13, CLK:1844396668
B:00002, W:06, SM:09, CLK:1844387312
B:00007, W:00, SM:13, CLK:1844396520
B:00005, W:12, SM:06, CLK:1844396640

B:00005, W:13, SM:02, CLK:24073638
B:00006, W:03, SM:04, CLK:24073536
B:00005, W:15, SM:02, CLK:24073642
B:00002, W:03, SM:05, CLK:24076530
B:00006, W:00, SM:04, CLK:24073572
B:00002, W:00, SM:05, CLK:24076570
```

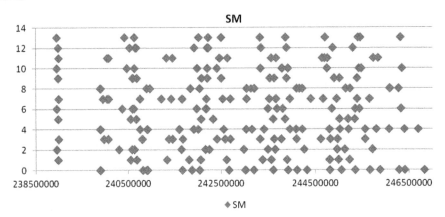

FIGURE 12.7

Warp execution by the 14 SMs (GTX470).

Here we're printing the block index, warp ID, SM the warp is executing on, and the raw clock value. You can simply redirect this output to a file and then plot a scatter graph. As we chose to place the device `printf` at the start of the kernel, it shows when each kernel is invoked.

In Figure 12.7, the SMs are shown on the vertical axis with absolute clock time on the horizontal axis. We can see all the SMs start at around the same time, except a few SMs that start a little later, again all together. We then see a mostly random distribution of timestamps as each block prints its details at the start of its execution. The distribution depends entirely on the program you execute and the time for external resources to become available, global memory being the primary example.

With multiple GPUs or multiple streams, we also have the issue of identification of where the message originated. This again can be simply handled by prefixing the message with a unique identifier. In several examples we have used a string created from the device ID string, `device_prefix`, to do exactly this when using multiple GPUs. However, the API for extracting this information is a host-side call, not a device-side call. This makes sense as we wouldn't want 30,000 threads each getting the device ID string, as it would be the same for all of them. Therefore, what we can do is provide this host-side information via global or constant memory. If we have one GPU, one stream, this is not necessary, but any nontrivial programs will be using both streams and multiple GPUs where available.

In the case of multiple GPUs, you will see a noticeable change in the clock values. Thus, it's quite easy to see the output streams are from different devices, but which came from device 0, 1, 2, or 3? For identical devices, we can't say. What if these messages originate from different streams on the same device?

Using the absolute TID (thread ID) value is sufficient to identify messages for single GPU kernels. However, a combination of device number, TID, and stream number is required where either multiple streams and/or devices are used.

The ordering issue is a problem in terms of viewing the output only. You should create a prefix in the following form:

```
GPU ID : Stream ID : TID : Message
```

With this prefix, it's possible to redirect the output to a file and simple sort using a sort that preserves the relative ordering. We then end up with all the messages, in order, for each GPU and stream.

Note that although `printf` is an easy way to display information at the host end, be aware that it's creating a 1 MB buffer in GPU memory and transferring that buffer back to the host upon certain events.

Thus, the `printf` output will be seen only under the following conditions:

1. At the start of a *subsequent* kernel launch.
2. At the end of a kernel execution if the environment variable `CUDA_LAUNCH_BLOCKING` is set (not recommended if using multiple GPUs or streams).
3. As the result of a host side–initiated synchronization point such as synchronizing the device, stream, or an event.
4. Blocking versions of `cudaMemcpy`.
5. Programmer-initiated device reset (`cudaDeviceReset` or driver `cuCtxDestroy` API calls).

Thus, in most cases you will see the output printed. If you do not, simply call `cudaDeviceReset` prior to exiting the host program or `cudaStreamSynchronize` at the end of the set of work from a stream and the missing output should appear.

Should you need a larger buffer, this can be set using the `cudaDeviceSetLimit` (`cudaLimitPrintFifoSize, new_size_in_bytes`) API call.

Version control

Version control is a key aspect of any professional software development. It does not necessitate using very expensive tools or huge processes that cover who can update what. In large projects version control is absolutely essential. However, even for single-developer projects, something that may apply to many readers, it is important.

Consider for a moment that debugging a 30,000-thread program is easy. If you laugh at this statement then you realize just how hard a task you are setting yourself up for by not versioning your program, either regularly or whenever a major point is reached. Programmers are generally a fairly overconfident bunch of people and can be sure at the outset that a "simple" change will work without problems. However, when it doesn't quite work to plan, remembering exactly the set of changes you made can be difficult. Without a working backup of the program it can be difficult if nearly impossible to get back to exactly the working version before the changes.

Most programs in the professional world are developed in teams. A colleague can be extremely helpful in providing a fresh pair of eyes with which to see a problem. If you have a versioned or baselined copy of the working code it makes it relatively easy to look simply at the differences and see what is now breaking the previously working solution. Without these periodic baselines it's not easy to identify the place where the error might be, and thus instead of a few hundred lines of code, you may have to look at a few thousand.

DEVELOPING FOR FUTURE GPUs
Kepler

The roadmap that NVIDIA has presented from Fermi and later versions is the Kepler GK104 (K10), the Kepler GK110 (K20), and the Maxwell. As of March 2012 the first of the Kepler releases was made, the GK104. This product was aimed squarely at the consumer market and lacked some of the features that some aspects of the HPC (high-performance computing) market would have liked to see, specifically significant dual-precision math support. Kepler GK110 will almost certainly be a far more HPC-focused product that will likely end up in some form or another as a consumer card. The GK110 is scheduled for release at the end of 2012, but the design is already in use internally at NVIDIA for development of the CUDA 5 release that will accompany it.

Let's look briefly at the changes Kepler brings to the table. First and foremost, it brings energy efficiency. The Kepler GTX680 has a TDP rating of 195 watts as compared with GTX580 at 244 watts. This is just over a 20% reduction in absolute power usage of the top-end single-consumer GPU. Looking more closely at the GTX680 it is actually closer to the GTX560 (GF114) in architecture than the GTX580 (GF110), being somewhat like an internally doubled-up version of the GTX560.

If, however, we look at power usage in terms of watts per gigaflop, then you see the Kepler GK104 outperforming Fermi GF110 by a factor of up to two. NVIDIA's own studies on common consumer games (NVIDIA, May 18, 2012) show an average of 1.5× better performance per watt. Many of today's games are highly complex, and thus it's reasonable to expect a comparable power usage profile on compute-based applications.

By being highly selective in terms of binning components, the GTX690 (a dual-GPU version of the GTX680) significantly outperforms even the GTX680 in terms of gigaflops per watt. A doubling or more in terms of performance per watt is a huge achievement on the part of the team at NVIDIA. The GTX690 is the basis of the Tesla K10 range. This is the first time a Tesla product will be a dual-GPU solution.

Although peak global memory bandwidth has remained the same from the GTX580 to the GTX680, we have now transitioned from PCI-E 2.0 to the PCI-E 3.0 specification. Thus, transfers to and from the card under a PCI-E 3.0 motherboard with a PCI-E 3.0–enabled CPU are double the speed of the PCI-E 2.0 400/500 series cards. This doubling of bandwidth should see significant speedups for certain PCI-E-limited kernels.

The Kepler GTX680/GTX690 moves us from the compute 2.1 level to the compute 3.0 level, with the Kepler GK110 being targeted as a compute 3.5 device. A summary of the new compute levels is shown in Table 12.4.

One of the major changes in Kepler was the elimination of the shader clock. Prior to Kepler, the GPU ran at a given GPU clock frequency and the shader clock was multiplied internally by a factor of 2. In previous generations, it was the shader clock and not the GPU clock that drove the execution of the CUDA cores within the device.

Clock rate is a significant driver of power consumption in any processor design. In eliminating the shader clocker, NVIDIA has to lay out double the number of CUDA cores per SM to achieve the same throughput. This tradeoff significantly reduced overall power consumption and allowed NVIDIA to push the core clock from 772 MHz all the way up to just over 1 GHz.

The Kepler GK104 design actually increases the number of CUDA cores by four. It doubles the number load/store units (LSUs), special functional units (SFUs), instruction dispatchers, and the size of the register file. The shared memory/L1 cache remains unchanged at 64 KB, but can now be split in a 32 K/32 K in addition to the usual 16 K/48 K split.

This choice is interesting in that a large amount of additional compute power has been added. If we look to previous generations, we see the move from the GT200 (compute 1.3) to the GF110 (compute 2.0) devices from 24 warps per SM to 48 warps per SM. The Kepler GK104 design increases the total warp count per SM to 64 and the total thread count per SM to 2048.

Table 12.4 New Compute Levels in Kepler

Description/ Device	G80 (GTX8800)/ G92 (GTX9800)	G200 (GTX280)	Fermi GF110 (GTX580)	Fermi GF114 (GTX560)	Kepler GK104/K10 (GTX680)	Kepler GK110/K20 (TBD)
Compute level	1.0/1.1	1.3	2.0	2.1	3.0	3.5
Max warps per SM	24	32	48	48	64	64
Max total threads per SM	768	1024	1536	1536	2048	2048
Total register size per SM in bytes	32 K	64 K	128 K	128 K	256 K	256 K
Max registers per thread	63	127	63	63	63	255
Max threads per block	512	512	1024	1024	1024	1024
CUDA cores per SM	8	16	32	48	192	192*
Max SMs per device	8	30	16	8	8	15
Max shared memory/L1 cache per SM	16 K	16 K	48 K	48 K	48 K	48 K
Max L2 cache per device	N/A	N/A	768 K	512 K	512 K	1536 K

Plus an additional 64 dual-precision units per SM.

The GTX680 claims a peak performance of 3 teraflops compared with the claimed 1.5 teraflops of the GTX580. This peak performance is based on executing floating-point multiply and add (FMAD) operations. Of course, in any real usage there is a huge variation in instruction makeup and memory access patterns, which ultimately determine real performance levels.

In addition, the Kepler GK104 now features dynamic clock adjustment where it will ramp down and up the clock according to the current GPU loading. We've seen this feature for years on the CPU side, which helps significantly in saving power, especially when the device itself is not in use.

In terms of instruction evolution, the major benefit we see is a shuffle instruction that allows communication between threads within a single warp. This is a huge benefit in that threads within a warp can now cooperate without the need to share data via shared memory. The final stages of reduction operations and prefix sum can be easily accelerated with such operations. Additional compiler intrinsics have become available for hardware-level shift, rotate, and access to the texture memory as a simple additional 48 K read-only cache without the overhead of having to write texture memory code. Four byte, packed vector instructions (add, subtract, average, abs, min, max) are also introduced.

The Kepler GK110 (K20) has some very attractive features from the compute perspective—the technologies NVIDIA refer to as dynamic parallelism, Hyper-Q, and RDMA. It also almost doubles the number of SMs per device and adds the missing double-precision floating-point units necessary for significant numbers of HPC applications. Initial (NVIDIA) figures indicate in excess of 1 teraflop of double-precision performance. The memory bus has been increased from 256 bits to 384 bits, which if we see similar clocks to the GK104, should result in a memory bandwidth in excess of 250 GB/s.

The first of these technologies, dynamic parallelism, allows us for the first time to easily launch additional work from a GPU kernel. Previously, this was implemented by either oversubscribing the thread blocks and leaving some idle or by running multiple kernels. The former is wasteful of resources and works poorly, especially for large problems. The latter means there are periods where the GPU is underutilized and prevents kernels from maintaining data in the high-speed shared memory/cache as this memory is not persistent between kernel launches.

The second of these technologies is Hyper-Q, which addresses the difference between the programmer exposed stream model and how it's actually implemented in the hardware. All streams up to and including Kepler GK104 are implemented in the hardware as a single pipe. Thus, a stream of kernels from stream 0 may not be intermixed with a stream of kernels from stream 1, despite the programmer explicitly specifying, via putting these kernels into separate streams, that they are independent work units.

Hyper-Q breaks this single hardware stream into 32 separate hardware queues. Thus, up to 32 streams from perhaps a set of a few hundred programmer-defined streams are available to be independently run on the hardware. The main benefit of this is in terms of loading the device. With 192 plus cores per SM, the granularity of an SM has increased considerably. The resources within an SM can therefore be wasted if small kernels are run that only partially load an SM.

Finally, RDMA (remote direct memory access) is also an interesting technology. NVIDIA has been working with certain vendors, noticeably on the Infiniband side, to improve the latency of GPU-to-GPU communications between nodes. Currently, the peer-to-peer function supports communication between GPUs within the node directly over the PCI-E bus. For cards and OSs supporting this, it avoids the need to go indirectly via the CPU memory space.

However, to send or receive data from a non-GPU device (e.g., an I/O device such as a network card), the best case is a shared area of pinned memory on the host. The RDMA feature changes that in that it allows the GPU to talk over the PCI-E bus directly to other PCI-E cards, not just NVIDIA GPUs. Currently, this is only supported for some Infiniband cards, but it opens up the potential for the use of other cards, such as direct data acquisition, FPGAs, RAID controllers, and the like, to be able to talk directly to a GPU. This will be an interesting technology to watch develop.

What to think about

Developing code that will run many years into the future, or at least be able to be run in the future, is always a difficult issue. The more something is tuned to be fast on one particular set of hardware, the less portable code will be in terms of future development. Thus, one strategy is to ensure any code you develop is parameterized so it can easily be adapted for future GPUs.

Often an application will be tailored to a particular architecture. Thus, you might have a code section such as the following:

```
if ( (major == 2) && (minor == 0) ) // Compute 2.0
 num_blocks = (96*4);
else if ( (major == 2) && (minor == 1) ) // Compute 2.1
 num_blocks = (96*2);
else
 num_blocks = 64; // Assume compute 1.x
```

Now what happens if a compute 2.2 or compute 3.0 architecture is released? In the sample program we'll drop through to the compute 1.x path (the G80/G92/G200 series). The users of your program don't want to replace their Fermi-class GPU with a new Kepler card and find your program runs slower or not at all on their brand-new graphics card. When writing such code, assume you may also come across an unknown computer level and cater for it accordingly.

With the move from G200 to Fermi there was a transition period, where authors had to reissue programs because the number of blocks executed per SM remained the same between generations, only the number of threads per block increased. If a kernel was already using the maximum number of blocks per SM, which allowed for the best instruction mix and thus good performance, no additional blocks got scheduled onto the SMs. Thus, the new hardware went unused and the existing software did not run any faster on the new hardware.

The major transition between G200 and Fermi was the need to increase the number of threads per block. The maximum number of threads per block, a property that can be queried, went from a maximum of 512 to 1024. At the same time the number of resident warps has increased from 24 (compute 1.0/1.1) to 32 (compute 1.2/1.3) to 48 (compute 2.0/2.1). Thus, it's likely in the future we'll continue to see such a trend, with blocks containing larger and larger thread numbers. Kepler was the first GPU architecture to also increase the block count per SM, doubling it from 8 to 16 blocks. Thus, the optimal number of threads, to schedule the maximum number of blocks, shifts back to 2048 threads ÷ 16 blocks = 128 threads per block.

We can work out the number of warps available from simply querying the number of threads and the warp size. The cudaDeviceProp structure returns warpSize and maxThreadsPerBlock. Thus, we can call cudaGetDeviceProperties(&device_props) API and then divide the number of threads per block by the number of warps to work out the maximum number of warps on a given GPU.

This approach would work well for Kepler GK104 and also the upcoming Kepler GK110. However, it does not take account of the changes in the programming model that the GK110 will bring. The dynamic parallelism aspect of the GK110, now that it's public, can clearly be planned for. NVIDIA showed some work at GTC (GPU Technology Conference) 2012, where it claimed this feature alone, primarily the elimination of the CPU control overhead, would leads to quite significant speedups on many codes. It also leads to greatly simpler forms of recursion, where the recursive part can increase the amount of parallelism as the number of nodes expands and contracts depending on the data that is encountered.

One important aspect that you can implement into programs today to run on Kepler hardware is the use of the dedicated 48 K read-only texture cache without the need to do texture memory programming. This will require only that you declare read-only pointers with the C99 standard ___restrict__ keyword, so for example:

```
void my_func(float * __restrict__ out_ptr, const float * __restrict__ in_ptr)
```

In this example by adding this keyword we're saying that any writes to the parameter `out_ptr` will have no effect on the memory region pointed to by `in_ptr`. In effect, we're saying that the two pointers do not alias one another. This will cause the reads via `in_ptr` to be cached in the texture cache, giving an additional 48 K of read-only cache memory. Potentially this could significantly reduce off-chip access to global memory and thus significantly improve memory throughput.

The Hyper-Q logic is also something you should think about in terms of what elements of existing kernels can be performed in parallel. For the first time task-level parallelism will be truly possible on the GPU. To prepare for this, if you currently run a series of kernels, split these into independent streams, one stream for every independent task. This will not adversely affect code performance when running on your current platform, but will prepare those kernels to execute better on Kepler once this feature becomes available.

Finally, the new K10 Tesla product is a dual GPU, based on the currently available GTX690 consumer card. As with CPUs, if you're using only a single core you're wasting 50% plus of the available compute capability. Thus, anyone planning to install the K10 product will need to move their existing code to support multiple GPUs. We covered this in Chapter 8. You'll need to think about where the data resides and if any communication between the GPUs will be necessary. Moving to a multi-GPU solution today will make the transition much easier and provide almost linear scaling for many applications.

FURTHER RESOURCES

Introduction

There are many CUDA resources available on the Internet and through a large number of universities worldwide. We run sessions for professionals wishing to learn CUDA on an individual or group basis. As such, I try to attend, in person or online, as many courses about CUDA as possible each year. As CUDA is a great passion of mine, I've read every book published to date on this subject. I'd, therefore, like to provide some information here about the various CUDA resources for anyone wishing to learn more about CUDA. This information is also available from our website *www.learncuda.com*, a portal for the various CUDA resources available worldwide.

Online courses

One of the great successes of CUDA is the commitment from NVIDIA to bring CUDA to a wider audience. If we look back in time, there have been many attempts to bring parallel programming to the mainstream and many languages designed to enable the use of parallel constructs. With the exception of perhaps OpenMP, and to a lesser extent MPI, all have failed. This is largely because they never escaped the niche group they were created for, did not have a major backer willing to invest in training, and were often restricted to a small number of machines owned by universities, governments, or corporations.

Thus, we start with one of the best resources for CUDA, NVIDIA's own page on training: *http://developer.nvidia.com/cuda-training*. Here you can access a number of recorded lectures from various universities, including:

ECE-498AL, *http://courses.engr.illinois.edu/ece498al/* — a course taught by Professor Wen-mei W. Hwu, author of the first major textbook on CUDA. Available from the 2010 course are lecture audio recording and slides.

Stanford CS193G, *http://code.google.com/p/stanford-cs193g-sp2010/* — a course run by Stanford University based on the ECE-498 course. Includes recorded lecture videos available via iTunes. Taught by Jared Hoberock and David Tarjan.

Winsconsin ME964, *http://sbel.wisc.edu/Courses/ME964/* — a course on high-performance computing applications in engineering, with links to lecture videos and a number of interesting guest lectures. Taught by Dan Negrut.

EE171 Parallel Computer Architecture, *http://www.nvidia.com/object/cudau_ucdavis* — an excellent course covering data-level parallelism, instruction-level parallelism, and thread-level parallelism from the architecture perspective. Taught by John Owens, University of California—Davis.

The next major source of online information is the recorded GPU conference archives. Usually every year NVIDIA holds a conference in San Jose, California, where they are based, called the GPU Technology Conference. These are actually held worldwide in various locations. About a month after the conference, the various sessions are uploaded to NVIDIA's GPU technology portal at *http://www.gputechconf.com/gtcnew/on-demand-gtc.php*. There are far too many sessions to attend since, like many conferences, sessions overlap with one another. You can view almost all of the sessions online going back a number of years. Also available are other conferences where NVIDIA has recorded sessions.

The keynotes, especially those by Jen-Hsun Huang, are always very interesting to listen to and give a great insight into the future of GPU technology. The keynote on the DARPA challenge by Sebastian Thrun shows just how wide the range of CUDA applications is, for example, with GPUs being used to autonomously control a car. Various talks by Paulius Micikevicius are available focusing on CUDA optimization, as well as one talk by Vasily Volkov on occupancy, which is also interesting to watch.

The next major source of online information is the archived webinars provided by NVIDIA that can be found at *http://developer.nvidia.com/gpu-computing-webinars*. The webinar series is aimed at registered CUDA developers. Registration is free and allows you access to the webinars live. Live attendance allows you to ask questions and provide feedback on a particular subject of interest. Sometime after the webinar is over, the archived versions usually become available. The webinar series tends to focus on new innovations in CUDA, the API, and may also have sessions on vendor-specific tools.

There are also many other resources available on CUDA and parallel computing. Visit *www.learncuda.com* for a complete list.

Taught courses

Many universities teach CUDA as part of parallel programming courses. Often it is taught alongside OpenMP and MPI, which are the dominant intercore and intranode programming models used today. NVIDIA provides a very useful tool to identify where CUDA is being taught around the world, so you can find a course near you: *http://research.nvidia.com/content/cuda-courses-map*. As of mid-2012, NVIDIA was listing 500 plus universities around the world teaching CUDA.

Books

There are a number of books written that cover CUDA. No single book will cover every aspect of CUDA and/or parallel programming. You may wish to read the following additional texts:

- *CUDA by Example* by Jason Sanders
- *CUDA Application Design and Development* by Rob Farber
- *Programming Massively Parallel Processors* by D. Kirk and Wen-mei W. Hwu
- *GPU Computing Gems*, Emerald and Jade Editions, by various authors

I've ordered these books in terms of how I'd rate them for accessibility to new CUDA/GPU programmers. All of these books are highly rated on consumer sites such as Amazon, so they are well worth the investment.

NVIDIA CUDA certification

The CUDA certification program is a program run by NVIDIA to allow you to demonstrate to a potential employer that you have achieved a certain level of competence in CUDA. It consists of a number of multiple-choice questions and a number of programming assignments that have to be completed within a given timeframe. The syllabus for the exam is covered at NVIDIA's website at *http://developer.nvidia.com/nvidia-cuda-professional-developer-program-study-guide* and *http://developer.nvidia.com/cuda-certification*.

The material you need to cover largely overlaps with the *Programming Massively Parallel Processors* textbook. The questions are highly programming focused. You are expected to have a good knowledge of CUDA, both in terms of being able to write a number of CUDA kernels from scratch and understanding what makes for efficient and high-performance code. This text you are reading covers many significant aspects of the certification exam, but not everything you might be asked. In many areas this text goes far beyond what is necessary for the certification. Throughout the text there are question and answer sections that require you to think and understand the examples provided in the various chapters. It is through working with such questions and adapting the examples so that you will gain the most understanding.

You will also be expected to keep abreast of new developments in CUDA that may not necessarily be listed in the syllabus but are covered by other aspects like webinars and training provided by NVIDIA.

CONCLUSION

You have finally reached the end of a book that attempts to cover CUDA from a practitioner's perspective. I hope you have learned a significant amount about CUDA, GPUs, CPUs, and how to write efficient programs.

I hope too that your view on GPUs and the use of CUDA is one of excitement. The older serial model of programming is dead. Parallel architectures, be it on a GPU or a CPU, are the future of computing. You are at a tipping point in history where parallel computing is finally gathering enough practitioners and is being driven from the computing industry as the only answer to increasing computational throughput.

Having to think as programmers in a parallel manner is becoming ever more the norm. Our everyday smart phones now have or are moving to dual-core processors. Most tablet-based PCs are dual core. Of those PCs used for gaming, the vast majority of the home PC market, some 92%, are now multicore machines. Just fewer than 50% of those machines are running NVIDIA GPUs (Steam, April 14, 2012).

CUDA has a huge potential to revolutionize parallel processing, both in the consumer arena and the business market. You can purchase a top-end consumer Kepler graphics card (GeForce GTX680) for around $500 USD. The GPU industry is still riding the curve of doubling performance every couple of years and looks set to continue this for at least the near future. It's an exciting time to be someone learning to program GPUs.

References

NVIDIA, "NVIDIA's Next Generation Compute Architecture: Kepler GK110." Available at *http://www.nvidia .com/content/PDF/kepler/NVIDIA-Kepler-GK110-Architecture-Whitepaper.pdf*, accessed May 18, 2012.

Steam, "Consumer Hardware Survey." Available at *http://store.steampowered.com/hwsurvey*, accessed April 14, 2012.

Index